"A very reada[...]
that you will [...]

"To Lasky...

"—Robert F. Kennedy, pure and simple,
was a political pragmatist, using his
experiences in national politics to win.

"—Robert F. Kennedy was a mush of
political thought: Joe McCarthy on one
end, the New Left on the other.

"—Robert F. Kennedy was on a mission.
He took up the torch from his assassinated brother and was determined to
take his ordained place. Come hell or
President Johnson.

"Lasky presents a convincing case, bolstered
by a wealth of sources, each one taking their
chances on the wrath of the Kennedy clan."
　　　　　　　—*Charlotte* (North Carolina) *Observer*

*Stephen Longstreet, Readers' Syndicate

**ROBERT F. KENNEDY:
THE MYTH AND THE MAN**
was originally published by Trident Press.

Also by Victor Lasky

The Ugly Russian

Published by Pocket Books

ROBERT F. KENNEDY

The Myth and the Man

by Victor Lasky

PUBLISHED BY POCKET BOOKS NEW YORK

ROBERT F. KENNEDY: THE MYTH AND THE MAN

Trident Press edition published November, 1968
Pocket Book edition published May 1971

This *Pocket Book* edition includes every word
contained in the original, higher-priced edition. It is printed
from brand-new plates made from completely reset, clear, easy-to-read
type. *Pocket Book* editions are published by Pocket Books, a division
of Simon & Schuster, Inc., 630 Fifth Avenue, New York, N.Y. 10020.
Trademarks registered in the United States and other countries.

Standard Book Number: 671-78013-1.
Library of Congress Catalog Card Number: 68-28365.

Printed in the U.S.A.

CONTENTS

FOREWORD

Tragic as was his untimely death, the fact remains that Robert F. Kennedy was a tough no-holds-barred politician constantly engaged in combat; and it does the truth an enormous disservice when his aggrieved friends seek to canonize him as a young idealist seeking power only for the sake of effecting reforms and insuring peace in the world.

Nor was he a Caspar Milquetoast when it came to winning votes. He was a professional political gladiator schooled in the rough-and-tumble of electoral combat, taking on all opponents with little regard for the political niceties. Not yet forty-three years of age, Robert Kennedy was one of the most feared men in American politics.

On the night of the California primary, when it became apparent he bested Eugene McCarthy, Kennedy happily told friends what he intended to do about the Democratic front-runner, Vice President Hubert H. Humphrey: "I'm going to chase Hubert Humphrey's ass all over America. I'm going to chase his ass into every precinct. Wherever he goes, I'm going to go."

Then he went downstairs to meet his death.

"Inevitably, perhaps," observed liberal columnist Marquis Childs, "the adulators are making Robert Kennedy in death larger than he was in life for all his extraordinary vitality, spirit and zest."

"Inevitably the legend of Robert Kennedy will swell," commented Max Lerner, "and inevitably the human being behind the legend will lose sharpness and become a blurred folk-hero. The process has already begun, and it will go further than is healthy, for Robert Kennedy—with all his vulnerabilities and strengths—was a striking human being. As Edward Kennedy

vii

put it in his eulogy of his brother, he does not need the legend to magnify him."

This book seeks to portray Robert Kennedy as he actually was—an earthy, colorful figure to whom little mattered but victory. Needless to say, this book was written while the Senator was alive. The final chapter, however, was added after the tragedy in Los Angeles.

Let the record show that the author did make an effort to interview Robert Kennedy. On May 15, 1967, he wrote the Senator for an appointment. Half a year later, on November 2, the Senator's press representative, Frank Mankiewicz (who happened to be an old friend of the author's from Los Angeles days) telephoned to say that the letter had been mislaid and that the Senator would see the author. A series of telephone calls ensued (at one time Mankiewicz reached the author in Cincinnati), but unfortunately no meeting with the Senator was ever arranged.

The author would like to thank the many people who so kindly cooperated in this project. Most of them, understandably, did not want their names publicized.

VICTOR LASKY

New York City

July 1968

ROBERT F. KENNEDY

1

Bobby

On a gloomy, rainy Sunday in New York, the grand, queenly Plaza Hotel was the scene of an extraordinary event. A group of Irish-Americans were picketing one of their very own. They frankly wanted to embarrass Robert F. Kennedy. Thus, one of the signs they carried read: HOW CAN A MAN WHO SUPPORTED JOE MCCARTHY DO THIS TO US, SENATOR?

It was an interesting question, but the Senator obviously wasn't replying as he bounded up the steps of the hotel. He had other things to do. That evening he was playing host to some five hundred of the party faithful, most of whom had paid $500 a ticket for the privilege of eating *filet mignon* with him and other high-ranking Democrats from across the nation. The funds were earmarked for the coffers of the near-bankrupt New York State Democratic Committee which, despite two years of RFK's attentions, had been unable to dislodge the Republicans from Albany.

There was little unity at the dinner. Just three days before, on March 2, 1967, Bobby Kennedy had delivered a major speech on the Senate floor criticizing President Johnson on Vietnam. And Democratic elder statesman James A. Farley had publicly called Bobby a saboteur of the nation's foreign policies. At the candle-lit tables, bejeweled ladies and their sun-tanned escorts were asking what Bobby's split with the President meant in terms of the future of the Party of the Common Man. No one really knew.

What unity there was was not disturbed by oratory. Violins played all over the Grand Ballroom. Comedian Alan King did his *schtick* just as he does at the Concord up in the mountains. And Andy Williams, who since Bobby's banishment of Frank Sinatra has become The Family's number-one entertainer, sang "Happy Days Are Here Again."

Outside in the drizzle, the conservative Hibernians kept picketing. "Bobby Kennedy is a lace-curtain Irish fink," they shouted as the police kept them moving around the Plaza fountain across the street. "Down with Surrenderniks!"

Making the most noise was self-styled ultra-rightist James F. Reilly who headed what he called the "Ad Hoc Committee Against Sending Blood to the Vietcong." Reilly had asked to meet with the Senator to discuss why he thought the Communist enemy was entitled to the blood of his countrymen. But Kennedy had declined.

What particularly annoyed Reilly was the fact that Kennedy, in preparing his Vietnam speech, had met with Staughton Lynd and Tom Hayden, stalwarts of the New Left who had defied State Department regulations in traveling to Hanoi. And he had also been seeing people like the guitar-playing singer of "protest" songs, Phil Ochs, who seemed quite taken with the Senator. "Why," said the New Left troubadour, "Bobby reminds me of a good gangster. Tough but on the right side."

James Reilly was, in fact, indignant. "Kennedy has the Irish Catholic vote in his hip pocket and now he's catering to the New Left," he told Joe Flaherty of *The Village Voice*, a nonconformist Greenwich Village weekly whose editors can't seem to make up their minds about Bobby.

"My God," Reilly went on, "my mother doesn't know what this man stands for. All she knows is that he's an Irish Catholic with a lot of kids, which means he doesn't practice rhythm. He's a Pope to these poor misinformed people—he should run for Pope."

What Reilly did not know was that Staughton Lynd and Tom Hayden were just as annoyed with the junior Senator from New York as he was. They had emerged from a lengthy interview (which Bobby had requested) convinced the Senator was in basic agreement with their position: namely, that if the U.S. really wanted to end the war it should accept the possibility of a unified, Communist-controlled Vietnam.

"We're in the same ball park," the Senator had told his visitors as they left his United Nations Plaza apartment overlooking the East River. But what had come out on the Senate floor was totally different from what Lynd and Hayden had envisaged. Though Kennedy had proposed a unilateral suspension of U.S. bombing of North Vietnam with the announcement that "we are ready to negotiate within the week," he had placed the primary blame for failure to obtain a peaceful settlement on the Communists in Hanoi and the Vietcong. And no self-respecting New Leftist will accept any thesis that does not pin most of the blame for the evils of the world on the United States, and, needless to say, the worst evil of all was the war in Vietnam.

In recent years, Robert F. Kennedy had found it necessary to score points with the proponents of the New Left, though on a personal basis he disliked the "beards," as he called them, intensely. "They're a first-class pain in the ass," he stated in private.

Like his brother, the junior Senator from New York felt decidedly "uncomfortable" in the presence of liberals who were forever demanding that he take far-out positions that in the long run could do him political damage. But, because of his close association with the late Senator Joseph McCarthy, Bobby felt he had no choice but to placate these still-suspicious elements. Thus, he sided with the civil libertarians on such issues as abolishing the Subversive Activities Control Board and favoring an Arlington National Cemetery burial for war hero Robert Glenn Thompson, who had been convicted and imprisoned for his Communist party activities.

And he appeared now to be breaking with President Johnson on Vietnam by urging direct negotiations with the National Liberation Front and a pause in the U.S. bombing of North Vietnam. True, the extreme Left criticized him for not going all the way and demanding withdrawal of U.S. forces. Nevertheless, he did establish an image as one of Lyndon Johnson's foremost critics on the war. In so doing, he deliberately sought to create the impression that the President's policies were far removed from those of his late brother's.

Actually they were not that far removed. The crucial decision to escalate from military advisers to combat troops in Vietnam was President Kennedy's. According to the official historian of the New Frontier, Arthur Schlesinger, Jr., President Kennedy had no alternative "but to work within the situation he had inherited." But what about the "situation" that President Johnson "inherited"?

Under President Kennedy's direction, the number of American troops in Vietnam had been increased from less than 800 to about 25,000. Moreover, President Kennedy assigned diplomatic and military personnel to Saigon who were fully committed to support of the regime headed by Ngo Dinh Diem.

It was a commitment fully shared by Robert F. Kennedy, then Attorney General of the United States and generally considered the second most powerful man in the Federal Government. And in 1962, while in Saigon, Bobby described President Ngo as a "brave and patriotic" leader of his people. "We are going to win in Vietnam," he said then. "We will remain here until we do win. . . . I think the American people understand and fully support this struggle."

Even after his brother's death, Bobby felt strongly about the necessity of saving South Vietnam from the Communists. He appealed to President Johnson to send him to Saigon as ambassador. He wanted to go where the action was, he said, but that was precisely why the President did not want him to go. The possibility of Bobby's getting hurt in a Communist-threatened capital troubled Mr. Johnson. The Kennedy family had had more than its share of tragedies, the President explained to friends.

Somehow, thanks to the rewriting of history by the court historians, the world at large has been led to believe that if President Kennedy were alive there would have been no war in Vietnam. But, as onetime Kennedy family friend Gore Vidal observed, "The mythmakers have obscured the fact that it was JFK who began our active participation in the war when, in 1961, he [began] the first of a gradual buildup of American troops. . . . And there is no evidence that he would not have persisted in that war for, as he said to a friend shortly before he died, 'I have to go all the way with this one.' He could not afford a second Cuba and hope to maintain the appearance of a defender of the Free World at the ballot box in 1964."

It was with considerable astonishment, therefore, that Lyndon Johnson observed Robert Kennedy's conversion from a "hawk" to a "dove" on Vietnam. For, whatever else could be said of the President, he is not naive. It was soon obvious that Bobby was seeking to outflank the President from the Left. The man who had been an assistant to the late Senator

Joseph McCarthy kept needling President Johnson for not being liberal enough. The man who had frowned on dissent during the Kennedy Administration was masterfully creating for himself—or having created for him—the image of the Great Dissenter.

As Peregrine Worsthorne, the distinguished editor of London's *Sunday Telegraph,* wrote after a 1966 visit to Washington: "Senator Kennedy, in effect, is seeking to promote his own personal career by undermining faith in the very policies which President Johnson inherited from his murdered brother."

Worsthorne was far from being a reactionary. He had, in fact, been an admirer of the late President Kennedy, whom he had known personally. But Bobby was something else again. Noting that the basic decision to escalate in Vietnam had been made by President Kennedy, Worsthorne observed:

"For the Senator to exploit its consequences to destroy his brother's successor might have struck Machiavelli as the epitome of princely conduct, but even he would not have imagined in his wildest fancies that such conduct could turn its practitioner into a popular hero.

"But this, it seems, is what is happening. Evening after evening on a recent visit to Washington one listened gasping to the liberals as they bemoaned President Johnson's lack of idealism and nobility, and lauded the Senator for precisely these qualities. The trouble is that they are prepared to see virtue even in the man who stabs him in the back."

The trouble also is that Robert F. Kennedy rarely—if ever—demonstrated the "idealism and nobility" so many liberals demand of their other messiahs. If anything, his record as Attorney General manifested an almost instinctive disregard for the "civil liberties" so highly prized by liberals. Rarely had any attorney general been so ardently devoted to wiretapping, mail covers and other violations of due process. Nor was it only people like Jimmy Hoffa or Roy Cohn who felt his vindictive sting. Several prominent newspapermen, including the author of a best-selling book critical of his brother's Administration, found themselves under investigation by Bobby's gumshoes. And Bobby ordered an audit of the tax returns of at least one Federal judge who had the temerity to criticize what he termed New Frontier efforts to "socialize" business. During the racial disturbances of the early sixties, Martin

Luther King's telephone conversations were monitored and transcripts sent to Bobby; subsequently, information was passed to a select few among newsmen and civil rights leaders regarding the Reverend Doctor's alleged ties to subversive individuals and groups.

While his brother was alive, Robert Kennedy was the terror of the New Frontier. There was the time when the then Attorney General literally "blew his stack" in arguing with top political reporter Earl Mazo over a series of stories he had written for the *New York Herald Tribune* on corruption in the Kennedy Administration.

"Bobby's so-called 'lecture,' as it has been described, was in reality a childish outburst," Mazo recalled. "He was so enraged about our coverage . . . that I expected at any moment he would throw himself on the floor, screaming and bawling for his way. Instead he paced back and forth, storming and complaining. It was something to see!"

Not that Bobby didn't believe in the right of dissent. All he wanted was to advise people on what to dissent about. This he made clear to none other than Chester Bowles following the fiasco of the Bay of Pigs. The then Undersecretary of State let it be known that he had opposed the anti-Castro operation but his views had been rejected by President Kennedy. This infuriated Little Brother. At a face-to-face meeting with Bowles, some twenty years his senior, Bobby poked the Undersecretary in the chest and snarled, "So you advised against this operation. Well, as of now, you were all for it." (Later, Bowles was "exiled" to an ambassadorship in New Delhi.)

But Bobby himself never liked such treatment. In 1966, at a Columbus, Ohio, fund-raising dinner, attended by 2,000 Democrats, Kennedy obviously was annoyed by his tablemate, Mayor Maynard Sensenbrenner, punctuating all his important points by punching Bobby hard on the arm. The Senator's tanned, weather-beaten face grew harder and darker until finally he leveled his glacier-blue eyes at the astonished mayor, saying coldly, "Don't you do that again!" His Honor, somewhat embarrassed, mumbled an apology.

Mrs. Alice Roosevelt Longworth, who has seen them come and go on the Washington scene for many decades, once kidded Bobby about one of his great mountaineering exploits. His face turned red with rage. "What arrangements have you made for your funeral?" he snarled.

Mrs. Longworth, who was then nearly eighty and had undergone a serious operation, was taken aback. "Why, I haven't thought about it," she replied. "I haven't made any arrangements."

"You mean," Kennedy went on in his heartless way, "you haven't even designated the pallbearers?"

"No, but I do know one thing—you and Dick Nixon will be seated in the front pew."

"Why?" asked Bobby.

"Because you are my two greatest disappointments."

Later, Mrs. Longworth said that though she was unhappy with Nixon's 1960 campaign performance—and had frequently told him so—the former Vice President had never been unkind to her. They are still good friends.

In recent years, it has been considered bad form in liberal circles to remind Bobby of his near-totalitarian proclivities. When J. Edgar Hoover, for example, proved beyond a reasonable doubt that Kennedy had gone overboard in promoting the use of wiretapping and various bugging devices, certain liberal publicists accused the FBI director of carrying on a vendetta against his former boss in the Justice Department.

Not that any of them tried to dispute the overwhelming evidence against Bobby. What they did say, generally, was that since his brother's tragic death, Bobby had mellowed considerably, that he had begun to develop some of the ease and grace which characterized his late brother and was losing his old image of the abrasive Little Brother. "When I first met him thirteen years ago," Theodore C. Sorensen, the late President's special counsel, told *Newsweek* in October 1966, "I would not have voted for him for anything. He was much more cocky, militant, negative, narrow, closer to his father in thinking than to his brother. Today I have no serious doubts about him. . . . I would vote for him for anything."

"Certainly he's changed," explained Edwin O. Guthman, his press secretary in the Justice Department, and now the national news editor of the Los Angeles *Times*. "But there is no new Bob Kennedy. He's just matured an awful lot in ten years. The snap judgments that characterized his youth are a thing of the past."

Then came the Manchester affair and once again the familiar Kennedy ruthlessness was demonstrated. Even his best friends were alarmed at Bobby's wild-swinging efforts to prevent publication of a book he had authorized in the first place. At one point, his attempt to intimidate the author caused William Manchester to cry out in dismay, "There's something wrong. This is not the brother of the man I knew. There's something definitely wrong here."

There was nothing wrong. Bobby was just being Bobby. He always found it difficult to curb his arrogance. It was too deeply ingrained. When things went wrong, as in the Manchester row, the furies possessed him. He could scarcely control himself. "Bobby hates the way I do," his father once said, and when it comes to hating, Joseph P. Kennedy has had few peers.

His facility for going in opposite directions at the same time was a standard Bobbyism. And it was increasingly recognized as such. Thus Bobby's seemingly forthright attacks on Johnson Administration policies have usually been followed by accusations of alleged misunderstandings by the press. No wonder the line that receives the biggest audience reaction in *MacBird* is when the actor portraying Bobby Kennedy says, "I basically agree with both positions."

Another standard Bobbyism was an unwillingness to do anything—unless forced to do so by circumstances beyond his control—that could conceivably rebound to the favor of a political rival. Kennedy, for example, viewed Mayor John V. Lindsay as his most serious threat in becoming the dominant force in Empire State politics, and described Lindsay as an "intellectual lightweight." That Lindsay did not think highly of the Senator is no secret either.

Thus, while perusing the small print of Federal legislation one day, a researcher discovered that New York City was entitled to $8,000,000 in housing money it wasn't getting. He went to Bobby and suggested that the Senator do something about it.

"Why should I help Lindsay?" was Bobby's immediate reply.

"When he talks about helping poor people," a former Kennedy aide has said, "you wonder if he means it."

Bobby mastered the art of shooting questions at people he wanted to impress with his great interest. Aside from the subtle flattery, the technique frequently helped him to avoid answering questions that might be awkward.

"When he first arrived in New York, I used to be pleased at how interested he seemed," one top city official has observed. "And I used to fill him in on all the background. But then I noticed that he seemed faintly bored or impatient although he never interrupted or cut me off. So instead of giving him a full explanation, I began giving him abbreviated, two- or three-minute explanations. He seemed just as satisfied with the short, superficial answers as the long, complete ones. So you figure it out. Does he really want to know or does he just like to ask questions?"

And you also begin to wonder whether Bobby meant all those things about advancing the Negro cause in the United States. The fact is that the Senator, despite his numerous injunctions to private industry to hire Negroes, hired few himself. Among Bobby's top staffers there were none. Late in 1967, he appointed one, Earl Graves, but as a liaison on Negro matters. And while Bobby constantly preached the necessity of further integration of the public schools, his own numerous progeny attended institutions where there are few Negro youngsters.

Thus, as is so typical, it was a case of doing what Bobby says, not what he does.

Kennedy's propensity for having it both ways—of eating his words and still having them—was nowhere better demonstrated than in the days before he decided that publication of *The Death of a President* was not in his political interest. Manchester at the time was negotiating the sale of magazine rights with both *Life* and *Look*.

When *Look* obtained them for the record price of $665,000, Manchester exuberantly telephoned the Senator at Hyannis Port. Bobby left the tennis court to come to the phone. "Great," Manchester later quoted the Senator. "Isn't that a record? *Look* has been so nice to the family and Henry Luce has been such a bastard."

Of course, the publisher of *Time, Life* and *Fortune* had been called worse things in his crowded lifetime, and Luce-baiting has long been a good old American pastime. Still Bobby was worried when the remark appeared in the press during the controversy over the Manchester book. Getting the *Time-Life* crowd angry with him could conceivably raise hob with his ultimate ambitions.

So, according to Frank Getlein of the Washington *Star,* he

sent a three-page handwritten letter to Luce specifically denying he had called the publisher a "bastard" and assuring him
that while he objected to "the prejudice and unfairness of
Time magazine as far as the Kennedys are concerned," he believed "this has not been true about *Life* magazine. We have
always felt that where you were personally involved we have
been treated fairly."

"Thus," as Getlein observed, "Bobby had whatever advantage an aspiring liberal politician gets from the routine side-
swipe at *Time*. Not content with that, he took the opportunity
to present himself to Luce as a friend and admirer. And, by
the simple expedient of writing his letter by hand, he managed
to have no copies to release to the press. . . . In reply, Luce
asked for conversations to review Bobby's charges of unfairness by *Time*, but this merely showed a lack of understanding
of what Bobby's letter was about. The review the publisher
asked for did not take place and neither Bobby nor his tame
academics bothered to deny publicly the quoted slur against
Luce."

Back in 1960, columnist Jim Bishop had sized up Bobby as
"an irritable and irritating little man [who] condemns and
praises men as though all of us were serfs on some big Kennedy estate." He was also "tactless, impatient, ruthless. . . .
When he concludes a short, confidential chat with a political
leader, the man is left with the feeling that his suit is hanging
in tatters and, if he doesn't do exactly as Robert tells him,
God will strike him dead. . . ."

Bobby may have been to the manor born, but he lacked
the grace and style usually associated with his late brother.
Actually wealth bred in him an arrogance which he found
difficult to suppress. He was frequently an ill-mannered boor.
He would think nothing of appearing shirtless among his
guests at his Hickory Hill home or disappearing in the middle
of dinner. Apparently, wife Ethel explained to him that this
wasn't conduct befitting a potential occupant of the White
House, for he markedly changed his ways. His friends, who
are forever commenting on how much he was "mellowing,"
say that—at long last—he learned the importance of manners. In novelist John O'Hara's eyes, however, Bobby remained "a pathetic figure . . . who turns on the charm when
he has none."

Charming or not, he demanded—and usually got—total

dedication from his staff, one of the largest on Capitol Hill. Their one complaint—whispered, of course—concerned the Senator's habit of taking off on a Thursday for a long weekend of fun and games, leaving them with lengthy assignments. And woe betide them if they hadn't completed their tasks by the time he returned. He was known to lose his temper and explode.

"You had to take a hell of a licking if you wanted to work for Bob Kennedy," says his former press officer, Ed Guthman. "But, it was worth it."

Not all of his employees felt the same way, however. Take the secretary who was called to Bobby's Carlyle Hotel suite one morning to take dictation, but found that her first assignment was to pick up the various articles of clothing strewn about the bedroom. Bobby was used to having servants pick up after him, but the young lady did not consider herself a house servant. She soon resigned.

The story got around and one of Bobby's most energetic apologists, William vanden Heuvel, took umbrage. Vanden Heuvel, a New York lawyer who hoped to become a big man in a new Kennedy Administration, told a TV audience that "all men in public life who have terrifically tough schedules, whether it's the Governor of New York or Senator Javits, have to ask their staff to do a number of menial tasks. . . ." Bill ought to know. He carried the Senator's shirts and picked them up on trips to several continents. Still it's a bit difficult to believe that Nelson Rockefeller or Jacob Javits ever asked their secretaries to pick up their discarded underwear.

Basically, Robert F. Kennedy was a humorless man. And he was aware of this deficiency. So he deliberately developed the type of self-deprecatory humor that Adlai Stevenson brought to contemporary politics. The only difference is that Stevenson usually made up his own jokes. Bobby relied on gag writers. In his 1964 campaign against New York's incumbent Senator Kenneth Keating, he paid a $10,000 fee to Gerald Gardner for an eight-week joke-writing stint. Gardner, who had written scripts for the satirical TV program *That Was the Week That Was,* provided him with "one-liners" aimed at projecting Bobby as warm and human, thus counteracting Republican charges that he was "ruthless."

It was during this campaign that Kennedy made his basic decision to turn to the Left. While he did win the election, he ran far behind President Johnson, for many important liberals refused to be convinced that he had changed radically from the days of his association with Senator Joseph McCarthy. They also frowned upon his close ties with the big-city "bosses." The list of pro-Keating liberals was impressive. It included author James Baldwin, *Nation* editor Carey McWilliams, Joseph (*Catch "22"*) Heller, David Susskind and poet Archibald MacLeish.

"A vote for Kennedy is not just a vote for a U.S. Senator," wrote leftist I. F. Stone in *I. F. Stone's Weekly*. "He acts as if the country owes him the White House."

Kennedy's problem, as he saw it, was to win over those intellectuals to whom—in the words of a *Nation* writer—his "cop's mentality," "mugger's instincts," and "emperor's ambition" were anathema. He approached the problem in typical Kennedy fashion; he surrounded himself with the best talent money could buy. Among others, he hired two young lawyers who had served in the Justice Department as his legislative assistants. Adam Walinsky and Peter Edelman were a far cry from the usual senatorial aides to be found on Capitol Hill. As Kennedy's "opening to the Left," they kept themselves *au courant* on what people like Jack Newfield were saying in papers like *The Village Voice*. They were constantly looking for "new ideas" in the pages of such left-leaning periodicals as *Dissent*. They even kept in touch with what the right wing was saying.

"Hip to the rhetoric of the New Left and the civil rights movement," Robert Scheer observed in *Ramparts*, "they [Walinsky and Edelman] have been invaluable in injecting choice phrases into Kennedy's speeches which have the effect of seducing left-oriented liberals without committing him to hard substantive positions for which he will be held politically responsible by the machine Democrats and Catholics who form his base. . . . What Bobby learned during the course of the [1964] campaign was that it was possible to gain liberal support without losing the other; for while 'bosses' care about the substance of power, liberals remain suckers for mere rhetoric."

One of the "suckers" was none other than the aforementioned Jack Newfield, author of *A Prophetic Minority*, a sympathetic study of the origins and development of the New Left. In 1964, Newfield had railed against Bobby and his senatorial aspirations. But two years later, writing in *The Nation*, he could hardly restrain himself in his praise of Bobby as a "new kind of liberal," one of those who eschew the "clichés of the old liberals, who remain tuned to the paternalistic federal bureaucracy" and their "simplistic slogans."

Though somewhat apologetic about projecting Kennedy as an existentialist statesman, Newfield really lost his sense of proportion in describing the Senator's "wit, rebelliousness, candor, glamour, activism and odd combination of tough-mindedness and compassion which the young find so attractive in other culture heroes like Bogart, Godard and Bob Dylan." He concluded his eulogy in a style worthy of an Elizabethan courtier: "The future is inscrutable, fate is capricious, facile prophecies are arrogant. But some day Robert Kennedy will lead his legions—the young, the black, the alienated, the romantic, the educated—to Armageddon."

The future was indeed inscrutable.

Meanwhile, Robert Kennedy kept saying the right (or is it the Left?) things so far as Jack Newfield was concerned. He supported every liberal cause, always managing to espouse a new New Frontier a shade beyond the boundaries of Lyndon Johnson's Great Society. A veritable Niagara of speeches and statements poured out of his offices. According to a *New York Times* report of May 26, 1966, "the largest quantity of continuous handouts that flow from any official quarter in Washington. . . . On one day alone almost a dozen statements and speeches by Kennedy on as many subjects were dispatched to the press." On another day, his speech on his trip to Latin America—which took two days on the Senate floor to deliver—arrived at newspaper offices in a package that weighed as much as a good-sized book.

"One is asked to admire his speeches on civil rights, on the racial question in South Africa, on urban redevelopment," commented Peregrine Worsthorne of the London *Sunday Telegraph*. "The list is endless. The quality of thought which they contain is embarrassingly reminiscent of the late Eleanor Roosevelt's column, with only one important difference. Whereas Mrs. Roosevelt radiated sincerity and human kindness—which excused the muddled thinking—Robert Kennedy's effusions have all their intellectual drawbacks without any of their redeeming warmth and spontaneity."

There was another difference. Mrs. Roosevelt wrote her own column, while Kennedy's words were rarely his own, which occasionally led to embarrassment. There was the time, for example, when Robert Kennedy told a New York Conference on Developing Nations that if he were describing the American economy to a Latin American student he would call it "electric socialism"—"not because that is what it is, but because to him it would describe us far more accurately than 'free enterprise system.'"

Explaining "electric socialism" further, Kennedy went on: "Knowing virtually nothing about U.S. politics or economy, for example, most [Latin students] are deeply suspicious of 'capitalism' which they identify only with the rapacious colonial control of their economy. They identify themselves, more than anything else, as 'socialists,' though their 'socialism' is in fact usually less daring than the platform of the Democratic party of the United States."

Actually, in writing the speech, Adam Walinsky had used the phrase "eclectic socialism." In preparing the big-lettered reading text, however, a secretary had hurriedly typed it as "electric socialism." Not that it mattered much, for the largely liberal audience thought it sounded good. Only Bobby seemed a bit bewildered. He never fully mastered the verbiage of dialectics.

As a rule, with his compulsion to be in the action and on the move at all times, Robert Kennedy did not have much time to preread the routine speeches prepared for him. For all work and no play would make Bobby a dull boy. It was not for him to sit around in the wee hours of the morning trading concepts with intellectuals like Peter Edelman and Adam Walinsky. Instead, he much preferred the company of the "beautiful people" and such glamorous screen stars as Candice Bergen and, until her death, Marilyn Monroe. A pretty girl columnist who had interviewed him aboard the family plane *Caroline* during the 1966 campaign ("When he got up to walk around, his pants—while they weren't hipsters'—fell down on his hips almost like a cowboy's," she disclosed) found herself besieged daily with gifts from the Senator until she was finally able to convince him that her boy friend might object.

Unlike his brother John, who became an inveterate reader during his various illnesses, Bobby had little taste for the world of ideas. He was not interested in reading long and complex works of literature. But he was aware of the political necessity of developing the kind of intellectual image his late brother projected. Thus, he was often photographed boarding a plane carrying books. But few reporters traveling with him ever saw him crack one.

He also arranged for the publication of books carrying his name. The latest, *To Seek a Newer World,* is hardly more than a collection of his largely ghost-written speeches. On its publication in late 1967, columnist Murray Kempton, normally an admirer of Bobby, was moved to comment on the junior Senator's *chutzpah* in obtaining an enormous advance (variously reported as ranging from $100,000 to $150,000) for rewriting the *Congressional Record.* The book consists of six essays, one of which—the chapter on slums—was obviously inspired by the speeches of Senator Jacob K. Javits. "For a pretense of unity," George F. Gilder wrote in a review in *The New Leader,* "the collection is shrouded with existential fatalism (quotations from Camus) and acned with poignant apostrophes to Youth."

Nor was Bobby any great shakes as an orator. His speaking style was wooden. His voice was too high and plaintive, his syntax too awkward, his posture too stooped, his manner too nervous and unsettling, his rhetoric often confusing.

As Attorney General, Bobby made the welcoming speech at a Harry Belafonte concert sponsored by the Foreign Student Service Council. Considering Bobby's own "dropout" propensities as a student—"I was completely unprepared and ill-equipped," he says, "when I left Harvard"—his latter-day interest in students and their problems was truly extraordinary. At any rate, Bobby told the audience, "You people are exemplifying what my brother meant when he said, "That's why my *brother* is President." More laughter. country but . . .'—well, anyhow, you remember his words."

The audience roared with laughter and Bobby's face reddened in embarrassment. When the laughter subsided, he said, "That's why my *brother* is President." More laughter.

That he "does rather badly with long formal expressions of ideas" was conceded by Murray Kempton. "The best ghost-writer has to damage him a little as the best dubber has to damage Belmondo. His style is the broken utterance, the suggestion. I cannot imagine a greater advantage in these times. Every formal utterance by now is a cliché. Adlai Stevenson took liberal oratory to the mountaintop in the fifties; and his disciples have been throwing themselves off it ever since. President Kennedy may have been the last American liberal it was possible to listen to without breaking into wild mocking laughter."

But that Bobby had a special appeal to collegians and teeny-boppers most Bobby-watchers acknowledge. He easily established rapport with the young. "His gentle pose in this world attracts the flower children," wrote John Speicher in the "mod" monthly *Cheetah*. "He even looks a bit like one."

But as Kenneth Crawford, an ex-youth himself, wrote in *Newsweek:* "Youth is an impermanent condition, almost always outgrown; each new generation adopts its own fads, different from its predecessors'; youth's half-formed political opinions are as varied as their elders' more hardened views. Young fogies are almost as common as old fogies."

And to at least one not unfriendly biographer, Kennedy's courtship of youth appeared both transparent and distasteful. "Although the young are important, their political opinions are the least important thing about them," *New York Times* editorial writer William Shannon wrote in *The Heir Apparent,* then added: His capacity "for exaggerating and romanticizing youth's role" is so great that sometimes "it is hard to say whether Kennedy is seeking the Presidency or the leadership of a new Children's Crusade."

Another curious aspect of Kennedy's personality was his extraordinary shyness. He disliked anyone's getting too close to him. There was little warmth in his icy-blue eyes or his fingertip handshakes. Though he took the buffeting of airport crowds with good grace, he visibly recoiled when someone tried to kiss him. There was one such moment in Cedar Rapids during the 1966 campaign when a drum majorette impulsively bussed him. Bobby sprang back with a look of horror. The poor girl, terribly embarrassed, did not know what to say. Obviously neither did Bobby.

The truth is that Bobby was not overly endowed with articulateness. Which may help explain why he studiously avoided verbal confrontations with such articulate opponents as William F. Buckley, Jr., who invited the Senator to debate with him on *Firing Line,* the conservative editor's syndicated weekly television show. According to Buckley, Bobby replied "to the effect that he would be too busy for the rest of his life." In early 1967, Bobby did appear on a question-and-answer TV program with the then newly elected Governor Ronald Reagan. By general consensus, Kennedy fared badly.

Few people in politics were overwhelmed by Bobby's charms, President Johnson least of all. To LBJ, Bobby was a "little s——." To Bobby, LBJ was an "s.o.b." And they had good reason to dislike each other vehemently. It was a dislike that goes back to the 1960 Democratic Convention in Los Angeles when Bobby sought to prevent LBJ from getting the Vice Presidential nomination. During the Kennedy years, Vice President Johnson felt—with considerable justification —that Bobby was "out to get me."

President Johnson had to contend with the memory of the Young Knight whom he succeeded. "I may not have style, but I get the bills passed," he said. Or, "I didn't go to Vienna and get down on my knees to Khrushchev." All of which got back to Bobby who, needless to say, was not at all pleased.

In the Senate, Bobby remained an outsider. By style and temperament he was light-years away from the Club—the Chamber's inner circle whose guiding lights viewed Bobby's disregard for hallowed traditions with distaste. The hard work that is required to get things done in the Senate was not to his liking. Bobby was also accused of "showboating" —using his seat in the Chamber as a stepping-stone to the White House. Even his liberal colleagues conceded—as one put it—that Bobby tends to neglect his Senate work for his political activities.

Actually, his attention span was most limited. He got restless and annoyed with the length and complexity of legislative proceedings. As his brother's number-two man, Bobby was used to barking orders on the phone and getting things done. Now things were different. As he recently explained, "It takes longer to get things done in the Senate than I like to see things get done."

His boredom was demonstrated at an executive meeting of the Senate Labor and Public Welfare Committee in July 1966. At issue was a resolution concerning a national airline strike. Bobby amused himself by passing notes to his brother, Senator Edward M. Kennedy; it was obvious that he couldn't have cared less. Finally, he had had enough. "Oh, hell," he exclaimed, "why don't you just flip a coin?" Then he strode out of the room. This, of course, did not endear him to his hard-working colleagues.

But he came to life when the lights and TV cameras were on. He thought constantly in terms of Walter Cronkite and the Huntley-Brinkley Report. And he got extraordinary TV coverage, far more than his senior colleague from New York, Jacob Javits, who needless to say was not very happy about it. Once Javits tried to get him away from a televised hearing on urban problems to a less-publicized committee session on a poverty bill. "You can have my proxy," Bobby snapped at his fellow New Yorker.

Despite his take-charge demeanor and brusque manner, Bobby did not have much luck influencing politics in his adopted state. He was singularly unsuccessful in New York City's 1965 mayoralty contest, in the election of his allies to leadership posts in the state legislature, or to the choice of a Democratic candidate to oppose Nelson Rockefeller's 1966 bid for re-election. His biggest success came in June 1966 in a relatively minor judicial contest when he helped bring about the election of a reform candidate as Manhattan surrogate.

That victory did not win him many friends among New York's Democratic leaders. "When party leaders are alone," a top leader told *The New York Times*, "three out of four hate him. They don't mention him by name. Everyone knows who they're talking about when they say 'that little s——,' well, they use a word they don't use in front of their wives."

But they were afraid of him. Having experienced the Kennedy drive for power through the years, they feared that sooner or later Bobby would occupy the White House. And that's where the power is, baby.

2

Run

On the basis of considerable firsthand observation, Gore Vidal, who shared the same stepfather with Jacqueline Kennedy, had this to say about Robert Kennedy early in 1963: "There are flaws in his *persona* hard to disguise. For one thing, it will take a public-relations genius to make him appear lovable. He is not. His obvious characteristics are energy, vindictiveness and a simplemindedness about human motives which may yet bring him down. To Bobby the world is black and white. Them and Us. He has none of his brother's human ease; or charity."

Bobby's reaction to Vidal was perhaps characteristic. He questioned the author-playwright's manliness.

That was the height of Bobby's scorn. For, if there's anything he could not abide in a man it's what he called "womanliness." It was almost a phobia. Once, seeking to bring together the feuding Amateur Athletic Union and National Collegiate Athletic Association, Kennedy snarled, "You're acting like a bunch of women."

Bobby also disliked losers. After Floyd Patterson lost the heavyweight championship, Bobby ordered the fighter's autographed picture removed from his office.

Asked about Vidal's hostility toward him, he once said, "Vidal got drunk at the White House. He said a few things about Jackie, my mother, and Ethel. He hasn't been back. It's sort of tough for someone who likes to go around pretending he has the latest White House gossip. He thinks I'm responsible."

After pausing, Bobby added, "He may be right."

Though Vidal was essentially correct in analyzing Kennedy's *persona*, how does one explain the extraordinary fervor that greeted the Senator wherever he went? It cannot all be put down to clever planning on the part of his "advance agents." He was, without doubt, as one Congressional leader put it, "a unique political phenomenon" or, in the words of a California Democrat, "the hottest political property around."

The main reason probably lay in the generally held assumption that, sooner or later, Bobby would become President of the United States. When Gore Vidal suggested this awesome possibility in a 1963 *Esquire* article, few professional politicians agreed. Certainly he had none of the mystique that surrounds a White House possibility or the stature that Americans tend to require of their Presidents. To most Americans he was still Little Brother, who had attained high position precisely because he was Little Brother, not because of any demonstrable competence.

Soon, of course, things were different. Growing numbers of Americans—with emotions ranging from joy to horror—believed in what William F. Buckley, Jr., had described as "the inevitability of Bobby." The powerful chairman of a major Senate committee, a Southerner wise in the ways of Washington, got a complaint from a veteran Democratic colleague that he was giving Kennedy preferential treatment despite his lowly ranking in the pecking order. "Oh, no," was the chairman's reply, "I treat him the same way I'd treat any future President."

As another Senator observed, "The Senate doesn't underestimate Bobby as they underestimated Jack, who was just another guy around here. Bobby has built-in standing. Who else gets in the news like he does? They take for granted he is a Presidential possibility, and no Senator wants to be on the wrong side of a future President."

Nevertheless Bobby kept saying, usually with a shy and toothy grin, that he was not laying plans to seek the Presidential nomination. "If I tried to, I'd destroy myself as a Senator. I'd be a basket case in three months."

In fact, as recently as January 30, 1968, Bobby breakfasted with a dozen newspapermen in Washington and stated with great conviction that he would not contest President Johnson for the nomination. Everyone was convinced he meant it. He permitted the newsmen to disclose that there were no "fore-

seeable circumstances" in which he would enter the race.
The young, ardent and ambitious crowd of liberal young
Democrats, who had viewed him as the nation's salvation and
Lyndon Johnson as almost the devil incarnate, was disap-
pointed and bewildered.

"Those admirers who expected Senator Kennedy to lead an
anti-Vietnam crusade within the Democratic party regardless
of the personal cost misread their man," said *The New York
Times.* "He may experiment in the way he has his hair cut or
float an interesting idea for a new social policy, but when it
comes to the crucial decision of politics and career, he remains an old pro."

Many of Bobby's admirers went to work for Senator Eugene
J. McCarthy, the Minnesota Democrat who, against seemingly
insurmountable odds, had boldly challenged President Johnson
in the New Hampshire primary as the "peace" candidate.
Much to everyone's surprise—probably including his own—
Gene McCarthy won at least a moral victory in New Hampshire on March 12. But he didn't have much time to savor it.
Less than twelve hours later, Bobby announced in Washington that he was "reassessing" his position. After a short
"reassessment," Bobby declared for the Presidency.

"It was," one Democrat told the Washington *Star's* Paul
Hope, "like a jackal coming to feast on the carcass after someone else had made the kill."

Bobby's motive was quite obvious: Unless he challenged
the President's vulnerability immediately, he might never survive as a credible Presidential challenger four years hence.
The fact that a relatively unknown politician like McCarthy
could do so well against Johnson convinced Bobby he could
take the nomination from the President at the forthcoming
Democratic National Convention in Chicago.

President Johnson had long expected Bobby's move. "Bobby Kennedy has been a candidate since the first day I sat
here," the President told a visitor shortly after the New Hampshire primary.

"That Bobby, he's something, isn't he?" was Gene Mc-
Carthy's immediate response.

Lyndon Johnson was vulnerable largely because of the
public disenchantment with a President who seemed incapable
of finding quick solutions for racial unrest and the Vietnam

quagmire. Thus the President left a political vacuum easily filled by Bobby.

Of course, Bobby had no quick solutions either, except for high-flown rhetoric to the effect that we were "not doing enough" either at home or abroad. Though his words sounded good, his new specific proposals were usually so astronomical in projected costs as to be virtually impractical. "Bobby does not understand the value of money," one liberal Republican colleague said. "He acts as if the public purse was there for him to disburse without regard to the taxpayer."

Nevertheless, a growing number of middle-class intellectuals, numerically insignificant perhaps but politically potent in the Democratic party, began looking to Bobby to lead them out of the Johnson wilderness. A Louisiana lady, overcome with the idea of a second Kennedy in the White House, wrote to the Senator: "A Kennedy in government represents the highest form of idealism and integrity. This admiration is only in part sentiment for your late brother. You are a force in your own right and many of us desire nothing more than Robert F. Kennedy as President. We are your people!"

Probably the biggest thing Bobby had going for him was the fact that he was so often referred to as "the brother of our martyred President." For the passage of time seems to have enhanced rather than diminished the glow of the JFK legend. No doubt, as Democratic Senator Vance Hartke of Indiana has observed, there is a "national guilt complex" over the events in Dallas, a sort of politics of expiation of which the chief beneficiary was Bobby. Part of this phenomenon has been a deep-seated longing for a return to the glamour of a White House occupied by Jack and Jackie, Caroline and John-John. A considerable number of Americans apparently will never be able to forgive President Johnson for replacing the style and grace of Camelot with the largely imagined gaucheries of his Texas cronies.*

"For many people," a savvy Washington political analyst told Newsweek, "Bobby embodies the dream of Camelot and the hope that it can one day be restored. There never really was a Camelot in Washington, but as long as people think there was, that's all that matters."

---

* Actually, according to a Johnson Administration count, there are fewer Texans in policy-level positions under LBJ than Massachusetts people during the Kennedy days.

"Certainly there's nostalgia aplenty in a Robert Kennedy appearance—some deliberately created, some entirely natural," reported *The Wall Street Journal's* Alan L. Otten during the 1966 campaign. "The voice is thinner than JFK's but the accent is the same, and so are the gestures—the finger jabbing through the air, the hand straying nervously to pat the hair."

Bobby played the game to the hilt, even to the point of passing out PT-109 tie clips. His speeches were sprinkled with references to his late brother—"President Kennedy believed . . ." or, "As President Kennedy once said. . . ." Addressing the Class of 1967 at Fordham University, Bobby reached a new height in ghost-written eloquence: "If there was one thing President Kennedy stood for that touched the most profound feelings of young people across the world, it was the belief that idealism, high aspirations, and deep convictions are not incompatible with the most practical and efficient of programs; that there is no basic inconsistency between ideals and realistic possibilities, no separation between the deepest desires of heart and mind and the rational application of human effort to human problems."

Thus revisited was the Camelot that never was.

Inaugurating a school in Brazil, Kennedy made this appeal in his brother's name: "Will you in the name of John F. Kennedy, after whom you've named this school, make an extra effort to wipe out illiteracy, to keep your children in high school, to send as many as you can to college?"

On that same Latin American trip, the shadow of John F. Kennedy once almost became macabre. Huge lunch-hour crowds had given Bobby an almost riotous welcome to the Argentinian city of Mendoza. He was visibly shaken by the frenzy. At first, he could hardly find words to explain his thoughts. After shaking his head, he finally said, "It was almost as if they saw something come out of Arlington."

His dead brother was rarely far from Bobby's thoughts. Once he showed a reporter how, because of all the handshaking he was forced to do, his right hand was wider than his left. "But," he added quickly, "my brother's was even wider."

Like JFK, Bobby was given to reciting statistics on the number of slum residents who get bitten by rats and the increase of malnutrition among the peasants in northeast Brazil. And, like his brother, he had a penchant for quoting from the great men of history and literature—George Bernard Shaw, Dante, Robert Frost, Oliver Wendell Holmes, Tennyson, Goethe, Churchill, Pericles and others. Bobby's memory bank stored up the quotations and statistics for use at a moment's notice.

The constant use of quotations also gave Bobby an appearance of cultural attainment, though actually there was little pretension in the Kennedys' cultural life. As Ethel Kennedy once explained, "I like films such as *South Pacific*, shows such as *My Fair Lady*, books like *The King Must Die*. We do not feel easy in the company of highbrows and we do not understand the first thing about music. I like jolly, happy things." And Bobby once told an interviewer his preference in motion pictures turns to "Westerns, mysteries [and] musicals," adding, "I don't like movies that turn out sad."

Sometimes this recently acquired fondness for the apt quotation came a cropper. Discussing the number of civilian casualties in Vietnam, he caused several of his Senate colleagues' eyebrows to raise when he said, "Describing the Roman campaigns of many years ago, Tacitus, one of their generals, said, 'We made a desert and we called it peace.'"

Tacitus, of course, was not a general but a famed Roman historian. It didn't seem to matter. As that little old lady said excitedly when the public-address system broke down on the town green in Marion, Iowa, "I can't hear what he said, but whatever it was, was right."

That was probably the most ambitious 1966 campaign trip ever undertaken by a freshman Senator. Operating independently of the Democratic National Committee, Kennedy toured the nation thanking the 1960 supporters of his brother, reminding them in the process that there was much that was left to be done in his brother's name.

"What should be the role of college students in political activity?" a pretty co-ed asked him one Sunday morning in Sioux City, Iowa. Bobby appeared to ponder for a moment, then replied, "Well, President Kennedy always liked to ask college students whether they wanted to be the anvil or the hammer."

To James M. Perry of *The National Observer*, who was traveling with the Senator, the answer was interesting. "First," he reported, "Kennedy managed to associate himself with his brother. Second, he seemed to be saying something profound. Whether the hammer-anvil business really is profound is probably irrelevant; the point is that Kennedy can summon, at a moment's notice, this sort of sentimentality-cum-mystical answer to almost any question. Nobody else can."

In many ways, according to Perry, Kennedy could be considered an outstanding practitioner of what Professor Daniel J. Boorstin calls the pseudo-event. "It wouldn't be hard to build an ordinary man into something superhuman, given such close relationship with a President who is now almost a legend. And the techniques of creating a pseudo-event are in evidence in the way that Bobby Kennedy has gained increasingly widespread recognition. There is a lot about him and what he has done in recent months that is *contrived*. The trips he has taken—to Latin America, to Africa—are calculated to keep him before the cameras and on the front pages. The speeches he has made, deliberately and carefully written to place him in a position just a little to the left of his party's leader, President Johnson, seem sometimes to be almost contrived."

An example of this premeditated publicity-seeking was his now-famous climb in March 1965 of an icy, windswept Yukon mountain that the Canadian Government had named Mount Kennedy in memory of the dead President. At 13,900 feet, it was then the highest unscaled peak in North America.

A few fusty critics complained that Bobby had no business climbing mountains when there was urgent business in the Senate. Moreover, on the eve of his departure, a civil rights crisis had flared.

According to the New York *Post's* James A. Wechsler, Bobby's most ardent defender in liberal journalism: "There will be those who say his decision was ill-considered, ill-advised, immature; one can almost hear the psychiatrists buzzing with diagnoses of obscure, elusive motivations ranging from 'death-urge' to other symptoms. I do not offer any quarrel with these learned comments; I share the judgment that this trip was neither necessary nor wise. What I contest is the suggestion that it was a lighthearted bid for headlines or a manifestation of capriciousness. It was in fact the dramatization of that strange blend of qualities—pride, dignity, vanity, combativeness, loyalty, tenacity, perhaps even a need for private reassurance—that renders this man so much more interesting and human than the stereotyped critiques of him, and so often infuriate his enemies."

As usual, Bobby was annoyed by the news coverage; but as

one member of the Kennedy family told *Time's* Nick Thimmesch: "If Bobby hates publicity as much as he says, then why, for heaven's sakes, does he go out and climb mountains?" * And what rendered Bobby's annoyance even more ludicrous was the fact that he permitted color photographs to be taken of every part of the ascent and wrote an article for *Life* magazine on his adventure.

Apparently, he had had second thoughts about the venture. For, according to Wechsler, he had confided his misgivings to a close friend. "But you must also understand," the friend told Wechsler, "that Bob has what might be called an existentialist streak in him—that he feels that when a challenge exists, and you have said you will meet it, you destroy yourself if you run away from it."

Things had gone too far actually to permit Bobby to pull out. From Whitehorse, a Royal Canadian Air Force helicopter flew him to a base camp 8,500 feet up the snow-covered slope of Mount Kennedy. With him were seven top-notch climbers including Barry W. Prather and James Whittaker, the first Americans to scale Mount Everest. Prather and Whittaker accompanied him on each step of the ascent.

"I began to climb," Kennedy later recalled in *Life*. "I remembered my mother's last words to me: 'Don't slip, dear,' and the admonition of a friend who had obviously never climbed: 'Don't look down.' And I remembered what my son, Joe, said on the telephone as I was about to leave Seattle: 'Good luck, Daddy. You'll need it.' And the reporter from a national newspaper covering the climb told me before I began that his paper had just completed my obituary. All of these splendid thoughts raced through my mind."

As he inched upward, his fear of heights nearly overcame him. He thought to himself: "What am I doing here? What can I do now?" He had no place to go but up. But the weather was good and, finally, with the help of the two experts, Bobby became the first man to reach the peak of Mount Kennedy at 1:00 P.M., March 24, 1965.

There, with copters full of news photographers buzzing overhead, Robert Kennedy planted the family flag in the ice,

---

* Thimmesch is the co-author, with William Johnson, of one of the first—and probably one of the best—of the so-called Bobby books. Entitled *Robert Kennedy at 40*, it was published in 1965 by W. W. Norton & Company of New York.

along with three PT-109 tie clips, an encased copy of JFK's inaugural address and a gold John F. Kennedy medallion. What should have been a most private moment became instead an excellent full-page color photograph in *Life*. And Bobby returned to Washington cracking jokes along the way. "I don't think I'll climb any more mountains," he announced. "I have nine children."

Ted Kennedy—the Senator from Massachusetts—joined in the fun. In congratulating his brother, Teddy observed "that he is not the first Kennedy to climb a mountain. I climbed the Matterhorn in 1957, which is higher. And I didn't need the assistance of the Royal Canadian Mounted Police."

Some weeks later members of the Explorers Club in Manhattan laughed uproariously when they viewed a five-minute color film of Bobby's conquest of Mount Kennedy. Richard Steel, a director of the club, was quoted in *Time* as saying, "When you see Bobby being carried 8,000 feet up the mountain by helicopter, then being carried the rest of the way between two professional climbers, a certain amount of gibing is to be expected."

But Bobby seemed to have a compulsion to keep proving his virility. The following November, while on his Latin American tour, he went on a fishing trip deep in an uncharted portion of the Amazon Valley. Andrew J. Glass, the Washington *Post* correspondent who accompanied the Senator, reported:

"It was dark and raining hard by the time we reached the edge of the lake. Just when we were ready to shove off with our guides, the tropical skies burst into torrents of water. Within seconds it became impossible to see six inches. . . . Only by putting our hands on one another's waists were we able to negotiate the 100 yards through the jungle to the nearest light—a native hut.

"The local guides also turned back, but Kennedy could not be persuaded to quit. While Tom Johnston [a Kennedy aide] bailed furiously amidships, [Richard] Goodwin took the forward seat and Kennedy pulled away—without a light and without a guide in the middle of the jungle. The rain was streaming down too heavily for Kennedy to see either of his two companions; occasionally he would yell to Goodwin to paddle on the other side.

"Forty-five minutes later, without having seen another boat

or landmark, the trio returned, triumphantly bearing four fish that had somehow been pulled into their canoe. The native guides solemnly said that they had never expected to see Kennedy or his companions again."

In Los Angeles early in 1963, Bobby, then Attorney General, was being driven by an FBI man and was late for an appointment. In bumper-to-bumper jockeying down the Freeway, Kennedy's Cadillac convertible was caught as the left-lane traffic suddenly congealed. Impatiently, Bobby stuck his face out of the window to probe the line of cars streaming by on the right. Spotting a Volkswagen-sized opening, he shouted, "Let's go!" The driver hesitated. "Come on!" Bobby yelled. "Come on!" The driver swerved the car to the right, and just in time. Bobby laughed: "You can't live forever."

During the 1960 Presidential campaign, Bobby wore his hair short. Later, his hairdo was a cartoonist's dream, puffing out on the sides over his ears and flopping down over his forehead in Beatlelike fashion. His forelock was made to order for cultivating his image as the spokesman for those who think young, and was also designed to hide what appeared to be a receding hairline. Obviously any sign of baldness could conceivably affect his reputation as the world's oldest living teenager.

"Watching Kennedy comb the incredible tangle is almost like watching an exercise in isometrics," wrote Jim Perry. "He tugs at the comb so hard that his muscles ripple."

Like his late brother, Bobby felt the need to shower several times a day, which is why Bill vanden Heuvel carried all those shirts whenever they traveled together. He dressed conservatively, as befits a member of the Senate, but wore elegant accessories—French cuffs, tucked handkerchiefs, tie clasps and cuff links. There was nothing "mod" about his clothes.

Lithe and spare, Bobby bounced as he walked. Though he claimed to be five feet ten inches tall, weighing about 170 pounds, one was always a little surprised at how little of him there seemed to be. One reason may be his poor posture. In contrast with JFK's commanding appearance, Bobby stooped forward, hunching his shoulders so that he seemed to be withdrawing into himself. In a pushing crowd, he looked small and oddly fragile. But this was deceptive. When he rolled up his sleeves, as he did frequently in his office, one saw the hairy forearms and brawny hands of a wrestler.

Bobby made a fetish of physical fitness. Look out! There he goes again! Throwing passes, sprinting, darting across the lawn, leaping, twirling, wheeee! He wanted everyone to play touch football, swim or play tennis. To him a flabby body was almost an unforgivable sin, as one chauffeur learned to his sorrow when he drove the Senator from the airport to Capitol Hill.

Having driven to within half a block of the Senate Office Building, he began to circle the block to avoid a one-way street, so he could drop the Senator right in front of the building. But Bobby would have none of it. "Here! Stop here! Good God, man, do you think we can't walk three feet?" Getting out, he poked his finger at the man's bulging stomach and said angrily, "You ought to walk more! Then you wouldn't be carrying *that* around with you."

He could also be vindictive to those who affronted any of his self-made images of decency. At a White House party during the years of the New Frontier, he saw a prominent New York writer, who happened to have been a childhood friend of Jacqueline Kennedy, with his arm around the First Lady. From the other side of the room, the then Attorney General rushed over and summarily removed the writer's arm.

"Oh, Bobby," said the embarrassed Jacqueline, "you're so sweet to want to protect me, even when protection isn't necessary."

Bobby couldn't let well enough alone. No drunken New York fag, he said loudly, was going to touch his sister-in-law while he was around.

Bobby prided himself on his toughness. Once, when he was Attorney General, he summoned the notorious New York hoodlum, Joey Gallo, for a talk in his ornate Justice Department office. "Jeez," a thoroughly flustered Gallo later recounted, "I walk into Kennedy's office and right away he gets mad at me. 'So you're Joe Gallo, the Jukebox King. You don't look tough. I'd like to fight you myself.' I hadda tell him I don't fight."

And Bobby's gall was almost proverbial. In October 1967, he canceled a long-scheduled speech before the AFL-CIO State Convention in New York. As a replacement he sent Theodore Sorensen, explaining that he had to be in Washington for a crucial vote on anti-poverty legislation. Much to their amazement those AFL-CIO delegates who read the

New York *Daily News* the next morning noted a front-page shot of Bobby at the first game of the World Series in Boston. A Kennedy could do things other legislators can't possibly hope to get away with.

But, at times, he seemed troubled by the extremes of emotion he aroused in people. "Why," he once asked a newsman in an unguarded moment, "do you think people don't like me?"

Bobby just couldn't seem to shake the adjective "ruthless." CBS News reporter Roger Mudd once asked him in a long television interview why he didn't try to be nicer since so many people thought him ruthless:

> KENNEDY: I do. Aren't I being nice to you?
>
> MUDD: Very nice.
>
> KENNEDY: See?
>
> MUDD: But most people have the view that—
>
> KENNEDY: Most?
>
> MUDD: Well, let's—I suppose that's unfair.
>
> KENNEDY: Yes.
>
> MUDD: But, people . . . think there's always an ulterior motive in what you do. Is that—
>
> KENNEDY: Is that what?
>
> MUDD: Is that—is that accurate?
>
> KENNEDY: No. What did you think I was going to say?
>
> MUDD: Is this something now that's gotten started and you can't do anything to stop it, the public image that you have?
>
> KENNEDY: I don't know.
>
> MUDD: How did it get started?
>
> KENNEDY: I don't know . . . I don't know . . . I don't know . . . I don't know.
>
> MUDD: The McCarthy thing, and the Hoffa thing, and the '60 campaign.
>
> KENNEDY: I suppose I have been in positions in which—but I don't know exactly. I don't know.

Obviously, Bobby was not one for engaging in public self-analysis. Nor is it likely that he ever spent much time analyzing himself privately. Obviously he considered self-analysis unmanly, and therefore bad.

His father, Joseph P. Kennedy, once made light of charges

that his son was "ruthless." "As a person who has had the term applied to him for fifty years," Old Joe said, "I know a little about it. Anybody who is controversial is considered ruthless. It's ridiculous. Any man of action is always called ruthless."

But not every man of action seemed as insensitive to other people's feelings as Bobby. He has been known to hold up the telephone and, while other people listen, silently mock his caller. At best, Bobby resembled F. Scott Fitzgerald's description of Gatsby: "an elegant young roughneck."

During Senate hearings on automobile safety, Kennedy took it upon himself to defend Ralph Nader, author of *Unsafe at Any Speed*. In so doing, he tangled with veteran Republican Senator Carl Curtis of Nebraska:

KENNEDY: What I don't understand is why you don't let Mr. Nader read his statement to find out if in fact—

CURTIS: I have no objection to his reading his statement.

KENNEDY: Then maybe we would understand his position— First, you admit you haven't read the book; and, secondly, you haven't heard his testimony. Why don't you listen to his testimony and then criticize?

CURTIS: I have no objection to hearing his testimony, but when he loses me with—

KENNEDY: With big words?

No matter how much one may disagree with a colleague, this is not the way one Senator is supposed to talk to another —at least, publicly. But Bobby was also paying off old scores. The Republican Senator had been one of his more persistent critics at the labor rackets hearings during the late fifties. And a Kennedy rarely forgets—or forgives—ancient slights.

Bobby paid off another old score in 1966 when he rudely walked out on a speech by the noted poet Archibald MacLeish at the dinner marking the 50th anniversary of the Pulitzer prize awards. He was there to represent his late brother who had won the coveted prize for his book *Profiles in Courage*. One can only speculate on how John F. Kennedy would have reacted to Bobby's performance. Whatever else could be said of him, Jack Kennedy had manners and a sense of dignity.

It was quite obvious when Bobby departed the crowded

Plaza ballroom that he was deliberately snubbing MacLeish. But why? Some months later, a diligent *Life* writer came up with the answer. An outspoken liberal, MacLeish had supported a Stevenson draft against John Kennedy in 1960; two years later he had tried to prevent Ted Kennedy's election as Senator from Massachusetts; and in 1964 he had given strong support to Republican Kenneth Keating in the New York Senate race. As someone who had tangled with Bobby told the *Life* writer, "Anybody who writes that he looks like a choirboy should burn in hell."

Rushing to Bobby's defense, as usual, was his devoted apologist, Jimmy Wechsler. According to the New York *Post* columnist, Bobby had not meant to insult MacLeish but was in a hurry to leave the ballroom because he was late for an appointment with Jacqueline Kennedy.

But the incident was reminiscent of another time when Bobby walked out of another dinner in 1955 when the late Edward R. Murrow arose to speak. The dinner was sponsored by the United States Junior Chamber of Commerce and Bobby was to be honored as one of the ten outstanding young men of the year. Only after Murrow had finished his speech did he return to the dais, where he told everyone within earshot that he had no use for that obscenity Murrow after what he had done to his good friend Joe McCarthy, a reference to a famous TV documentary in which Murrow had excoriated the Senator from Wisconsin.

That there was a good deal of Joseph P. Kennedy in Bobby was once conceded by the Founding Father himself. "Bobby is more direct than Jack," Old Joe said in 1961. "Jack has always been one to persuade people to do things. Bobby tends to tell people what to do. But Bobby—in the things he has had to do—couldn't always take the time to persuade someone.

"Bobby is very decisive. He resembles me much more than any of the other children. I make up my mind very quickly and go ahead and get it done. Bobby is the same way, so I suppose he gets a lot of that from me."

But getting things done was no longer as simple as when he was Attorney General of the United States. Jack was in the White House then, and Bobby was the second most powerful man in the Federal Establishment. Though apologists claim that Bobby matured, and no doubt he did to some extent, the fact remains that he did not use power as ruthlessly as he did in the past because he no longer had that much power. Lyndon Johnson, the man he probably hated most in the world, had taken over the White House. And that's where the power is, baby.

3

Family

Robert F. Kennedy was exactly four years of age when he became a millionaire. The year was 1929 and his father, already a millionaire many times over, bestowed upon his children identical trust funds. Through the years, the elder Kennedy has added more to the funds, and this, of course, does not include his vast holdings in various family enterprises.

These holdings are supervised from a suite of offices on the thirtieth floor of New York's Pan Am Building. There dozens of financial experts work under the direction of Bobby's brother-in-law, Stephen E. Smith, to make certain that the family fortune continues to grow. One interested observer from time to time is Joseph P. Kennedy who, despite his stroke, still enjoys the hustle and bustle of moneymaking. Still in a wheelchair, the Founding Father finds it difficult to participate in the critical decisions. But he is happily aware that his fortune is in good hands.

It was a fortune accumulated primarily in the stock market, motion pictures, real estate and the liquor business. In the roaring bull market of the twenties, Joe Kennedy was less the speculator than the manipulator. With a ticker by his side, and a dozen or so telephones before him, he was a genius at seducing, confusing and panicking the stock-buying public.

Unlike other Wall Street plungers, he got out of the market in time. "Only a fool holds out for the top dollar," he explained to a perplexed friend who apparently felt the bull market would go on forever.

By the summer of 1929, Joe had disposed of most of his holdings and when stock prices began to crack in September, he was in a safe position. He had only contempt for those who had lost fortunes.

Joe had invested in a chain of New England theaters in the mid-twenties, and became involved in the production end of motion-picture making. This meant he spent considerable time in Hollywood without his family. He quickly made a name for himself as a moneymaker by concentrating on production of dozens of adventure-type films, mostly Westerns. But he ran into trouble with an expensive film, *Queen Kelly*, starring Gloria Swanson. Ahead of its time, the film had some far-out sex scenes.

"Joe told me he was shocked, horrified and stunned," Hollywood columnist Florabel Muir reported many years later. "Realizing the irreparable harm it could do to him as a leading Catholic layman, he ordered the entire 800,000 feet of film hidden away in a vault. . . .

"Would John F. Kennedy have enjoyed a political career that took him to the White House if *Queen Kelly* had got into the nation's theaters? Would Joe have become an Ambassador? Would the course of history have been changed?

"Perhaps we are living in a more grown-up world. Miss Swanson, at sixty-seven, is one of the remarkable women of her generation. But, recalling her close friendship with Joe Kennedy in her heyday as a star, you wonder. . . ."

Joe and Gloria were, indeed, close friends. They became, in the vernacular of the times, "constant companions." They were often seen together at parties and dinners in Hollywood or New York. They were so close that when Miss Swanson disclosed she had adopted a son she said she had named him Joseph in the producer's honor. But in years to come, when she came on bad times, her efforts to borrow money from the fabulously wealthy Kennedy to support young Joseph fell on deaf ears. Thus ended a beautiful friendship. But when the White House loomed as a possibility for John F. Kennedy, Joe sent a former secretary to warn Miss Swanson, an outspoken Republican, against saying anything that might hurt Jack's chances.

After creating RKO, he had decided that he had had enough of Hollywood. He was forty years of age and about $6,000,000 ahead when he cashed in at the end of 1928.

Old Joe entered real estate during World War II. His agent, John J. Reynolds, estimated he made over $100,000,000 by wheeling and dealing in property. Under his guidance, it was Kennedy's practice to move into a promising situation, exploit it and then quickly move out. Typically, he purchased one property at 59th Street and Lexington Avenue for $1,900,000, then sold it for $6,000,000. He had put up only $100,000 in cash to make the deal. On another occasion, a New York State Supreme Court Justice described the Kennedy family as "greedy" in paying "less than its fair share of taxes" on a piece of property Old Joe eventually sold to New York City at great profit.

Needless to say, Joseph P. Kennedy made many enemies along the road to fortune. And some of them tended to transfer their hatred of Joe to his sons. "My God," Bobby told a closed meeting in New York in 1964, *"I'm* running for the Senate, not my father."

One of those Joe angered was Edwin Weisl, a wealthy Wall Street lawyer now in his seventies and a powerful man in New York politics. An old friend of Lyndon Johnson, Weisl is now the President's man in Gotham and a Democratic National Committeeman. Of gentlemanly mien, the soft-spoken Weisl is not given to grudges. But he could never forgive Joe Kennedy's hot temper, buccaneer manner and anti-Semitic outbursts during some business negotiations over thirty years ago.

That is why Weisl adopted a lukewarm attitude toward Bobby's entrance into New York politics in 1964. And when Bobby challenged Lyndon Johnson for the Presidency in 1968, Weisl charged that Bobby had "a lust for power" and a "burning ambition [that] cannot stand being denied the top honor of the Presidency."

There was a great deal of Joe Kennedy in Bobby. Father Joe has long made it clear that he never had much use for people who finish second. In his credo it really didn't matter how you won. Old Joe's never-give-the-other-guy-a-break attitude was reflected in Bobby when he leaped into the 1968 Presidential race the day after Senator Eugene McCarthy scored impressively in the New Hampshire primary.

It was on November 20, 1925, that Robert Francis Kennedy first saw the light of day in a fashionable two-story house on Naples Road in the Boston suburb of Brookline.

The Francis in his name is of no particular significance. His mother simply felt that every child should have a middle name and Francis was as good as any other. His brother Joseph Jr. was already ten years of age and John was eight. Four girls—Rosemary, Kathleen, Eunice and Patricia—followed the two older boys. Jean was born shortly after Robert. Teddy did not come along until 1932.

Thus, Bobby's formative years were spent as the little brother among five sisters. For a time, his parents worried about this predominantly female influence. Rose Kennedy once explained, "He was the smallest and thinnest, and we feared he might grow up puny and girlish. We soon realized there was no fear of that."

In the spring of 1926, some months after Bobby's birth, the family moved to New York. Forty years later, Senator Robert F. Kennedy told a student audience in South Africa, "My father left Boston, Massachusetts, because of the signs on the wall that said NO IRISH NEED APPLY." What Bobby neglected to point out, however, was that the senior Kennedy hired a private railroad car to take his family, servants and belongings to their new home in Riverdale, a well-to-do community that sometimes forgets it's part of the Bronx.

Old Joe himself helped contribute to the legend by complaining bitterly of the "social and economic discrimination" faced by the Irish in Boston. Since others of Irish origin did not react to Boston with the same vehemence, it may be assumed that other factors may have influenced the Kennedy departure. Boston, after all, is a staid, conservative city and definitely not the place for an ambitious man to make a lot of money in a hurry. For, as Joe Kennedy put it on another occasion, "Boston is a good city to come from but not a good city to go to. If you want to make money, go where the money is."

Bobby had no distinct memories of the rambling white cement-and-stucco building at 5060 Independence Avenue in Riverdale, though during his campaign for the Senate, he made a much-publicized visit to the old homestead, hoping to knock down the "carpetbagger" issue raised by his Republican opponent.

He was not yet four years old when the family moved from Riverdale to an imposing brick Georgian mansion at 294 Pondfield Road in the wealthy New York suburb of Bronx-

ville. The estate, which had five acres of clipped lawns and
well-tended gardens and has since been broken up, cost close
to $250,000. But by then Joe Kennedy could well afford it.
As a summer residence he also bought a rambling eighteen-
room house at Hyannis Port on Cape Cod, overlooking Nan-
tucket Sound. Later—during the Depression—Joe bought still
another rambling structure in Palm Beach for the Clan's
winter vacations.

During his repeated absences, Joseph P. Kennedy relied
on his wife to raise the children, so Rose Kennedy was really
the major presence in their early years. A devout woman, she
taught the children their catechism and heard their prayers.
She also saw them off to school—at least the older ones. But
as she later told the Queen of England, she arose early for
the first six of her children—"but when seven, eight and
nine came along I thought 'this can go on forever' and I
rolled over and went to sleep. . . ." There were always plenty
of servants around including a nurse and a governess.

She also maintained meticulous records concerning the
various ailments of her children as well as other data. Discussing the now-famous card file, a *Reader's Digest* reporter
in 1939 wrote: "I picked a bunch of the cards. They were
Robert's. The date and hour of his birth were recorded, his
weight day by day and then month by month. Every illness
was there, the dates when he had chicken pox, mumps (both
sides), mild scarlet fever, whooping cough, and when his
tonsils and adenoids were removed." (Ethel Kennedy keeps
the same kind of card file on her ten children.)

Needless to say, neither Kennedy nor his family suffered
any deprivation during the Depression. The children were so
isolated from the world that they were scarcely aware of
breadlines and Hoovervilles. Jack Kennedy, who was thirteen
at the time and enrolled in Canterbury, the only parochial
school he ever attended, wrote to his dad in the fall of 1930:
"Please send me the Litary [*sic*] Digest, because I did not
know about the Market Slump until a long time after, or a
paper. Please send me some golf balls. We just finished breakfast and am going to chapel in about two minutes."

Though rarely at home, Joe still managed to make himself
a major force in his children's lives. "His personality was
so strong, his ideas so definite, his view and outlook so determined, that he dominated our home and our lives," Bobby

once reminisced. "[Yet] this man with such a strong personality . . . consciously retreated to the background so the spotlight would be on his sons. . . . The most important thing to him was the advancement of his children. . . . I can say that except for his influence and encouragement, my brother Jack might not have run for the Senate in 1952, and there would have been much less likelihood that he would have received the Presidential nomination in 1960. I would not have become Attorney General, and my brother Teddy would not have run for the Senate in 1962."

Teddy puts it this way: "My first consciousness of how important Dad was to me began when I was allowed to crawl into bed with him in the morning and listen to him read 'Donald Duck.' From our earliest days, I think all the Kennedy children were made to feel that our father's principal interest in life was his family. As the youngest, it appeared to me that the family was his only interest."

These recollections were contained in a book of privately printed tributes to Joseph P. Kennedy entitled *The Fruitful Bough*. In all, one hundred and thirteen friends—including Marlene Dietrich, Richard Cardinal Cushing, and Justice William O. Douglas—contributed. The editor was Teddy Kennedy, who began work on the project while he was recovering from a 1964 plane crash.

"Hot water was my department, business was Joe's department," Rose once said. Joe left all corporal punishment to Rose and she applied it particularly to Bobby. "I used to spank him with a ruler," she told audiences during her son's 1964 race for the Senate.

Only when Rose had exhausted every other means of persuasion would she call in her husband to deal with the boys. She recalled that during a "particular phase," when Jack was in boarding school, "he had a little difficulty with discipline. He and some of the boys . . . gave a lot of trouble to the headmaster. . . . He was generally a nuisance and was wasting his time and the time of a lot of the masters."

At this point the patriarch intervened. "His father was called in, and things did begin to pick up then. Jack paid more attention to his studies and applied himself, and so it was really a turning point in his life."

There was also an important secondary influence on the younger children—Joseph Jr. "My brother Joe took the greatest interest in us," said Bobby. "He taught us to sail, to swim, to play football and baseball." (In later years, it was Joe Jr. who coined the phrase "Kennedy clan.")

In the shadow of Joe was Jack, two years his junior. They were altogether different. According to the senior Kennedy, Joe was "more dynamic, more sociable and easygoing" while Jack "was rather shy, withdrawn and quiet." Their father had originally envisioned his oldest son as the politician in the family and young Jack as either a writer or a teacher.

Joe and Jack, so close in age, fell into a natural rivalry and would fight constantly. Bobby recalls one terrible squabble which so frightened him and his sisters that they huddled upstairs while his older brothers slugged it out downstairs. The elder Kennedy didn't mind. He was convinced that such rivalry could only strengthen character. But against *outsiders* they were taught to stand united and firm—to win at all costs.

Nor was the will to win confined to the boys in the family. Eunice Kennedy, too, reflected her dad's passion to be first. A visitor to the Kennedy household at Hyannis Port recalls an occasion when Eunice and her sisters took their sailboat well out in the Sound for a race. Moments before the event began, he heard Eunice's voice carrying across the water: "All right now! Everyone say a Hail Mary!"

There is also the story of a Greater Boston schoolteacher who regularly won in races against the Kennedy boys with an odd-looking sailboat he had assembled himself. To say that Father Joe was infuriated is putting it mildly. He bought new equipment for the boys and gave them pep talk after pep talk. Nevertheless, the lowly teacher continued to win. When the boys finally managed to beat him, Joseph P. Kennedy was once again a happy man.

About this time, Joe Kennedy hired a tall, thin, native Cape Codder as "skipper" of the Kennedy flotilla which eventually consisted of five sailboats and a motor launch. (Later on, the family acquired the yacht *Marlin* which had been built for Edsel Ford in 1930.) According to Cape historian Leo Damore, the skipper "was used to catering to the milder whims of a seasonal gentry at Osterville, which attracted a more staid, genteel breed of summer aristocracy. In comparison the Kennedys seemed 'raw and crude.' The relationship was to last—with one long interruption during the years of Joseph P. Kennedy's ambassadorship—a total of three stormy years, providing the most direct confrontation between the Kennedys and a Cape Codder determined 'not to let them get away with anything.' Neither enjoyed it very much."

First, there was the secondhand power boat which Joe Kennedy had turned over to the new skipper, claiming it had had a complete overhaul and was in perfect working order. The skipper took one look and disagreed. He pointed out that the engine's screws had rusted over, which meant that the boat had not been touched in years. When the vessel was finally put in the water, it promptly began to sink. But as Damore noted, "Kennedy—who had already earned a local reputation as 'opinionated,' 'hard as nails' and 'an impossible man to work for'—refused to admit that he had made a bad bargain." Insisting that the boat could still be made seaworthy, Kennedy ordered it refloated and towed to a nearby repair yard. Much to his mortification, it sank at the entrance to the boatyard.

Another of the skipper's tasks was to be "boss of the kids." Years later he told Damore that he regarded Joe Jr. as "the only one in that bunch you could talk to." He was aghast at the conduct of the young ladies "brought down from Boston to share uproarious sails aboard the Kennedy fleet of boats. Nor did he approve of the children's habit of stepping from their boats and flinging articles of clothing as they progressed down the pier, in the expectation that someone else would pick up after them."

According to Damore, some Cape Codders could not respect the Kennedys because they "never said thank-you" and looked upon an employee as "just a machine to work." The locals also complained of the low wages the Kennedys paid and of "always having to ask for my money."

One Hyannis seamstress refused to hand over a sail she had spent hours repairing unless she was paid on the spot. "That'll be seven dollars," she told the Kennedy chauffeur when he arrived to pick up the sail. He said he had not brought any money. "No money," the seamstress replied, "no sail."

The chauffeur was furious. He argued that the race was about to begin. But the seamstress refused to be budged and finally the chauffeur rushed home to get the seven dollars. "But," says the seamstress, "it was the last sail that was ever brought to me again."

Bobby did not take to sailing the way his older brothers did. Even during the early days of World War II, when competition was slight, Bobby did poorly in regattas. Skippering Jack's boat *Victura* in 1942, Bobby placed thirteenth out of the fifteen boats racing.

Carrying out his father's injunction to "win, win, win" was not always easy for Bobby. Eight years younger than Jack, he was the smallest of the Kennedys. He had the poorest physical coordination and the least interest in intellectual pursuits. In order to be included, he was always scrambling to catch up.

Agreeing with this evaluation is K. LeMoyne Billings, who has been a friend of the Kennedy family ever since he roomed with Jack at Choate in the mid-thirties. Billings, currently an advertising executive in New York, said in 1961, "Teddy and Jack are much more alike in their natural attributes. Jack always has been a good public speaker. The same is true for Teddy. Both are very natural and easy in their dealings with other people. But for Bobby speaking and dealing with people have been difficult. Everything has come much harder for Bobby. He has to work harder."

4

Childhood

"The first time I remember meeting Bobby," John F. Kennedy once said in all seriousness, "was when he was three and a half, one summer at the Cape."

In the long shadows cast by his glamorous, extroverted older brothers and sisters, Bobby was all but overwhelmed. He always had to try harder. "I was the seventh of nine children," he once explained. "And when you come from that far down, you have to struggle to survive."

"He was the little brother, the one who got beaten up by his big brothers," a family friend recalled recently. "It's on his mind and he often says now that he's going to bring up his children differently. When he was little, it was always 'Robert, go fetch the ice cream.' And he was always fighting with Jack over the radio—the Senator liked jazz . . . and Jack didn't."

"He's feisty and strong-tempered," still another family confidante has observed. "But remember he was the runt of a pretty competitive family. It's a matter of a couple of inches of tibia."

Jack Kennedy was about twelve years of age when he first recalled "meeting" Bobby at Hyannis Port. It was there that the entire family, including Father Joe, would generally get together for long summer vacations. At Palm Beach the family would assemble for abbreviated winter vacations, usually around Christmas-New Year's time. But whether at Palm Beach or Hyannis Port, there was always the incessant clatter of the ticker tape on the veranda. With several telephones at hand, Father Joe rarely allowed family affairs to interfere with business.

Even in later years Joe Kennedy found it necessary to do considerable traveling. But on the major holidays there would be family gatherings at both Hyannis Port and Palm Beach.

Since her husband's incapacitation by a stroke in December 1961, it has been Rose who has done most of the traveling. Still slim and beautiful despite her age, Mrs. Kennedy spends considerable time in Paris and New York, going to all the better parties. She was one of the more animated guests at Truman Capote's much-celebrated 1966 masked ball at the Plaza.

All through a lifetime crowded with unusual experiences, some bitter, Rose Kennedy has managed to find comfort in her deeply felt religion. A daily communicant at St. Francis Xavier in Hyannis, she rarely missed early Mass. Sundays without fail the entire family went to church.

"I wanted them to form a habit of making God and religion a part of their daily lives, not something to be reserved for Sunday," she has said.

As far as Bobby was concerned, Rose feels she has been eminently successful. "Bobby was always very devout," she once said, "probably the most devout of all the children." Never was he known to question any of the tenets of his faith. With him there were none of the doubts that occasionally assailed John F. Kennedy.

His mother had even hoped that Bobby might decide to become a priest. And for a time, as a youth, he did give it serious consideration. And Bobby has remained as devout as ever. In later years, he has frequently filled in as altar boy —serving without ritual error—whenever the priest was short of acolytes.

With Bobby lost to the priesthood, Mrs. Kennedy then hoped that her youngest, Teddy, might get the call. But it was not to be. Many years later, Rose showed an audience a photograph of the entire Kennedy ménage visiting the Vatican in the late thirties. "With all these spiritual advantages," she said, "I had hoped that Teddy would grow up to be a priest—but he met a beautiful blonde one night."

Robert Kennedy was never much of a student. He attended a Bronxville nursery school, a private school for the first and second grades, and a Bronxville public school for the next three. According to his wife Ethel, Bobby flunked third grade and was forced to repeat it. The school administrator at the time, Julia Markham, remembers Bobby as a "nice little freckle-faced kid, his hair some shade of brown, a regular boy. He needed no special handling. . . . It seemed hard for him to finish his work sometimes. But he was only ten after all. . . ." His mother later recalled that Bobby was an "average student."

"He didn't read very much when he was young," she added. "He was one of the ones I had to keep urging to read."

The Kennedys kept largely to themselves. They played no major role in community affairs. Bronxville, at the time, was not known for an excessive tolerance of the *nouveaux riches* and many of the neighbors tended to frown on the senior Kennedy's notoriety as "the wolf of Wall Street." Perhaps this was the reason that little Bobby was rarely asked to parties at the homes of other rich Bronxville kids.

Because he received only a modest allowance, young Bobby decided to supplement his income by selling *The Saturday Evening Post* and the *Ladies' Home Journal* to his Bronxville neighbors. Soon he lost his enthusiasm. He took to covering his route with magazines stacked in the back seat of his family's chauffeur-driven Rolls-Royce. Finally, the entire venture floundered.

As a youngster, Bobby indicated no aptitude for any particular career. A Cub Scout, he showed a love of the outdoors. All he was interested in was athletics and animals. In fact, he had a beloved pet pig—Porky—which followed him wherever he went. And he raised rabbits to sell—"just plain white rabbits, the kind that have a lot of babies."

It was Bobby who taught his younger brother, Teddy, to ride a bicycle. "I was put on the two-wheeler and pushed down the hill between a set of trees," Ted Kennedy later recalled. "Inevitably I crashed at the bottom." Another recollection of the Massachusetts Senator is of Bobby and the chauffeur's son making parachutes out of sheets in order to jump off the roof of the Bronxville house. "The chauffeur's son broke a leg. Bob never jumped."

Otherwise, Bobby was like any other little rich kid who never had to worry about creature comforts. As his mother put it, "There was never much trouble with Bobby, less than with any of the other children. His health was always good and he always seemed well adapted to whatever situation he was in." When he was ten, however, he did have a brief bout with pneumonia which irritated him profoundly because it came at the height of the summer swimming and boating season at Hyannis Port. He was rushed to a Boston hospital.

Bobby's thirteen-year-old sister Patricia had just undergone an appendectomy at the same hospital. One of her nurses was a young lady named Luella R. Hennessey, who recalled that the children were on different floors, each with around-the-clock "specials," a total of six nurses between them.

"As they got better," Miss Hennessey later wrote, "they did a great deal of telephoning to one another. These conversations usually started when I was out of Pat's room for a tray of medication. They ended in the middle or changed to whispers and giggles as soon as I opened the door. Pat kept suggesting that I go to Bobby's room about something or other, and Bobby constantly sent his nurses to see her. The two of them, it turned out, were making up their minds which of us they wanted to take home to Hyannis Port. Finally, they chose me . . . out of the six."

After that, Miss Hennessey traveled with the family and took care of many of the Kennedy grandchildren.

"Bobby was always very cooperative," his mother also recalls. "I can't think of even a small crisis when we couldn't convince him what was right. There was never any problem on where he was going to school, for example." There had been a problem with Jack, who had wanted to go to Princeton instead of Harvard, despite his father's wishes. Probably he wanted to get away from the shadow of his older brother, Joe, who was already at Harvard.

Nor did his mother ever recall Bobby in any open disagreement with his father, although she noted that young Joe and Jack would "sometimes take sides against their father."

In her syndicated memoirs, Rose Kennedy contends that her husband never sought to force his views on any of his sons. "I recall an incident involving Joe Jr. that illustrates this, and makes a point that I have always thought interesting. When Joe Jr. returned from his visit to Russia, he talked much to his father and all of us about his trip. He said he thought there might be some merit in the Soviet ideology. His father staunchly defended the capitalistic system.

"Jack, who was two years younger than Joe, listened intently," Mrs. Kennedy continues. "He came to me one day and said he thought that Joe Jr. 'understood the situation better than Dad.'

"I told Mr. Kennedy about this, half jokingly, and he replied, 'I don't care what they think about my opinions. I can get along. As long as they stick together, they will be all right.' He considered it a great asset for brothers to remain united."

Actually, the discussions at the dinner table were not so sanguine as Rose makes out. As Jack Kennedy later recalled, both his father and older brother were hot-tempered and their debates occasionally grew heated. During one exchange, Joe Jr. angrily left the room. On another occasion, Joe Sr. stalked away.

Old Joe, of course, had been an original New Dealer. He was the first Wall Streeter of any consequence to hop aboard Franklin D. Roosevelt's bandwagon. He felt that Roosevelt had the strength to lead the nation out of the doldrums of the Depression. He was worried that the economic crisis would generate pressures which could easily explode into violent revolution. And that would mean the end of the Kennedy fortune.

Kennedy contributed $25,000 to the Roosevelt campaign, lent another $50,000 and raised an additional $100,000 among his moneyed friends. At the deadlocked 1932 Democratic National Convention, he urged his reluctant friend William Randolph Hearst to support FDR on the fourth ballot, thus clinching the nomination for the squire from Hyde Park.

But there was no immediate payoff. FDR, in choosing his Cabinet members, ignored Kennedy. Old Joe's disappointment turned to deep indignation. He was at his foulmouthed best in castigating anyone for a lack of gratitude.

In February 1933, Raymond Moley, one of Roosevelt's closest advisers and a leading brain truster, spent several days at Kennedy's home in Palm Beach. "There I heard

plenty of Kennedy's excoriation of Roosevelt, of his criticisms of the President-elect, who, according to Kennedy,
had no program—and what ideas he had were unworthy of
note. There must have been hundreds of dollars in telephone
calls to provide an exchange of abuse of Roosevelt between
Kennedy and W. R. Hearst. The latter by this time was
wondering why he had ever supported Roosevelt in the final
hours before the nomination.

"There was little I could do in 1933 either to pacify
Kennedy or to move Roosevelt to offer some substantial
recognition of his obligation," Moley continued. "But while
I never developed a real affection for Kennedy, I sympathized with his disappointment. Our friendship reached
a point when during the Hundred Days Kennedy invited
me for lunch in New York. . . . After a few preliminaries,
Kennedy came down to the business he had in mind. He
said that my status in Washington required a certain
standard of living that my limited private means could not
sustain. Therefore, how would it be if he solicited some
of his friends to contribute to a fund to provide me with
the means to live as I should?"

Moley told Kennedy that though he appreciated his interest, he was earning more than enough. His refusal of
help, he wrote later, "in no way impaired our relationship
and the matter was not mentioned again, although I saw
Kennedy often in the years that followed."

It was Moley who eventually convinced FDR to name
Kennedy the chairman of the newly organized Securities
and Exchange Commission, the SEC, an appointment that
was greeted with incredulity by the liberal community.

But Kennedy did a superb job in launching the regulatory
agency. After returning to private life, he formed a businessmen's organization to support FDR for a second term in
1936. And in his book, *I'm for Roosevelt,* written with the
assistance of Arthur Krock of *The New York Times,* he
castigated "irresponsible wealth" for its "unreasoning" opposition to the New Deal's social reforms.

Many of Kennedy's neighbors at Hyannis Port were infuriated by the book when it was published in August of
that election year. "My father hit the ceiling," a former
resident recalls. "He'd built his own company himself and
earned every dollar honestly. He felt that the stock-market

speculators—'the get-rich-quick boys,' he used to call them —who had managed the stock pools and driven up prices, then deserted the market to make millions had been responsible for the crash in the first place. Now, one of them had written a book about how wonderful everything was going to be if government regulated business."

Old Joe couldn't have cared less. What he wanted, he wrote Roosevelt, was a handwritten note from the President acknowledging receipt of the book. He wanted the note for the sake of his children. Several months later, after several reminders, FDR sent such a letter. "Dear Joe," it began. *"I'm for Kennedy!* The book is grand. I am delighted with it. . . ." Kennedy framed the note and hung it in his Hyannis Port living room for all to see.

It was important to Joe Kennedy that his children meet the high and mighty of the world, and he went out of his way to arrange such meetings. "Bobby was only five or six when his father became interested in Mr. Roosevelt's political campaign and from that time on he met most of the major figures of the Roosevelt Administration," Rose Kennedy has recalled. Later on, when her husband was Ambassador in England, Bobby "met Churchill and Eden and lived in the Embassy where he was constantly in contact with politics."

And when he was not yet ten, Bobby received the following letter in Hyannis Port:

DEAR BOB:—

Your Dad has told me that you are a stamp collector and I thought you might like to have these stamps to add to your collection. I am also enclosing a little album which you may find useful.

Perhaps sometime when you are in Washington you will come in and let me show you my collection.

My best wishes to you.

The letter was signed Franklin D. Roosevelt.

It hangs today just inside the front door of Bobby's home in McLean, Virginia.

Mrs. Kennedy also believes that her children's interest in politics was whetted by regular family discussions. "There was a constant review of events," she recalls, "whatever was pertinent at the time. I kept a chart and bulletin board where clippings for discussions were posted." The discussions usually occurred at family dinners and "because in large families the older ones hold forth, we divided the children into two groups, so the younger children moved up." Bobby, she said, always took an active role.

But these famous family conversations (in later days pictured as almost a junior Algonquin round table) were primarily concerned with the personalities and techniques of politics, rather than with substantive issues.

In 1937, Joe Kennedy was appointed Ambassador to the Court of St. James's. Most Britons were delighted and amused by the improper Bostonian, his lovely wife, and their many children. (The two older boys, Joe and Jack, attending Harvard, were to join the family that summer.) "His bouncing offspring make the most politically ingratiating family since Theodore Roosevelt's" commented *Life* magazine. "Whether or not Franklin Roosevelt thought of it beforehand, it has turned out that when he appointed Mr. Kennedy to be Ambassador to Great Britain he got eleven Ambassadors for the price of one."

Back home, the Kennedys had become celebrities. They were even being satirized in a Broadway musical. Jack, writing from Harvard, informed his parents that he had just seen Victor Moore and Sophie Tucker in *Leave It to Me* and "the jokes about us got by far the biggest laughs whatever that signifies."

Bobby, then twelve, and Teddy, six, were enrolled in the Gibbs School, an exclusive London day school. The girls—Eunice, Pat and Jean—were transferred from the Sacred Heart Convent School in Noroton, Connecticut, to the Sacred Heart Convent School in Roehampton, England. Rosemary, whom her mother wanted to keep a close eye on, was enrolled at the nearby Visitation Convent.

Kathleen, having finished school, soon made her debut at a dinner and reception at the Embassy. She was a poised young lady of eighteen, and her main job now was to assist her mother as hostess at the Embassy. "Kick," as she was nicknamed, became one of the most popular girls in London society. "Every time you turned around," Luella Hennessey was to recall years later, "there was an Honorable Such-and-such or Lord Something who had come to see her. Even then, I thought the one she liked the most was the Marquess of Hartington, son and heir of the Duke of Devonshire.

"In the afternoons," Miss Hennessey continues: "when Bobby and Teddy came home from school, Betty Dunn and I sometimes took them for walks. We always followed the custom that their mother had initiated when the children were toddlers, that of stopping in church to say a few prayers. Mrs. Kennedy believed it was a good way of impressing upon young minds the fact that God isn't only for Sundays."

Bobby and Teddy, as well as the other children, attended most of the Embassy receptions. This was part of the Ambassador's desire that they meet "high-class" people. Bobby and Teddy also occasionally attended parties at Buckingham Palace for Princesses Elizabeth and Margaret Rose.

The children's doings were grist for the mills of gossip-hungry London newspapers. The press couldn't carry enough of their bright sayings. The *Daily Mail* reported that, on hearing his father addressed as "Your Excellency," little Teddy had asked, "Is that your new name, Daddy?" and the *Evening News* published a cartoon showing a motor bus outside the United States Embassy with the caption: MR. KENNEDY TAKES HIS FAMILY TO THE THEATER.

The palatial, thirty-six-room Embassy at No. 14 Prince's Gate in Grosvenor Square had been a gift to the American people from J. P. Morgan. Elaborately furnished in the period of Louis XVI, it had a household staff of twenty-three, plus three chauffeurs. A long marble terrace, running the length of a large formal garden in the rear, was used by the children for bicycling, thus solving in part the exercise problem. The Ambassador also purchased seven horses so the family could ride together.

"Obviously," Rose Kennedy recalled years later, "we had a superior entry to nearly everything. If we went to the races we watched from the owners' boxes. We all had tea with the Queen. The children got a great deal out of it."

During their stay in England, most weekends were spent at Ascot, where the Ambassador had rented a house. The family went to St. Moritz during the winter holidays, and the children concentrated on improving their skating and skiing. "I remember Bobby was so pleased when he won one of the races in St. Moritz, while we were there in

1939," his mother recalls. Summers were spent on the
Riviera, in a villa high in the hills back of Cannes with a
breathtaking panoramic view of the blue Mediterranean.

With the exception of young Joe, the entire family went
to Rome in March 1939 to attend the crowning of the new
Pope. President Roosevelt had asked Ambassador Kennedy
to attend. It was a signal honor, indeed. It was the first
time the United States had ever been represented. And
what made it all the more enjoyable was that the Kennedys
were acquainted with the new Pope, Pius XII, who as Cardinal Pacelli had once visited their Bronxville home. The
Pope recalled this at the private audience he granted the
family.

In short, it was a heady, opulent life for the Kennedys.
As Ambassador Kennedy remarked to his wife when they
dressed to dine at Buckingham Palace with King George and
Queen Elizabeth, "It's been quite a journey from East Boston, hasn't it, Rose?"

5

War

Hardly had he arrived in London, as his nation's most important diplomat abroad, before Joseph P. Kennedy began to voice views on international affairs that would haunt his sons—and even threaten their political ambitions—in years to come. As recently as December 4, 1967, President Johnson—angered by Robert Kennedy's continuing criticism of his Vietnam policy—ad-libbed a comparison between those who sought a fast and simple way out of the Vietnam War and those who had refused to believe that Fascism represented any menace in the thirties.

"They are looking for the fire escape and the easy way out," the President said, "and they were doing that in the time of Mussolini and Hitler."

Once before, Lyndon Johnson had used Joe Kennedy's views to get at one of his sons. In a last-ditch effort to pull delegates off John F. Kennedy's bandwagon at the 1960 Democratic National Convention, the then Senate Majority Leader had told various delegates, "I never thought Hitler was right. I was never any Chamberlain umbrella-policy man."

The fact was that in 1938 the newly arrived Ambassador had, indeed, established quick rapport with Prime Minister Neville Chamberlain, the former Birmingham hardware manufacturer who rarely appeared without his umbrella.

The possibility that Joe Kennedy had White House ambitions had become the subject of considerable speculation in Washington. In fact, Ernest K. Lindley even wrote an article for *Liberty* entitled "Will Kennedy Run for President?" Since

Roosevelt was barred by precedent from seeking a third term, the Ambassador, according to Lindley, might emerge as a contender, doubly urged by the President and big business.

The Ambassador was actually a dedicated isolationist who sincerely believed that Nazi Germany could win any war. Also, he was troubled about what might happen to his family should America enter the conflict. He did not want any of his four sons killed in a foreign war.

War clouds, meanwhile, were gathering. Hitler's jackbooted legions, after the *Anschluss* with Austria, appeared on the verge of gobbling up Czechoslovakia. About this time, the Ambassador proposed to deliver a speech in Scotland, the draft of which stirred up a storm at the State Department. For what Kennedy proposed to say was: "I can't for the life of me understand why anybody would want to go to war to save the Czechs," and only on a direct order from FDR did he strike the extraordinary sentence from his speech.

Kennedy's free-wheeling made him few friends among his more dignified colleagues in the U.S. diplomatic corps. In his recently published *Memoirs,* George F. Kennan recalls an episode when he was Second Secretary at the Embassy in Prague in 1938:

"In those days, as the German forces advanced like encroaching waves over all the borders of Bohemia, no trains were running, no planes were flying, no frontier stations existed. Yet in the midst of this confusion we received a telegram from the Embassy in London, the sense of which was that our ambassador there, Mr. Joseph Kennedy, had chosen this time to send one of his young sons on a fact-finding tour around Europe, and it was up to us to find means of getting him across the border and through the German lines so that he could include in his itinerary a visit to Prague.

"We were furious. Joe Kennedy was not exactly known as a friend of the career service, and many of us, from what we had heard about him, cordially reciprocated this lack of enthusiasm. His son had no official status and was, in our eyes, obviously an upstart and an ignoramus. The idea that there was anything he could learn or report about conditions in Europe which we did not already know and had not already reported seemed (and not without reason) wholly absurd. That busy people should have their time taken up arranging his tour struck us as outrageous. With that polite but weary punctiliousness that characterizes diplomatic officials required to busy themselves with pesky compatriots who insist on visiting places where they have no business to be, I arranged to get him through the German lines, had him escorted to Prague, saw to it that he was shown what he wanted to see, expedited his departure, then, with a feeling of 'that's that,' washed my hands of him—as I thought.

"Had anyone said to me then that the young man in question would some day be the President of the United States and that I, in the capacity of chief of a diplomatic mission, would be his humble and admiring servant, I would have thought that either this person or I had taken leave of his senses. It was one of the great lessons of life when memory of the episode returned to me, as I sat one day in my Belgrade office, many years later, and the truth suddenly and horribly dawned. By just such blows, usually too late in life, is the ego cut down to size."

Meanwhile, the inordinate publicity the Ambassador had been getting in the American press led FDR to suspect—and with good reason—that Kennedy was feeding selected Washington correspondents news items not included in the Embassy's official reports to the State Department. The disaffection between the President and his envoy began to grow.

"The young man needs his wrists slapped rather hard," FDR told his Secretary of the Treasury, Henry Morgenthau, at one point.

On September 29, 1938, the fate of Czechoslovakia was decided at Munich. A general war appeared to have been averted. Returning home to England, the Prime Minister held high a piece of paper and told his relieved people, "I believe it is peace in our time."

Several weeks later, Ambassador Kennedy strongly defended the Munich pact at a Trafalgar Day dinner. His speech provoked a furor in both Britain and the United States. And it did little to enhance the Ambassador's standing in the eyes of the President.

In early 1939, Walter Lippmann visited Ambassador Kennedy in London. Following this not-so-historic meeting, Lippmann attended a private dinner party at which he repeated the Ambassador's remark that not only was war coming but that England would lose it.

Whiskey in one hand, cigar in the other, Winston Churchill replied eloquently, ". . . Yet supposing (as I do not for one moment suppose) that Mr. Kennedy were correct in his tragic utterance, then I for one would willingly lay down my life in combat, rather than, in fear of defeat, surrender to the menaces of these most sinister men. It will then be for you, for the Americans, to preserve and to maintain the great heritage of the English-speaking peoples. It will be for you to think imperially, which means to think always of something higher and more vast than one's own national interests. . . ."

Finally and inevitably came the war Kennedy feared with all his heart. On September 1, 1939, Hitler's armies moved into Poland. On the morning of September 3, Chamberlain showed Kennedy the speech he would deliver in a few hours declaring war against Germany. Kennedy wept as he read, "Everything that I have worked for, everything that I have hoped for, everything that I have believed in during my public life has crashed in ruins."

After notifying the State Department, Kennedy telephoned the White House. "It's the end of the world," he told Roosevelt over and over. The President attempted to soothe him, but Kennedy kept repeating, "It's the end of everything."

There was to be no sleep for the next few days. The Canadian-bound British liner *Athenia* was torpedoed in the Atlantic by a German submarine, and the Ambassador sent his twenty-two-year-old son Jack to Glasgow to interview the surviving Americans. Shortly after this he and Rose decided that the family should return home to Bronxville.

The younger children entered American schools, with Bobby going to St. Paul's. After a brief stay at the Episcopal school, he was transferred to Portsmouth Priory, a Catholic prep school in Rhode Island.

According to Randolph S. Churchill: "Kennedy not only spread defeatism and despondency in London and Washington as to Britain's capacity to defend herself; he was also indiscreet enough in private gatherings to speak loudly—and often in vitriolic terms—about the President's policy. The British, who knew by this time that Kennedy was no friend of theirs, naturally took steps to see that this information was not withheld from Roosevelt."

About this time, Jack Kennedy published his first book. He had spent part of his junior year in Europe, occasionally working for his father at the Embassy, and had returned to Harvard imbued with his father's view of the European situation and written a senior thesis entitled "Appeasement at Munich: The Inevitable Result of the Slowness of the British Democracy to Change from a Disarmament Policy."

Arthur Krock, who helped get it published as a book, suggested the title *Why England Slept*. Another family friend, publisher Henry Luce, wrote the foreword.

Among those the Ambassador sought to impress by sending them copies were Queen Elizabeth, Winston Churchill and Harold Laski.

"The reviews have been swell," the Ambassador wrote Professor Laski, asking for a blurb.

But the Socialist scholar refused to endorse the book. He profoundly disagreed with Jack Kennedy's analysis of why England was unprepared for the war. "For while it is the book of a lad with brains," Laski wrote in reply, "it is very immature, it has no real structure, it dwells almost wholly on the surface of things. I don't honestly think any publisher would have looked at that book of Jack's if he had not been your son, and if you had not been Ambassador."

Twenty-seven years later, when the letter was published in the Washington *Post's* Sunday magazine, Laski's widow, Frida, had this to say: "In 1948 Jack met my husband, and to his credit the first thing he said was 'How right you were about my book. I do wish I had never written it.' Probably this gives a better glimpse of his character than the forgotten book."

On October 23, 1940, after thirty-three months of service, Ambassador Kennedy flew home. Supporters of Wendell Willkie, the Republican Presidential candidate, spread the story that Kennedy was returning home to bolt the Democratic ticket and publicly condemn FDR. But before the Ambassador could say anything, he was whisked off to Washington for a confidential chat with the President. What transpired between the two was never fully disclosed, but Kennedy emerged from the White House pledged to FDR's re-election.

In 1960, John F. Kennedy was asked whether it was true that FDR had gotten his father's support in 1940 by offering him the nomination in 1944. Kennedy laughed and said, "I don't know—my father certainly thought he had."

Shortly after the election, the Ambassador received three

newsmen in his suite at Boston's Ritz-Carlton. To say he was indiscreet is putting it mildly. He revealed his uncompromising isolationism; predicted that "national socialism" was coming to Great Britain; and took potshots at Winston Churchill, the King and Queen, and Eleanor Roosevelt.

Kennedy talked on and on and, as it transpired, talked himself right out of public life. The furor raised by publication of his remarks led to his immediate resignation as Ambassador. Anti-Kennedy elements on both sides of the Atlantic—and they were by now legion—were overjoyed.

In London's *News Chronicle*, A. J. Cummings wrote: "While [Kennedy] was here, his suave, monotonous style, his nine over-photographed children and his hail-fellow-well-met manner concealed a hard-boiled businessman's eagerness to do a profitable business deal with the dictators, and he deceived many decent English people."

As a political force, Joseph P. Kennedy was finished, and he knew it. Whatever hopes the Ambassador had had in politics would have to be transferred to his sons.

6

School

Robert Kennedy had a vivid memory of what he was doing on December 7, 1941, the day the Japanese attacked Pearl Harbor. Then sixteen years of age, he was lounging around the dormitory at Portsmouth Priory when he heard the news on radio. The neatly combed, fuzzy-faced Bobby immediately telephoned his father in Palm Beach. The elder Kennedy, since resigning as Ambassador, had been conducting almost a one-man keep-America-out-of-war campaign. Now that campaign was over. What he had feared most had finally come to pass.

Swallowing his pride, he immediately telegraphed President Roosevelt: IN THIS GREAT CRISIS ALL AMERICANS ARE WITH YOU. NAME THE BATTLEFRONT. I'M YOURS TO COMMAND.

There was no immediate response from the President.

Some months later word leaked out that Joe Kennedy was being considered for a major appointment in the maritime industry. The opposition from liberals was bitter. The head of the CIO's National Maritime Union, Joseph Curran, declared, "If you want to win the war you don't put in a key spot, like shipping, a man who wants to make peace with Hitler." And questions were even raised about Kennedy's courage during the Nazi air raids on London.

All through the war years, in fact, Joe Kennedy was beset by what he angrily denounced as "vicious" accusations in the public prints. He was accused of being almost everything —a Nazi sympathizer, an isolationist, a reactionary, a turncoat, a Roosevelt-hater.

With Joe Jr. and Jack away, Bobby was the only son still

around who could understand his father's ordeal. Teddy, at nine, had no comprehension of the implications of the war. As Bobby since recalled, he fully shared his father's views against intervening in foreign wars. But he added, "I don't remember that anyone asked my views."

Both of Bobby's older brothers, who pretty much shared the same isolationist sentiments, had volunteered for service prior to Pearl Harbor. Joe Jr., putting aside his chosen career, became a Navy flier, and Jack tried to join the Army, but he was rejected because of a football injury to his back. However, he finally convinced the Navy that he was still serviceable. Chafing under the boredom of shoreside assignments, Jack used his father's influence with then Undersecretary of the Navy James V. Forrestal (whom the Ambassador had known on Wall Street) to get himself transferred to PT boats. As skipper of PT-109, Jack Kennedy became one of the war's most publicized heroes. The story of how his boat was rammed and shattered by a Japanese destroyer and how he led the survivors to safety was told and retold in magazines and books and finally in a full-length Warner Brothers technicolor film production. The enormous publicity did Jack little harm in his climb up the political ladder.

Bobby's three years at the Portsmouth Priory were not marked by any outstanding scholastic achievements. The fact that he excelled in sports did not impress his father, who was becoming increasingly concerned lest low grades prevent Bobby from qualifying for college. After reading the riot act, the Ambassador had his son transferred to Milton Academy, a secular school near Boston. Naturally shy, physically slight and still no scholar, Bobby compensated by a grim determination to succeed. "It was much tougher in school for him than the others—socially, in football, with studies," a Milton classmate recalls. But he did manage to obtain grades good enough to get him admitted into Harvard.

But before his graduation, Bobby signed up as a naval officer candidate. His father watched proudly as Bobby took the oath. On November 14, 1943, from the South Pacific, Jack wrote a letter of comic congratulations:

"Dear Robert," Jack's letter read. "The folks sent me a clipping of you taking the oath. The sight of you up there, just as a boy, was really moving particularly as a close examination showed that you had my checked London coat on.

I'd like to know what the hell I'm doing out here while you go stroking around in my drape coat, but I suppose that what we are out here for, or so they tell us, is so that our sisters and younger brothers will be safe and secure—frankly, I don't see it quite that way—at least, if you're going to be safe and secure, that's fine with me, but not in my coat, brother, not in my coat. In that picture you looked as if you were going to step outside the room, grab your gun, and knock off several of the house-boys before lunch. After reading Dad's letter, I gathered that cold vicious look in your eye was due to the thought of that big blocking back from Groton. I understand that you are going to be there till Feb. 1, which is very nice because it is on the playing fields of Milton and Groton, and maybe Choate, that the seeds will be sown that in later years, and on other fields, will cause you to turn in to sick bay with a bad back or a football knee.

"Well, black Robert, give those Grotties hell and keep in contact with your old broken down brother. I just took the physical examination for promotion to full Looie. I coughed hollowly, rolled my eyes, croaked a couple of times, but all to no avail. Out here, if you can breathe, you're one A. and 'good for active duty anywhere,' and by anywhere, they don't mean El Morocco or the Bath and Tennis Club, they mean right where you are. See you soon, I hope. Jack."

One August afternoon in 1944, Joseph P. Kennedy was informed that his beloved oldest son had been reported missing in action. Joe Jr. had volunteered for a dangerous mission—to fly a "drone" plane toward a German target on the Belgian coast. He and his co-pilot were to bail out before the radio-guided plane was to reach its destination. But before they could parachute into the Channel, the plane exploded. Their bodies were never recovered.

Young Joe's last known words to anyone were exchanged with Ensign James Simpson, who was checking the PB4Y Liberator just before takeoff: "I shook hands with Joe and said, 'So long and good luck, Joe. I only wish I were going with you.' He answered, 'Thanks, Jim, don't forget, you're going to make the next one with me. Say, by the way, if I don't come back, you fellows can have the rest of my fresh eggs.' We never saw him again."

Young Joe was awarded the Navy Cross posthumously.

Joe Jr.'s heroic death convinced Bobby that he was wasting

his time. After several months of training at Bates College in Lewiston, Maine, he had wound up at Harvard in the V-12 program. The lectures bored him and he was afraid he would end up sitting out the war on some college campus. As Jack had done, he went to Washington to see James Forrestal, now Secretary of the Navy. Before long, the nineteen-year-old Bobby got his wish and was released from the officers' training program. As a seaman second class, he was assigned to the *Joseph P. Kennedy Jr.,* a sleek 2,200-ton destroyer named for his dead brother.

Bobby's naval service consisted of six dismal months in the Caribbean, mostly chipping paint as his ship cruised peacefully in the placid waters. About the only action he saw was a fistfight with a Puerto Rican—over what he does not recall—he once confided to José Torres, the Puerto Rican boxer. As a result of that encounter, Bobby still walks around with a scar on his forehead.

The fact that he had not seen combat annoyed him greatly. In mid-1946 the twenty-year-old Bobby took a trip through South America with LeMoyne Billings, who had roomed with Jack at Choate and has remained a family friend ever since. "The war was still fresh in people's minds down there," Billings recalls, "and they'd ask where we had been, what we'd done. Bobby didn't have anything to say. I used to kid him about it. He didn't think it especially funny."

Bobby had his first taste of politics in the spring of 1946. This was during the primary contest for Congress in Boston's Eleventh District, in which his brother Jack was one of nine Democratic contestants. At first, Jack was not overly interested.

"It was like being drafted," Jack later told Bob Considine. "My father wanted his eldest son in politics. 'Wanted' isn't the right word. He demanded it. You know my father."

Twenty years of age and recently out of the Navy, Bobby was assigned to manage a campaign office in East Cambridge, an industrial area in which Jack's major opponent, Mayor Mike Neville, was particularly strong. On occasion Bobby would close the office to play softball with the neighborhood kids in a park across the street. But most of the time he walked around the largely Italian neighborhood shaking hands, eating spaghetti and telling voters what a wonderful brother Jack was. And a war hero, too.

Bobby worked under the direction of Lem Billings, one of a dozen or so of Jack's friends from school or PT days who came flying into Beantown from all over the country to help "Shafty," as Jack was then known.

Masterminding the campaign from a suite in the Ritz-Carlton was Joseph P. Kennedy. In directing the publicity and advertising efforts, Old Joe played heavily on his son's war heroism. A *Reader's Digest* condensation of John Hersey's *New Yorker* article on PT-109 and its heroic commander was mailed to every voter in the district.

John F. Kennedy received almost as many votes as his eight opponents combined; the general election in the fall was a mere formality.

7

Harvard

The war, his brother's successful entry into politics and his trip to South America had not noticeably sharpened Robert F. Kennedy's scholastic aptitudes. At Harvard, which he reentered in the fall of 1946, he finally managed to scrape through to a Bachelor of Arts degree, but without demonstrating any superior talents in his chosen major—Government. In fact, he did not seem to make much of an impression on any member of the Government faculty.

"He was a fly-by-night character and didn't pay much attention to academic work," says one retired professor. "Jack, by contrast, worked hard."

"Bob was a very energetic fellow," another former Harvard official recalls, "but studies weren't his exciting point. He liked to play around rather than work. . . . Bob had his own interests at Harvard. It wasn't studying. The Kennedy tribe is quite a gang, but you always have to ask yourself how far they would have gotten without $300,000,000, or whatever it is, behind them."

It was a question that was to keep plaguing the Kennedy boys as they moved up the political ladder.

Bobby himself was the first to concede that the groves of Academe never enthralled him. Except for athletics, he showed little interest in college activities. Though he was a member of the Catholic, Spee and Hasty Pudding clubs, he much preferred the company of fun-loving athletes.

"I didn't go to class very much," he has since said. "I used to talk and argue a lot, mostly about sports and politics."

Politically, Bobby considered himself a Democrat. But

party allegiance was as much a family matter as anything else. In those days he emulated his father in despising Harry S Truman and his Fair Deal. Yet he considered Henry Wallace's Leftist challenge to Truman in 1948 "outrageous." And like his father, he could barely conceal his contempt for the late Franklin Delano Roosevelt.

Bobby claimed FDR had made "deals" in the international arena beneficial to the Soviet Union. In many ways, his thinking in those years also reflected his brother Jack's views as a young Congressman. The "Massachusetts Democrat," as Jack then preferred to be labeled, rather than "liberal" or "conservative," had also publicly denounced Roosevelt for having failed to comprehend the true nature of insidious Communism. But at this stage of Bobby's life all that really mattered was football.

He had captained the freshman football team when he was a V-12 student at Harvard. And Henry Lamar, freshman coach since 1931, remembers Bobby very well. "Bob didn't have any great God-given ability, nor great physical stature, but he had great determination," the coach recalls. "You'd have had to kill him to make him quit. He had a temper which he tried to keep under control. He had a determined and belligerent look. His attitude was always 'We'll settle this thing right now and I'm willing to go all the way to do it.' "

On his return to the campus in the fall of 1946, Bobby made the varsity squad as an end. Ken O'Donnell (who was to become President Kennedy's appointments secretary) later said that because of his small size and inexperience, Bobby had "no right to be on the varsity team" and made it strictly on guts.

Ken's brother, Cleo A. O'Donnell, who was captain of the 1946 team, recalls that Bobby didn't play much that season. But he did play briefly in the November 23rd game against Yale—The Game—and, thus, was entitled to wear the big red "H" letter on his sweater, an honor that had eluded both of his older and bigger brothers. According to Cleo, Bobby was good on defense but needed improvement as a pass receiver.

Throughout the summer of 1947, Bobby practiced on the beach. For hours on end, the O'Donnell boys would throw passes at Kennedy. "He'd catch them until our arms fell off," said Cleo. "His never did." Bobby's efforts paid off; he was in the starting lineup in the first game of the 1947 season against Western Maryland.

He played well, making one of the eight Harvard touchdowns. The following week he suffered a nasty leg injury in a scrimmage, and for weeks sat on the bench, his leg heavily taped. Then came the day of The Game against Yale and Bobby wondered whether he'd get a chance to play. On the last play of the game, with Yale leading 31 to 21, Bobby was sent in as right end.

The idea had been for Harvard to kick the ball to the left so that Kennedy would not be involved. But the ball went wobbling to Bobby's side of the field and as a Yale man grabbed it, Bobby went after the Yalie. "It was one of the high points of my life," he said later.

"Except for war," Bobby told a meeting of college coaches in Pittsburgh some years later when he was Attorney General, "there is nothing in American life—nothing—which trains a boy better for life than football."

Not even a Harvard education, apparently.

On graduating from Harvard in 1948 (he never picked up his diploma), Robert Kennedy headed for the Near East for a close-up of the Arab-Jewish war. He wrote four articles for the Boston *Post* in which he predicted that the Jews would win because they were "hardy and tough." And but for the grace of God, he might have become another Kennedy fatality. He had intended to ride in a convoy from Tel Aviv to Jerusalem but ran into a British tank captain who had known his sister Kathleen in London. The tank got through all right, but the Jewish convoy, with which he originally planned to travel, was virtually wiped out by Arab raiders.

"The loathing and hatred between Arab and Jew was an all-consuming thing," he wrote years later. "It was impossible in those days to talk to any representative on either side without becoming immediately aware that every person on both sides had been caught up in the conflict. Men had lost their reason."

Bobby's Grand Tour also included visits to Egypt, Lebanon, Turkey, Jordan, Syria, and Germany. He got into Czechoslovakia but was refused a visa to Hungary, where he was thought to be a Catholic spy assigned by Francis Cardinal Spellman to make contact with anti-Communist Cardinal Mindszenty.

Bobby had, in his own words, "led a pretty relaxed life." As he later explained, "I just didn't know anything when I got out of college. I wanted to do graduate work, but I didn't know whether to go to law school or business school. I had no attraction to business, so I entered law school."

Because of his Harvard grades, Bobby had difficulty getting into law school. Finally, he was accepted by the University of Virginia, where he gave his legal address as the Harvard Varsity Club, his home address as Hyannis Port and his father's occupation as "banker."

Bobby entered law school in September 1948. As at Harvard, he set no worlds afire. By his own later appraisal, he was "a barely average student." In 1951 he graduated 56th in a class of 125. And, as at Harvard, he did not pick up his law school diploma.

One professor, who taught him at the time, claims to "have no recollection of him in *class* at all." But he does recall Bobby from his extracurricular activities. "He was very brash —he seemed to think most people weren't worth his time. He didn't want to waste time and was thinking ahead. I don't think he had any thought of just being a lawyer."

Professor Charles Gregory, who instructed Bobby in labor law, does recall him in class. "Bob had lots on the ball, but he would never set the Thames on fire scholastically . . . but then he had lots of other activities, so it was hard to judge what he could have been like if he had given more time to work. . . . He wasn't one of the students who talked much in discussion times. You have to work harder than he did to stick your neck out. He listened. You can't talk unless you've worked."

Bobby did achieve one scholastic triumph. He wrote a thesis on the Yalta agreements, which won a place in the Law Library's treasure trove as one of the best submitted in the 1950–51 seminar. It reflects an even harsher attitude toward Franklin Roosevelt's role at Yalta than his father's.

While Bobby remained dead set against "appeasing" the Soviet Union, he put up a strong defense of his father's prewar position on Nazi Germany. "I was surprised that he defended the Munich Pact," says Law School Dean Hardy C. Dillard. "He said it gave Europe a chance to rearm. He was not at all unsympathetic to the appeasement approach."

Bobby lived in a small cottage down by the railroad tracks

which he shared with a classmate, George Tierney (who was later to marry one of Ethel's sisters). A classmate recalls, "Bobby was considered just another rich kid and nobody paid much attention to him. But he did make a name for himself when he invited Joe McCarthy down to lecture at the Forum. Bobby had a big party for him, and this outraged the campus liberals."

This was during the winter of 1950–51. Bobby did much to reinvigorate the Student Legal Forum which, because of a paucity of "name" speakers, had been in the doldrums the previous seasons. Most of the speakers he invited were friends of his father. They were of all shades of political opinion. The most controversial, needless to say, was Senator Joseph McCarthy.

McCarthy's appearance was anticlimactic. About the only excitement came when the Senator ordered Seal, the University mascot, from the auditorium, saying he would not compete with a dog for the attention of the audience. Introduced by Bobby, McCarthy was comparatively mild in his speech. He said that the United States Army was being "run by politics" and "political generals" and urged that Chinese Nationalist troops be sent from Formosa to fight the Chinese Reds in Korea. And he declined to accept a challenge that he repeat from the platform his Senate floor charge that Owen Lattimore, a former State Department consultant, was a Communist agent.

Bobby's first speaker was Thurman Arnold, the old New Dealer who had been in charge of antitrust activities for five years under Franklin Roosevelt.

Other speakers included Supreme Court Justice William O. Douglas, *New York Times* columnist Arthur Krock, RCA President Frank M. Folsom, Subversive Activities Control Board Chairman Seth W. Richardson, James M. Landis, Congressman John F. Kennedy, and Ralph Bunche.

In inviting Bunche, the first Negro to win a Nobel prize, Bobby had no idea he would cause a storm in Charlottesville. Segregationists howled about having a "nigger" invade the lily-white campus. But the school authorities finally approved Bunche's appearance and the top United Nations official was accorded a cordial welcome.

In his speech, Bunche lashed out at an isolationism which he said "has come out of hiding and has even become respectable again." Bunche named no names, but a previous speaker at the Forum had described the veto-ridden United Nations as "a hopeless instrumentality" for preserving peace. And Bunche apparently had taken umbrage.

The previous speaker had been Joseph P. Kennedy.

The elder Kennedy had called on the United States to "get out" of Korea. Not only that; he had advocated that the U.S. remove its presence from Europe itself, even if it meant that Communist hordes would overrun Europe. He was willing to give up Berlin immediately. "Today," he went on, "it is idle talk of being able to hold the line at the Elbe or the line at the Rhine. Is it not best to get out now? The truth is that our only real hope is to keep Russia, if she chooses to march, on the other side of the Atlantic. It may be that Europe for a decade or a generation or more will turn communistic."

Conceding that his views probably would be labeled "appeasement," he insisted "that the word would be used mistakenly." And he asked, "Is it appeasement to withdraw from unwise commitments to arm yourself to the teeth and to make clear just exactly how and from where you will fight? If it is wise in our interest not to make commitments that endanger our security, and this is appeasement, then I am for appeasement."

It was obvious that Old Joe had learned little from the lessons of World War II.

In 1951, Bobby made a round-the-world tour with his brother Jack and his sister Pat. It was an exhausting trip, one that included "study stops" in the Middle East, Pakistan, India, Indochina, Malaya and Korea. The young Congressman interviewed numerous world leaders including General Dwight D. Eisenhower at SHAPE headquarters near Paris; India's Prime Minister Nehru; Pakistan Prime Minister Liaquat Ali Khan and Israeli Prime Minister Ben Gurion. It was Bobby's job to photograph his brother in deep conversation with all these celebrities. The pictures, which were to be used in Jack's forthcoming campaign, turned out well. Bobby had become an able photographer.

But the trip nearly ended in tragedy in the Far East. Jack, who had undergone a spinal operation that had failed to heal properly, suddenly took so ill that he was flown to a United States military hospital on Okinawa with a temperature above 106 degrees.

"They didn't think he would live," Bobby recalled later.

By this time, Bobby was a married man. During his last two years at Harvard and his first two at Virginia, he dated Ethel Skakel, the sixth of seven children of George Skakel, a self-made millionaire. The Skakel family was very conservative and Roman Catholic and Ethel had attended the very best parochial schools. Both of Ethel's spirited parents died in a private plane crash in 1955, leaving George Skakel, Jr., in charge of the huge family enterprise.

George Skakel, Jr., died in September 1966 in a private plane crash in Idaho.

Ethel's fate was entwined with the Kennedys even before she met Bobby. At Manhattanville College of the Sacred Heart in Purchase, New York, she was the roommate of his younger sister, Jean (who later married Stephen Smith), who was confident that Ethel would be "crazy about my brother Bob." Ethel first met Bobby in 1944 during a skiing vacation at Mont Tremblant in Canada. She was seventeen and Bobby was two years older. "I thought he was divine," she says. The only trouble was that Bobby appeared to be smitten with her older sister Pat, until two years later when she married Irish architect Luan Peter Guffe.

During a vacation from school in 1946, Ethel hit the campaign trail for Jack Kennedy in Boston to help the Kennedy women win votes for their brother. It was her first taste of politics and she loved it. Several years later, Ethel wrote her senior English thesis on Jack's book *Why England Slept*, and received an A. Eventually, she won Bobby, too.

On Saturday, June 17, 1950, the two were married—as *The New York Times* reported the next day—"in a garden setting of white peonies, lilies and dogwood in St. Mary's Roman Catholic Church" at Ethel's home in Greenwich, Connecticut. Congressman John F. Kennedy—still unmarried—was best man. Among the ushers and guests were fifteen members of the Harvard football team on which Bobby had played.

Following the honeymoon in Hawaii, the newlyweds rented a three-bedroom cottage near the law school campus, where they entertained a good deal, usually on weekends. By now, Ethel had been around the Kennedys long enough to know she faced a strenuous life. But she enjoyed every moment of it. It was more than a compliment when the elder Kennedy said that while Ethel may not have been born a Kennedy she certainly "acts like a Kennedy." With her exuberance, competitiveness and love of sports—she even played hockey—the new Mrs. Kennedy quickly fitted the mold for "vigah" on the distaff side of the Clan.

Ethel's impulses are all positive and partisan. She is defensive about any criticism leveled toward the Kennedys. She is more of a "Kennedy"—if that is possible—than the Kennedys themselves. To her the world is made up of "goodies" and "baddies." In her view, that means people who are either for the Kennedys or against them. (People like the writer of this book are among the "real bad baddies," according to Ethel.)

Ethel Kennedy has been described as an authentic American primitive—artless, informal, happy and spontaneous. She has a wary, quick wit and flings about such words as "terrific," "marvelous" and "fantastic." She is completely uninhibited. Once, at Hyannis Port, while welcoming a younger member of European royalty, she sprayed his shirtfront with a can of pressurized shaving cream.

And at the dinner party in honor of the Dowager Duchess of Devonshire in the tiny dining room at Hickory Hill which could hardly contain the thirty guests, Ethel bowed her head to say grace and startled her guests by concluding: "And please, dear God, make Bobby buy me a bigger dining-room table."

Those were the good old days of the New Frontier when such luminaries as Pierre Salinger and Arthur Schlesinger, Jr., found themselves pushed, fully clothed, into the Kennedy swimming pool. His dignity seemingly undisturbed, Pierre came up wringing wet, but with his thick cigar still clenched between his teeth. Cracked Barry Goldwater, "When Bobby sends out invitations to a formal party, they read 'black tie and snorkel.' "

But Ethel doesn't like to discuss these highly publicized moments of New Frontier existence. "The only thing I can say," she has stated, "is that it is probably a mistake having the dance floor right next to the pool. It's awfully unfortunate because I think it probably hurt Bobby."

Like her mother-in-law, Ethel is deeply religious. During the 1960 campaign, she would get out of bed at 6:30 A.M. to attend Mass before starting the day's schedule. She is concerned that her children have a strict Roman Catholic up-

bringing. As of mid-1968, Ethel and Bobby have produced ten
children, most of whom bear names reflecting family mem-
ories or a fondness for friends. They include: Kathleen
Hartington (born July 4, 1951); Joseph Patrick III (Septem-
ber 24, 1952); Robert Francis, Jr. (January 17, 1954); David
Anthony (June 15, 1955); Mary Courtney (September 9,
1956); Michael LeMoyne (February 27, 1958); Mary Kerry
(September 8, 1959); Christopher George (July 4, 1963);
Matthew Maxwell Taylor (January 11, 1965); and Douglas
Harriman (March 24, 1967).

The size of her family—and when it will stop increasing
nobody really knows—delights Ethel. "I was one of seven
myself," she has said, "and I think a big family is good for
children. They have to learn to get along together. In the
family tradition, they also have learned that they are Kennedys. Bobby is determined to instill in the children the competitive spirit handed down by his father." A newspaperman,
watching him push his children on a swing, heard Bobby
exclaim, "Come on, let's swing higher and see if we can't set
a new record. A Kennedy shouldn't be scared."

Ethel's own competitiveness was once demonstrated when
her oldest daughter, Kathleen, asked her mother, "Which is
it better to be, on the offensive or the defensive team?"

"Well," her mother replied, "both are good, but Mommy
likes offense best. That way you can make touchdowns."

The children, who obviously have inherited their parents'
vitality, are also keenly aware of their political role. It is said
that while at the ski resort at Aspen, Colorado, the oldest
child, Kathleen, implored her brother Joey, who was cutting
up, to "remember your age, manners and Boston accent."

When this failed, she invoked the ultimate reprimand.
"Joe," she commanded, "do be quiet! You are losing votes
like this!"

8

Lodge

Such are the ironies of American politics that had it not been for the late Senator Joseph McCarthy's friendship with the Kennedy family, John F. Kennedy might never have become President of the United States. For, by refusing to go to Boston to campaign in behalf of Jack's Republican opponent, Henry Cabot Lodge, Jr., in the 1952 senatorial race, Joe McCarthy all but assured a Senate seat for John Fitzgerald Kennedy. If Kennedy hadn't won in 1952, he wouldn't have become President in 1960.

Senator McCarthy disclosed his decision not to campaign for his Republican Senate colleague while dining at the home of William F. Buckley, Jr., in the fall of 1952. "The phone rang for McCarthy," Buckley recalled ten years later, "and when he came back to the dining room he told us glumly that he had just been confronted with a dilemma. The caller was a member of Lodge's campaign staff, with a request to McCarthy that he go to Boston and make a speech in behalf of Lodge's re-election. McCarthy felt that as a dutiful Republican he had a formal obligation to go.

"On the other hand, he explained, Lodge had always opposed him in the Senate, most noticeably during the period of the Tydings investigation. By contrast, Jack Kennedy had always been friendly to him, and he counted him as a covert supporter—and Mr. Joe Kennedy, he said, had contributed money to McCarthy's anti-Communist campaign. . . .

"Suddenly he shot up, went to the phone, came back with an expression of overwhelming self-pleasure. 'I cracked that one,' he said impishly. 'I told them I'd go up to Boston to speak if Cabot publicly asked me to. And he'll never do that —he'd lose the Harvard vote.' "

McCarthy's prediction was correct. Lodge never asked for his help. And McCarthy stayed out of Boston. As it turned out, Jack Kennedy beat Lodge by some 70,000 votes, a slim majority which McCarthy most surely could have offset had he campaigned for Lodge. The Wisconsinite was the number-one hero of practically all of the Boston Irish, most of whom unequivocally supported his anti-Communist crusade. "Which makes McCarthy a dynasty-maker, doesn't it?" commented Bill Buckley. "His enemies must remember to add that to the list of his sins."

So certain was Senator Lodge of being reelected that he didn't bother to campaign until very late in the game. He had devoted most of his time to assuring Dwight D. Eisenhower the Republican nomination for President.

Joe Kennedy never had any doubts that his son would win. In fact, it was Old Joe who advised Jack to take on Lodge. "When you've beaten him, you've beaten the best," he told Jack. "Why try for something less?" He based this advice on the best intelligence money could buy. For a year and a half he had been receiving in-depth reports from a pair of well-paid advance workers who had toured the state, taking soundings and romancing local politicians. "You wonder why we're taking on Lodge," Old Joe told a friend. "We've taken polls. He'll be easier to beat than Leverett Saltonstall."

Normally, a veteran of Massachusetts politics would have been named as Jack's campaign manager. But, since Kennedys trust only other Kennedys, Bobby—on his father's instructions—was brought in ostensibly to run the campaign. After his graduation from law school in 1951, Bobby had been interviewed by several prestigious law firms in New York, but had shown little interest. Instead, with the help of Joe McCarthy, he had obtained a $4,200-a-year job as a Justice Department attorney in the division dealing with internal security. Transferred to Brooklyn, he was assigned to a special Federal grand jury investigating tax frauds, corruption and bribery.

Then twenty-six years of age, Bobby bade farewell to friends and colleagues at the Brooklyn Federal Building and told a reporter for *The New York Times,* "I hate to leave such an interesting assignment as I have had in Brooklyn for the last three months. But I think I owe it to my brother Jack to return to Massachusetts and do my part before the Democratic primary in September. Of course, I think Jack is going to be the Democratic nominee and the new United States Senator from Massachusetts."

As sister Eunice has since said, "All this business about Jack and Bobby being blood brothers has been exaggerated. First there was a big difference in years. They had different tastes in men, different tastes in women. They didn't become really close until 1952, and it was politics that brought them together. That's a business full of knives. Jack needed someone he could trust, someone who had loyalty to him. Jack knew he had a person like that with Bobby around."

In announcing Bobby's appointment as campaign manager, Jack Kennedy noted his brother's tender years and said wryly, "If I need somebody older there's no need to go outside the family. I can always get my father." The Ambassador would probably have been delighted; but as one of the most controversial men in the nation, he knew he would be too great a liability. Instead, he decided to remain in the background, using Bobby as a beard.

Bobby's arrival as campaign manager was not exactly greeted with joy at Kennedy headquarters. "When Bobby came in," one insider recalls, "we knew it was the old man taking over. What had Bobby done up to that time politically? Nothing. Not a damn thing. And all of a sudden he was there as campaign manager, waving the banners."

It soon was made painfully obvious that Bobby knew very little about Boston. A celebrated local politician paid a visit to the newly opened Kennedy headquarters and was amazed to discover that no one, not even the candidate's manager, knew who he was. "You're asking me who I am?" the pol shouted. "You mean to say nobody here knows me? And you call *this* a political headquarters?"

As the politician continued to be abusive, Bobby angrily told him to get the hell out.

Another day a group of Boston pols walked into headquarters to offer their services, and Bobby said sure, suggesting that they could stuff envelopes with campaign literature. Looking askance at each other, they turned and walked out, never to return.

Governor Paul Dever, running for re-election, sought to link his campaign with John F. Kennedy's for a united Democratic assault on the Republicans. But the Kennedys believed in playing an independent game. They wanted no part of Dever. So Bobby was dispatched to Dever's office to tell him so. From all accounts, he was "snotty" about it. The Governor cut him short and angrily showed him to the door, then telephoned the Ambassador: "I know you're an important man around here and all that, but I'm telling you this and I mean it. Keep that fresh kid of yours out of sight from here on in."

Jack Kennedy, who tried to soothe such ruffled feelings, later observed, "Every politician was mad at Bobby after 1952, but we had the best organization in history. And what friend who was really worthwhile has he lost? I can't recall."

Bobby's attitude was this: "It doesn't matter if they like me or not. Jack can be nice to them. I don't try to antagonize people. But if they aren't getting off their rear ends, how do you say that nicely?"

Everyone of consequence connected with the campaign knew, of course, that the man to see with any problem was none other than Joseph P. Kennedy, comfortably ensconced as usual in a suite at the Ritz-Carlton Hotel beside a battery of telephones. And wherever there was Old Joe, there was money.

"Cabot was simply overwhelmed by money," Dwight D. Eisenhower has since said. "There was simply too much money spent."

Statements such as these irritated the Kennedys.

"We had thousands of workers around the state," Bobby says, "and I don't think there were more than six paid employees in the entire campaign. I mean that. The other campaigns—the Dever campaign, for example—had many more paid employees."

It was obvious that Bobby had little idea of what was going on behind the scenes.

Old Joe had hired the best talents money could buy. Among them were James Landis, the former Harvard Law dean; Ralph Coghlan, former editorial writer of the St. Louis *Post-Dispatch;* John Harriman, financial writer for the Boston *Globe;* and a youthful Sargent Shriver, who had once worked for *Newsweek* but in 1952 was one of the top executives of the Kennedy-owned Merchandise Mart in Chicago. (The following year "Sarge" was to marry Eunice Kennedy.)

And, in the final analysis, could a price really be placed on the Ambassador's own extraordinary talents?

Old Joe directed the enormous publicity effort himself. Distributed throughout the state were one million copies of a campaign tabloid featuring drawings of Lieutenant Kennedy rescuing his shipmates in the South Pacific PT-109 incident. On another page was a photograph of Joe Jr., captioned: JOHN FULFILLS DREAM OF BROTHER JOE WHO MET DEATH IN THE SKY OVER THE ENGLISH CHANNEL. And inserted in each paper was a copy of the familiar *Reader's Digest* article by John Hersey.

The Kennedy women, mother Rose and sisters Eunice, Pat and Jean, were roaming every corner of the state, describing Jack's virtues at numerous receptions. At one such event, some 8,600 cups of tea were consumed. And Cabot Lodge, following his defeat, was convinced it was "those damned teas" that had done him in.

Though heavy with child, Ethel Kennedy made her debut as a campaign speaker. After addressing an audience in Fall River, Ethel drove to Boston where she had her second child, Joseph Patrick III, the first male of a new generation of Kennedys. (The year before, Ethel had given birth to Kathleen.) The Lodge campaign, needless to say, was not aided any when the then Archbishop Cushing baptized the baby in a well-publicized ceremony just before the election.

Where the Kennedy campaign was most effective was in outflanking Lodge from both the Left and the Right. This could be done easily because Jack Kennedy's own positions were highly ambiguous. Thus, the candidate could and did point to his general support of the Truman Administration's Fair Deal domestic policies. But, at the same time, he argued persuasively that he was more sympathetic to the foreign-policy views of Senator Robert A. Taft than was Cabot Lodge.

One of the more remarkable campaign documents issued on Bobby's instructions was a forty-page "study" which, in effect, sought to demonstrate that Lodge was "soft on Communism." The document, for example, accused the Republican candidate of "straddling on the big issue of the guilt or innocence of Owen Lattimore, John Service and Philip Jessup. . . ." It also contended that "the outstanding question in [Lodge's] case as well as the Administration's, is why there has not been more of an awareness for a strong anti-Communist policy in the Far East."

All of which was shrewdly calculated to appeal to the conservative Republicans still rankling over Cabot Lodge's role in promoting Eisenhower over Taft.

Joe Kennedy, who had meanwhile contributed secretly to the Taft campaign, arranged for the formation of "Independents for Kennedy" to persuade outraged Taftites to vote for his son. The feeling of many conservatives was that the elder Kennedy, with his pronounced right-wing views, would exercise a steadying influence on his son. The fact that the *Chicago Tribune* had described Jack as a "fighting conservative" did him little harm among rock-ribbed Republicans.

After talking with Joe Kennedy, Basil Brewer, publisher of the influential New Bedford *Standard-Times* and Taft's pre-convention manager in Massachusetts, called on his readers to support Jack Kennedy. As a result, Kennedy carried New Bedford by an astounding 21,000 votes, almost one-third his plurality, while Governor Paul Dever squeaked through by 328 votes.

Joe Kennedy's behind-the-scenes activities were no secret in the Jewish community. And Lodge's people sought to tie the father's wartime views to his son. They published leaflets reprinting captured Nazi documents which purported to describe Old Joe's conversations with Nazi diplomats. The leaflets were headed: GERMAN DOCUMENTS ALLEGE KENNEDY HELD ANTI-SEMITIC VIEWS.

"We were in a real bind with respect to the Jewish people," says Phil Fine, a lawyer and Kennedy worker. "At first, we didn't have a soul with us."

Fine then introduced the candidate to Jackson J. Holtz, who had returned from the Korean War, and he became chairman of Kennedy's "Jewish Committee." Holtz also had lunch with Old Joe. Later Fine remarked, "I don't see eye to eye with Joe about anything and I doubt that Jack does. I wouldn't vote for Joe at any level. . . ."

At Joe Kennedy's request, Congressman John McCormack —who was very popular among Boston's Jews—also spoke in behalf of young Kennedy in Jewish districts. And at

McCormack's request, Franklin Delano Roosevelt, Jr.—then a Congressman—flew to Boston to speak for Jack.

"Jack was in serious trouble in the Jewish districts because of the rumors that the old man was anti-Semitic," Roosevelt recalls. "But more than that, Lodge had a real record with the Jewish voters. I went in and McCormack told me afterwards that I swung the Jewish vote over big to Jack and it was just about the margin of victory. He probably would have won anyway, I'm sure, but it helped. Jack never dropped me a note about it, but McCormack did."

Jack made his biggest breakthrough at a dinner attended by some three hundred Jewish leaders at the Boston Club. Though he spoke well and forcefully, he sensed a lingering doubt in the audience. "What more do you want?" the candidate finally pleaded in exasperation. "Remember, *I'm* running for the Senate, not my father." That did it. The audience broke into loud applause.

Generally, liberal sentiment was lukewarm toward Jack Kennedy. The candidate brought in Gardner "Pat" Jackson, a Bostonian whose liberal credentials went back to the days of Sacco and Vanzetti. After considerable effort, Jackson obtained an ADA endorsement for Kennedy. But labor endorsements were more difficult to get since Lodge had long played ball with the unions.

Jackson, however, learned who the real boss was when he sought to get his candidate to sign a statement assailing McCarthyism. Though Jack was willing, his father refused to permit it. Old Joe vehemently denounced Jackson and his "sheeny friends" for "trying to destroy my son." The statement was never issued.

Several years later, Old Joe told an interviewer that attacking Joe McCarthy would have meant political suicide.

Joe Kennedy left no stone unturned in his all-out effort to obtain conservative support for his son. Thus, the Republican Boston *Post* surprisingly endorsed Jack; and it was later disclosed in a Congressional probe that Joe Kennedy had made a post-election loan of half a million dollars to the now-defunct newspaper.

On Election Day the entire Kennedy organization across the state was mobilized to get voters to the polls. Bobby himself drove a dozen elderly citizens to their voting places. Then, after a leisurely dinner with his father at the Ritz-Carlton,

Bobby went to campaign headquarters for what he knew would be a long, tense wait. Soon after the polls were closed, the early returns gave Eisenhower a fast, strong lead across the nation, and Massachusetts was no exception.

Hour by hour, the returns in the Kennedy-Lodge race swayed back and forth. With the outstate (outside the Greater Boston area) results coming in, the Kennedy margin began to dwindle. It looked as if Lodge might ride in on Ike's coattails. The mood at Kennedy headquarters turned to gloom. One political hack told Bobby, "You're dead. You've lost."

But Bobby knew better. They were being beaten in the small cities and towns, but they were doing five percent better across the state than previous Democratic candidates. And this, his father's experts had assured Bobby, would make the difference. At eight o'clock in the morning, Henry Cabot Lodge conceded. While Eisenhower swamped Stevenson in Massachusetts by 210,000 votes and Governor Dever lost to Christian Herter by 15,000, Kennedy's margin over Lodge was 70,000—a stunning upset.

And no one was more overjoyed than Joseph P. Kennedy, who had masterminded the whole thing. The Ambassador placed a call to Joe McCarthy to congratulate the Senator on his own overwhelming victory in Wisconsin. "The family will always be grateful to you, Senator, for what you did for Jack," Joseph P. Kennedy assured Joe McCarthy.

9

McCarthy

According to Bobby Kennedy, the first time he ever laid eyes on Joseph R. McCarthy was at the University of Virginia when he invited the Senator to address the Student Legal Forum of which he was president. Be that as it may, they soon became the best of friends. When Bobby's first child, Kathleen, was born on July 4, 1951, he and Ethel asked McCarthy to be the godfather.

Bobby was always loath publicly to bemoan the evils of "McCarthyism" in a manner wholly satisfying to his new-found friends in the liberal community. For whatever else is said of Bobby, one thing about him stands out crystal-clear: He was loyal to his close friends.

In more recent years, of course, Bobby decidedly changed his once-militant views on the Communist threat. He espoused views—such as favoring contributions of blood plasma to the Communist guerrillas in Vietnam—which not too many years ago he would have regarded as near treason. One seasoned observer who viewed Bobby's ideological metamorphosis with absolute astonishment was his old friend, the Pulitzer prize-winning journalist Marguerite Higgins. Shortly before her untimely death, Miss Higgins recalled—with nostalgia— "those long, angry letters I used to get from Bob when I stopped over in Hong Kong en route to the Korean War in 1952–53.

"His usual handwritten letters," she wrote, "requested hard information about the dastardly British who, we both agreed, were being very naughty in letting potentially important gear— trucks, tires, certain steel bolts—be sent through Hong Kong to our enemy, Red China, which was busy killing thousands of Americans on Heartbreak Ridge and elsewhere in Korea.

"In those days RFK was a sensible middle-of-the-road sort
—a 'whose-side-are-you-on-anyway' kind of man. Those were
clearer, better days. . . .

"After JFK's death Bobby felt a need to cultivate the
liberal Left which had mistrusted him correctly. He had to
carve himself a niche to the left of LBJ."

Bobby's new-found liberalism has also been ascribed by
friends, in part, to the waning influence of his father, whose
stroke in December 1961 left Old Joe in a semiparalyzed
condition. Others, less kindly, call it opportunism pure and
simple. They contend that in his single-minded pursuit of the
White House, Bobby believes that he must cater to the liberals
whose company he once abhorred. This was, after all, pretty
much the strategy applied by brother John in his successful
propulsion into the White House.

Jack Kennedy had instinctively shrunk from the bitter
controversy that raged over the head of Joseph McCarthy. So
much so that when Bobby talked about joining McCarthy's
staff, following the 1952 election, his brother said he had
tried to talk Bobby out of it. Their father's views prevailed,
however. Old Joe Kennedy liked McCarthy, liked what he
was doing to combat "atheistic Communism," and felt there
was a future for Bobby on the McCarthy Committee.

Frequently, McCarthy—then a bachelor—was seen in the
company of two of the Kennedy girls, Pat and Eunice. There
was increasing speculation that McCarthy might marry one
of them. But the Senator had his eyes on his attractive secretary, Jean Kerr, whom he eventually married. Nevertheless,
one can only wonder how the course of history might have
been changed if Joe McCarthy had become John F. Kennedy's brother-in-law. Under those circumstances, would
Jack Kennedy have made it to the White House?

Joseph P. Kennedy had asked McCarthy to give Bobby a
job with the Senate Committee on Government Operations and
its Permanent Subcommittee on Investigations when the
Senator had become its chairman after the November 1952
election. Bobby had thought the McCarthy Committee was
the place where the action would be and where he could make
a name for himself. "I felt the investigation of Communism
was an important domestic issue," he later explained.

Actually, the job Bobby wanted was Chief Counsel for the

Permanent Subcommittee on Investigations. But McCarthy explained to Old Joe that he had already hired a young New Yorker named Roy Cohn. As an assistant U.S. Attorney, Cohn had won a name for himself by helping prosecute the Government's espionage case against Ethel and Julius Rosenberg, who had been found guilty in 1951 of charges of having passed U.S. atomic secrets to the Soviet Union.

Bobby then agreed to join the three-man staff of Francis Flanagan, an ex-FBI man who was general counsel of the McCarthy Subcommittee. The understanding was that Bobby would conduct his own investigations and hearings, answering directly to the Senator—and not to Roy Cohn. Before too long it was obvious that Kennedy disliked Cohn with extraordinary passion, and their strained relationship was to lead to a feud as enduring as that of the Hatfields and the McCoys.

Bobby's first investigatory chore for McCarthy had to do with the alleged homosexual influx into the State Department. Another of his early cases involved Government-purchased palm oil that had hardened and could not be removed from storage tanks. Neither was very rewarding. Then he turned to the problem of East-West trade, a subject of great interest to his brother, who had labeled such activity "trade in blood."

On May 9, 1951, Congressman John F. Kennedy, in fact, had introduced a bill in the House to ban shipment by the United States or by any foreign country of strategic war matériel to Red China or the British port of Hong Kong. Kennedy's bill would have banned "American economic or financial assistance . . . to any foreign country which exports or permits to be exported such materials to China or Hong Kong."

Late in May 1953, Bobby testified before the McCarthy Subcommittee. He announced that in 1952, while American boys were fighting Red Chinese troops in Korea, 193 ships flying flags of the Allied nations had made at least 445 trips to the Chinese mainland. Moreover, in the first three months of 1953, at least 100 British-owned ships had engaged in trade with Communist China. And he wound up with this shocker: two British ships had actually carried Chinese Communist troops along the China coast.

Bobby's testimony caused Democratic and Republican committee members alike to explode in anger. To Senator John

L. McClellan, the Democrat from Arkansas, it was proof positive that Britain's trade with Communist China at least equaled, and perhaps offset, its contributions to the Korean War. Republican Senator Everett Dirksen of Illinois asked, "Is it a fair assumption that we are not trying to win the war?" And Senator McCarthy said, "It seems unbelievable, unheard of . . . that a nation would have ships owned by its nationals transporting the troops to kill its own soldiers."

The distinguished columnist of *The New York Times* and old Kennedy family friend, Arthur Krock, cited the probe as "an example of Congressional investigation at the highest level, with documentation given for every statement represented as a fact and opinions expressed dispassionately despite the provocations of what is disclosed."

The British did not think so, however. The British Information Services in Washington insisted that the China trade involved "no goods of strategic importance to Communist China"; that, in fact, most of the one hundred ships Kennedy had referred to had arrived in Chinese ports "in ballast," i.e., to pick up cargo rather than to discharge it. And in London, the head of the British shipping firm that allegedly transported Red troops said, "It's a horrible lie—it just did not happen."

Democrats on the McCarthy Subcommittee saw in this a good way to embarrass the brand-new Eisenhower Administration. They called on the chairman to write to the President complaining about British trade with Red China and to demand a statement of President Eisenhower's views on such commerce. McCarthy thought this was a good idea and asked Bobby Kennedy to prepare such a letter, which was read over the telephone to McCarthy, then in Bethesda Naval Hospital for a checkup.

After the Senator approved it, Kennedy took the letter to the hospital for McCarthy's signature. Later that evening, he delivered the letter to the White House, along with a copy for Vice President Richard M. Nixon.

"As I now recall the letter," Nixon said recently, "it was a terribly exaggerated rendering of the actual facts of East-West trade. But, of even more significance, it constituted a declaration of war by Senator McCarthy against the Eisenhower Administration."

The Administration had been in power less than five months and Mr. Nixon sought to head off what perhaps was inevitable—an all-out break between McCarthy and the new President. He telephoned the Senator at the hospital. "Joe, I am not trying to act the censor. But remember you are a Republican Senator and that this is a Republican Administration. Your letter constitutes a tremendous bonanza for the Democratic opposition. Why play their game?"

The ailing Senator appeared to be convinced. "Okay, Dick. I trust you, but I don't trust those other bastards in the Administration."

McCarthy then asked Nixon to retrieve the disputed letter before it was "officially received" by President Eisenhower. Senator McCarthy's decision angered—and embarrassed—young Kennedy. Bobby felt that the episode constituted a repudiation of all the good work he had done in exposing the "perfidy" of America's so-called allies. His anti-British bias at this time was almost as deep as that of his father.

Shortly, McCarthy turned over to Chief Counsel Roy Cohn control of the entire subcommittee staff, and Robert Kennedy was fit to be tied. Bobby gave the Senator an ultimatum: either he would be given Cohn's job as Chief Counsel or he would resign. McCarthy urged Kennedy to stay on until something could be worked out.

Years later, in his book *The Enemy Within,* Kennedy wrote that under Cohn and his sidekick G. David Schine, "most of the investigations were instituted on the basis of some preconceived notion by the Chief Counsel or his staff members and not on the basis of any information that had been developed. Cohn and Schine claimed they knew from the outset what was wrong; and they were not going to let the facts interfere. Therefore no real spadework that might have destroyed some of their pet theories was ever undertaken. I thought Senator McCarthy made a mistake in allowing the committee to function in such a fashion."

Thus, Kennedy very carefully exonerated Senator McCarthy on the issue of "McCarthyism." Instead, he pinned the blame for any excesses on Roy Cohn and David Schine.

To give some maturity to his youthful staff, McCarthy, meanwhile, hired J. B. Matthews, a former researcher for the House Un-American Activities Committee, as his Director of Investigations. Bobby, who thought the appointment was "superb," was named Matthews' chief aide. The understanding was that he would work directly for Matthews and not for Cohn. Bobby told Matthews that as much as he admired McCarthy he could not understand why the Senator had not summarily dismissed Cohn and Schine who, he claimed, had made a laughingstock of the subcommittee in their investigations of left-wing books in overseas libraries of the United States Information Agency. He said that as long as Cohn remained, he had no future with the subcommittee; that, in fact, he was thinking of moving out West—perhaps to a state like Nevada—where he could establish residence and run for Senator. Massachusetts was out of the question because his brother Jack had that state sewed up. Nevada had a tiny population and he thought with some hard work and "a lot of handshaking" he could obtain the Democratic nomination for Senator.

Matthews had hardly settled into his new office when an article of his was published in the *American Mercury*. It began with this sentence: "The largest single group supporting the Communist apparatus in the United States today is composed of Protestant clergymen."

The article caused a brouhaha. Divines of all faiths called Matthews' attack on the loyalty of Protestant clergymen unjustified and deplorable, and shortly President Eisenhower charged that Matthews had shown "contempt for the principles of freedom and decency." Within an hour of the President's statement, McCarthy asked for Matthews' resignation. The three Democrats on the subcommittee—Arkansas' John McClellan, Washington's Henry Jackson and Missouri's Stuart Symington—had already staged a walkout on the grounds that the chairman was hiring staff members without consulting any of them.

Bobby did not resign until a month later, when it became obvious that he would not get Cohn's job. His resignation had nothing to do with the angry walkout staged by the three Democrats. "Although an effort was made in some quarters to bolster the claim that Kennedy, too, had quit in anger, he himself vehemently denied the allegation," John Kelso, a Washington correspondent, wrote in the Boston *Post* after a long talk with Bobby.

In fact, it was Chairman McCarthy who announced Kennedy's resignation. A press release from the Senator's office publicized the exchange of letters between them:

July 29, 1953

DEAR SENATOR McCARTHY:

Please accept my resignation as assistant counsel and deputy staff director of the Senate Permanent Subcommittee on Investigations, effective as of the close of business July 31, 1953.

With the filing in the Senate of the Subcommittee report on Trade with the Soviet bloc, the task to which I have devoted my time since coming with the Subcommittee has been completed. I am submitting my resignation at this time as it is my intention to enter the private practice of law at an early date.

I have enjoyed my work and association on this subcommittee and I wish to express to you my appreciation for the opportunity of having served with your group.

Please accept my sincere thanks for the many courtesies and kindnesses you have extended to me during these past seven months.

Sincerely yours,

RFK:gm

/s/ ROBERT F. KENNEDY

Hon. Joseph R. McCarthy,
United States Senate
Washington 25, D.C.

Two days later Senator McCarthy responded:

July 31, 1953

Mr. Robert F. Kennedy,
Senate Permanent Subcommittee on Investigations
Senate Office Building
Washington, D.C.

DEAR BOB:

This is to acknowledge receipt of your letter of resignation.

I know it is needless to tell you that I very much regret seeing you leave the Committee. In accordance with our conversation, I sincerely hope you will consider coming back later on in the summer to complete the project with Mr. Flanagan and the full Committee.

From discussing your work with other members of

the Committee, I can tell you that it was the unanimous feeling on the part of the Senators that you were a great credit to the Committee and did a tremendous job.

With kindest regards, I am

Sincerely yours,

/s/ JOE

McC:dr

Joe McCarthy, Chairman
Senate Permanent Subcommittee
on Investigations.

Though it may have been Bobby's "intention to enter the private practice of law," he wound up instead working for the Commission on the Organization of the Executive Branch of the Government—the so-called Hoover Commission—on which Joseph P. Kennedy had been serving since 1947. The Ambassador had become a warm friend of Herbert Hoover, whom he found a congenial soul whose conservative views were more to his liking than those of the Fair Dealers. The Commission had been organized to propose ways and means of curbing waste and confusion in Government, and the elder Kennedy invariably sided with Mr. Hoover in disputes with the more liberal Commissioners.

Actually Bobby was employed by his father, as his chief assistant. But, compared with the excitement of the McCarthy Subcommittee, the work was dull, and Bobby made no secret of being bored. Most of the other chief assistants were young lawyers like Bobby, but he rarely mixed with them or participated in their round-table discussions.

Occasionally he might lunch with one of his confreres. One of them, now a Republican legislator in the Midwest, recalls, "I never thought he liked the work. I had the impression that this was an interim period for him, that he hoped to be doing something else, something more exciting." Bobby had been assigned to analyze the Weather Bureau.

Bobby did spend time with Herbert Hoover. He later described the former President as having "a greater knowledge of government generally than any man I'd ever known." He added, "I greatly admired him. Most of the time, there were not many people around and so I had a chance to work with and talk with him personally. It was a wonderful experience."

That Bobby was going through a most difficult period psychologically was confirmed by a close friend. "He wanted to achieve. He had proved himself in the 1952 election, but he wasn't able to find anything to get his teeth into. The McCarthy era was frustrating. There were many clashes with Roy Cohn. But even that period was more interesting than the one that followed—the one on the Hoover Commission. He was dissatisfied with the Hoover Commission. He was rather cross much of the time in those days, with his family, and his friends. Bob normally is one of the most pleasant persons to be around. But he just wasn't himself in that period."

That Bobby had his mind on things other than government economies was shown by a letter he wrote to *The New York Times* in which he ranged himself with the conservatives of both parties who favored the adoption of the Bricker Amendment to limit Presidential treaty-making powers and to increase the authority of Congress in the foreign-relations field. The amendment, which President Eisenhower opposed, stemmed from a conservative determination to prevent a repetition of the agreements made by the Roosevelt and Truman Administrations in Tehran, Yalta and Potsdam.

When first introduced by Ohio's Republican Senator John Bricker, the amendment was co-sponsored by sixty-two Senators of both parties. A respected member of the Senate, Bricker was troubled over what he believed was a tendency in leading governmental circles to consider treaty-making as a means of effectuating domestic reforms—reforms in areas traditionally regarded as solely within the province of the separate states—and warned against imposing "socialism by treaty."

As the months passed, the argument grew more bitter. It divided the Eisenhower family, as the former President later wrote in his *Mandate for Change:*

"My brother Edgar, a lawyer who always liked to refer to himself as a 'constitutional conservative,' argued hotly—so far as an argument by letter can be so characterized—that the amendment was absolutely necessary to save the United States from coming disaster. My own opinion was that the contrary was true. Being a lawyer, he felt somewhat frustrated that I could not agree with him on a legal matter, but my best retort was that the subject was far above legalistic interpretation in importance. Both of us felt so strongly about the amendment that by common consent it was finally dropped as a subject of correspondence between us."

In his letter to the *Times*, Bobby took issue with an editorial entitled "Senator Bricker's Backers." The editorial claimed that Bricker's supporters were worried "lest some future President and a misled two-thirds of some future Senate produce another Yalta." As far as the *Times* was concerned, "If Russia had honorably and honestly carried out its part of these agreements Yalta might be remembered with reasonable satisfaction."

Not so, retorted Bobby, and he virtually repeated the arguments he had made in the thesis he had written at the University of Virginia. Again he berated Franklin D. Roosevelt for making agreements with the Soviet Union "with inadequate knowledge and without consulting any of the personages, either military or political, who would ordinarily have had the most complete knowledge of the problems involved. [Averell] Harriman and [Harry] Hopkins were his sole advisers on the question of whether Russia should be brought into the war and what post-war problems would be created by our concessions to her."

"I believe," Bobby concluded, "the United States Senate, if this matter had been put up to them, would have done a more thorough job."

Up at Harvard, Arthur Schlesinger, Jr., read Bobby's letter with growing indignation. In his own answer to the *Times*, he described Bobby's epistle as "an astonishing mixture of distortion and error." Schlesinger then vigorously proceeded to defend Franklin Roosevelt.

"These facts are easily ascertainable," Schlesinger continued. "How, then, can Mr. Kennedy imply with a straight face that the decision to secure Russian participation was taken without consultation with the military authorities?

"Mr. Kennedy's larger point is apparently that the Bricker Amendment would be a fine thing, because it would subject Executive actions like the Far Eastern agreement at Yalta to Congressional debate. His argument, on the contrary, brilliantly illustrates the futility of the Bricker Amendment. . . ."

By this time, Joe McCarthy had contrived a truce with the three Democratic Senators who had walked out of his subcommittee, and Joe Kennedy approached Senator Mc-Clellan, a fellow member of the Hoover Commission, and asked him to put Bobby on as minority counsel. The Arkansan, after consulting with his fellow Democrats, agreed.

After five months with the Hoover Commission, Bobby resigned in February 1954. "I am sorry to hear you are leaving us," Mr. Hoover wrote. "I realize, however, that there is little to do until the task forces have reported and that a restless soul like you wants to work."

Bobby's new job with the McCarthy Subcommittee was to work directly with McClellan, Jackson and Symington. But conflict with Cohn was inevitable. One well-publicized episode occurred during the questioning of Mrs. Anna Lee Moss, a Negro woman whom Cohn—on the basis of information supplied by an underground FBI informant—identified as a card-carrying Communist. Mrs. Moss, a low-echelon employee of the Army Signal Corps, denied this under oath.

Cohn said there was considerable evidence to demonstrate Mrs. Moss's membership in the Party, but that the evidence was secret and he could not produce it publicly. Senator McClellan then bitterly decried "convicting people by rumor and hearsay and innuendo."

Mrs. Moss did admit, however, that a man named Robert Hall had once delivered the *Daily Worker* to her home. According to Cohn, Robert Hall was the top Communist party organizer in the District of Columbia. But when Mrs. Moss said that the Robert Hall who had appeared at her home was a Negro, a newspaperman slipped Bobby Kennedy a note. There then ensued the following colloquy:

MR. KENNEDY: Was Mr. Hall a colored gentleman, or—

MRS. MOSS: Yes, sir.

MR. KENNEDY: There is some confusion about it, is there not, Mr. Cohn? Is the Rob Hall we are talking about, the union organizer, was he a white man or a colored man?

MR. COHN: I never inquired into his race. I am not sure. We can check that, though.

MR. KENNEDY: I thought I just spoke to you about it.

MR. COHN: My assumption has been that he is a white man, but we can check that.

SENATOR SYMINGTON: Let us ask this: The Bob Hall that you knew, was he a white man?

MRS. MOSS: He was colored, the one I knew of.

SENATOR SYMINGTON: Let's decide which Robert Hall we want to talk about.

MR. KENNEDY: When you spoke about the union organizer, you spoke about Rob Hall and I think we all felt that was the colored gentleman?

MR. COHN: I was not talking about a union organizer, Bob. I was talking about a Communist organizer who at that time, according to public record, was in charge of subscriptions for the *Daily Worker* in the District of Columbia area.

MR. KENNEDY: Evidently it is a different Rob Hall.

MR. COHN: I don't know that it is. Our information is that it was the same Rob Hall.

SENATOR MCCLELLAN: If one is black and the other is white, there is a difference.

MR. COHN: I think that might better be something we should go into and get some more exact information on.

MR. KENNEDY: I think so too.

The Democratic Senators enjoyed Cohn's obvious discomfiture. They roared with laughter when Mrs. Moss was asked whether she had ever heard of Karl Marx, and replied, "Who's that?"

When she left the stand, Symington brought the hearing to an emotional climax. "I may be sticking my neck out . . . ," he cried. "I think you're telling the truth. If you're not taken back into the Army [job] . . . I am going to see that you get a job."

Eventually, Mrs. Moss was cleared by Defense Secretary Charles E. Wilson and was given a job as a typist in a finance office away from the Pentagon. Four years later, though no one cared by then, Cohn could have claimed vindication. The Subversive Activities Control Board finally unveiled its secret evidence and reported "the Communist Party's own records . . . show that an Annie Lee Moss, 72 R. St. SW, Washington, D.C., was a Party member in the mid 1940's."

It was during the McCarthy-Army hearings that Roy and Bobby nearly came to blows. At issue in the highly publicized, nationally televised hearings was the Army claim that McCarthy and his staff had tried to obtain preferential treatment for G. David Schine when he was drafted into the Army. According to an Army report, Cohn had once threatened to "wreck the Army" if his sidekick were not assigned as he directed.

In his testimony, Senator McCarthy mentioned as one of Schine's qualifications the "Schine plan" for psychological warfare which he had submitted to the State Department. Waving a copy of the "Schine plan," Senator Jackson leaped to his feet and asked McCarthy about one item in the "plan." It had to do with using girly pinups in the battle against Communism.

"We can all laugh on that one, I think, Senator," said Jackson.

"I couldn't subscribe to every item here," McCarthy replied defensively.

Throughout the interrogation, which became more and more sarcastic, Kennedy kept passing notes to Jackson from a rear-row seat. As the day's session recessed, Cohn strode purposefully toward Kennedy, who was gathering up his documents. Cohn said something and reporters heard the following exchange:

KENNEDY: Don't you make any warnings to us about Democratic Senators.

COHN: I'll make any warnings to you that I want to— any time, anywhere. Do you want to fight right here?

KENNEDY: Get lost.

COHN: You have a personal hatred for one of the principals.

KENNEDY: If I have, it's justified.

COHN: Do you think you're qualified to sit here? Do you think you're qualified?

As Bobby strode off through the rapidly gathering crowd, Cohn told newsmen, "Oh, we've got a real cute kid here."

Later Bobby claimed that Cohn had threatened to "get" Senator Jackson for having once written something "favorably inclined toward the Communists." Cohn vehemently denied having said any such thing and repeated his charge that Kennedy was indulging his "hatred" for him. "I can produce evidence," Cohn told reporters, "that Kennedy said he hated me and was going to get me during these hearings. He made a special trip to someone in McCarthy's office to deliver that message a week before the hearings began.

"While Kennedy is entitled to his personal opinion about me, I certainly don't think it's either fair or just for one who has stated he has a personal hatred for a principal in a case to help in supposedly impartial presentation of that case."

On that "special trip" to McCarthy's office, Bobby also told McCarthy's secretary to inform the Senator that, no matter what happened at the hearings, he still admired the Senator.

Eventually the Army-McCarthy hearings ground to a halt. They had presented a pretty sordid spectacle. It was obvious that Senator McCarthy had fought a losing battle. It was also obvious that the Army itself was invested with a pretty sorry leadership. With the hearings over, Bobby prepared a seventy-eight-page summary of the evidence, which was accepted by both Republicans and Democrats. Both sides agreed that Senator McCarthy had been wrong in permitting Roy Cohn to pressure the Army in behalf of G. David Schine whose services, the Senators contended, were hardly indispensable.

Senator McCarthy emerged relatively unscathed, though his once-powerful influence, particularly among his fellow Republicans, was unquestionably diminishing. Kennedy's attitude was charitable. Robert E. Thompson and Hortense Meyers, in their friendly biography of Bobby (*Robert F. Kennedy: The Brother Within*), quote him:

"He got so involved with all that publicity—and after that it was the Number One thing in his life. He was on a toboggan. It was so exciting and exhilarating as he went downhill that it didn't matter to him if he hit a tree at the bottom. Cohn and Schine took him up the mountain and showed him all those wonderful things. He destroyed himself for that—for publicity. He had to get his name in the paper. I felt sorry for him, particularly in the last year, when he was such a beaten, destroyed person—particularly since many of his so-called friends, realizing he was finished, ran away from him and left him with virtually no one.

"I liked him and yet at times he was terribly heavy-handed. He was a very complicated character. His whole method of operation was complicated because he would get a guilty feeling and get hurt after he had blasted somebody. He wanted so desperately to be liked. He was so thoughtful and yet so unthoughtful in what he did to others. He was sensitive and yet insensitive. He didn't anticipate the results of what he was doing. He was very thoughtful of his friends, and yet he could be so cruel to others."

In many ways, Bobby might have been describing himself.

On December 2, 1954, by a vote of 67 to 22, the United States Senate voted to censure Senator McCarthy. The dramatic vote took place after hearings into the Senator's conduct were completed by a Select Senate Committee headed by Utah Republican Senator Arthur Watkins. The resolution charged that McCarthy (1) had refused to co-operate with the Senate Committee on Privileges and Elections in its investigations of the Senator's tangled financial affairs; and (2) had acted insultingly toward the Watkins Committee by, among other things, accusing its members of assisting the Communist conspiracy.

Ironically, had McCarthy so desired, he could have had a lesser reprimand. Senator Everett M. Dirksen, Republican of Illinois, had worked out a compromise resolution saying that while the Senate did not condone what McCarthy had done, nevertheless there were no rules forbidding it. The Dirksen proposal then suggested that the Senate should appoint a committee to study barring similar behavior.

The resolution sounded good to McCarthy's lawyer, Edward Bennett Williams, who later wrote: "Senator Goldwater and I begged McCarthy to accept the resolution. We pleaded, but McCarthy was adamant. He said he would not ask his friends in the Senate to vote that they did not condone what he had done. He said he knew they did condone it and did approve it. If he could not win, he said, he wanted to lose with his twenty-two friends. Senator Goldwater and I came back to my home in the early hours of the morning convinced that McCarthy's judgment was bad and that he had rejected his only chance to stave off defeat. We went back to the Capitol that day, but the fight against censure was all over. McCarthy was beaten.

"Many times since," Williams continued, "it has been written that the Senators' censure marked the end of McCarthy, that it broke his spirit and left him a bitterly disappointed man. In my opinion, nothing could be more remote from the truth. He rejected a clear invitation to stave off censure. From the first he regarded it as inevitable, and when it came he wore it as a badge of courage. He showed no disappointment and no regret."

One Senator who failed to vote on censure was John F. Kennedy. The reason, he was to keep insisting all the way to the White House, was that he had been in a New York hospital undergoing spinal surgery. But, for many liberals, this was not good enough. They contended that he could have gone on record either for or against censure.

"To understand my situation," he explained in 1956, "you must remember that my father was a friend of Joe's, as was my sister Eunice, and my brother Bobby worked for him. So I had all those family pressures."

For Bobby Kennedy there was no personal problem. He continued to remain on good terms with Joe McCarthy. However, as a result of the 1954 elections in which the Republicans lost control of Congress, McCarthy was no longer chairman of the Government Operations Committee and its Permanent Subcommittee on Investigations. The new chairman was John L. McClellan, the austere Democrat from Arkansas, who immediately named Bobby as Chief Counsel.

Roy Cohn was no longer around. He had returned to New York to launch a private law practice. Having lost Cohn, Joe McCarthy felt closer to Bobby than he did to his own Republican minority counsel, James Juliana. But Joe had lost his old fire, and there were few fireworks emanating from the committee he had once chaired.

How Bobby felt about McCarthy can be determined from a conversation in the spring of 1956 between Bobby and an Assistant United States Attorney in the Eisenhower Administration, who today is a Wall Street lawyer. According to the lawyer, the conversation which took place at a Washington party went like this:

KENNEDY: The trouble with you Republicans is that you have done away with the very best man your party has.

LAWYER: Who is that?

KENNEDY: Joe McCarthy.

LAWYER: You must be kidding.

KENNEDY: I am not kidding. I think so well of the man I made him a godfather of one of my children.

10

McClellan

In taking over the chairmanship of the Government Operations Committee and its noisy stepchild, the Permanent Investigations Subcommittee, Senator John J. McClellan made it clear that he would continue to investigate Communist activities as "an even greater menace" than governmental waste, inefficiency and corruption.

Because of the nationally televised Army-McCarthy hearings, McClellan had become a national figure. In the closing moments of the raucous hearings, all the principals had made final remarks, each cornier than the next, geared for the TV cameras. Only McClellan had placed the thirty-six days of hearings in proper perspective. Said the Arkansan, "No one of us should forget the events which precipitated these hearings constituted some of the most disgraceful events in the history of our government." It was a plague-on-both-your-houses approach, but it scored among most Americans.

In January 1955, on assuming the chairmanship of what had been the McCarthy Committee, McClellan announced his intention of cleaning up once and for all the case of the former Army dentist, Dr. Irving Peress, who had been called a "Fifth Amendment Communist" by ex-Chairman McCarthy. For almost a year, the Peress case had hovered like a restless phantom over the Army-McCarthy hearings, the Watkins Committee hearings and the censure debate on the Senate floor. It had left in its wake a trail of unanswered questions.

"The case stinks to high heaven," the twenty-nine-year-old Bobby told the Army brass.

Peress, a New York dentist drafted into the Army, had invoked the Fifth Amendment during a routine loyalty investigation. He then held the rank of captain. The Army recommended his dismissal but paper-shuffling had delayed his discharge, and somehow he was promoted to major before he received an honorable discharge on February 2, 1954. Two weeks later, Senator McCarthy had leaped into the case.

In reopening it, Chairman McClellan not only wanted to set the record straight but also to demonstrate that Democrats could be as tough on the Communist issue as their Republican critics.

"When those who come before the committee resort to the Fifth Amendment," McClellan told Allen Drury, then with *The New York Times,* "they command no respect from me, as individuals. I respect their right to resort to it if they feel they must, but it carries with it an implication I am compelled to consider, and not favorably. A man who cannot face competent authority and say he has no affiliations with any subversive organizations has no right to employment with the Federal Government in a sensitive or any other position."

Actually, there was no way to "get" Peress, who was back in New York filling teeth as a civilian. But the McClellan Committee did "get" the Army. After a week-long hearing, in which McClellan curbed McCarthy's attempts to refight his war with the military spokesmen, the committee issued a report concluding that "some forty-eight errors of more than minor importance were committed by the Army in connection with the commissioning, transfer, promotion, and honorable discharge of Irving Peress."

The report, written by Bobby and his aides, was a damning indictment. It cited numerous instances in which the Army was "deceptive" and had practiced "gross impositions" on legitimate Congressional investigators. Pronouncing himself more than satisfied, Senator McCarthy praised Bobby by dubbing the report "a great tribute to the staff of the committee." But, by then, most of the country was apathetic to the subject.

Another case that was cleared up was the one involving

lax security practices at Fort Monmouth, New Jersey. Mc-
Carthy had been subjected to heavy attack when he conducted hearings into alleged Communist infiltration into
that supposedly top-security installation. Now, however, the
McClellan Committee—in an investigation conducted by
Bobby Kennedy—found that no fewer than thirty-three
security risks had been discharged from Fort Monmouth, the
vast majority in the wake of the McCarthy inquiries and
in acknowledgment of them.

Summarizing the year's work, a report prepared by Bobby
for the Permanent Investigations Subcommittee read, in
part: "Investigation and testimony established that the Communist party has successfully infiltrated national defense in-
dustries and is in a position to acquire vital information
concerning our military secrets and our military effectiveness.
The employment of Communists in defense facilities is a
clear and present danger to the national security. Many investigations conducted by the staff in connection with this
subject have never been made part of executive or public
hearings, and a great deal of additional investigation is
contemplated in this regard."

The Permanent Investigations Subcommittee struck pay
dirt again when it conducted hearings on several conflict-of-
interest cases that plagued the Eisenhower Administration.
The most spectacular dealt with Secretary of the Air Force
Harold E. Talbott. For several months, Bobby and his staff
secretly probed the Secretary's relations with a New York
engineering firm, Paul B. Mulligan & Co., Inc., in which
Talbott had been permitted by Congress to retain an interest. There were rumors that the subcommittee had
evidence that Talbott had indeed solicited business for Mulligan.

"I did not," the Secretary told newsmen.

But a few days later, *The New York Times* published a
selection of letters—presumably from the subcommittee files
—which had been written by Talbott to industrialists suggesting that they consider retaining the Mulligan company.
Did Bobby "leak" the damaging letters to the *Times?* This
was the charge leveled at the Chief Counsel by Republican
Senator George H. Bender of Ohio.

Conceding he was the only one who had handled them,
Bobby flatly denied Bender's accusation. "I don't think you

should say it if you don't know, Senator," he said. "I resent it."

But the damage to Talbott had been done. After a vigorous cross-examination by Bobby, Talbott—still protesting his innocence—decided to resign. Two years later, Talbott died in Palm Beach of a cerebral hemorrhage, the victim— his widow claimed—of one of Bobby's witch-hunts.

Another investigation had to do with payoffs in government purchases of military uniforms. Among the witnesses was a Mrs. Mella Hort, formerly a contract administrator for the Government's military purchasing agency in New York. She had been accused of having accepted a $2,000 kickback from a manufacturer of uniforms. Confronted with the discrepancies between her public and executive testimonies, Mrs. Hort accused Bobby and his chief aide, Carmine Bellino, of having "closeted" her in a "hot room," where she was "browbeaten, badgered and kicked around." When Bobby and Bellino had finished with her, she said, "I would have sworn to almost anything." In fact, they made her so "hysterical," she continued, "I'd have sworn I put the crack in the Liberty Bell."

The inquiry was successful insofar as it helped produce six fraud convictions.

In the summer of 1955, Bobby toured the central Asian area of the Soviet Union with Supreme Court Justice William O. Douglas, a trip five years in the making. Douglas had first mentioned it in 1950 when he spoke at Bobby's Student Legal Forum at the University of Virginia. But it had taken four years of constant pressuring of the Soviet Embassy in Washington to obtain a visa permitting him to enter the Communist fatherland. Back in 1949, the Soviet press had published charges that Douglas was "spying" on the Russians when he had gone mountain climbing in the Near East.

At Douglas' request, a visa was also issued to Kennedy, and in late July Bobby met Justice Douglas and the then Mrs. Douglas in Tehran. They entered the Soviet Union from the south and began what Bobby was to describe as "a great adventure." Some of the areas they visited had had no Western visitors since the 1917 Bolshevik *coup d'état*. If anything, the trip made Bobby more of an anti-Communist. Wherever they went they were convinced that "our conversations were always monitored."

And their request to visit Karaganda, a city in Kazakhstan, was hardly facilitated. In fact, their Soviet escort took them everywhere but Karaganda.

"Ultimately," reported Bobby, "after we had worked our way back to within a reasonable distance of Karaganda, we were told that orders had come from Moscow that we were not to be allowed to visit that city at all. When we arrived in Moscow, we found out that Karaganda is the site of the most notorious slave-labor camps in the Soviet Union."

Bobby also reported that he and Douglas had talked with various Soviet judges and court officials. "Of course, there is no habeas corpus and there are no jury trials. By a provision, never publicly repealed, the MVD can still move groups of the population to correctional labor camps for the general good of the state. They can extend a man's sentence after he gets there without bringing him before a court."

Returning to Washington, Bobby provided Central Intelligence Agency officials, who had briefed him before he left, with an in-depth report of what he had seen, whom he had talked to, and told them his general impressions. He also gave the intelligence agency copies of photographs he had taken, as well as hundreds of feet of motion-picture film. Justice Douglas, however, saved his impressions for his book, *Russian Journey*.

Bobby's bitterness toward the Soviet Union was reflected in speeches he made at Georgetown University, at a Notre Dame Alumni Association communion breakfast at New York's Waldorf-Astoria, as well as in an interview published by *U.S. News & World Report* in October 1955:

"Communism retains its basic evils whether it is the Khrushchev type or the more oppressive Stalin type. . . . They haven't relinquished any of the real power, and the ordinary citizen feels the full extent of it—even to where a factory or farm worker cannot leave his job without permission of his superiors—in other words, the state. . . ."

Bobby said it was beyond his comprehension why some American liberals professed an affinity for the Communist system since it was so diametrically opposed to liberal principles.

The final *U.S. News & World Report* question was this:

"Do you think with all our troubles and all our friction and all our defects, we may be better off than they are?"

"I think anybody who doesn't think so should take a trip there," Bobby replied. "I am hopeful that what happened at the Geneva Conference and what will happen at the meetings of the foreign visitors will mean peace for us all. However, on the basis of what I saw and learned in Russia, I am very distrustful that we will get anything other than smiles.

"We are dealing with a Government to whom God, the family or the individual means nothing, and whose practice it has been in the past to make promises and treaties to serve their purposes and to break them when it has been to their advantage. It can only be suicidal for us during this period, on the basis of smiles, to strengthen Russia and weaken ourselves."

Interviewed by International News Service, Bobby also assailed the Soviet-American exchange programs instituted by the Eisenhower Administration. He claimed that as a result of Soviet agricultural experts' visits to the United States, the Russians had been able "to jump a ten-year gap. . . . We should not be blinded by the bear's smile," he said.

On returning to the McClellan Committee, Bobby announced that his staff would begin an investigation of payments by the Veterans Administration to GI trade schools allegedly run and staffed by Communists. Then he returned to his favorite subject—the question of East-West trade. The report he had prepared for the McCarthy Committee—which had won Bobby so much publicity—had apparently done little good. There was more East-West trade than ever.

According to Bobby, the extent of Western trade with Communist China was "astonishing" and he denounced the Eisenhower Administration for relaxing Allied restrictions on shipments of strategic goods to potential enemy nations. He said that American approval of a British sale of 200 million pounds of copper wire to the Soviet Union was "almost unbelievable." The McClellan Committee had been conducting hearings into the removal of embargoes on nearly two hundred strategic items. But various Federal agencies were hiding behind "executive immunity" by declining to answer questions concerning these items.

"The Russians know what items are off the list, and so do the rest of the European nations," said Bobby. "Why can't the American public get the same information?"

In a letter to the *Times*, Bobby concluded that the sale of these items might be profitable to some people in the West, but insisted that such profits were offset by other disadvantages. "We might also keep in mind that during the nineteen-thirties, when there were nine or ten millions unemployed in the United States, the profits that came from the sale of scrap steel to Japan were undoubtedly economically helpful to some of our citizens. The lives that that economically profitable trade cost the United States during the nineteen-forties should have taught our allies and ourselves a lesson. It apparently has not."

Yet five years later, with his brother in the White House, Robert Kennedy was in the forefront of those arguing for increased trade with the Soviet bloc.

The year 1956 was most important in the lives of the Kennedy family. It was the year when John F. Kennedy sought the Democratic nomination for Vice President. And it was also the year that Theodore Sorensen, JFK's administrative assistant, promulgated the thesis that one of the Senator's greatest assets was that he was Roman Catholic. Because it might seem too self-serving if he distributed it in his own name, John Kennedy arranged for the document to be sent out by Connecticut State Chairman John Bailey. Thus, it came to be known as the "Bailey Report."

Historically it was of enormous significance since it presaged what was to become John F. Kennedy's major strategy for winning the Presidency. An extraordinary document, it declared:

"The Catholic vote is far more important than its numbers—about one out of every four voters who turn out—because of its concentration in the key States and cities of the North. These are the pivotal States with large electoral votes, which vary as to their party support and several of which are inevitably necessary for a victory in the Electoral College. And the strength of the Catholic vote within these States is considerably increased by the findings of Gallup and others that Catholics consistently turn out to vote in greater proportions than non-Catholics. . . . In short, even a Catholic nominee for President would be judged by most people on his qualifications for the office—and it is apparent that a Democratic Catholic Vice Presidential nominee, though admittedly prejudice would be stirred, would lose no electoral votes for the ticket simply because a handful of Southerners or Republicans would not support him."

In short, a Catholic candidate, solely on the basis of his religion, would bring more votes to the ticket than he would lose.

Ironically, much of the opposition to Kennedy came from professional Catholic politicians who believed that—as one of them said to Adlai Stevenson—"America is not ready for a Catholic." And the older party leaders generally wanted no part of young Kennedy. Harry S Truman, for example, said whenever anyone mentioned Jack Kennedy he couldn't help thinking of "that old bastard," Joseph P. Kennedy, operating behind the scenes. Sam Rayburn, the powerhouse from Texas, told Stevenson, "Well, if we have to have a Catholic, I hope we don't have to take that little —— Kennedy. How about John McCormack?"

Liberal Democrats were appalled at the idea because of Kennedy's failure to take a stand on McCarthyism. They recalled that Kennedy had written a book entitled *Profiles in Courage* in which he said, "Few, if any, face the same dread finality of decision that confronts a Senator facing an important call of the roll . . . when that roll is called he cannot hide, he cannot equivocate, he cannot delay. . . ."

Along with that failure, Kennedy had to listen to considerable literary criticism such as Eleanor Roosevelt's widely quoted comment that the Senator should "show less profile and more courage." And though an instant commercial success, *Profiles in Courage*, nevertheless, got a mixed press. Critic Alfred Kazin, for example, wrote that the book reminded him "of those little anecdotes from the lives of great men that are found in *Reader's Digest*, Sunday supplements, and the journal of the American Legion." But most readers apparently enjoyed the book.

When *Profiles in Courage* was awarded a Pulitzer prize, it proved to be a valuable weapon in the Kennedy-for-Vice-President drive. Autographed copies were mailed to leading Democrats around the country.

One thing was becoming more obvious: the closer Stevenson got to the convention, the more difficult it became for him to decide on a running mate. For one thing, he was troubled by Kennedy's health; JFK had had a serious back operation and, according to rumors, was suffering from Addison's disease. And other things disturbed the Stevenson camp. For example, the rumor that Kennedy had made a substantial contribution to Richard Nixon's 1950 Senatorial campaign against Helen Gahagan Douglas.

A ruffled Ted Sorensen hastily denied this, saying it must have been Jack's father. It is true that Joseph P. Kennedy had made a substantial contribution to Nixon's campaign. But it is also true that John F. Kennedy had walked into Nixon's Congressional office in mid-1950 and handed the then Congressman's administrative assistant, William Arnold, a personally signed check for $1,000 as a campaign contribution. And later that year, at a Harvard seminar, he had made it clear that he was happy over Nixon's victory. Mrs. Douglas, he said, "was not the sort of person I like working with on committees."

Actually, Jack had another reason for helping Nixon. Despite such rewriters of history as Arthur Schlesinger, Jr., Jack Kennedy and Dick Nixon were good friends. They had been sworn into Congress on the same day, and had worked together on the House Education and Labor Committee. Jack had admired Nixon's work in exposing Alger Hiss, and their views were similar on other matters, too—until the White House bug bit Jack.

Another criticism was no longer often voiced—the fact that he was a "swinger." Many stories had circulated about him when he was a bachelor, but on September 12, 1953, Jack had taken unto himself a bride, a shy, wide-eyed beauty named Jacqueline Bouvier. The marriage was performed by then Archbishop Cushing in a picture-book extravaganza in Newport with a boyish-looking Robert Kennedy as the best man.

There were seven hundred guests at the nuptial Mass, ranging from Marion Davies to Alfred Gwynne Vanderbilt, and nine hundred at the reception that followed.

As much as she disliked politics and politicians, Jacqueline was excited about her husband's quest of the Vice Presidential nomination. Though expecting a child, she decided to attend the National Convention in Chicago, staying with the Sargent Shrivers. Meanwhile, Bobby's right to be a delegate to the Democratic National Convention had been challenged by Robert P. Donovan, of East Boston, who protested to the Election Division of the Secretary of State's office that Bobby was "not a legal resident of Massachusetts."

Donovan charged that Bobby "purportedly" lived at 122 Bowdoin Street on Beacon Hill, noting that this was the same home address given by Senator Kennedy. Donovan said it was a two-room apartment and added, "How the Senator, his wife, Robert and his wife and three children can all squeeze in, I don't know." He contended that Bobby lived in either Connecticut, Washington, Virginia or West Palm Beach, although he might possibly be a summer resident at Hyannis Port.

"The same goes for his brother," Donovan declared. "This is a big farce. Robert Kennedy should and will be ruled off the ballot."

Perhaps Bobby should have been, but he wasn't. Donovan's protest was thrown out on a technicality by the state ballot law commission. The technicality was his failure to submit a certificate of party enrollment when filing his protest. Donovan insisted he had not been informed of the requirement. But the commission chairman said the requirement could not be waived.

At Adlai Stevenson's request, Jack Kennedy made his nominating speech. A line attacking Nixon got the biggest applause. As expected, Stevenson was renominated without difficulty. And when he threw the Vice Presidential nomination up for grabs, there was an immediate ground swell for Jack. Adlai's decision caught the convention off guard, and the Kennedys had only overnight to corral votes. It turned out to be one of the most frenzied nights in recent campaign history.

Bobby took charge of a tiny group of Kennedy workers—most of them family members. Under his direction, sister Eunice was assigned to appeal to the Mississippi delegation. Bobby himself tackled Senator John McClellan and other friends among the delegations. Brother-in-law Sargent Shriver worked on his home state of Maryland. And Connecticut

Governor Abe Ribicoff and State Chairman John Bailey worked on the New York delegates.

Their chief refrain was "It's either Estes Kefauver or Jack Kennedy; and you don't want Kefauver, do you?" The argument was persuasive. Many Southern delegates didn't cotton to Kefauver because of his deep commitment to civil rights, while some Northerners were alarmed about his anticrime investigations which uncovered close ties between big-city Democratic machines and racketeers.

The first ballot showed Kefauver with 483½, Kennedy 304, Senator Albert Gore of Tennessee, 178; New York's Mayor Robert F. Wagner 162¼, and Humphrey 134½. Kennedy, watching the balloting on television, was amazed at the unexpected strength he showed in such Southern states as Georgia, Louisiana, and Virginia, and in Nevada. Then came the report that Kefauver was on the way to see Humphrey. "Get up there and intercept Hubert," Kennedy told Sorensen. "Tell him I'd like to see him, too."

Sorensen ran into Humphrey's floor manager, Representative (more currently Senator) Eugene McCarthy. "Jack wants Hubert to come over to see him," said Sorensen.

"Not a chance," was McCarthy's reply. "Up in Minnesota we're Protestants and farmers." (McCarthy, a Catholic, was alluding to Jack's two alleged major handicaps: his religion and his agricultural voting record.)

Bobby stood on the floor of Convention Hall and watched as the devastating Kefauver comeback continued. State after state began switching from Humphrey to Kefauver. Soon it was all over. Kefauver had won the nomination.

Out on the Convention Hall floor, Bobby was observed in a boiling rage, but eventually he calmed down. "It really struck me then," he said later, "that it wasn't the issues which mattered so much, it was the friendships. So many people had come up to me and said they would like to vote for Jack but they were going to vote for Estes Kefauver because he had sent them a card or visited in their home. I said right there that as well as paying attention to the issues we should send Christmas cards next time."

Jack Kennedy, who had suffered his first political defeat, flew off to France to visit his father on the Riviera. Bobby went to Hyannis Port.

Taking a leave of absence from the McClellan Committee, Bobby spent seven weeks traveling with Adlai Stevenson. Though carried on the rolls as special assistant to campaign director James Finnegan, he had little to do. But he wanted to learn everything he could about national campaigning. He observed Stevenson's performances carefully —and was appalled. The Democratic Presidential candidate made little effort to stir up the crowds at his whistle-stops, and Stevenson and his staff showed little interest in cooperating with the press. The candidate often ruined his television speeches by rushing through the final pages as if air time was about to run out. But the most serious problem lay in the division of command between Finnegan and Paul Butler, the Democratic National Chairman. For the most part, Bobby remained alone and silent during those seven weeks, hardly speaking to anyone. When reminded of this years later, Bobby said, "I was learning what not to do."

Once Bobby came to Adlai's rescue at Lewistown, Pennsylvania, when Stevenson was unable to deliver a whistle-stop speech because a group of noisy youngsters were loudly chanting "I like Ike" and other Republican slogans. "You people are making so much noise," Adlai told them, "that I don't know whether I'm teaching a third-grade class or giving a political talk."

Bobby lured the kids away to a railway siding and began to tell them a story. So that Adlai might finish his speech unmolested, he persuaded them to have a footrace. The prize he offered was a choice of a big Adlai button or a quarter. An onlooker said that Bobby seemed a bit stunned when the winner chose the quarter. But at any rate, Adlai did finish his speech. Which may have been Bobby's major contribution to the campaign.

That the Kennedys' political fortunes remained on his mind was demonstrated by a statement to reporters in Little Rock, Arkansas. Bobby mentioned his family's gratitude for the Southern support given Jack at the recent Democratic National Convention. "My family is so grateful to the South for supporting John that we sing 'Dixie' after we say grace before eating."

After learning what he could from a firsthand look at the Stevenson campaign, Bobby returned to Washington, where he found that his good friend Joseph McCarthy was suffering from a serious liver ailment. In the Senator's last months, Bobby frequently called on him to try to sustain his morale. His loyalty to the Senator in a time of adversity won for Bobby the everlasting gratitude of Mrs. McCarthy. Since she remarried they have remained close friends.

On May 2, 1957, Joseph R. McCarthy died in the Naval Medical Center at Bethesda, Maryland. Bobby attended the funeral in Washington, then flew out to the Senator's hometown of Appleton, Wisconsin, for the interment. It was the end of the McCarthy era. The Kennedy era was about to begin.

11

Hoffa

For two years, as Chief Counsel of the McClellan Committee, Bobby "had shown that he knew how to dramatize hearings," reported Pulitzer prize-winning reporter Clark Mollenhoff. "But he also had shown signs of unsteadiness. He sometimes lost his temper, and occasionally a little-boy impetuousness marred his performance. Members of the press were inclined to give a major part of the credit for those successful investigations to Carmine Bellino, Jerome Adlerman, Alphonse Calabrese, and other older, more experienced members of the staff."

Mostly the press viewed Bobby as just the kid brother of Senator John F. Kennedy, who had barely lost the nomination for Vice President at the 1956 Democratic Convention. "Others regarded him as the socialite millionaire son of Joseph P. Kennedy, who was best known as a conservative Democrat and former United States Ambassador to England," wrote Mollenhoff in his book, *Tentacles of Power*. "It was general knowledge that Bob Kennedy had been given one million dollars at the age of twenty-one, and had married the equally wealthy Ethel Skakel. He did not have to work for a living. He was likable, but he was not a politician. He had a tendency to use acid sarcasm, and he was inclined to be irritable or rudely blunt when he was crossed."

It was Mollenhoff who finally convinced Bobby that pay dirt might be uncovered in a probe of the hierarchy of the International Brotherhood of Teamsters. But when Mollenhoff first broached the subject in early 1956, young Kennedy did not seem overly interested. For one thing, several other

Congressional committees had probed into Teamsters' affairs and apparently uncovered nothing more startling than some suspicious wheeling and dealing on the part of a then little-known international vice president named James Riddle Hoffa.

During his McCarthy days, Bobby had come to know Edward Bennett Williams, the noted criminal lawyer who later served as general counsel of the International Teamsters. Bobby admired Williams for his brilliant defense of Mc-Carthy during the Watkins Committee hearings, and for a time they were good friends. And one of Ed Williams' law associates, with whom Bobby also became well acquainted, was Edward T. Cheyfitz, who had been a Communist in his youth.

Young Kennedy was plainly fascinated by Cheyfitz' many wondrous tales of life in the Communist party. Cheyfitz shocked Kennedy when he said that he had run into Walter and Victor Reuther in the Soviet Union in 1933; and that the two brothers had written shortly thereafter a glowing tribute to the Communist system. Bobby apparently was horrified that such people had gained enormous power in the labor movement—but that was before he came to realize how much he and his brother would need Walter Reuther. Reuther was also a power in Democratic politics.

At that time, Cheyfitz was public-relations man for Team-sters' president, Dave Beck. In this capacity, he invited Bobby to tour the brand-new five-million-dollar Teamsters Build-ing, the "marble palace," as it then was known, in Washing-ton. Beck, it happened, was not there that day, but Bobby met Beck's attractive and efficient secretary, Ann Watkins, as well as several other top Teamsters officials.

As Bobby himself later told the story, he was much im-pressed with what he saw. He was overwhelmed by Beck's office. "It was as big as it possibly could have been without being an auditorium," he wrote. "I genuinely admired the view from the big bay windows across the park to the Cap-itol. It was all very friendly."

So friendly, in fact, that Bobby promised to arrange for "my brother, the Senator," to send over an autographed copy of *Profiles in Courage* for Dave Beck. This was done later in the day.

Mollenhoff, who, as a reporter for the Cowles publications,

had been blasting away at the Teamsters, kept "bugging" Bobby about a possible investigation. "As I tried to stimulate Bob Kennedy's interest in the labor racket inquiry, his mood blew hot and cold," Mollenhoff said. "I didn't know what to make of it . . . I assumed he was just another young lawyer who didn't want to take on the job of fighting the labor racketeers. I didn't blame him completely, for there were few prosecutors with the interest and the courage to investigate labor rackets. It was a thankless task in many ways. Undiscriminating newspaper cartoonists, editors and the uninformed voters were apt to accept the premise that those who prosecuted labor leaders were anti-labor."

By now John F. Kennedy had decided to try for the Presidency. He knew he needed the liberals if he was to succeed in obtaining the Democratic nomination in 1960. Consequently, at first, he was not too happy when brother Bobby finally decided to look into labor's abuses. Even Old Joe, anti-labor to the core, voiced misgivings, and even suggested that Bobby resign as counsel. He argued that Jack's chances for the Presidency would be damaged if any anti-labor tag were pinned on Bobby.

But Bobby remained firm. This was something he wanted to do. It would give him the limelight, he argued, and more-over it would benefit Jack in the long run. Later, of course, he was proved right. The investigation was authorized unanimously by the Senate on January 30, 1957. Headed by Senator McClellan, a special committee was voted a budget of $350,000 and a staff composed of twenty investigators and twenty-five accountants. Later that staff was more than doubled.

John F. Kennedy, however, was still having qualms. He had been warned by Majority Leader Lyndon Johnson that if he was to be a serious contender in 1960, it would be smart to stay off such a committee. But the fact that "Bobby has worked terribly hard on this investigation, he believes it is important and he wants to do it," as Jack Kennedy told Clark Mollenhoff at the time, finally convinced him.

It was one of John F. Kennedy's more astute decisions.

Clark Mollenhoff was probably the first newsman to forecast fame for Bobby Kennedy. Two days before the first hearings of the Select Committee, he wrote: "The mop-haired and boyish-appearing little brother of Senator John Kennedy is on the move." The article in the Cowles newspapers was highly flattering, referring to Bobby's status as a "millionaire," his father's many millions and the "political prominence of the family." But to Mollenhoff's amazement, he discovered that young Kennedy was displeased with the piece.

"Why do you reporters have to bring politics, family and my money into it?" Bobby snapped angrily. "Those things aren't important." Bobby indicated he wanted to stand on his own feet.

Things were pretty routine on the committee until February 14, 1957, when Bobby received a call from a New York lawyer named John Cye Cheasty: "Mr. Kennedy, I've got information that will make your hair curl."

"What's it about?"

"I can't discuss it on the phone."

The next day Cheasty told his story in Kennedy's office in the Senate Office Building as Bobby munched on a cheese sandwich and took notes. It was a startling story, indeed. What Cheasty reported was that Jimmy Hoffa had offered him $18,000 to "infiltrate" Kennedy's staff and pilfer secret information from the files. Hoffa particularly wanted to know what the committee had on him.

Asking Cheasty to wait, Bobby strode into the office of Chairman McClellan. After hearing the story, the Arkansas Democrat drawled, "This is a job for the FBI."

Fifteen minutes later FBI Director J. Edgar Hoover entered the Senator's office. Meanwhile, a quick check had been made on Cheasty. FBI agents soon pieced together his background: Cheasty, forty-nine, lived in Brooklyn with his wife and five children . . . had served with the Internal Revenue's intelligence unit . . . Navy intelligence officer in World War II . . . retired as Naval Commander in 1951, following heart attack . . . in recent years had done part-time legal work from Wall Street office . . . no derogatory information in FBI files. . . .

The implications were enormous. Hoffa, tough as he was, had always been careful. Had he slipped with Cheasty? The FBI decided to find out. It set a trap—with Cheasty as the bait.

Meanwhile, Bobby had a problem. He had agreed to dine with Hoffa at the home of Eddie Cheyfitz, the redheaded lawyer and public-relations man. Now he had qualms about breaking bread with Hoffa. But he agreed to go ahead after J. Edgar Hoover advised him that canceling the dinner— Hoffa was flying in from Detroit—might look peculiar.

Arriving in Washington February 19, Hoffa had proceeded to Cheyfitz' office in the Hill Building. First order of business was an off-the-record interview with Ed Lahey of the Chicago *Daily News*. (The next day Lahey warned Bobby not to underestimate Hoffa. "I was surprised at Kennedy's confidence," Lahey said.) Second order of business was a phone call from Cheasty, who arranged to meet Hoffa at the corner of 17th and I Streets, N.W. There—under FBI observation—Cheasty gave Hoffa the names of witnesses to be subpoenaed by the committee.

When Bobby left his office that night for Cheyfitz' home, he had already received a report of this FBI surveillance.

As they sized each other up for the first time, Bobby said to Hoffa, "From what I've heard about you, maybe I should have worn my bulletproof vest."

Hoffa grinned. "I only do to others what they do to me, only worse."

They sat down to a roast-beef dinner—the three of them— and talked about many things. Neither Bobby nor Hoffa drank. Cheyfitz asked many of the questions—about Hoffa's widely reported associations with the underworld, for example. Hoffa conceded he had underworld associates, including labor racketeer John (Johnny Dio) Dioguardi, but said he was entitled to his own choice of friends. He assured Bobby he was tough, plenty tough, but "strictly legal."

Just before 10:00 the phone rang, a prearranged call from Ethel Kennedy. "Better hurry up," chided Hoffa. "She probably called to see if you're still alive."

Within hearing distance of Cheyfitz and Hoffa, Bobby said, "I'm still alive, dear. If you hear a big explosion, I probably won't be."

Hoffa broke into a loud guffaw: "Bob's got a real sense of humor."

"It was a real pleasant dinner," Cheyfitz later told this writer. "We broke up early when Bob had to leave. And I drove Jimmy to the airport."

Talking to Clark Mollenhoff a few days later, Bobby said, "I'd heard he was a likable fellow, but that he was tough.

He talked so much about how tough he was that I had difficulty believing he really was tough."

But as Hoffa recalled the meeting, "I can tell by how he shakes hands what kind of fellow I got. I said to myself, 'Here's a fella thinks he's doing me a favor by talking to me.' "

Meanwhile Cye Cheasty was officially sworn in as a staff member and assigned to New York, supposedly to look into racketeering in the building trades. He kept feeding Hoffa a stream of innocuous FBI-screened information, but after a while Jimmy demanded something more. He urged Cheasty to seek a transfer to Washington. The FBI thought this a good idea—and on March 8, Cheasty was able to report to Hoffa that he was being transferred. Events now began to move more rapidly.

On March 10, Hoffa arrived in Washington for a trade-union conference, and with Jimmy in Washington, the FBI decided to make its big move.

At 7:00 P.M., March 12, Cheasty met Hoffa in the park across the street from his hotel, the DuPont Plaza. A motion-picture camera manned by two FBI agents filmed the scene, as other agents posed as passersby. Cheasty handed over an envelope containing carefully screened documents. He and Hoffa shook hands. In doing so, the FBI claimed, Hoffa slipped money to Cheasty. Both then went their separate ways.

The next day, March 13, just ten minutes before the committee was to resume hearings, Bobby received a call from the FBI, requesting an immediate conference. At 2:15 P.M. McClellan and Kennedy departed for what they told reporters was a "routine discussion of a legal matter not connected with the hearing." The meeting in McClellan's office began five minutes later. Present, besides the Senator, Bobby and two FBI agents, was Assistant Attorney General Warren Olney III, head of the Justice Department's Criminal Division.

Legally, to arrest Hoffa, the documents had to be on his person, so Cheasty arranged an 11:00 P.M. meeting. Blissfully unaware of the trap about to be sprung, Jimmy dined at the Sheraton-Carlton Hotel with seven Republican Congressmen from Michigan. He left early, he told them, to attend a conference with officials of the Machinists Union.

Bobby ate alone with his wife at their home in Hickory Hill. "All evening I knew Bobby was restless," Ethel later told a newsman. "He said he was waiting for an important call from Senator McClellan. He wouldn't tell me what it was all about."

Senator McClellan didn't leave his office that evening. He ordered his dinner sent in. J. Edgar Hoover, who was calling the shots from his office, was in constant radio communication with his men staked out around the DuPont Plaza Hotel, at that time one of Washington's newer hostelries. The glass-walled lobby, clearly visible from the street, was crowded with labor officials. The air was heavy with cigar smoke and the hearty laughter of those who had dined well.

At 11:00 Cheasty arrived in an FBI-driven cab. He got out and waited. Hoffa appeared five minutes later, accepted the documents and entered the hotel. As he started into a self-service elevator, six men surrounded him. Hoffa was startled, but he did not resist. An FBI agent quickly frisked him and removed the incriminating documents.

Eddie Cheyfitz, who was in the lobby, thought some goons were taking Jimmy for a ride. He rushed to a phone to call the FBI, and was told about the arrest. He then called his partner Edward Bennett Williams, who hurried down to the District Courthouse to arrange for Hoffa's release on bail.

Bobby, meanwhile, had arrived at the courthouse with Ethel. Hoffa joshed with the Kennedys, they later reported, and said he had read they liked to ride horses every morning. "Bet I'm a better horseman," he quipped, adding that he usually got his exercise doing pushups. "I can do thirty-five," Hoffa boasted. "How many can you do?"

Bobby said he could do more.

But Hoffa had another version of the meeting: "I said, 'Listen, Bobby, you run your business and I'll run mine. You go on home and go to bed. I'll take care of things. Let's don't have no problems.' He was very unhappy because I called him Bobby. He's a kid, a spoiled kid."

Bobby was asked what he would do if Hoffa were acquitted, and replied, "I'll jump off the Capitol dome." It was a remark he would eventually regret. For Edward

Bennett Williams, after a brilliant defense resulting in an acquittal for Hoffa, sent Bobby a parachute, a gag the recipient failed to appreciate. Afterward he no longer considered Williams a friend. Hoffa's defense was that he had hired John Cye Cheasty as a lawyer; there had been no intent to bribe.

But Bobby, infuriated by the acquittal, noted that the defense had played to the eight Negroes on the twelve-member jury. For example, former heavyweight champion Joe Louis put in a personal appearance in the courtroom to "see what they're doing to my good friend, Jimmy Hoffa." Louis and Hoffa put on a display of affection that could hardly have been missed by the jurors. Other questionable tactics were also used to convince the Negro jurors that Hoffa was almost a "soul brother."

"What Kennedy did not note," later commented Professor Albert A. Blum in a *New Leader* review of Bobby's *The Enemy Within,* "was that these eight jurors may have been aware that the charges against Hoffa developed out of a committee headed by a Senator from Arkansas, whose great concern for civil liberties and for the right to vote within unions did not appear to extend to Negroes in his own state. Hoffa did not particularly need the help of Joe Louis in this case."

Almost immediately Bobby put his gumshoes to work. They discovered several tie-ins between the former heavyweight champion and Jimmy Hoffa. Investigator Walter Sheridan was dispatched to Chicago, to talk to Louis, but how all this could be justified, except as the use of a Senate committee for punitive measures, baffled civil libertarians.

"The former fighter was a lonely figure," Bobby reported later. "Walt found him in a third-floor apartment, sitting in a chair and reading a newspaper, with both the radio and the television going. . . . Joe Louis had been one of my heroes when I was a small boy. I had requested Walt to ask for the former champion's autograph for my son, whose name also is Joe."

At the end of the interview, Sheridan made the request. "I'll do it for his son, but not for him," Louis said. "Tell him to go take a jump off the Empire State Building."

But Bobby never called Louis to testify publicly. The reason was his pity for the ex-champ who, Bobby felt, had been unaware of what he had done by going to Washington. Perhaps a more practical consideration was that the charge of "intimidation" would have arisen as a result.

But Bobby did score one significant victory in his campaign against crooked labor leaders. He managed to destroy Dave Beck. Millions of Americans watched their TV sets with amazement as the once-powerful labor baron, his eyes downcast, resorted constantly to the Fifth Amendment. "It was like shooting rats in a barrel," commented Hoffa, who viewed the proceedings with equanimity. For he was well aware that Beck's downfall meant his own election as international president of the Teamsters.

Bobby pursued the enemy with the uninhibited joy of a youngster playing sheriff in a cowboys-and-Indians game. A writer for *The Saturday Evening Post* reported that "a certain gaiety pervades the office. . . . A while back on [Bobby] Kennedy's birthday, the staff held a party in the office. They gave him a pair of cowboy gloves, a cap gun and a whodunit game."

A week before the Teamsters convention that was certain to elect him as Beck's successor, Jimmy Hoffa was called before the committee. It was soon clear that although Beck had been no match for Bobby, Hoffa was. He was ready, willing and more than able to put up a fight. As Hoffa later put it, "I didn't intend to play patsy for the Kennedys' political ambitions."

From the start, Bobby's pursuit of Hoffa had all the elements of a personal vendetta. His zealous efforts to skewer Hoffa at times seemed second only to his desire to get his brother elected President. Unlike Beck, however, Hoffa disdained the use of the Fifth Amendment and invariably beat Bobby down in any argument.

Hoffa, not overly modest, has explained how he usually managed to get the upper hand during Bobby's relentless and interminable questioning. "Oh, I used to love to bug the little bastard," he told this writer in August of 1966. "Whenever Bobby would get tangled up in one of his involved questions, I would wink at him. That invariably got him. 'Mr. Chairman,' he'd shout, 'would you please instruct the witness to stop making faces at me?' "

Hoffa laughed and laughed.

The record amply demonstrates that Hoffa often did manage to make a monkey out of the crusading committee counsel. Once Bobby asked him what he had done with some Minifons (tiny tape-recording devices) which Jimmy had purchased:

> HOFFA: What did I do with them? Well, what *did* I do with them?
> KENNEDY: What did you do with them?
> HOFFA: I am trying to recall.
> KENNEDY: You could remember that.
> HOFFA: When were they delivered, do you know? That must have been quite a while.
> KENNEDY: You know what you did with the Minifons and don't ask me.
> HOFFA: What did I do with them?
> KENNEDY: What did you do with them?
> HOFFA: Mr. Kennedy, I bought some Minifons and there is no question about it, but I cannot recall what became of them.

The verbal sparring continued for a time, then:

> HOFFA: Well, I will have to stand on the answers that I have made in regards to my recollection and I cannot answer unless you give me some recollection, other than I have answered.

Criticism of his tactics as Chief Counsel of the "Rackets Committee" (Select Committee on Improper Activities in the Labor Management Field) has always irked Bobby. For example, he responded with heat to the British writer, Anthony West, when he raised questions about his inquisitorial tactics.

In a letter to the Montreal weekly, *Saturday Night,* which had published a West article in early 1959, Bobby wrote in part: "If Mr. West was working for us and made a report on a situation similar to the one that I read in your magazine, as we are interested in facts, I would fire him because of incompetency."

To which West replied: "After noting that these [words], with all their evidence of the command of language and of the common sense of the writer, are the work of the Chief Counsel of a select committee of the United States

Senate, the reader is invited to consider an important difference between Mr. Kennedy and your correspondent. While Mr. Kennedy devotes three and a quarter columns of this magazine to calling him a liar, an ignorant booby and an incompetent reporter, he cannot bring himself to quote one single complete sentence written by your correspondent.

"As your correspondent has said before, this sort of trickery and disregard for the truth is what may be expected of Mr. Kennedy. It is not to be expected from a lawyer with any sense of ethics of his profession, or from a man in the responsible position of Chief Counsel to a Senate Committee. The combination of contempt for the truth, contempt for legal processes, and temperamental instability [is] shown as clearly in his letter as in his conduct of his office. . . .

"Mr. Kennedy has been remarkably unlucky in getting indictments, and still more unlucky in getting convictions, out of his committee's findings. His facts, so carefully nourished and cherished, tend to wilt when exposed to a courtroom atmosphere, just as the witnesses who produce them tend to fade under cross-examination by defending counsel."

And Bobby was absolutely livid when *The New Republic* questioned his qualifications in an article entitled "The Case Against Him for Attorney General." Yale Law Professor Alexander M. Bickel did not make an issue of Bobby's lack of legal experience or his youthfulness, but said that the committee "with Mr. Kennedy in the lead . . . embarked on a number of purely punitive expeditions" and engaged in "relentless, vindictive battering" of certain witnesses. The professor detailed several cases of Counsel Kennedy in action. One was the questioning of Joseph F. (Joey) Glimco, the president of Chicago Teamsters Local 777, often arrested but seldom convicted:

KENNEDY: You got your citizenship and abused it; did you not?

GLIMCO: Fifth Amendment.

KENNEDY: Did you ever do anything to help the union membership, one thing? You don't care anything about yourself and these other people who are gangsters and hoodlums, do you? And you defraud the union . . . ?

GLIMCO: I respectfully decline to answer because I honestly believe my answer might tend to incriminate me.

KENNEDY: I would agree with you.

MCCLELLAN: I believe it would.

KENNEDY: You haven't got the guts to [answer], have you, Mr. Glimco?

GLIMCO: I respectfully decline . . .

MCCLELLAN: Morally you are kind of yellow inside, are you not? That is the truth about it?

GLIMCO: Fifth Amendment.

Professor Bickel commented: "Mr. [Robert] Kennedy's exercise of power to destroy or damage individuals was not subject to such safeguards as the right to cross-examination and the right to an impartial judge who is not at the same time also the prosecutor. . . . What is one to make of the way both the Senator and Mr. Kennedy took it upon themselves to denounce Glimco at the end? This was the language of a judge passing sentence, not of legislators looking for facts to guide them in their law-making."

Or there is the answer of Attorney General William P. Rogers when Bobby complained that the Justice Department had not acted on several citations for contempt which he had sent over. Rogers' reply was that the citations were so poorly drawn that they would not stand up in any court of law. And in a letter to Representative Thomas M. Pelly of Washington, Kenneth Rosengren, a lawyer and a Democrat, wrote: "It was common knowledge among lawyers that young Kennedy was inept and unskilled in both direct and cross-examination. He constantly argued and quarreled with the witnesses. His fumbling and stumbling frequently caused the proceedings to become a Pier 6 shouting contest, rather than an inquiry."

One such shouting match occurred in July 1959. In questioning Louis Goldblatt, secretary-treasurer of the International Longshoremen's and Warehousemen's Union (ILWU), Bobby said, ". . . our information is that you have been a member of the Communist party. Will you tell the Committee when you left the Communist party?"

It was, as Goldblatt's lawyer quickly noted, "a loaded question."

Chairman McClellan leaped in, as he often had to do, to rescue Bobby. "I will ask it so it is not loaded," the Chairman said. "The question is, are you now a member of the Communist party?"

After haggling about the pertinence of the question to the inquiry, Goldblatt finally declared, "On advice of counsel, I refuse to answer that question. . . ."

Then Bobby started in on Hoffa:

KENNEDY: Now, does it concern you at all that the leadership of the Longshoremen's Union were expelled in 1950 by organized labor because they were Communist-dominated?

HOFFA: Mr. Kennedy, I am very familiar with politics in organized labor leading to the expulsion not only of the ILWU but the Teamsters. . . . Harry Bridges has never been convicted by a court. . . .

KENNEDY: This was a report, Mr. Chairman, of the executive committee appointed by President Murray to investigate charges against the International Longshoremen's and Warehousemen's Union. Their findings were that the ILWU "has consistently and without a single deviation followed the sharp turns and swerves of the Communist party line and sacrificed the economic and social interests of its membership to that line."

HOFFA: Of course you know that is ridiculous because they have the highest hourly wage for their people in their classification that you will find. You know it is ridiculous. They have a pension and welfare and a very wonderful medical center for the people. They just recently built a beautiful hall.

KENNEDY: The Teamsters up at least until 1957, January 1957, had also followed a very critical position of the Longshoremen's Union on the West Coast, and held that Harry Bridges and that union were following the Communist line.

HOFFA: I am not responsible again for politics in our union. . . .

KENNEDY: Is there any question in your mind that Mr. Goldblatt is a Communist, Mr. Hoffa?

HOFFA: I don't know whether he is or not, but that is not the question. If I am dealing with Goldblatt I deal

with Goldblatt like our Secretary Herter deals with
Khrushchev, on the basis of what is good for the
American worker, the American citizen, and I am not
in bed with him.

KENNEDY: I don't think the comparison quite holds.

HOFFA: This is what you think.

Bobby also triumphantly reported to the committee that
in contrast with the Teamsters, the East Coast longshoremen had refused to become part of any deal with Harry
Bridges. "However," as Paul Jacobs, in a *California Law
Review* analysis of the McClellan Committee, observed,
"Kennedy neglected, at the time, to also point out to the
Committee that the East Coast longshoremen he used as an
example of political virtue had been expelled from the AFL-
CIO for being dominated by racketeers at the very time they
were expressing their righteous horror at the idea of being
associated with Communists."

Jacobs, a consultant of the Center for the Study of
Democratic Institutions at Santa Barbara, also noted:

"The Committee was not above also using anti-union
employers to discredit the Teamsters or capitalizing on a
witness' recourse to the fifth amendment on some questions
to ask other unrelated ones knowing that the fifth amendment would be used again in answer. . . ."

A Teamster lawyer, David Previant, has listed the kinds
of "guilt" he claimed Bobby Kennedy used against the union:
"We had guilt by association, guilt by marriage, guilt by eating in the same chop house, guilt by the general counsel's
amazement, guilt by somebody else taking the Fifth Amendment, guilt by somebody else refusing to testify. But we
think the 'doozer' was the one that happened when the
Committee was taking testimony concerning a criminal
case in which eight defendants were tried for eleven weeks;
the jury was out only eight minutes and came in with the
verdict of 'not guilty.' The police detective who helped
prepare the case said the prosecution felt it was not a fair
trial. The Committee nodded in sympathy and agreement.
This is guilt by acquittal."

But if some attorneys came away feeling that Bobby, as
one of them put it, was "a sadistic little monster," others

felt differently. One, significantly, was Joseph L. Rauh, attorney for Walter Reuther and the UAW:

"He was trying to be a fair investigator and any abuses were not due to 'vindictiveness,' but to his lack of experience. If it sometimes led to abuse of witnesses, it sometimes led to witnesses like Hoffa getting away with murder. The technique of questioning is an art, and Bobby wasn't experienced at it—he didn't know how to go for the jugular. Far from browbeating Hoffa, it was more of a case of Hoffa browbeating *him*."

Bobby Kennedy also involved himself in behind-the-scenes activities to "get" Hoffa. Bobby took an active role in the maneuverings that resulted in the formation of a court-imposed Board of Monitors which was supposed to help clean up the Teamsters. On May 17, 1959, Bobby invited to his father's Park Avenue apartment two of the thirteen rank-and-file Teamsters whose lawsuit had led to the monitorship, and told them that he had evidence that one of the monitors, Larry Smith, had sold out to Hoffa. He then suggested they vote to replace Smith with a former FBI agent named Terence F. McShane.

Steve Milone, one of the Teamsters, was shocked. In an affidavit, he later testified:

"I told him that I was not going to vote to oust Larry Smith on this hearsay evidence. Mr. Kennedy got very excited; he said that he had never said he would use that type of evidence to oust Lawrence Smith. I said to Mr. Kennedy, you said exactly that. You have been telling me about this hearsay evidence and these witnesses you can't bring forward. On those grounds you are asking me to vote to oust Larry Smith and join up with you. I said I would not do it.

"Mr. Kennedy then said to me you are a liar. I told him I wasn't a liar and that I knew what I was talking about. Kennedy said to me, you are a son of a bitch.

"This coming from Bob Kennedy really shocked me. I said to him that if you will step outside or down the street and repeat the remark I'll flatten you. Kennedy said you will what? I said you heard me. I'll give you one more opportunity to step outside and repeat it, and I'll guarantee I'll flip you."

The would-be combatants nearly came to blows but were

separated by Walter Sheridan and Terence McShane, who had sat silent during the meeting. When he left the apartment, Milone continued in his affidavit: "Bobby came out and put out his hand to apologize. I refused to accept it. He said he had been called a son of a bitch many a time. I said maybe you are one, but I'm not."

Paul Jacobs concluded his 1963 *California Law Review* article with these observations:

"Jimmy Hoffa and the Teamsters Union are the antithesis of what I believe a union leader and a union ought to be. But my feelings about Hoffa are only important insofar as they affect what I write about him. Robert Kennedy's behavior toward Hoffa is of far greater significance, for Kennedy is not a private citizen—he is a public servant, and what he does about Hoffa involves not only himself but the very Government itself. As staff counsel for the McClellan Committee and as Attorney General, he acts in a public capacity in the name of every citizen. As a result he is open to judgment about *how* he exercises that responsibility.

"The Kennedy-Hoffa feud has many political and moral dimensions which need examination, but it seems clear to me that the McClellan Committee's direct involvement . . . in the affairs of the board of monitors went far beyond the committee's specific mandate and the general mandate of Congressional committees. The evidence demonstrates to me that the committee and its staff, under Robert Kennedy's direction, trespassed heavily upon the rights of Hoffa and the union.

"It is a cliché and a truism that the most important civil rights are those of our enemies—of the people with whom we disagree. And so, although I have nothing in common with Hoffa, the union leader, Hoffa, the citizen, is me. His rights are the same as mine and require the same protection."

When he became Attorney General, one of Bobby's first acts was to put together what later became known as the "Hoffa Brigade." Walter Sheridan, who had been one of Bobby's chief investigators, was assigned as the leader. The Brigade had only one mission—"to get Hoffa."

12

Goldwater

From its inception, Robert F. Kennedy ruled the Rackets Committee with an iron hand. He ran it as his own private domain. Chairman McClellan would be consulted—but usually as an afterthought. "Bobby didn't consult us," the then Senator Barry Goldwater says. "We would arrive for hearings and there we would find witnesses called by the Kennedys without our knowledge."

And during an executive session, when Republican Senator Homer Capehart once asked Bobby about the progress of a jukebox investigation in his home state of Indiana, Bobby not only refused to reply but turned his back. The angry Capehart turned to Chairman McClellan and said, "John, that little snotnose turned his back on me when I asked him a legitimate question. Why don't you do something?"

Obviously embarrassed, the chairman did nothing.

There was little doubt that John McClellan was enjoying the limelight, but he wore it well. (Like the Kennedy brothers, the chairman usually showed up in a blue shirt for the TV cameras.) Not so long ago, he had been just another Senator. Now he was a national figure. Not bad for a boy born on a farm in Grant County, Arkansas, who "never saw the inside of a law school," and was admitted to the practice of law at the age of seventeen by a special act passed by the legislature.

Barry Goldwater recalls that Bobby frequently became flustered in grilling labor hoods or their lawyers. "When the going would get rough, John McClellan was likely to take over the questioning, thus saving Bobby from embarrassment."

Once Bobby was questioning Dave Beck, the International Teamsters president, about $9.65 in union funds that had been used to purchase five dozen diapers. When Kennedy asked who they were for, Beck took the Fifth Amendment, but volunteered, "I'll guarantee you, Mr. Kennedy, they weren't for me."

The crowd roared with laughter as Bobby spluttered.

But Chairman McClellan interjected, "I have my doubts about that last statement."

The crowd roared again.

Executive sessions of the committee were frequently tense. Once Senator Goldwater remonstrated with Carmine Bellino, the committee's accountant investigator, for not having spent more time examining the books of Walter Reuther's United Automobile Workers. Under questioning, Bellino conceded he had given less than two days to checking the UAW's finances. Goldwater, who viewed Reuther as just as dangerous as Hoffa, angrily wanted to know how it was possible for an accountant, no matter how able, to do a conscientious job on a major union's books in that short a time.

Bobby Kennedy exploded. "Are you questioning my integrity?" he shouted. Leaping from his chair, fists clenched, he advanced on the Senator from Arizona.

"Fortunately," Goldwater drily recalls, "Jack Kennedy leaped up from his chair, grabbed Bobby from behind, and prevented him from hitting a United States Senator."

On the whole, however, Goldwater got along better with Bobby than did the other Republicans on the committee. In fact, on several occasions, he saved Bobby's job for him. There was the time, for example, when the other Republican Senators thought they finally had "the arrogant little bastard" boxed in. But at a Republican caucus, Barry used all his persuasive talents to argue his colleagues out of demanding Kennedy's resignation. "Basically what I told them," recalls Barry, "was that Bobby was a young man and that he was entitled to make an occasional mistake."

The Barry-Bobby relationship was not wholly a one-way street. "Bobby had been most helpful to me during my 1958 campaign for re-election to the Senate," says Goldwater.

The political weather vanes pointed to a Goldwater defeat. Governor Ernest McFarland, his Democratic opponent, was making capital out of Barry's unorthodoxy. He had broken with the liberal elements in his party, bitterly denouncing President Eisenhower's domestic policies as "dime-store socialism." He had called for firmer anti-Communism in foreign policy and protested Federal intervention in school integration squabbles.

"Things sure looked bad for a time," recalls Goldwater. "But, out of the blue, Bobby Kennedy came to the rescue."

The rescue was the information that in one of his gubernatorial races McFarland had accepted a $4,000 contribution from Jimmy Hoffa's Teamsters Union. This was material Bobby had uncovered in the course of his work on the McClellan Committee.

"And, brother, did I use that particular piece of information!" says Goldwater. "That, plus Walter Reuther's announced opposition to me, helped turn the tide in my favor. Of course, I was grateful to Bobby. . . . That's why, despite our differences, I did my best to keep him from being fired."

One of those differences was Bobby's obvious unwillingness to do battle with Walter Reuther. But the Kennedys were well aware of Reuther's enormous power within the Democratic party. They had seen it in action at the 1956 Democratic National Convention when Reuther dumped Averell Harriman in favor of Adlai Stevenson. More personally, they had felt it when Reuther had switched to Estes Kefauver for the Vice Presidency. The lesson of 1956 had not been lost on the Kennedys, now committed to going all the way to the White House. And under Bobby's guidance, the McClellan Committee concentrated its fire almost exclusively on the Teamsters and the old-line AFL unions, most of whose leaders had long records of supporting Republicans.

This behind-the-scenes feuding had come to a political head as early as July 1957 when *Newsweek* reported: "Several Committee Republicans suspect—but won't charge publicly as yet—that Robert Kennedy's conduct of the labor-rackets probe helps promote, in effect, the ambitions of Walter P. Reuther—a fact which would not lead Reuther to oppose Bobby's brother, Sen. John F. Kennedy, for the nomination in 1960.

"Robert Kennedy has ignored continued demands for an investigation of Reuther, GOP members say privately. And they further emphasize the coincidence that the labor leaders subjected to the Committee's sharpest attacks are the ones who have stood in the way of Reuther's domination of American labor."

Barry Goldwater has since recalled that the McClellan group "never got around to investigating David Dubinsky and his Garment Workers" either, though "their names came up a couple of times."

Nor could Barry Goldwater get anywhere with his request for an investigation of another of the leading members of the AFL-CIO hierarchy. Several weeks later, Goldwater asked about the status of the investigation and Bobby, almost as an afterthought, replied that Ken O'Donnell, his administrative assistant, had asked the labor leader in question about the allegations. The AFL-CIO bigwig replied that they were false. The investigation was terminated.

Bobby brooked no interference from staffers. "Either you agreed with him 100 percent and all the time or you were an enemy," one recently recalled. Bobby apparently trusted only three subordinates—Walter Sheridan, Carmine Bellino and a former magazine writer named Pierre Salinger. In his memoir, *With Kennedy*, Salinger narrates with evident satisfaction how he invaded a union official's home in Seattle without a warrant to search for missing Teamsters records. The story, which also involves the seduction of a maid, is funny, but it raises a question as to the propriety of the tactics used by Bobby's people in the pursuit of evidence.

Bobby even had his own wiretap expert. He was "bug-crazy," a former staffer recalls, and even "bugged" staff members in the field. Two Republican staffers, Jack McGovern and Vern Johnson, were delving into United Auto Workers affairs in Detroit, and discovered an eavesdropping device in the closet of their Sheraton-Cadillac hotel room. After shouting expletives into the "bug," they ripped it out of its hiding place.

Staff members in Washington, particularly on the Republican side, suspected that their telephone conversations were being monitored, and Robert Manuel, the minority counsel, made it a point never to discuss anything of consequence within his own office. He would make his phone calls on the outside. "And sometimes I wondered whether *those* phones weren't being tapped," he recalls. "Bobby always seemed to be aware of what we were doing."

Wiretapping isn't cheap; and the question arose as to whether Joseph P. Kennedy might be paying the bills. The suspicion was that the Ambassador was underwriting private investigators around the country to make his sons look good. On dozens of occasions, Bobby would open up hearings with transcripts and/or recordings. Invariably, his explanation was that the material had been graciously provided the committee by local police or private detectives. He never did explain where he obtained the recordings of Hoffa's telephone conversations he played before the committee as a means of refreshing Hoffa's memory.

Bobby's speeches were well covered in the communications media. And they reveal a great deal about his attitudes in the late fifties. At the University of Notre Dame in February 1958, for example, he said the nation faced disaster unless "we reinstill the toughness and moral idealism which guided George Washington a hundred and sixty years ago." Bobby charged that one out of every ten prisoners of war in Korea had "informed on his fellow prisoners on at least one occasion"; that one of every three had "collaborated to some extent with the Red Chinese." "There was," he observed, "a complete lack of self-discipline; there was very little real understanding of the United States, its history or principles, and there was no real strong belief in anything—the Army, family, religion, or even themselves."

It was a speech that could have been made by Barry Goldwater.

In April 1958, Bobby addressed the annual Patriots' Day dinner of the Massachusetts Council, Knights of Columbus, at which he was awarded the Council's annual Lantern Award for outstanding patriotism. The presentation was made by Archbishop Cushing, who likened young Kennedy to early Massachusetts patriots. "He is a Massachusetts man," said the Archbishop, "and therefore a reminder that New England is still producing men of vision, integrity and leadership."

The prelate recalled that the award the previous year had gone to FBI Director J. Edgar Hoover for his "brilliant work" in combating Communism, adding that the two awards "symbolize the close relation between the two evils these two men are fighting."

Inevitably, there was talk of a political career for Bobby. His name kept popping up as a potential candidate for Attorney General of Massachusetts, a stepping-stone to the

governorship. But invariably, he told newsmen that his political aspirations were "zero," adding, "There is only room
for one Kennedy." And that was the name of the game as
far as all the Kennedys were concerned—taking over the
White House for Jack.

John F. Kennedy soon began to play a bigger role in the
affairs of the committee. At the hearings, Bobby frequently sat
alongside his brother. The resemblance was strong. "Each has
a big shock of unruly hair," reported *The New York Times* in
a profile of Bobby, "but the younger Kennedy parts his on
the right, the Senator on the left."

It was *Parade* that first called the team a "brother act," suggesting to its readers: "Keep an eye on those young Kennedys
of Massachusetts." The article, by Jack Anderson and Fred
Blumenthal, concluded: "And always, behind the Kennedy
'brother act,' is Old Joe Kennedy—a natural political force in
himself."

But the "brother act" had its problems. Jack and Bobby
could not appear to be anti-labor lest they lose the liberal
support absolutely indispensable in JFK's drive for the Presidential nomination. At the same time, they could not appear
to be pro-labor lest they lose conservative support—particularly in the South. With absolute brilliance, they managed
to achieve these seemingly incompatible objectives.

By concentrating on Dave Beck and Jimmy Hoffa, they established themselves in the public mind as shining knights dedicated to driving corrupt and venal leaders from the house
of labor. The fact that Beck and Hoffa were at constant odds
with the UAW's Walter Reuther did not hurt. For liberals,
both in and out of the labor movement, were pro-Reuther.

To some Republican members of the committee, it appeared
that Reuther was calling the signals, at least so far as the committee's inquiry into UAW affairs was concerned. A former
Congressman on the UAW payroll was a frequent visitor at
the counsel's office, where he consulted not only with Bobby
but with his administrative assistant, Kenneth O'Donnell.
Thus, Reuther was well aware of almost everything that went
on inside the committee. Bobby's collusion with Reuther
was further demonstrated during the hearings into the Kohler
and Perfect Circle strikes in which UAW-instigated violence
had become a subject of national controversy.

From the beginning, it was apparent to Republicans that Bobby was loath to investigate these strikes or anything else of a derogatory nature pertaining to Walter Reuther. As Goldwater, Capehart, South Dakota's Karl E. Mundt and Nebraska's Carl T. Curtis put it in a minority report: ". . . we are deeply disappointed that the Chief Counsel, who had been delegated broad authority, was not only reluctant, but actually refused in more than one instance to probe into areas which would have fixed the responsibility for the clear pattern of crime and violence which has characterized and has generally been associated with UAW strikes.

"From the very outset of the UAW investigation, it became apparent that the Committee faced an awkward, if not an impossible situation growing out of the natural conflict-of-interest situation in which its Chief Counsel found himself. When investigating unions other than those affiliated with the leadership of Walter Reuther, the Chief Counsel worked effectively and cooperatively with all members of the Committee—Democrats and Republicans alike. But whenever an investigation touched upon the domain of Walter Reuther, an altogether different procedure was followed. Throughout the course of the investigation, a double standard of Committee morality prevailed: one procedure was employed for the unions not connected with Walter Reuther and a different procedure was employed for the investigation of the activities of the United Automobile Workers. . . ."

There can be little doubt that the vast files on corruption collected by the Rackets Committee, at great cost to the taxpayer, gave Bobby an invaluable weapon in brother Jack's drive for the White House. As Roland May of the York [Pennsylvania] *Gazette and Daily* noted: "The forays of the Kennedy sleuths . . . into St. Louis, Chicago, Gary, Philadelphia, Manhattan, Brooklyn, the Bronx and Miami were followed by a remarkable swing of Democratic politicians in the areas to the Kennedy Presidential cause. And unions involved did the same."

Early in 1960, an irate Bobby Kennedy barged into the office of Jameson G. Campaigne, editor of the *Indianapolis Star,* to complain bitterly about editorials critical of Jack Kennedy's relations with Walter Reuther. At first, Campaigne didn't think Bobby was serious. After a time, the astonished editor realized that he was.

"Aren't the charges true?" Campaigne asked.

"Like hell they are. They're designed to hurt my brother. And, anyway, Reuther is a good guy."

Later, William Moore of the *Chicago Tribune* wrote that "the Kennedy brothers, thinnest-skinned politicians in the rhinoceros hide game," flatly denied the accusations. They called in Moore—"not in anger but in ostensible sorrow that anyone should think such a thing." According to Moore, Bobby said, "Our father didn't raise us that way."

13

Plans

It was at Bobby Kennedy's house in the family compound at Hyannis Port that the final plans were devised for John F. Kennedy's race for the Presidency. A lot had taken place since Jack and Bobby had angrily left Chicago after Estes Kefauver had narrowly taken the Vice Presidential nomination. It had been Jack's first major political defeat and he had taken it hard. "He was hurt, terribly hurt," recalls Florida's Senator George Smathers. The following day he flew to the French Riviera to join his sympathetic father. Meanwhile, Jacqueline Kennedy had flown off to Newport to be with her mother.

Jack was out yachting on the Mediterranean when his father received a transatlantic call from Bobby that Jackie had lost the baby. She was almost in her eighth month of pregnancy. (It was Jackie's second miscarriage, the first occurring early in her first pregnancy in 1953.)

The fact that Jack had not broken any speed records getting to his wife's bedside occasioned considerable interest. The gossip columnists wrote that the Kennedy marriage was on the rocks. Drew Pearson reported that the Kennedys were estranged. And *Time* reported one widely circulated story to the effect that Joe Kennedy had made a million-dollar deal with Jacqueline to keep her from divorcing Jack. "In the gossip circle they moved in," gossiped *Time*, "it was an open secret that the Kennedys' married life was far from serene."

But Old Joe did have a long heart-to-heart talk with his son about the obligations of a husband to his wife. "Most importantly," wrote George Carpozi, Jr., in his *The Hidden Side of Jacqueline Kennedy,* "Papa told Jack that he had to do something about dispelling the rumors that he was a playboy and was carrying on with other women. The Old Man . . . told Jack that the only way to avoid such gossip about himself was to spend more time with Jackie—at home and in public."

In July 1957, David Barnett, then Washington Bureau chief of North American Newspaper Alliance, reported that Jacqueline Kennedy was "expecting" again. He added: "A child will put an end to some of the recurring rumors that the youthful Mr. Kennedy and his beautiful wife are not getting along so well."

Jackie had her baby at the New York Hospital, and this time Senator Kennedy was there. She was delivered by Caesarean section of a seven-pound, two-ounce daughter (whom they named Caroline after Jackie's sister, Caroline Lee Bouvier) at 8:15 on the morning of November 27th. Ten days later they took the child home.

For the most part the rumors then died out, but to make certain, the Kennedy camp arranged for a short TV documentary to be shot showing Jack's home life with Jacqueline and their newborn daughter.

Jack Kennedy was so certain of winning his campaign for re-election as Senator in 1958 that Massachusetts Republicans were having difficulties finding someone to contest him. The late Bill Cunningham, conservative columnist for the Boston *Herald,* suggested that the Republicans endorse him, too. Since the Republicans "can't possibly lick him," wrote Cunningham, and "they couldn't borrow a better man . . . why not make it unanimous?"

In the end, the Republicans did find a patsy, a relatively unknown lawyer, Vincent Celeste, who still lived on the top floor of a North Boston three-decker tenement. Campaigning emotionally against the Kennedy wealth, Celeste pictured himself as a man of the little people. "I'm running against that millionaire, Jack Kennedy," he repeatedly told folks on his handshaking tours. "What right do Kennedy and his brother Bobby have to sit in judgment on labor without ever doing a day's work in their lives?"

As usual, Old Joe was operating behind the scenes from an apartment on Beacon Street which he had rented for that purpose—staffed by political operators on his payroll.

Teddy Kennedy bore the title of campaign manager. A Boston newsman reported that he operated out of "the most plush political headquarters Boston has ever seen" and that the young bachelor "is customarily surrounded by a flock of young beauties."

After leaving Harvard University under a cloud, having had a friend take a Spanish examination for him, Teddy spent twenty-two months in the Army, then returned to graduate from Harvard and the University of Virginia Law School. Shortly after the 1958 election, he married the blond, willowy and hazel-eyed daughter of a Manhattan advertising executive. They were married by Francis Cardinal Spellman a year after they had met at a tea at Manhattanville College, where Joan was a student. Teddy, who had gone there to dedicate a gymnasium that the family had donated, had little difficulty spotting the young lady who had spent a college summer appearing on commercials for the Perry Como and Eddie Fisher television shows.

On election night John F. Kennedy was in his father's hotel suite, listening to the returns. They were incredible. He was reelected by a margin of 874,608 votes, the greatest landslide scored by any candidate for any office in either party in the history of Massachusetts. Moreover, it was the largest margin received by any Senatorial candidate in 1958.

In addition to doctrinaire liberals, the big-city bosses and officeholders in the Eastern metropolises—many of them Catholic—also had their qualms about Jack as a Presidential candidate. Outside the East, such powers in the party as former President Truman and House Speaker Sam Rayburn anticipated a showdown at the 1960 convention that would put the youthful interloper in his place. JFK's religion, youth and inexperience hurt him generally with these pros.

Another who viewed Operation Kennedy with alarm was Adlai E. Stevenson. In San José, Costa Rica, he told two reporters—he later said he had thought the conversation was off the record—that "the amount of money being spent" by the Kennedys "is phenomenal, probably the highest amount spent on a campaign in history." When an infuriated Kennedy called on Stevenson for an explanation, the two-time Democratic Presidential candidate told Jack he had been misquoted. But Adlai had a constant problem in not being quoted correctly, and The New York Times, which had published the quotes in question, let them stand without retraction.

Other groups within the Democratic coalition were none too happy either. Among Negro leaders, Kennedy's ambivalence about civil rights had rooted a suspicion of political expediency not easy to erase. Jack was still staking his chances for the Presidential nomination on his ability to rally a substantial Southern bloc—as he did for the Vice Presidency in 1956.

Negro suspicions, however, erupted into outright hostility in June 1959 when Alabama's Governor John Patterson— "admiring Bob's racket-busting and Jack's vigor," as Ted Sorensen put it—announced he favored Kennedy for the Presidency. Bobby had first met Patterson the year before when he flew to Montgomery to deliver a speech about corruption and gangsterism in labor management. So impressed was the young Governor that he invited Kennedy to address the state legislature. But Bobby had a prior engagement in Washington that he said he couldn't break.

"We got along very well," Bobby recalls. "Patterson was our first break in the Solid South."

Patterson endorsed Jack after he and an associate, Sam Englehardt, a leading light in the super-segregationist White Citizens Council, breakfasted with the Senator in Georgetown—thirteen months before the National Convention. Patterson's announcement did not shock Jack Kennedy, but its timing did. The well-laid plan had been for him to wait a year before making his endorsement and then ascribe his choice to grassroots sentiments.

One of Dixie's more outspoken foes of civil rights, Patterson once enlivened a gubernatorial race by waving a blown-up photograph of a Negro being pummeled at a Little Rock disturbance and exclaiming, "This is how I will treat them if you make me your Governor."

Ironically, one of his opponents in the 1958 race was George Wallace, the future Governor of Alabama, who sought to make political capital out of the revelations published in the Montgomery *Advertiser* that John M. Patterson had the support of the Ku Klux Klan and called its leader Robert Shelton a "friend."

Wallace, in a statewide telecast from Decatur, said:

"My opponent . . . has now been found wrapped in the

bed sheet with the Grand Dragon of the . . . Klan . . . The Grand Dragon is one Robert Shelton, a twenty-eight-year-old man living at 1710 East 15th Street in Tuscaloosa. . . .

"At present the Klan in Alabama is still controllable. It is still discredited by the crimes and brutalities it committed as it rode the night in the past. . . . If my opponent is elected . . . the Klan will have achieved a success that might attract many thousands of new members. . . . My opponent's election would put starch in all those dirty sheets. . . . Let John Patterson tell the people of Alabama the following: (1) that he repudiates the votes of the Klansmen, as I do; (2) that, if elected, he would steadfastly oppose repeal of the 1949 Klan anti-masking law. . . . There are a lot of pistol-toters and toughs among the Klansmen, though all Klansmen are by no means bad men. . . ."

When asked to comment on the Patterson endorsement, Jack Kennedy said, "I haven't seen it, so I better let it go."

But Patterson kept singing Kennedy's praises. "If elected, Senator Kennedy will be sympathetic to the problems of the South."

Roy Wilkins, of the National Association for the Advancement of Colored People (NAACP), said, "It is very difficult for thoughtful Negro leaders to feel at ease over the endorsement of Senator Kennedy by Governor Patterson." *

Thurgood Marshall, general counsel for the NAACP, who today sits on the United States Supreme Court, was another who said that Kennedy had never explained satisfactorily why he had breakfasted with "the number-one segregationist of the South, even worse than [Governor] Faubus [of Arkansas]."

Bobby's advice to his brother, in effect, was to "play things cool," to say nothing that might lose Southern votes to Lyndon Johnson who, it was becoming increasingly apparent, was also seeking the 1960 Presidential nomination.

Bobby, not yet thirty-four, resigned from the McClellan Committee on September 10, 1959. Almost immediately, he began work on a book about his work as a Senate investigator of labor corruption, entitled *The Enemy Within*. To assist Bobby, John Seigenthaler took leave from the Nashville

---

* Arthur Schlesinger's Pulitzer prize-winning account of the New Frontier, *A Thousand Days*, fails to mention the Patterson endorsement. Sorensen's memoir contains a fleeting reference.

Tennessean, where he had a justified reputation as a top-notch investigative reporter. Later there were published reports (including one in *The New York Times*) that Seigenthaler had done most of the writing. This Seigenthaler flatly denies, and considering the style, the book may well have been mostly Bobby's handiwork.

Arthur Krock, who appeared to like the book, wrote its foreword. But Telford Taylor, a prominent New York lawyer, was not overenthusiastic in his review in the *Herald Tribune Book Review:*

"The characterizations are anything but subtle. Good guys are clean-cut, square-jawed, and open-faced; bad guys are shifty-eyed, gross and slick-haired. Whether these overtones of Dick Tracy are the product of Mr. Kennedy's natural diction or of the acknowledged journalistic assistance of a Tennessee newspaper man, the result will not commend itself to the sophisticated reader. . . ."

Taylor also noted that Bobby didn't have much to say about the late Senator Joseph McCarthy. "It would be interesting to read of Mr. Kennedy's experiences on Senator McCarthy's staff, but they are not related here. It might be enlightening to read the author's opinions on the many and controversial issues of security and liberty that Senator McCarthy so sharply projected, but whatever Mr. Kennedy's views on this score may be, they are not to be found in his book."

The book, generally well-received, became a best seller. And Hollywood even showed an interest in it. Bobby and Twentieth Century-Fox agreed to a contract, but Joe Kennedy, the old showman, would not accept certain clauses. "But your son, the Attorney General, said *he* was satisfied with the way that clause was drawn," said a surprised movie executive.

Snapped Kennedy, "What the hell does he know about it!"

The contract was revised.

On October 28, 1959, the high command of the Kennedy team met in Bobby's home in Hyannis Port. Joseph P. Kennedy was silent for the most part. Bobby and Teddy were there, as were Ted Sorensen and Kenneth O'Donnell, who had just resigned from the McClellan Committee; Hy Raskin, advance man for Adlai Stevenson's two unsuccessful campaigns; and Larry O'Brien, a Massachusetts publicity man and compiler of a manual entitled by insiders "How to Get Kennedy Elected to Anything." Also present were Louis Harris, a Kennedy pollster; Connecticut State Chairman John Bailey; brother-in-law Steve Smith; Marjorie Lawson, a Washington lawyer in charge of proselytizing Negroes; Dave Hackett, an old family friend; John Salter, an aide to Senator Henry Jackson; and Pierre Salinger.

Senator Kennedy spoke for three hours without notes, charts or a map. According to Sorensen, it was a brilliant performance.

This was the meeting at which it was decided that Jack had no alternative but to go the primary route in order to convince the pols who run conventions that he was a vote getter outside Massachusetts and that his "religious affiliation" and youthful appearance were not political liabilities. And with Joseph P. Kennedy beaming his approval, Bobby was assigned to take charge of the primaries.

As usual, the Kennedys trusted no one but their own.

14

Primaries 1960

The Kennedys went after the Presidency with a well-polished and powerful political machine, fueled by Joe Kennedy's millions (some say the costs to the family ran as high as $7,000,000) and sparked by an inexhaustible Bobby to whom nothing mattered but the election of his brother. This he made clear to leaders of the reform Democrats in New York who were warring with the regular Democratic organization. "I'm here to elect a President of the United States," Bobby barked at former Senator Herbert H. Lehman, Mrs. Eleanor Roosevelt and other reform leaders. "I don't give a damn what happens to any of your people afterward. . . ."

No one present at that meeting has ever forgotten the shocked looks of the liberal elder "statesmen," Lehman and Mrs. Roosevelt. "He's a nasty little man," Lehman said later, and there were many who agreed with him.

John F. Kennedy officially announced his candidacy for the Presidency on January 2, 1960. He was then forty-two years of age. His most likely opponents appeared to be Hubert Humphrey, though few were really taking him seriously; Missouri's Stuart Symington, who couldn't seem to get off the ground; Lyndon Baines Johnson, who had already selected Jack as his Vice Presidential running mate; and Adlai Stevenson, hopefully waiting in the wings polishing up his prose.

Three days after he announced, Kennedy got a big boost when Governor Michael V. DiSalle surprisingly handed Jack Ohio's sixty-four delegate votes six months before the convention. DiSalle had never before demonstrated any particular affection for Jack Kennedy.

The Kennedy forces had worked on him for nearly a year. Conversations with Jack had finally convinced him that he had no alternative but to support Kennedy. Then Bobby very nearly blew the deal. He tried to lay down the law to the Governor.

"In the late fall of 1959," DiSalle has since reported, "I met briefly with Robert Kennedy and John Bailey at the Drake Hotel in New York to discuss the details of how and when I should make my public declaration. It was quite a stormy session.

"Bobby Kennedy, demonstrating his fierce single-purposed devotion to his brother, wanted to know the mechanics and timetable of the announcement, while I was just as determined to keep the specifications to myself.

"The agreement," continues DiSalle, "was possible as a result of the level-headed intervention of John Bailey. Bailey, who has since been functioning as Democratic National Chairman, was then helping candidate Kennedy in the basic job of making nationwide contact with political leaders.

"Without Bailey's all-important mediation at the Drake Hotel conference, Jack Kennedy might have felt himself engaged on three fronts—Ohio, Wisconsin, and West Virginia as well—and the required effort might have changed the outcome in at least one of these states.

"From that day on, Bobby Kennedy and I had frequent contact in the furtherance of Jack Kennedy's nomination and election. I never ceased to marvel at his unfailing energy and dedication, even at the risk of great physical damage to himself. . . ."

DiSalle met privately with Jack Kennedy at an airport motel in Pittsburgh where Kennedy apologized for his brother's undiplomatic behavior, explaining that Bobby "was still young and has a lot to learn." The deal for DiSalle's support was finally made.

"What could I have done?" DiSalle pleaded with friends. "Those Kennedys play real rough."

Several weeks later, Joseph P. Kennedy took the Empire State Express to Albany. He went to see Daniel (Uncle Dan) O'Connell, the Albany County Democratic Chairman. The

O'Connells had controlled upstate New York Democratic politics for half a century.

When Kennedy asked O'Connell's help, the crusty veteran balked a bit, remarking that Jack was only forty-two years old. "He's a little young, isn't he?"

"He is," Old Joe conceded, "but I'm seventy-two and I want to be around to enjoy it."

Uncle Dan assured the elder Kennedy of his machine's support.

The Ambassador was also assured the support of Charles Buckley, the boss of the Bronx, and at New York's Brook Club he also met with bosses Joe Sharkey of Brooklyn and Peter Crotty of Buffalo. Ben Wetzler, a Buckley man and secretary of the State Democratic Committee since 1946, began to make the rounds of upstate county committee meetings, discreetly passing the word that Jack Kennedy was Buckley's choice for President.

Joe, Jack and Bobby were filled in regularly on what was taking place in New York. By October 1959, the machine support for Kennedy in New York had become so impressive that the candidates felt it wise to cancel a scheduled appearance before the Lexington Democratic Club, the pioneer reform organization, lest he alienate certain old friends. And in the spring of 1960, Buckley formally urged the New York State Democratic organization to jump aboard the Kennedy bandwagon. At a dinner to which he had invited all sixty-two county leaders, Buckley arose and endorsed Kennedy in his presence and predicted he would receive all but a few of the delegation's votes. Soon the bandwagon was crowded.

As Bobby told the New York *Post's* Pete Hamill following Buckley's death in January 1967, "During the convention, Lyndon Johnson and Sam Rayburn had lined up their friends in New York. They thought they had at least thirty delegates. They wanted them for the first ballot. And they said it would go to us on the second ballot. There wasn't any second ballot, of course. And Lyndon said later, 'I thought Carmine [De Sapio] and [Mike] Prendergast ran New York. I found out it was someone named Charlie Buckley.' "

Bobby laughed as he recalled those never-to-be-forgotten days. Oh, Bobby went on, Charlie Buckley was a "rogue," but you just had to love him.

Also corralled was Chicago's Mayor Richard Daley.

Through the family-owned Merchandise Mart, Old Joe wielded enormous economic clout in the Windy City.

The Kennedy strategy for the primaries had been laid out with shrewdness and resourcefulness. Wisconsin was to be the scene of the first major electoral battle. The chief competitor, Hubert H. Humphrey, seemed hardly a terrifying threat, but the Kennedy forces kept insisting that Jack was the underdog. Bobby, in fact, announced that things looked so tough in the Badger State he had advised Jack against running. After all, Wisconsin was "Senator Humphrey's back yard."

Friendly political analysts like Joseph Alsop and the Baltimore *Sun's* Thomas O'Neill picked up the refrain. But one columnist who wasn't buying the "underdog" bit was Murray Kempton. He wrote:

"Jack Kennedy goes against Hubert Humphrey in the Wisconsin primary with most of the money, most of the charm, most of the killer instinct, and, we might assume, most of the potential votes.

"He also has in his back pocket a private poll made for him by Louis Harris, which showed him, as of six weeks ago, with a lead in eight of Wisconsin's 10 districts and 60 percent of the vote. Knowing this, he insists on talking like the Colgate coach the week before the Syracuse game."

Still protesting about the tremendous risks he was running, Jack Kennedy announced that he would enter the Wisconsin primary. But from the start, it was obvious that Humphrey didn't stand a chance.

"It's in the bag," Bobby was overheard telling a group of Wisconsin partisans by a CBS correspondent, who rushed to his microphone with his exclusive story. When this came to Bobby's attention he went into an uncontrollable rage, sought out the correspondent and denounced him as a "Stevenson Jew." The correspondent, who did happen to be Jewish, squared off for a fight.

But Jack Kennedy insisted that Bobby apologize. He then took the correspondent off to a private lunch, where apparently he mollified him. Had the episode been reported at the time, it might well have cost John F. Kennedy the Presidency. At least it would have cost him much of the crucial Jewish vote. For memories of Father Joe's intemperate ethnic outbursts had not wholly faded away.

Meanwhile, Hubert Humphrey kept referring to his "humble origins." He said that the drugstore in Huron, South Dakota, in which he worked as a boy, was still in his family. "I have a brother, too," Humphrey said. "But he's too busy running the drugstore to campaign for me."

One of Humphrey's top supporters, Senator Eugene McCarthy, after observing Bobby's rough tactics in the primaries, later described Jack Kennedy as an "amiable lightweight," who would not have gone very far if he had not been so well-financed.

As the zero hour approached, the entire clan hit the road. Mrs. Peter Lawford, Mrs. Stephen Smith and Mrs. Sargent Shriver, Rose, along with other imported relatives and friends, were streaming into the Badger State.

"I cannot win by competing in glamour or in public relations," grumbled Humphrey. "The Kennedy forces are waging a psychological blitz that I cannot match. I'm not the candidate of the fat cats. . . . I feel like an independent merchant competing against a chain store."

Meanwhile, behind the scenes, the Ambassador had spent considerable time on seeking the support of William Loeb, publisher of New Hampshire's largest newspaper, the Manchester *Union Leader*. Loeb, probably the most outspoken conservative publisher in the United States, later reported:

"A detailed study of Joe revealed to us one of the most completely amoral individuals that I ever had anything to do with. The only good thing I could say about Joe was that he certainly was a hard-driving individual and at over seventy years of age he was selling Jack as if he were a young man of thirty selling customers."

Mort Sahl, whose socially significant and politically advanced humor had caught the nation's fancy, was contacted by Joseph P. Kennedy. "I would like you to write some stuff for my boy," the Ambassador said.

The call wasn't a complete surprise, for Sahl's manager also handled Peter Lawford, and Sahl had become a member of the fringe group who surrounded the family. He was flattered, and agreed to write gags for Kennedy without recompense but on the understanding that his role would be unpublicized.

"I'd jot them down whenever I thought of them and pass them along through different people," he recalled years later.

"Once I scribbled a few of them on an envelope and gave them to Pat Lawford at an airport. Another time I was on location making a movie and I drove 150 miles to find a Western Union office to turn in my jokes. When Kennedy came to California to round up delegates, he appeared at a big political dinner. I wrote his gags. . . ."

But after Kennedy defeated Nixon, Sahl stopped writing jokes for the new President and instead made JFK his target. After all, he explained, he had needled President Eisenhower and Vice President Nixon all through the fifties. And the natural subject for jests in the sixties was the New Frontier.

And that's when the gags hit the fan. His agent told him he had been to dinner with Lawford and some of the Kennedy family. "He told me that one of them said, 'He [Sahl] isn't one of us.' "

Another Kennedy friend approached him at a Miami hotel and angrily told him, "You are more vicious with the President than you ever were with Nixon."

Sahl said that suddenly his agent couldn't find work for him, especially on TV, where he had been doing quite well. "He kept telling me, 'Nobody wants you. You've made lots of enemies.' And Lawford told me, 'It would have been so nice if you would have laid off.' "

When the final break came, said Sahl, his agent and Lawford warned him, "You are going to get it. You'll see."

In one year, his income dropped from $400,000 to $19,000. Unable to find work, Sahl felt he was being blacklisted. When he voiced his suspicions, his friends in California—most of them liberals—said it was all in his mind.

The Kennedy coffee hours, organized by a cousin from Boston, proved to be as great a success in Wisconsin as they had been in Massachusetts. One woman summed up for *U.S. News & World Report* what she thought the Kennedy kaffee-klatsches had done for the Senator:

"We ladies go back home and talk about Senator Kennedy—gossip over the back fence, if you want to call it that. We talk him up to our in-laws and friends. If it hadn't been for that little coffee get-together this morning, we wouldn't have been thinking very much about this primary that's coming up. Now we have Kennedy on our minds."

Bobby ran the main headquarters in Milwaukee, the tight, systematized organization that had become a Kennedy trademark. In Milwaukee alone, there were 30,000 volunteers among its approximately 750,000 inhabitants.

Brother Teddy, in between speeches, stuffed envelopes, passed out literature at factory gates, shook thousands of hands, presided at an ice-fishing contest; and one day outside Madison he distinguished himself (and reaped reams of publicity) by taking off on his first ski jump, soaring seventy-five feet and crashing into the spectators. Meantime, Bobby zoomed around the state, horrifying audiences with the news that Jimmy Hoffa was prepared to spend $2,000,000 to keep "my brother, the Senator," out of the White House.

Humphrey denounced the opposition for raising such an issue. He even questioned the right of the Kennedy "boys" to pose as racket busters. He said it was one thing to serve on a Senate committee, and another to fight rackets as mayor of Minneapolis, as he himself had done. He reserved his sharpest barbs for Bobby.

"You're looking at a man who has fought the rackets all his life," roared Humphrey. "And I did so before some of the people who are doing all the talking about rackets were dry behind the ears. Whoever is responsible deserves to have a spanking. And I said spanking because it applies to juveniles."

Bobby also made the decision to discourage Frank Sinatra from coming to Wisconsin. No reason was given for the decision, but Sinatra at the time was involved in a bitter controversy following the disclosure that he had hired a Communist writer, one of the Hollywood Ten, to write a scenario for him. There was an uproar in patriotic circles and actor John Wayne addressed an open letter to Senator Kennedy, asking him how he felt about his "crony" hiring a "Commie." The Kennedys were also worried about Sinatra's associations with underworld figures. It was widely reported that he owned four percent of the action at the Sands Hotel in Vegas.

Nevertheless, though the Rat Pack leader was not present, his voice boomed out from Kennedy sound trucks all over the state in a rousing rendition of "High Hopes," a campaign song written by Sammy Cahn and Jimmy Van Heusen:

> *Everyone is voting for Jack*
> *'Cause he's got what all the rest lack. . . .*

Also "disinvited" were Sinatra's business partner, Peter Lawford, and Sammy Davis, Jr. As Peter later explained, "Senator Humphrey's boys had passed out pamphlets saying Jack's glamorous friends from Hollywood were coming to bedazzle the voters. Jack's advisers thought it might cause hard feelings so we didn't go into the state."

Meanwhile Bobby could not help commenting on the few "big names" that showed up from out of the state to help Humphrey. Take the case of Jackie Robinson. The former baseball star, who had flown out to Milwaukee to stump for Humphrey, reported:

"When I alighted from the plane, the Senator was there to greet me before he left the airport to campaign in cities in the northern part of the state. I was greatly shocked at what one of his assistants told me. It seems the Kennedy camp had accused Senator Humphrey's committee of paying me money to come out to campaign for Humphrey's nomination.

"I frankly admit I was very angry. In the first place, when I believe in a man and his principles the way I believe in Senator Humphrey, I would have lost respect for his entire campaign if there had ever been even a mention of payment. . . . He has consistently refused to tailor his principles to placate anyone, regardless of whether or not it costs him his chance at the nomination. When a man takes a stand like that, he doesn't have to buy my support.

"When I inquired as to who had put out such a story, a Milwaukee newspaperman replied that Senator Kennedy's brother, Robert, had told him personally that I had been paid to join Humphrey's camp. I want right here to emphasize what I told that reporter. Whoever originated such a story is a liar."

Bobby never did reply directly to the man who had called him a liar.

Neither candidate reached any great heights of eloquence in their numerous effusions. "If either Kennedy or Humphrey made one serious, considered speech on the great national issues, it was, so far as my reading of the newspapers goes, not reported to the nation," complained the dean of pundits, Walter Lippmann.

The Kennedys sought a large Republican vote. As Miles McMillin observed in the Madison *Capital Times:* "No one has been willing to estimate how much of the crossover will be religiously motivated, but there seems little doubt at this point that Kennedy will be the chief beneficiary, largely because of the skillful and quiet way his organization has exploited the religious factor."

Then, toward the end, vicious anti-Catholic literature poured into the state. Marquis Childs reported that it was sent "largely to Catholics and often to individuals in care of the local chapter of the Knights of Columbus. While they seem to have originated with the lunatic fringe, the effect is naturally to create sympathy for Kennedy. . . ."

Humphrey's people demanded an investigation. But the damage had been done.

Later *National Review* charged that the literature had been circulated by one of Bobby's hatchet men, Paul Corbin, who was named an assistant to Democratic National Chairman John Bailey in 1961. According to *National Review,* "Corbin was involved in an anonymous mailing of virulently anti-Catholic literature to Catholics from a mail drop across the line in Minnesota, with such success that many of them, with a sort of negative Pavlovian reflex, voted for Kennedy."

For an unbelievable hour or so, after the Wisconsin polls closed on April 5, Humphrey led his rival by some 4,000 votes. At the hotel where the Kennedy forces had gathered, there was gloom. Holed up in a suite, receiving returns as they were being phoned in, were Bobby Kennedy and pollster Lou Harris. Suddenly the tide turned. Jack Kennedy was ahead, and the trend soon appeared irreversible.

Final returns showed Kennedy winning six of the state's ten election districts by 56 percent of the vote. If anything, the results demonstrated that an attractive, hard-campaigning Catholic candidate could count on a powerful Catholic vote cutting across party lines. For Catholic Republicans by the thousands crossed over to register their protest against the "hate" literature flooding the state.

In West Virginia the game grew rougher than ever. The primary turned out to be one of the bitterest contests in recent campaign history. In a state where less than five percent of the population is Catholic, the religious issue quickly came to the fore. Largely forgotten was the fact that West Virginia went overwhelmingly for Catholic Al Smith in the 1928 primary.

The way the Kennedys kept bringing up the Catholic issue led one Humphrey worker, a Catholic himself, to say to the AP's Arthur Edson, "Jack's workers tell the voters here if they don't vote for him, they're bigots. In Wisconsin, they kept telling the Catholics they had to turn out to prove that a Catholic could roll up a big vote. How in the hell can you keep up with arguments like that?"

Bobby once more accused Senator Humphrey of conniving with Jimmy Hoffa. And Jack chimed in with a charge that Hoffa had given "direct orders" to the local Teamsters to support Humphrey. "Jimmy Hoffa," said the Senator, "gave the orders to join the gang-up against my candidacy here because he knows that if I am successful here I will win the Democratic nomination."

By now the Kennedys had dug up a New Deal heirloom to match Humphrey's claims that he was dedicated to following the FDR tradition. Campaigning in the depressed parts of the state was Franklin D. Roosevelt, Jr., and every time he mentioned "my father" he raised a storm of applause. Not-so-young Roosevelt, for a time, had been a registered public-relations agent for the Trujillo dictatorship in the Dominican Republic and a distributor for Italian cars in Washington. Now the talk was that he was seeking a political comeback.

In a state with a high percentage of war veterans, FDR Jr. extolled his candidate as "the only wounded veteran" running for President. But on April 27, he added, "There's another candidate in your primary. He's a good Democrat but I don't know where he was in World War II."

The implication was plain. The following day the Washington *Star* quite properly described Junior's statement as "a new low in dirty politics." Humphrey, married and the father of three children, had tried to enter the Navy but had been rejected for a physical disability.

Jack Kennedy failed to repudiate the Roosevelt remark. And Roosevelt construed Kennedy's silence as passive approval. On May 6, four days before the polls opened, FDR Jr. revived the issue, this time blasting Humphrey as a "draft dodger."

Whereupon Senator Kennedy issued a statement disapproving the injection of Humphrey's war record into the primary campaign. But later that night, at a Charleston rally, he said that no one had made "a greater contribution to the discussion of issues" than Franklin D. Roosevelt, Jr.

Eventually Roosevelt apologized to Humphrey. Both in person and in writing, Junior assured the Minnesotan that his primary statements were "unnecessary and unwarranted."

Six years later, when FDR Jr. ran for Governor of New York on the Liberal party ticket, he was asked about his smearing of Hubert Humphrey.

"The only thing I can say *publicly* about this," he told Jerry Tallmer of the New York *Post,* "is that it was based on so-called reliable information which was made available to me; and that it was used in the heat of the closing days of a vital and decisive primary; and that when I found it was unwarranted I went to Mr. Humphrey and not only ate crow but asked for his forgiveness."

Privately, however, he admitted that the "so-called reliable information" about Humphrey's wartime draft status had been given him in dossier form by Robert F. Kennedy. "And Bobby left me holding the bag," said Roosevelt bitterly.

Finally, what one Charleston newspaper described as "one of the worst name-calling campaigns in the history of Presidential politics" came to a merciful end.

On primary day, John Kennedy returned to Washington and that evening saw a movie. All through the day Bobby sat tense and irritable in Kennedy headquarters, a former barbershop in the basement of the Hotel Kanawha in Charleston. When the returns began coming in, Bobby relaxed and about midnight telephoned his brother, suggesting he fly to Charleston. Humphrey, he reported, was about to concede.

It was drizzling when Bobby strode through the streets to pay his call on Humphrey. Arriving at his headquarters, Bobby approached the loser's wife, Muriel, who turned her back, refusing to greet him. To this day Muriel has not forgotten Bobby's outrageous treatment of her husband.

Meanwhile, Hubert, tears in his eyes, was telling his weeping workers that he was pulling out of the Presidential race for good. Then both men walked the wet streets together to the Kanawha Hotel where they heard Jack Kennedy make his victory statement. At a press conference, the victorious candidate said, "I believe we have now buried the religious issue once and for all."

The final returns, showing Kennedy with 220,000 to Humphrey's 142,000 votes, confounded the experts. Kennedy carried all but seven of the state's fifty-five counties. "It just proves you can't trust bigots," was the morning-after comment of Baltimore *Sun* correspondent Howard Norton.

Accusations of Kennedy vote buying were openly published in the press. "One of the most corrupt elections in county history" was a typical newspaper charge.

The FBI, on investigating, filed a report of nearly 200 pages with the Justice Department. Jack Kennedy demanded to know whether the Administration planned to use the FBI "as a political weapon."

The Justice Department denied a published report that an indictment of Bobby Kennedy was under consideration. The entire matter was dropped when the Eisenhower Administration decided against opening itself to accusations of political persecution.

The Kennedys were within grasp of the big prize.

15

Convention 1960

There were times, even after West Virginia, when the Kennedys were discouraged. Though they had piled up majorities in seven primaries (of which only two, Wisconsin and West Virginia, could possibly be described as contests), they still had failed to convince any significant segment of liberal opinion that "the man for the sixties" was truly John F. Kennedy. And there was increasing talk of a possible Stevenson-Kennedy ticket.

It was Bobby who suggested that his brother talk with Adlai Stevenson. On May 21, 1960, Senator Kennedy went to the Stevenson farm in Libertyville, Illinois, and after the usual pleasantries got to the point. Stevenson could have any job he wanted if he would support Kennedy. But Adlai politely said "no," pointing out that it would "look like a deal." Later, he told his speech writer William Attwood that he wasn't sure he even wanted to be Secretary of State under Kennedy. The truth was that Adlai Stevenson did not much admire John F. Kennedy.

According to Herbert J. Muller, in *Adlai Stevenson: A Study in Values:* "Considering him at best too inexperienced in foreign affairs, Stevenson resented all the more the rude pressures on him by the Kennedy crowd. For on the record to date the Senator from Massachusetts was much more clearly an ambitious politician than a great young statesman. He had made some name for himself during his eight years in the Senate by a few speeches, such as a bold one criticizing French policy in Algiers, but in recent years he had been too

154

busy politicking in preparation for his campaign to work hard at the job he had been elected to do; Republicans would needle him about his frequent absences from the Senate. . . ."

Within the family councils, Old Joe had long been insisting that, despite his disavowals, "that son of a bitch" Stevenson was running and had been running ever since the 1956 debacle. Jack was now inclined to agree. He was afraid that Adlai would be egged on by such diehards as Eleanor Roosevelt to openly contest for the nomination, and the pressures on Kennedy to accept the Vice Presidency would then become unbearable.

From the start, Kennedy had made it abundantly clear that he would not accept second place.

In his present mood, *Newsweek's* Benjamin Bradlee told William Attwood in June 1960, "Jack will walk out of the convention if he doesn't get the nomination."

Bradlee, a close friend of Kennedy's, thought Attwood should meet with Kennedy, if only to maintain communications. So less than a month before the convention, Attwood had dinner with the Kennedys and Bradlees at the latter's Georgetown home. After some small talk, Kennedy got to what was troubling him: What the hell was Adlai up to? The day before, Stevenson had announced he was not a candidate.

"I explained," Attwood later wrote, "that Stevenson wanted to keep the party united but, despite the urging of his supporters, would do nothing to get the nomination or prevent Kennedy or anyone else from getting it."

Kennedy replied that he had the nomination "virtually sewed up" and that Stevenson's actions, or non-actions, could only aid Johnson and Symington. No matter what happened at the convention, Jack added, there would not be a Stevenson-Kennedy ticket. He would release his delegates to someone like Symington before he would let that happen.

Attwood suggested that if the delegates did end up by choosing Stevenson, they would surely draft Kennedy for the second spot. "I wouldn't take it," Jack answered in a hard, flat voice. "I'm campaigning for the Presidency, period."

"Not even knowing it would make Nixon's election inevitable?" asked Attwood.

Before Jack could reply, Jacqueline—who had said little up to then—suddenly spoke up: "Let Adlai get beaten alone!

If you don't believe Jack, I'll cut my wrists and write an oath in blood that he'll refuse to run with Stevenson!"

Attwood told Jacqueline he was convinced.

A few days later, Attwood delivered a memorandum of the conversation to Stevenson in Chicago. When Adlai finished reading it, he burst out, "How could I ever go to work for such an arrogant young man?"

Another party luminary who considered Kennedy arrogant was Harry S Truman. So disturbed was the former President about the probability of Kennedy's nomination that he launched a last-ditch effort to prevent it. On July 2, in a nationally televised press conference from Independence, Missouri, Truman attacked the forthcoming convention as a "prearranged . . . mockery . . . controlled . . . by one candidate." And he accused Kennedy's overzealous backers of having pressured and stampeded delegates. In short, he implied that the Kennedy money had been improperly utilized to win the nomination.

Lyndon Johnson had sat out the primaries, hoping that Humphrey would stop Kennedy, at least in West Virginia. As Eliot Janeway, a former Johnson admirer, put it in his recent book, *The Economics of Crisis,* "The Kennedy legend has blandly alleged that his nomination expressed a universal mandate from the public and politicians alike. In fact, it was an exercise in bandwagon-building. Kennedy gambled on his ability to pyramid a string of decisive primary victories into a public-relations simulacrum of an invincible mandate. If Johnson had had the will and fortitude to enter the Indiana primary in early May 1960, he might have defused the rocket that Kennedy sent flaring into the political skies in Wisconsin and West Virginia. Instead, smarting and sulking under the criticism of the liberals, Johnson retreated into legislatively effective but politically unintelligible power combinations with the Republicans—a pattern prophetic of his operation as President."

Two weeks before the convention, Henry Luce arrived at Richard Nixon's office for lunch. The *Time-Life* publisher said he had just seen Lyndon Johnson and was sorry he hadn't had time to accept his invitation for a highball and a chat. "Let's ask Lyndon to join us," said the Vice President, and soon the conversation got around to Jack Kennedy.

For the next half hour, Johnson reviewed the many things

he had done to push and promote the political welfare of the young candidate, yet Senator Kennedy and members of his family often sought to embarrass him—especially since 1956 when Jack began running for President and saw in Johnson a potential competitor.

Typical of these anti-Johnson maneuvers was the rumor, a few weeks earlier, that had swept the Texas State Democratic Convention about Lyndon Johnson's suffering another heart attack. Johnson contended it had emanated from the Kennedy camp and was designed to make his health an issue. "It was that little bastard, Bobby," said Johnson.

A Washington columnist later bore this out. During the convention, Bobby Kennedy had run into Bobby Baker, then Senate Majority Secretary, in the lobby of the Biltmore Hotel in downtown Los Angeles, he reported. The two of them had decided to have breakfast together, and as the meal neared its end, Baker had said to Kennedy, "You know, Bobby, Lyndon doesn't mind any of these things you've been doing to him and saying about him except for one thing. He couldn't quite forgive that story that was put out in Dallas, Houston and Austin just before the Democratic Texas Convention that Lyndon Johnson had just died of a heart attack. The Houston *Post* got three thousand phone calls in one day, and Lyndon just didn't think that was quite cricket."

"You don't mean to say you think we would do a thing like that?" remonstrated Bobby Kennedy.

"When that story crops out in the three biggest cities of Texas on exactly the same day, one day before the Texas convention and your brother Teddy is in Texas," replied Baker, "what do you expect us to think?"

According to Drew Pearson, Bobby had slammed two dollars on the table to pay for his share of the breakfast and walked out.

On July 5, Lyndon Johnson formally announced for the Presidency. In the accustomed tradition, he hit hard at the front-runner, Kennedy. He warned that the "forces of evil," meaning global Communism, "will have no mercy for innocence, no gallantry toward inexperience."

On his way to the West Coast, Johnson was asked about Bobby's prediction that the outcome would be decided five hours before the convention opened. Lyndon's reply: "There are countries in the world where such pure arrogance is customary in politics. This is not that kind of country."

The New York Times put it this way: "If Robert F. Kennedy, the brash young man who is fighting with no holds barred for his brother's nomination, is right, the Democratic prize-winner at Los Angeles will be determined this weekend, before the Convention even opens its doors. . . . In the old days these decisions were traditionally made in the smoke-filled room. In this electronic age we tend to think of those stuffy hotel rooms as somewhat *démodé;* but the smoke remains as thick as ever."

The New York Times estimated Jack was 160 votes short of the 761 needed to win, but the Kennedy team, led by Bobby, oozed confidence. Kennedy had strength in almost every section of the nation. There was, for example, North Carolina's delegate and Governor-elect Terry Sanford. Without consulting other delegates from his state, he surprisingly announced for Kennedy.

Sanford had been considered a Johnson man. But, according to Drew Pearson, who is one of Lyndon Johnson's friends:

". . . some time before, Sanford had sent word to Senator Johnson through his former schoolmate, Robert Redwine, who works in the Senate, that he would be for Johnson. Redwine added that Sanford was running up some big campaign expenses and needed financial help. Johnson replied that he was against taking sides in primaries.

"Later Bobby Kennedy . . . made a quiet trip to North Carolina. Sanford had rolled up $106,000 of campaign expenses in his first primary—more than was spent by all three of his opponents. . . . After Bobby Kennedy's visit, Sanford suddenly cooled toward Johnson, the man he wanted to support and the man from whom he asked campaign contributions. Johnson sent one of his aides to North Carolina to see him. But things had changed. The future Governor was cool as a cucumber. He was not interested in Johnson, he was not interested in campaign funds. He did say he would call Johnson the day after his final primary."

He never did. Arriving in Los Angeles on Friday, July 8, Sanford went to Kennedy headquarters for a final conference, where it was agreed that while Sanford would give Jack Kennedy his overall endorsement, he reserved the right to disagree on single specific issues like civil rights. At 9:00 A.M.

the next day, Sanford made his announcement in the Biltmore Bowl, where the press was headquartered. The wires across the nation soon crackled with the news that Jack Kennedy had breached the South, supposedly the safe domain of Lyndon B. Johnson.

The Kennedys made deals with other Southerners. In 1961, Georgia's Governor Ernest Vandiver disclosed that he had obtained a pre-election pledge from the candidate that he would never send troops to Georgia to enforce school desegregation and he now supported Kennedy. And working hard for Jack behind the scenes were Governor John Patterson of Alabama and Senator James Eastland of Mississippi.

A special drive was being made among the uncommitted Dixie delegations by Robert B. Troutman, Jr., an Atlanta businessman who had been at Harvard Law School with Joe Kennedy, Jr. Anti-Johnson literature accused the Texan of being a "traitor to the South" because of his activity in behalf of civil rights legislation. The word was passed along that Jack had sided with the South in a crucial civil rights debate in 1957.

John Kenneth Galbraith and Arthur Schlesinger, Jr., meanwhile, were assuring fellow liberals that Jack had matured greatly in recent years and that his credentials as one of them could no longer be questioned.

The well-organized Kennedy operation reached into each of the fifty state delegations spread throughout the vastness of Los Angeles. From Room 8314 of the Biltmore Hotel a shirt-sleeved Bobby directed strategy from a small table near a window overlooking Pershing Square.

On Bobby's orders, each delegation was double-checked, then triple-checked. "I don't want generalities or guesses," he said. "There's no point in fooling ourselves. I want the cold facts. I want to hear only the votes we are guaranteed on the first ballot."

Trouble developed in the Minnesota delegation which had been teetering in Kennedy's direction. It was reported that a strong Stevenson sentiment had swept the delegation. Arthur Schlesinger, Jr., was sent in to talk to the delegates. "I found them resentful over the intense pressure of the Kennedy people and particularly mistrustful of Bobby Kennedy," Schlesinger later wrote.

Schlesinger, Jr., had been among the first of the so-called intellectuals to board the Kennedy bandwagon. As he confessed to James Reston that spring, he was "nostalgically for Stevenson, ideologically for Humphrey, and realistically for Kennedy." And the convention turned out to be one of the "most agonizing" weeks in his life, he later recalled. Stevensonians accused him of being a "turncoat opportunist." He had another problem. His wife Marian was working for Adlai.

"Can't you control your own wife," wrote Bobby in a memo to Schlesinger, "or are you like me?"

Arthur's mother also announced for Adlai, but the tall, stately gray-haired lady was not so passionate about it as was her daughter-in-law. "In a way," she said, "I suppose it is good that Arthur is working for Senator Kennedy. If Kennedy is nominated and elected, he'll certainly need Arthur's brilliance in the White House."

Bobby's day usually began at 8:00, with a conference with the top forty "pros" who made up the Kennedy organization's hard core. After summing up the latest developments, Bobby would be on the phone with Jack. The talks usually centered around the two main questions: Were the Kennedy-committed delegates standing firm? Were they picking up enough to bring a first-ballot victory into sight? Usually the news was good.

Several times a day Bobby would talk with Father Joe, who was hiding out in the Beverly Hills home of former film star Marion Davies. But the Ambassador was making his influence felt throughout the convention. Old Joe did make the scene at one party, however. He turned up at Frank Sinatra's plush pad in Beverly Hills.

For the rest of the convention, Sinatra and Peter Lawford prowled the floor, ostensibly on missions for Kennedy. The back of Sinatra's head was painted black to prevent the television cameras from picking up the high gloss of his bald pate.

In the *New York Herald Tribune,* political writer Earl Mazo reported: "One of the intriguing sidelines of the Democratic Convention is the frantic effort of Frank Sinatra and other Hollywood friends of Senator Kennedy to keep a searing feud between the Senator's father and an in-law from breaking into the open. Lady Lawford, mother of Kennedy's brother-in-law, Peter Lawford, has been sounding off to some reporters about her intense dislike for Joseph P. Kennedy. . . ."

Interviewed by former Governor Goodwin Knight on a Los Angeles TV station, Bobby was asked his thoughts on the highly controversial Connally Amendment. Bobby, who was already being touted as the Attorney General in a Kennedy Administration, confessed he had never heard of it. "Frankly, that's not my province. I'm just on the team and Jack's the captain."

Playwright-columnist Morrie Ryskind, who was watching the performance, was amazed. "What do you do against naïveté like that?" he asked. "I even forgave him—for the moment—the things he had done as counsel for the Labor Committee. After all, a kid who had never heard of the Connally reservation could hardly be expected to know what went on in the goon squads that were used in the Kohler strike."

Nor did Bobby exhibit too much concern over civil rights. He has since freely admitted that this was an area in which he became interested only in more recent years. "I won't say I stayed awake nights worrying about civil rights before I became Attorney General," he has said.

At the convention, however, Robert Kennedy supported a strong civil rights plank after a member of the Platform Committee urged him to do so on the grounds that "you're not getting the Southern delegates anyway, and so you have nothing to lose there and plenty to win in the North."

Without reading the document, Bobby said, "It's a tough plank, eh? All right, we'll support it."

And the next morning he handed down the line to his key men: "This plank must be passed without a word changed— not a word." What it said didn't matter so long as it could propel Jack into the White House.

When the delegates began to arrive, they found the Kennedys, their in-laws, relatives and friends everywhere. Ethel had flown in from Boston with her four eldest children, headed by eight-year-old Kathleen. On the same plane were sisters-in-law Jean Smith and Joan Kennedy. Their husbands were already on the scene. Eunice and Sarge Shriver had arrived earlier; and Pat and Peter Lawford, of course, lived in nearby Santa Monica. Mother Rose was at the Marion Davies villa with Old Joe.

By the time Lyndon Johnson arrived on a sultry, smoggy July 8, Los Angeles was a Kennedy town. But the tall Texan did not act as if it was. He announced he was ready to do battle with the man with the "Madison Avenue toothpaste smile," and he denounced the Kennedy camp for its "constant, crude efforts to smear candidates with guilt by association." This was a reference to Bobby's claims that Jimmy Hoffa was backing Johnson.

"I really think," Johnson told a packed press conference in the Biltmore Bowl, "that Mr. Kennedy, his father, and his brother have been running against Mr. Hoffa for several years now . . . the closer we get to the nomination, the hotter their breath becomes." But at the same time, he indicated he would not reject Senator Kennedy as a Vice Presidential running mate. "The Vice Presidency is a good place for a young man who needs experience," he observed.

But Lyndon Johnson, old pro that he was, knew that the only hope of stopping Kennedy was a deadlock and that would require bolstering Adlai Stevenson's candidacy. Johnson had no particular affection for Adlai but, as they say, politics makes strange bedfellows.

The Kennedy forces, meanwhile, were troubled by the amount of pro-Stevenson sentiment. Over 10,000 people—the largest demonstration in the airport's history—showed up to greet the twice-beaten standard-bearer when he arrived at Los Angeles' International Airport late in the afternoon of Saturday, July 9. Seeking to nip the Stevenson movement in the bud, the Kennedy people asked Adlai to nominate the youthful Massachusetts Senator for President. But the proposal died on the vine. "Just like always," Bobby said, "he can't make up his mind."

Bobby was visibly annoyed by the pro-Stevenson demonstrations outside the convention hall. Thousands of Adlai supporters were parading and yelling, *"We want Stevenson!"*

Bobby, who had transferred his operations to a model cottage near the Sports Arena, reported to his brother that the demonstrations were nothing to be concerned about. But what did give Bobby momentary concern was the twenty-minute, ear-splitting demonstration Tuesday night when Adlai Stevenson made a surprise appearance at the convention hall, presumably to join the Illinois delegation of which he was a member. Finally, when things quieted down, Stevenson made a short speech.

Thanking the delegates for their welcome, Adlai said, "After getting in and out of the Biltmore and this hall, I know whom you are going to nominate. It will be the last survivor." The audience laughed, but it obviously wanted more. Adlai was not about to give them what they wanted. And Bobby, watching the spectacle on television, breathed a little easier.

Earlier that day, he had a real scare. Governor Edmund G. (Pat) Brown had lost control of the California delegation, with 31½ votes going to Stevenson and 30½ to Kennedy.

Bobby fumed. Joe Alsop quoted Bobby as describing Brown as a "leaning tower of putty." Brown, of course, had made a deal with Jack to deliver the California delegation in return for Jack's staying out of the California primary.

Then came another blow. Hubert Humphrey, after conferring with Lyndon Johnson, gave his eleventh-hour support to Adlai Stevenson. He had previously indicated he would back Kennedy. "You know you can never bank on Hubert," Bobby commented bitterly.

Following the convention, when most politicians would have let bygones be bygones, Bobby cornered Humphrey and bluntly told him, "I'm going to get you."

By Wednesday, Lyndon Johnson knew he didn't stand a chance for the nomination, yet right down to the final moments he roamed various state caucuses, bitterly assailing his young rival. He referred to the Kennedy's wealth, Joe Kennedy's prewar isolationism, and Jack's record on McCarthyism.*

But it was too late. Lyndon Johnson returned to his suite at the Biltmore and, even before the nominating speeches had begun, started thinking of the telegram of congratulations he would be sending that night to Jack Kennedy.

The last burst of anti-Kennedy defiance came when Senator Eugene McCarthy of Minnesota placed in nomination the name of Adlai E. Stevenson. It was, observers agreed, the best speech of the convention. "Do not turn away from this

---

* When the campaign got under way, Jack Kennedy told intimates—according to *Newsweek*—he had made a bad mistake in not taking a firm public stand against the late Senator McCarthy. "Had I known then that I was going to run for President," the nominee said, "I would have gone on crutches to vote for censure."

man," McCarthy pleaded. "He spoke to the people. He moved their minds and stirred their hearts. . . . Do not leave this prophet without honor in his own party. Do not reject this man."

At the conclusion, the hall exploded into the noisiest, most determined demonstration of the convention. The aisles were jammed with supporters far in excess of the organized demonstrators for Kennedy, Johnson or Symington. But Bobby quickly discovered that the Kennedy delegates had not been affected. He phoned Jack at his hideout: "Don't worry, we're in."

During the balloting, Bobby directed operations from the cottage outside the Arena. He phoned one of his floor "commandos" to ask the Governor of New Jersey to give his votes to Kennedy. But Robert B. Meyner, a distant relative of Adlai's by marriage, had been angered at Joe Kennedy's wooing of northern New Jersey political bosses earlier in the year; the internal dissensions he had created threatened Meyner's control of his party's state machinery.

"Meyner's going to stand pat," the commando reported. "He doesn't think we can make it the first time around and will take the votes himself as a favorite son."

Bobby's response was unprintable. (Meyner paid the penalty following the election. After visiting the White House, the ex-Governor disclosed he was not getting a job on the New Frontier.)

By the time the roll call reached the state of Washington, Kennedy's total neared 700. Washington made it 710. Realizing that Wyoming's fifteen votes could end the contest, Bobby telephoned his younger brother Teddy. "Get over to Wyoming and tell them if we can get their fifteen, Wyoming will cinch the nomination of the next President."

Wyoming at that point had only ten votes for Kennedy. The TV cameras focused on Ted Kennedy bearing in on Wyoming's chairman, Tracy McCraken. McCraken threw up his hands and roared, "Let 'em all go." And that was it. By the first ballot's end, Kennedy had 806 votes, Johnson 409, Symington 86, Stevenson 79½.

The next morning Bobby was up bright and early. At 9:30 he conferred with twenty-five slightly dazed state chairmen and stressed one of his favorite political themes—the importance of a voter-registration drive. "The key to our whole campaign," he said, "is a national registration drive. I know everyone says this every two years or every four years. This is going to be different, because this time it's going to be done."

Later he met with Arthur Schlesinger, Jr., who stressed the need to "conciliate" the Stevenson people and get them involved in the campaign. "Arthur," Bobby told him, "human nature requires that you allow us forty-eight hours. Adlai has given us a rough time over the last three days. In forty-eight hours, I will do anything you want, but right now I don't want to hear anything about the Stevensonians. . . ."

Most of Thursday was devoted to the selection of a running mate for John F. Kennedy. More than half-a-dozen party luminaries believed they would be tapped for the number-two spot, because that's what the Kennedys had led them to believe. "If they [the Kennedys] called a meeting of all the people to whom they've promised the Vice Presidency, they couldn't find a room in Los Angeles big enough to hold it in," said Oklahoma's Senator A. S. Mike Monroney, who had headed up the Stevenson effort.

When the Washington *Post* published "reliable reports" that Lyndon Johnson was also in the running, Joseph Rauh, who headed the District of Columbia delegation, rushed to Bobby. Nothing to it at all, Bobby replied; his brother's choice most definitely would not be Johnson. And Jimmy Wechsler was told by Schlesinger that it would be "safe" to report to the readers of the New York *Post* that Kennedy had made no final determination on a running mate but "Johnson definitely isn't on the list."

By Thursday morning, however, reports to the contrary were flying around the Biltmore Hotel. One of those who tried to find out the truth was columnist Robert G. Spivack. Almost by accident, he met Jack Kennedy as he came out of his suite. "I asked him point-blank if Senator Johnson had been offered the nomination," Spivack later recalled. "He shook his head and whispered 'no.'"

On his way down to the press bullpen to file his story, Spivack encountered an old friend, Governor David L. Lawrence of Pennsylvania. He told Lawrence what Kennedy had just told him. "Bob," Lawrence said in his fatherly way, "don't write it."

"Why not, Governor?" Spivack asked.

"Because it's all set for Lyndon Johnson. It has been for days. We've all known it and I'm for it. He's a very able man, but he also can unite the party and give us a chance to win. Arvey [Jacob Arvey, the Illinois National Committeeman] is also for it."

Several hours later what Lawrence told Spivack was confirmed. Following the convention, Lawrence told Spivack that the reason he had wanted Lyndon on the ticket was that he was not optimistic about the chances of a Kennedy victory. "Johnson," he said, "may be able to save the ticket."

Many months later, Spivack asked Jack Kennedy about his answer to the columnist's question and why he replied as he did. Kennedy shrugged and said, "That's politics."

To this day, no clear, authoritative explanation has emerged about that momentous day, July 14, and how Lyndon Johnson came to be picked as Kennedy's running mate. Jack Kennedy never told the full story. In fact, he made this cryptic remark to Pierre Salinger a day or two after the convention: "The whole story will never be known. And it's just as well that it won't be."

It is conceivable that Jack Kennedy never knew the whole story himself. Reporters at the scene, including this writer, were given widely varying accounts of what had occurred. Lyndon Johnson, for example, told three different stories to as many reporters within the space of three hours.

"What happened in Los Angeles in 1960 no longer matters," wrote Douglas Kiker in *The Atlantic* six years later. "What matters now is what Johnson believes to have happened. . . ."

And Lyndon Johnson believes that Bobby moved heaven and earth to keep him off the ticket. There can be little doubt that Bobby was dumbfounded when his brother informed him that Lyndon Johnson was high on his list of possible running mates.

"When Johnson's name was selected," Bobby said several years later, "I pointed out to my brother that this was going to be very hard to explain to many of our supporters. Johnson had tried to block us, to fight us all the way, and the fight had unfortunately gotten personal in the final stages. I was afraid the news of Johnson's selection to be Vice President would cause the Walter Reuthers and others to collapse. . . ."

Eventually at least a dozen versions of this laying on of hands were published. All of them had this in common: Johnson regarded the young and handsome Kennedy as an ingratiating interloper, and Kennedy viewed Johnson as a political necessity. Without him there was no hope of carrying the South. And without the South, Kennedy knew he had no hope of winning.

For weeks close friends from the South had been telling him that. And, at the convention, Northern party leaders including Governor Abraham Ribicoff of Connecticut and New York's Carmine DeSapio had shown concern that Kennedy's nomination had only nine and one-half votes from Southern states.

What apparently clinched it for Johnson was a meeting of Southern governors with Jack the morning after the nomination. The meeting was held at the suggestion of Bob Troutman.

Years later, Ribicoff agreed that what the Southerners told Kennedy helped to nail down the decision.

"Afterward," said Ribicoff, "Governor [Mennen] Williams [of Michigan], who had not been invited to the meeting, voiced his objections to having Mr. Johnson on the ticket. He said he would lead the opposition to Johnson's nomination on the convention floor.

"Everything had been smooth to this time. Then tempers began to rise. It was a very delicate situation. The Southerners were ready to bolt the convention.

"I made a little talk in which I said that, next to Mr. Kennedy, Senator Johnson was the strongest man in the party, and that the Democrats ought to put their best ticket into the field. Gradually, the meeting quieted."

Kennedy himself probably put it best when asked by a disturbed Adlai Stevenson why he had picked Johnson. "Because," said the candidate, "I want to win."

Jack suggested that Bobby total up the electoral vote of Texas and other Southern states that Johnson's name presumably would carry for the Democratic ticket and he would understand. This was the argument used by their father, who, in the meantime, had telephoned Johnson to urge him to become Jack's running mate. And once his brother had made a firm decision, Bobby said later, he went along.

Joe Rauh, who in addition to being chairman of the tiny but noisy District of Columbia delegation was Walter Reuther's lawyer, told all and sundry that Bobby had "double-crossed" him.

A floor fight appeared to be shaping up for that evening. But Jack Kennedy was aware of the realities of political life. He had no compunction about ignoring these anguished cries from the liberal-laborite bloc. They still made him feel uncomfortable, but he had come to understand them. He was well aware of their almost pathological aversion to Richard Nixon. He knew there would be no significant defections.

And, in the end, he was proved right.

Jack Kennedy then made a decision that was to have fateful implications for the future. He sent his brother to talk to Johnson. At first, Bobby did not get to see Johnson. Instead, he talked to the late Speaker Rayburn, Johnson's chief confidant and adviser. Rayburn, who had a low boiling point and hadn't wanted Johnson to take the Vice Presidency in the first place, snarled at Bobby, "Sonny, if we want to talk to any Kennedy about the Vice Presidency, it won't be with you."

Philip Graham, publisher of the Washington *Post* and a Johnson admirer, reported that Johnson had been "considerably on edge" and "in a state of high nerves" when he failed to hear from Kennedy, who had promised to call, and when Bobby again showed up at the Johnson suite, Bobby reported the impending troubles on the floor and asked whether Johnson might prefer to withdraw and become Democratic National Chairman.

Then, at Rayburn's order, Phil Graham was asked to phone Jack. Coolly, Jack replied, "Bobby's been out of touch and doesn't know what's been happening." He assured Graham that Lyndon Johnson was indeed his candidate for Vice President. Because of this episode Lyndon Johnson believed that Bobby had indeed done all he could to prevent his candidacy.

The fact remains that Bobby has never been candid about his role in these fateful hours. One version of Bobby's meeting with Johnson was published in Schlesinger's *A Thousand Days*.

According to the Pulitzer prize-winning historian, Schlesinger quotes Johnson as practically begging to be named as Kennedy's running mate: "I want to be Vice President and if the candidate will have me, I'll join him in making a fight for it."

The truth is that Johnson said nothing at all to Bobby. It was Sam Rayburn who had done the talking. Nor does Schlesinger's suggestion that Jack Kennedy had offered the nomination believing "that there was practically no chance Johnson would accept" hold much water.

According to Ted Sorensen, it didn't happen that way at all. In a *Meet the Press* interview in February 1964, Sorensen —who had far better access to Jack Kennedy than Schlesinger —denied that Kennedy's decision had been made with reluctance or because of pressure.

"I was not surprised [by the decision]," said Sorensen, "because I had long known of President Kennedy's feeling about Lyndon Johnson and had in fact been one of many who recommended Mr. Johnson as President Kennedy's running mate should he be nominated. . . . I think it was a logical and happy choice both for the campaign and the country."

Kenneth Galbraith, always the realist, thought so too. The six-foot-eight professor moved among the liberal delegates who were exploding with anger over the choice of Johnson. "This," Galbraith explained, "is the kind of political expedient Franklin Roosevelt would never have used—except in the case of John Nance Garner."

After a long, wearying and chaotic day, the Johnson nomination was rammed through. On Bobby's orders, there was to be no opportunity for dissent. Johnson was nominated in a controversial voice vote which was greeted by boos from all parts of the vast arena. "Soapy" Williams and Joe Rauh kept yelling, "No!"

Jack and Bobby were tired and depressed as they sat around the swimming pool at the Marion Davies villa discussing the day's events. The rancor which had greeted the Johnson nomination had finally got through to them. At that moment their father, wearing a fancy smoking jacket, appeared in the doorway.

"Don't worry, Jack," he said. "In two weeks everyone will be saying that this was the smartest thing you ever did."

Which is exactly what they were saying in two weeks.

16

Campaign 1960

The morning after their triumphant return from Los Angeles, Bobby called his bleary-eyed staff together in Hyannis Port and announced there was no time for relaxation. Washington's Senator Henry Jackson had agreed to an interim appointment as Democratic National Chairman—a post that, under normal circumstances, would have put him in charge of the campaign—but he quickly learned that at most he was a titled figurehead.

It was Bobby who "learned" him. Bobby, while still in Los Angeles, had quickly asserted his authority, and Jack himself had confirmed it. From then on, the Democratic National Chairman was rarely heard from during the campaign. As so many others had discovered, he found out that the Kennedys trusted few outsiders.

The reason he had been named was to soothe his feelings, ruffled by his failure to obtain the Vice Presidential nomination. And soon the Kennedys sought to appease another party power, "Soapy" Williams of Michigan, who had bitterly, but futilely, sought to prevent Lyndon Johnson's nomination. Originally, it was thought that "Soapy's" wrath might be assuaged if his state chairman, Neil Staebler, was named executive secretary of the Democratic National Committee, but when news of this leaked out, a deputation of important Southern leaders called on Bobby.

They said they were opposed to the appointment because Staebler would be doing the bidding of UAW President Walter Reuther, no particular hero in Dixie. So as a compromise,

Mrs. Margaret Price, national committeewoman from Michigan, was named vice chairman of the National Committee.

This, of course, meant the dismissal of Mrs. Katie Louchheim, one of the best-known women in the Democratic party and a tower of strength in the women's division. But she was just in the way, and Bobby, in his inimitable fashion, told her so.

Accepting the inevitable, Mrs. Louchheim asked, "Isn't there anything you want me to do? I'd be glad to help out in the campaign."

"Are you arguing with me?" Bobby snapped at a lady twenty years his senior. "Are you trying to tell me what to do?"

"Why, of course not."

"Then get out. You're through!"

After a few days in Hyannis Port, Bobby hustled himself down to Washington, where he took over an office at National Committee headquarters. He looked over the staff that had accumulated over the years and was appalled at the inefficiency he discovered. "When we first took over," he says, "there were at least one hundred workers, and only one girl who could take dictation."

Bobby's immediate instinct was to fire the lot of them, hire new people and begin afresh. But a lot of influential Democrats had placed friends on the staff, and would have been offended. Besides, there wasn't time. So instead Bobby began to hire new people.

By mid-campaign, the staff had overflowed into dozens of offices in five Washington buildings, each packed to the transom with workers. Mimeograph machines and tables choked the corridors. "Everybody's working like hell," one of Bobby's aides told *Time*. "Some of them don't know what they're doing, but they're working like hell."

And they worked like hell because it was being whispered around Kennedy headquarters from coast to coast that "Little Brother is watching." Or, at least, one of his trusted subordinates was watching. For Bobby had dispatched thirty regional coordinators to as many states to insure that everything that could be done was being done.

Meanwhile, Bobby assembled the top elite of Operation Kennedy. These veterans included top organizer Larry O'Brien, scheduling coordinator Ken O'Donnell and press agent Pierre Salinger. Brother Teddy was dispatched to San Francisco, where he assumed command of all campaign operations from the Rockies to the Pacific Coast. From Denver, Bobby summoned lawyer Byron R. (Whizzer) White, the former Colorado University All-American and Rhodes scholar, to head the volunteer Citizens for Kennedy-Johnson.

Before he had left Hyannis Port, Bobby had received Jack's final approval for his crash program to register new voters. "The Democrats are there," said Bobby, "and if we are going to win this election, we just have to reach them." He reasoned that labor unions could help mightily in getting people registered without violating laws concerning political expenditures. Unions like Walter Reuther's Auto Workers would be only too happy to pick up the tabs. Which they were.

Behind this highly publicized registration drive was Bobby's belief that 70 percent of the habitual non-voters would vote Democratic if registered and taken to the polls. When asked by a *Newsweek* reporter where he obtained his estimates, Bobby snapped back, "These are not estimates. They are facts and figures."

Statistical studies had actually been made in every state under the direction of Bobby's friend Representative Frank (Fearless) Thompson, Jr., of New Jersey, whom he had named director of the drive. The hard-driving Thompson did an excellent job. When the election was over, Bobby cited as one of the "important factors" in the victory "the work that was done on registration and getting out the vote on Election Day. . . ." Bobby estimated that an additional 10,000,000 voters had been registered.

The campaign had not taken off as Bobby had hoped. Jack's acceptance speech had been hardly inspiring and received a generally bad press.

The speech was memorable only because it was the first time Kennedy had publicly used the phrase "New Frontier." The candidate had first heard it at a Boston cocktail party that June, held in the apartment of a member of the Kennedy academic advisory group. Shortly after Jack had arrived, he was cornered by Walt Whitman Rostow, an economic historian at the Massachusetts Institute of Technology, who said in effect, "I've got the slogan—the New Frontier." Kennedy, who had long been seeking a brief but vivid phrase along the lines of Roosevelt's "New Deal," bought it immediately.

Actually Rostow's contribution was probably the most important made by any of the hundreds of intellectuals who gravitated around the Democratic candidate.

"In the end," as he told Dick Nixon in a post-election meeting in Florida, "I found myself relying more and more on Sorensen, who was with me on the campaign tour and who therefore could react to and reflect up-to-the-minute tactical shifts in our basic strategy."

In the weeks following the nomination, Jack made his peace with Eleanor Roosevelt and Harry S Truman. Both, however, gave him lukewarm endorsements.

Back in Washington, he sought to reassure some of his disgruntled Southern colleagues that they need have no fears about the "far-out" Democratic platform.

One of the Senators to whom he paid a visit, accompanied by a now obsequious Lyndon Johnson, was Virginia's Harry F. Byrd, Sr., of Virginia. The nominees told Byrd they did not go along with the platform plank calling for abolition of state right-to-work laws. They also promised no new civil rights legislation, despite Democratic platform pledges.

At Kennedy headquarters, Bobby was cracking the whip like a plantation overseer. "I don't even have to think about organization," marveled Jack. "I just show up. Bobby's easily the best man I've ever seen. He's the hardest worker. He's the greatest organizer. He's taken no time off. He's fantastic. He's living on nerves."

Bobby was also living on the absolute conviction that he and Jack would be victorious in November. And he intended to do everything possible in his single-minded way to insure that victory. Campaign workers across the land might complain about Little Brother's battering-ram methods. But when some of these complaints reached Jack he told a friend, "Bobby has the strong support of his staff and the people who really want to do some work and help us. . . . There's nothing you can do about the people who complain. They don't like me either. They don't like our success."

Bobby was unconcerned. He announced repeatedly he wasn't running in a popularity contest. And basically, he was doing Jack's bidding. Even when they were unable to consult with each other, he quickly and instinctively knew what to do. The two brothers, in effect, had an extrasensory communications system going with each other. When the Senator was unavailable, staff members would "clear it with Bobby," and few staffers would dare argue. All hands were well aware that he spoke for the candidate.

Jack was the one man to whom Bobby readily deferred. This did not mean he always concurred. "He expresses himself volubly, not to say repetitiously," an associate told the New York *Post's* Irwin Ross. "Then all concerned discuss the matter with Jack. Bobby quietly expresses his reservations. Jack hands down his decision. If it goes against Bobby, there's not a peep out of him. He cheerfully goes forth to carry it out."

Bobby never made any effort to compete with his brother on an intellectual level. "He is not at home with abstract concepts," a friend told Ross. "He's fundamentally a doer. Bobby's political ideas are Jack's political ideas."

One of the things that gave Bobby considerable annoyance was that people around the National Committee tended to refer to the candidate as Jack. He sent around a memorandum to all concerned that the candidate was always to be referred to as "Senator Kennedy." There were still lingering concerns about Jack's image as a mature statesman. And after conferring with Jack, Bobby notified Frank Sinatra and Walter Reuther it would be best if they made themselves scarce. This didn't mean they couldn't operate behind the scenes, but any publicity about their efforts could only be harmful.

Reuther, needless to say, played the Kennedy game. He even discovered hidden virtues in Lyndon Johnson's "reactionary" background.

Frank Sinatra was more difficult to convince. Speculation about what role Sinatra might play in the campaign had begun at the Democratic National Convention. True, the Rat Pack had been most valuable to the Kennedys. They had all done considerable drumbeating for the candidate and raised large sums of money for him in the lush acres of Beverly Hills and Bel Air. But, the Kennedys soon came to realize, they had also cast a shadow over the candidate which could easily hurt him. When it leaked out that the Pack privately referred to the Senator as "Jack the Ripper," that was it.

Old Joe had flown off to Cap d'Antibes on the French Riviera for a short vacation and he refused to grant interviews. An intrepid *Newsweek* correspondent swam up to him in the warm waters off his rented villa and engaged him in conversation, but the Ambassador, somewhat taken aback, said he would have nothing to say prior to the election.

All the other Kennedys were working hard, except Jacqueline Kennedy, who could not campaign because she was in her final months of pregnancy. Though reporters had speculated whether Jack's beautiful wife, a creature of the *haute couture* and of the jet set, would be a political liability, Bobby has always maintained she was a political asset. "We came out of that Los Angeles convention looking like a hard, tough family juggernaut," he says, "but in her few gentle low-key TV appearances, Jackie softened that image and put the spotlight back where it belonged—on Jack and his family."

Jackie's brother-in-law, Prince Stanislas Radziwill, flew in from London. Lee Bouvier's second husband came from a family that had once been the wealthiest in Poland. "Stash" Radziwill spoke to Polish-American communities in the big cities and Bobby was later to tell a cheering crowd in Kraków that his brother owed his election to the votes of these Polish-Americans.

How much good Eunice Shriver did during the campaign is arguable. "People who enjoy criticizing the rich and the prominent find her a relatively easy target," observed Robert A. Liston in *Sargent Shriver: A Candid Portrait*. "She is outspoken, often tactless, sometimes rude." She was almost primitive in her tribal instincts. Once, while walking along Park Avenue, she encountered an old friend, a young business executive whose picture had appeared in *Fortune* that month as one of Nixon's hardworking supporters.

"Traitor," she hissed and strode quickly away.

On August 25, 1960, Bobby Kennedy received a 125-page report from the Simulmatics Corporation offering predictions on how different parts of the electorate would respond to various situations. The predictions were based on the findings of a so-called "People Machine," actually an IBM 704 computer into which had been fed interviews with some 100,000 voters. The interviews were divided into 480 "voter types" such as "Midwestern, small-town, poor, Catholic, female" and "Western, metropolitan, Jewish male."

The story of how this device—described by Professor Harold D. Lasswell of Yale as a "breakthrough . . . comparable to what happened at Stagg Field"—was secretly programmed for use in the campaign and was first mentioned in the January 1961 issue of *Harper's*, in an authoritative article entitled "People-Machine" by free-lance writer Thomas B. Morgan, who had served as a volunteer press adviser to the draft Stevenson movement in Los Angeles.

Bobby was most interested in one segment of the report. To the question "What if the religious issue becomes embittered close to Election Day?" the computer reported:

". . . Kennedy today has lost the bulk of the votes he would lose if the election campaign were to be embittered by the issue of anti-Catholicism. The net worst has been done. If the campaign becomes embittered he will lose a few more reluctant Protestant votes to Nixon, but will gain Catholic and minority group votes. Bitter anti-Catholicism in the campaign would bring about a reaction against prejudice and for Kennedy from Catholics and others who would resent overt prejudice. It is in Kennedy's hands to handle the religious issue during the campaign in a way that maximizes Kennedy votes based on resentment against religious prejudice and minimizes further defections. On balance, he would not lose further from forthright and persistent attention to the religious issue, and could gain. The simulation shows that there has already been a serious defection from Kennedy by Protestant voters. Under these circumstances, it makes no sense to brush the religious issue under the rug. Kennedy has already suffered the disadvantages of the issue even though it is not embittered now—and without receiving compensating advantages inherent in it."

The Kennedy brothers already knew the political potency of The Issue. After all, beginning with the Bailey Report in 1956, they had learned to use it to superb advantage. Beyond question, it helped Jack get the nomination in Los Angeles. And now, almost predictably, Jack would repeatedly urge the voters to forget his religion.

Once again, the Kennedys were also running against Hoffa. Jack himself announced, early in the campaign, that he was "extremely glad" that Jimmy Hoffa's union was not "supporting me in this campaign." And he was happy, too, that the Communist-influenced Longshoremens Union was also opposed.

A *New York Times* dispatch suggested that the Democratic candidate apparently "thought he had a good campaign issue, linking Mr. Nixon to the leadership of these two unions. It is an argument that Robert Kennedy made frequently during the Democratic primary campaigns, in which Mr. Hoffa was accused of providing money to help the 'Stop Kennedy' movement."

Bobby, meanwhile, was also playing the religious issue for all it was worth. In Stevenson's home town of Libertyville, he announced that his brother's Catholicism had become a major issue in the South. He went on to say again that his brother had not been questioned about his religion when he went into the Navy.

"Of course he wasn't," commented the *Chicago Tribune,* "but why orate about these matters in Illinois if the issue is more important only in the South? Mr. Kennedy's managers must have come to the conclusion that he has more to gain by keeping the issue alive than by agreeing with Mr. Nixon to drop it. . . . These calculations may be correct but it is no credit to Mr. Kennedy. . . . He is promoting exactly the kind of voting that he professes to deplore and which men of good will, regardless of religious affiliations, genuinely do deplore."

Bobby was busy reporting that the Republicans were spending at least $1,000,000 on anti-Catholic literature. Toward the end of the campaign, on nationwide television, he said that while Nixon was not to blame for the hate campaign, "there are a number of Republican headquarters, for instance the one in San Diego, one in Pennsylvania, one in Florida, there are a number across the country that are issuing anti-Catholic literature, and doing it quite openly." (After the campaign the Fair Campaign Practices Committee disclosed that an intensive investigation had failed to substantiate these charges.) Then what Bobby literally had been praying for came to pass. Dr. Norman Vincent Peale and a group of Protestant clergy issued a 2,000-word statement voicing concern over the possibility of a Catholic President.

The Peale episode could not have been arranged better by Bobby himself. The Democrats leaped on the statement as absolute proof of GOP bigotry. Dr. Peale, after all, was a well-known Republican.

Jack Kennedy replied to the Peale statement in a speech

before a group of Protestant ministers in Houston. Basically, he said that he would resign from the Presidency rather than take orders from the Vatican.

"It was not widely noticed, though it is a charming confirmation of John Kennedy's genuine innocence of the Roman coils," wrote William F. Buckley, Jr., "that in answer to one minister who asked him how he could reconcile his protestations of liberalism with the drastically anti-liberal encyclical 'Syllabus of Errors,' Mr. Kennedy (who was to earn a record as the best-briefed candidate in the history of Presidential convention) gave an answer that would have amused novitiate Catholics and anti-Catholics alike:

"The 'Syllabus,' Mr. Kennedy replied . . . was concededly still a part of church doctrine' [it isn't] but on the other hand, the encyclical was from 'several centuries in the past.' [It was promulgated in 1864.]"

Nevertheless, the Houston meeting was a decided plus for Kennedy. Bobby arranged for repeated TV showings of a film version of the confrontation in cities with large Catholic populations.

Commented the Catholic *Commonweal:* "While we see that it may be desirable to distribute to Protestants who misunderstand and fear Catholicism [the film] . . . we see little need to show the film before Catholics who, presumably, have no such fears."

Not all Democrats bought this Kennedy strategy. Matthew E. Welsh, who feared that raising the issue in Indiana could defeat him for Governor, dispatched an aide, Clinton Green, to meet Bobby when he arrived for a day-long series of speeches in southern Indiana. On the way in from the airport, Green relayed Welsh's fears. "I might as well have been talking to that wall over there," he later said. "He listened and he didn't say anything. But you know what he said [in his speeches]."

What he said on fourteen different occasions, rarely varying his pitch, was exactly what the local Democrats had asked him not to say. Over and over, Bobby attacked religious intolerance. When the day's ordeal was over, Clinton Green said, "I realized that the Kennedy people had come to a conclusion, and were taking a calculated risk. They were going to talk about religion. They were the ones who brought up the religious issue and kept it alive. It wasn't the Republicans."

Tristram Coffin, in the *New Leader*, wrote a wrap-up piece on the campaign in which he noted that Bobby "leads a crew of tough, young, energetic Irish politicians who, in the words of one observer, 'don't give a bloody damn about philosophy, logic or altruism. Bobby only wants to know, "How many votes will this bring Jack?" He is already thinking ahead to 1964. Bobby is utterly and completely loyal to his brother, and would jump off the Washington Monument or cut a man's throat if he thought it would help Jack. Bobby, too, is a genius at organization and at digging up buried bones.' "

Bobby's dedication to his brother frequently damaged his effectiveness. Because of his hard line with such liberals as Eleanor Roosevelt and Herbert Lehman, a half century his senior, he only widened the breach between the reformers and the regular Democrats. Finally, an agreement was reached whereby Bobby was to stay out of New York. Acting in his behalf, however, was William Walton, a close friend of Jacqueline Kennedy, who had formerly been a newspaperman on the defunct *PM*, and later *Time*. But despite Walton's intervention, reports from New York indicated that the campaign was slow in getting started. The liberals and reformers still hadn't "bought" Lyndon Johnson, and once again reports of the alleged pro-Nazism of Joe Kennedy were making the rounds.

As a remedy, the Kennedys authorized a National Conference on Constitutional Rights and American Freedom to meet in Manhattan, with—of all people—Hubert Humphrey as chairman. Humphrey had every reason not to accept the invitation. He was facing a tough fight for re-election in his own state. And Bobby, at the Los Angeles convention, had rebuked the Minnesotan and had vowed revenge in terms many thought would never be forgiven. But Humphrey told reporters everything had been patched up. "In fits of emotion," he explained, "some things may have been said that should not have been said. But Bob and I got together for dinner in Washington."

In a New York radio interview with Barry Gray, Bobby excoriated his brother's enemies in a free-swinging hour-long appearance. They included everyone from Jackie Robinson to Southern Democrats, to pollsters, doctors, airline executives and, as was not entirely unexpected, Dick Nixon.

Bobby assailed the Southern Democrats for having blocked "progressive legislation," identifying as the chief culprits Virginia's Senator Harry F. Byrd and Congressman Howard W. Smith, who had been serving in the House of Representatives since Bobby was five years old.

He also charged that the medical profession had sabotaged medical care for the aged by raising "the false cry of socialism." He wanted to know why Nixon was not being interrogated on how his religious views would affect his attitudes on public questions, and deplored the Republican candidate's alleged attempt to take political advantage of a scheme to bring African students to the United States. It was quite a show.

He particularly criticized Jackie Robinson for having dared to question his brother's commitment to civil rights. "Of course my brother had breakfast with Governor Patterson [of Alabama]," Bobby exclaimed angrily. "Why shouldn't he? He's interested in votes from all sections of the United States."

Bobby had come to the Barry Gray program with a dossier on Jackie Robinson compiled by several of his investigators, and he used it to deliver a sharply personal attack on the former baseball star.

Robinson's reply was immediate and scorching: "If the younger Kennedy is going to resort to lies, then I can see what kind of campaign this is going to be. I don't see where my company has anything at all to do with his brother's having had breakfast with the head of the White Citizens' Council and the racist Governor of Alabama."

Bobby's criticism of Southern Congressmen on the Barry Gray Show also aroused considerable anger. When South Carolina and Florida leaders complained about what Bobby had said about the South, Jack Kennedy told them that the remarks were "unfortunate." He said his brother was "young and very hotheaded," and he implied that he already had had words with Bobby. He assured the Southerners that it wouldn't happen again.

Meanwhile, after studying the Lou Harris polls, Bobby advised his brother to stop stressing the Quemoy-Matsu issue. It had been Jack's suggestion that the United States should "make it clear that we should not engage in the defense" of these tiny islands off the coast of mainland China. Quemoy and Matsu were under the control of the Chinese Nationalists based on Formosa.

The best indications were that Kennedy had suffered on this issue; that, in fact, it had given the Nixon campaign a much-needed shot in the arm. Nixon, of course, did not favor handing over these tiny offshore islands to the Chinese Communists.

The Harris polls also indicated that the American people were truly concerned about the spectacle of a Castro-controlled Cuba thumbing its nose at the United States. "I found in my trips around the United States," Bobby reported, "that the major problem in everybody's mind is this question of Cuba and what's going to be done ninety miles off our coast. It has become a bastion for the Soviet Union."

Jack Kennedy decided to hammer hard on Cuba. "I wasn't the Vice President who presided over the communization of Cuba," he said at Jacksonville, Florida.

"I'm not impressed with those who say they stood up to Khrushchev when Castro has defied them ninety miles away," he said again at Evansville, Indiana.

In mid-campaign, Kennedy issued a statement urging direct intervention in Cuba: "We must attempt to strengthen the non-Batista democratic anti-Castro forces in exile, and in Cuba itself, who offer eventual hope of overthrowing Castro. Thus far these fighters for freedom have had virtually no support from our Government."

What made the statement shocking was that Kennedy had been briefed by the Central Intelligence Agency about the surreptitious training of anti-Castro Cubans for eventual invasion of Cuba. Nixon quickly determined from the White House that Kennedy had indeed been briefed, but there was little he could do about it. "For the first time and only time in the campaign," Nixon said later, "I got mad at Kennedy personally."

The vehemence of the editorial reaction, particularly from liberal sources friendly to him, frightened Kennedy. "I really don't know what further demagoguery is possible from Kennedy on this subject," commented Murray Kempton, "short of announcing that, if elected, he will send Bobby and Teddy and Eunice to Oriente to clean Castro out."

Kennedy quickly changed his line, berating Nixon for supposedly distorting his views and "attacking me for things I never said or advocated." What he advocated, he told Nixon in a telegram, was that "all available communications . . . and the moral power of the American government" be used "to let the forces of freedom in Cuba know that we are on their side."

Again the Kennedys had succeeded in having it both ways.

And they used the same strategy on civil rights. Up North, people like Harlem's Adam Clayton Powell (in Kennedy's presence on one occasion) were accusing Nixon of having failed to repudiate an endorsement by the Florida Ku Klux Klan. While Jack's pal, Florida Senator George Smathers, who had been named Kennedy's campaign manager for all of the South, was busily accusing Nixon of having once held an honorary membership in the National Association for the Advancement of Colored People.

The fact is that between the West Virginia primary and the nomination in Los Angeles, the Kennedy camp had no civil rights strategy. It did have a civil rights expert, Harris L. Wofford, Jr. One strategy that Wofford submitted to Bobby was quickly rejected. It called for placing Negroes on Jack Kennedy's personal staff, not as civil rights advisers, but in charge of other areas. "The time isn't right," Bobby said. "We'd lose the election."

Wofford proved invaluable to the Kennedys. According to Sorensen, he conducted high-level negotiations with "the flamboyant but effective" Adam Clayton Powell to obtain his support. What was "negotiated" was never disclosed, but Powell, who had been charging that Jack Kennedy "had a bad civil rights record for a man from Massachusetts," suddenly announced his "full, all-out support." And one of the first things Bobby did after becoming Attorney General was to drop a long-standing charge of income-tax fraud against Powell.

The St. Louis *Post-Dispatch,* one of the Middle West's most liberal newspapers, termed the Justice Department's action "a disgrace." "We wonder," the paper editorialized, "whether the young Attorney General, who is said to burn indignantly at the sight of justice obstructed, really believes that justice has been done in the case of a key Congressman who campaigned effectively for his brother last fall, in St. Louis among other places.

"Two of Mr. Powell's office secretaries went to jail, convicted of tax evasion after testimony that they paid kickbacks to Mr. Powell for the privilege of holding their jobs. The kickbacker goes to jail and the accused recipient of the kickback goes free; does that sound like justice? . . . It would be nice to know what Robert Kennedy thinks about it all."

If Bobby ever gave it any thought, he did not say so.

And when Dr. Martin Luther King was arrested, along with seventy-eight others, for having invaded an Atlanta department store and staged a "sit-in," Kennedy remained silent. A few days later all the Negroes were released except Dr. King, who was peremptorily sentenced on a technicality to four months' hard labor at the State Penitentiary at Reidsville. Harris Wofford heard rumors that Nixon had asked the White House to do something about the case and wanted to beat the Republicans to the punch. He suggested that Jack Kennedy telephone Mrs. King in Atlanta and inform her of his concern. But Bobby would have none of it.

Wofford then telephoned Sargent Shriver in Chicago. Shriver thought the idea a good one and immediately drove to the motel at O'Hare Airport where his brother-in-law was staying the night. After a quiet talk, he persuaded the candidate to make the call. Kennedy talked to Mrs. King and assured her not only of his concern but of his intervention, if necessary.

When Bobby learned of the call, according to an eyewitness, "he literally blew his stack." "There goes the election," he shouted. "We've lost the South. We blew it!"

Later that day, a still-angry Bobby met his brother at LaGuardia Airport. Jack calmed him down, and ordered him to get in touch with George D. Stewart, Georgia Democratic party secretary. It was at Stewart's suggestion that Bobby telephoned Judge Oscar Mitchell, who had sent King to jail. Bobby made the call, and afterward the Reverend Dr. King was released. And at Stewart's suggestion, Judge Mitchell told reporters that it was Robert Kennedy who had intervened in King's behalf, while Vice President Nixon had done nothing.

Nixon later conceded that this might have cost him the election. But he pointed out that Bobby's conduct "was unethical," though he agreed King should never have been jailed. "As a lawyer I know if you call a judge in a case, you're guilty of contempt and this is a violation of canons of legal ethics." Strangely enough *The Nation* agreed. After the election it wrote: "Robert Kennedy's direct communication with the judge was improper, but the uproar which might have been expected failed to develop. . . ."

Ironically, the role the Kennedys played in freeing Dr. King did not at first penetrate Negro communities. So with financial help from several large unions, Wofford prepared and distributed in predominantly Negro areas two million copies of a four-page pamphlet headed: " 'No Comment' Nixon Versus a Candidate with a Heart, Senator Kennedy." The extraordinary thing was that Robert Kennedy received most of the credit for Dr. King's release, even though he practically had to be bludgeoned into getting involved.

And finally the American people voted, 69,000,000 of them in fifty states. It was the largest turnout in American history. At Hyannis Port, a command post had been set up in Bobby's house in the compound. That night, the house swarmed with staffers and Kennedys. All the brothers and sisters—Bobby, Ted, Jean, Eunice and Pat—and their husbands and wives—were there. The first state to report was Connecticut. A Kennedy sweep was in the making.

At about 10:30, when a landslide appeared inevitable, Jacqueline Kennedy whispered to her husband: "Oh, Bunny, you're President now!" But her husband replied, "No . . . no . . . it's too early yet." By midnight, the euphoria in the Kennedy camp began to dissipate as it became evident that the race was still undecided.

Shortly before 4:00 A.M. (1:00 A.M. in L.A.), a tired Dick Nixon appeared on TV. His statement fell short of an outright concession, although he conceded if "present trends" continued, his opponent would be elected. Jack Kennedy decided to go to bed, but Bobby stayed up all night, keeping in touch with crucial areas across the country.

Actually, Bobby was surprised and disappointed by the closeness of the election. The official tabulation showed that Kennedy had defeated Nixon by a mere 119,450 votes. Counting write-in and other votes for minority tickets, he did not even receive a majority of the total votes cast. The official tally gave Kennedy 34,227,096 votes and Nixon

34,107,646, with 303 electoral votes for Jack and 219 for Nixon. Senator Byrd of Virginia received 15.

In the end, Kennedy squeaked out a victory from a coalition of Northern big-city bosses, labor and urban minorities, plus—thanks to Lyndon Johnson—a large number of votes from the South. He received some 78 percent of the Catholic vote, 70 percent of the Negro vote and 80 percent of the Jewish vote, which meant lopsided majorities in the big cities, enough to carry the states where they were located.

Hardly had the votes been counted before complaints poured in—particularly from Illinois and Texas—that the election had been "stolen." "Ridiculous," scoffed Bobby Kennedy. "A tempest in a teapot." But all three major Chicago newspapers agreed that the charges had some substance. As the *Tribune* put it, "the election of November 8 was characterized by such gross and palpable fraud as to justify the conclusion that [Richard Nixon] was deprived of victory."

Kennedy had taken Illinois and its 27 electoral votes by less than 10,000 votes and, as usual, most of the alleged vote-stealing occurred in Democrat-controlled Cook County. Many city precincts reported more votes than were actually cast on the basis of ballot requests. Eventually the election board of one precinct was convicted of fraud.

Responsible Texans estimated that from 100,000 to 150,000 ballots were actually cast that were never accounted for. Since Kennedy carried the state by less than 50,000, these ballots might easily have changed the result. In his *Look* article, "How to Steal an Election," Richard Wilson wrote that in one Texas precinct where only 86 persons received ballots, the results showed Kennedy 147; Nixon 24. All over Texas, similar irregularities occurred. And similar charges were made in Pennsylvania, Missouri and New Jersey.

From all over the country, Nixon was being besieged with demands that he contest the election. But looking into the legal aspects of the situation, he discovered that it would take at least a year and a half to get a recount in Cook County, and that there was no procedure whatever for getting a recount in Texas. Nevertheless, many of his closest friends and associates continued to urge him to seek a recount. In the end, Nixon finally decided against it because of the chaos it would have created in government.

A week after the election, Kennedy called on Nixon, who

was vacationing in Key Biscayne, Florida. The President-elect appeared anxious to make a conciliatory gesture in the interests of national unity.

Kennedy, cordial and candid, told Nixon that he did not believe in some of the more radical promises made in the Democratic platform, and that as President he did not intend to carry them out. As far as "socialism" was concerned, he said he did not propose to destroy the American free-enterprise system under which his father had been able to accumulate a fortune estimated at $400,000,000.

Bobby, meanwhile, flew off with his wife for a much-needed vacation in Acapulco. En route he telephoned the United States Ambassador, Robert Hill, in Mexico City. The Ambassador was in the midst of an important conference and Bobby was forced to wait. After ten minutes, Bobby hung up in disgust.

Bobby did not contact the Embassy again and let it be known he didn't think too highly of an Ambassador who had the temerity to keep him waiting. Hill, an efficient and well-informed diplomat about to retire, was miffed that the brother of the President-elect had not tried to get in touch with him again. He dispatched a starchy note to Bobby offering him a briefing on the Cuban situation.

Things got even more fouled up when the Kennedy party stayed at the Acapulco home of a close associate of former President Miguel Alemán. The current Mexican President was Adolfo López Mateos, who had not been speaking to Alemán for some time, and he let it be known that he was deeply hurt over Bobby's failure to pay his respects.

Bobby told newsmen, "I would love to meet President Mateos [sic] and would love to have a briefing from American Ambassador Hill. They are both fine gentlemen. However, I feel it would be presumptuous for me to act otherwise than as a visitor to Mexico with no official capacity."

By the time Bobby returned to Washington, he was preparing for the Senate hearing on confirmation of his appointment as Attorney General. It was a controversial appointment, to say the least, and Bobby knew he would be in for a lot of criticism. The President-elect had asked any number of consequential people what they thought of the appointment. One of those was Speaker Sam Rayburn, and in so many words, Rayburn had told Kennedy that it was "a bad appointment."

Bobby himself had checked people for their opinions. He visited the retiring Attorney General, William P. Rogers; then dropped in to see J. Edgar Hoover. The FBI Director was cordial and thought the new Administration could do a great deal about the war on crime. Later, Bobby lunched with Supreme Court Justice William O. Douglas, who did not take to the idea at all. But finally, after considerable doubts, Bobby accepted the post.

The President-elect announced his appointment and before long the flak began to fly.

The New York Times was particularly bitter: "It is simply not good enough to name a bright young political manager, no matter how bright or how young or how personally loyal, to a major post in Government that by rights (if not by precedent) ought to be kept completely out of the political arena. . . ."

The *Chicago Tribune,* on the other side of the political fence, wrote: "The obvious thought of nepotism is not what is disturbing about the elevation of Bobby, for the Kennedy family is rich and its members don't need federal jobs to keep off the bread line. But Bobby is marked in particular degree with that streak of ambition and ruthlessness which is a characteristic of the clan. His political infighting to grab the nomination for his brother showed that few holds are barred. He could use his powers vindictively."

The New York *Post* happily endorsed the appointment (on the grounds that Bobby might put J. Edgar Hoover in his place) and the late conservative columnist George Sokolsky, an old friend of the senior Kennedy, thought the appointment a splendid idea. According to Sokolsky: "Robert built his own career without particular aid from brother John. His career is that of a tough, ruthless prosecutor. And that is precisely what is needed in the Attorney General's office which has not been too effective in recent years. . . ."

In short, the appointment did not exactly inspire dancing in the streets of Washington.

One of the charges against the future Attorney General was that he had never so much as tried a case in court. Addressing the Alfalfa Club in jest, the President-elect said, "I can't see that it's wrong to give him a little legal experi-

ence before he goes out to practice law." Later Bobby told
him he didn't think the remark was very funny. Jack replied that people liked it when he kidded himself. "Yes,"
Bobby observed, "but you weren't kidding yourself. You
were kidding *me*."

The hearing before the Senate Committee on the Judiciary
into Bobby's qualifications had been billed in the public
mind as the Great Spectacle. And an hour before Bobby was
to appear, spectators began to line up outside the hearing
room. Some Republicans had promised fireworks. But, as
it turned out, there weren't any.

Bobby, looking suitably tense and pale, displayed a variety
of moods. He gave his answers with care. One moment he
would be intense and his face would darken with anger as
he talked about the labor racketeers; the next, when some
Senator would crack a joke, his face would be all smiles.
The only note of protest was sounded—though very mildly
—by Senator Everett Dirksen. Reluctantly the Illinois Republican read into the record numerous clippings criticizing
Bobby's youth (he was then thirty-five) and his lack of
experience in private practice.

What was extraordinary was that Bobby had hardly to
utter a single word in his own defense. It was all done for
him by the Democratic senators who, one after the other,
issued a series of ringing testimonials. Connecticut's Thomas
J. Dodd said that as a private lawyer he had dealt with
Bobby, then chief counsel of the McClellan Committee, and
had found him "an extremely competent lawyer, and a man
of fair mind and one who treated a lawyer as I believe a
lawyer should be treated. . . ."

It was all very friendly. After the public hearing the
Senators trooped into a private anteroom led by the solidly
pro-Kennedy Jim Eastland of Mississippi. Five minutes later,
Eastland emerged from the executive session and announced
to the press that the committee had voted unanimously to
approve the nomination.

The nation's new chief law enforcer immediately assigned
a trusted group headed by Walter Sheridan to "get Hoffa."
And the following story circulated in Washington, thanks
to Maxine Cheshire of the Washington *Post*.

Ethel Kennedy, while riding with her children near the

national Capitol, was stopped by a red light. She pointed to a building on the hill. "What's up there?"

"The Teamsters Union," responded four or more little Kennedy voices.

"And what do they do there?"

"Work overtime to keep Jimmy Hoffa out of jail."

"And?" Ethel prompted.

"Which is where he belongs!" was the delighted response.

The Kennedys had finally taken over Washington.

17

Attorney General–I

Shortly before taking the oath as Attorney General, Bobby Kennedy told an AP reporter that he intended to divorce himself from active politics while serving as the nation's chief law official. "I am in the midst now of detaching myself from the political arena," he said. But he indicated it was not a simple task. "You can't be the campaign manager of Senator Kennedy today, and be out of politics tomorrow. It takes a bit of time."

The truth was that Bobby was JFK's weather vane for politics and his sounding board for decisions. The Attorney General kept in close touch with political situations all over the country. When aides would bring political questions to the President, he invariably said, "Why don't you check it with Bobby?"

Hardly had the New Frontier been established on the banks of the Potomac when the word went out that Bobby was the man to see. He even took over the dispensing of enormous political patronage in the Post Office Department while he was Attorney General.

According to J. Edward Day, who was Postmaster General during the first two years of the Kennedy Administration, Bobby "passed on applicants for the top appointive positions in the Department. . . . He took an occasional interest in appointments to intermediate jobs in the Department and in those who were going to sell or lease property to the Post Office. . . .

"When we had a major internal crisis in the Department in 1962, it was Bobby who came over from the Justice

Department personally to straighten the problem out. . . .
When too many members of the White House staff were giving orders to various people in the Post Office Department,
it was decided that the liaison between the two offices should
consist of one man. Bob Kennedy named that man. . . ."

Also there were numerous Federal judgeships to be appointed. During the Eisenhower years, Congressional Democrats had refused to expand the overworked Federal bench
—gambling on a Democratic victory in 1960 to assure
those prize plums for loyal Democrats. True, a campaigning
JFK had solemnly assured the American people that the
judgeships would go only to the best-qualified, regardless
of their political affiliations. But, somehow, under Bobby, the
best-qualified invariably turned out to be Democrats.

At Bobby's suggestion, President Kennedy's very first appointment as a Federal judge was Mississippi's William Harold
Cox, a pal of Jim Eastland's and an outspoken segregationist. Shortly after he ascended the bench, Judge Cox refused to accept an appeal from five Freedom Riders who
had been convicted in the state courts for breach of peace.
Referring to the civil rights workers as "a bunch of chim-
panzees" the Kennedy-appointed judge added, "Their status
as interstate passengers is extremely doubtful. Their destination was Jackson, but their objective was trouble."

Others whom Bobby suggested included such men as
Louisiana's Judge E. Gordon West who, while upholding
the Supreme Court's 1954 school ruling, dubbed it "one of
the truly regrettable decisions of all time," and Georgia's
Judge J. Robert Elliott, who once said, "I don't want those
pinks, radicals and black voters to outvote those who are
trying to preserve our segregation laws and traditions."
Arthur Schlesinger's rationale was that the appointments were
"an effort to placate" the chairman of the Senate Judiciary
Committee, Jim Eastland, in order to make possible the
appointment of the NAACP's Thurgood Marshall to a Federal judgeship.

Almost from the advent of the new Administration Bobby
had taken over the Democratic National Committee, firing
those he described as "dead wood," and installing his hench-
men. One of those he named to a key post at the committee was his old hatchet man from primary days, Paul
Corbin, who became a special assistant to Democratic Na-

tional Chairman John M. Bailey. The title could have meant almost anything; what it meant, in practice, was that Corbin was deeply involved in patronage. And, as far as he was concerned, only committed Kennedyites would get the jobs as long as he was around.

Paul Corbin had an incredible background. On August 24, 1961, the Milwaukee *Journal* began a series of articles based on considerable digging into Corbin's background. According to the *Journal:* "Paul Corbin's political power—apparently derived from Attorney General Robert F. Kennedy—in the Democratic National Committee has caused growing wonder, especially in Wisconsin, in view of his political history, which includes working hard with Wisconsin Communists some fifteen years ago." And Corbin had also been a buddy of the late Senator Joseph McCarthy, according to the *Journal*.

Following publication of these articles, the House Un-American Activities Committee conducted hearings in executive session. Thirteen witnesses were questioned, including Corbin, who appeared July 2, 1962. He said he was born in 1914 on a farm near Winnipeg, and that he first came to the United States in 1934 when he married his first cousin in Brooklyn. He admitted having entered the U.S. illegally in 1935, using his brother's name and birth certificate while telling immigration authorities that he was U.S.-born.

"Is it true," he was asked, "that you endeavored to conceal your true identity when you entered this country because of your Communist affiliations?"

"I was never a member of the Young Communist League of Canada," he replied. "I was never a member of the Communist party of the United States."

But several witnesses testified otherwise. John Dominick Giacomo of Milwaukee, a field representative for the United Steelworkers of America, testified that during 1946 or 1947 Corbin asked him several times, "Why don't you join the Communist party?"

"Corbin is a mouthy sort of individual," Giacomo told the Committee. "He is an egotist. He is domineering, he is forceful, he is a pathological liar. He is just about everything that a fine, upstanding citizen would not want to be . . . he holds nothing sacred."

An admitted ex-Communist and president of the Black

Hawk Publishing Company, who had been in partnership with Corbin at one time in Rockford, Illinois, testified that Corbin had told him he had been a member of the Young Communist League in Canada. He said Corbin "was always associating with people" who were known to be members of the Communist party.

Corbin told the committee, "That man is a liar."

Asked if he was issued a Communist party registration card bearing the number 62908, Corbin replied, "How do I know? I wasn't a Communist."

Corbin claimed to have joined the Marines in 1943, fought at Saipan and Okinawa, and received an honorable discharge in 1945. He became a naturalized United States citizen while on military duty, and returned to Wisconsin after the war, where he became a friend of Senator Joe McCarthy. In fact, Corbin was photographed embracing the famed Communist-hunter at the American Legion State Convention at Green Bay in 1950. At this time, Corbin was making speeches about the "Truman war" in Korea, calling on the Administration to "untie the hands of General MacArthur," and demanding that the atom bomb be dropped on Red China across the Yalu River.

"I was a Marine," Corbin testified. "I knew what the score was, and I knew the Reds were our enemies."

Though the House Committee made no formal findings, it did refer the entire record of the Corbin case to the Justice Department for possible perjury action, in view of conflicting testimony. Later, a Justice Department spokesman said no grounds for action were found. And, on Bobby's instructions, Paul Corbin remained on the payroll of the Democratic National Committee.

On February 1, 1961, the Attorney General named a thirty-six-year-old New York lawyer, Edwyn Silberling, to head the Justice Department's new Section on Organized Crime and Racketeering. A graduate of Harvard Law School and a World War II Air Force veteran, Silberling boasted a formidable legal background, having served five years as an assistant district attorney in New York under Frank S. Hogan. He also gained fame as the prosecutor in the notorious Mickey Jelke call-girl case which rocked New York City and the nation in the early fifties. It was Silberling's work on a

Citizens Committee for Kennedy in 1960 that drew the Kennedy clan's attention to the aspiring young lawyer.

To join Bobby's "pet project," Silberling gave up a salary of $25,000 with Hogan for one of $16,000 at the Justice Department. Silberling eventually formed a staff of fifty lawyers to work in the field with the ninety-one United States district attorneys (and FBI men) throughout the nation.

According to Silberling, the "Get Hoffa" drive remained in the hands of Bobby Kennedy, though the unit within the Criminal Division of the Department was nominally headed by Walter Sheridan. "That was rather odd, you know—Sheridan wasn't a lawyer—he didn't have any legal training but he was handpicked by Bobby."

Asked why Bobby hated Hoffa with such passion, Silberling suggested it was largely the way the Teamsters chief had made him look foolish during the interminable McClellan hearings. "Bobby wasn't too much on the law—had not practiced it very often—and actually didn't care much for a legal career. During his work as counsel for the McClellan Committee, Hoffa made Kennedy look pretty bad. Bobby never forgave him for this."

Silberling, who served two years with the Department before resigning, said that day by day Bobby was spending less and less time in the Attorney General's office. "Bobby just wasn't cut out to be a lawyer," said Silberling. "He is a fine politician and after a time he wasn't bothering too much with the leadership of the Justice Department."

Actually, Bobby had brought in some fine people to run the Department. As his number-one aide, Bobby named Byron "Whizzer" White, later President Kennedy's first appointee to the Supreme Court. Former law professor Nicholas D. Katzenbach, who had been Assistant Attorney General, then moved into "Whizzer" White's post as Deputy. Burke Marshall, once a member of Dean Acheson's law firm, was Assistant Attorney General in charge of the Civil Rights Division. Another law professor, Archibald Cox, was Solicitor General. John Woolman Douglas (Senator Paul Douglas' son) headed the Civil Division, while Ramsey Clark (Justice Tom Clark's son) ran the Lands Division.

In the March 28, 1961, issue of *Look* there was an interview with Bobby in which he responded to a query concerning his position on legislation to permit wiretapping: "We are studying this question carefully. No conclusions have been reached. If such legislation were passed, my feeling is that the use of legal wiretaps should be limited to major crimes such as treason, kidnaping and murder. In each instance, however, it should only be done with the authority of a Federal judge. We would still have to request permission for a wiretap, exactly as we must now do to get a search warrant. . . . I would not be in favor of its use under any circumstances— even with the court's permission—except in certain capital offenses."

Actually Bobby's "studying" of the problem was anything but an academic exercise. He had already quietly authorized J. Edgar Hoover to approve installation of listening devices not only in internal security cases but also to obtain intelligence about crime. Other agencies, too, were deploying electronic equipment and were encouraged to expand surveillance of criminal suspects by Bobby's zest for combat against mobsters from coast to coast.

On February 24, 1961, Internal Revenue Commissioner Mortimer M. Caplin dictated these confidential instructions to regional commissioners: "As part of the Government's drive against organized crime, the Attorney General has requested the Service to give top priority to the investigation of the tax affairs of major racketeers.

"In conducting such investigations, full use will be made of available electronic equipment and other technical aids, as well as such investigative techniques as surveillance, undercover work, etc."

While Caplin did not specify what "electronic equipment" he was referring to, it surely was reasonable for IRS agents to assume that he meant listening devices. And nowhere in the directive was there the usual warning against wiretapping.

In recent years, Bobby has flatly denied any knowledge of all this. He swears to God Almighty—with appropriate hedges—that he never authorized any illegal eavesdropping. But Ed Silberling takes issue with him. Now a lawyer in Mineola, on Long Island, he says that J. Edgar Hoover sent the Attorney General numerous intelligence reports, sometimes as many as three or four a week, and that the information contained in them was obviously gleaned from bugs. "When you see direct quotes or language in the vernacular," he said, "you'd have to be pretty thick not to conclude that some came from overheard conversations."

Not only did Bobby approve wiretapping and other eavesdropping devices, but he set up a special confidential three-man squad to handle such activities. All three had been in the employ of the McClellan Committee. One was put on the Justice Department payroll, a second on the White House payroll, and a third on the payroll of the Immigration and Naturalization Service.

Bobby's crusade did succeed in scaring some underworld lords out of the rackets. And the Justice Department did set new records in mobster convictions, though more minnows were netted than big fish. But, as Silberling recently noted, "many convictions of top hoodlums obtained under Kennedy are now being reversed by higher Federal courts on one technicality or another."

And Bobby sent a bill up to Congress to legalize wiretapping. Federal agencies would have been allowed to employ wiretapping in cases involving murder, kidnaping, extortion, bribery, traffic in narcotics, and organized crimes such as gambling, in addition to matters of national security. Under the Kennedy bill, all the local police would have needed to tap phones in the same kind of cases, with the exception of those involving organized crime, was to obtain court permission.

The entire liberal community rose up in arms. At a hearing of the Senate Judiciary Committee, ADA's Joe Rauh said that passage of the bill "would constitute a knockout blow to the right of privacy of American citizens." And Lawrence Speiser, representing the American Civil Liberties Union, told the Senators that the bill was an unnecessary law-enforcement tool inimical to the spirit of a free society: "A fundamental principle is at stake. A hallmark of totalitarian societies is that the people are apprehensive of being overheard or spied upon."

The upshot was that the Kennedy bill never reached the floor.

The ACLU, among other critics, also censured Bobby for supporting legislation sponsored by the House Un-American Activities Committee, aimed at depriving five million workers in defense plants of the right to confront accusers in loyalty proceedings. The bill was defeated in the House under the leadership of then Congressman John V. Lindsay of New York.

As Attorney General, Bobby was also chairman of the President's Committee on Juvenile Delinquency. Information Officer of the Committee was a twenty-five-year-old newspaper reporter, Pat Anderson. Here are Anderson's impressions of the then Attorney General: ". . . a strange, complex man, easier to respect than to like, easier to like than to understand; in all a man to be taken seriously. His love for humanity, however real, seemed greater in the abstract than in individual cases. He was no intellectual, but he was more receptive to other men's ideas than most intellectuals. But even as you made excuses for his weaknesses, there was the fear that you were doing more than he would do for you."

This was the man who rushed to his brother's side the terrible night of the Bay of Pigs disaster. "I've got to be with him," Bob told Ethel at a state dinner at the Greek Embassy. "I know he needs me." At the White House, Bobby waited to be alone with the anguished President. "They can't do this to you," he told his brother. "These black-bearded Communists can't do this to you."

The Communists and their allies throughout the world set up a worldwide clamor, once again picturing the United States as the number-one imperialist power. And President Kennedy responded by taking an aggressive tack. Addressing the American Society of Newspaper Editors, he said that "we do not intend to abandon" Cuba to the Communists. Rather, he proposed outright unilateral intervention, should "the nations of this hemisphere fail to meet their commitments against outside Communist penetration. . . . Should that time ever come, we do not intend to be lectured on 'intervention' by those whose character was stamped for all time on the bloody streets of Budapest."

Thus was enunciated the Kennedy doctrine for the Western Hemisphere. But four years later, when President Johnson evoked the doctrine and dispatched a military expedition to the leftist-threatened Dominican Republic, one of his leading critics was none other than the new Senator from New York, Robert F. Kennedy.

Following the Bay of Pigs, it was not easy for President Kennedy to snap out of his despondency. "This is the first time that Jack Kennedy ever lost anything," an aide told a reporter. But Old Joe was on the phone almost daily trying to rally his son's spirits. At one point, the Ambassador said, "Oh, hell, if that's the way you feel, give the job to Lyndon!" He told Jack that the fiasco, traceable to gross errors of judgment, was the best thing that could have happened this early. It would give Jack the opportunity to make necessary changes in his Administration.

Kennedy moved in quickly to avert a bruising debate on his abilities as the leader of the free world. He conferred with Richard Nixon, Barry Goldwater, Nelson Rockefeller, Herbert Hoover and Dwight D. Eisenhower. In effect, he obtained from each a promise not to make a painfully partisan issue of the fiasco.

At the same time, Kennedy assigned brother Bobby to head a group to investigate the role of the CIA in the disaster. Other members were General Maxwell Taylor, CIA Director Allen Dulles and Admiral Arleigh Burke.

It was Bobby who urged his brother to replace Allen Dulles with John A. McCone. McCone, a Republican, was an interesting choice. In Arthur Schlesinger's words, he "had the reputation of a rigid cold-warrior who viewed the world in moralistic stereotypes." As a regent of the University of California, he had bitterly criticized those professors who had supported Adlai Stevenson's position on a nuclear test ban during the 1956 campaign.

The investigation had also convinced Bobby of the need for the United States to develop effective techniques to combat Communist "wars of liberation." He became the leading nonmilitary proponent of the policy known as counter-insurgency. This, according to columnist Frank Getlein, "means letting them have it whenever and wherever they raise their Commie heads."

The problem of guerrilla warfare fascinated the President, too. He read the classic texts by Mao Tse-tung and Ernesto (Ché) Guevara and suggested that top United States military men read them. And he insisted on training an increasing number of Army Special Forces to combat the Communist guerrillas in the field. "The President directed—over the opposition of top generals—that the Special Forces wear green berets as a mark of distinction," wrote Ted Sorensen. "He wanted them to be a dedicated, high-quality elite corps of specialists, trained to train local partisans in guerrilla warfare, prepared to perform a wide range of civilian as well as military tasks, able to live off the bush, in a village or behind enemy lines. He personally supervised the selection of new equipment. . . ."

To Bobby, South Vietnam seemed a most promising place for proving America's ability to withstand Communist tactics. The Attorney General agreed wholeheartedly with his brother's decision to send in the Green Berets. And while touring the Far East with Ethel in early 1962, he painted a relatively rosy picture of the world at a Hong Kong press conference. He said that the Communists had more problems than the West and "there is great promise for us." Asked about the war in South Vietnam, he replied, "The solution there lies in our winning it. This is what the President intends to do."

A week later, on a brief stopover in Saigon, Bobby said, "This is a new kind of war, but war it is in a very real sense of the word. It is a war fought not by massive divisions but secretly by terror, assassination, ambush and infiltration.

"Hanoi may deny its responsibility but the guilt is clear. In a flagrant violation of its signed pledge at Geneva in 1954, the North Vietnamese regime has launched on a course to destroy the Republic of Vietnam. . . .

"We are going to win in South Vietnam. The United States will remain here until we win."

The escalation of the war in Vietnam had already begun. President Kennedy had stated clearly and firmly, "The United States is determined that the Republic of Vietnam shall not be lost to the Communists for lack of any support which the United States can render."

JFK had taken this position despite the impassioned entreaties of John Kenneth Galbraith not to send American combat troops to South Vietnam. "A few," the professor advised Kennedy in 1962, "will mean more and more and more." And, for once, his forecast proved flawless. From less than 800 U.S. troops, the number under Kennedy increased to 25,000. Today, under LBJ, it is over 500,000.

A British correspondent in Saigon asked Bobby, "American boys are dying out here. Do the American people understand and approve of what is going on?"

"I think the American people understand and fully support this struggle," Bobby replied. "Americans have great affection for the people of Vietnam. I think the United States will do what is necessary to help a country that is trying to repel aggression with its own blood, tears and sweat."

But when he left the Justice Department in 1964, Bobby was not overly happy about three years of counter-insurgency. "We have made a beginning," he said. "We have achieved some notable successes, but we have not mastered the art of counter-insurgency. More importantly, perhaps, in a practical sense, we have not perfected the technique of training foreign nationals to defend themselves against Communist terrorism and guerrilla penetration. This kind of warfare can be long-drawn-out and costly, but if Communism is to be stopped, it is necessary. And we mean to see this job through to the finish."

Within a year, a "new" Bobby was expressing doubts that the United States should see the job "through to the finish." He began to take public issue with the Johnson Administration's conduct of the war.

In August 1961, columnist Mary McGrory asked the Attorney General to sum up the first six months of the Kennedy Administration.

"I am not pessimistic," Bobby said, "but when you look around the world the problems are almost overwhelming. We are on the defensive. But I think we're moving ahead, inch by inch. I guess in a situation like this if you're holding your own, you're making progress."

All Bobby would say about the Cuban disaster was: "Obviously, it would have been better if it hadn't happened but it would have been disastrous if he [the President] had not learned the lesson of Cuba."

Another plus resulting from the setback was the naming of Maxwell Taylor as White House military adviser. Bobby, after working with the retired General for two months during the CIA inquiry, grew quite fond of him and recommended him to the President as "a tough, incisive, well-organized, articulate, taciturn, self-confident expert."

In January 1963, when the Bay of Pigs was little more than a horrible memory, Bobby Kennedy flatly denied the generally held assumption that at the last minute JFK had reneged on a solemn pledge to provide air cover for the 1,500 Cuban invaders as they landed from the sea.

"There never was any plan to have U.S. air cover," he told

David Kraslow, Washington reporter for the Knight newspapers. "There never was any promise. . . ."

The item prompted a swift Republican counterattack. According to then Senator Barry Goldwater, Bobby's remarks were an excellent example of "news management." Then the Arizonan asked the Senate, "Has this practice of the Administration now been extended to the rewriting of history? . . . I myself talked with President Kennedy . . . and I certainly got the impression that an air cover had been part of the original invasion plans."

Then a Florida newspaper editor said that President Kennedy had disclosed a month after the ill-fated Cuban expedition that he had ordered air cover canceled. Jack W. Gore, of the Fort Lauderdale *News,* said JFK had told him and other Florida newspaper executives at an off-the-record briefing that UN Ambassador Adlai Stevenson was concerned that "any such action would make a liar out of him in the United Nations."

All had kept the story out of print.

"What Attorney General Robert Kennedy hoped to accomplish by coming out at this late date and denying that any air cover had ever been planned, the *News* cannot fathom," Gore wrote. "When the brother of the President, however, conducts an official autopsy of the sorry affair and makes official comments which are in direct contrast to the words of the President, the *News* feels that any off-the-record pledge which might apply must be removed in the quest for truth."

Top Pentagon officers privately bridled at Bobby's remarks. They took particular umbrage at the Attorney General's contention that "the plan [for the invasion] that was used was fully cleared by the CIA and the Joint Chiefs of Staff. It was war-gamed at the Pentagon in whatever manner they do these things."

But, as a high-ranking officer told *Newsweek,* "If Bobby Kennedy says it was war-gamed, he does not understand the term. If it had been war-gamed, it might never have happened. . . ."

For their part, most of the Cuban veterans of the Bay of Pigs remained convinced that the United States had suddenly withdrawn the air cover. Many of them, ransomed out of Cuban dungeons, angrily accused President Kennedy of having betrayed them.

One extraordinary thing about the Bay of Pigs was the President's handling of the press. As early as October 1960, according to Pierre Salinger, JFK read press accounts of how the United States was training a brigade for action against the Castro regime, and was livid. "I can't believe what I'm reading!" JFK told Salinger. "Castro doesn't need agents over here. All he has to do is read our papers. It's all laid out for him."

Following the Bay of Pigs, the Kennedy Administration's credibility gap increased. And the Administration, Bobby in particular, was not averse to using strong-arm methods to curb criticism.

In the April 1963 issue of *The Atlantic*, Hanson W. Baldwin, military analyst of *The New York Times*, contended that "the blatant methods used by the Administration and its tampering with the news deserve considerably more criticism and discussion than they have received."

Under Robert Kennedy, the freewheeling use of Federal agents to investigate leaks grew to menacing proportions. Some of the most respected Washington correspondents experienced "the treatment," which included visits by Federal agents to their homes, tapping of telephones, shadowing of reporters, investigations of their friendships, and other forms of intimidation.

The President's ambivalence toward freedom of the press was nowhere better demonstrated than in the grim, dark days following the Bay of Pigs. Before the American Newspaper Publishers Association on April 27, 1961, JFK admonished, "Every newspaper now asks itself, with respect to every story: 'Is it news?' All I suggest is that you add the question: 'Is it in the national interest?' . . . And should the press of America consider and recommend the voluntary assumption of specific steps or machinery, I can assure you that we will cooperate wholeheartedly with those recommendations."

The paradoxical nature of JFK's reaction to the press was further illustrated when the President told Turner Catledge, executive editor of *The New York Times*, "If you had printed more about the [Bay of Pigs] operation you would have saved us from a colossal mistake." Kennedy also told the late Orvil E. Dryfoos, then publisher of the *Times*, "I wish you had run everything on Cuba. . . . I am just sorry you didn't tell it at the time."

The irony is that as a candidate seeking the Presidency, JFK had promised to end unlimited secrecy in government and to tell the truth to the American people. By any standards of measurement, however, things got worse, not better, under the New Frontier.

One book that particularly aroused Bobby's ire was this writer's *JFK: The Man and the Myth,* a critical account of the life and works of President Kennedy. After the book zoomed to the number-one position on the nation's best-seller lists came a revelation that the Justice Department had undertaken an investigation of the author. At first, under prodding from then Senator Kenneth Keating of New York, Attorney General Kennedy flatly denied that he had ever authorized such an investigation. Later—after evidence was produced— Bobby finally conceded that an "overzealous" official had launched the probe without his approval. It was also learned that the FBI had been asked to conduct the investigation but that J. Edgar Hoover had refused to involve the bureau in what was strictly a "political vendetta." As it turned out, the "overzealous" official was one of Bobby's Senate committee investigators with a penchant for wiretapping, who was now on the payroll of the Immigration and Naturalization Department. Which led the author to ask where Bobby intended to deport him—to Staten Island, perhaps?

One of the chores assigned this snooper was to determine whether the author could be tied in with subversive activities. He scoured various government dossiers for information but blundered by signing an official request for such information from the Senate Internal Security Subcommittee. One of its members immediately informed the author that one of Bobby's boys was poking around the files.

The upshot was that several Western Democratic State Chairmen charged the author with being an ex-Communist (which was untrue), and Democratic National Chairman John Bailey, in effect, described the author as a "Birchite" (also a falsehood). The New Frontier obviously had graduated from the "burning" of books to the "burning" of authors.

On one occasion, John F. Kennedy got so angry with dispatches critical of the United States position in Vietnam filed to *The New York Times* by David Halberstam that the President sought to get him fired.*

A whole book could be written on the extraordinary lengths to which the Kennedys went to whip the press into line. Representative Bob Wilson, a California Republican, said on the floor of the House, "I know of one instance where a publisher was invited to the White House where he was wined and dined . . . and then was asked to go down the street to the Department of Justice, where he had a conference with the President's brother. The conference had to do with a possible antitrust violation. So, the orders soon went out—and we have this on good authority—that the critical columnists and newspapermen on this particular paper were to let up on their criticism of the New Frontier."

According to Wilson, other reporters and columnists who were critical of the Administration were offered "very cozy and very attractive jobs. One columnist told me that he was offered a very exciting job in the State Department. He turned it down. Shortly thereafter his income-tax returns were being checked."

Another who began having tax troubles was Jim Bishop. "They started about the time that Robert Kennedy became the Attorney General. I wrote a story and said he acted as though the rest of us were working on his old man's plantation. After that, audits. There is, of course, no connection between the two except the hysterical, or rather, historical." But probably the most incredible of all were audits of the tax returns of Richard M. Nixon and his campaign manager, Robert H. Finch, shortly after they returned to California following the 1960 defeat. Their returns were in order.

"We do not necessarily see each other very often," the President said in 1962, "but I know that when Bobby wants to talk to me, it is about something important. He has his department running well with a good deputy in Byron 'Whizzer' White." Actually, Bobby kept in constant touch with the President by phone.

Bobby's freewheeling in government was demonstrated fol-

---

* Halberstam tells this astounding story in his *The Making of a Quagmire*, a book to which Arthur Schlesinger, Jr., refers in his Pulitzer prize-winning *A Thousand Days*. But, typical of Schlesinger's covering up for the Kennedys, the former Harvard historian makes no reference to JFK's effort to get Halberstam dismissed.

lowing the assassination in the Dominican Republic of dictator Rafael Leonidas Trujillo. Anarchy threatened in the tiny Caribbean nation. With President Kennedy off in Europe for his meeting with Nikita Khrushchev, Bobby moved into a command post in the State Department. The great fear was that the Communists would seize the Dominican Government. To prevent such a tragedy, Bobby ordered a United States fleet of warships, loaded with battle-ready Marines, to sail close to Santo Domingo in a show of force.

When the Communists began raising the Berlin Wall in the summer of 1961, President Kennedy cut short a cruise and raced back to shore. "Get Rusk on the phone," he ordered. "Go get my brother."

At the time, Arthur Schlesinger, Jr., described Bobby's extraordinary role as follows: "Bobby has been a kind of troubleshooter for the President in many fields. No Attorney General in history, for instance, has sat in on as many State Department meetings. He's certainly closer to the President than anyone else, and the President has great reliance on his judgment—he feels more secure about any situation if Bobby is involved in it. This doesn't mean that the President agrees with him all the time. . . . Not only the President depends on him, but often, when some of us here in the White House see things that ought to be done, we call on Bobby."

However, Bobby's unorthodox behavior during the flap over steel prices in the spring of 1962 aroused considerable concern. FBI agents had been dispatched in the middle of the night to interview newspaper reporters on some aspects of the steel story. Columnist Max Lerner found the episode "distasteful" and smacking of a "police operation." The Richmond *Times-Dispatch* described it as an "indefensible abuse of personal power by a hired public servant."

After Bobby instituted antitrust proceedings against the steel companies, Big Steel capitulated and rescinded the price hikes.

The dual role played by the White House and the Justice Department during the seventy-two hours of the steel "crisis" served to demonstrate that there really were two Kennedys to deal with. What is particularly significant about Bobby's emergence as the number-two man—or as one wit put it, the number-one-and-a-half man—was that Joseph P. Kennedy planned it that way. "There was never a tougher one than

Joe Kennedy, nor a more unscrupulous opponent," commented the late Robert Ruark. "Young Bobby, even more than Jack, shows more outer smudges of the parental stamp, but there is a lot of he-coon in the hide of the new President. He strikes me as practically cold all the way, with a hard blue eye on Valhalla."

Now, Old Joe had his heart set on seeing his youngest son, Teddy, a United States Senator. Jack Kennedy, at first, was said to be opposed. He had enough problems by then. Anyway, both Jack and Bobby argued, Teddy's young; he can wait a couple of years.

But Teddy couldn't wait. True, his tender years and total lack of qualifications were bound to evoke considerable resentment. As someone observed, "Ted wants a Senate seat the way other young men want a Jaguar." But logic loses its power to persuade when it runs counter to the ambitions of a Kennedy.

"You boys have what you want now, and everyone else helped you work to get it," Old Joe told Jack and Bobby. "Now it's Ted's turn. Whatever he wants, I'm going to see he gets it."

Soon after reaching his thirtieth birthday, the minimum age requirement for a United States Senator, Edward Moore Kennedy announced his candidacy. There was no problem about the incumbent, Benjamin A. Smith II, who had been keeping the seat warm for Teddy. True, Smith had acquired a liking for the job, but there was little he could do. He had agreed to vacate as soon as Teddy was old enough to run.

Teddy, who had graduated from law school only three years before, had taken an interim job as assistant district attorney in Suffolk County, Massachusetts. His candidacy stunned State Attorney General Edward J. McCormack, Jr., who had been elected by an impressive 400,000 majority in 1960. The favorite nephew of Speaker John W. McCormack, he was a seasoned political veteran at thirty-nine and had built a solid record in a state perennially rocked with scandals. He also had the support of most of the state's intellectual community. Professor Mark DeWolfe Howe of Harvard Law School (a former adviser to John F. Kennedy) described Ted Kennedy's candidacy as "both preposterous and insulting."

Under brother-in-law Steve Smith's direction, Teddy's managers made it clear to each of the 1,719 delegates they had better hop on the bandwagon before they got run over. The word was also passed along that, win or lose, Teddy would be in charge of the state's patronage from the Kennedy Administration.

"It's pressure, pressure, pressure, post office, post office, post office," complained McCormack's father, "Knocko." But the lure of a postmastership was only one of the pressures. It was alleged that one McCormack delegate was being investigated for income-tax irregularities; that a member of another delegate's family was facing deportation charges. The effect of all this was summed up by one delegate after conferring with the youngest Kennedy: "Teddy's been an assistant district attorney for a year or so. He's completely unqualified and inexperienced. He's an arrogant member of an arrogant family." Then, smiling, he added, "And I'm going to be with him."

Lacking the Kennedy resources, Ed McCormack concentrated on his opponent's obvious lack of experience. He even needled Ted into two televised debates.

"And I ask," said McCormack concluding the first, "if his name was Edward Moore—with his qualifications, with your qualifications, Teddy—if it was Edward Moore, your candidacy would be a joke, but nobody's laughing because his name is not Edward Moore. It's Edward Moore Kennedy. . . ." Shaken to his very core, Teddy turned his other handsome cheek and said nothing.

Though at first most observers felt that the youngest Kennedy had fared badly, it turned out that this slashing attack had created sympathy for Teddy, particularly among women voters. And when it was all over, Teddy ran away with the primary, some 69 percent of the vote.

A frustrated Ed McCormack announced he was through with politics. "If this is politics, if they can get away with this, then I don't want any part of politics."

The New York Times described Teddy's victory as demeaning to the dignity of the Senate and the democratic process. James Reston put it this way: ". . . the Kennedys have applied the principle of the best man available for the job to almost everyone but themselves. Teddy's victorious headlines are resented [in Washington] because he is demanding too much too soon on the basis of too little. . . . What is particularly surprising about all this is that the Kennedys do not see this line of criticism at all, and in fact deeply resent it. They have invoked the new pragmatism, but cannot see that, where the family was concerned, they applied the old nepotism." But both Bobby and Jack knew from past experiences that such bitter criticisms would soon pass and be forgotten.

The previous December, Old Joe had suffered a stroke in Palm Beach. He was left partially paralyzed and unable to speak. It was Bobby who phoned his brother at the White House to tell him the sad news. The President, who had just spent a few days with his father in Palm Beach, immediately returned aboard the Presidential jet, *Air Force One*, accompanied by Bobby and sister Jean. From all over the nation the Clan gathered.

Within a few weeks, Old Joe began physical therapy aimed at recovering the physical functions he had lost. But the Ambassador, even with that rambunctious spirit, was never to fully recover.

For the Kennedy brothers, this came as a particularly hard blow. Now they would be entirely on their own.

18

Attorney General–II

In November 1961, Jimmy Wechsler of the New York *Post* called on the Attorney General at his offices in the Department of Justice building. Bobby had just turned thirty-six years of age, though he looked younger. He was in shirt-sleeves, his collar carelessly loosened, and his hair drooped over his forehead.

"On the day before I saw Robert Kennedy," Wechsler reported, "Arthur Schlesinger, Jr., told me of his deepening respect and affection for him, and of his hopes for his future. On the day after, by curious accident, I taped a television debate with George Sokolsky and, as we conversed afterward, Sokolsky spoke in similarly warm terms; he had come to know young Kennedy during the McCarthy days, and believes he will one day be a pillar of conservatism.

"It could be said this simply proves Bobby Kennedy is all things to all men. More subtle analysis would suggest that his identity has not yet fully evolved; he is a man very much in transition, groping for many answers. That both Schlesinger and Sokolsky should find him personally appealing is testimonial to his charm, which is great. But beneath the surface there is a struggle for his political soul which may be one of the large dramas of the coming years. . . ."

That Bobby Kennedy had not yet fully achieved an identity at thirty-six must have struck some of Wechsler's readers as incredible. Most men that age have developed their ways of thinking and their philosophies. Most know whether they are liberals or conservatives or somewhere between. But Bobby brought no clear-cut political philosophy to his job as Attorney

General, let alone any distinction in the law. Both friend and foe agreed that he was devoted only to his brother's cause, and that he fitted no particular slot because he measured each issue by its political dividends.

The one big idea he brought into the Justice Department was his proposal for a National Crime Commission. In *The Enemy Within* he described it: "This Commission would serve as a central intelligence agency, a clearing-house to which each of the seventy-odd federal agencies and the more than 10,000 local law-enforcement agencies throughout the country would constantly feed information on the leading gangsters. The Commission would pool and correlate all its information on underworld figures and disseminate it to the proper authorities."

But J. Edgar Hoover was opposed and so went on record: "Nothing could be more dangerous to our democratic ideals than the establishment of an all-powerful police agency on the Federal scene." Moreover, the FBI Director objected to giving such information to local law authorities, some of whom were believed to have strong ties with underworld elements.

Nor, on taking over as Attorney General, was Bobby a civil rights crusader. "He leaves the impression," a Washington *Star* reporter wrote at that time, "that the political hazard of alienating the South by pushing too hard on integration outweighs any other ardor he might otherwise feel for advancing Negro rights."

Bobby did not place civil rights at the top of the list when asked by *Look's* Peter Maas what areas of law enforcement he intended to emphasize. Maas also asked, "What would your position be if you were confronted by another Little Rock?"

"I don't think," Bobby replied, "we would ever come to the point of sending troops to any part of the country on a matter like that. I cannot conceive of this Administration's letting such a situation deteriorate to that level. In my judgment, examining the facts, we could have handled the situation with U.S. marshals, who have a fine record and are equipped to handle the job."

But in 1962 at Oxford, Mississippi, President Kennedy was forced to send in an estimated 15,000 Federal troops and U.S. marshals to end the riots that swept the campus area when a Negro, James H. Meredith, sought admission to the University of Mississippi. Two persons were killed; scores were injured; and hundreds were arrested. At Little Rock no one had been killed or seriously injured.

Bobby's number-one interest was still Hoffa; and Jimmy was beginning to feel the heat. The Justice Department kept issuing a steady stream of press releases telling about new indictments or sinful incidents involving Teamsters officials. And Bobby himself kept feeding favored reporters anti-Hoffa material, a questionable practice at best when the labor boss was under indictment. Bobby, as Senator Mc-Clellan recently observed, "knew the value of publicity. I don't have to tell you that. He liked publicity more than I do, but he was good at using it. . . ." What he did not say was that Bobby, while counsel for the McClellan Committee, had become so outspoken in his press releases that the Senator had requested they be cleared by him before they were passed out.

"Our phones are tapped and our hotel rooms are bugged," Jimmy complained to reporters. "We'd make remarks just to see and the government attorneys would know the next morning what we said. We're building a new $800,000 office building in Detroit and they come to me and say the whole place is wired and bugged. I say, 'Hell, whaddya expect? Go on and finish the building.' They go to school and investigate my kid. He's a good kid, if I do say so. They go around to his friends and say, 'How many suits of clothes has Jim Hoffa got? How much money does he carry around in his pocket?' They gave orders to every airline office in the country—when Hoffa makes a reservation, call the nearest FBI office and give the time he takes off and the time he arrives. You wouldn't believe some of the creepy stuff they are pulling."

Walter Sheridan, head of the "Get Hoffa" detail, denied having anything to do with this. Sheridan said he would never dream of doing anything that crude. But Sheridan had been ordered by Bobby to nail Hoffa. Bobby's pride was at stake.

During the 1960 campaign, Jack Kennedy had stated flatly, "An effective Attorney General, with the present laws on the books, can remove Mr. Hoffa from office." But by the end of 1962, Bobby had proved to be as ineffective as any of his predecessors—despite the extraordinary lengths to which the Justice Department went. And the suspicion was growing that either Bobby had no case or that he was too inept to prove it in court.

Commented columnist Richard Starnes, "For all I know, Hoffa may be guilty of wholesale mopery. But is the Attorney General entitled to dedicate the immense power of the federal government to chucking him in jail? I've followed Hoffa's career with some passing interest, and all I can swear to of my own knowledge is that he makes lousy speeches. He may set fire to orphan asylums for kicks, but does this deprive him of the right to due process?"

Eventually, Jimmy Hoffa got his comeuppance. On March 4, 1964, he was found guilty in Chattanooga on charges of having tried to bribe three jurors during a 1962 trial in Nashville. But none of the hundreds of men Bobby had assigned to "get" Hoffa had turned the trick. Instead, Hoffa had been convicted largely on the testimony of an informer, Edward Grady Partin, released from a Louisiana jail in 1962, to become a trusted member of Hoffa's Nashville entourage. He became bartender, errand boy, bag carrier, general factotum; and all the time he was telling Bobby's boys what Hoffa was saying.

Hoffa's conviction was upheld in December 1966 by the Supreme Court by a four-to-three decision. Chief Justice Earl Warren, for the minority, contended that Partin's testimony should have been rejected as an "affront to the quality and fairness of Federal law enforcement." The majority ruled that "the use of secret informers is not per se unconstitutional."

Bobby's "Get Hoffa" squad were so jubilant they threw a private cocktail party at a Georgetown restaurant. They gave the boss a fitting gift for the occasion—a leather wallet embossed with the words used by the jury foreman pronouncing Jimmy Hoffa guilty. "You don't know how long I've been waiting for this," said Bobby.

In early 1962, President Kennedy sent Bobby and Ethel on a four-week good-will trip around the world. Even before they left, the trip became the subject of great controversy. The Cleveland *Plain Dealer* commented editorially: "Not only does the trip imply the President doesn't have confidence in his appointed diplomats but young Bobby's trek gives the impression the United States, internally, is in great shape —such great shape that the head law man can take time out to size up the rest of the world and straighten out the kinks. This is contrary to what Bobby has been shouting for the past year. He has been pleading for tougher laws and more power to combat interstate crime. He has said that things are in a mess, crimewise, in our country. . . . We wonder what Bobby can find out in Europe, Africa, Asia, the Middle East, the Far East that Ave, Chester, Soapy, or any of the other traveling specialists couldn't uncover and we wonder if this trip, no matter who pays for it, really is necessary?"

Then Congressman John Lindsay wrote to Secretary Rusk demanding an official explanation for the Attorney General's trip. The letter suggested that Bobby was "untrained and without background in the business of diplomacy" and that the trip made Congressmen who seek a bipartisan approach to foreign policy wonder "where the channels of policy lie.

"We question whether it is necessary for you and your office to be either burdened or embarrassed by freewheeling foreign missions on the part of highly placed amateurs who do not have the background, training, language ability or capability to carry on the enormous burden of diplomacy in the context of today's long struggle. . . . Far better that the man who holds the highest legal office in the country spend time familiarizing himself with the meaning of the rule of law."

Rusk replied by stating that Bobby had gone on the trip "at my personal request and urging," and that he had "eminent qualifications for the mission."

Commented the New York *World-Telegram:* "We'd say the American public was more than charitable in accepting the appointment of Robert Kennedy, with his comparative youth and inexperience, as the nation's top legal officer. But we think it is much too much to expect the public to abide him as a super-Secretary of State, in which his inexperience is total.

"We are not so naive, and neither is Mr. Lindsay, as not to know the practical answer—that the Attorney General happens to be the President's brother. Nor can anyone be unaware of the obvious effort to groom Robert Kennedy as the President's alter ego, factotum and even, some say, prospective successor."

Before leaving Washington, Bobby told reporters, "I was asked to go by the State Department to indicate that the

United States is not, as described by the Communists, run by a tired and old government." Also in the Kennedy party were a family friend, Mrs. Donald Wilson, wife of the Deputy Director of the United States Information Agency; the Attorney General's administrative assistant, John Seigenthaler; Brandon Grove, representing the State Department; and four reporters and a photographer.

The day after he arrived in Tokyo, that sprawling metropolis was hit by a minor earthquake. But this was to be the least of Bobby's problems. Everywhere he went he was heckled and jeered at by leftist students. Arriving at Waseda University, he was greeted by loud shouts of *"Cuba Libre"* from anti-American elements. When he started to speak, the heckling in the auditorium was so loud he could not be heard. Angrily, Bobby pointed his finger at one of the jeer-leaders and challenged him to a debate. The heckler climbed up on the stage and, with Bobby holding the microphone, read a long denunciation of the United States.

When the youth had finished, Bobby tried to make his rebuttal but the electric power suddenly failed and the mike went dead. The mood of the crowd grew uglier and at U.S. Ambassador Edwin O. Reischauer's suggestion, the Kennedy party slipped out the back door.

The Reporter observed all this with growing amazement: "Suppose that Pat Nixon rather than Ethel Kennedy had been quoted as asking the Japanese, 'Did I read that your cats have no tails?' or 'Do the Japanese use snuff?' Suppose that *The New York Times* had written of Richard M. Nixon rather than Robert F. Kennedy that the students 'loved his slang ("You're crazy," "Pick up your marbles," "The hell with you"),' although to be sure 'the effectiveness of this tough talk is another question.'

"Fairly or unfairly, the anti-Administration press would have had a lot of fun. What solemn criticism of freewheeling diplomacy and reminders of the gravity of the world situation would have followed the news that an official of the Eisenhower Administration who had been stoned, splattered, or publicly heckled abroad had returned to find, as a Washington paper reported, that his staff had put a Welcome sign 'on his chair with an egg splattered on one side reminiscent of an egg thrown at him in the Far East'?"

The egg had been hurled at the University of Indonesia in

Djakarta, where after Bobby's speech there had been a spirited question-and-answer period. One student suggested that the United States annexation of Texas was similar to Indonesia's seizure of West New Guinea. "Some Texans might disagree," Bobby replied, "but I think it [the Mexican War] was unjustified. It was not a very bright spot in our history. Not one to be very proud of."

Needless to say, a lot of Texans disagreed. The *New York Herald Tribune* did, too. "Forget the Alamo," an editorial stated, "but let Bobby be brought home, promptly."

In India, Arthur Schlesinger joined the Kennedy entourage. He accompanied Bobby as far as Berlin, helping out with his speeches. West Berlin gave the Attorney General a tumultuous welcome in a new outpouring of the isolated city's faith in the United States.

And Bobby responded in kind. "Difficult times are ahead of us all over the world, but we are going to win," he told a throng of 150,000 Berliners. "West Berlin, although it lies on the edge of a totalitarian system, will not be attacked, because an attack on Berlin will be the same as an attack on New York, Chicago, London or Paris.

"You are our brothers and we will stand by you."

Everywhere Bobby had gone he had told newsmen, "We are going to win in Vietnam." But suddenly Vietnam was no longer the big issue; Cuba was. And Cuba was to provide the most horrifying crisis the Kennedy brothers would ever face.

Senator Kenneth Keating had first sounded the warning that the Soviet Union was building missile bases in Cuba. The New York Republican, in a series of ten speeches on the Senate floor, kept insisting that the United States was in danger. But President Kennedy had scoffed at these "alarmist" rumors. The United States, he said, had seen no evidence of a Soviet buildup in Cuba. Typically, Bobby, by now home from his world junket, ordered an investigation into where Keating was getting his information.

Fearing his office was "bugged," the New York Senator began conducting his important business elsewhere. (This writer, for example, discussed certain problems with the Senator in the corridor outside his office.) But on October 15, 1962, John F. Kennedy learned the bitter truth. Senator Keating, it turned out, was absolutely right. High-flying

U-2 planes, photographing every foot of Cuban terrain, had come up with some incredible photos of bases for long-range ballistic missiles nearing completion.

On consulting with Bobby, the President called together a crisis squad that came to be known as the Executive Committee (ExComm) of the National Security Council. Bobby, obviously acting for his brother, ran the ExComm sessions with his usual rudeness. Complained Adlai Stevenson, "Bobby was like a bull in a china shop."

Much has been said about Stevenson's "softness" on Cuba, but Bobby's role as leader of the "peace" faction has generally been overlooked. Much to the amazement of his fellow consultants, Bobby argued with passion against former Secretary of State Dean Acheson's proposal for blasting the missiles out by a series of air strikes.

He warned that bombing the sites would create a "Pearl Harbor in reverse" and would "blacken the name of the United States in the pages of history."

Acheson patiently pointed out that a "surgical" strike would not only eliminate the missile bases but would lead to the toppling of the Castro regime and rid the Western Hemisphere of a major Communist threat. But most of the ExComm members argued for a "quarantine," a naval blockade to prevent Soviet freighters from landing missiles in Cuba. The President agreed and on the evening of October 22, a grim JFK reported to the world on television the existence of the missiles and called on Nikita Khrushchev "to halt and eliminate this clandestine, reckless and provocative threat to world peace."

The world trembled on the brink of nuclear holocaust.

Left-wing peace groups all over the world staged demonstrations, and Bertrand Russell, after calling the President "a murderer worse than Hitler," cabled the President: YOUR ACTION DESPERATE. THREAT TO HUMAN SURVIVAL. NO CONCEIVABLE JUSTIFICATION. CIVILIZED MAN CONDEMNS IT. WE WILL NOT HAVE MASS MURDER. ULTIMATUMS MEAN WAR. I DO NOT SPEAK FOR POWER BUT PLEAD FOR CIVILIZED MAN. END THIS MADNESS.

The madness ended, however, when Chairman Khrushchev agreed to remove the missiles. Whether or not he removed all of them is still a matter of considerable controversy. But Bobby believes that this eyeball-to-eyeball confrontation with Khrushchev is one of the New Frontier's greatest achievements.

Some experts doubt this. Cyrus L. Sulzberger wrote in *The New York Times* five years later: "The Cuba confrontation was a historic watershed but the U.S. didn't gain much from it save prestige, and that intangible fades fast. More significant was a decision by General de Gaulle, who then stood firmly beside us, to reduce the chances of ever again having to take a similar risk. Since 1962 he has deliberately cut France's alliance ties outside Europe and has chosen a stance close to neutrality on major issues."

Later, Nikita Khrushchev—now deposed as Soviet Number One—claimed in an NBC telecast that it was he, not JFK, who had been the winner in the missile confrontation. "If rockets had not been installed, would there be a Cuba now?" said Khrushchev. "No, it would have been wiped out. We took our rockets and bombers away in exchange for President Kennedy's promise not to invade Cuba."

The December 8, 1962, *Saturday Evening Post* contained an article by Stewart Alsop and Charles Bartlett entitled "In Time of Crisis," which purported to give the inside story of the ExComm meetings during the two weeks of the missile crisis. According to the article, after the consensus had been reached favoring a naval blockade, there was only one dissenter—Adlai Stevenson. A top official was quoted as saying that Stevenson "wanted another Munich. He wanted to trade Turkish, Italian and British missile bases for the Cuban bases. . . . There seems to be no doubt that he preferred political negotiation to the alternative of military action."

The article created a furor. Many newsmen, knowing colleague Charles Bartlett's close ties with the President, assumed JFK had fed Bartlett the material with the hope that Stevenson would resign. Naturally, Stevenson was boiling mad. He publicly denounced the article as setting "some kind of record for irresponsible journalism," and privately told Arthur Schlesinger that if the President wanted his resignation he need not have acted in such a "circuitous" fashion.

Schlesinger denied that the President had had anything to do with the article, or that the President sought Adlai's resignation. But though he "limped to Stevenson's defense"

—as *Time* put it so well—the President never fully disavowed the Alsop-Bartlett piece.

Stevenson's years with the Kennedys had not been particularly happy ones. There can be no doubt that JFK distrusted his Ambassador to the United Nations, so much so that Stevenson always felt that he was surrounded by Kennedy spies. "It's something like Orwell's *1984,* if you please," Stevenson once told his sister, "Buffie" Ives. " 'Big Brother Is Watching You!' Informers seem to be everywhere."

But even world problems seemed comparatively minor compared to the storm clouds the Kennedys faced over civil rights. For the first two years of the New Frontier, they had been extremely prudent. They had decided that the Congress would not buy any new civil rights legislation, so instead they concentrated on making more effective use of voting-rights statutes already on the book.

Jack Kennedy had promised the millennium to Negro voters when he campaigned for the Presidency in 1960. He had castigated the Eisenhower Administration for failing to do enough. He had promised to abolish discrimination in housing with a "stroke of the pen." But not until November 1962 did he get around to fulfilling this promise, only after Negroes had taken to mailing him pens as sarcastic reminders. And Negroes were still dissatisfied because of the executive order's limited scope.

As election year 1964 drew closer, the Kennedys tried even harder to solve the civil rights dilemma without really offending anyone. But in June 1963, their old friend, Martin Luther King, compared the Kennedy record with that of the Eisenhower Administration and said that the New Frontier had merely substituted "an inadequate approach for a miserable one." And Whitney Moore Young, Jr., executive director of the National Urban League, urged the President to "place human rights above regional politics" and to "exhibit the kind of guts that he himself described in his book, *Profiles in Courage.*"

Bobby was truly bewildered by such belligerence. He had honestly believed that Negroes, generally, felt a deep gratitude to the Administration. To find out what was wrong, he asked author James Baldwin to assemble a group of "Negroes other Negroes listen to." He wanted to meet them. "No poli-

ticians. I don't mean Adam Clayton Powell, or even Martin
Luther King."

On May 24, 1963, such a meeting was arranged at Joe Kennedy's New York apartment at 24 Central Park South. It
lasted two hours and forty-five minutes. Among those present
besides Bobby and Baldwin were singers Lena Horne and
Harry Belafonte, playwright Lorraine (*A Raisin in the Sun*)
Hansberry, psychologist Kenneth B. Clark and a white actor
named Rip Torn.

"I don't know why I'm here," confessed Torn, "maybe because I'm a Southerner." And it wasn't long before Bobby
too was wondering why he himself was there. Instead of gratitude, he encountered a shouting, finger-shaking barrage of
anger, disappointment and impatience. At one point, he
snapped, "I'm not going to sit here and listen to that kind of
talk."

When it was all over, James Baldwin said, "Bobby was a
little surprised at the depth of Negro feeling. We were a little
shocked at the extent of his naïveté."

"This was one of the most anguishing experiences I've ever
had," added Dr. Clark. "If this was the best white America
had to offer, then God help us. . . . There was a real lack of
communication. It was macabre. . . ."

Bobby believed the group was thoroughly misinformed.
"They don't know anything," Bobby later told court historian
Arthur Schlesinger, Jr. "They don't know what the laws are—
they don't know what the facts are—they don't know what
we've been doing or what we're trying to do. . . . It was all
emotion, hysteria. They stood up and orated. They cursed.
Some of them wept and walked out of the room."

The morning after the meeting, James Baldwin reported
trouble with his phone. In her book, *The Furious Passages of
James Baldwin*, Fern Marja Eckman quotes him as having
told her: "I could make calls only with the greatest difficulty
because my line was loaded with clicks, growls and bleeps to
such an extent, in fact, that in the course of a single telephone
call, I was cut off four times—which I reported indignantly
to the operator. My conclusion, not unnaturally, was that
my phone was being tapped."

Finally, in mid-1963, the Kennedy Administration did propose new civil rights legislation. The package consisted of
four proposals that would: (1) extend the life of the Civil

Rights Commission for four years; (2) fortify voting rights; (3) give the Attorney General broadened authority to intervene in school-segregation cases; (4) ban discrimination in hotels, motels and restaurants.

Former President Eisenhower, whom Kennedy called in in the hope of obtaining Republican support, later told a partisan gathering in Hershey, Pennsylvania, "To Republicans, 'the rights of men' is a living doctrine. To our opponents, it is a campaign catch-phrase, a political gimmick to be cunningly exploited as part of the great mosaic which presents a public but deceitful image, known far and wide as concern for the common man—protection of the poor—champion of the people."

Meanwhile, in March 1962, Bobby's adversary from McClellan Committee days, Senator Carl T. Curtis, charged on the floor of the Senate that the Government-controlled General Aniline & Film Corporation was being used to provide "patronage" for friends of the Kennedys. General Aniline had been seized from Germany at the outbreak of war and had been operated since then by the Attorney General. Shortly after Bobby had taken office, according to the Nebraska Republican, General Aniline had switched its $1,500,000 advertising account to a Madison Avenue agency whose vice president was a close personal friend of the Kennedys, K. LeMoyne Billings, Jack's roommate at Choate.

Bobby replied that the selection of a new advertising agency was "a decision by management executives of General Aniline. I congratulate them on the excellence of their choice."

"What more political influence can come from close to the White House?" asked the Nebraskan.

As Attorney General, Bobby also had the right to appoint the entire board of directors of General Aniline, and as vice chairman he appointed William Peyton Marin, who listed himself in *Who's Who* as "legal counsel for Joseph P. Kennedy and family; general counsel for the Joseph P. Kennedy enterprises." Others named to the board were Ross D. Siragusa, president of the Admiral Corporation; Hal Clancy, managing editor of the Boston *Traveler;* and Joseph N. Lyons, Boston insurance executive—all friends of Joe Kennedy.

Bobby, it must be made clear, was well within his rights to name his friends to the board. But the new Attorney General could be faulted for using what Senator Keating was to call "poor judgment," for this was another example of "government by crony."

Then in March 1963, the Justice Department announced that it had reached an agreement with Interhandel A. G., a Swiss holding company, for the sale of General Aniline. Interhandel was also the Swiss front for the German firm of I. G. Farben. Because I. G. Farben had used slave labor during the Nazi days, four Attorneys General prior to Kennedy had refused to settle with Interhandel despite pressure from Interhandel lobbyists. But acting in behalf of Interhandel was Prince Radziwill, Jacqueline Kennedy's brother-in-law, who was on the Swiss firm's payroll as a lobbyist.

According to Senator Keating, there was a distinct odor about the deal. In a Senate speech, the New Yorker suggested that "any settlement of this magnitude deserves close scrutiny to make certain that it is in the best interests of the United States."

When JFK was in the White House, Bobby followed a policy of ignoring Vice President Johnson as much as possible, speaking to him only when it was unavoidable. At times he went out of his way to embarrass the Veep. There was the occasion when the Attorney General barged in on a meeting of the President's Committee on Equal Employment Opportunity over which Lyndon was presiding.

Bobby's first words were "I have just come from the President." And with that, he took over, demanding of all the participants what they had done about employing Negroes. It was the old snarling Bobby, glaring at officials, demanding answers and shutting off those who protested they needed more time. Then he left abruptly. Lyndon Johnson, who had sat through it all with his eyes half closed, said nothing and also left.

"The Vice President looked like a beaten man," one of the participants later recalled.

Lyndon Johnson was then in the depths of a Vice Presidential depression. For some months, beginning in February 1962, someone in the Kennedy group had been passing out to newsmen material for stories that tended to downgrade his competency. In private conversations, the Vice President blamed Bobby for most of his trials and tribulations. And when a Washington gossip column listed competitive candidates for the Vice Presidency, Johnson claimed the piece had been planted by Bobby.

There was great merriment at a party at Hickory Hill when some of Bobby's friends gave the Attorney General an LBJ voodoo doll in which to stick pins. And some years later, Senator Abe Ribicoff of Connecticut recalled that "some of the young people around the White House did not treat Vice President Johnson with the respect he was entitled to and did not accord him his proper place in the Administration."

"During his Vice Presidential tenure," Arnold Beichman was to write later, "Johnson's loyalties were surely tried. He had an unhappy idea that he was being followed, that his wires were tapped. What outsiders can only sense is how black were those days for him and the dark foreboding about his political future. What is now said in Washington—and which has not been publicly confirmed—is that, as soon as he became President, Johnson ordered an end to widespread wiretapping. With good reason, Johnson is for the right to privacy."

As late as October 1963, Lyndon Johnson told a United States Senator he did not believe he would be Jack Kennedy's running mate in 1964. He complained bitterly that the Kennedy brothers were "sadists." He said they were responsible for the many reports being published about his being "dumped" the following year.

President Kennedy, at a press conference, flatly denied any plan to drop Johnson. But in her recent book, *Kennedy and Johnson*, Mrs. Evelyn Lincoln, JFK's secretary, claimed the President had, indeed, spoken of his intention of getting rid of Vice President Johnson.

"Who is your choice as a running mate?" she had asked President Kennedy.

"At this time," the President replied unhesitatingly, "I am thinking about Governor Terry Sanford of North Carolina. But it will not be Lyndon."

19

Aftermath

For Robert F. Kennedy the world had come to an end. He had held up well in the days immediately following the assassination when overnight he had become the head of the Kennedy family. His father, still unable to speak, could only listen to his son's consoling words on the telephone. For Jacqueline Kennedy, Bobby was a source of strength. For the slain President's children he had become a substitute father. But Lyndon Baines Johnson was in the White House. Gone was the New Frontier. Hail to the Great Society!

Then Bobby began to crumble. He appeared to sink into deep melancholia. When after two weeks he returned to his office in the Justice Department, his associates immediately noticed the changes. His eyes were puffed. His hair was a little too long. His face contained new lines. And he had lost so much weight that his clothes appeared too large for him.

Though he came in daily, he worked irregularly. Ed Lahey, the veteran correspondent of the Knight newspapers and an old friend, was—in his column of December 13—the first to quote the Attorney General directly after the assassination. Lahey asked what Bobby's plans were. "I just don't know," he replied. "I suppose I'll stay here until the civil rights bill gets through Congress. After that, I don't know."

President Johnson asked Bobby to take on his first—and last—troubleshooting assignment. Indonesia's President Sukarno was making belligerent noises about breaking up the newly created Federation of Malaysia. He was against the Federation, Sukarno said, because it was a "neo-colonial" device to maintain British control and bases. He also wanted to exclude

United States military installations from the Philippines.

Tokyo was chosen as the meeting place because of the mellowing influence the Japanese capital seemed to have on the Indonesian leader. In Tokyo, Sukarno was free from the pressures of Djakarta, and he seemed to admire the charms of Japanese females. Bobby's pitch, in effect, was that Sukarno would be cut off from United States aid should Indonesia continue her aggressive activities. He thought he had persuaded Sukarno to agree to a cease-fire and to begin talks with Malaysian leaders.

But hardly had Bobby boarded a homeward-bound plane when Sukarno retracted his pledges. He told a howling mob of 15,000 in Djakarta that he intended to crush Malaysia. "Onward, never retreat!" he shouted. "Indonesia may change its tactics but our goal will remain the same."

On arriving in London for conferences with the skeptical British, Bobby insisted that Sukarno seemed "genuinely willing" to settle the dispute. Asked if he thought Sukarno could be trusted, Bobby said, "Yes, I think so." Back home, Bobby delivered his report to Lyndon Johnson, and the President praised the Attorney General for having "carried out his assignment constructively and with real achievement."

Gradually Bobby emerged from the shadows of despair. "There isn't that hollow look in the eyes," a New York politician told Murray Kempton, "and the talk just doesn't turn automatically back to his brother the way it did a little while ago." Now he was talking about staying on for a year, indicating he could get along with Lyndon Johnson. But things were different. No longer were there numerous calls from the White House; and J. Edgar Hoover began to report directly to the President.

Hugh Sidey, after visiting with the Attorney General, wrote in *Life:* "No matter how normal things seem back at the Justice Department, the pain of John Kennedy's death for his brother is still soul-deep. In the quiet moments his mind comes back and back to President Kennedy. That memory is all-important. Bob Kennedy is concerned that the right national attitude be retained of the three years of the New Frontier. . . . Bob believes that many of the most important things are the intangibles—the rebuilding of the world's confidence in America, the rekindling of America's own self-confidence, the leadership given to a young and vibrant generation all around the world. And they came not in any single massive step but in small increments—more military strength, a booming economy, the pleas for peace, the dedication to excellence and firmness toward Communism."

The Kennedy legend had begun and Bobby was heir to it. He wanted nothing to sully that legend. Thus Bobby encouraged Ted Sorensen and Arthur Schlesinger to write books about what they had observed in the White House. And he signed a contract with a little-known writer, William Manchester, to do a book on the assassination itself.

Four days after the tragic event, Bobby had directed Pierre Salinger to telephone the New York offices of North American Newspaper Alliance from Hobe Sound, Florida, where the Attorney General was spending several days. The newspaper syndicate had announced an eight-part series based on a book by Gene Schoor entitled *Young John Kennedy*. Salinger told NANA that Bobby personally would sue if any of the material differed in the slightest from what was in the original Schoor book. The Attorney General then got on the phone and confirmed Salinger's warning. Only later did NANA learn that the Kennedy family had given Schoor certain other information which had not appeared in the book. Bobby apparently feared that some of this might be included in the NANA series. Needless to say, the series was adulatory.

One of the first things the Johnsons discovered when they moved into the White House was that the white mantel of the bedroom had a new inscription. It read: IN THIS ROOM LIVED JOHN FITZGERALD KENNEDY WITH HIS WIFE JACQUELINE DURING THE TWO YEARS, TEN MONTHS AND TWO DAYS HE WAS PRESIDENT OF THE UNITED STATES.

This was directly under an original plaque which read: IN THIS ROOM ABRAHAM LINCOLN SLEPT DURING HIS OCCUPANCY OF THE WHITE HOUSE AS PRESIDENT OF THE UNITED STATES. MARCH 4, 1861–APRIL 13, 1865.

Jacqueline, needless to say, was anticipating the verdict of history.

"Would you believe it?" President Johnson asked a leading Washington correspondent.

One of President Johnson's major problems was his feeling he was being forced to compete with the myth of his predecessor's "greatness." The adulatory rhetoric had, indeed, gotten out of control. The truth is that the JFK image was floundering before his untimely death.

"There is a vague feeling of doubt and disappointment in the country about President Kennedy's first term . . . ," wrote James Reston in *The New York Times* a week before the assassination. "He has touched the intellect of the country but not the heart. . . . There is clearly a feeling in the country, often expressed by middle-aged women, that the Kennedys are setting standards that are too fancy, too fast, and as one woman said in Philadelphia, 'too European.' "

"In general," commented *The New Republic,* "the Kennedy performance is less impressive than the Kennedy style." Kennedy was having so many difficulties with Congress that his abilities as a strong executive leader were being questioned. His leadership in foreign affairs was described as "disappointing" by the London *Times* and "ineffectual" by *Le Monde* of Paris.

"Would it be sacrilegious to whisper that John F. Kennedy—for all his charm, his style, his intelligence—was not quite the 'great President' almost everyone feels obliged to say he was?" wrote literary critic Irving Howe in the *New York Review of Books.* "To enter this dissent in no way affects the grief that every decent person feels at the President's death. After all, even not-so-great Presidents, like not-so-great human beings in general, have a right to live out the natural course of their lives."

When he finally pulled himself out of his depression, Bobby had a long talk with a newspaper friend of the family. It was obvious that to the Attorney General the New Frontier had been something special—so special, in fact, he wanted to see it continued.

Wherever he went, Bobby invariably talked about his brother. He was able now to achieve a rapport with his audiences that he had never had before.

Even before the end of the official period of mourning, Bobby Kennedy-for-Vice-President boomlets cropped up across the country. In New Hampshire, a write-in campaign developed—or was created—by the mysterious Paul Corbin, still with the Democratic National Committee.

Corbin's activities were no secret to the White House, whose chief occupant had become increasingly concerned that he would be outpolled by Bobby in the primary. Word went out from the President that Corbin be dismissed from the National Committee. But Corbin remained in New Hampshire on the payroll of the Joseph P. Kennedy Jr. Foundation.

The President ordered new efforts to bolster his votes in the Granite State. And he certainly needed them. For the final primary vote showed Johnson looking weak, indeed, with only 29,635 votes to Bobby's 25,861 write-ins.

Though reports of the feud between them grew stronger, Bobby was doing everything possible to minimize them. For he had decided he wanted to become Vice President, though all indications were that Lyndon Johnson didn't want him. It was even said that LBJ's buildup of Sargent Shriver was designed to deflate brother-in-law Bobby's political balloon.

From his ivory tower, that oracle of oracles, Walter Lippmann, examined Bobby's bid for the Vice Presidential nomination: ". . . the Vice President must be chosen with complete awareness that at any time . . . he may suddenly become the President. It would, I believe, be deeply disturbing to the people of this country if President Kennedy's brother got to the White House because of a political maneuver in the Democratic convention. I think many would resent it. The possibility that this could happen would be a grave liability in the election.

"The greatest service that can be done to the memory of John F. Kennedy is to finish what he began. . . . No greater disservice could be done than to feed the suspicions of the many who admired President Kennedy but thought his family were over-active.

"Robert Kennedy is not ready to be President of the United States. But at his age and with his very remarkable political gifts, he has every right and much reason to aspire to be the President some day. The only self-respecting way to go about that is for him to earn his own way, not to inherit the office from his brother."

The St. Louis *Post-Dispatch* added: "With all due respect to Robert Kennedy, granting that he has been an excellent Attorney General, an able counselor to his brother and a tested champion of civil rights, still the facts remain that he is only thirty-eight years old, that he has risen to power on a brother's coattails, that his government experience prior to 1961 consisted solely of investigative work for senatorial committees, and that he has yet to establish himself on his own merits as a man fit to carry the highest responsibility in the most powerful country in the world."

By now, many New Frontiersmen had already resigned. Arthur Schlesinger, Jr., could hardly wait to get out. In fact, the day after the assassination, he had asked John Bailey whether there was any way to deny the new President the nomination at the forthcoming convention. The Democratic National Chairman replied, "It might be technically feasible, but the result would be to lose the election for the Democrats."

Not all of JFK's appointees left, however. Several remained with the new President. Lawrence O'Brien, who had been Special Assistant to the President for Congressional relations, was named Postmaster General. And what astonished O'Brien was the fact that many Kennedyites regarded him as a renegade who had gone over to the usurper. And John Kenneth Galbraith had also remained on good terms with Lyndon Johnson and even written some speeches for him. He was described as a "rat fink" by people close to Bobby.

McGeorge Bundy had stayed on as Special Assistant to the President for national security affairs. Though his primary area was foreign affairs, Bundy was troubled about the messy brawl that was developing around the Vice Presidential nomination. He stuck his neck out by suggesting to Johnson that Bobby might make a fine running mate. But Lyndon thumbed him down, and suggested he call Bobby and recommend that the Attorney General "leak" to James Reston that he was voluntarily withdrawing from the running. As Bobby himself said later, "I'm afraid he hasn't been a very good friend."

The pro-Bobby pressures had meanwhile built up to a point where the President was forced to make a move. The Bobby problem, if left alone, was not going to go away, and Johnson was afraid he might lose control of the one big decision to be left to the delegates—the choice of his running mate.

For one thing, Chicago's powerful Mayor Richard J. Daley, a friend of the Kennedy clan, had made it known he favored Bobby. And it was rumored that Jacqueline Kennedy had assured Bobby that she would do anything he wanted to help him win. It was even said she was willing to make an appearance at Atlantic City to help stir up enthusiasm at the convention. To top it all off, a massive tribute to JFK was being planned, and such a spectacle was bound to start an instant bandwagon for Bobby.

Almost from the beginning, Jacqueline Kennedy had cold-shouldered the President. This first became obvious when she refused to attend the memorial services for her husband on December 22, 1963, at which President Johnson paid tribute to JFK. (For that matter, no other Kennedy turned up at the services, held at the Lincoln Memorial.) Indeed, Jacqueline refused every invitation from the White House, including one from Mrs. Johnson asking her to come to the dedication of the Jacqueline Kennedy Rose Garden, adjacent to the executive offices. At one point, President Johnson even offered Mrs. Kennedy the post of Ambassador to Mexico, but she turned it down on grounds of being in mourning.

LBJ disposed of the problem by calling in the Attorney General on July 29, 1964, and telling him forthrightly that he was out of the running as Vice President. "You have a bright future, a great name, and courage," he read from a piece of paper in front of him, "but you have not been in government very long. I have given you serious consideration, but find it inadvisable to pick you."

Bobby did not argue, but did say that the Kennedy family would not be overly happy if the President selected Sargent Shriver. Within the family, of course, there is a sense of priority, and brother-in-law Sarge is way down the list. As he left the President's office, Bobby Kennedy turned and said, "I could have helped you a lot."

"You are going to help," replied Lyndon Johnson.

20

Decision

To the bitter end, Robert F. Kennedy had hoped for the Vice Presidency. It would have been a stepping-stone toward his dream of one day succeeding his beloved brother in the White House. But now the dream was shattered.

Also ended was the fabulous era that had become known as the New Frontier, the gay and glittering time of brothers, sisters, romping children, Jacqueline Kennedy and Arthur Schlesinger, Jr., and the exciting parties. It was now LBJ, Ladybird and Texas. And Bobby knew that there was no place for him in this hearty new world of Stetsons and barbecues.

An illuminating insight into Bobby's state of mind at this time is provided by an interchange during his briefing of some top Justice Department aides. "Where do we go from here?" one of them asked.

"Well," the Attorney General said with a wry smile, "I think we had better go out and form another country."

Bobby had been well aware that he was not one of President Johnson's favorite people. But the manner in which the President had erased Bobby from consideration was unprecedented. He had merely announced he had decided it would be inadvisable to choose as a running mate any member of the Cabinet or anyone who had been regularly meeting with the Cabinet. Then he excised these names specifically: Bobby Kennedy, Secretaries Rusk, McNamara and Freeman, Peace Corps Director Sargent Shriver and UN Ambassador Adlai Stevenson.

The humor of the situation was not overlooked by

Bobby. Addressing a group of Democratic Congressional candidates, he said that he had written to his fellow Cabinet members saying, in effect, that "I am sorry to have taken so many nice guys over the side with me."

Among Bobby's friends there was little levity. United Press International reported that the Attorney General was having some difficulty in cooling off members of his family and associates who made no secret of their bitterness toward President Johnson. And columnist Joseph Kraft, a close friend (in 1960 he had been one of JFK's speech writers), took this dire view: "Perhaps the President will now come up with a choice for Vice President who has all the attributes of the Attorney General. Still, the manner of dumping, if not the decision itself, inspires misgivings. It suggests the President never has had any real understanding of the Attorney General. And that blind spot casts a shadow over the whole future of American life."

Johnson's friends got in a few licks, too. One of them, talking to columnist Marguerite Higgins, observed: "You know, it could have been different. If in November, Attorney General Kennedy had said something like this: 'Thank God we have as our leader a man chosen by President Kennedy. Let's rally behind President Johnson—my brother's choice —and get on with the job.' If Bob Kennedy had said something like that, you could not have pried the two apart with dynamite."

On July 31, 1964, President Johnson's press secretary, George Reedy, made a date for lunch at Washington's elegant Sans Souci with Tom Wicker of *The New York Times*, Eddie Folliard of the Washington *Post* and Douglas Kiker of the *New York Herald Tribune*. Its purpose was to brief the three newsmen on why the President had decided to dump Bobby. At the last minute, however, the President decided to do the briefing himself.

Wicker was already seated in the restaurant, but the others were notified of the change in plans before they had left their offices.

It was obvious from the start of the lobster-and-watermelon luncheon at the White House that the President was elated over how he had eliminated the Bobby problem. He showed the correspondents telegrams he had received from all fifty of the Democratic State Chairmen vowing support.

What of course had really occurred was that the leader of each state delegation had been called and told, in effect, "I've done it. Are you with me, or against me?" And there was little else they could do but immediately vow allegiance to the President.

The more the President talked the more he threw caution to the winds. No longer did he demonstrate the reticence he had previously affected in discussing the Kennedys. He even mimicked Bobby's discomfiture—"This is the way he gulped on hearing he was not going to get the Vice Presidency." It was quite apparent that the President had truly enjoyed putting "the little snotnose" in his place.

The next morning the three newsmen published guarded accounts of the luncheon. Tom Wicker, in the *Times,* reported "on the highest authority" that Kennedy "was eliminated from consideration . . . because of the racial crisis and because President Johnson had concluded that the Attorney General would hurt the ticket in crucial areas more than some other candidates." Moreover, President Johnson felt, Bobby was decidedly unpopular with businessmen because of the role he had played in the steel-price rollback of 1962. And numerous conversations with political leaders had convinced the President that there was a general reluctance to see a "Kennedy dynasty" particularly in view of Bobby's youthfulness. Not that he did not have strengths, but the weaknesses outweighed the strengths, in the President's estimation.

In a matter of hours, Bobby had a full account of what the President had told the three newsmen and began to fume. He had been given to understand that his meeting with the President would be off the record, and now the whole town was talking about it. A few days later he told the President so to his face, and when the President denied talking to anyone, Bobby exploded. He ended up calling the President a liar.

It is one of the primary laws of politics that no one calls the President of the United States a liar, at least to his face. No one had ever called President Kennedy a liar, though he had occasionally veered from the truth. It just isn't good manners. But apparently the common courtesies do not apply where Bobby is involved.

In Buffalo, Peter J. Crotty, chairman of the Erie County Democratic Committee, announced that President Johnson's action left Bobby "available for a draft" as a candidate for the Senate from New York. Crotty, along with John F. English, the young ambitious leader in Nassau County, had been the chief instigator of such a candidacy the previous spring, when they had circulated private polls purporting to show that only the Attorney General could beat the Republican incumbent, Senator Kenneth B. Keating.

Kennedy had not discouraged them at first. In fact, he had even assigned his brother-in-law, Steve Smith, to make an exploratory tour around New York State to sound out the sentiment in his behalf. The slender boyish-looking Smith, then thirty-six years of age, had reported that Charles A. Buckley, the Bronx boss who had done so much to get John F. Kennedy the Presidential nomination, was agreeable. Only Daniel P. O'Connell, the political czar of Albany County, appeared reticent because of his close ties to New York Mayor Robert F. Wagner.

"Bobby knew what was going on," an associate reported. "But at the time he genuinely didn't know what he wanted to do. The Senate was just one option. Bobby really saw his future in the executive or administrative—not the legislative—end. He thought the Vice Presidential thing would go right down to the wire."

But it hadn't, and now Bobby knew that a political future with the Johnson Administration was out of the question. What should he do? He had by then reached a major personal decision: He wanted to remain in government.

On Friday, July 31, Kennedy took off for Hyannis Port where he spent the weekend conferring with a group of old friends including Dave Hackett, now a trusted aide in the Justice Department; Averell Harriman, Undersecretary of State for Political Affairs (who had privately been boosting the idea for months) and the inevitable Arthur Schlesinger, Jr., whose overpowering hatred for Johnson exceeded even Bobby's.

"That was the weekend Bobby looked down the deep well," one insider reported. And what he saw was simply that he had no alternative. New York was wide-open for takeover. A vacuum of leadership had been created among

New York Democrats with their brand of boss-ridden, feud-ridden, small-bore politics. "This is a marriage of necessity," one Kennedy intimate said candidly at the time. "They need a candidate and Bob wants to stay in government."

Not that Bobby particularly liked New York. For Bobby, New York City wasn't even a nice place to visit. "I don't like cities generally," he told a *New Yorker* writer. "The part of New York I like the best is Central Park—especially the zoo. If the [1960] election had turned out differently and if Mr. Nixon hadn't made me Attorney General, I'd probably be making short trips to New York only to visit the zoo."

For years Bobby had resided at Hickory Hill in Virginia, had voted from Hyannis Port and had just been named a Massachusetts delegate to the Democratic National Convention soon to open in Atlantic City. But, to a Kennedy, these were not insurmountable obstacles.

One of Bobby's problems was the highly vocal Reformers in the New York Democratic party. Not only did they look upon him as a carpetbagger but, even worse, as much too conservative. Anyway, most of them wanted Adlai Stevenson as their candidate, though, as usual, Adlai could not make up his mind. Besides, the Reformers were well aware that it was their archenemy Charles Buckley, the aging, crotchety "boss" of the Bronx, who gave Bobby the go-ahead on running in New York.

Then Buckley called a secret meeting of the "bosses" to work out plans for "securing" the nomination for Bobby. Peter Crotty, John English and Bobby's brother-in-law Steve Smith were present, along with Brooklyn leader Stanley Steingut, a bitter foe of Mayor Wagner. Somehow the details were leaked out and published in an exclusive story in the New York *Journal-American*.

"That meeting was a political masterstroke, but it was a public-relations disaster," a leading Democrat recalls. "It helped create the image of Bobby as the candidate of the bosses."

Sensing disaster, the Kennedy forces decided to try to get the reluctant Adlai Stevenson, still the number-one love of the Reformers, to announce his support of Bobby. Steve Smith was dispatched to the United Nations Ambassador's

Waldorf Towers apartment, but Stevenson's reaction to the Kennedy proposal was one of pure anger. "Stevenson was livid," a friend recalls. "He complained about 'steamrollers' and refused to cooperate."

Apparently, Stevenson was still interested in running himself. He had had his fill of the United Nations and was tired of apologizing for foreign policies which he privately deplored. Moreover, such good friends as Mary Lasker, widow of the advertising executive, and Alex Rose, chief strategist of the Liberal party, had been urging him to run. But in the final analysis, as the Kennedy forces well knew, he would revert to his traditional indecision. By the time Mayor Wagner got around to asking whether he wanted to become a candidate, Stevenson said no, that he had no wish to be considered a "stop-Kennedy man."

Mayor Wagner himself was in a bind. A Lyndon Johnson man, he had no particular love for Bobby, who represented a threat to his role as the most influential Democrat in the state. Besides, the Mayor had battled hard since 1961 against "bosses" Buckley, Crotty and Steingut. Welcoming Bobby into New York would mean working with these old-time bosses, which Wagner wanted no part of. Also upsetting was a feeling that Bobby's victory might eventually prevent him from running for Governor.

Wagner's decision was made no easier when Harlem's mercurial Adam Clayton Powell, in one of his boastful moods, told newsmen at his Abyssinian Baptist Church that "Steingut, Buckley, Crotty and I will decide who will be the next U.S. Senator, or at least the Democratic nominee." The Reverend Congressman pointedly observed that he had urged Bobby to run three months ago. (Later, during the campaign, Bobby was asked why he did not run for the Senate in Virginia where he actually resided. "Because Charles Buckley and Adam Clayton Powell couldn't sponsor me in Virginia," Bobby quipped.)

The Powell statement caused consternation in the Kennedy camp, where the repercussions were fast and furious. The Queens Democratic leadership was upset. Upstate Democrats were chagrined. The anti-Kennedy bias of the Reformers was reinforced. And Bobby was forced to sit through a lecture by Mayor Wagner about running around with the wrong politicians.

A few days later Bobby dropped a bomb in the Mayor's lap. He told reporters that under no circumstances would he come into New York without "the express approval of the Mayor." The statement, of course, was designed to smoke the Mayor out. But when asked by newsmen whether he would give that approval, Wagner cagily replied, "If he is available, he is the type of person who would make an exceptionally fine candidate. . . ."

That night Bobby took off on a cruise along the coast of Maine on the *Palawan*, a 54-foot, mahogany-hulled yacht belonging to Thomas J. Watson, Jr., chairman of the International Business Machines Corporation. Going along for the ride, besides Watson, were Navy Undersecretary Paul B. Fay, Jr.; Donald Wilson of the U.S. Information Agency; columnist Rowland Evans, and Ethel Kennedy. Fortunately, there were also a skipper and a mate aboard, thus eliminating the obstacle to navigation that Bobby afloat normally represented. (The previous summer, as he and Teddy and their wives and friends left North Haven, after dragging anchor, catching cables and swiping moorings, the harbor master was heard to remark, "If they run the country the way they run that boat, I'm getting off.")

Only later did Bobby learn what the *Times* had to say about his candidacy. It was enough to make him want to buy the paper in order to personally fire editorial page editor John B. Oakes. The editorial was entitled "But Does New York Need Him?" and read:

"We seem to have been premature when we congratulated Attorney General Robert F. Kennedy in late June for the wisdom of his decision that 'I will not be a candidate for United States Senator for New York.' It was learned last night that, having been locked out as a Vice Presidential hopeful, Mr. Kennedy will look for a New York job.

"Why he has any special claim on New York to rescue him from non-office is a mystery. His sponsorship is hardly the cream of the party. . . .

"After some arm-twisting, apparently, Mayor Wagner and State Democratic Chairman William H. McKeon are being cajoled into adding at least the lip-service of more respectability to the list of those willing to go along with a Kennedy candidacy. . . .

"The real issue, of course, is not where this leaves Wagner, but whether New York is so poverty-stricken for United States Senate material of authentic residence that it has to import a young man so obviously non-resident that he is just about to be a Massachusetts delegate to the Democratic National Convention. The constitutionality of Mr. Kennedy's running in New York does not seem to be in doubt; the question of state law is being raised, but is not likely to disqualify him. His utter innocence as to New York State problems should.

"The cold fact is that Mr. Kennedy appears to have decided that his ambitions will be best and most immediately served by finding a political launching pad in New York State. If his brother were not already representing Massachusetts in the Senate, Mr. Kennedy undoubtedly would have run in that state. But to run now would mean that he would have to elbow out another Kennedy. Thus Mr. Kennedy apparently needs New York. But does New York really need Bobby Kennedy?"

The bitterness toward the *Times* in the Kennedy camp was ill concealed, though in talking with a reporter, Steve Smith said, "Bobby has never been worried about what Scotty Reston and 'Punch' Sulzberger think. It's a big joke for the paper of Ochs and Sulzberger to write about nepotism. Anyway, Democrats normally win without support of the newspapers."

If so, Bobby was on his way, for he was getting the cold shoulder from other distinguished newspapers all over the state. A survey of editorial opinion in twelve showed nine opposed to his candidacy, two in favor and one neutral. The pro-Kennedy papers were Dorothy Schiff's New York *Post* and Hearst's *Journal-American,* strange bedfellows indeed.

Largely forgotten in all the excitement was the fact that an upstate Democratic Congressman, Samuel S. Stratton, had been running hard for the Senate nomination for nearly two years. Speaking in his behalf, Schenectady County Chairman George Palmer warned, "Naming an outsider for Senate in New York could set a precedent which would later be exploited by reactionary well-heeled Republican conservatives. . . . What is to stop a reactionary oil or mining tycoon from deciding that he would like to buy himself a Senate election in some small and poor Republican farming state?"

Stratton vowed a fight to the finish. He could hardly believe that anyone—even a Kennedy—could come into the state and be permitted to walk off with the big prize. But, as the Washington *Post* observed editorially, ". . . the Kennedy family displays a resolute indifference to the political axioms that guide the decisions of humbler folk."

More realistic was ultraliberal Congressman William Fitts Ryan, representing Manhattan's upper West Side, who also had had plans to seek the senatorial nomination. No fool, Ryan knew the ball game was over. Throwing in his bat, he endorsed Bobby.

Also unhappy about Bobby's arrival on the New York scene had been four other elected Reformers: State Senator Manfred Ohrenstein, Assemblymen Albert H. Blumenthal and Jerome Kretchmer, and City Councilman Theodore S. Weiss. But these gentlemen also saw the handwriting on the wall. They, too, fell in line, issuing a statement praising Bobby's "leadership in achieving the Civil Rights Act" (for which, incidentally, they could as easily have lauded Republican Senator Everett Dirksen, who actually had more to do with its passage). "His grasp of urban issues equips him ably to represent the State of New York," the statement continued. "We believe that no one will be fooled by the desperate efforts of a few discredited bosses to use the Attorney General's candidacy for their own selfish purposes."

Not all Reformers fell in line, however. Center of the opposition was the Lexington Democratic Club, an upper East Side Reform group whose members refused to be conned. Led by the militant Lisa Howard, a blond television news reporter, the group circulated copies of the famous March 1963 *Esquire* article in which Gore Vidal said, "Bobby's view of men and actions is a good deal closer to that of Barry Goldwater than it is to that of President Kennedy."

Bobby was concerned about this lack of enthusiasm and assigned William F. Haddad, a former Peace Corps executive who had been an unsuccessful Reform candidate for Congress earlier in the year, to woo them. Liberal party's Alex Rose and David Dubinsky also spent considerable time on the phone telling people to forget all the bad things they had heard about Bobby, that actually he was a nice liberal *boychik* and—more important—would win. A great deal of effort also went into seeking Mrs. Herbert Lehman's support of Kennedy. But Mrs. Lehman had a long memory. She could not forget how brusquely "that little man," as she called him, had treated her late husband during the 1960 campaign.

But the trouble was that the Reformers did everything but line up Democratic delegates behind a stop-Kennedy candidate. True, they called on Mayor Wagner and demanded he "do something," and he listened patiently as their spokesman, Arnold L. Fein, enumerated the arguments against Bobby. But all the Mayor would say was that he still had not made up his mind.

"We confess to a certain amount of sympathy with Bob Wagner," editorialized the *New York Herald Tribune*. "New York's three-term Mayor, the supposed strong man of state and city Democratic politics, the slow-motion Reformer who still hasn't exterminated the bosses, the amiable citizen who wanted to be U.S. Senator or Vice President or perhaps Governor, is now almost certainly at that painful point where he is compelled to approve Bobby Kennedy. . . .

"The local Democrats, feuding as always, needed a candidate. And Kennedy needed a fresh base of operations for the future. He made the gesture that Wagner must give his blessing, in itself a disguised bit of arrogance commanding party unity. But the Mayor's political control has never been completely effective, and thus he is in the unhappy predicament of having to yield to hostile boss clamor, the emotion of the Kennedy name, and above all the persistence of the carpetbagging intruder himself. For if Wagner doesn't graciously cooperate, the prospect at this late stage is that Bobby Kennedy would appropriate the Senate nomination anyway.

"That's why we express sympathy for Bob Wagner. . . . But for our state there is a greater challenge than partisanship. What originally seemed a bad jest has come to pass. The non-resident Bobby Kennedy covets New York as his own, as so much personal necessity in furthering his restless purposes. This is to assert that a Kennedy must have what he wants, that a Kennedy is indispensable and never mind about the hawk tactics in snatching the New York nest. And this is the gall so raw that it had to be conceived in the outsider's mind."

By now the Mayor well knew the game was over. He was aware that Bobby had more delegates than he needed to capture the nomination. The Kennedy forces oozed confidence as they had on the eve of the 1960 convention. The reason, as one Kennedy intimate said at the time, "was the oldest reason in politics—you can't beat somebody with nobody, and the anti-Kennedy people had nobody."

Finally, on August 21, after two weeks of hesitation and dozens of strategy meetings, the Mayor walked into the reception room at City Hall, sat down under a John Vanderlyn portrait of James Monroe and announced that he was endorsing Robert F. Kennedy for Senator. Reading solemnly and slowly from a typescript, Wagner praised the Attorney General as a man of "personal eminence" and "great achievements."

The morning after Wagner's statement, the *New York Herald Tribune,* in an editorial entitled "Surrender to the Carpetbagger," commented:

"There wasn't a spot for Mr. Kennedy elsewhere, so he invited himself in as the new boss of New York Democratic politics. . . . It is bossism gone mad in the obeisant welcome of a carpetbagger, however distinguished, who thinks he is indispensable. In the election of a Senator, we in New York owe the first obligation to ourselves as a state rich in home-grown talent. New York is not an undeveloped territory, waiting to be civilized through a Kennedy colonization."

The good, gray *New York Times* also lost its cool. Noting that Bobby had assured Wagner that he wanted to work with him for the party's "revitalization and democratization," the *Times* said: "This may satisfy the Mayor, but it is not likely to satisfy many other New Yorkers until it is accompanied by a specific repudiation of leaders like Boss Buckley of the Bronx, whose rule would have ended long ago if he did not have the effusive endorsement of all the Kennedys whenever a challenge arose. The Attorney General never manifested much passion for reform in Massachusetts. . . .

"All that is left now is for young Lochinvar to fly here, symbolically purge himself of Massachusetts residence by announcing his withdrawal as a delegate from that state at next week's Democratic National Convention and then wait for a supine New York State convention to hand him the toga September 1."

Which is pretty much what did occur. On August 25, Robert F. Kennedy formally entered the race. With his wife on his left and Mayor Wagner on his right, the Attorney General made his announcement on the lawn of Gracie Mansion, the Mayor's tree-shaded 200-year-old official residence facing the East River. Bobby's hands trembled slightly as he read his statement in a voice that seemed to bring the singsong inflections of his dead brother's voice echoing from the past. Reporters noticed that he had the same shock of unruly, sandy-colored hair, specked with a bit of gray at the temples. He wore a black pin-striped suit and black tie, which made him look older than his thirty-eight years. His wife, expecting her ninth child, wore a lavender maternity dress.

In his statement, Kennedy acknowledged that the carpetbagger issue would be one of the most difficult facing him in the campaign. He tried to soften the issue by describing himself as a man "who has left the state and who has only recently returned," mentioning his father's Park Avenue apartment and his early schooling in Bronxville.

"But I do not base my candidacy on these connections. I base it on the belief that New York is not separate from the nation in the year 1964. I base it on the conviction that my experience and my record equip me to understand New York's problems and to do something about them. I base it on the fact that the greatest state in the union must play a leading role at the Federal level in solving these problems. And I wish to play a part in that effort."

Senator Keating, campaigning upstate, said he "welcomed" Bobby to New York. "Indeed, as his Senator, I would be glad to furnish him a guidebook, road map, and other useful literature about the Empire State which any sojourner would find helpful."

Leaving Gracie Mansion, Bobby flew to Atlantic City to get acquainted with members of the New York delegation. He had already resigned as a member of the Massachusetts delegation. First stop was Averell Harriman's fifth-floor suite at the Ritz-Carlton, where for the next hour and a half the

Kennedy team—Ethel, Bobby, Steve Smith, William vanden Heuvel and Ed Guthman—held court for a procession of New York pols and well-wishers. The press was barred.

And for good reason. For in trooped such Democratic "bosses" as Charley Buckley and such labor leaders as John J. O'Rourke, president of the New York Teamsters. What was extraordinary about O'Rourke's presence was that in his book, *The Enemy Within,* Bobby had blasted him as "a Hoffa-Dio friend."

"O'Rourke is the Teamster voice in New York today and he is the man on whom the responsibility falls for ridding the Teamsters Union of 'The Mob.' He isn't capable of doing the job. In May, 1959, he himself was indicted on charges of conspiracy, coercion and extortion in connection with the juke-box business in New York. . . . Before I left he promised that he would take specific steps to get rid of one particularly corrupt Teamster in the New York area. He didn't keep his word."

One intrepid photographer managed to sneak into the Harriman apartment and photographed Bobby huddling with various cigar-chewing characters. But he was forced to give up his film. And after that experience, Boss Buckley decided to stay away. As Bobby himself put it following Buckley's death, "When I was running for the Senate, he refused to see me, to pose for pictures with me, anything like that. 'I want you to win,' he said. 'You have to stay away from me.' "

Later in the afternoon, the Kennedys turned up at a reception given by the New York delegation. Thousands had literally fought their way into a modest-sized ballroom in the Ritz-Carlton. Extra guards were hastily posted and at one point no one—even with a ticket—was permitted in. Columnist Mary McGrory, unable to obtain admission, telephoned Steve Smith, who escorted Miss McGrory and several other correspondents past a heavyset, perspiring guard. Miss McGrory shook her finger at him and declared, "You know what you're going to do? You're going to keep him from getting elected."

Celebrities were everywhere. The New York *Post's* publisher Dorothy Schiff tried to converse with the ubiquitous Arthur Schlesinger, Jr.; Mrs. Anne (Henry II) Ford and her daughters rubbed elbows with people not in the Social Register. Also present were Serge Obolensky, leader of the "Russian Rat Pack," Eddie Fisher, Carmine De Sapio and Steelworkers President David J. McDonald.

Quieting the crowd briefly, Bobby shouted, "This is very well organized as it is now, and I hate to change it. But we're going to try to have a receiving line." And finally such a line was formed, with Bobby, Ethel and Mayor Wagner shaking hands for two hours.

Asked by reporters how Bobby would treat the "carpet-bagging" issue, Ethel evidenced annoyance. She noted that her husband had spent twenty out of his thirty-eight years in New York. She tried hard to think where Bobby went to school in New York, then exclaimed in exasperation, "I hate facts." Nor did Ethel know too much about their home in Glen Cove, Long Island, which Bobby had rented as a New York residence. Steve Smith had told her, she said, it had "lots of rooms . . . you know . . . and a big lawn."

Probably the happiest man at the reception was Averell Harriman, whose boyish enthusiasm about the Kennedy candidacy made him appear, in the eyes of some jaded observers, "a silly old man." As he stood coatless near the receiving line, perspiration reaching even the knot of his tie, he waved happily to his friends in the press. Asked about Bobby's chances, he replied, "You have the answer here. We haven't had such a voice in the Senate since Herbert Lehman."

Bobby was supposed to leave that evening for Washington. Instead, he idled in the Harriman suite for two hours, while his advisers debated whether or not he should take the convention by storm that night in an effort to obtain the Vice Presidential nomination. Those present included Mrs. Harriman; Steve Smith; Walter B. Coleman, who ordinarily accompanied Mayor Wagner on his rounds but who had stuck with Bobby since his arrival that afternoon; former Ambassador to New Zealand and Mrs. Anthony B. Akers; William vanden Heuvel; Theodore White; and Peter Crotty, the Buffalo boss.

In the end, Bobby decided against the move.

Thursday was Kennedy's big day. It had begun with appearances at breakfast of six state delegations—Kentucky, West Virginia, California, Illinois, Wisconsin and New York. Almost everywhere Bobby said the same things, told the same jokes, and evoked the same hearty responses. He told the delegations to back the Johnson-Humphrey ticket as the best way to perpetuate the ideals and programs of his brother. He repeated the joke about the astronaut who feared that when he got to the moon he would be called a "carpetbagger." The issue, obviously, was weighing on his mind.

Jacqueline Kennedy finally made her long-awaited appearance. Again there was a mob scene at a reception given in her honor by Ambassador Harriman. Bobby stood by her side as Jackie—tanned and fresh from a Mediterranean vacation—greeted almost 6,000 delegates and guests. Actor Frederic March read some of JFK's favorite prose and poetry—including Alan Seeger's poem that begins, "I have a rendezvous with Death/At some disputed barricade. . . ."

Jackie said very little, but when she spoke her words typified the Kennedy line. In her soft, whispery voice, she said, "Thank all of you for coming—all of you who helped President Kennedy in 1960. May his light always shine in all parts of the world."

Lyndon Johnson was temporarily forgotten, and the day was to end in an emotional scene, the likes of which had never before been seen at any National Convention.

For sixteen minutes, 5,000 delegates and alternates stood and cheered after Washington's Senator Jackson introduced Bobby. Wave upon wave of cheering and applause surged over the huge auditorium as Bobby occasionally uttered, "Mr. Chairman—" Then came shouts of *We want Bobby!* After ten minutes of this, a Texas delegate grumbled to Mary McGrory, "He's a resourceful young man; he could stop this if he wanted to."

But Bobby quite obviously did not want to. Some delegates said it was really an outburst of affection for the slain President and sympathy for his family. "It was a means of expressing the feeling, emotion and sentiment for the great tragedy, the assassination of President Kennedy," observed Governor John Connally of Texas. "I think this was the way they had to show it."

In front of the Massachusetts delegation was the Texas delegation, most of whose members sat reading newspapers as the rest of the gigantic throng whooped it up. Then Joan Kennedy, who had left her husband Teddy in a Boston hospital to replace Bobby in the Massachusetts delegation, put her hands on the shoulders of a Texan seated in front of her and pretended to try to lift him. It was too much. He got up with a sheepish grin and was joined by the others.

Bobby, looking younger than his years, stood hunched at the podium. Then he began to speak. He thanked the delegates "for all that you did for President John F. Kennedy." His eyes dimming with tears, he went on: "I realize that as an individual we can't just look back, that we must look forward. When I think of President Kennedy I think of what Shakespeare said in *Romeo and Juliet:* ' . . . *when he shall die, / Take him and cut him out in little stars, / And he shall make the face of heaven so fine, / That all the world will be in love with night, / And pay no worship to the garish sun.'* "

Then he introduced the documentary film about his brother which Lyndon Johnson had so cannily rescheduled from the first to the last day of the convention in order to head off any demonstration to force him to take Bobby as his running mate. The film touched what few heartstrings Bobby had left unplunked.

A twenty-minute memorial put together by Wolper Productions, the film was fresh and artfully edited. There was the haunting spectacle of the Presidential funeral and the echo of the dolorous drums. There was JFK at his inauguration ("ask not what your country can do for you"), signing the test-ban treaty and preparing America's defenses during the tense days of the Cuban missile confrontation. Finally, there were intimate scenes of President Kennedy with his children, greeting Caroline and John-John at an airport, trying to get his son to hold a buttercup under his chin.

Between Bobby and the film, the delegates were undone. They let their tears flow one last time. And as Mary McGrory wrote, "They knew that, somehow, a convention totally dominated by Lyndon B. Johnson had been captured by a Kennedy."

Johnson knew it, too. Moments after the film had been completed, the President walked into his special box, from which Bobby had watched the film. As the delegates broke into cheers and the band broke into "Hello, Lyndon," the President shook Bobby's hand. Bobby and Ethel then moved to the rear of the Presidential box, but the President quickly motioned them forward, and they sat in the front row as the evening continued.

Bobby had one more convention to attend, this one at New York's 71st Regiment Armory at 34th Street and Park Avenue. The atmosphere was dank and noisy as the delegates to the New York State Democratic Convention came to choose their candidate.

The nominations began. It fell to Mayor Wagner to put Bobby's name up for consideration. "Let me now be personal and confessional," the Mayor said. "It is no secret that not long ago I entertained some doubts about the wisdom of Mr. Kennedy's being the candidate. . . . In response to those doubts, Mr. Kennedy gave—not to me alone, but to the party and the public—certain commitments. My doubts have been resolved. I think that all doubts should, by now, be dissipated. . . . I believe that Bob Kennedy is clearly our most outstanding candidate. . . ."

As the Mayor spoke, many of his friends were prowling the convention floor, shaking their heads. "They said," R. W. Apple, Jr., reported in the *Times,* "that this was the end of the Mayor's dominant position in state Democratic politics."

The Mayor lashed into Ken Keating as a "false liberal" but one who would be difficult to beat. Wagner described the Senator as "a beater of war drums" who seriously embarrassed "the efforts of President Kennedy to contain and manage the delicate and dangerous situation in Cuba. . . . Senator Keating is no laughing matter. He must be defeated."

Representative Otis G. Pike, Democrat of Suffolk County, nominated Sam Stratton. "Time after time," he said, "we have managed to snatch defeat from the jaws of almost certain victory. Our party in this state has been, is, and will be sick, sick, sick, until we make some changes. There are two paths that we can follow to rebuild and revitalize this party. We can try to build it from the top down, or we can try to build it from the bottom up. . . . To those of you who have said privately, 'I know the principle is wrong, but I think he's a winner,' my candidate would say, sadly, 'I understand.' But principles are like muscles—if you don't use them, they atrophy, they wither and they die."

The delegates were hot, and most of them wanted to get the proceedings over with. In the late afternoon the roll was called. By the time New York County had cast 97 votes for Bobby, the contest was over. The final vote was 968 to 153.

After a twelve-minute ovation, marred only by the raising of signs reading BOSTON NEEDS BOBBY and GO HOME, BOBBY, RFK finally spoke. And from what he said, the Kennedy strategy was clear: He intended to hit the "carpetbagger" issue head on, much in the manner that his brother had used in the religious issue in 1960.

"I grew up in New York, my family has had a home here for forty years and I have lived here a longer period of time than any other place. My work has been in Washington and I have had ties to Massachusetts. . . .

"And despite what has been written and said, my candidacy establishes no precedent. There have been similar cases around the country and even here in New York. The first Senator from the State of New York, Rufus King, was from Massachusetts! And he served this state well.*

"Further, for every citizen who is a New Yorker by birth there is one who is a New Yorker by choice, or whose parents were. I am in the second category, but so was Thomas E. Dewey."

Kennedy served notice that he would attempt to picture his opponents—Senator Keating and the Conservative party candidate, Professor Henry Paolucci of Iona College—as the creatures of Barry Goldwater, somewhat overlooking the fact that Keating had refused to endorse the GOP Presidential nominee.

"I am for Lyndon Johnson," he shouted. "I am against Barry Goldwater. No other candidate for the Senate from New York is willing to make either statement. I do not have to walk a tightrope between my party and my principles."

That the Attorney General had the same appeal to teen-age girls as his brother had had soon became evident. As Bobby left the armory he was mobbed by bystanders, most of them teen-agers, who broke through police lines to get to him. One teeny-bopper stopped abruptly, turned to a friend and shouted happily, "First Peter Lawford and now Bobby Kennedy—this is really too much."

Murray Kempton, a bemused spectator, later commented

---

* The difference was that King had come to New York to get married and not for political reasons. After making his home in New York, he ran for the State Assembly and was elected. Later, he became the first member of the U.S. Senate from New York.

in *The New Republic:* "And so the Democrats of New York have offered the electorate not so much a choice as an echo. It is not an echo against which, in fairness, any man of reason should be asked to run."

21

Campaign 1964

But before the campaign began, Bobby faced the necessary formality of officially resigning as Attorney General. There was the usual exchange of hypocritical letters. Bobby wrote saying how sorry he was to be leaving the President's Cabinet, and the President replied that his regret over the Attorney General's resignation was "tempered with satisfaction" because "you will soon be back in Washington where I can again call upon your judgment and counsel." (As it turned out, Bobby did return but somehow Mr. Johnson never seemed to find it necessary to call upon him for his "judgment and counsel.")

Handshaking at a rally of some 2,500 high-school kids assembled to pay him a farewell tribute made Bobby half an hour late for his farewell appointment with the President. But Lyndon Johnson was still smiling when Bobby walked into the White House with his pregnant wife Ethel. For about an hour they were in seclusion. Little is known about their conversation. Later it was disclosed that, among other things, Bobby had made a strong plea that Nicholas Katzenbach be named as his successor. LBJ said he would think it over.*

Understandably, these were difficult moments for Bobby Kennedy. For nearly three years he had been, next to his

---

* Justice Department sources said at the time that, because of RFK's endorsement, Katzenbach did not stand a chance for the Attorney Generalship. Highly touted for the job was Leon Jaworski, a prominent Houston attorney and close friend of the President. But LBJ, as usual, was to confound the tipsters.

brother, the most powerful man in Washington. Now he was asking a favor of a man whose guts he hated; moreover, of the man who had kept him from the Vice Presidency and whose very presence in the Oval Office reminded him of the tragedy in Dallas. Finally, reporters and photographers were admitted to record the farewell scene. Lyndon sat in his rocker, with Ethel and Bobby—looking uncomfortable on a sofa—on his right. The photographers asked for a handshake picture. Bobby diffidently extended his hand. Johnson rose and extended his. During all of this, not one intelligible word was uttered.

At a brief news conference in the White House driveway, Bobby said, tight-voiced, "We went in and said goodbye to President Johnson. He was very kind to President Kennedy and very kind to me and all those of us who had any dealings with the White House."

Had his working relationship with the White House been changed under LBJ?

"Obviously, there would be a difference—because of the different relationship. . . . He has treated me with the utmost courtesy and the greatest kindness, as he has treated all members of my family."

Well, what about the July 30 confrontation at which LBJ dashed his hopes for the Vice Presidency?

"Too much has already been written about that. . . . And anyway in the John F. Kennedy Library you can read all about it later on."

What about his own designs on the White House?

"I think there's someone there. [It came out 'they-ah' in the reminiscent inflection.] I keep reading that and I never see any statement that he is willing to move out. I think he'll be there for some time."

The next day Bobby was back in New York to launch a whirlwind campaign around the state. Over the Labor Day weekend, he was swamped by hundreds of bathers on Long Island's beaches. Then, in a three-day swing around "the Southern tier," he made fifty-one stops in twenty-one cities, where he got such an overwhelming response that people began to refer to "poor old Ken." And with good reason, for "poor old Ken" could hardly compete with Bobby as a crowd gatherer. Bobby drew 2,000 people to Ken's 24 in Ogdensburg. Tardily arriving just before 1:00 A.M. in Glens Falls,

Bobby found 4,000 people, more than one-fifth the population, waiting for him. It was a nice example of what the Kennedy people liked to call "turning lemons into lemonade."

The crowds appeared to do more screaming than listening. And their median age seemed below the legal voting age. "If I had my way," Bobby invariably told the teen-agers thronging around him, "I'd lower the voting age to six."

The techniques were familiar and reminiscent; when Bobby had been JFK's campaign manager he had often stated that appealing to the emotions was basic to political success. The recruiting of screaming, screeching youngsters, the deliberate exploitation of the good looks of the numerous Kennedys, the use of "jumpers and shriekers" were all part of deliberate planning. The idea was to ensure turnouts so overwhelming that the opposition would be demoralized.

But such distinguished columnists along the campaign trail as Robert G. Spivack and Marquis Childs wondered whether he was getting anywhere with this approach. "A highly emotional campaign of little substance" was the way Spivack described it, and Marquis Childs made these comments: "No one except the Beatles stirs up such frenzy as Bobby Kennedy. . . . But the question he himself asks—how much does it mean?—gets at the heart of the matter. Around him is the aura of the fallen leader. . . ."

No doubt, of all Bobby's assets, none was more important than his name. It evoked memories that were warm, alive and deeply emotional. And there were times when he sounded so much like his slain brother that it was almost eerie.

But Bobby was now a celebrity in his own right. His image had been established by appearances on the Jack Paar television show—the personality that seemed so boyish, shy, and troubled about the ills of mankind. His face appeared etched with tragedy—and women's hearts went out to him.

"I love being with Bobby and seeing how the crowds react to him," said Ethel Kennedy. "It's very exciting and wonderful, he can stir such magic. It really is sort of like the Beatles."

But Marquis Childs observed: "Thoughtful individuals who would ordinarily vote Democratic have doubts. They feel the Kennedy candidacy has been too abruptly and crudely stage-managed. The feeling is related to doubts about the candidate's character—he is too ambitious, too ruthless, overly zealous."

In a typical short appearance he did not even bother to debate Keating's record, as the Republican incumbent had urged him to do. Instead, he would shout, "I am for President Johnson!" (*Applause.*) "I am for Senator Humphrey!" (*More applause.*) "I am against Goldwater!" (*Tremendous applause.*) Or he would claim he was the only senatorial candidate willing to say he was against Goldwater. Technically this was true since Keating, despite his failure to back the Republican candidate, did not indulge in anti-Goldwater speeches, and the third candidate, Professor Henry Paolucci, fielded by the Conservative party as a last-minute substitute for Clare Boothe Luce, was an ardent Goldwater supporter.

Keating would hit back, again and again, telling his audiences, "If my opponent isn't good enough for President Johnson—a man he knows well and who knows him—he isn't good enough for the people of New York, whom he knows hardly at all."

Invariably, Bobby would invoke the aura of his brother's ideals, referring to John F. Kennedy at least two dozen times in a typical twenty-minute oration. Statistics, classical quotations, artful local references, appeals to "face up to our problems" tumbled out in breathless volleys.

"But," commented the Albany *Times-Union* on September 10, "there were few specifics about what Bobby Kennedy can do for New York that Ken Keating hasn't already done and can't do better in the next six years. Indeed, some legislative goals Kennedy favors were being fought for on the Congressional battleground by Ken Keating while Bobby still served on a Senate committee staff."

Rarely were the Kennedy crowds carried away by the candidate's oratory. "Usually they pay little attention to what he says," Homer Bigart reported in *The New York Times*. "They have come out to see him and, if possible, touch him. He can evoke shrieks of pleasure from women and girls, who predominate in the crowds, simply by running his hand through his tousled hair."

That Bobby was campaigning more on personality than on ideas was obvious. Why get involved with issues when the polls showed him a runaway winner against Keating? Despite the upstate Republican's many years of service in the state, he was far less recognizable to the public. Besides, the Democrats plus the Liberal party (which had quickly endorsed Bobby) gave him a heavy voting edge.

And, of course, there was the fledgling Conservative party, which was feeling its oats. Its little-known candidate was draining off votes from Keating. The Conservatives were angry with Keating for failing to support Goldwater.

If Keating faced opposition from the Right, his opponent faced dissension on the Left. Gore Vidal and television reporter Lisa Howard established a spirited group called "Democrats for Keating" and soon enlisted 120 prominent people anxious to defeat Bobby. Among them were actor Paul Newman; Niagara Falls Mayor E. Dent Lackey; Mrs. Marshall Field; *Nation* editor Carey McWilliams; movie producer Joseph L. Mankiewicz; Mrs. Agnes E. Meyer; television impresario David Susskind; Robert K. Bingham, then managing editor of *The Reporter;* actor Walter Abel; Bill Todman of Goodson-Todman Productions; authors Barbara Tuchman and Joseph Heller; and—of all people—historian Arthur Schlesinger, Sr.*

In a statement announcing the formation of Democrats for Keating, Vidal and Miss Howard asserted: "We cannot, in good conscience, support Robert Kennedy for the Senate seat from New York. We believe that one of the great myths of current American politics is the widespread belief that Robert Kennedy is a liberal. We believe he is anti-liberal and disturbingly authoritarian. . . . In the weeks ahead, our Committee will work to bring these facts to the attention of New York voters."

One of the facts the committee brought to public attention concerned actor Paul Newman, whom Bobby had wanted to play his counterpart in a film version of *The Enemy Within.* But when Newman told Kennedy he was going to narrate a documentary film based on the Army-McCarthy hearings entitled *Point of Order,* Bobby castigated him and said that

---

* Arthur Schlesinger, Jr., without direct reference to his distinguished father, had this to say in a letter to *The New Republic:* "I despair of persuading those who have hopelessly committed themselves to the devil theory of Robert Kennedy. I can only remind them that many of them were saying exactly the same things about his brother in 1959–60. Events, I believe, convinced them once that they were wrong, and I am sure that events will convince them again; but how many times do we all have to go through this experience?"

Newman knew nothing of what went on during the McCarthy era. A quarrel ensued.

Then there were the immortal words of Jack Newfield (a future Bobby biographer) in an article published in the Socialist *New America:* "I think Kennedy, if elected, would reshape the New York State Democratic Party in his own image. It is not that he will back the bosses in the factional fight with the Reformers, but that he will import his own people—and family—from New England and Washington—like FDR Jr.—and anoint the most opportunistic elements of both factions as his deputies. . . . I have covered Kennedy on the stump twice within the past week and found him dull intellectually, and dependent on his brother's legend and on schoolboy charisma for his appeal. I think he would make a middling Democratic Senator—like Ribicoff or Muskie—bereft of creativity or independence, and overly intent on building a national organization loyal to him and his inevitable bid for the White House."

Bobby's response to his detractors was this: "These people hate everything and everybody, even each other."

But he did not give up trying to win over the liberals to his cause. Arthur Schlesinger, Jr., at Bobby's request, was holding forth before liberal audiences, trying to cajole the reluctant to fall into line.

Schlesinger, joined by John Kenneth Galbraith, turned up to rally the "intellectual vote" at a party given by Bill vanden Heuvel at his West Side digs in the grand old Dakota apartment house. Everybody was there, or at least some seventy luminaries including John Gunther, Paddy Chayefsky, Leonard Bernstein, Lauren Bacall, Gloria Vanderbilt and Abe Burrows. And last but not least, Jacqueline Kennedy.

Schlesinger made one of his shorter addresses, and the audience seemed to enjoy every hour of it. "I am here in the absence of Gore Vidal to make some remarks about Bobby Kennedy," Artie began. He emphasized the fact that Senator Keating was no intellectual, leaving the implication that Bobby was. And he cited numerous historical precedents to demonstrate that carpetbaggers often make good senators.

Jackie Kennedy, hardly able to suppress a yawn, slipped away before Galbraith was introduced. Towering and listing to one side, the six-foot-eight former Ambassador to India said that while he would have put the words "more eloquently and cogently," he was certain that "in your heart you know Arthur's right."

Before the evening was over, Arthur Kopit, the young playwright (*Oh Dad, Poor Dad*), made it loudly clear that he was for Keating. George Plimpton, editor of *Paris Review*, shoved Kopit over a sofa. "You see, the swimming-pool syndrome is still with us," quipped Kopit, as he stuffed his cigar into Plimpton's drink.

From the beginning, the Kennedy campaign had all the earmarks of improvisation. Bill Haddad, Bobby's official link to liberals, told a reporter that "everything is being done on the run. This campaign got started very late and it's very disorganized." So disorganized, in fact, that there was at least one miscalculation: Bobby's "nostalgic visit" to his boyhood home in the Riverdale section of the Bronx.

Reporters and photographers rushed to the two-story house overlooking the Hudson River, and Bobby showed up with his three-year-old nephew John-John in tow. He explained he wanted the youngster, who was carrying a red stuffed dolphin, to see the house his father once lived in and to visit the nearby Roman Catholic church where he had been confirmed.

But this attempt to remove the carpetbagging issue from the campaign misfired. Republicans, needless to say, were outraged. And some Democrats privately agreed Bobby was exploiting the late President's son. The candidate knew he had blundered. He did not argue the point.

David Susskind declared, "Bobby Kennedy's running for the Senate is not only an immoral grab for power, but his using his late brother's son in the campaign is a terrible violation of good taste. Anybody who cannot see this for what it is is a dolt."

Jack English, the Nassau County Democratic leader, thought the criticism unfair. "It wasn't that way at all," English asserted. "He isn't the type of man who would exploit any child—least of all his brother's. You have to understand the man to understand why he would take that child on such a trip. He feels that he must be a father to Jack's children. He has taken over the role completely. He handles their finances and Jackie's, too. She has to lean on him, and because he is the kind of man he is, he willingly accepts the responsibility. I just think that he felt he was neglecting Jack's children because of the campaign and decided to take one morning out and give John-John an airing."

"Well," responded Averell Harriman, "whether he meant it or not, it was stupid, pretty damned stupid."

As a result of this episode, Bobby decided against bringing Jacqueline Kennedy openly into the campaign. He had asked leading Democrats what they thought of the idea, and most were opposed. But Bobby's wife, three sisters, and mother poured tea for, drank coffee with, made speeches to, shook hands with, signed autographs for, and were "at home" to an estimated 60,000 New York women. The star, as always, was Mrs. Joseph P. Kennedy. At one reception in a New York hotel ballroom, Rose introduced her son by commenting that she could tell many things about him, but now she would only say that Bobby worked very, very hard.

"You know," Bobby replied, "my brother Jack and I never wanted to appear on a platform with her, because she's the real campaigner. She's been campaigning for something like seventy-two years. . . . Was it for Grover Cleveland's Administration or maybe Lincoln's that you began, Mother?"

One Sunday Bobby unexpectedly left the reviewing stand and joined a parade of some 100,000 Polish-Americans celebrating Pulaski Day. Ken Keating remained in the stands and viewed Bobby's exhibition with obvious distaste. As did the man in charge, Francis J. Wazeter, head of the Polish-American Congress. He explained that in the twenty-eight-year history of the parade no political candidate not of Polish birth or extraction had ever marched. "Mr. Kennedy," Wazeter told reporters, "has been the first one for purely selfish political reasons to break this tradition."

Bobby's response was that such comments were to be expected from a Goldwater Republican. Moreover, he claimed he had been invited by his Polish neighbors in Glen Cove to march with them. A week later, Bobby turned up at another Pulaski Day celebration, this one in Buffalo.

Probably the most ridiculous statement Bobby issued in the campaign was one in commemoration of the eightieth anniversary of the birth of Eleanor Roosevelt.

"Mrs. Roosevelt was a generous friend, a candid adversary and a grand American," said Bobby. "When she died a great light went out all around the world."

Noting that President Roosevelt had given his father "his

first opportunity for public service," he added, ". . . the ideals of progressive democracy which President and Mrs. Roosevelt so superbly embodied were deeply formative influences on the lives of my brothers, my sisters and myself."

Many extraordinary things are said to win votes—but this was probably the most extraordinary.

John, Eleanor Roosevelt's youngest son, said he resented Bobby's "use of my mother's name for his selfish ends and the implication that she would have sanctioned his candidacy for the U.S. Senate." Added Republican Roosevelt, "I recall that in the 1960 Presidential campaign, in one of the few meetings Robert Kennedy ever had with my mother, he subjected her and her longtime ally in the cause of good government, Herbert Lehman, to the arrogance and rudeness for which he is so well known."

The Kennedy campaign, of course, was well fueled with funds. Money was no problem, a top Kennedy adviser explained. "I think it's significant that we haven't got around to appointing a campaign treasurer yet." And early in the campaign, two separate but duplicate campaign organizations came into being in New York, one guided by Steve Smith, the other by Edwin Weisl, Lyndon Johnson's chief operative in the state.

The Smith operation was an elaborate one dominated by old family friends and former associates. Working directly under Smith were Carmine Bellino, Bobby's accountant-investigator of labor-rackets days; Dave Hackett; James S. Ottenberg, an early theoretician in the Reform Democratic movement, who was now in charge of the voter-registration drive; and Thomas Corcoran, a nephew of the "Tommy the Cork" of New Deal days and operator of a ski school in Aspen, Colorado.

Quartered separately in three suites at the Chatham Hotel were William vanden Heuvel, who was responsible for drafting position papers on major issues; Milton Gwirtzman, a lawyer-turned-speech-writer; press director Debs Meyers and ex-newscaster Tom Costigan who handled radio and television. Lem Billings acted as liaison man with Papert, Koenig, Lois Inc., the avant-garde advertising agency retained by the candidate.

"We'll show the candidate talking on street corners and in natural situations," said Frederic Papert, the agency's chairman. "No studios. No gimmicks. No 'creativity.' We want to reveal the man, not conjure up an image."

Directing the scheduling operation out of the Chatham were Justin Feldman, a New York lawyer active in Democratic politics, and Joe Dolan, who had been Bobby's administrative assistant in Washington. Under them were seven regional coordinators including Walter Sheridan, who had been in charge of the "Get Hoffa" operation in the Justice Department. Also, there were thirteen advance men—who went into a city four or five days before Bobby to prepare the ground for him. And generally to be found with Bobby as he traveled on the family plane, the *Caroline,* were Edwin O. Guthman, his Justice Department press secretary; Bernard J. Ruggieri, formerly Mayor Wagner's legislative assistant; and Dean Markham, a Harvard football teammate and an old friend.

Markham's job was to get Bobby through crowds, while Ruggieri provided data on the areas the candidate was visiting. (In the campaign's early days, the candidate's lack of knowledge of local conditions was appalling. On a visit to Fire Island, the candidate was forced to ask a local politician just what county he was in.)

And operating out of a floor at 730 Fifth Avenue was the research program directed by William Haddad, where dozens of lawyers, journalists and assorted researchers were put to work scouring Ken Keating's voting record over the many years. Their object was to destroy the Senator's credentials as a liberal. Eventually the numerous research papers were combined to form a study entitled "The Myth of Keating's Liberalism."

The first genuine issue to creep into the contest had to do with the controversy over long-distance bussing to achieve school integration. Senator Keating, asked about his position, said that while "everyone knows I am a strong advocate of racial integration in the schools," he was "opposed to compulsory bussing of children long distances from their neighborhoods."

Not to be outdone, Bobby chimed in with a statement contending "it doesn't make sense to move children from one place to another and bring down the level of education so that everyone is more equal."

The reference to making people "more equal" aroused

enough civil rights advocates to compel Bobby's aides to claim misquotation; except there had been no misquotation, only clumsiness.

"We regret," editorialized the New York *Post*, "that Mr. Kennedy did not follow his original instinct and steer clear of involvement in what he described as a 'local matter.'"

Meanwhile, the Keating people were busy too, mounting an all-out offensive against the "opportunistic, arrogant carpetbagger, seeking to exploit New York in pursuit of ruthless Presidential ambition."

Bobby sought to answer suspicions that he regarded the Senate election merely as a stepping-stone to the Presidency.

"Let's assume that I want to be President of the United States," he told students at the University of Rochester. "In the first place, truthfully now, I can't go any place in 1968. We've got President Lyndon Johnson . . . and I think he's going to be re-elected in 1968.

"Now we get to 1972. That's eight years. Assume that I am still using it [the Senate seat] as a power base. I'm going to have to be re-elected in six years.

"If I'm re-elected—if I have done such an outstanding job and I really want to be President, I'm going to have to do a tremendous job for the State of New York, for the people of the State of New York. . . . Then, if I have done such an outstanding job in eight years that people just demand all over the country that I be a Presidential candidate, I don't see how New York suffers."

One thing Keating had going for him was an understanding of New York's complicated ethnic mixture. Bobby was unable to develop the instincts that Keating possessed after eighteen years' experience. In Jewish areas, for example, Keating had long been a familiar figure. It was often said that the Senator carried a *yarmulke* (skullcap used in Hebrew rites) in his pocket. He seemed to enjoy sampling kosher hot dogs, pickles and cheese blintzes on his walking tours. One sign greeting him on the lower East Side read: KEATING AND ISRAEL GO TOGETHER LIKE BAGELS AND LOX.

Bobby candidly told Homer Bigart of *The New York Times* that political leaders in heavily Jewish neighborhoods had warned him to expect moderate-to-heavy Jewish defections. The extraordinary thing was that four years earlier New York's 2,500,000 Jews had given nearly 90 percent

of their votes to his brother. There were a number of explanations. For one thing, Ken Keating had long been interested
in Jewish affairs—attending hundreds of bar mitzvahs and
ground-breaking ceremonies, and speaking out forcefully on
Israel and the plight of Soviet Jewry. "Jews consider Keating
a *gute goy*—a good Gentile with nothing behind his sleeves,"
a Yiddish journalist observed. "How do you repay a man
like that—with stones?"

Furthermore, many Jews looked on Bobby as a ruthless
young man. Moreover, he tended to remind people of his
father. "Jews liked Jack Kennedy because he reminded them
of Franklin D. Roosevelt," claimed one ethnic expert. "Bobby
doesn't really remind them of anyone they like. He may be
on the right side—but that's all."

So Bobby went out of his way to court the Jewish vote.
He also turned up, wearing a *yarmulke*. And he learned how
to eat blintzes.

"Where Bobby Kennedy goes completely wrong," wrote
columnist Robert Spivack, "is in thinking he can impress
Jewish voters by saying that in 1948 he stood atop a tank
during the Palestinian hostilities, or by now saying that he
agrees with those at the Ecumenical Council who wish to
exonerate modern Jews for responsibility in the execution
of Christ. Such an appeal is so obvious it is offensive."

Keating, meanwhile, played on Jewish suspicions by charging that Kennedy, while Attorney General, had made a "deal"
to sell off part of the Government-held General Aniline &
Film Corporation's assets to a Swiss holding company once
operated by Germany's I. G. Farben, a notorious exploiter
of Jewish slave labor. Keating had instead proposed selling
the assets—some $200,000,000 worth—to private U.S. inter-
ests.

Bobby immediately branded the charge a "smear" and demanded an apology. But, as Spivack noted, "If Senator
Keating was totally or partially wrong, one might have
thought Kennedy would welcome a chance to show him up
and explain in detail just what the settlement involved.
Senator Keating is certainly within his rights in insisting that
Mr. Kennedy cannot just run on his brother's record; his
own record as Attorney General, including other possible out-
of-court settlements, are proper subjects of campaign comment."

At the same time Bobby was reported to be running into as many problems with Italians as with Jews. A *New York Times* survey indicated that Kennedy's role, as Attorney General, in releasing testimony by a notorious hoodlum named Joseph Valachi had placed undue emphasis on gangsters with Italian names. Italian-American organizations accused Bobby Kennedy of possessing an alleged anti-Italian bias.

Political analysts in the Keating camp were convinced that their man was profiting from anti-Bobby resentment in the Italian community, so Keating stepped up his attack. The Senator accused his Democratic opponent of having "directed the entire thing" on the Valachi hearings as a "publicity stunt."

On October 12—Columbus Day—Bobby angrily counter-attacked in Buffalo. He said that Keating's efforts to picture him as the villain in the televised crime hearing was typical of the Senator's "hit-and-run" tactics throughout the campaign. He said that Keating had demonstrated this tactic first "by accusing me of making deals with Nazis, then of accusing me of a sellout of the Negroes and of being anti-Italian." Bobby heatedly denied that he was responsible for the Valachi hearings. "These hearings were held by a Senate committee. . . . I had no basis on which to make a refusal. Such witnesses are always furnished to Senate committees."

"Kennedy," reported Frank Lynn in the New York *World-Telegram & Sun*, "has been portrayed as 'a friend' in Jewish areas and remained silent on the subject in non-Jewish neighborhoods; he has sung 'We Shall Overcome' in Negro areas and remained silent on civil rights upstate and he has let loose with the Polish song '*Stolat*' in Polish areas."

Many liberals, who had never voted for a Republican before, announced they would cast their ballots for both Ken Keating and Lyndon Johnson. One of them was the noted civil libertarian Morris Ernst, who wrote in *The Villager*:

"I'm in trouble. . . . I have concluded, for the first time in a half century, that I have not the heart to support my party candidate. Even though many think he was an efficient Attorney General I am sorely troubled because Robert Kennedy, more than any local official in my lifetime, has been an enemy of Due Process. . . .

"A lad of arrogant ambition, ruthless and shrewd, believing in the evil concept of winning for winning's sake, has decided to be our Senator. . . . I sense no popular demand for him. Even if he were familiar with our local societal standards, I would resent the mere arrogance of his attempt to capture a political party of our State. . . . I look with disdain on his disavowal of his first and greatest local backer, Congressman Buckley; I will never know what naïveté drove Wagner to think that if Bobby wins the Senatorship, he would not own the Democratic Party in New York, and use it to grab other gold rings on the Bobby-go-round. He is the same Robert Kennedy who was a lawyer on the staff of Senator McCarthy at the peak of the Senator's knifing of Due Process."

By October, Bobby knew he was in a fight for his political life. The easy victory the early polls had indicated now appeared to be slipping away. A great deal of sympathy appeared to be building up for the genial Keating as he doggedly campaigned from one end of the state to the other. And on October 14, R. W. Apple, Jr., reported in the *Times* that Robert F. Kennedy had radically changed the tenor of his campaigning. "No longer does his campaign have the flavor of a personal-appearance tour by a movie star; no longer does he seem to be relying on glamour and nostalgia to win votes; no longer is he reluctant to comment on his opponent's record."

Now Bobby no longer campaigned alone but toured with such Democratic stalwarts as Adlai E. Stevenson, W. Averell Harriman and Mayor Wagner. And major figures in the Truman, Kennedy and Johnson Administrations were asked to help counter the support of Keating by Dwight Eisenhower, Tom Dewey and Dick Nixon. An endorsement by Harry S Truman was released, and it was remarkable because it scarcely mentioned Kennedy. The statement merely stressed the importance of having "a Senator of his own party representing the key state of New York. Senator Wagner was a strong right arm to President Roosevelt, and Senator Lehman was always at my side no matter how rough the going."

But the real tipoff on Kennedy's plight was a change in campaign posters. In the early weeks of the campaign, they had read: LET'S PUT ROBERT KENNEDY TO WORK FOR NEW YORK. Now they exhorted voters to GET ON THE JOHNSON-HUMPHREY-KENNEDY TEAM and photographs showing Johnson and Kennedy shaking hands suddenly made their appearance at Kennedy headquarters.

All this was bitter medicine for Bobby Kennedy to swallow. But the truth was that Bobby's touch-and-go chances depended in substantial part on how wholeheartedly Lyndon Johnson worked in his behalf. "After spending several days around New York State and in the city," wrote Marguerite Higgins, "it is perfectly plain that Bobby's chances are being hurt by the not-so-subtle whispering campaign to the effect that LBJ would be secretly delighted to see the Kennedy clan take a trouncing. Everywhere in the state, a visitor runs into this contention that LBJ is really gunning for a Johnson-Keating victory."

Bobby needed Lyndon (who, the polls indicated, would win by a landslide in New York) and Lyndon knew it. This, of course, was the irony of ironies. And the President reveled in the thought. He had not forgotten Bobby's argument that he was needed on the national ticket to help re-elect Johnson President.

Actually, Johnson would not have been overly distressed had Bobby been knocked out of the box. The President not only disliked Bobby but he liked Ken Keating and hated to see him ousted from the Senate by "the young snot." A tip-off on the President's attitude was that when Bobby asked Daniel Patrick Moynihan, an Assistant Secretary of Labor, to come to New York to help out on the problem of minorities, he wasn't in New York twenty-four hours before he was ordered back to Washington, ostensibly to assist with LBJ's own efforts.

But when the S O S came through, LBJ decided to go to New York. It was not the most pleasant of tasks. As Marianne Means, of Hearst Headline Service, reported: "President Johnson went into New York State although he was certain to carry it big himself and did not really need to appear at all. He stood with Robert Kennedy in the spots where Kennedy needed it most. And after the Johnson visit, the polls showed Kennedy's popularity on the rise.

"President Johnson did not help Robert Kennedy . . . because he suddenly developed a liking for him. Lyndon Johnson helped Robert Kennedy for an entirely personal reason. He did it out of memory of John F. Kennedy.

" 'I paid him back,' he explains simply."

As Election Day neared, Bobby launched a massive assault on Keating. He declared, "It is instructive to note that Senator Keating's record surpassed in conservatism even that of Georgia's Senator Talmadge and Louisiana's Senator Ellender. . . . Keating sat back without doing anything while America saw a major political party captured by extremists of the Right." Exactly what Bobby thought Keating should have done about the nomination of Barry Goldwater he did not explain. The fact was that if anyone "captured" a nomination it was Bobby Kennedy.

Then the Kennedy people hit at Keating with newspaper advertisements reading: BY RIGHT-WING STANDARDS, KEATING IS AN ULTRA-CONSERVATIVE. The ads berated Keating for not having rejected an "award" in 1961 from Americans for Constitutional Action, the right-wing counterpart of Americans for Democratic Action. A subhead read: MR. KEATING CHOOSES TO FORGET HIS RIGHT-WING AWARD.

As Bruce Felknor, then executive director of the Fair Campaign Practices Committee, later noted in his book *Dirty Politics:* "It has been suggested that indexes often are misleading: Keating's ACA conservatism rating has been exceeded on occasion by the Administration's leader in the Senate, Mike Mansfield, among others. To paint a man as an ultra-conservative by rummaging in his past until one finds so flimsy a support for the charge is dishonest enough, but this episode was simply one hit-and-run assault in a long series."

There were charges that Keating had been *against* aid to education, *lukewarm* toward the nuclear test-ban treaty, *against* area redevelopment legislation, minimum wage law extension, school lunches, drug price legislation, Federally aided public housing, and that Keating had never "added a comma" to the Civil Rights Act of 1964.

"The distortions of the Keating record," wrote Felknor, "were accomplished with such facility, and such economy of documentation, that they bear close inspection, for they amount to a classic example of how to use isolated excerpts of an incumbent opponent's record against him."

Picking an opponent's selected votes and declaring that they are the rule, rather than the exception, is of course an old political trick. Senator Javits commented "about this practice of selecting a handful of isolated votes out of hundreds, generally on complicated amendments, in an effort to discredit a Senator's whole record. Any legislator's public record can be besmirched by such a tactic. One could say, for example, that in 1963 Senator Humphrey voted on the same side of an issue with Senator Goldwater on forty-seven occasions! It is true, but what does it prove without accurately specifying the issues and the situation on each vote?"

What Javits described as "a reckless disregard for facts" was pinpointed by a document called "The Myth of Keating's Liberalism." Millions of copies of this document were finally distributed and, apparently, it had a considerable impact on New York's liberal-minded voters.

"Keating has opposed federal aid to education since 1947," the leaflet read. "In 1961 he voted to deny $2.55 billion for teachers' salaries and school construction." True, Keating had voted against this bill. But in so doing, as he explained at the time, he felt it cheated New York of its fair share of Federal funds, and that it did nothing to prevent Southern states from using its grants to perpetuate segregation in the schools. A scrutiny of the record shows that Keating, in fact, had supported one amendment and offered another himself to correct what he called "fatal flaws."

Another absurd Kennedy contention was that neither Keating nor his colleague, Senator Javits, had "added a comma" to the Civil Rights Act of 1964. While these two outspoken legislators may not have added a *comma,* the record clearly demonstrates that much of the ultimate language of the act was introduced by the two New York Senators in seventeen civil rights bills they jointly introduced in the 87th and 88th Congresses. Moreover, both were loudly praised by Democratic Majority Leader Mike Mansfield for their roles in obtaining its passage.

Also extraordinary was the claim that Keating had voted against a Kefauver amendment on "dangerous and overpriced drugs." This was a plain falsehood. First of all, the amendment was tabled, not voted down. And the motion to table was offered by the Democratic Majority Leader. Also significant was the fact that the amendment was not included in President Kennedy's own recommendations to strengthen the drug bill. The plain fact is that Keating voted both to release the Kefauver bill from the Judiciary Committee on which he served, and for its final passage on the floor of the Senate.

The Reporter, a magazine of informed liberalism, was aghast at what the Kennedy "mythmakers" were trying to do to Ken Keating. In its pre-election issue, it proclaimed in part: "The considerable talents of the persons who have been putting out this sort of baloney in behalf of the former Attorney General have also been used to make Mr. Kennedy look like the greatest civil libertarian since Justice Hugo L. Black. But we have a judgment from the American Civil Liberties Union on his first two years as Attorney General:

" 'Capitol Hill observers cannot recall any previous effort of such intensity by any administration for wiretap legislation.'

"We also have it from the record that while the Attorney General was pushing for unsupervised wiretapping, Keating was pushing for bills with judicial safeguards. None of this seems unduly troubling to the Kennedy camp's litterateurs. Our favorite example is a recent brochure that does in fact make mention of Kennedy's bill to legalize wiretapping. It is called: 'Robert Kennedy's Bill to Prohibit Wiretapping.' . . .

"Mr. Kennedy had recently been at pains to point out that he left the McCarthy Committee because he did not approve of its procedures and because he was disappointed that McCarthy himself had not upheld commitments he had given concerning those procedures. He has added that he worked on matters not directly connected with the witch-hunt campaigns. The record again contradicts a good bit of this, and 1953, the year when he joined the committee, was pretty late in the McCarthy game to be accepting the Wisconsin Senator's assurances.

"Still until his campaign against Keating took on its present unsavory quality, we were prepared to assume that Kennedy had come to understand what was amiss in this sort of thing, one of many who just took a long time to do so."

The charge that got the greatest political mileage, however, was Bobby's contention that Keating had ridiculed the nuclear test-ban treaty and had come to its support only when its passage seemed assured. As *The Reporter* observed:

"We counted fourteen separate [Keating] speeches on its behalf prior to passage, a finding that did not surprise us since we recalled that Keating had in fact been one of the co-sponsors in the Senate of the proposed treaty almost two months before it was negotiated in Moscow."

On October 22, Keating wrote a three-page letter to Bruce Felknor of the Fair Campaign Practices Committee, and complained bitterly about Kennedy's "incredible false-hoods." Ironically, the Fair Campaign Practices Committee had already injected itself in the campaign in a manner entirely unrelated to Keating's charges.

A pamphlet entitled "The Strange Death of Marilyn Monroe," written by right-wing "investigator" Frank A. Capell, and replete with references to "sex-depraved V.I.P.s," had just been published. The 71-page document suggested that the glamorous actress's death was not the result of suicide, but rather a murder arranged by Bobby Kennedy (in cahoots with the Communists) after an unsatisfactory affair with Miss Monroe.* And the Fair Campaign group had reason to believe that the Capell pamphlet would be given wide circulation in New York during the Senate campaign. They routinely contacted the Keating people and obtained an immediate and forthright repudiation of the scurrilous document.

Bobby, of course, quickly denied the allegations of distortions contained in Keating's letter. "Everything that I've said about his voting record is documented right out of the Congressional Record," and he added he would "continue to attack" the Keating record.

After studying the documentation provided by Keating, Bruce Felknor got off a strongly worded letter to Bobby: "Mr. Keating has provided documentation of his complaint . . . which demonstrates conclusively that your description of his position on the Test Ban Treaty is not only false and distorted, but also appears to be either a deliberate and cynical misrepresentation or the result of incredible carelessness. . . . I trust you will be able to correct this grievous flaw in your research operation that this dishonest and unfair distortion reveals."

---

* Capell later was forced to apologize to Senator Thomas Kuchel after he and several others had been convicted for a vicious libel of the California Republican.

The letter was personal and confidential and meant for Kennedy's eyes only. But because of a series of unplanned and accidental developments described by Felknor in *Dirty Politics,* it was published in the *New York Herald Tribune* and all hell broke loose.

Finally, the committee—against its better judgment—formally apologized to Kennedy, after withdrawing the Felknor letter, which was trumpeted by Bobby's aides as a complete vindication of Bobby. After the election, in interviews granted the *Times* and *Herald Tribune,* Bobby admitted he would have lost to Keating had the Felknor letter not been withdrawn.

Felknor had this to say in *Dirty Politics:* "The Kennedy-Keating saga should not be construed as a suggestion that the new Senator from New York is personally or deliberately dishonest, any more than any candidate who lets excesses and distortions by his staff represent him in public. But it does suggest that every candidate should be alert to the possibility, the danger, that eager aides, more concerned with scoring points than with presenting facts fully clothed, can make him seem a sophistic, deliberate, and cynical twister of his opponent's record."

Bruce Felknor, of course, was being kind.

By this time, Bobby knew he had won the ball game. The polls, most notably that of the New York *Daily News,* showed him comfortably ahead. Only one problem remained —the question of a face-to-face meeting on television. Both Kennedy and Keating insisted the other was ducking the confrontation. Finally, Keating purchased a half hour of TV time on WCBS. He announced that, in view of Kennedy's unwillingness to debate, he would debate an empty chair with Bobby's name on it.

In turn, Bobby purchased the half hour following Keating in order to reply; then just as Keating was about to go on the air the evening of October 27, he showed up at the CBS studios announcing, "I want to go in and debate Senator Keating."

Norman Kramer, a WCBS-TV official, blocked his way, as he had earlier blocked newsmen wishing to enter the studio. Later, on his own half hour, Bobby said he was shocked at the "political trickery" Keating used in connection with the non-debate.

Bobby was asked, "If you wanted to get in to debate him at 7:30, why didn't you get there at 7:15 before the program was under way?"

"I just thought I'd come at 7:25," Bobby replied. "He said he wanted me there at 7:30 and I was there at 7:30."

"When did you tell CBS you'd be there?"

"I didn't tell them."

"Did you advise Keating you were coming?"

"No," Bobby said, "I did not."

Two hours later, Bobby was breaking up campaign audiences: "There were Javits and Keating on television really giving it to this empty chair. I've never seen either of them better. They kicked that chair all over the room. And there I was trying to get in. But Senator Keating had a guard (or three guards) bar me from the studio."

That this was untrue did not seem to inconvenience the former Attorney General. He was having a grand time ridiculing the dignified Senator Keating. For Keating the episode was a disaster. And the Senator knew it. But he fought gamely to the end.

22

Junior Senator

On election night, the Kennedy family gathered at Jean and Steve Smith's elegant duplex apartment at 950 Fifth Avenue. The candidate was there, watching returns in an upstairs bedroom. He was edgy. It had been a long day for Robert F. Kennedy. He had awakened at 4:00 A.M. in his eleventh-floor suite at the Carlyle and dressed quickly, anchoring his tie with a clip carrying the PT-109 insignia left over from his brother's Presidential campaign. Then, accompanied by two aides, he had ridden through the silent streets of Manhattan for several hours of shaking hands with Democratic precinct workers.

At the Delightful Coffee Shop on 116th Street and First Avenue, a precinct captain jovially told the candidate, "Yaw gonna dew awright here."

"That's what we will find out today," the candidate replied in his flat Boston accent.

True, the polls showed Bobby well ahead. Yet, as the day wore on, the candidate appeared to be under tension. For, as he well knew, the polls had been wrong before. And if they were wrong, his ambitions could be terminated on this day, in a state where they called him an outsider, an interloper and a carpetbagger. A week and a half before Election Day, in a conversation with the late columnist Dorothy Kilgallen, Bobby had wondered out loud, "If I lose, do you think there's some small college that will take me on as a teacher?"

A *Herald Tribune* reporter, Paul Weissman, assigned to follow Bobby around on Election Day, reported the candidate's thoughts as follows: "Had the old criticism that he was a ruthless, arrogant young man stuck? That campaign ad signed by John Roosevelt, saying Eleanor Roosevelt would never have voted for him, would that hurt? The Jewish vote? Did his victory in the non-debate help enough? And the rest of it, all the talk and the screaming teenagers? And IF he won in the end, would it be only a shirt-tail triumph, riding home now behind the Texan they had beaten and then made Vice President in 1960?"

Returning to the Carlyle, Bobby changed his suit and took his family to the Bronx Zoo. The crowds were big and they annoyed him. "Ed," he told press aide Guthman, "this is impossible. I mean they [the children] are not going to get to see anything." But he did not leave until the photographers got pictures of himself and his children at the elephant pit. These would be substituted for the traditional Election Day shots of the candidate entering the voting booth.

Then, in the privacy of his hotel suite, he tried to relax. It was difficult. He could not help recalling that four years ago he had been the center of the hectic activities at Hyannis Port, taking telephone bulletins and sifting scribbled messages. Today the only message was from his eldest daughter Kathleen: "Dear Dad, you better beat Keating—or else!"

Two hours before the polls closed, the candidate was on the move again. He drove to 1040 Fifth Avenue, where he visited Jacqueline Kennedy, left with young John-John and later stopped at his father's apartment at 24 Central Park South. Old Joe had had a bad setback two weeks before, but—as Bobby later told a friend—"he was so excited about the election he had to come to New York, even though he isn't very well."

At 8:15 that night Bobby arrived at the Smiths' apartment. Shortly after the polls closed at 9:00, the first report came in: he was running slightly ahead of Keating but far behind Lyndon Johnson. Averell Harriman, who sensed the uncertainty, shouted to Ethel not to worry; Bobby would win big. But Bobby was not overly certain.

At 9:20, Bobby stood up impatiently. "I can't find out anything here," he announced. He and Ethel headed downtown to the Democratic command post at the Statler-Hilton, where in a suite packed with assorted Kennedys, friends, top-ranking politicos and celebrities, the candidate learned that his lead over Keating was widening.

Brother Ted called from Boston to announce he was receiving 81 percent of the Massachusetts vote. "What I'm doing here," Bobby cracked, "must be rubbing off on you." For the first time that evening, he laughed. He took a call from Pierre Salinger who was trailing in his race with George Murphy in California.

"Of course," chronicled Dorothy Kilgallen the next day, "the private Kennedy suite was a living demonstration of what to wear while waiting for your candidate to win. Eunice Kennedy Shriver was chic in a black top, black and white polka dot skirt, and watermelon pink sash; Jean Kennedy Smith looked lovely in white silk with an aquamarine sash and white satin shoes; Marlene Dietrich looked rather like Mata Hari in black with a velvet headband . . . and [Gary Cooper's daughter] Maria Cooper, busily sketching the scene on a small pad, was encased in a sheath of American beauty satin. Shelley Winters, arriving late, wore a dotted-net hat above a dark crepe dress. When she discovered she did not have a Pierre Salinger emblem among the many campaign buttons arrayed across her neckline, she had a friendly gentleman inscribe 'Pierre Salinger' on her bosom with a ballpoint pen."

A face appeared on the television screen. "I have just sent the following wire to Bob Kennedy," Ken Keating began. The room exploded with cheers. "We made it!" Marlene Dietrich cried out throatily. When Keating finished, Governor Nelson Rockefeller took the microphone to praise the fallen politician. "He ran a million and a half votes over the party—unprecedented."

Bobby smiled. "Gee," he said, "he's making me feel bad."

Everyone laughed. Champagne corks popped. Ethel kissed Bobby. And the tension was over. Shortly afterward a call came from the White House. What Lyndon Johnson told the Senator-elect was never disclosed.

There remained the traditional chore of making a victory statement before party workers assembled in the Grand Ballroom. Though he thanked his helpers all the way down to people who licked envelopes for him, Kennedy failed to thank the man who had done most to make his victory possible—Lyndon Baines Johnson. Nor did he express any gratitude to Hubert Humphrey, who had made a special trip to the garment center to speak in his behalf. As for the leaders of the Liberal party, Alex Rose and David Dubinsky, Kennedy ignored them, too. Then he made it all the worse by calling Dubinsky from an airport to apologize.

In his victory statement Bobby said, "We started something in 1960, and the vote today is an overwhelming mandate to continue." Looking straight at the TV cameras, Bobby concluded, "This is what I dedicate myself to in the next six years."

Kennedy's failure to mention LBJ's name did not go unnoticed. Society columnist Betty Beale of the Washington *Star* was particularly horrified. She conceded that thanking the President for his assistance might not be customary. "But in Bobby's case, in view of the strained relationship between the two and the fact that the President quickly responded to his urgent requests to come to New York and campaign for him, it would have been a gracious thing to express gratitude for his support."

Scripps-Howard columnist Richard Starnes next day labeled Bobby one of "the great coattail riders of history . . ." who "could not have won except for the greatest political convulsion in history."

Still and all, a victory is a victory, no matter how it be fashioned.

Analyzing his loss for the post-election issue of *U.S. News & World Report*, Keating contended that the "decisive factor" in his defeat "was the massive victory by President Johnson, who carried New York State by more than 2.5 million votes—away beyond expectations."

Actually, LBJ carried New York State by a record margin of 2,669,597 votes. The official count was 4,913,156 for Johnson to 2,243,559 for Barry Goldwater. Kennedy defeated Keating by 719,693 votes—3,823,749 to 3,104,056. The Conservative party candidate Henry Paolucci received 212,216 votes.

Obviously Kennedy owed his victory less to his own vote getting than to Lyndon Johnson. Despite the magic of the Kennedy name, he ran over a million votes behind LBJ. Nelson Rockefeller had been correct in contending that the white-thatched Keating had been "rolled under in a national landslide." Or, as *The New York Times* put it in a grudging editorial of congratulations, "[Kennedy] fought hard for the office with toughness and skill, but it was the anti-Goldwater sentiment resulting in a Johnson landslide that carried him to victory. . . ."

Hardly had the last vote been counted, however, when talk of Bobby for President began among newsmen and Kennedy fans. Sputtered Weisl, LBJ's man in New York, "He'll have to prove himself first as a Senator."

Though Bobby concealed his dislike of Weisl, at least publicly, the family's hostility was made manifest in a post-election sum-up by Charles Bartlett, a close friend of the late President Kennedy.

Bartlett described Weisl as "the only significant holdout among top New York Democrats" in all-out support for Kennedy, and continued: "Weisl nurses a dislike for the Kennedys that apparently goes back to a business difference with Joseph P. Kennedy many years ago. Weisl was not always helpful and as he voted Tuesday, he predicted 'more than the usual amount of ticket-splitting' in behalf of Keating.

"But Weisl is a lawyer-businessman and not a politician. It could be said of him, as it was once frequently said of Robert Kennedy, that he does not fully comprehend the useful give-and-take of politics. Kennedy has had a graduate course in politics in recent months. He has blossomed as a campaigner, mellowed in his outlook, and moved in the direction of his brother's philosophy that an enemy is not necessarily an enemy until death."

The "line" that Bobby had changed from a ruthless little monster, mellowing as he more fully understood the foibles of mankind, was one of the poignant little fables assiduously being spread by Kennedy partisans. The only trouble was that it wasn't true.

In a strikingly frank interview given two days before the election on the understanding that it would not be published unless he won, Bobby said of Keating: "If he hadn't attacked me, I would have had a hell of a time with him. If I were him, I would have remained aloof and talked about my record and said, 'Here is this ruthless young man trying to come into this state and take my job.' If he had done that, I don't know what I would have done. He had been very fatherly toward me in Washington, and I couldn't go after him, unless he started in on me first."

In Bobby's view, Keating made three major tactical errors: (1) "making people consider me the underdog"; (2) making "charges that couldn't stick . . . that I made a deal with a huge Nazi cartel . . . that I'd run out on the Negroes"; and (3) appealing too openly for Jewish votes, thereby alienating many Jews who were ready to vote Republican.

Asked what had helped him most, Bobby replied: "the general public impression" that Keating had locked him out of a proposed TV debate, and his own "TV spots showing that I was something more than a Beatle."

Asked about his debate with Keating on the Barry Gray radio show, Bobby had said he hadn't wanted to win. "I just didn't want to lose. The last guy who won a debate was Pierre—he knocked George Murphy all over the studio—and you know what kind of shape he's in now."

"I am convinced that Bobby was the chief factor that beat Pierre," a prominent California Democrat was later quoted in *The New York Times.* "Pierre ran very well in the primary. But the minute Bobby got into the New York race there was a shift in the California situation. . . . Bobby's entrance heightened Californians' sensitivity to a belief that the whole thing was a Kennedy power play. Too many Kennedys and close allies were trying to get into government. Californians decided they didn't want California to be a tail on the Kennedy dog."

Two days after the election Bobby, Mayor Wagner and Senator Javits paid a visit to the Pentagon to urge that there be no more layoffs at the Brooklyn Navy Yard. Javits, who had been invited so that the session might have a bipartisan tone, warned Defense Secretary McNamara, "He [Kennedy] is going to cause you a lot of trouble; he has got to get a lot for New York."

The meeting was the outcome of a campaign pledge Bobby had made to Navy Yard workers. He had assured them that if elected he would quickly talk to McNamara about their jobs. Well, he did see McNamara but apparently failed to convince him. A short while later, McNamara announced he was phasing out not only the Brooklyn Navy Yard but three other military installations in the New York area as well.

So the man who had promised he could "do more for New York" struck out his first time at bat.

After the meeting with McNamara, Bobby drove to Capitol Hill to pay his respects to Congressional leaders. Wagner headed for the *Caroline* to await the flight back to New York. But Bobby remained on the Hill an hour longer than expected, and the Mayor was forced to cool his heels. The "power struggle" had begun.

When the Senate convened, Bobby ranked ninety-eighth in seniority, sixty-seventh among sixty-eight Democrats. But there was little doubt about whom the gallery had come to see be sworn in. Bobby did not look particularly happy when he and Senator Joseph D. Tydings of Maryland were ushered to two rear seats on the Democratic side. "I had better seats for *Hello, Dolly*," he later quipped.

At first, Bobby had only temporary quarters—four rooms of the suite from which he had dislodged Ken Keating. But he decorated them with true flair, putting up paintings by Bernard Buffet and William Walton. He also temporarily displayed a present he had received while in Indonesia—a stuffed, snarling Bengal tiger. But there were too many invidious wisecracks about its resemblance to the Tammany tiger. "Angie," Bobby finally said to his secretary, Angela Novello, "we'll have to get rid of this tigah."

Next day, it was removed.

Bobby's arrival in the Senate was an event for another reason. Senate historians remarked that it was the first time that two brothers had taken the oath of office as Senators together and, moreover, the first pair of brothers to serve together in the Senate since 1803, when the joint tenures of Dwight Foster of Massachusetts and Theodore Foster of Rhode Island ended.

It was Teddy's first appearance in the Capitol since he had broken his back in a plane crash the previous June. He wore a steel brace under his dark blue suit, but his face betrayed no pain, though his injuries had immobilized him for months. With Bobby a step ahead, Teddy moved stiffly but briskly into the caucus room where the Democratic Senators were meeting prior to the noon swearing-in. First to spot Teddy was Mississippi's John Stennis, who bellowed: "Mighty glad to have you back, boy!" Missouri's Stuart

Symington grabbed Teddy's hand and Georgia's Richard Russell walked over to warn him to take care of his back.

Teddy was touched by this outpouring of affection. It was a far cry from the almost hostile reception he had been accorded two years earlier. Then, with few exceptions, the Senators had regarded him as a lucky upstart who had invaded their sacred precincts thanks to the coattails of his brother Jack. Many of them had waited for him to stumble, but the young Senator from Massachusetts had heeded Jack Kennedy's warning. He had kept out of the spotlight, generally avoiding interviews and photographers.

As was traditional, the Kennedy brothers were escorted down the aisle for the swearing-in by colleagues from their home states: Bobby by Jacob K. Javits and Teddy by Leverett Saltonstall, both Republicans. Teddy later played host at a packed reception in his office, while his aides clucked nervously about the strain on his back; Bobby headed for his home in nearby Virginia, where nearly one hundred guests were awaiting him at a buffet lunch.

That night Bobby returned to sit side by side with Teddy during LBJ's State of the Union message. For LBJ it was a memorable effort. He now emerged fully as his own man; it was his first address to Congress that failed to mention John F. Kennedy. "No longer are we called upon to get America moving," he said. "We *are* moving." Here the television cameras picked up the pensive Kennedy brothers applauding haltingly.

The contrast between the two brothers was sharp. Teddy has always been friendly and outgoing; Bobby seemed taut, withdrawn, ill at ease. Occasionally he would attempt to soften that image. At a Women's National Press Club salute to the new Congress, for example, he used humor. "I want to assure you that I have no Presidential aspirations," he said, pausing—"nor does my wife, Ethel Bird."

With the inevitable interviewers, Bobby was guarded and distant. Asked for his impressions of opening day at the Senate, he said, "I was remembering and regretting the situation that gave rise to my being there. That affected everything. But I would not be here unless I had wanted to come, and I'm deeply committed. I expect my manners to be good. And I have no complaints." His relations with LBJ, he said, were good.

But they were not so good as Teddy's. The President thought the younger Kennedy "a bright youngster who has all the earmarks of a comer." During Teddy's six-month stay in a Boston hospital, the White House called weekly. "How's my campaign goin' up there, Teddy?" the Chief Executive would invariably ask.

Determining which brother's outlook was brighter had become a favorite conversational gambit at Georgetown cocktail parties. There was even talk about an eventual split between Bobby and Teddy over the Presidency. But most people who knew the Kennedys thought this nonsense.

"If Bobby wants it," said one longtime friend from Massachusetts, "Ted'll step aside and let him have it. He told me that one night. We sat in the car in front of the apartment and he said, 'Look, there isn't any question about it. That's the way it is in the family. If Bobby is in a position to go and he wants it, that's the way it will be.' So that's the way it *will* be. . . ."

But, for the moment, Bobby's biggest problem was not how to become President but how to exercise his newfound leadership in New York State politics, where the party was fragmented into warring groups. Leader of the party was Robert F. Wagner, still Mayor of New York City, and for Bobby to gain control proved easier said than done.

The Johnson sweep had carried the Democrats to control of both houses of the New York State Legislature, and before long a leadership struggle broke out between pro-Wagner and pro-Kennedy forces. Both groups were hungry. "It has been estimated that about one-third of the Legislature's $12 million budget represents pure patronage—once defined by a Tammany leader as pay for a job you don't perform," political writer James Desmond observed. That was worth fighting for. But in Democratic caucuses the Wagner group was able to muster enough votes to prevent any takeover.

Bobby quickly became disgusted and decided to remain aloof from the tedious, almost comical battle that had tied up the legislature for weeks. He made no further move to support his Albany forces in the continuing struggle for control of the leadership, and it was at this point that Bob Wagner moved in. The cagey Mayor made known his staunch opposition to the two candidates put up by the Kennedy forces: State Senator Julian Erway, of Albany; and the Mayor's sworn enemy, Assemblyman Stanley Steingut of Brooklyn.

"No ticket thrown against him could have been more suitable to Wagner's purposes," James Desmond commented. "Erway, a gentlemanly conservative of sixty-five, was *ipso facto* unacceptable to the reform and liberal elements that support the Mayor, and they proceeded to assassinate his character with a violence of which they must today be ashamed. Steingut, son of the last Democratic Speaker of the Assembly and a young man in a hurry, had already been classified by the Mayor as one of the 'bosses' who were ruining the party."

The Kennedy people were unable to line up the required votes in the Senate or Assembly. The Wagner people concentrated their fury on Erway, whom they charged with being anti-Negro. In all, there were fifty-four roll calls—twenty-eight in the Assembly and twenty-six in the Senate. The result was that for nearly five terribly embarrassing weeks the legislature was leaderless and actionless. The great Democratic opportunity to demonstrate their capacity for governing a hitherto Republican-dominated state was rapidly being lost. But the glimmering opportunity to embarrass the Democrats was not lost on the Republicans.

Word went out from Governor Rockefeller to "stop Kennedy," and displaying extraordinary political discipline, the Republican minorities joined the Wagner forces. First, Republican Senator John Hughes of Syracuse calmly introduced a resolution calling for the election of Democratic Senator Joseph Zaretzki as president of the upper house. The anti-Wagner Democrats fought frantically, but eight hours later twenty-five Republicans joined fifteen Democrats to elect Zaretzki. The following day forty-six Republican assemblymen and thirty-five Wagner Democrats elected Anthony Travia as Assembly Speaker.

The way the Kennedy Democrats fumed one might have thought the end of the world was at hand. They screamed that an unsavory deal had been cooked up by the "Wagnerfellers" and the "Rockycrats," but no "deal" was necessary to explain the Rockefeller-Wagner coalition. Wagner, for the time being, had saved his political skin. And Rockefeller—looking toward

1966 when he knew he would face a tough race for re-election as Governor—now had the way cleared for passage of his legislative program.

Bobby Kennedy, somewhat aghast as he surveyed the Democratic wreckage from afar, commented in Washington, "It is unfortunate that things have developed to the point that the leadership of the Democratic party is decided by the Republicans. It's going to be very, very difficult to resurrect the party."

Because he had remained quiet during the Albany row, Bobby escaped relatively unscathed. Then he pulled a monumental blunder. He sent letters to Zaretzki and Travia, warning them that "dealing out patronage like so many cards off the top of the deck" would weaken the party in New York.

"It has come to my attention," wrote Bobby, "that telephone calls have been made to various political leaders around the state asking them to fill positions on the basis of patronage. Especially in light of the injury which we must agree has been sustained by the Democratic Party as a result of the long leadership impasse, I feel constrained to bring to your attention my opposition to filling jobs without paying careful attention to the ability of the men selected for the jobs." The Senator "assumed that these positions would be filled on the basis of merit." ("The way it was always done in Massachusetts, or in Virginia?" *The New York Times* scoffed editorially.)

In this frosty letter, Bobby haughtily proposed that a "talent hunt" for personnel be conducted the way his late brother had sought recruits for the New Frontier following the 1960 election. "This operation, in which I participated along with Sargent Shriver and others, brought such distinguished men as David Bell, Douglas Dillon and Robert McNamara to the Government," and he wrote that talent should be sought on a nonpartisan basis.*

Anthony Travia was particularly stung because nowhere in the Kennedy letter was there a word of congratulations to either Zaretzki or himself on their elections to party leader-

---

* Later in the year, Bobby and Teddy fought a losing battle in Washington in behalf of confirmation of old family friend Francis X. Morrissey as a Federal judge, despite the fact that both the Massachusetts and American Bar Associations dubbed him as distinctly "unqualified."

ship. The Assembly Speaker said he would not be drawn into a controversy with Bobby, but not only did Zaretzki deny Kennedy's charges, the spunky bantamweight legislator fired back a letter (written by Mayor Wagner's speech writer Julius Edelstein) of his own:

"The fears you have expressed really have no basis in fact, and the reports you cite have no relationship to anything which has actually taken place. . . . I'm sure that you already know from your brief experience in the legislative branch of the federal government that there is a difference between the legislative staff positions and positions of administrative duties in the executive branch of the government." He said he agreed with the contention that jobs should be filled on the basis of merit rather than politics, but he questioned whether "the specific procedure you recommend has ever been used by Congress or even by you in filling the staff positions in your own office in the United States Senate."

The more Travia thought the matter over, the angrier he got. He, too, sent off a letter to Senator Kennedy. "Senator," he concluded frostily, "out of respect for your office and expectation of the closest cooperation in the future in legislative matters of common concern, I have refrained in this letter from the spirited reply that might have been justified. There is, however, a tradition of comity between legislative bodies. I would not undertake to tell you how to run your office."

Anti-Kennedyites had a field day. *The Reporter* published what it described as the text of a letter to Senator Zaretzki "that was not written by U.S. Senator Robert F. Kennedy, although it bears certain superficial resemblances to the one he did write."

DEAR SENATOR ZARETZKI,

IT HAS COME TO MY ATTENTION THAT IN THE DAYS SINCE YOU AND MAYOR WAGNER PULLED THE RUG FROM UNDER ME, YOU GUYS HAVE BEEN GIVING OUT JOBS TO PEOPLE WHO WERE ON YOUR SIDE RATHER THAN ON MY SIDE IN THE RECENT CONTEST TO SEE WHO COULD GET CONTROL OF THE STATE LEGISLATURE. SHAME ON YOU, SENATOR ZARETZKI! FRANKLY, I HAVE NOT SEEN A MORE FLAGRANT USE OF POLITICAL PATRONAGE SINCE 1961

WHEN SOME SEGREGATIONISTS WERE APPOINTED FEDERAL
JUDGES IN THE DEEP SOUTH ON THE ADVICE OF THE THEN
ATTORNEY GENERAL OF THE UNITED STATES.

SINCE THIS IS A STATE MATTER WHICH I HAD PLANNED
TO HAVE TAKEN CARE OF FOR ME BY MY FRIENDS IN THE
LEGISLATURE, I HAD HOPED TO REMAIN UNINVOLVED. BUT
I SEE THAT YOU ARE UNWILLING TO PLAY THE GAME AC-
CORDING TO MY RULES, SENATOR ZARETZKI, AND SO I HAD
NO CHOICE BUT TO COME OUT LOUD AND CLEAR AGAINST
CHEAP WARD-LEVEL POLITICKING. WHAT WE NEED UP
THERE IS A HIGH-CLASS TALENT SEARCH LIKE THE ONE
MY BROTHERS-IN-LAW AND I RAN A FEW YEARS BACK TO
PUT THE HARVARD FACULTY ON THE FEDERAL PAYROLL.
STEVE AND SARGE KNOW MORE ABOUT HOW TO GET A DOL-
LAR'S WORTH OF VOTES FOR A DOLLAR'S WORTH OF PAT-
RONAGE THAN YOU RIBBON CLERKS WILL EVER KNOW.

AND JUST KEEP ONE THING IN MIND, ZARETZKI—
THINGS COULD BE VERY DIFFERENT A YEAR FROM NOW,
AND MY BROTHERS-IN-LAW AND I ALL HAVE VERY GOOD
MEMORIES

> YOURS FOR PARTY UNITY,
> A FRIEND

The Republicans, needless to say, also had a field day.
For Rockefeller it was a sort of revenge for the merciless
hammering Bobby had been giving him in Washington. In
his first public statement as the junior Senator from New
York, Bobby was pointedly critical of the role the Rocke-
feller Administration was playing in the affairs of the tottering
New Haven Railroad, a principal commuting line for New
Yorkers.

A few days later, in his maiden speech on the Senate floor,
Bobby again ran roughshod over Rockefeller policy. The
issue up for Senate consideration was a $1.1-billion aid bill
designed to relieve poverty in the eleven-state region known
as Appalachia, a program that had been several years in
the making.

Generally, freshmen in the seniority-conscious United States
Senate are expected to know their place, and most of them
are only too happy to keep their feet planted under their
desks until they learn the ropes. But Bobby was no ordinary

newcomer, and he quickly demonstrated he had no time to waste on Senate etiquette.

President Johnson himself had telephoned various Senators (including Teddy Kennedy of Massachusetts) to dissuade them from offering amendments to obtain such funds. Teddy decided not to offer his amendment, but Bobby disregarded the President's desire to keep the bill within financial bounds.

Up he popped, only to be recognized as "the Senator from Massachusetts" by the presiding officer—New Mexico's Senator Joseph M. Montoya, who as a fellow liberal Democrat and newcomer should have known better.

"Mr. President," Bobby began, "will the record show that it is the Senator from New York?"

Then Bobby proposed that the aid-to-Appalachia legislation be amended to make thirteen New York State counties eligible under the program. The episode illustrates Bobby's ambivalent attitude toward any program. The previous December he had urged upstate New Yorkers in the same thirteen counties to solve their problems locally; now he was accusing Rockefeller of being notably lukewarm and "shortsighted" in refusing to grab these Federal funds.

(Rockefeller, in fact, was vigorously opposed to having New York included in the Appalachia program, feeling acceptance of such funds would damage the state's reputation for a vigorous, expanding economy. And the Governor doubted that the program's emphasis on rural highway construction could be of real benefit.)

Caught momentarily off guard was New York's senior Senator, Republican Jacob Javits, who quickly showed his youthful confrere what *Time* described as "a bit of fancy footwork." He noted that Bobby had not bothered to name the thirteen counties he wished included. Agreeing this was a good idea, Bobby amended his amendment. Then, Javits—no slouch as a parliamentarian—observed that, as in all Appalachia-aid states, any program in New York would require consultation with and the approval of its Governor. Again Bobby agreed, sending up another amendment to his amendment. The amendment was then passed by voice vote.

Though the *New York Herald Tribune* the next day credited Bobby with "a personal coup," there were those in the Senate—including Democrats—who saw in the maneuver a "nasty ploy." "Traditionally," commented columnist Paul

Healy in the New York *Daily News,* "it is not considered good form for a freshman Senator to buck his own state's government. Senatorial courtesy also dictates that a junior Senator consult with his colleague before proceeding with an amendment that affects their state."

Javits was barely able to conceal his irritation, and from then on the senior Senator hardly ever refrained from one-upping his junior partner. When Bobby told the presiding officer he would "yield" the rest of his time on an amendment, Javits advised him in a loud voice to "reserve" it instead. An embarrassed Bobby agreed. Another time Javits informed him an amendment was "loosely drawn" and Bobby was forced to agree. It was enlightening to see the former Attorney General of the State of New York giving lessons to the former Attorney General of the United States.

Bobby plowed in on yet another state issue—a bill, which the Governor opposed, to make New York's minimum wage $1.50 an hour, rather than the Federal minimum of $1.25. Rockefeller opposed the bill on the ground that it would drive business out of the state. Bobby then needled Rockefeller on something they had in common and in abundance—wealth: "I know I couldn't get by on $1.50 an hour and I doubt if Mr. Rockefeller could."

Meanwhile, Bobby's relations with Javits were getting no better. In those early weeks there were far more examples of irritation than of smooth cooperation between the two. For example, there were Bobby's announcements—formerly made jointly by Javits and Keating—of government contracts for New York firms. The practice of making joint announcements was followed by Senators from most other states, including Senator Teddy Kennedy and his then Republican colleague Leverett Saltonstall.

But with President Johnson's help, Javits managed to get even. Javits learned that Bobby was flying to Syracuse to announce a $483,610 war-on-poverty grant for that city, and —failing to get poverty czar Sargent Shriver's approval to jump the gun with an announcement—phoned the White House. With the President's approval he then called the biggest Syracuse newspaper. An hour before Bobby's press conference, the paper was already reporting the grant as "announced by Senator Javits' office."

Also causing friction were committee assignments. As a result of the failure to coordinate, Javits and Bobby served together on two major committees—Government Operations, and Labor and Public Welfare. Usually Senators seek to have their states represented on as many committees as possible. Finally, after numerous stories were published about their strained relations, Bobby and Javits met privately for forty minutes in a room off the Senate floor and agreed to put an end to their intensifying conflict.

"Robert Kennedy is not acting like a freshman Senator," observed columnist Roscoe Drummond three months after the election. "He is acting like a Kennedy. He isn't shackling himself with petty protocol which says he mustn't speak on the floor for months and not move until his seniors beckon."

But Bobby was definitely not acting the way Jack or Teddy had acted during their early Senate days. Both had been cautious in speech and had deferred to their elders. Jack and Teddy played the game cautiously and by the book.

Robert F. Kennedy also began "going to the Left" in an undisguised maneuver to "build a distinction" between himself and President Johnson. He even took on his brother-in-law Sargent Shriver in an effort to score points against the Johnson Administration. Shriver was testifying before a Senate Education subcommittee, and the junior Senator did not hesitate to accuse him and the Administration of sponsoring a loose and overlapping package of bills. "When you do that," he scolded, "you are asking for trouble."

Strangely enough, according to Roscoe Drummond, Bobby was also cementing relations with a number of Southern Democratic Senators, including the powerful chairman of the Judiciary Committee, Senator James O. Eastland of Mississippi. Drummond reported that Senator Eastland was now remarking to colleagues, "Bobby suggests this," "Bobby thinks that," etc.

What was Bobby up to so early in the game? No one knew for sure, but Drummond suggested: "[He] is smoothly, ably and shrewdly marshaling his forces within the Senate to win just as quickly as possible an ascendant position in the power ranks of the Democratic party. He is moving in daringly, but not recklessly. He is not wasting one second with polite protocol. He is not signing up for any matches where the odds are too great. He is building his political base and widening his political influence."

Obviously Bobby Kennedy was not waiting for destiny to beckon—he was helping it along.

23

Feud Watching

Despite his obvious inability to cope with the jungle of New York politics, Bobby moved in quickly to score points as an activist legislator. But exactly what he accomplished as a go-go Senator, in terms of practical achievements, is of course debatable. And for all his headline-grabbing proclivities, he was to remain an outsider in that amorphous, indefinable, but powerful organism of government called the Senate Club. Perhaps this was not too important in terms of his ultimate ambitions; after all, JFK in his Senate days was unable to penetrate that exclusive establishment.

Actually, with few exceptions, most Senators had viewed Bobby's arrival with distaste. Politics had little to do with their feelings. Jealous of their power and of the power of the Senate, they also shared an abiding affection and respect for the defeated Ken Keating. Keating had been a valued member of the Senate Establishment; and his former colleagues of both parties deeply regretted the cruel trick of fate that had befallen him. Naturally, they harbored a perfectly understandable human resentment against the man who had bet on a sure thing and won.

Barely two months after taking his oath as Senator, Bobby suffered lumps even outsiders seldom experience on Capitol Hill. It occurred when Roy Cohn and his lawyer, Thomas A. Bolan, had been subpoenaed to testify about a "mail cover" that had been placed on both of them while Cohn was being tried on charges of obstruction and perjury in a stock fraud case. After two trials, Cohn had been acquitted.

Heading a subcommittee was Senator Edward V. Long, a

Missouri Democrat who had long led a passionate crusade against "invasions of privacy" by government agencies, and assisting him as counsel was Bernard Fensterwald, Jr., a protégé of the late Senator Estes Kefauver.

When Bolan completed his testimony on the mail cover—a procedure whereby the Post Office Department scrutinizes the mail of certain individuals to find out whom they are corresponding with—he was asked by Fensterwald whether he had ever submitted an affidavit to a Federal judge that was not accepted.

Bolan said he had, and described an affidavit that told how he had subpoenaed *Life's* files for an article the magazine had published under the title "Roy Cohn: Is He a Liar Under Oath?" and in the same files discovered correspondence between Henry Suydam, of *Life's* Washington bureau, and E. K. Thompson, *Life's* managing editor.

Senator Long then asked that the affidavit be read into the record. According to the affidavit, the Suydam memorandum outlined a proposal in March 1961 by the then Attorney General Robert F. Kennedy. The *Life* bureau chief had been invited to Kennedy's office one Saturday to meet Sam Baron, a Teamsters official described as "honest . . . idealist . . . disillusioned and disgusted with the corruption he saw around him." "Kennedy," the Suydam memo continued, "said he had suggested to this man that he make his break via an article in *Life* in the form of a personal exposé of Hoffa. . . . Kennedy feels perhaps melodramatically, perhaps not, that the man's life would be in danger if word leaked out of his intentions. . . . I gave my word."

At the time, of course, Hoffa was under indictment.

Eventually, on July 20, 1962, *Life* published such an article, signed by Baron but ghosted by a staffer, entitled "I Was Near the Top of Jimmy's Drop-Dead List." And, according to Bolan: "The import [of the memo] was the setting up of a whole cloak-and-dagger operation between Mr. Robert Kennedy and the top men in *Time* and *Life* to do an exposé of Mr. Hoffa. . . ." He further alleged that the article on Roy Cohn also "had its genesis in the offices of the Attorney General."

After the affidavit was read, Senator Long said he was "shocked" to hear that a top Justice Department official would be trying to plant a story derogatory to an individual awaiting trial. "This thing smells to high heaven," the Senator said. "It is rather obvious from your testimony that the Department of Justice was definitely attempting to try in the press the same persons, Mr. Cohn and Mr. Hoffa, that they were prosecuting in the courts. To me this is a very serious charge."

The matter seemed so serious to Long that he proposed it be brought to the attention of the entire Judiciary Committee, and when Bobby learned from newsmen what had transpired, he could scarcely contain his fury when he called Senator Long: Why hadn't he been informed that charges were to be made against him? Bobby then raised the question of whether Long had knowingly violated the unwritten law of senatorial courtesy by permitting the charges to be made without informing him. Long maintained it had all come as a surprise to him, and invited Bobby to testify the following day.

The next morning Bobby strode into the hearing room and took the stand. "There was an implication across the country that I acted improperly and I resent it," he snapped.

"I can understand that you would," replied Senator Long, but he declined to back down from his previous day's statement that he was "shocked" at the allegations.

Bobby then testified that he had known Sam Baron when he was Chief Counsel of the McClellan Committee and Baron was supplying information about Hoffa and also acting as an undercover man for the FBI on corruption within the Teamsters Union.

"He was in fear of his life," Bobby went on. "He felt that if anything happened to him, if he was killed, that he wanted to make sure that his story was told. He asked me to put him in touch with somebody who would relate what he had undergone as a Teamsters official. . . . I made that arrangement. I did nothing else. It was my understanding that if anything was published, it was going to be published if anything happened to him—if he was killed or in some way beaten."

Bobby said that "nothing in fact was ever published until Mr. Baron . . . was physically beaten by Mr. Hoffa," and Hoffa was arrested in the District of Columbia in May 1962 after Baron charged him with assault.

Baron's story was published by *Life*, sixteen months after

the Suydam arrangement. Bobby's argument, therefore, was that he had done nothing more than place Baron in touch with the magazine.

Fensterwald persisted. "This," he asked, "was an arrangement whereby [as] I understand it, you were putting what would normally be described as a 'fink' in touch with *Time-Life* to write a magazine article?"

"Normally described as what?" snapped Bobby.

"Fink. F-I-N-K."

"I never heard of that."

"A stool pigeon. Does that word strike a chord?"

"I thought it was a citizen who was reporting information and evidence in connection with legal activities."

"That is correct," said the counsel. "That would be a very good definition."

"I thought Baron was a citizen who was reporting information and evidence in connection with illegal activities," Bobby continued. "Let me say that I am shocked to hear that. I think there have been a lot of loyal people that provide information to the United States Government in connection with Communist activities, underworld activities, narcotics activities, at great risk to their own lives."

"And it is also your position, sir," Fensterwald snapped back, "that it is proper for the Attorney General to take such people, even while a case is under investigation and indictment, and attempt to see that their testimony is printed in the public press rather than taken to court?"

With television cameras focusing on him, Bobby could barely contain his anger. "That is not the way it was done. I never did anything like that. That was the implication of the testimony yesterday and this article was not published. As I understand it, there was no evidence or information ever given to any magazine by the Department of Justice. . . ."

With that exchange—and an impromptu lecture to Long and Fensterwald on investigatory manners—Bobby made bigger headlines than had his antagonists. However, as *Newsweek* noted: "For all his air of outrage and injury, his own account of the Baron episode hardly differed significantly from the one reflected in the [Suydam] memo."

But the Washington *Star* attacked the subcommittee counsel for his treatment of Bobby. "Mr. Fensterwald," its editorial contended, "attacked him as if he were a middle-range hoodlum or a profiteering war contractor refusing to give evidence. It may be assumed that Senate employees like Mr. Fensterwald do not turn into tigers without some indication from above that growls and the baring of fangs are acceptable."

James Wechsler took a similar tack. "Robert Kennedy has earned the enmity of Messrs. Hoffa and Cohn," he wrote in the New York *Post*. "He will survive and perhaps derive a certain pride from such hostility; his defense of Baron was spirited and effective.

"But surely the full Senate Judiciary Committee should examine the circumstances under which Baron was so vulgarly maligned by counsel Fensterwald in the alleged process of investigating violations of individual civil rights."

But Kennedy's own behavior provided critics with an opportunity they had long awaited. The Toledo *Blade*, for example, bristled: "Isn't it rather late for Bobby Kennedy, of all people, to be complaining about implications and insinuations, which were his chief stock in trade when he was often employing the investigating powers of Congress for political advantage?"

But, in all this attack and counterattack, the main point brought out by the hearings was all but lost. And that had to do with the allegations that an Attorney General had been instrumental in planting highly prejudicial magazine articles against two individuals under Federal indictment. The *Chicago Tribune* suggested the allegations demanded "the fullest kind of investigation by the responsible committees in Congress. It is one of the most serious charges ever made against a high officer of government. . . .

"Lawyers and judges recently have been trying to make much of representations that pre-trial publicity in newspapers impairs the chances of defendants in criminal trials to get a fair hearing. There has been a random cry that restraint should be placed on the press and that lawyers, prosecutors, and defendants should not be quoted. . . .

"But the activities attributed to the man who was attorney general of the United States make this whole position look silly. The chief law officer of the federal government stands charged with manufacturing publicity against men his agents proposed to try before the defendants were permitted their day in court. Why don't the bar and the judicial arm start investigating Mr. Kennedy, and why doesn't the Senate start considering the conduct charged to him?"

These were good questions. They have yet to be answered. Perhaps one reason is that, under the "club" rules of the Senate, members are supposed to say nothing derogatory about each other. Whether this includes mention of acts that occurred before a Senator became a Senator or just what he does while he *is* a Senator has long been a matter of considerable dispute. At any rate, Chairman Long's threat to present the allegations to the Judiciary Committee seemed to evaporate into thin air.

At almost every turn—or so it seemed in those days—Robert F. Kennedy appeared to be deliberately involving himself in political disputes with one person after another. But most amazing to people in his own party was the manner in which the junior Senator began to openly take potshots at the President of the United States. That there had long been friction between Lyndon Johnson and the Kennedy tribe—most particularly Bobby—came as no surprise. Even the society pages were contributing to the increasing talk one heard about the Kennedy-Johnson feud. And all because Mrs. Perle Mesta decided to give a party for the Senate Majority Leader, Mike Mansfield, the same night Teddy was celebrating the fifteenth wedding anniversary of the Robert Kennedys.

Mrs. Mesta, Ambassador to Luxembourg under Harry Truman, was known to be unfavorably disposed to the Kennedys. During the glittering days of the New Frontier, when Washington party life was at an elegant high, she had never once been invited to the White House. Perhaps the Kennedys had never forgiven her for having backed Lyndon Johnson for the Presidential nomination in 1960 and then—*mirabile dictu*—for having switched her allegiance to Richard M. Nixon. (Though she never explained the switch, one reason may have been her displeasure with young JFK for turning up at her 1949 dinner for President and Mrs. Truman wearing, as she put it, "brown loafers with his tuxedo.")

But once the Great Society replaced the New Frontier, Mrs. Mesta, an Oklahoma oil heiress and the inspiration for the musical comedy *Call Me Madam,* was back in the social swim and being invited to the White House. Like the Kennedys, the Johnsons rarely forget their friends.

As Nan Robertson of *The New York Times* put it, Washington became "the Confused Society" as "an amused Washington waited to see who would be the hostess with the mostest."

Most social experts agreed the Kennedy party had to be ahead on points, what with ten Senators, four Ambassadors, two Cabinet members, a smattering of "beautiful people" from New York and some 300 guests.

Those in the Mesta inner circle claimed *nolo contendere,* arguing that had President Johnson been in town, he surely would have been at Mrs. Mesta's. "And you know," a Washington society leader informed the *New York Herald Tribune's* Gwen Gibson, "where the President goes—that's the test of who's who in Washington."

But was this the social showdown everyone had been expecting? Mrs. Mesta said the whole idea was preposterous. It was merely her annual party for the Senate Majority Leader. In fact, she liked the Ted Kennedys. They were good friends and very charming people. Why should she try to sabotage their affair?

But after the ball was over, Mrs. Mesta explained casually that she also had had four Ambassadors and their wives. "Let's see . . . I had Greece, I had Spain, I had Peru, I had Kuwait . . . Representative Albert Thomas of Texas . . . some people from New York, the producer of *Glass Menagerie,* Mr. Christy, is it, Orrin Christy? I didn't keep a guest list. It was not a large affair at all. No entertainment. Just Devron [a Washington combo specializing in the monobeat music known as "the bureaucratic bounce"]. You know when you have six or seven Senators you don't need entertainment."

Among the Senators was Jacob Javits, with his glamorous wife Marion, who tried to place things in perspective. "I am absolutely convinced," she explained, "that Mrs. Mesta didn't give the Kennedy party a thought when she planned her dinner. Hers was a pure 'Perle party.' I accept that completely, despite what they're saying."

Asked whether they had gone to the Kennedy party later, Marion replied, "No. We weren't invited. But come to think of it, we've never invited the Kennedys to one of our parties."*

Mike Mansfield, always the diplomat, told Mrs. Mesta's guests the contretemps was much ado about nothing. Lifting a glass, he proposed a toast: "To Mrs. Mesta, still the hostess with the mostest." A short while later, the Mansfields took their leave and headed for the Ted Kennedys' in Georgetown.

A huge tent had been erected in the garden. The music was by Lester Lanin and his fashionable orchestra. There were flamenco dancers imported from the Spanish pavilion of the New York World's Fair and a shaggy-haired combo with guitars. There was also Senator Gale McGee of Wyoming, who stood outside the Kennedy home counting the guests as they arrived. Every now and then he would shout to Ted Kennedy on the porch, "Who's ahead, Perle or—?"

The Robert Kennedys, accompanied by the Chet Huntleys, arrived fashionably late in an open-top white convertible, its right rear fender bashed in from an old accident. Art Buchwald, puffing his ever-present cigar, was there. (Later, he was to chronicle l'Affaire Kennedy-Mesta as "the most important crisis in Washington in the last six months.") And the big New York contingent included Mrs. John R. Fell, the William vanden Heuvels, the junior S. Carter Burdens and the Frederick Cushings. Mrs. Herve Alphand, wife of the then French Ambassador, was also on hand to add additional glamour. And, of course, most of the Kennedys and their spouses were there. Mother Rose arrived on the arm of film maker George Stevens, Jr.

The row over the Mesta party has been reported here merely for its humorous overtones, but the truth is that while the Kennedy brothers may not have declared open war against Lyndon Johnson, they were engaged in guerrilla

---

* The Javitses had been in the bad graces of the Kennedys ever since Mrs. Steve Smith saw Marion carrying a copy of this writer's *JFK: The Man and the Myth,* in September 1963. "What are you doing with that terrible book?" asked JFK's sister. "Why," replied Marion, "I'm quoted in it." And so she was. The book contains Mrs. Javits' description of one of JFK's parties at the White House: "Before departing," she said, "the President graciously asked my husband to bring me to Washington more often. With all respects to New York, he jocularly observed that Washington was a much jazzier town these days." And that was the last time, during the Kennedy reign, that Marion and Jack were invited to the White House.

warfare against the President's legislative program and foreign policy.

For example, in the first eighteen months following his election, Teddy Kennedy was hardly heard from. Then, in his first major speech, he in effect challenged the White House by proposing to broaden the Administration's voting-rights bill to include a ban against poll taxes in state and local elections.

According to the Administration, the amendment was of doubtful constitutionality. Senate Democratic Leader Mike Mansfield and Republican Leader Everett Dirksen combined forces to oppose it. But they were opposed by a band of liberal Senators led by Teddy Kennedy, who had lined up thirty-eight co-sponsors for his amendment. Bobby, who operated behind the scenes, did not formally join the co-sponsors because, he explained, he did not want it to look like a Kennedy-vs.-Johnson battle—which Washington cynics quite realistically insisted it was. The Kennedy clan was out in force for the showdown. In the Senate gallery were Teddy's wife Joan, sister Eunice Shriver, and Bobby's wife Ethel. Temporarily presiding over the session was Bobby himself.

Leading off the debate was Everett Dirksen, who asked, "If Congress can tell the states by statute this afternoon that they cannot impose a poll tax, why not tell them they cannot impose a cigarette tax or any other tax?" But Mike Mansfield had another worry. The entire voting-rights bill might be endangered.

Teddy floor-managed the amendment with the skill and finesse of a veteran. He had done his homework, with the notable assistance of several Harvard Law professors. In the debate, unbending in his leather back-brace and moving slowly with the help of a silver-tipped cane, he spoke gracefully from notes: "It is a settled constitutional doctrine that where Congress finds an evil to exist, such as the economic burden in this case, it can apply a remedy which may affect people outside the evil."

Teddy's appearance reminded many of John F. Kennedy. Indeed, on the Senate floor, he was the image of his late brother—pronouncing "Alabamer" in twangy codfish-cake accents, right index finger stabbing the air, left hand tugging at coat pocket.

In the tense roll-call vote, Teddy came within four votes of defeating the Administration. Yet it was a fluke victory for LBJ: Liberal Democrats Eugene McCarthy, Vance Hartke, Joseph Montoya and Clinton Anderson had all been bludgeoned into voting the Administration line. For the Kennedys it was an honorable defeat.

Bobby then pushed for an amendment that would outlaw state requirements that voters pass an English literacy test. Non-English-speaking Puerto Ricans in New York, which has such a requirement, would thus qualify. Bobby sought to persuade his senior colleague, Jack Javits, to co-sponsor the bill. But Javits found the bill to be constitutionally defective. It was Teddy who mediated the dispute between them, and convinced his older brother that he should accept Javits' modifications. Actually, one reason for Javits' attitude was probably that he himself had introduced a similar bill in 1962 with no success.

In the Senate debate, Bobby freely conceded that the vast majority of the voters who would be added to the New York City voting rolls under the amendment would be loyal Democrats. But that, he added, was no reason to deny them the right to vote. The only taunt during the debate which made both Kennedy and Javits squirm came from Senator Thruston Morton. The Kentucky Republican reminded his colleagues that New York "has a Republican Governor and a Democratic legislature and has been preaching for years to the rest of us around the country as to how to run things."

"Don't you think they could work this out in Albany?" Morton asked.

But not all liberals were overjoyed by the passage of the amendment. Writing in *The New Republic,* Yale Law Professor Alexander M. Bickel noted that New York had long "known the evil of monolithic bloc-voting by homogeneous nationality groups beholden to one powerful leader and virtually inaccessible to anyone else." At the same time, Bickel contended that "the Kennedy-Javits amendment . . . is . . . an undesirable—in the last analysis, an irresponsible—addition to the voting-rights bill before the Congress."

Bickel asked why the two New Yorkers had not directed their reforming effort toward the state legislature, then in session in Albany. "It is unlikely that a measure which both Kennedy and Javits thought worth their while to support in the Senate, with some fanfare, could not be put through the New York Legislature. Theirs are ruling names in both parties in the state. It must be that the Senators did not much care where they achieved their purpose, in Washington or in Albany. But that is precisely what matters. This is too big and diverse a country to be governed in every detail from Washington."

Hubert Humphrey had a difficult time adjusting to the Kennedy onslaught. Under White House guidance, the Vice President, of course, opposed the amendment. But what made his lobbying against the proposal so incongruous was the fact that for years he had vociferously favored outlawing of all poll taxes.

Hence, the Kennedy clan felt that it was one-up on Humphrey in the race toward the White House.

"I mean really," exploded William F. Buckley, Jr., in his syndicated column. "Can you really picture Teddy losing sleep at night because you have to pay a buck and a half to vote in Virginia?"

Slowly but surely the Kennedys were scoring points among those liberals who were growing disenchanted with the hardline foreign policies being pursued by the Johnson Administration. Bobby, particularly, made liberals sit up and take notice when he cautiously questioned the Administration's military intervention in the Dominican Republic.

The President had dispatched United States Marines to the troubled land with the cry that it was "just like the Alamo." The President had also privately asserted that handing the Dominican government back to the ultra-liberal Juan Bosch "would be like turning it over to Arthur Schlesinger, Jr." But from the moment the United States intervened in the Dominican Republic liberals were outraged.

The New York Times, as usual, fulminated. Harshly critical articles appeared in all the liberal magazines. *The New Republic,* for example, complained: "Mr. Johnson's tough action is cheered loudest by those who want only strong-man rightwing governments in Latin America." It was, to these liberals, a horrible betrayal of everything John F. Kennedy had urged in his Alliance for Progress.*

---

* Not all liberals were opposed to intervention, however. Walter Lippmann and Wayne Morse surprisingly endorsed the President's Dominican policy.

Stung by the criticism, President Johnson told a labor conference in Washington on May 3, 1965, "We don't propose to sit here in our rocking chair with our hands folded and let the Communists set up any government in the Western Hemisphere."

Some observers saw this as a snide thrust at the late President Kennedy, but there is no evidence to support it. It is no less difficult to believe that so cool a political cat as Bobby, even had he interpreted the remark as a slur on his brother's memory, would have permitted it to provoke him into an unintended strategic shift. Whatever the reasons, three days later Robert F. Kennedy did attack the President's Santo Domingo policy on the Senate floor, following it up by a press interview.

Joining those of his colleagues who insisted that a vote for the President's $700,000,000 supplemental military appropriation did not imply endorsement of White House policy in Santo Domingo, Bobby declared, "Our determination to stop Communist revolutions in this hemisphere must not be construed as opposition to popular uprisings against injustice and oppression just because the targets of such popular uprisings say they are Communist-inspired or Communist-led or even because known Communists take part in them." To sharpen the point, Bobby inserted into the Congressional Record a dispatch from James Norman Goodsell of the *Christian Science Monitor* claiming that "the top rebel command is in the hands of non-Communist elements who fiercely proclaim their opposition to Communism."

This did not mean he opposed United States intervention as such, Bobby explained in an interview. But, he added: "I think there should have been consultation prior to any action we would take in the Dominican situation. I don't think we addressed ourselves to the implications of what we did in the Dominican Republic." According to Bobby, President Johnson should have consulted the Organization of American States (OAS) before sending in the Marines.

A newsman asked Bobby whether he thought the Bay of Pigs (a New Frontier adventure in which the OAS was *not* consulted in advance) had been a more successful foray in Caribbean diplomacy, but the Senator answered, disarmingly, "I don't think we handled that one particularly well."

With the passage of time, however, it has become obvious

that President Johnson—whatever his other faults—did handle the Dominican crisis fairly well. He did what he had to do. As a result, the Communists were thwarted in their efforts to develop another beachhead in the Caribbean. At least that's what John Bartlow Martin, JFK's Ambassador to the Dominican Republic during the power vacuum following the assassination of dictator Rafael Trujillo, believes. Martin, also a close friend of Bobby Kennedy, forsook diplomacy following President Kennedy's assassination. In April 1965, when Santo Domingo exploded again, Martin was dispatched by LBJ to serve once more in that hapless country. In his perceptive memoirs, *Overtaken by Events,* Martin—without doing so directly—disputes Bobby's version of Dominican events:

"I have no doubt whatsoever that there was a real danger of a Communist takeover," Martin wrote. "Given the circumstances that existed at the time, President Johnson had no choice but to send troops." If he had not done so, the Castroites, in all probability, "would have spread the rebellion throughout the republic and in the end established a Communist-dominated government."

The ultimate vindication of the U.S. involvement came in the fall of 1966 when the last American soldier pulled out of the Dominican Republic. By then, the people had held a free and fair election, establishing a new constitutional regime that brought that troubled nation a measure of stability.

If Martin had any criticism of U.S. policy, it was that Washington should have been more forthright in helping the anti-Communist generals fight the Castroites to a standstill. "Once we had decided we were in the republic to stop Communism," he wrote, "we should have stopped pretending neutrality."

But this ambivalence on the part of the Johnson Administration could be ascribed, in part, to the onslaught of the largely liberal critics who accused the President of yielding to panic, being trigger-happy, using gunboat diplomacy and despoiling the American image around the world. And it was these same liberal critics, disaffected by President Johnson's hard line in global affairs, whom Robert F. Kennedy was desperately seeking to impress. These were the people who had long distrusted Bobby. And, from their point of view, with good reason. Despite all the rewriting of history, Bobby's ties with the late Senator McCarthy are a fact of life which cannot easily be erased from certain liberal memories.

"As a matter of fact," commented William Buckley, Jr., "Senator Kennedy's views on Latin American politics are much less interesting than the fact that he adopted them. When Lyndon Johnson declined to make Mr. Kennedy Vice President, Kennedy had to (a) retire, or (b) come into Washington with his own mandate and, consistent with his high station, set up a rival establishment. He won election as Senator, arrived in Washington, and waited. He would either go to the left of the President, or to the right of the President, and there set up his own magnetic field.

"The President took the initiative by moving right (at least in foreign policy) whereupon Senator Kennedy immediately moved left. He has staked out his position there, and instantly, and almost automatically, the forces of equilibrium go into motion, and the regularizations begin. Kennedy comes out against Johnson's policies in Vietnam or at least moderately so. Johnson, says Bobby, has not put sufficient emphasis on the 'political and diplomatic aspects of the problem.' The political-and-diplomatic-aspects-of-the-problem is presumably defined as those aspects Bobby used in his notoriously unsuccessful treatment of Sukarno in previous years."

Bobby's views on Vietnam were of a piece with his views on Santo Domingo. He gave generalized support to the Administration's efforts in Vietnam, but urged that Washington should work for "honorable negotiations" between the warring Vietcong and the South Vietnamese. Addressing the Senate on May 6, 1965, he said, "I believe that we have erred for some time in regarding Vietnam as purely a military problem when in its essential aspects it is also a political and diplomatic problem. I would wish, for example, that the request for [military] appropriations today had made provisions for programs to better the lives of the people of South Vietnam. . . ."

Brief as the allusions were, the Kennedy speech was quickly interpreted as a criticism of the Johnson Administration whose partisans made no secret of their belief that, if anything, "the mess in Vietnam" was part of the JFK legacy left the new President. Which, in fact, it was. But Bobby was no longer talking about the necessity to "win in South Vietnam" as he had done when his brother was in office. One can only wonder what his reaction would have been during his brother's Administration had some maverick Senator proposed a coalition with the Communists.

By now, the press was full of "dope" stories concerning an LBJ-RFK feud. John O'Hara, then writing a syndicated column, opined that "there must be sleepless nights in the White House when the President wishes he could replace Bobby with a genial, tractable man like Charles de Gaulle." Every speech uttered by the junior Senator from New York was being widely examined for anti-Johnson barbs. The Bobby-watchers even got excited about a speech Bobby *almost* made to the International Police Academy about counter-insurgency.

The advance text warned that the anti-Communist struggle in South Vietnam—and elsewhere—could not be won through military force alone and urged the government to put more emphasis on political solutions to the problem of achieving stability in the world. It also warned that a government forced to bomb its own cities could not be a government for long, adding that "victory in a revolutionary war is won not by escalation, but by de-escalation."

Inevitably the speech was seized upon as a harsh critique of the Administration's policies in Vietnam. But the speech was never delivered in its original form. Newsmen, who had read the handout the day before, began questioning the Senator. Bobby had second thoughts. He decided to strike out some of the more pungent passages, even though the afternoon papers, in their early editions of July 9, 1965, had published headlines (as in the case of the New York *World-Telegram*): RIFT WITH JOHNSON WIDENS: KENNEDY RIPS VIET POLICY.

Probably Bobby's biggest blunder on Vietnam, one that would give him many uncomfortable moments, came at a press conference at the University of Southern California on November 5, 1965. He had been asked at a news conference whether he disapproved of a student group's plans for sending blood to North Vietnam, and replied, "I'm willing to give blood to anyone who needs it."

A newsman then asked him if he believed blood should go to the North Vietnamese when they were "killing our troops."

"If the Red Cross is making a drive for blood and feels that [giving blood to North Vietnam] can be helpful," he replied. Asked if he favored some left-wing students' plans to ship American blood directly to Hanoi, he added, "I'm talking about through an organization like the Red Cross. . . . If it's a blanket question of would we furnish blood to North Vietnam, I think that's in the oldest tradition of the country."

Bobby did not go all the way with the New Leftists then running amok on several California campuses. Asked if he thought that anti-Vietnam demonstrators had gone too far, he replied, "Yes, I think they have. For example, where they won't let those with opposite views speak. Or where violence is used."

And asked if he thought draft-card burners had gone too far, he replied, "Yes, I think that also. If a person feels that strongly and wants to make that kind of sacrifice, he can go and burn his draft card and take the consequences. But I don't agree with it personally."

Almost predictably, Kennedy's "blood" remarks set off a small furor. Though generally they remained silent, most Democrats were unhappy. Republicans, of course, were more outspoken. Barry Goldwater, for example, termed the remarks "closer to treason than to academic freedom." His voice rising in anger at a Republican conference in Albuquerque, he said, "It's appalling to me that the press of the nation hasn't jumped down his throat. I've known a lot of Irishmen. I've never known an Irishman who would help our enemies."

The New York Post, as usual, rushed to Bobby's defense with an editorial titled " 'Treason' or Humanity?" And it asserted that "the charge of 'treason' is harsh and terrible. That Goldwater employs it as a form of political debate is a measure of his reckless irresponsibility. His distortion of Senator Kennedy's words on the subject of giving blood to the North Vietnamese only compounds the scandal."

The Chicago Tribune reminded Bobby that "it was not the United States or the people of South Vietnam who launched aggression; it was the totalitarian regime of Ho Chi Minh in Hanoi. The United States is not prosecuting a war of conquest; the Communists are. The United States is fighting for the freedom of a people under attack; the Communists are bent on the subjection of the same people."

The Tribune felt that Bobby's remark about sending blood to Vietnam was "one of the most ill-considered statements of the year."

And apparently, on second thought, Bobby agreed. For, through an aide, he let it be known that he believed shipping blood to North Vietnam through other than an international organization was "possibly illegal under the neutrality act and the trading with the enemy act."

Complaints from constituents were numerous. The standard reply was sent back by Bobby's administrative assistant Joe Dolan: "Senator Kennedy has always opposed any direct action by groups in this country to send blood or other supplies to the North Vietnamese."

Bobby Kennedy's next blast was delivered in what, to his mind at least, was a "major speech" on foreign policy.

"The need to halt the spread of nuclear weapons must be a central priority of American policy," he said. "Of all our major interests, this now deserves and demands the greatest additional effort."

He proposed that Red China be invited to attend the Geneva disarmament talks in the hope of achieving agreement to halt the proliferation of nuclear weapons, and before jammed Senate galleries quoted liberally from statements made by President Kennedy who, he observed, by obtaining a test-ban treaty shortly before his death, had taken "the first step in a journey of a thousand miles. We have not yet taken the second step."

The implications were unmistakable.

"This seems hard and even unfair criticism to an Administration that has been working on the problem for years and is now preoccupied with the crises in Vietnam and the Dominican Republic . . . ," James Reston of *The New York Times* noted, and White House reaction was quick and snappish.

"Of course," then press secretary George Reedy snapped, "we are glad Senator Kennedy is also interested in this field." He noted that President Johnson had named a task force some time ago to look into ways to keep nuclear weapons out of trigger-happy lands. That task force, headed by Roswell L. Gilpatric, had handed in its report to the President the previous January.

According to columnist Robert G. Spivack: "What happened was that identical language in the speech delivered by Kennedy on nuclear proliferation was included in the U.N. speech prepared for the President. This was not only a breach of manners on the part of the State Department, whose speech-writers were working on the President's address. It had all the earmarks of pressure on the President by junior officials to make sure their ideas were made government policy.

"The White House liked the ideas but not the methods used to put them over. The President would not permit himself to be maneuvered into the position of 'me-tooing' the maiden speech of New York's junior Senator. But even more than that, he did not relish having the language suggested by speech-writing subordinates peddled, as it were, to someone else if they were rejected by the White House.

"When any President fails to make clear to subordinates that he takes a dim view of such behavior, he soon discovers that every speech-writer becomes his own policy-maker. Johnson has made his displeasure very clear. The anguished howls of those who tried to outflank him are the sounds you now hear."

Columnist Marguerite Higgins, who had known Bobby when he was an ardent McCarthyite Red-baiter, could hardly contain her amazement at the enormous shift in Bobby's thinking. And she wrote that she had little doubt "that an intelligent man like RFK knows perfectly well that the nonproliferation treaty as proposed—which he has raised to an issue of universal urgency—would be a sham. Russia has nuclear weapons today. To whom are they going to give those nuclear weapons? Peking? Poland? Albania? In signing such a treaty, the Russians would really be (tongue in cheek, presumably) agreeing not to do that which they had no intention of doing and every vital national interest in avoiding.

"For our side," Miss Higgins continued, "nonproliferation, especially if it were combined with a ban on even sharing nuclear knowledge, would shut out our key partner in Europe—the Germans—and cause a festering sore inside the alliance that would probably cause Khrushchev, even in his forced retirement, to dance his famous jig.

"And finally, how times change. Here we have Robert Kennedy, who objected so bitterly more than a decade ago to trading with the Peking enemy, announcing that he believes furnishing blood to North Vietnam would be 'in the oldest tradition of this country.' But think how such shipments of blood from Americans would affect Communist Hanoi.

"Sending blood is a very special thing—a sign of sympathy. Doesn't this give aid and comfort to the enemy? Such false humanism may win RFK the squeals and the jumps of the Vietniks, quite apart from the fact that it harms vital American interests. Will such 'trading with the enemy' reflect well in the long run statesmanship of RFK?"

Bobby's growing ambivalence toward Vietnam was demonstrated again on NBC's *Meet the Press* December 5, 1965, when he urged a thorough discussion in Congress before the Administration sent more troops to Southeast Asia. At the same time, he said he "basically" supported the President's Vietnam policy. But he had "reservations about whether we are doing enough in the economic and political field."

Bobby kept up a stream of "proposals" on Vietnam, echoed by brother Teddy. President Johnson, however, did not appear to be listening. But though it feigned disinterest, the White House was watching every Kennedy maneuver with the fascination of a cobra weaving to a snake charmer.

24

Latin Trip

As President Johnson's first year drew to a close, there could be little doubt that he faced the not-so-loyal opposition of the Kennedys and their many allies within the Democratic party. The Kennedyites, particularly the intellectuals among them, had drifted away to other climes, making no secret that they considered That Man in the White House little more than a usurper. "The Kennedy years were magic, and the magic lasted all the time he was President," the wife of one of them explained to British newsman Michael Davie. "But this man—he's creepy."

Davie had spent the summer of 1965 in Washington writing a series of articles for *The Observer* of London on "the most powerful man in the world," Lyndon Baines Johnson. The articles—which later became a book, *LBJ: A Foreign Observer's Viewpoint*—constituted a sympathetic but candid portrait of that complicated man who was President of the United States. Probing the President's political successes and failures, Davie concluded that while the President's failures at the time were trivial they included failing to coax Jacqueline Kennedy into the Johnson orbit. "Mrs. Kennedy," Davie reported, "despite regular, solicitous telephone calls from the White House, has declined to respond to Johnson's advances; instead, a widowed queen in exile, she waits on Fifth Avenue for the restoration of the dynasty to the throne."

But if the dynasty is restored, it will be Ethel Kennedy (with whom she has little affinity) and not Jackie who will occupy the center of the stage. There cannot be two First

Ladies in the White House. Yet the fact that she is doomed to be discarded by her brother-in-law should he become President has not deterred Jackie from doing all she can to further Bobby's political fortunes. And because they frequently holidayed together, often without Ethel, there had been rumors that something untoward was going on. The truth is the bond with Jackie has no romantic undertones. It stems from the time of her miscarriage in August 1956 when Jack failed to interrupt his Mediterranean cruise but Bobby, dropping everything, rushed to the hospital to handle matters for Jackie.

"Life was so disorganized," Jacqueline once said of her early married years. "We never had a home for five years. Politics was sort of my enemy as far as seeing Jack was concerned. I was alone almost every weekend while Jack traveled the country making speeches. It was all wrong." And following her husband's death, Jacqueline Kennedy felt strongly that she had let him down in life. It became an absolute fixation with her that she should not fail him in death.

Robin Douglas-Home, a nephew of Britain's former Prime Minister Sir Alec Douglas-Home, put it this way: "She thought—wrongly—that she had failed her husband in his life, had failed to give him the full, unstinting support she could have given and that he expected her to give. But now, *now,* she was determined to give him, posthumously, all that support. And more. She was trying to make good her imagined deficiencies during his lifetime. And the clearest and easiest way to do this was to help her brother-in-law, whom she clearly identified with her husband, to carry on re-creating the dreams so dear to her husband and which he had been prevented from achieving by his premature death."

Robin Douglas-Home, a White House visitor during the Kennedy years, was a man to whom Jackie turned for long talks which lasted late into the night. On these occasions Jackie apparently talked quite freely and at times—as it turned out—indiscreetly. "I became her own personal emotional blotting paper, able to soak up and absorb the problems, the frustrations, the paradoxes of her life," Douglas-Home explains.

Douglas-Home's candid assessment of Mrs. Kennedy was

published in the February 1967 issue of *Queen,* a British monthly catering to sophisticated ladies. This was soon after the unedifying brawl over the William Manchester book. The not unexpected result was that Mrs. Kennedy informed friends that Douglas-Home was no longer welcome in her home.

Douglas-Home disclosed that in a conversation Mrs. Kennedy defended Lyndon Johnson against his aspersions. "Oh, he's not as bad as all that," she exclaimed. "After all, he's got all Jack's advisers. So how can he go wrong?" And she went out of her way to praise the Johnsons for being so kind about allowing her to take her time about moving out of the White House.

Three months later she was interviewed for ten hours by William Manchester. By now she had a more jaundiced view of Lyndon Johnson. According to Douglas-Home, "she began to think that her murdered husband was being forgotten and that Lyndon Johnson was being praised as a President who could get legislation through Congress that her own idolized husband had merely dreamed about getting through Congress. It was then, I think, that she temporarily lost her balance. . . . Furthermore, the solid support and constant proximity of Robert Kennedy during the post-assassination months must have led her to believe that the best way of serving her dead husband was to back his brother—his rightful political heir—and to further his cause in any way she could."

Bobby reminded him of a bird dog, said Douglas-Home. "Tell him to go into a thicket and sniff after pheasant and that's what he'll do. He'll keep on doing it until he's succeeded. If he gets elected President on that kind of reputation, that's fair enough. But I don't think he should do it on an emotional tidal wave of JFK's mythology. I think that Jackie should remove herself from this bandwagon because she is not cut out for it."

Meanwhile, the bird dog was not doing too well in his relations with influential New York Democrats. He publicly disparaged the work of the state legislature under the leadership of Joseph Zaretzki and Anthony Travia. "The business of parties is not just to win elections," he said at a Brooklyn Democratic dinner. "It is to govern. And a party cannot govern if it is disunited. . . . We have so far failed our test.

We have failed because we have forgotten the lessons of the campaign. We have allowed our campaign unity to dissolve in quarrels within the party."

Spunky little Joe Zaretzki angrily termed Bobby's attitude "divisive," adding that he had done nothing to heal the breach in the party and that, moreover, he had swallowed "hook, line and sinker" the Republican contention that upstaters must have predominance in the legislature to prevent New York City from controlling the state.

One sign of Democratic disunity was the unwillingness of Mayor Wagner to accept Bobby's choice for head of the Federal anti-poverty program in New York, William J. vanden Heuvel, a Kennedy frontiersman who had been tentatively appointed to the post by Poverty Corps Director Sargent Shriver. One reason City Hall was down on vanden Heuvel was that he had worked hard to keep Wagner from getting the mayoralty nomination in the 1961 Democratic primary. Vanden Heuvel never did get the job. But, informally, he was on Bobby's team, acting in his behalf in ticklish political situations and carrying the Senator's bags on his travels abroad.

Then came a minor disaster, the first of several indications to come that the Kennedy name in and of itself does not always rub off on other candidates. When handsome, forty-three-year-old liberal Republican John Lindsay, going nowhere in the United States Congress, announced he would seek the mayoralty at the head of a "fusion" ticket—that is, with Democratic and Liberal party running mates—Mayor Wagner, for reasons both political (he might lose) and personal (to remarry and rest), bowed out of the contest. This opened the way for a bruising primary contest in which Abraham D. Beame, Comptroller of the City of New York, beat Wagner's boy, Paul R. Screvane, and two Reformer types. About which the irrepressible Murray Kempton wrote as follows:

"The internal Democratic struggle in New York has lately come to be described as one between activists loyal to Senator Robert F. Kennedy, and activists loyal to outgoing Mayor Robert F. Wagner. This is about as useful as saying that *Madame Bovary* is a book about a woman who likes boys. There is small indication, for one thing, that Senator Kennedy is particularly loyal to the people who are loyal to him—most of them are comparative strangers—and even less indication that Mayor Wagner is loyal to his loyalists.

"Senator Kennedy, in any case, would have serious conflicts in being that loyal; the local Democrats who defer to him as against Mayor Wagner stretch all the way from Congressman William Fitts Ryan, focus of the more intense desire for liberal reform, to former Congressman Charles F. Buckley of the Bronx, the last visible symbol of resistance to reform of any sort.

"Beame won the support of what remains of the old-line Democratic organization which Mayor Wagner sorely wounded during his transitory manifestation as a reformer in 1961. Beame therefore has to be described as a Kennedy candidate. . . ."

But the "Kennedy candidate" went roundly down to defeat at the hands of John Lindsay in a campaign made notable only by the emergence of William F. Buckley, Jr., as the Conservative candidate. As Kempton had also noted, Abe Beame was "the Jewish candidate running in a city where the best sort of candidate to offer Jewish voters is a forward-looking Yale Episcopalian. Lindsay happens to fill the bill." And Kennedy's contributions to the Beame campaign could hardly be described as inspiring. His major point, in campaign speeches, was that "Abe Beame, the Democrat," could do more for New York because in Washington "the heads of agencies and committees are Democrats."

The New York Times, once again aghast at Bobby's effrontery, labeled this type of appeal "a remarkable indictment of the Johnson Administration. It suggests, for example, that Sargent Shriver, the head of the anti-poverty program and a Democrat, would be less sympathetic and helpful to New York if its Mayor were a Republican. . . . It suggests that President Johnson, Vice President Humphrey and Senator Kennedy himself would not be so helpful to the Mayor of the nation's largest city if he were of a political faith different from theirs. . . ."

The Beame people made no secret of their feelings that Kennedy had not given his all in behalf of their candidate. For example, on the last day before election, Bobby was sent into Irish Catholic neighborhoods where Bill Buckley appeared to be making strong inroads. The Senator attacked the problem in his own style and, as a *New York Herald Tribune* reporter noted: "the style didn't meet with favor from the Beame camp." The tone was set at Bobby's first stop in the Bronx. "I ask for your support for the Beame ticket," he told a small crowd. "Now, we'll clap at the end of that."

There was applause.

"The Republican party gave you Herbert Hoover, Harding, Coolidge and Rockefeller. Everybody boo."

There were boos.

"That's it," Bobby concluded.

Another rally, arranged by the Bronx Democratic organization, was held near a parochial school. Many of the students were waving banners and shouting Bill Buckley slogans. Bobby professed amazement that they could be for the Conservative candidate. "He's going to have school on Saturday," the Senator jested to the youngsters. "He's going to have the nuns hit you with a ruler. A real loud boo for Buckley!"

Later, when informed of the Beame camp's dissatisfaction with his performance, Bobby asserted, "I was just having a little fun with the children."

Many Reformers were aghast at the spectacle of Bobby beating the drums (or trying to) for regular Democrat Beame against a progressive Republican like Lindsay. With Wagner no longer in official life, Bobby had become the major figure in the party and this was the first exhibition of his leadership. Jimmy Wechsler, for example, opined: "As the state's Democratic Senator, Robert F. Kennedy's role in the campaign was consistent with political protocol. Yet even he engaged in excesses of simulated enthusiasms that diminished his own stature especially among dedicated young voters and enhanced the impact of Lindsay's extraordinary personal triumph."

To make matters worse, it was only after the campaign was over that Bobby learned that Abe Beame and his advisers had consulted with his mortal enemy Roy Cohn on several occasions. In fact, one conference had taken place shortly after the same group had met with Bobby himself.

And on Election Day there was one final embarrassment. Bobby and Ethel were challenged at the voting booth on the ground that they were not legal residents of that election district. The challenge was made by City Councilman

Theodore Roosevelt Kupferman, a law partner of Robert Price, Lindsay's campaign manager.*

The Kennedys had had to wait for over an hour at a public school on East 81st Street after Kupferman said, "I challenge your right to vote, because I don't believe you're a resident of this district." If looks could kill, Kupferman would have been struck dead. The Kennedys glaringly filled out an affidavit claiming that they maintained a residence at the Carlyle Hotel, and election officials finally allowed them to vote.

"It's a nice publicity stunt for that smart guy," Bobby said.

That night the Kennedys gathered at the duplex of brother-in-law Stephen Smith, as they had done a year earlier, to watch the election returns. Jacqueline Kennedy was there, as were Rose Kennedy and other members of the family, friends and campaign aides.

After it was apparent that Beame had lost, Ethel reminded Bobby he needed some rest. And so, off to bed.

The following day the political pundits appeared divided on whether or not Bobby had been hurt by the debacle. Mary McGrory did not think so. She thought Bobby had "walked away from the wreckage of Democratic hopes in the New York City election without a visible scratch." Others wondered whether, with Lindsay's election, Kennedy any longer had a monopoly on youth and glamour. By and large, the Reformers forgave Bobby's participation in the campaign on the ground that, as a party man, he had no alternative. "Besides," commented Miss McGrory, "his lightsome pleas rather confirmed their feeling that there was not a great deal to say about Beame. All agree that Kennedy is now not only free but obligated to take a strong line in party affairs."

But, if Bobby felt so obligated, he went about it in a peculiar way. Two days after the election, he flew off to the West Coast for some speaking engagements and then on to South America for three weeks, hardly the strategy of a man anxious to inject himself into the bloody warfare of the Democratic clubhouses.

Nevertheless, from Buenos Aires, of all places, Bobby

* Kupferman was to win Lindsay's Congressional seat within a few months in a tight contest with Kennedy-supported Orin Lehman.

announced that he intended to assume personal leadership of New York State's Democratic party on his return from South America. *New York Times* correspondent Martin Arnold, traveling with Bobby, said the Senator had "told friends" (the "friends" obviously being the reporters present) that he intended to steer clear of the intraparty squabbling so common in New York State. One reason he did not want to get involved was to avoid the issue of "bossism." "Now," Arnold reported, "Mr. Kennedy is said to be convinced that whatever he does he will be associated with the so-called bosses by certain sectors of the press and public. If he is going to be hit with the brush, he feels he might as well paint the house."

Almost immediately after Bobby's trial balloon went up, New York City Council President-elect Frank D. O'Connor shot it down with a sharp shaft characterizing Kennedy as only *one* of the state's leading Democrats. O'Connor, who had received the biggest vote of any candidate in the 1965 citywide elections, including even John Lindsay, further stated that it would be "a group of us" who would chart the party's policy and future.

"Privately," reported Dominick Peluso in the New York *Daily News,* "most of the top Democrats throughout the state endorse the O'Connor barbs leveled at Senator Kennedy's grand design to make the state party his personal preserve.

"But none of them, thus far, has dared publicly to join O'Connor's ranks because of Bobby's reputation—whether deserved or not—for seeking political vengeance against those who oppose his will.

"On the other hand, it is interesting to note that no one has rushed forward to support the view that Kennedy should wear the leadership mantle."

Meanwhile, Bobby was racing around South America advising the natives how to run their affairs and interfering in local politics to the extent that the State Department made no secret of its concern. Even before he had left on his tour, he had got into a violent argument with officials at a State Department briefing on Latin America. The principal confrontation was between Kennedy and Jack Hood Vaughn, then Assistant Secretary of State for Inter-American Affairs.*

---

* More recently, Vaughn has headed the Peace Corps.

What set Bobby off was Vaughn's suggestion that he explain to Latin Americans why the United States intervention in the Dominican crisis had been necessary. "I will like hell," said Bobby.

Bobby was also annoyed when Vaughn quoted a statement made by President Kennedy to the effect that the United States could not afford to be bound by a non-intervention policy when the national security was at stake. The statement had been made during the Cuban crisis, at a time when Bobby was sitting in the White House advising his brother, Vaughn further noted. Bobby angrily made clear he did not believe his brother had meant to justify anything like the Dominican affair.

Persons present in Vaughn's office reported that another dispute centered around the question of how well U.S. aid policies in Latin America were doing at the time as compared with the Kennedy years. Among other things, Bobby was told how the United States had "frozen" soft-term loans to Peru a year before because of a continuing dispute between that country and the International Petroleum Company over oil properties which the Peruvians were threatening to nationalize. Bobby said he did not believe that aid programs should be an instrument of foreign policy, particularly in a dispute involving a private company such as IPC, a Standard Oil Company subsidiary.

Vaughn replied that he did not agree with the manner in which "your brother" cut off aid to a Peruvian military junta that had staged a bloodless coup in 1962 to prevent a leftist party electoral victory. Bobby bridled at Vaughn's use of the expression "your brother" and bitterly demanded that Vaughn refer to him as "President Kennedy."

The two men also argued over President Kennedy's decision to cut off aid to the Dominican Republic when Juan Bosch was overthrown by a military coup in September 1963.

"It became perfectly obvious that the Administration did not want Bobby to make the Latin American trip," the Chicago *Daily News* later quoted a Kennedy partisan.

The differences grew so acrimonious that Kennedy stalked out of Vaughn's office. Both men obviously felt they were too far apart to continue the discussion. Later Bobby told a newsman, "It sounds like we're all working for United Fruit again."

Bobby's aides, though conceding that the Senator's five-nation, twenty-one-day trip was partly in search of Stateside publicity, insisted that he was really interested in Latin American problems. It was Bobby's first major visit since 1946 when, released from duty as a seaman second class aboard the destroyer *Joseph P. Kennedy Jr.,* he had spent six weeks touring the continent. (In December 1962, he had flown to Brasilia for a brief visit to express President Kennedy's displeasure with the leftist and inflationary policies of the then President João Goulart.) This time, however, Kennedy was accompanied by an entourage of Presidential proportions. In fact, as Andrew J. Glass later noted in *The Saturday Evening Post,* Bobby's "Latin hosts assumed he was there to gather experience for a Presidential contest against Lyndon Johnson. At nearly every stop cheering throngs threw rose petals at his car and chanted *'Presidente, Presidente'* as he rode by."

BOBBY KENNEDY HAS OPENED HIS PRESIDENTIAL CAMPAIGN was the headline in *Expreso* of Lima, Peru.

"I am not thinking of running for the Presidency," Bobby informed reporters at almost every press conference. "I have a high feeling for President Johnson. He has been very kind to me. I would support his bid for re-election in 1968, and I strongly wish to campaign for him."

Glass was one of a dozen or so newsmen who accompanied the Kennedy party, which included Bobby's longtime secretary Angela Novello; Adam Walinsky, who wrote his speeches; Richard Goodwin, former aide to both Presidents Kennedy and Johnson; John Seigenthaler, now editor of the Nashville *Tennessean,* who acted as *de facto* press secretary; and Thomas Johnston, a New York-based aide who, among other things, paid the bills.*

Also traveling with Bobby was New York attorney Bill vanden Heuvel, who alternated as bodyguard and researcher.

---

* At times aide Johnston neglected to pay. One such occasion occurred in Buenos Aires when bills totaling over $1,000 went unpaid, to the embarrassment of U.S. Embassy personnel in the Argentinian capital. The creditors put up a howl; and the Ambassador himself paid certain bills, lest there be unfavorable publicity. Finally, after considerable correspondence between Buenos Aires and New York, the Kennedy office paid its debts in mid-May 1966—eight months after they had been incurred. The bills were for monogrammed handkerchiefs for Bobby, a bullhorn, a Plaza Hotel tab for his staff (Bobby stayed at the Embassy residence) and other odds and ends. By the time they were paid, depreciation of the peso had greatly reduced them.

Ethel Kennedy brought along several friends including Judy Harris, an old school chum, and Mrs. Frederick Ames Cushing, a part-time volunteer in Bobby's Manhattan headquarters. And a good time was had by all—except for a few unpleasant episodes.

One of these occurred at the University of Chile in Concepción, where Castroites and assorted leftists spat upon and pelted the Senator. "Go home, go home, you Yankee son of a whore," the Communists shouted at Bobby. Then the frenzied comrades sang the Chilean national anthem and followed it up with the Cuban anthem. Bobby stood up for both.

For ten minutes he remained silent. The shouts were deafening and the curses—as Andrew Glass noted—were no longer printable. After several attempts to speak, Bobby challenged the Communists. "Let one of them come down here and debate me," he shouted. "I challenge you to a debate! I am willing! Will you test your ideas before the students of this university?"

"Assassin!" screamed back the Communists. "Murderer!"

Ethel Kennedy, a man from the Embassy at her side, looked on wide-eyed as an American flag was set afire by the Communists. The Embassy man giggled nervously, according to Andrew Glass. "Don't you laugh when the American flag is being burned," Ethel said sharply. And wiping spittle from the corner of his eye, Bobby told his aides, "Let's go. We've done what we came to do."

Wherever he went in Latin America, Bobby seemed to go out of his way to tangle with the brass—native as well as American. At times the Senator showed a lack of courtesy, as when he canceled a formal dinner with a provincial Governor arranged by the Embassy at Bobby's request. His excuse was that he wanted to rest. The State Department people on the scene also felt the edge of Bobby's impatience. And they weren't any too happy about what they considered the inordinate demands of his thoroughly inconsiderate staff.

"I wouldn't vote for Bobby Kennedy if he were the last American on earth," exclaimed one frustrated information officer, suddenly ordered to translate, mimeograph and deliver copies of a speech to a distant student rally—and in less than three hours.

Arriving in Lima, Bobby was infuriated when only minor

crowds were on hand to greet him. The Embassy cited "security precautions" as the reason for withholding word of his arrival until the last minute, but according to Glass, Kennedy's staff "was convinced that U.S. Ambassador J. Wesley Jones had held back in hope of scoring brownie points with Lyndon Johnson."

The next day, leaving Ethel behind to do the school and hospital circuit, Bobby flew to Cuzco, the Inca capital high in the Andes. Getting off the plane, he spotted a crowd of some 2,000 Indians and mestizos waiting behind a barbed-wire fence. Ignoring a bouquet-carrying welcoming committee, he shook hands with people through the barricade—much to the consternation of the police. After a triumphant ride downtown, the Kennedy party got a once-over-lightly tour of the gable-roofed city and then headed for a vocational training school run by the Army, where Bobby tangled with a two-star general who was guiding him through the buildings.

Later that day, flanked by Spanish and Quechua interpreters, Kennedy spoke to some 300 peasants in a mountainside village about 50 miles from Cuzco. "There are people outside this village who are on your side, who wish you well. The people of America want to help get your children educated, your homes built, and your fields made fertile. And I want you to know that they are proud to be associated with your village."

Several times Bobby tried to thank his audience in Quechua, but the tongue-twisting sounds eluded him, and finally he switched to his two-word Spanish vocabulary: *"Moochas gratchas,"* which the interpreter translated for the still-puzzled audience as *"Muchas gracias."*

At another village, Bobby watched children perform a harvest dance to the wailing sounds of Indian music and cross-examined a dozen Peace Corps volunteers about their work. Ostensibly, Bobby had flown to the area for a firsthand examination of how the Alliance for Progress was faring. He gamely downed a cup of *aguardiente,* a raw sugar-cane liquor, but passed a glass of the brown, unappetizing-looking beer called *chicha* to Dick Goodwin, who grinned and said, "I am expendable."

That evening, looking haggard with weariness, Bobby was back in Cuzco for a meeting with leftist college students. The questions, not unexpectedly, were bitterly anti-American.

"Sometimes," Bobby sighed at one point, "I wish somebody said something nice about the United States."

The day ended on a typical Kennedy ploy: caught in a crush of admirers, the Senator extricated himself by racing vanden Heuvel a block and a half to the hotel. He won by two yards.

Bobby celebrated his fortieth birthday party at the São Paulo home of wealthy American friends. After dinner, Ethel handed out party favors from a paper bag, explaining what each one signified. There was, for example, a paper U-2 plane that, according to Ethel, Lyndon Johnson had ordered to spy on Bobby's progress in Latin America.

Throughout the trip, Bobby was kept informed by his Washington-based press secretary on how he was faring on television and in the newspapers back home. "In South America Kennedy never left the headlines, and radio stations suspended their regular programs to provide blow-by-blow reports of his movements," Andrew Glass reported. "But Kennedy was upset, because—back home—the clippings were scanty and the 'play' subdued."

The reason for the subdued attention back home was the fact that Bobby was saying the same things over and over again wherever he went. For example, when asked about United States policy in Santo Domingo, Bobby invariably noted that he had opposed United States intervention there. "But it must be seen in its proper perspective," he went on. "We have no territorial demands there, we want no military base there, we will get out as soon as there is an election even if a Communist is elected."

The New York *World-Telegram* commented: "He is entitled to his opinion, of course. He might be right. But Kennedy should realize, even if his hearers do not, that mere freshman Senators do not make important foreign-policy decisions. And that only the President has the authority to announce such a commitment."

Though Bobby repeatedly announced that "I have come to learn," the evidence suggests that the Senator did more talking than listening. His preconceived notions of Latin American affairs were buttressed by a large loose-leaf briefing book entitled *Easy Answers to Hard Questions*. Prepared by Adam Walinsky, the "answers" were largely based on liberal notions that Latin America was being victimized by American business—e.g., the United Fruit Company. United Fruit—that left-wing symbol of exploitative free enterprise—apparently troubled Bobby no end. In Rio de Janeiro he told 4,000 students at Catholic University, "If all we do is complain about the universities, criticize the government, carry signs, make speeches to one another, and then leave to take a job with United Fruit . . . and then not pay any attention to those who need our help, then we have not met our responsibility."

This glib association of the United Fruit Company with poverty, and the overlooking of the readily available facts concerning the benefits accruing from such American investments, is typical. But then one must remember that Bobby was well into his thirties before he himself discovered poverty in the hills of West Virginia during the 1960 Presidential primary contest.

Bobby also lashed out at "the incredible hypocrisy" of rich liberals who talked about social revolution but did very little about it. Invariably before student groups he would say, "A revolution is coming—a revolution that will be peaceful if we are wise enough, compassionate if we care enough, successful if we are fortunate enough—but a revolution will come whether we will it or not. We can affect its character, we cannot alter its inevitability."

Headlined one Rio newspaper: KENNEDY PREACHES REVOLUTION!

In the closing days, Bobby and his party were cutting uphill through a sugar-cane field in northeast Brazil when they came across a slender, baby-faced cane cutter. When Bobby asked how much he was paid, the boy replied through an interpreter, "Twenty-five hundred cruzeiros [$1.25] a week." Angrily Bobby turned on the plantation agent and exploded. "Now don't you think that this is outrageous? Don't you know you are making way for your own destruction?" Then, turning to the puzzled worker, he said, "I only hope for the sake of all Pernambuco landowners that they improve your living conditions and that you remain with them on reasonably friendly terms. If they don't, they won't last very long."

Commented *National Review:* "The company's management representative is not reported to have snapped back that cane cutters are earning wages substantially in excess of those earned by Mr. Kennedy's grandparents even at a time when the American economy was advanced over the present stage of the Brazilian economy. There is no excuse for wages that are artificially low as the result of monopolistic exploitation; but there is no way in the world to increase wages beyond the capacity of an economy to produce. Latin America is dirt-poor, and will only rise from wretchedness through hard work—and through political stability. . . ."

Though, as Bobby repeatedly said, he had "come to learn" and not to intervene in local political affairs, he urged Chilean workers to support the social reforms of President Eduardo Frei Montalva, a Christian Democrat. And after meeting with Frei, he reported, "Of all the heads of government I've met around the world and all their administrations, I am as much impressed with this group as any I've seen." However, when it came to Brazilian President Humberto Castelo Branco, whose government had saved a major nation from a Communist takeover, Bobby made clear his displeasure. In Rio he ostentatiously avoided the President. Instead, he was photographed with a soccer star. Only after touring the country did the two meet, and reporters were quick to note that the meeting was short and perfunctory.

Since the military seizure of power, President Castelo had been weeding out Communists and their sympathizers from all walks of Brazilian life. His efforts to quell Communist agitation, needless to say, led to the usual charges that he was hampering freedom.

"What do you think of our government?" a student asked Bobby.

"There's a good deal of criticism of North Americans for their intervention in the internal affairs of other countries," the Senator responded. "Of course," he added with an almost imperceptible smile, "you know where I stand: I believe in freedom of speech, freedom to criticize. . . ." When he finished, the applause was loud and clear.

Venezuela was the last stop on the long, tiring trip, and the Senator's arrival in Caracas touched off an anti-American demonstration in which students exchanged gunfire with the police. Several buses were burned in separate parts of the city, which led one Venezuelan cynic to observe, "Any more visits by distinguished Americans and we're not going to have much transportation left."

The last day, Bobby visited President Raúl Leoni, spoke at

a labor rally, and paid the by-now customary visit to a slum. And then it was all over. He flew home.

James Wechsler of the New York *Post* called to inquire whether the Senator had received an invitation from any State Department official for a report on his expedition, and Bobby told him he hadn't. Wechsler was apparently laboring under the illusion that Bobby had something new in the way of information to impart to America's foreign-policy makers. But the record clearly demonstrates that the Senator had not. "I've seen or heard little that I haven't been briefed on," the Senator told one newsman toward the end of his trip. "But coming here was as important for understanding this region as spending a month in West Virginia to learn about U.S. poverty. . . . I think we should become associated with the more progressive elements in the hemisphere rather than being momentarily safe and, in the long run, sorry."

Vice President Nixon had come back with similar conclusions in 1958. The Alliance for Progress, which actually originated in the closing days of the Eisenhower Administration, was founded on the need to do business with "the more progressive elements in the hemisphere." But it is easier to express such sentiments than to translate them into action. Whenever the United States proposed reforms, the Latin Americans would get on their high horses and claim that the Americans were attempting to interfere in their domestic affairs.

"Perhaps," wrote columnist Robert G. Spivack, "the real value of the trip was the spitting episode for its reverse effects. Undoubtedly it illustrated to Kennedy that sworn enemies of the U.S. do not understand or care to learn about the fine differentiations of politics and personality that separate him from the Johnson Administration.

"Certainly Kennedy, like Senators Mansfield, Fulbright or Morse, has a perfect right to disagree with Administration foreign policy and to work as hard as possible to change it. However, when Mansfield, Fulbright or Morse travel abroad, they rarely make speeches or comments to the press. . . . How [Kennedy] might have reacted had some young Senator gone abroad, while his brother was President, and taken a disdainful attitude toward the Administration is not difficult to imagine. . . .

"When lawmakers who are at odds with any administration

carry their differences outside the country, there is an inclination to ask, 'Was this trip necessary?' "

A half year later, in May 1966, Senator Kennedy finally delivered his long-awaited report on Latin America. It was a 20,000-word speech which took Bobby two days to read to the Senate. Whereas fifty-three Senators had turned up to listen to Bobby's nuclear proliferation speech the year before, there were never more than five Senators present (all Democrats) to hear his views on Latin America. And most of the time only the presiding officer was on hand.

But every Senator had been provided with a copy of the speech. It ran to 54 pages of single-spaced typewritten copy on long legal-size paper, complete with six other pages summarizing the document. Nothing was overlooked. The whole packet was delivered to reporters days in advance. The networks were advised, and video tapes were cut on the key passages, all aimed at the national news shows.

"The public relations aspects of this exercise," wrote James Reston of the *Times,* "are very similar to the techniques established during the period when John F. Kennedy was mounting his campaign for the Presidency after the 1956 election. Once the areas of political opportunity are identified, the scholars are mobilized. The evening seminars continue at his country house in Virginia. The writers are brought in and the speech is finally launched with all the care of a major advertising campaign."

For the most part, however, the speech proved a dud. While Bobby's colleagues were too polite to say so publicly, most of them privately thought it far too long. And in analyzing the text for *The New York Times,* correspondent Richard Eder observed: "Considering the work and consideration that went into preparing it and the expectations it aroused, Senator Kennedy's two-day exposition . . . reached what has been termed some remarkably unremarkable conclusions."

The speech contained the familiar litany of Latin American squalor: Illiteracy is 50 percent in some countries and is increasing; half the population never reach their fourth birthday; incomes are often under $100 a year, which would be worse than destitution here and means not-so-slow starvation there. He urged a greater emphasis on education and land reform, and recommended doubling U.S. capital assistance and the establishment of a private investment code that would stress local sovereignty as well as give a guarantee to American investors. He asked for a selective reduction in military aid, strong efforts to encourage democratic governments, fuller consultation with Western Hemisphere partners before any such decisions to intervene as in the Dominican Republic.

In one area he was fairly bold. He went beyond many members of his own church to advocate the offer of U.S. funds for family planning in Latin America. At their present rate of population growth, the 230,000,000 Latin Americans would, Senator Kennedy said, be 363,000,000 by 1980. "We cannot compel Latin Americans to practice birth control. This would only inflame suspicions that we seek to keep them underpopulated and weak. But we should stand ready to help; we should encourage any efforts they undertake to make themselves more aware of their problem . . . and we should help them make the decision that is truly in the interest of their people and serves the goals of the Alliance. . . ."

No comment was forthcoming from the White House, though some political analysts were interpreting the speech as containing mild slaps at the President. For his part, Vice President Humphrey regarded it as "a good speech." But Humphrey aides were quick to say that Hubert Horatio had said many of the same things in his sixteen years in the Senate, and had advanced similar proposals in a *Foreign Affairs* article just prior to the 1964 Democratic Convention.

At the State Department, it was conceded that Kennedy had sent an advance copy to the then Alliance for Progress coordinator Lincoln Gordon. "It's obvious," one source said, "that there were things in the speech Gordon was not fully in accord with. After all, it is critical of him at some points. But Gordon felt that, on balance, the speech was not as supercritical as he had been led to expect."

In Mexico there was strong reaction. Deputy Manuel Origel Salazar of the offical government party—Partido Revolucionario Institucional (PRI)—said, "Mr. Kennedy does not know what he is talking about when he refers to Mexico. We accept that there may still be a lot of shortcomings in Central and South America, but not in Mexico, where important goals have been achieved in raising the farmers' living standards. We also accept that there are still some problems here and that we must do our best from day to day to remedy them, but we will do so without political guidance from anyone."

The last phrase was the crux of Latin American criticism of the junior Senator from New York, according to a story filed by the late Jules Dubois, then dean of American correspondents in Latin America. Writing in the *Chicago Tribune*, Dubois contended that Latin Americans "dislike what they regard as his political meddling in Latin American affairs. . . . Kennedy's utterances on Latin America are traced to the fact that during his visit last year he sought out only the radical left and ignored the members of the business community and political leaders who may have been moderates, right of center or conservatives.

"Had he taken the time (he spent four days touring the Amazon) to discuss the problems of free enterprise and social reforms with those members of the business and political community, he would have left Latin America with a more balanced and a more objective picture that would have prevented him from making some of the statements that have cropped up in his Senate speeches. . . ."

Another view was provided by a veteran career diplomat who said of Bobby's tour of Latin America that he could not imagine a "worse way to promote international good will." Ellis O. Briggs did not mention Kennedy by name in a New York speech, but he left no doubt about whom he was speaking. "The hospitable good neighbors must have heaved a sigh of relief audible from Puerto Rico to Puerto Montt [in Chile] when a youthful Senator returned to the United States last autumn without upsetting a Latino applecart or smearing himself with anything more detergent than ripe *aguacates* [avocados]."

Briggs had retired from the diplomatic service in 1962 after a forty-one-year career. He had been Ambassador in four Latin American countries—the Dominican Republic, Uruguay, Peru and Brazil—since 1945; he had also been Ambassador to Czechoslovakia, Greece and Spain, as well as Ambassador to Korea during the war and the armistice negotiations. The occasion of his speech was the acceptance of an award from The American Foundation, a group whose aim is helping American nations to get along together. Deriding Bobby's actions, he observed, "In a reverse situation, an invading foreigner who presumed to harangue a North American audience about civil rights, the slowness of desegregation, or inadequate taxes would be lucky to escape with a shirt on his back. He would almost certainly lose his *bombachas* [a Spanish word for breeches]."

25

Moving Leftward

One trait possessed by Bobby Kennedy in abundance is summarized in the Yiddish word *chutzpah*. The *Random House Dictionary of the English Language* defines the expression as "unmitigated effrontery" or "impudence," and a good example of a man with *chutzpah* is the son who after murdering his parents goes before the judge to plead for leniency on grounds that he is an orphan. A good example of Bobby's *chutzpah* was the way he intervened at almost the last minute in New York City's unprecedented two-week-long transit strike that virtually crippled the metropolis in January 1966.

Actually the Senator's intervention was unnecessary, as the strike was on the way to being settled. But the purpose of the Kennedy ploy was obvious. Bobby wanted to take some credit for the settlement without performing a solitary thing to deserve it.

The strike had begun in the early hours of January 1. Later that morning John V. Lindsay—whom Bobby views as a competitor for the affections of the liberal community—took the oath of office as the one hundred and third Mayor of the city. In his inaugural address on City Hall steps, beneath a coffin-gray sky, Lindsay blasted the walkout as "an unlawful strike against the public interest . . . an act of defiance against eight million people."

The leader of the transit workers, Michael J. Quill, told Lindsay in effect to go to hell. A few days later Quill was arrested, convicted for precipitating an illegal strike, and jailed. But except for a brief telegram to Lindsay offering "any assistance" that might be helpful in settling the dispute, Robert F. Kennedy appeared to have lost his tongue. The man who voiced an opinion on just about any subject, could not, for once, decide what to say.

James A. Wechsler, his admiring chronicler, claimed that the transit strike had "placed Senator Kennedy on a spot on which he would almost certainly be damned if he acted and no less bitterly condemned if he didn't. There were some urging him to fly into the city and even conduct a dramatic personal visit to Mrs. Mike Quill; there were others imploring him to remain silent. . . ."

Bobby remained silent. And his silence did not go unnoticed. Letters condemning his unnatural forbearance were published in the newspapers. "Where's Bobby Kennedy?" they asked. Also there were the gags. Asked why Bobby hadn't intervened in the transit dispute, a television newscaster responded, "Maybe because he hasn't heard about it yet." *

Then, just as the subway strike was about to grind to a dreary end, Bobby, fresh from a skiing expedition, made a surprise appearance at City Hall to confer with Mayor Lindsay. The purpose of the visit was never made clear. To this day, Mayor Lindsay claims to be uncertain why the junior Senator had decided to pay him a call.

During their forty-minute conference, Lindsay briefed the Senator on the latest developments in the strike. From time to time, as the Mayor described the situation, the Senator would interrupt with a question. Then both men emerged and talked to the press. They stood side by side, smiling into a bank of television lights. Lindsay, who spoke first, said he was "delighted to have the junior Senator from New York as our guest here at City Hall," and that he considered the visit "a sign that all good men pull together in times of difficulty."

---

* During Gotham's fantastic garbage strike, when 100,000 tons of garbage piled high on the city's streets in February 1968, the usually voluble Bobby managed to stay away from the city and to avoid comment on the illegal strike that brought on a row between Mayor Lindsay and Governor Rockefeller. At one point, he turned up looking for poverty in eastern Kentucky. One reason he kept his mouth shut was the fact that the striking union, the Uniformed Sanitationmen's Association, had been in his corner in the 1964 Senate race. Hardly a profile in courage. Rather a profile in caution.

Asked for his view, Bobby began, "Well, I think I have no original thought on it." When Bobby was asked a second question, the Senator said, "I don't think there's anything further that I can add that will help the situation."

The impromptu press conference lasted five minutes.

Bobby then repaired to the office of City Council President Frank D. O'Connor where he unburdened himself of some criticism of the Mayor. He said the Mayor was guilty of bad timing in not asking a mediation panel to propose a strike settlement "forty-eight hours ago." (Earlier in the day, Lindsay had directed the three-man mediation panel to draw up their own terms for a settlement.)

Asked by reporters later whether the idea to request a solution from the panel was his or Lindsay's, the Senator replied, "That doesn't matter." And asked if he thought the Mayor had exercised poor judgment in the negotiations, Bobby said, "That sort of thing doesn't help."

Lindsay was angry when he heard about Kennedy's comments. "That boy sure knows how to play rough," the Mayor told a friend. But, publicly, a spokesman for the Mayor said that Lindsay would have no comment.

Despite Bobby's intervention, the strike was settled the next day. And satirist Art Buchwald, in a column entitled "Bobby Saves the Day," wrote: "Sources close to Mayor Lindsay say the Mayor's warmth and gratitude to Senator Kennedy for coming in at the end of the strike has never been higher. The Mayor just has no words to express it."

Ten days later the Mayor again refused to comment when Bobby objected strenuously to Lindsay's hogging the publicity in connection with cleaning up a rubble-strewn lot in the southeast Bronx. The Mayor had obtained considerable coverage in the newspapers and on TV, by shoveling aside debris, tossing a football to neighborhood children, and announcing he would shortly order a "vest-pocket park" constructed on the site.

Bobby, after reading about it in the Sunday papers, was furious. No one had mentioned the fact that he had had a prior interest in the park. "The idea that the place had suddenly been discovered as if it was brand-new was amazing," Kennedy aide Tom Johnston told reporters. "The Senator was shocked." In fact, the day before Lindsay's visit, Bobby had presented Parks Commissioner Thomas P. F. Hoving with a scale model of a "dream" park for the site. "That scale is in Hoving's office right now."

The scale model had been constructed without publicity or reimbursement by architect John "Rod" Warnecke, who had designed the memorial to President Kennedy at Arlington. According to the plans, the park would contain an Air Force jet, a fire truck, a swimming pool, a baseball field and places for climbing. Bobby had planned to raise private funds for the project. Johnston said the Senator was "up there a number of times during the past year, without photographers. We didn't want publicity because we didn't want to build up people's hopes."

Speaking for the Lindsay Administration, Hoving said there certainly was no desire to "horn in" on a Kennedy project. "I deeply regret if Senator Kennedy is upset by the publicity this cleanup received," he said. He added he would be willing to assume the blame. "I would be delighted to be the goat, if this is going to lead to a good recreation facility."

The New York *World-Telegram* ran this short editorial: "Senator Robert F. Kennedy, who has been pretty successful personally and politically, is pouting because Mayor Lindsay got some mileage out of an idea he says was his.

"Relax, sir. You're still young, no elections are immediately ahead, and there's plenty of room for praise and blame for everyone in New York's governmental jungle, from parks to transit and in between."

Bobby didn't think so. He wanted all the credit he could get, even when it meant breaking an agreement with New York's senior Senator. Javits had been under the impression that Bobby had agreed to issue joint announcements whenever a major defense contract went to New York or a Federal agency made a major grant in the state. And announcements of a number of relatively minor awards had been put out in both their names. But often, when the dollars were numerous or the local impact significant, Javits learned of the grants through newspaper stories that featured his junior colleague's name prominently.

Javits, annoyed, took his complaints to the White House, Vice President Humphrey and Robert C. Weaver, Secretary of the Department of Housing and Urban Development. "In all cases," the *New York Herald Tribune* reported, "Senator Kennedy's methods have been deplored, but presumably there is no way to demand a change, if indeed one is desired."

Two incidents, particularly, had provoked Javits' wrath. On one, Bobby had taken John L. Sweeney, Federal co-chairman of the Appalachia program, on a tour of Southern-tier counties during which several aid projects were announced. And on a similar swing through northern New York, with Kennedy by his side, Eugene P. Foley, Director of the Economic Development Administration, announced grants aimed at opening up the economically stagnant area to further Federal funds.

There was little doubt that these upstate activities were effective in building up Bobby's image as the Senator who could really get things done when Federal funds were needed for local projects. And Javits was not willing to take this kind of *chutzpah* lying down. New York's senior Senator took to the airwaves to voice his differences with Kennedy. Javits felt that Bobby was "really beginning to press the system to its outermost limits," and he vowed that he intended to see "what can be done about making these announcements more objective."

Commented Ted Lewis in the New York *Daily News*, "It would not be fair to say that Senate life has become unbearable to Javits since Kennedy became his New York colleague last year. But Javits did work in complete harmony with Bobby's predecessor, Kenneth B. Keating, partly because Keating was a Republican, but mostly because Javits had an equal share of the limelight without having to battle for it as he has with Kennedy. . . .

"Actually, of course, Bobby, it is felt here, is in a much more advantageous position all around. In the first place, just because of the magic of the Kennedy name, whatever he does has the effect of overshadowing Javits. Secondly, when he utters words of wisdom in the Senate he is sure to get more national attention than Javits ever could have reason to expect. This is because Bobby's prospects for the future are much more glamorous. He is young. Talk naturally concerns his White House chances in 1972.

"Can another Kennedy be President someday? is a question that provokes discussion at any social or political huddle.

"How can Javits possibly compete in the same arena with a Kennedy? Well, Javits has clearly decided to take on that

Herculean task. And it is admitted on all sides that, though defeat is likely, he gets better than a passing grade for simply trying."

It was a titillating game to watch. After Bobby made his swing through Latin America, Javits followed suit, making a far more extensive tour. On his return, however, Javits was called in to see the President and report on his findings, as Kennedy had not been. Nevertheless, Bobby received the lion's share of publicity. For a long time, Javits could not become reconciled to the unfairness of the press coverage.

Bobby also renewed his feud with Nelson Rockefeller. This time the Senator accused the Governor of gross neglect of the mentally retarded in state institutions, some of whom, he claimed, were "worse off than animals in a zoo." The quarrel had to do with whether Rockefeller had availed himself of available Federal funds appropriated for the retarded. It was Bobby's point that Rockefeller simply hadn't got around to filling in the necessary forms. And it was Rockefeller's point that such grants call for matching grants from the supplicant state, and that the Empire State had its own problems and was spending its money as best it could. Moreover, the Governor angrily contended that Kennedy was trying to set himself up as a "political broker" on Federal funds, adding, "Never before in history has a Senator injected himself this way."

Bobby retorted that the Governor was "jeopardizing the future of children and others for the benefit of his own political administration."

The upshot was that Rockefeller said he would set up a staff in Washington to make sure the state got all Federal money available. And Bobby named an eight-man committee to develop plans to tap Federal surpluses he believed were in the offing. Both, however, switched their positions on Federal aid when it came to aiding the New Haven Railroad, whose Manhattan-bound commuters would be left stranded if the railroad were permitted to discontinue its passenger service.

Rockefeller told an Interstate Commerce Commission hearing that, in his judgment, "there is no real or lasting solution to the total problem of the New Haven Railroad" without Federal aid. Bobby, who had previously complained that the state was not tapping all the available Federal funds for mental-health programs, took the reverse view. He said that the fate of various bills in Congress in 1965 made it clear that "the Federal Government will not be the immediate source of salvation" for the New Haven, that state and local governments would have to shoulder most of the public burden.

In his testimony before the ICC, Rockefeller took another jab at Kennedy. He said that in grappling with the New Haven's difficulties, a joint state and Federal committee had been set up at one point with "an aide to the then Attorney General, Robert Kennedy," as a member. The Governor stated, to the accompaniment of titters, that the aide "attended one meeting and then never was heard of again."

But Bobby kept hitting away at Rockefeller for other alleged derelictions. He hit at one point by contending that the Governor's veto of a statewide primary bill was aimed at preventing Senator Javits from becoming the 1966 Republican gubernatorial candidate. "It is quite clear that if he had not vetoed the bill there would be a statewide primary and Javits would be running for Governor," Bobby said, simulating sorrow over the fate of his senior colleague. (Javits had previously indicated that he might be interested in contesting Rockefeller for the nomination.) Bobby also charged that the number of narcotics addicts in New York State had doubled under Governor Rockefeller. He opposed the Rockefeller program for compulsory treatment of addicts and stated that what he called the Governor's plan to "sweep the addicts off the streets" would cost hundreds of millions of dollars and fail to solve anything.

On February 19, 1966, Bobby very nearly came to an open break with the Johnson Administration over Vietnam. The junior Senator had been watching the television proceedings of the Senate Foreign Relations Committee hearings in his office. As the questioning droned on, Bobby restlessly paced the floor and found himself talking back to the boob tube. Finally, he decided he had to say something about what was dominating the thoughts of many Americans. And when Bobby decides to say something, he has at his disposal a squad of speech-writers who in this case worked around the clock to produce a lengthy statement, which Bobby read at a well-attended Saturday press conference.

It made the usual appeal for the right of dissent. In so

doing, of course, Bobby placed himself on the side of the angels. "The greater the issue, the larger the stakes, the more passionately debate has raged, in the Senate and across the land. Abraham Lincoln was reviled for opposing the war of 1848. . . . Those who saw the storm, and tried desperately to prepare the nation for World War II, were cursed as warmongers, enemies of mankind, subverters of democracy—and worse."

Thus, in one paragraph, Kennedy managed to praise anti-war and pro-war elements at the same time.

The reference to Lincoln was bad history, of course. There wasn't any war in 1848. The Mexican War terminated in 1847. Lincoln made his anti-war speech on January 2, 1848. And Lincoln made a special point of saying that he had thought he should remain silent until the war ended. He also pointed out that he had voted for all necessary supplies and support for the troops.

But the passage in the Kennedy statement that aroused the most controversy was: "Whatever the exact status of the National Liberation Front—puppet or partly independent—any negotiated settlement must accept the fact that there are discontented elements in South Vietnam, Communist and non-Communist, who desire to change the existing political and economic system of the country. There are three things you can do with such groups: kill or repress them, turn the country over to them, or admit them to a share of power and responsibility. The first two are now possible only through force of arms.

"The last—to admit them to a share of power and responsibility—is at the heart of the hope for a negotiated settlement. It is not the easy way, or the sure way; nor can the manner of the degrees of participation now be described with any precision. It may come about through a single conference or many meetings, or by a slow, undramatic process of gradual accommodation.

"It will require enormous skill and political wisdom to find the point at which participation does not bring domination or internal conquest. It will take statesmanship willing to exploit the very real differences of ambition and intention and interest between Hanoi and Peking and the Soviet Union. It may mean a compromise government fully acceptable to neither side."

What Bobby was saying, in effect, was that one way to end the war was to guarantee in advance that the Communist guerrillas would be seated in a coalition government, which ran counter to the White House contention that it was self-defeating to make any concessions in advance of negotiations. Secretary of State Rusk, in fact, in his appearance the previous day before the Foreign Relations Committee, had repeatedly made clear his opposition to a coalition government by citing the experience with such a venture in Laos where, he asserted, the Communists had not abided by the concept of neutralism.

The Kennedy statement also was at odds with the position enunciated before the same committee by General Maxwell D. Taylor, who though an adviser to President Johnson had remained a close personal friend of Bobby. Taylor testified that it was the United States' objective to apply enough military power to force the Communists to accept an independent and non-Communist South Vietnam.*

When Chairman J. William Fulbright said that he regarded this as requiring unconditional surrender and that he wished the Administration would seek "a compromise to stop the slaughter," General Taylor asked, "How do you compromise the freedom of fifteen million South Vietnamese people?"

The Administration was not long in responding to Bobby's statement. McGeorge Bundy, then White House Special Assistant on national security affairs, reminded Bobby that in 1963 President Kennedy had warned against coalition governments when he said in Berlin, "I am not impressed by the opportunities open to popular fronts throughout the world. I do not believe that any democrat can successfully ride that tiger." And Undersecretary of State George Ball used the terms "absurd" and "impossible" in discussing Bobby's proposal. Moreover, if adopted, it would lead "in a very short time" to a Communist government in Saigon.

Vice President Humphrey, in New Zealand on the last stop of an Asian tour explaining U.S. policy, angrily replied, "I don't believe in writing a prescription for the ills of

---

* Typical of Bobby's pragmatic nature was the fact that he had named his ninth child after Maxwell Taylor. Bobby is unique in that he is probably the only politician whose political gyrations can be measured by the names of his progeny, or by their godfathers, as in the case of the late Senator McCarthy.

Vietnam that includes a dose of arsenic. It would be something like putting a fox in the chicken coop. Or to put it another way, it would be like installing an arsonist in the fire department. If my advice is asked, I will oppose it."

Some read into the harsh Humphrey comment the beginnings of a 1972 contest for the Democratic Presidential nomination. But according to the well-informed Ted Lewis:

"Sure, Humphrey blew his top! Certainly his nerves were strained from his exhaustive jet swing around the Pacific! . . . But what was really upsetting, yet couldn't be put on the record, was that Kennedy's proposal . . . undercut Humphrey's mission itself. Both in Vietnam and particularly in Thailand, officials were concerned about the U.S. softening its attitude toward the Vietcong. Humphrey thought he had successfully reassured them. Then came the Kennedy move.

"No wonder Humphrey blew his stack. . . ."

Editorial opinion was about as expected. *The New York Times* saw in the Kennedy statement "less a criticism of the President's policies than an invaluable contribution to the decision-making process." But the *Times* foreign affairs columnist, Cyrus L. Sulzberger, concluded that "both Peking and Hanoi must have gained fresh encouragement by the joining of our Know-Nothings with our Know-It-Alls." Kennedy, he observed cuttingly, would have been "more honest to suggest abandoning Vietnam without even bothering to negotiate."

Simultaneously, Bobby found himself being hailed as the new leader of the Senate's doves, and was even editorially embraced by the Communist *Worker*. RFK JOLTS WHITE HOUSE, read a *Worker* headline, GAINS POPULAR SUPPORT. And out in California, the ultra-liberal California Democratic Council's convention booed references to LBJ and Humphrey while a denim-clad activist shouted *"Viva* Bobby Kennedy!"

Bobby, however, claimed to be unimpressed by this sudden burst of affection from the Left. "They used to picket me," he observed wryly, and when informed of the California cheers, said, "Those are the people with the picket signs and beards—aren't they? I don't want the support of the beards."

Bobby took issue with the conclusion reached by many columnists, liberal and conservative alike, that he was deliberately and calculatedly swinging sharply to the Left in order to

fill the vacuum left by a Hubert Humphrey moving toward
the center. In his background talks with newsmen, he noted
that he had deliberately avoided an alliance with J. William
Fulbright and others attacking the President's policy. "I am
not their Wayne Morse," he insisted, contending that in his
statement he had "carefully made it clear—I didn't talk in
generalities—I made it clear as I could that I supported the
President in the military effort." He also disclosed that he had
"communicated this position to the Russians," a reference to
the fact that he had met privately with Soviet UN Ambassador Nikolai Fedorenko to disabuse him of any notion that
the Democratic party was divided into a Johnson wing (pro-
war) and a Kennedy wing (anti-war).

Fundamentally, Bobby insisted, he was not in tune with the
basic precepts of the peace movement. He did not see the
American commitment in Vietnam as a blunder (to do so
would, after all, constitute a repudiation of Jack Kennedy's
foreign policy). Nor did he view U.S. bombings of the North
as immoral. In fact, he planned to support the supplemental
authorization for more funds to support the U.S. troops in
Vietnam.

The furor had plainly surprised the Senator. It was obvious
that Bobby—unless he was being completely Machiavellian—
did not understand the reasons for it. But by advocating a
coalition to run South Vietnam in the interim before elections
were held, Kennedy had gone further than anyone in Washington—even critics like Senator Fulbright. Fulbright clearly
recognized this when he told newsmen the next day that he
thought the composition of an interim government might
better be the subject of negotiations.

With the confusion increasing, Bobby cut short a skiing
holiday in Stowe, Vermont, to return to New York and
Washington, he said, not to clarify his own position but to
reply to his critics. And on Tuesday, February 22, three
days after he made his original statement, Kennedy began
to publicly retreat.

Speaking on NBC-TV's *Today* show and at press conferences, afterward, Bobby said he "hadn't thought" his proposals were very different from those of the Administration.
His only aim was to clarify the "confusion" among Administration officials—to which White House press secretary Bill

Moyers stiffly retorted, "I don't think it is the Administration that is confused."

In full retreat, Bobby called for help from his old friend, General Maxwell Taylor. Taylor obliged him, but in the process only added to the confusion. The General suggested that Bobby didn't mean to say what he had, in fact, said. He explained that Bobby was thinking of giving representation to "discontented elements in South Vietnam, including the Communists" only *after* free elections had been held. Taylor added that he personally did not favor "negotiating" the Communists into a coalition government without elections. Otherwise, he professed that Kennedy's position was "very, very close to what I consider my position."

It quickly got closer. After talking things over with Bill Moyers, Bobby called yet another press conference. This time he said that he was not advocating that the Vietcong "automatically" be given a share of power in any interim Saigon regime. All he was saying was that the United States should not "shut the door" on a Vietcong role at a future conference or even in a future government, else there might never be negotiations.

Said Moyers, "If Senator Kennedy did not propose a coalition government with Communist participation before elections are held, there is no disagreement." At that point, finally, Bobby's reversal was complete. "I find no disagreement between what Mr. Moyers said and what I have said."

But a few days later, Moyers took to evasive tactics. Asked if he felt that Kennedy was now in agreement with the Administration's position, the press secretary replied, "That is not for me to say. That is for Senator Kennedy to say."

But Bobby wasn't saying much more than "There has been some advantage in free discussion." But he disputed those critics who contended he had fudged or backed down on his original statement. "Maybe," he said, "I'll do better next time." And he smiled enigmatically.

Liberal pundit Max Lerner opined: "The disarray surrounding Senator Kennedy's proposal . . . was partly due to the clumsiness of trying to stage a debate through press conferences and TV shows on one side and press secretaries on the other. . . . But partly also it was due to the fact that few public figures (and Kennedy is no exception) have had a chance to think their way through the touchy problems of a peace conference and what would follow it. Compared with this the Vietnam jungle is a grove."

It remained for *Newsweek's* Kenneth Crawford to sum up the contretemps: "It is impossible to classify the Bobby Kennedy who emerged from last week's peace-in-Vietnam episode. He could be dove, hawk, fox in the chicken coop or just a mixed-up kid. While it was going on he was all but smothered by the embrace of doves. When it was all over the hawks hoped he was back on their roost. . . .

"However, there were some who contended that he had been pretty foxy and others who applied the old gag that he had thought things over carefully before going off half-cocked. Those who said he had been confused like a fox pointed out that, while committing himself to nothing much, he had nevertheless left the impression that he was somehow more for peace than the Administration—an impression that serves well his political interest in carving out an independent clarification on the sunny side of the peace issue. Others said his ultimate clarification of previous clarifications indicated that his confusion had been all too genuine. . . .

"Kennedy may have revealed more about himself than about his attitude toward the war in Vietnam. But even this is uncertain. One couldn't be sure whether he had been canny or careless in making a suggestion which was bound to create a furor. On several recent occasions he had betrayed an itch to get into the big debate on the side of the doves either because he thought he had something to contribute or something to gain, or both. But always before he had drawn back, perhaps in deference to the judgment of his late brother. President Kennedy not only decried coalitions with Communists but escalated military intervention in the hope of saving South Vietnam."

Lyndon Johnson had what appeared to be the last word. At a Freedom House dinner in New York, there were moments when the President appeared to be delivering a stern lecture to Bobby, seated a few feet away from him on the Waldorf-Astoria dais. The President recalled the words of John F. Kennedy as if to underline the message: "Let every nation know, whether it wishes us well or ill, that we shall pay any price, bear any burden, meet any hardship, support any friend, oppose any foe to assure the survival and success of liberty."

Newsmen had been told that the President's speech was not a "reply" to Bobby. But Bobby seemed to get the point as he sat on the platform, grimly staring ahead and rarely applauding. As Atra Baer reported in the New York *Journal-American,* "Had there been a mosquito glued to his palm, that mosquito would have taken the slapping around and emerged intact, unsquashed and not even slightly rumpled."

Bobby's presence at the dinner had been unexpected. Along with all New York members of the Congress, he had been invited by the President to fly to New York to listen to his speech. And Bobby decided to go at the last minute. "I got on *Air Force One,* the big Presidential jet," recalls Republican Congressman Theodore Kupferman, "and there was Bobby Kennedy huddled in the corner by himself. Since he claims to live in my district, I went over to talk with him. We got along fine, even though he recalled my contesting his right to vote. As we were about to land, someone—I think it was Bill Moyers—came up and asked if Bobby would like to drive into town with the President. Bobby indicated he had other plans. But he must have thought better of it. For he did drive in with the President."

What they talked about was not overheard. But one thing appeared certain: whatever was said, there was to be no surcease in the growing feud between RFK and LBJ. For in April 1966, Senator Kennedy took on the Administration over its mishandling of the poverty programs—and in the process criticized brother-in-law Sargent Shriver, director of what the Republicans dubbed "the Great Society's poverty empire." Both houses of Congress had been reverberating with charges of "scandal" in the anti-poverty war which according to the Republicans was costing $53,489,000 for salaries of "newly entrenched bureaucrats."

Congressman William H. Ayres, the ranking Republican of the House Education and Labor Committee which handled poverty legislation, said, "Word has gotten around among civil servants that the big money is in poverty." And from the Senate floor, Republican Milward L. Simpson of Wyoming exposed what he described as such a shocking laxity in the poverty program's hiring practices that Bobby was moved to exclaim, "I think the Senator has brought to the attention of the Senate and of the country a situation which is really intolerable."

A week later Bobby was hitting at the Johnson Administration from another angle. He accused the White House of instituting budget cuts that would hit the poor the hardest. Speaking in Accord, New York, the Senator dubbed the cutbacks "unfortunate" and "disturbing." He denounced the Administration for what he alleged was its failure to follow through in areas of education, school lunches, housing and other such programs.

The President was severely wounded by Bobby's contention that he was neglecting the Great Society in favor of Vietnam. Two days later, in a largely ignored speech in Baltimore, Johnson again blasted Kennedy without mentioning his name. He laid it on the line to Bobby and, by inference, stressed how much more he had done for the people than had his predecessor. Among other things, he said, "I'm not funding all the programs I got action on last year. The reason I'm not is that it would take $3 billion extra on my budget. More than that, it takes trained personnel . . . you can't just push a button and have a whole working program." And, he emphasized, "we shall not be stampeded into unwise programs. . . ."

The strongest response to the Kennedy speech came from Representative Joseph Y. Resnick, an upstate New York Democrat. Resnick accused Bobby of making "a completely irresponsible statement" and "talking like a demagogue." He said that Kennedy "should know full well that President Johnson is doing all he can."

"President Johnson got all these programs passed," the Congressman added. "President Kennedy tried to and failed."

In an effort to undercut Bobby, the Johnson Administration authorized two speeches by Defense Secretary McNamara which sounded as if they were lifted from the pages of *The Nation* and *The New Republic*. In the first, before the American Society of Newspaper Editors at Montreal, McNamara proposed that "every young person in the United States give two years of service to his country—whether in one of the military services, in the Peace Corps, or in some other volunteer development work at home or abroad."

Four days later, in a commencement address at Pittsburgh's Chatham College, McNamara took the offensive on another issue of great appeal to Kennedy's youthful admirers—the right of dissent, even in time of war. The Defense Secretary was all for it. And in so doing, McNamara alluded to Plato, Goethe, Blake, Kierkegaard, Kafka, Huxley, Orwell, Ortega y Gasset and Simone de Beauvoir. He romped around in medieval Latin, touched on St. Jerome, the Chinese sages, and Dr. Strangelove, and spoke of the "renaissance of meta-physics" and the "calculus of relevancy." He suggested that the major problem of twentieth-century man was not the "over-management," but rather the "under-management" of his social problems. It was a speech that could have been written by one of Bobby Kennedy's ghost-writers.

Despite accumulating evidence to the contrary, the men around Johnson continued to insist that, as far as the President was concerned, there was no "feud" with Bobby. "I've got no quarrel with Bobby," the President was quoted as saying, "and he should have no quarrel with me. He is of a different generation." (At times, Kennedy himself spoke in private of the "generation gap" between himself and LBJ.)

Meanwhile, Bobby inevitably set off a fresh round of speculation over his long-term political aspirations by taking off in June 1966 for a much-publicized twelve-day swing through Africa. But on the eve of his departure, LBJ tried to steal Bobby's thunder by deploring white supremacy in Africa in a speech to black African Ambassadors.

"It was his first speech on African policy since he became President and the first by an American Chief Executive on the subject since John F. Kennedy spoke briefly on 'Africa Day' in 1961," editorialized *The New York Times*. "Mr. Johnson's remarks . . . were doubtless aimed at countering a feeling widespread in Africa that the Administration is no longer genuinely interested in that continent. Cynics will wonder if the attention given to Senator Kennedy's forth-coming visit to South Africa may also have been a factor."

Months before, Bobby's trip to South Africa had been enveloped in controversy. There could be little doubt that in the eyes of the official Government at Pretoria, his impending visit was as welcome as a mild plague.

After considerable top-level consultation, the regime decided to grant visas to Kennedy and his wife, Mrs. Stephen Smith, Mrs. Peter Lawford (recently divorced from her actor husband), and members of the Senator's staff. At the same time, the South Africans announced that no foreign newsmen would be permitted to accompany the Senator. The Government stated that since Kennedy's trip was "of a purely private nature . . . it is not regarded as necessary to permit the entry of publicity teams."

Needless to say, Kennedy had not conceived his trip to South Africa as a good-will mission. As the Washington *Post* observed: "The target of his personal diplomacy is not the Verwoerd government but rather the country's restless students as well as its seething and aspiring multitudes of have-nots. There is, too, the vast political audience back home."

"Must I," Kennedy responded, "stop traveling because someone will say I'm after publicity?" The Senator contended that he had always been interested in Africa and merely wanted to learn about that continent's problems firsthand.

The regime headed by the late Prime Minister Hendrik Verwoerd, meanwhile, was doing all it could to limit Kennedy's impact. It imposed a five-year "ban"—social and political excommunication without stated cause or trial—on twenty-one-year-old Ian Robertson, head of the student organization that had invited Kennedy to South Africa. Robertson was restricted to the Cape Town area and ordered not to teach anywhere in the country. Thus, Kennedy was due to arrive with a massive publicity buildup unwittingly handed him by the white supremacist regime. It was a setup much to Bobby's liking.

Bobby and his party stopped off in London on their way to South Africa. While in the British capital, the Senator gave a completely off-the-record "deep background" interview to several American correspondents. He said little of South Africa, but a great deal about Vietnam, a subject that appeared to dominate his thoughts.* In substance, this is what he told the correspondents:

The American bombings of North Vietnam should be called off. Although he had originally favored the air strikes, he now felt they were no longer serving any useful political or military purpose. In early 1965, the bombings were justified as a means—probably the only one available at the time —of shoring up South Vietnamese morale and making it clear the U.S. was determined to prevent a Red takeover. But now, a year later, it had become clear that the strikes were failing

---

* A year later, Bobby denounced the use of such background briefings by United States officials.

in their objective of slowing down the infiltration of North Vietnamese regulars into the South. Therefore, he now favored concentration on a new politico-military strategy designed to win the war in the only place where it could be won—in South Vietnam. By winning the war, he said, he did not necessarily mean an outright military victory, rather the creation of a set of conditions in which a viable popular government could be established in South Vietnam and the United States permitted to withdraw with honor.

Kennedy said the Johnson Administration was divided on the subject of the air strikes. The Joint Chiefs of Staff and "powerful elements" in the State Department advocated an extension of the bombings; while Undersecretary George Ball led the doves and Defense Secretary McNamara harbored grave doubts about the wisdom of further escalation. Bobby emphasized he did not favor outright withdrawal. He was in the middle of the spectrum, supporting the President's policies with considerable reservations. He thought the President had badly missed the bus in refusing to accept the Vietcong in its own right at the conference table. But he conceded he saw little hope that Hanoi would agree to negotiations in the near future.

Having disposed of Vietnam, Bobby took off for South Africa, where the scene at Johannesburg's Jan Smuts Airport was bedlam. Several thousand students had turned out and vociferously welcomed him, then carried him to an airport platform where he read from a prepared statement. Despite the fact there were no black Africans in the throng, Bobby noted that some 20,000,000 Americans were of African descent—"from the same cultural and racial origins as most of you." Two girls held up a huge black-and-white banner proclaiming WE LOVE YOU BOBBY, and a poster saying YANKEE GO HOME brought boos and hoots.

The South African Government was not represented at the airport, but U.S. Ambassador William M. Rountree was there. He drove the Kennedy party to the Embassy to spend the night. As a matter of fact, the only South African representatives Bobby saw during the trip were policemen ordered to prevent untoward incidents.

For his part, Bobby shook every hand in sight. But on June 6 a misunderstanding with one of the common people almost created an incident. At Jan Smuts Airport, as he was ready to leave for Cape Town, Bobby walked over with outstretched hand to an African airline gasoline attendant named Paulus. The black man took fright, uttered a muffled scream and fled for his life. Paulus later said, "I thought the white baas [boss] was going to hit me."

"Kennedy was puzzled," reported George Laing in the New York *Daily News*. "He could not understand that for a black man to accept the greeting of a white man as an equal would be to brand himself in the eyes of the ever-present security police as 'a cheeky boy' at the very least, one to be watched closely in the future." Nor could he comprehend "that of the thousands of Africans who were to catch a glimpse of him, not one in a hundred would know his name, what he stood for, where he came from."

Laing, the only American newspaperman to beat the ban on visiting correspondents, had spent a year in South Africa as a working journalist. Therefore, he readily recognized "the fear in brown eyes." "I remembered," wrote Laing, "that when I left the country I gave a small present to the aged African who worked in my home as a houseboy . . . I wanted to shake hands in farewell. The man refused, saying softly: 'The walls have eyes and ears. To take your hand would be dangerous.'

"I tried to explain all this to the Senator. At first he did not understand. But in Cape Town he understood very well. . . ."

In Cape Town, Bobby called on Ian Robertson, the "banned" student leader who had invited him to South Africa. He presented the youth with a copy of John F. Kennedy's *Profiles in Courage,* autographed by Jacqueline Kennedy and himself. Before entering Robertson's modest digs in midtown, Bobby looked around the room and asked, "Is this place bugged?"

"Yes, I think so," Robertson replied.

With that, Bobby jumped into the air several times, coming down hard on the floor. He explained that the vibrations would disturb the bugging mechanism for fifteen minutes.

"How do you know that?" Robertson asked the Senator. Pausing for a moment, Kennedy replied, "I used to be Attorney General."

Bobby's most enthusiastic reception came at the University of Cape Town where his speech on academic freedom was stopped many times by applause—at one point for more than a minute. Bobby indirectly compared South Africa with Nazi Germany, and he bluntly uttered two words rarely heard in the white-dominated nation—"racial inequality." He said, "There is discrimination in New York, apartheid in South Africa and serfdom in the mountains of Peru. People starve in the streets of India; intellectuals go to jail in Russia; thousands [of Communists] are slaughtered in Indonesia; wealth is lavished on armaments everywhere. These are differing evils. But they are the common works of man."

Then, in ringing tones, he called on the students to share a common determination to wipe away such unnecessary suffering. "Moral courage," he concluded, "is a rarer commodity than bravery in battle. . . . Yet it is the one essential, vital quality for those who seek to change a world which yields most painfully to change."

One of Bobby's few outspoken critics was Blaar Coetzee, Deputy Minister of the Bantu Administration. In a Durban speech, Coetzee said, "This little snip [Kennedy] thinks he can tell us what to do. He has only been in the country for three days and already he has the audacity to tell us what the remedies to our problems are. . . . We will not be intimidated by America or England. We are growing militarily stronger every day and we could eat any other African state for breakfast."

The pro-Government Afrikaans press was generally antagonistic. *Die Burger*, for example, said that the visit had degenerated into an "election campaign . . . with high-sounding slogans aimed at the yearning for justice and brotherhood . . . [a] somewhat ominous spectacle." The English-language papers were more friendly. The opposition *Rand Daily Mail* said the Kennedy visit had been "the best thing that has happened to South Africa for years. . . . It is as if a window had been flung open and a gust of fresh air has swept in."

In London, however, the *Daily Express* took issue with Bobby's suggestion that the white man had done little to help Africa.

"Well, Mr. Kennedy," replied the British daily, "among other things the British brought peace and justice.

"They ended the slave trade and tribal wars.

"They saved the lives of millions who would otherwise have died as a result of famine, neglect, or battle.

"The population of just one British colony, Kenya, increased from under four million to more than eight million during the period of British rule—in remarkable contrast to the sad decline of the red Indians in North America."

Back home Bobby was receiving a generally good press. The Senator's office had distributed copies of the Cape Town speech far and wide. Excerpts were published, as befits a historic document, in *The New York Times*. And the Washington *Star* observed: "Those with a cynical turn of mind may think that the New York Senator was not oblivious to the impact of his remarks on Negro voters in the United States. It does not follow, however, that the speech can have no effect in South Africa. Any society which permits this kind of criticism is not impervious to change. And every effort to encourage the liberalization of South Africa's racial policies is, in our view, highly commendable."

But, as luck would have it, the news of Bobby's African safari was overshadowed by the ambush of James Meredith on a Mississippi highway. Meredith, the Negro who desegregated the University of Mississippi in 1962, suffered what a hospital official termed superficial wounds of the head, neck, shoulder, back and legs. Nevertheless, the episode relegated Bobby's African adventures to secondary press coverage. And this, needless to say, was annoying to the publicity-conscious Kennedy.

The Senator next spoke at Simonsberg Fraternity on the campus of the University of Stellenbosch, South Africa's oldest Afrikaner university and regarded as a citadel of the nation's apartheid policies. He said that the United States was not interested in telling South Africans how to run their country. America, the Senator said, just looked for one sign from South Africa that it planned greater freedom for all.

One student, speaking with a heavy Afrikaans accent, asked the Senator what he would do if he ever discovered that God was a black man. Bobby paused, looked directly at his questioner, and said, "If He is, you'll be in serious trouble." *

---

* Bobby's *Look* article summarizing his South African findings was entitled "Suppose God Is Black." In it he fails to credit the Stellenbosch student for suggesting the theme. Instead, he narrates how at the University of Natal in Durban he learned how most of the whites belong to a church that teaches apartheid as a moral necessity. And he quotes

On Bobby's final day in South Africa, he toured the streets of Johannesburg's African township of Soweto. Thousands of blacks, having heard wondrous tales of this strange white man who wanted only to shake their hands, took to the streets to greet the "bwana." As his car drove slowly through the black ghetto, Bobby stood on the roof, waving to the crowds like a political candidate. He seemed embarrassed when the blacks surged forward in an uncontrollable mass, shouting, "Master, Master."

"Please," he implored, "please, don't use that word."

But it was the only word of praise and gratitude they knew.

The following morning, he flew north to equally tumultuous receptions in the black-ruled nations of Tanzania and Kenya. In Dar es Salaam, capital of Tanzania, his first public appearance was at the headquarters of the Tanganyika African National Union (TANU), the nation's only political party. Hundreds of Tanzanians gathered in front of the headquarters to hear Bobby, whose first word of greeting was "Uhuru!" (Swahili for "Freedom!") except that what came out sounded more like "O'Hara." He tried again and got it right. "Well," he joked, "you can't say I didn't try."

Despite the excessive humidity, Bobby appeared to be in good spirits. Inside TANU's Central Committee rooms, the Senator spoke briefly with party executives. Again he jested. "I know you have a one-party system in this country," he said. "That's the kind of system I would like to establish at home."

On his arrival, he was presented with two gifts—a zebra-skin drum and a carved ebony elephant. The latter elicited the obvious remark about its being the symbol of the other party back home. "Every time I will look at this elephant, I will think of you," Bobby said. "But I assure you it will be the only elephant in my house."

Later he was received by President Julius Nyerere in his Moorish-style whitewashed official residence overlooking the bay. An exchange of gifts was the occasion for the inevitable banter. Bobby gave Nyerere a PT-boat pin and the President pinned a torch emblem of TANU on Bobby's lapel. "Now,"

---

himself as having said, "But suppose God is black. What if we go to Heaven and we, all our lives, have treated the Negro as an inferior, and God is there, and we look up and He is not white? What then is our response?" According to Bobby, "There was no answer. Only silence."

said Nyerere, "I want to make you a member of the party. There are no dues."

Repeating his earlier quip, Bobby said, "I know you have only one party. We could use that kind of system in the United States."

According to press reports, his major speech in Dar es Salaam was stumbling and ineffectual. His hands trembled and he read his text awkwardly. *Newsweek* correspondent Angus Deming reported that Bobby's "rapid Bostonese was quite beyond the comprehension of many of his listeners. Nevertheless, afterward he was mobbed and cheered all the way to his car."

Then after a three-day non-hunting safari in East Africa's huge game reserves, the Kennedy party flew into Nairobi, capital of Kenya. Bobby lunched with President Jomo Kenyatta, paid a brief visit to Parliament and addressed a student group. In his speech, the Senator again claimed that white men "bear heavy responsibility for many of Africa's present difficulties." And he added that strife and injustice remained deep and difficult problems in the United States. "Our revolution, like yours, has far to go."

During a televised news conference, Bobby discussed his experiences in South Africa. He said that American businesses operating there should push for racial equality, but he conceded the position of foreign businessmen was "delicate and difficult." One newsman remarked that many American industrialists with investments in South Africa were also major contributors to the Democratic party. Would the Senator try to change their policies when he returned home?

The next day, Bobby arrived in Addis Ababa, where he had a private talk with Ethiopia's Emperor Haile Selassie, patted a cheetah outside the Emperor's palace and addressed an audience of high-ranking diplomats and members of the Organization of African Unity. In this speech, he castigated both sides in the cold war for having failed to find common ground for controlling the spread of nuclear weapons. The great powers, including the United States, he said, "are simply not doing enough, not trying hard enough, not sacrificing enough to arrive at an agreement."

Bobby urged the Africans to take worldwide leadership in ending the deadlock on nuclear arms control. "You must now take the lead and restore the flagging energies of governments and their negotiators."

The Reporter later commented: "Considering the sad and frequently tragic record of the new African states in misgovernment and non-government, the suggestion staggers the imagination. The most charitable thing that can be said about this episode is that the Senator, in his eagerness to remain young, proved childish."

Arriving in New York, Bobby sounded more temperate. He said he would oppose any cutoff in trade with South Africa. The greatest sufferers, he said, would be the blacks, and "the economic boom in South Africa has been the greatest force in breaking down apartheid." It has taken the United States "such a long period of time to accomplish what's right that we should keep this in mind on any criticisms of South Africa."

Several days later, the ruling Kenya African National Union party in Nairobi officially criticized this statement: "This is the line peddled by apologists for apartheid especially by vested interests who fear their own investments will be harmed by a policy of sanctions."

Airport newsmen then queried him about comments made by Senator Wayne Morse the previous day. The maverick Democrat from Oregon, interviewed on *Kup's Show* in Chicago, had announced he intended to oppose the renomination of President Johnson at the 1968 Democratic National Convention and that he "wouldn't hesitate to support" Kennedy instead, if the New York Democrat continued to be critical of the war in Vietnam. Bobby's response was: "I have no plans to run for anything but the Senate in 1970 and I support President Johnson in 1968."

Arriving in Washington, he reiterated his support of President Johnson's re-election and, when informed that Barry Goldwater had said he was already running for President, Bobby quipped, "He hasn't always been accurate, and he's not this time." He was also asked whether he agreed with a statement attributed to his newly appointed press aide, Frank Mankiewicz, formerly with the Peace Corps. Mankiewicz had been quoted as having said that United States foreign policy makers were displaying "an unbelievable smugness and blandness."

"I don't agree," Bobby said, and after a hasty huddle with

aides, he returned and added, "He's not on my payroll yet; he doesn't work for me."

And thus ended the fifteen-day trip. Exactly what it had accomplished besides keeping Bobby in the news was difficult to estimate. One thing was certain, however. Whatever its merits, the Johnson Administration was not overjoyed about the possible diplomatic repercussions. The trip was widely interpreted in black Africa as a positive indication that the United States favored immediate change in South Africa, even to the point of black rule.

The actual U.S. position was described from Africa by Albert J. Meyers of *U.S. News & World Report:* "U.S. diplomats in Africa are emphasizing that Washington is not advocating any such swift change, and that, if the black countries think so, they are bound to be disappointed. Some diplomats believe the Kennedy visit has sharpened the division between white and black Africa and between the U.S. and South Africa, and that the trip, therefore, was ill advised."

Malcolm Muggeridge, still as irreverent as ever, may have had the last word on the Kennedy trip in *Esquire:* "I think with considerable disgust of [Kennedy's] performance in South Africa, which would have been so much more impressive if a similar demonstration had first been mounted in Alabama. There, it might subsequently have cost electoral votes; in South Africa it cost nothing but the hopes perhaps of those who turned out to cheer." *

After Bobby's return he discovered—much to his dismay— that he was being accused of being part of an anti-Negro conspiracy. The charge resulted from his unexpected intervention in an obscure New York judicial primary. The New York Democratic organization, known as Tammany Hall in less self-conscious days, had nominated State Supreme Court Justice Arthur G. Klein, an organization man, for the patronage-laden plum of County Surrogate. And as frequently happens in New York, Tammany chieftain J. Raymond ("The Fox") Jones and his Republican counterpart, Vincent F. Albano, agreed to make the judicial nomination bipartisan.

---

* Actually, Bobby had been to Alabama, where he spoke at the University of Alabama. He was applauded for one minute when he declared Negroes had an equal right to education and all other benefits of American society. There were no boos or catcalls such as were greeting the President's spokesmen on so-called liberal campuses.

The argument traditionally has been that such pacts freed judgeships from domination by one party or party boss. But, on a practical basis, they also give both parties a share of the patronage.

The spoiler in this comfortable arrangement was Alex Rose, the boss of the Liberal party and *macher* in New York politics generally. Alex had early begun to heckle the GOP to continue the Republican-Liberal coalition that had produced Mayor Lindsay's fusion victory the previous November. But the Republicans clearly preferred to "fuse" in this instance with the majority Democrats. As part of this skirmishing, the Liberals nominated a registered Republican judge for Surrogate. Rose's efforts were further aided by newspaper editorials criticizing Justice Klein's links with old-line Democratic leaders. And Mayor Lindsay, upset over the furor resulting from the Republican endorsement of Klein, said, "I certainly do not feel very happy about it."

The situation was machine-made for Bobby's benefit. There had been a decided coolness between Bobby and both Rose and the Reformers because of the Senator's willingness to play ball with New York's machine bosses. Less than a year before, Alex Rose had been telling friends it had been a mistake for his organization to have endorsed Kennedy for the Senate. "He was not one of our people," Alex had said, according to *The New York Times*.

Joining the chorus of indignation, Kennedy huddled with Liberal partyites and Reformers. The Liberals dumped their earlier nominee, the Reformers deserted Klein, and the new coalition plumped for Justice Samuel J. Silverman, a Klein colleague on the bench. Bobby let it be known that he personally talked Silverman into running. The Senator's intervention thus converted what otherwise would have been an obscure contest into front-page news.

Among other things, the Senator's decision pitted him openly for the first time against J. Raymond Jones, the New York County Democratic Chairman. Since Jones, a Negro, could be characterized as a "boss," an "anti-boss" posture was hardly likely to injure Bobby's image. According to psychologist Kenneth B. Clark, the prominent Negroes rallying behind Klein had tried to alert Bobby "to the clear danger that the racial issue would be raised by his entering a conflict of this kind with J. Raymond Jones in New York County, at the same time that he refuses to enter any conflict with the regular Democrats under Buckley in Bronx County and Steingut in Brooklyn."

The six-week campaign itself was most unjudicial. "It was," as *Newsweek* reported, "in fact, squalid." Bobby complained to newsmen that the Klein nomination was "tainted by the suspicion of corruption or a deal"—but, despite repeated challenges, the Senator never produced any evidence. Ironically, Klein's first government job had been as an SEC lawyer under Joseph P. Kennedy. Now, much to his amazement, he found his nomination opposed by Kennedy's son.

The Klein forces counterattacked. The charge was made that the Silverman effort was really aimed at J. Raymond Jones because he was a Negro.

There had been bad blood between Jones and the Kennedy clan for some time. Jones, the only Negro County Chairman in the United States, had held out for Lyndon Johnson at the 1960 convention. And tolerance for past opponents is not a Kennedy family trait. However, Jones himself never accused Bobby of racism. But he chided the Senator for "disrupting" the Democratic party, adding, "And if there were any deals as the Kennedy people suggest, the deals were all on the other side, where Kennedy met with Rose and then the Reformers to satisfy the combinations of boundless burning ambitions, the ruthless quest for power, a vendetta to seize control."

Asked if Kennedy was planning to oust him as county leader as a major step toward taking over the state's party, Jones said, "Yes I do and everyone else in Harlem thinks so."

(On March 10, 1967, Jones resigned as Tammany chief.)

Not all Reformers, however, sided with Bobby. A minority led by Francis W. H. Adams, Reform leader emeritus and former Police Commissioner, echoed Jones's cry that Bobby's entrance into the primary contest was nothing more than "a political power grab." Adams told a press conference that in backing Silverman, Bobby had moved in with "all his money, power and prestige" in an effort to capture the Reform movement.

The principal issue, Bobby said, was the "integrity of the judiciary." Yet, in the midst of this self-styled "crusade" the Senator submitted the name of one of his early sponsors in

New York State, Peter J. Crotty, for clearance by the American Bar Association's Committee on the Federal Judiciary. Though the committee found Crotty "not qualified," none of his newfound friends among the Reformers could work up much indignation about Bobby's promotion of his Buffalo friend. The "not qualified" tag effectively eliminated Crotty from consideration for a Federal judgeship.

The Klein forces also recalled that "the integrity of the judiciary" had been raised by the Kennedys' nomination of Francis X. Morrissey to be a Federal judge the previous fall.* All of which led columnist Henry J. Taylor to observe that "Bobby Kennedy sounds as sanctimonious as Sadie Thompson."

"Of all the causes espoused by the Kennedy brothers, reform of their own state parties has not been their favorite," reported Martin F. Nolan in *The New Republic*. "Senator Robert has begun to move in this field in New York, but at the very same time his younger brother Edward was washing his hands of Massachusetts primary politics. . . . The advice given Teddy to stay aloof from the Massachusetts scene came from the same mentors now counseling Robert Kennedy to engage himself in party reform in New York, specifically, William J. vanden Heuvel and Milton S. Gwirtzman. . . . Both were involved in Teddy's decision to support Francis X. Morrissey for a federal judgeship last fall. They are now working actively, along with Stephen Smith, the famed brother-in-law, for a Kennedy judgeship candidate in Manhattan. . . .

"The counsel given both brothers by common advisers makes room for only one strong leader and puts Teddy in the back seat. But if the 'Making-of-the President' syndrome is removed from their roles in party leadership, the Kennedys appear as different men. Bobby, with ten years' experience in big-league politics and a lingering reputation for ruth-

* The Morrissey episode recalled a statement made by President Kennedy when he signed a bill creating additional judgeships. He said, "I want for our courts individuals with respected professional skill, incorruptible character, firm judicial temperament, the rare inner quality to know when to temper justice with mercy, and the intellectual capacity to protect and illuminate the Constitution and our historic values in the context of a society experiencing profound and rapid change." Yet the record shows that of President Kennedy's first eighty-eight appointments to the Federal bench, eighty-eight went to Democrats.

lessness, is moving gingerly in a situation ripe for take-over. Teddy, at age 34, seems lost in the paleolithic vastness of Massachusetts politics."

The six-week surrogate contest followed the tried-and-true Kennedy formula. While the Klein forces operated out of a modest four-room suite in a midtown hotel, the Kennedy-Silverman combine had fifteen rooms and ample financing. Directing the campaign, as usual, was brother-in-law Stephen Smith. William vanden Heuvel and William Haddad were busy on the phones. Jerry Bruno, of Bobby's staff, and Milton Gwirtzman, an aide to Teddy, were also there. Teddy turned up one night at the Kennedy-Silverman headquarters while Bobby was off in Africa. Decked out in dinner jacket, he had come by, he said, to "bless" the volunteer workers. Also on hand was Andrew W. Hatcher, the former assistant press secretary under President Kennedy. Actor Henry Fonda was on the radio with spot announcements and even James Meredith did his bit by announcing his support of Silverman.

But the real campaigning did not begin in earnest until Bobby began electioneering up and down the sidewalks of New York with a diffident Silverman at his side. He exhorted volunteers to "win for integrity and the city of New York." It was a brutal schedule indeed. Every day he shuttled back and forth from Washington, working in the Senate by day, campaigning as the sun began to go down.

As Manhattan's voters went to the polls that muggy day, J. Raymond Jones again assailed Bobby Kennedy's role as "despicable." The voting was light, and Silverman beat Klein by a vote of 70,771 to 47,625, all but insuring his victory in November (after which he was pledged to try to abolish his job by merging the Surrogate's Court with the State Supreme Court). Before the night was over, Bobby savored the fruits of victory at the Sheraton East Hotel where the campaign workers had gathered. After Silverman thanked everyone, Bobby began to talk.

"I would like to make a few personal remarks," he said, grinning. "I remember well that Sunday when I called him [Silverman] to see if he would run. And he said, in a ruthless kind of way [laughter]—it's true—he said, 'Just you remember, Mr. Kennedy, Silvermans don't finish second!" (Loud laughter.)

Bobby then introduced some of the people who had made

it all possible. He began by saying, "I would like to introduce a relative, a beloved figure who is replacing me on the American horizon, ruthless, mean Stephen Smith. . . ." The room of sweating people cheered, and then it was all over.

Over at the Commodore, Justice Klein tearfully conceded defeat. "Unfortunately," he said, "there are certain things that we can't beat."

"What things?" he was asked.

"Money is the most important thing," Klein replied.

There could be little doubt that the primary was a telling personal victory for Robert F. Kennedy.

"Until their present alliance," editorialized *The New York Times,* "Senator Kennedy was weaker among the Reform elements of his party than in any other segment of New York's Democracy. Most of the Reform wing resented his entry into New York State politics two years ago as that of a carpetbagger, and disliked and mistrusted his close ties with old-line party bosses. . . .

"Now Senator Kennedy has, at least for the moment, become a hero of the Reformers—at any rate, those in Manhattan. This does not mean that he has become a Reformer himself. Senator Kennedy is a very practical politician who in the past has dealt with some pretty distasteful holders of power and will doubtless continue to do so. His recent submission of Mr. Crotty's name to the Department of Justice as a candidate for a Federal judgeship was not reassuring. But at the same time the Senator has now publicly identified himself with at least one local fight for good government."

Bobby's political future never looked brighter. In one stroke he had managed to (1) whip both Tammany Hall and the Republicans, (2) put luster on a still-unclear liberal image, and (3) consolidate his personal power to a point where New York Democrats would most likely accept his judgment on the selection of an opponent for Governor Rockefeller in the fall.

Or so it seemed to such political analysts as Rowland Evans and Robert Novak, whose column contained the following intelligence: "The upshot is that any New York Democrat with an anti-Kennedy image suddenly becomes automatically ineligible for the Governor nomination—ruling out former Mayor Wagner as a dark horse possibility. Moreover, it greatly increases the chances that Kennedy will intervene in the Governor's race before the September convention in Buffalo.

"Kennedy will do nothing immediately that would look like an over-obvious follow-up to the victory in the Surrogate race. There is, however, at least a possibility he will endorse Eugene Nickerson, the County Executive of Nassau County, for Governor. But inside the Kennedy camp, there is serious doubt whether Nickerson is a sure winner capable of catching front-running Frank O'Connor, President of New York City's Council. A more cautious politician than is generally recognized, Kennedy does not like to play long shots. . . ."

Having disposed of the "bosses," Bobby, Ethel and seven of their nine children headed for Idaho's rapids-filled "River of No Return"—the Salmon. There they were joined by astronaut John Glenn, singer Andy Williams' wife and LeMoyne Billings. Everyone piled into a World War II rubber landing craft for a wild trip down nearly 100 miles of boiling rapids of the Middle Fork of the river. "The place is full of dangerous rocks and swirling eddies," *Time* reported. "So naturally every time a guide stood up to see what lay ahead, some fun-loving Kennedy would push him overboard." Fortunately, no one was hurt.

"The biggest problem," expedition leader Don Hatch later maintained, "was keeping Ethel's wig box right side up through the rapids."

Bobby insisted on negotiating the final forty miles all by himself in a kayak. "It was great," he said later. After four days of this, Bobby and family took off for Canada, where the Senator was scheduled to open the annual Calgary Stampede. Considering Bobby's enthusiasm, there were some Canadians who half expected the Senator to come busting out of a chute on a bronco.

Perhaps he was talked out of it.

26

Government-in-Exile

In the April 2, 1966, issue of *The New Republic*, Andrew Kopkind reported: "Kennedy is not capturing a bloc, or putting together a coalition, or hewing out a program. What is happening is less dramatic; around him are gathering people in government and outside who in the very loosest sense constitute a Kennedy Party. . . . The Kennedy Party could be an antiwar government-in-exile. It already is a home for many of the New Frontier officials who were ripped untimely from their jobs. There is a kind of 'shadow Cabinet' which Kennedy uses both for ideas and to a lesser extent for political activity."

However, only when the bitter controversy developed over the *Look* serialization of the William Manchester book on the Kennedy assassination did the *dramatis personae* of Bobby's "inner circle" become evident. "The Kennedy goon squad" is the way *Look's* editors labeled the Kennedy representatives who argued the Senator's case. The list included Edwin O. Guthman, John Seigenthaler, Burke Marshall, Richard N. Goodwin, Arthur Schlesinger, Jr., and Theodore Sorensen. These were some of the people Manchester apparently referred to when he said, "The Senator is surrounded by people who have hitched their wagon to his star . . . people who are betting their futures on another Kennedy Administration, who are willing to do anything."

Goodwin, Sorensen and Schlesinger had served John F. Kennedy. Two of them, in fact, had written best-selling memoirs of the Kennedy years. All three had found it impossible to work for Kennedy's successor. At least one—

Schlesinger—despised Lyndon Johnson with an irrational passion ill-befitting a two-time Pulitzer prize-winner. Guthman, Seigenthaler and Marshall were young men whose primary loyalty had always been to Robert F. Kennedy. All had been in the Justice Department and had been at Bobby's side in the battles to convict Jimmy Hoffa and to integrate the Universities of Mississippi and Alabama.

It was in 1957 when Bobby, then chief counsel of the Senate rackets committee, first met Guthman in Seattle and Seigenthaler in Nashville. Both were newsmen who had been assigned to uncover corruption in the Teamsters. Guthman, in fact, had won a Pulitzer prize for doing so.

In 1961 Guthman came to the Justice Department as press secretary to the Attorney General and for three years was chief custodian of Bobby's public image. Guthman's main preoccupation, it seemed, was to reply to charges of Bobby's "ruthlessness" by countering with background briefings on "the real Robert Kennedy," the Attorney General who not only fought crime, but helped Negroes and served as principal adviser to his brother in the White House.

Seigenthaler, who had had much to do with preparing Bobby's best-selling book, *The Enemy Within*, entered the Justice Department as Kennedy's administrative assistant. He remained with Bobby for two years and then resigned to become editor of the Nashville *Tennessean*. Guthman, however, did not leave until Bobby was safely ensconced as Senator. Then in May 1965 he became national news editor of the Los Angeles *Times*. Like Seigenthaler, he left Kennedy reluctantly—for more money. But both men have the essential Bobby quality—absolute loyalty. And both are always on call whenever the Senator wants them. They were the first two men Bobby asked to read the manuscript of *The Death of a President*.

"You have to go through something with Bob Kennedy before you have a relationship with him," Guthman once observed to Richard Reeves of *The New York Times*. "And relationships are everything with him. It's hard to explain but it's straight. He's absolutely honest with you." According to Reeves, Guthman and Seigenthaler "are somewhat typical of the kind of men Bobby likes." Rugged, they give the impression they could still fit into their old football uniforms.

"So many of Kennedy's guys look like Marlboro men," another reporter has observed.

Burke Marshall, Assistant Attorney General for the Justice Department's Civil Rights Division under Kennedy, does not exactly fit the football mold. Shy and introspective, he was an outstanding Washington antitrust lawyer when Bobby invited him, in January 1961, to join his team. Marshall took his oath of office from a notary public—rather than face the glare of public attention.

After leaving the Justice Department, Marshall became vice president and general counsel of International Business Machines. Based in New York, Marshall played the role of the anonymous "Kennedy family spokesman" during the battle over The Book. But probably the most important hold-over from John F. Kennedy's team was Richard Naradof Goodwin.

He is tall, dark and rumpled. During the 1966 campaign, a group of reporters who did not know him watched as he boarded a California-bound plane with Bobby. They fell to speculating as to who he might be and decided he was an Italian newspaperman with a hangover.

It was during that transcontinental flight that Goodwin told a reporter, "One of the reasons I'm with Kennedy is that he's one of the focal points that afford intellectuals the opportunity to get their ideas into the arena of public affairs . . . there's something about him—a modern quality —that reflects the tempo of the times. He's the most profound man in public life today. It's not just that he's willing to talk to John Kenneth Galbraith or Robert Lowell, it's that he's willing to talk to Galbraith about poetry and Lowell about Vietnam." *

During the Manchester controversy, Goodwin earned himself a special place on the list of the *Look* "Kennedy goon squad." But Goodwin wasn't at all troubled. "He had the air of a fanatic, believing wholeheartedly in the absolute justice of the Kennedy position," one of the *Look* people

* Poet Lowell, a pacifist, spent several years in a Federal penitentiary rather than fight in World War II. He gained some notoriety when he publicly refused an invitation from President Johnson to read his poetry at the White House because of his opposition to the war in Vietnam. During the 1960 primaries, Lowell traveled with Senator Eugene McCarthy.

reported. Born in Boston in 1931, the son of an engineer, Goodwin was graduated *summa cum laude* from Tufts University in 1953 and some years later from Harvard Law School, where he was president of the *Law Review*. In both, he was first in his class.

In 1958 he became a law clerk for Associate Supreme Court Justice Felix Frankfurter, a post that opened many doors in the nation's capital. The following year, Goodwin became an investigator for the House Subcommittee on Legislative Oversight, which was looking into rigged television quiz shows. He left the subcommittee after writing an article on the investigation for *Life*.

In 1959, Goodwin jumped on the John F. Kennedy bandwagon, surprising many people with his flair for political speech-writing. When Kennedy took office, he named Goodwin as his Assistant Special Counsel. Though he did not speak Spanish, Goodwin became an adviser on Latin American affairs. But his dabbling in foreign policy managed to irritate a good many professionals in the State Department.

He showed himself naïve, to say the least, when he met with Cuba's Communist theorist, Ernesto "Ché" Guevara, during the Punta del Este conference of 1961. Returning with a Cuban flag and a humidor of Havana cigars, Goodwin contended he had not entered into any substantive discussion with Ché. But the episode was to have serious repercussions among Latin American statesmen who, rightly or wrongly, suspected he had. It was Goodwin who turned out the basic draft of JFK's famed Alliance for Progress speech. In fact, he coined the slogan.

So abrasive was Goodwin on occasion that President Kennedy was forced to move him out of the White House. In 1962 Barry Goldwater demanded that he be fired. Among other things, Barry insisted that Goodwin, together with Adlai E. Stevenson, Arthur M. Schlesinger, Jr., and Chester Bowles, had "consistently urged a soft policy toward Communism, both in Cuba and elsewhere throughout the world." Though Kennedy exiled Goodwin to the Peace Corps, the President kept in close touch with him. At his death, Kennedy was preparing to announce his reappointment to the White House staff, this time as his Special Consultant on the Arts.

President Lyndon Johnson "borrowed" Goodwin from the Peace Corps to write speeches. Indeed, Goodwin coined the phrase the Great Society for Johnson, and wrote the speech defining its aims. But Goodwin kept up his alliance with Bobby Kennedy and even accompanied him on his trip to South America.

In 1965 he left the White House to become a senior fellow at Wesleyan University (and, ironically, William Manchester's neighbor) for $15,000 a year, half his White House salary. President Johnson gave him a gracious send-off, declaring that his services had been "a blessing to the country."

Though called back to the White House from time to time, Goodwin virtually burned any bridges to the Johnson Administration with a September 17, 1966, speech excoriating LBJ's handling of Vietnam. Before the ADA's national board, Goodwin contended that the President's policies had reduced the chances of a settlement while increasing the risks of a war with Red China.

Although given to nonconformist opinion, Goodwin refuses to countenance any heretical notions regarding Bobby Kennedy. He is almost unable to control himself when he runs into critics of the Senator. For example, Goodwin angrily remonstrated with Nick Thimmesch, co-author of *Robert Kennedy at 40*, a fine 1965 book that was greeted with excellent reviews. He objected to such passages as: "As Americans consider Bobby Kennedy for the Presidency now, many will have a feeling of ambivalence, of uncertainty. They will see many of the traits they demand of a President and many they could not allow. They do not want a weakling, and Bobby is not one. Neither do they want a man who shoves people around, and Bobby has done that. They want a leader, and Bobby is. But they do not want a man who takes his followers for granted, and Bobby has done that, too. They want a man who understands the anatomy of crisis and can make decisions without personal involvement. Bobby can do that. But they do not want a man who is impetuous and easily angered. And Bobby has been that, too.

"Indeed, Americans must wonder whether Robert Kennedy is a man who should be trusted with the Presidency."

Goodwin encountered Thimmesch at a party at, of all

places, Steve Smith's New York home, and the former White House adviser loudly demanded to know just what in hell an enemy of Bobby's was doing there. "I was invited," Thimmesch countered. There were heated words. Fortunately, cooler heads prevailed. The antagonists were separated. Goodwin, of course, personified what Bobby Kennedy liked most in a supporter—undeviating loyalty and a desire to battle to the death for the Restoration.

Also integral parts of Bobby's "government-in-exile" were Arthur Schlesinger, Jr., and Theodore Sorensen. After leaving Washington, both took jobs in New York—Schlesinger as a professor at City University of New York and Sorensen as a partner of a prestigious law firm. And hardly a day passes that Bobby is not on the telephone with both, seeking advice and guidance. "Sorensen and Schlesinger are his utility infielders," a Kennedy aide once told Richard Reeves. "They can play any position. He checks with them on everything he's doing to see what they think. Schlesinger gives him the liberal judgment and he tempers it with his own instincts."

Schlesinger's attitude toward Bobby has changed considerably from the mid-fifties when the then Harvard professor considered John F. Kennedy's kid brother little more than a "pipsqueak McCarthyite." Today Schlesinger views Bobby as the new white knight of American liberalism. He also saw Bobby as a means of once again getting close to a position of power. For Schlesinger admires power.

President Kennedy never took him too seriously when it came to policy making. Primarily Schlesinger was Kennedy's bridge to the intellectual community, some of whose rambunctious spirits were continually berating the President for his timidity in installing an instant and total liberal-type society.

Arthur Schlesinger (he prefers it pronounced *Shlayzinger*) was born in October 1917 in Columbus, Ohio—the eldest son of Elizabeth and Arthur Meier Schlesinger. Mrs. Schlesinger is collaterally descended from the nineteenth-century American historian and statesman George Bancroft. Schlesinger, Sr., after a stint at Ohio State, went on to teach United States social and intellectual history at Harvard in 1924. He died in 1965 at the age of seventy-seven.

In Cambridge, the Schlesinger family lived in a Georgian-style brick house that overflowed with books. And young Arthur tried to read them all. After attending public schools, he was packed off to Exeter. Something of a prodigy, he was two years younger than most of his classmates and already an outspoken liberal. And Exeter is decidedly conservative. An indifferent athlete, Schlesinger spent most of his time with books. "He wasn't one of the boys," a classmate recalls.

Graduating at the age of fifteen, Schlesinger took time off for a year-long tour of the world with his parents and brother (now a historian-researcher for the Colonial Williamsburg restoration project). When they returned, Schlesinger entered Harvard as a classmate of the late Joseph P. Kennedy, Jr., whom he recalls as a bright, amiable guy who might have gone far in politics—but not as far as brother John. Graduating in 1938, Artie went off to England for a year's study at Cambridge.

In 1940, Arthur married Marian Cannon, daughter of Harvard physiologist Walter B. Cannon. During World War II he served with the Office of War Information in Washington, and later with the Office of Strategic Services in Europe. After a brief spell as a free-lance writer, he returned to Harvard as an associate professor.

To his rambling, brown-shingled home on Irving Street came a steady stream of visitors. Novelist Mary McCarthy, a longtime friend, recalls, "There always seemed to be someone in the spare bed." Of the many people she met on Irving Street, however, not one was a Republican. "Arthur just doesn't like Republicans," she noted. "There is a certain amount of cowboys-and-Indians about it."

At twenty-eight, Schlesinger became the *Wunderkind* of the academic world with the publication of *The Age of Jackson,* which won a Pulitzer prize. At the time, Schlesinger viewed American history as the story of "a perpetual tension in society, a doubtful equilibrium, constantly breeding strife and struggle." It was, in his view, an "irrepressible conflict . . . the struggle on the part of the business community to dominate the state, and on the part of the rest of society, under the leadership of 'liberals,' to check the political ambitions of business." Needless to say, he disliked businessmen —"a group that has invariably brought national affairs to a state of crisis and exasperated the rest of society into dissatisfaction bordering on revolt."

His views have undergone extraordinary changes. In more recent years, he concedes that American businessmen "share with American liberals a basic faith in the free society. I have more confidence now than when I wrote *The Age of Jackson* in their intelligence and responsibility." Typically Schlesinger feels not the slightest embarrassment in this shifting of position. He claims that revision "is a permanent process in the writing of history."

In 1947 Schlesinger helped found Americans for Democratic Action, after taking the Far Left to task for "following the policies of the Soviet Union."

During the 1952 and 1956 Presidential campaigns Schlesinger was a speech writer for Adlai Stevenson, and his crushing defeats at the polls greatly disturbed Artie. "Stevenson came along too soon," he observed in 1957. "Americans, after a generation's buffeting by depression and war, had to have a breathing spell. Even by 1956 they had not had their fill of inertia."

Schlesinger then returned to completing his massive *Age of Roosevelt*. In four years he produced three volumes, all of which turned out to be best sellers. The project was a difficult one. As Schlesinger observed, "It's much harder than writing history that's long past. For *Jackson*, the source material was limited and all the witnesses were dead. There was no one to pop up and say, 'You were wrong—I was there.'" (Which was to happen later with the publication of Schlesinger's memoir of the Kennedy years, *A Thousand Days*.)

After some initial doubts, Schlesinger worked hard for John F. Kennedy in 1960. His major contribution was a slender volume entitled *Kennedy or Nixon: Does It Make Any Difference?* He also turned up in intellectual circles from Greenwich Village to Berkeley arguing with diehard Stevensonians that they had no choice—agonizing as it was —but to vote for Kennedy. Schlesinger did an effective job.

Kennedy actually used Schlesinger sparingly on the campaign trail. Not only had the Republicans made him into a bogeyman, but he had a manner irritating to nonintellectual audiences. Though generally liked by people who knew him, he frequently created unfavorable impressions among others.

Thus, New York Democratic leaders were upset in 1960 by Schlesinger's slashing, belittling attack on Al Smith, Jr. —son of the 1928 Democratic Presidential candidate and a Nixon supporter—on the Barry Gray radio show. "Schlesinger may have won the argument, but he most certainly lost us votes," a highly placed Democrat asserts.

Following the election, President Kennedy invited Arthur to join the new White House team. "With his horn-rimmed glasses and floppy bow ties, his retreating hairline and advancing waistline, the slightly built man with the professorial air hardly looked the part of the New Frontiersman," *Time* observed, and at the White House, he quickly discovered that at best his ability to influence events was marginal.

Much of his time was devoted to churning out lengthy memorandums, which President Kennedy generally ignored. For one thing, they often showed—in the words of another Kennedy aide—"bad judgment." A case in point was reported, following JFK's death, by UPI's White House correspondent Merriman Smith. According to Smith, Kennedy, in talking to a visitor, once held up a Schlesinger memo and remarked, "Look at that, will you? Seven single-spaced pages. And what a lot of blankety-blank. I dearly love this man. He has a fine mind and some fine ideas, but in this case . . ." According to Smith, the President's voice then trailed off and he shook his head ruefully, a slight smile crossing his face. Then Kennedy added, "He is proposing that I conduct myself as Franklin Roosevelt did in 1933, but this fellow can't get through his head that first, I'm not FDR and this is 1963, not 1933; that what was fine for Roosevelt simply would not work today for a simple reason —in 1933, Roosevelt faced one central problem, the depression, and he could take more liberties with domestic matters than I could possibly enjoy today. Also, in 1933, there were no nuclear bombs or missiles or jet aircraft or cold war."

With that, John F. Kennedy balled up the Schlesinger memorandum and threw it carelessly toward the wastebasket.

On another occasion, Kennedy told columnist William S. White, "Arthur has nothing to do with making policy. He works over there"—indicating the East, and nonoperating, wing of the White House—"and he is a good writer, period."

Schlesinger, of course, was never part of the President's inner group, as was, say, Ted Sorensen, though a reading of *A Thousand Days* might give a contrary impression. Schlesinger was only on the periphery of power, though from the very beginning he did savor its perquisites and pleasures. Shortly after being named a Special Assistant to the fledgling President of the United States, Schlesinger debated with William F. Buckley, Jr., in Boston. According to Buckley, his adversary made a "grand entry into the lecture hall twenty minutes late, escorted by screeching police cars—it obviously hadn't taken long for Mr. Schlesinger to acquire princely habits."

Once, Schlesinger offered to resign. As the most visible liberal in the Kennedy entourage, he had come under bitter attack. Walter Winchell, for example, wrote: "Schlesinger is haunted by intellectual snobbery, dominated by arrogance . . . as power-mad as he is venomous . . . a threat to fundamental American concepts." And Henry J. Taylor, in a Scripps-Howard column entitled "Schlesinger Should Go," exhumed a 1947 contribution by the professor to a *Partisan Review* symposium on "The Future of Socialism." This was the article, incidentally, in which Schlesinger excoriated Joseph P. Kennedy's views as going "beyond the normal limits of political incompetence." Barry Goldwater had also begun to go after Schlesinger; and in California a group of conservatives founded the Organization to Remove Schlesinger from Public Life.

Feeling he had added troubles to the Administration at a time when the President had enough on his mind, Schlesinger informed JFK that he was ready to leave.

"Don't worry about it," Schlesinger quotes Kennedy as having told him. "Everybody knows what Henry Taylor is like. No one pays any attention to him. All they are doing is shooting at me through you. Their whole line is to pin everything on the professors—you, Heller, Rostow. When the market fell, *Time* put Heller on the cover, not Dillon. Don't worry about it. This is the sort of thing you have to expect."

When Lyndon Johnson took office following the assassination, Schlesinger reported to the White House as requested. Hands were shaken, cordialities exchanged, commitments expressed, but after one hundred days of having little to do (and being afraid his telephone was tapped), Schlesinger resigned and his East Wing office was quickly taken over by another certified intellectual, Professor Eric Goldman of Princeton.

After spending two weeks as a judge at the Cannes Film Festival, Schlesinger began working nine hours a day churning out *A Thousand Days,* taking time off only to help Bobby Kennedy in his New York senatorial campaign. When the book was finished, he had more time to devote to *la dolce vita.* (By this time he and his wife Marian had separated.) In New York he was seen everywhere—from Sardi's to Arthur. Everywhere he went he was immediately recognized as a celebrity. He met everyone who counted, even Jacqueline Susann. He was a frequent escort of Jacqueline Kennedy to the more fashionable places; she had liked Arthur from the first. For a professor, he seemed to have an unusually wide acquaintance among actors, artists, poets, and miscellaneous wits.

For Ted Sorensen, the eighteen months spent writing *Kennedy* constituted an emotional catharsis. "I worked on the book from the minute I got up in the morning until I couldn't hold my head up any longer," he says. "The book ran me. It dominated my life. I stayed up more nights than I had during all the crises in the White House. It got to such a point that I couldn't sit down to read a newspaper for a few minutes in the evening without feeling guilty." This was the book JFK himself might have done had he lived, Sorensen suggested.

Sorensen first met John F. Kennedy in 1953, shortly after JFK became Senator. And though he was to become one of Kennedy's most important aides, Sorensen toiled faithfully in the shadows all the years Kennedy was in the Senate. In the White House, he became better known—but generally he avoided the spotlight. Next to Bobby Kennedy, he undoubtedly was the President's closest adviser. He was also described as the President's "intellectual blood bank," "alter ego," and "frontal lobe."

Sorensen was the first of the top Kennedy aides to leave the Johnson Administration. There had been no ill will or hidden antagonism prompting Sorensen's decision. Unlike Schlesinger's, his relations with Johnson had always been amicable, and he decided to leave primarily because each time he saw a man other than John Kennedy sitting in the President's Oval Office he felt a mild sense of shock. Though

Johnson was genuinely sorry to see Sorensen go, he understood how difficult it was for him to remain. "Reluctantly and regretfully I accept your resignation . . . ," Lyndon wrote. "But I accept your decision, appreciative of the motivations which led to it. . . ."

"Johnson tried to be very nice to me," Sorensen recalls, "and he *was* very nice. He wanted me to stay and I agreed at first, but I knew it could never be the same and I never expected to stay. I had given eleven years of my life to John Kennedy, and for those eleven years he was the only human being who mattered to me."

After submitting the manuscript to his publisher, Sorensen began grappling with the problems of his future. Offers of important jobs poured in. But it was difficult for him to decide what to do. Finally, after talks with Bobby Kennedy and Roswell Gilpatric, the former Deputy Secretary of Defense, Sorensen made his decision. In January 1966, he became a full partner in the prestigious law firm of Paul, Weiss, Rifkind, Wharton and Garrison. Important for Sorensen, it was "a firm that would *encourage,* not just permit, me to be active in public affairs."

And active he became. He lectured weekly at Princeton's Woodrow Wilson School of Public and International Affairs and became an editor-at-large of the *Saturday Review* (frequently participating in that magazine's editorial sessions). He also was named chairman of the State Democratic Advisory Committee, a member of the executive board of the national Lawyers' Committee for Civil Rights Under Law, a member of both the John F. Kennedy Institute and the Memorial Library at Harvard and a frequent speaker at luncheons and dinners in New York and elsewhere.

His wide-ranging activities led the state's politicians to conclude that he might be seeking public office, possibly as Senator, but Sorensen repeatedly denied he had any intention of running for the Senate. Still a lot of people thought that such denials were merely the proper ritual for a man running for office. "There's not a possibility of my becoming a candidate," Sorensen told Terence Smith of *The New York Times.* "But given his background," the *Times* reporter observed, "it is difficult to believe that he will not someday be back in government, perhaps in an appointed office, if not an elected one."

Following the assassination, his relationship with Bobby became "close," according to Sorensen. "He and I are friends. I'm in touch with him from time to time. I try to assist him when I can be of help. Robert knows he can count on me for advice and help whenever he needs it. He also knows I won't hesitate to give him bad news." This sets Sorensen apart from most of the people around Bobby, who rarely take issue with the Senator. For example, almost to the last, it was Sorensen who strongly advised Bobby against contesting LBJ for the 1968 nomination, a move vociferously recommended by the Senator's legislative assistants, Adam Walinsky from Yale Law School, and Peter Edelman from Harvard Law School.

Both Edelman and Walinsky were Bobby's "opening to the Left." Joe Alsop, in fact, contends that "Senator Kennedy's staff intellectuals tend to resemble exceptionally brilliant leaders of the Menshevik Youth League. . . ." And Robert Scheer reported in *Ramparts:* "They read the academic journals and *The Village Voice* and are among the small minority of legislative assistants who can differentiate between Julian Bond and Stokely Carmichael."

Walinsky, in particular, was great at supplying the New Left rhetoric for Bobby's speeches. But, unlike Edelman, he has many critics on the Hill, one of whom described him as "nasty and brilliant, in that order." The brash young Walinsky, who likes to boast about being Bobby's top speech-writer, happily refers to his critics as "those clucks." All he cares about is the approbation of Robert F. Kennedy.

Edelman, a year younger than his colleague, is far less controversial. He is known as the quiet Kennedy man who does most of the research and drafting of legislation. He has worked on such programs as narcotics addiction, cigarette advertising, voting rights for Puerto Ricans, New Haven Railroad commuter service, aid to education, Appalachia, and Hudson River conservation. He also drafted speeches, mainly on domestic matters. The two of them have known each other since mid-1963 when they became special assistants at the Justice Department.

Walinsky makes no secret of his far-out views. He believes in radical changes in social and economic conditions, insisting that the United States "can now afford to reshuffle its priorities." And he believes that Lyndon Johnson's Great Society

programs have come up with too little too late. Needless to
say, he thinks the United States ought to get out of Vietnam.

"It is therefore not surprising that Walinsky at times draws
Kennedy toward more radical positions, particularly on such
issues as the Negro upheaval in the ghettos, United States
policy toward Latin America and the war in Vietnam," observed Andrew J. Glass and Leroy F. Aarons in the Washington *Post*. "On the other hand, Walinsky is apt to moderate his
own views in exercising his uncanny ability to write 'for the
Senator's ear.' And Kennedy, for his part, has more than
once inserted a paragraph or two in a Walinsky speech text
to forestall headlines proclaiming a new Kennedy assault on
the Johnson Administration."

All this was viewed with a sort of bemused tolerance by Joe
Dolan, the senior man on the staff. As such, Dolan supervised
the daily activities of staff members, who worked in seven
crowded rooms in the Senate Office Building. Joseph F. Dolan,
a New Yorker in his mid-forties, was graduated near the top
of his class at St. John's Law School. He is also an alumnus of
Bobby's Justice Department.

Bobby's press secretary, Frank Mankiewicz, joined the staff
in June 1966, resigning a $25,000-a-year post as regional
director of the Peace Corps for Latin America to do so.
Mankiewicz, who is in his early forties and a nephew of
movie producer Joseph Mankiewicz, met Bobby late in 1965.
Six months later Bobby "called me up and suggested I come
over and talk," Mankiewicz recalls. "I said 'yes' pretty
quickly."

He handled over a hundred calls a day from the press, plus
numerous requests for exclusive interviews from representatives of domestic and foreign newspapers, magazines, radio
and television stations. Mankiewicz' problem was not so much
getting publicity for The Boss as trying to shape the resulting
deluge of words into a more favorable image. He also was an
alarm system, checking speeches or statements prepared by
Walinsky and Edelman to make sure the Senator didn't say
anything that might be politically damaging.

Another influential adviser was Bill vanden Heuvel, the
New York attorney who served under Bobby in the Justice
Department. Easygoing and voluble, vanden Heuvel made it
a practice to appear on New York's various radio and tele-

vision "talk" shows to argue with Bobby's critics. And he did a pretty good job of it.

Vanden Heuvel's affinity for men of power is extraordinary. Prior to joining Jacob Javits' law firm, he had been special counsel to New York Governor Averell Harriman and a partner and aide of General "Wild Bill" Donovan, the Republican lawyer who had headed the Office of Strategic Services during World War II. At one time he had also cast his lot with the political fortunes of State Comptroller Arthur Levitt who, in 1961, was allied with Tammany boss Carmine de Sapio in a fruitless effort to unseat Mayor Robert Wagner.

Vanden Heuvel has done pretty well since he left Rochester, New York. In December 1958, he married Jean Stein, the vivacious daughter of Jules Stein, chairman of the board of Music Corporation of America (MCA). They are, without doubt, two of New York's most "in" people.

Vanden Heuvel, however, was a trusted aide. During the Manchester affair it was he who flew off to Germany to attempt to persuade a magazine to delete material offensive to the Kennedys. More recently, he served as Bobby's top man at the New York State Constitutional Convention, a frustrating job that would have wearied lesser men.

Nevertheless, vanden Heuvel arouses resentment. As Andrew Glass and Leroy Aarons reported: "His privileged place near Kennedy is an irritant to some of the Senator's supporters in the Reform Democratic camp, who dislike his little-disguised personal drive for public office."

Contacts built up in the days of the New Frontier continued to serve Bobby. He had probably the finest political intelligence system available to a United States Senator. Some of these contacts were highly placed in the Johnson Administration, the most notable being former Defense Secretary McNamara. Others were more reticent about their relations with Bobby. But the RFK people go out of their way to insist there was no such thing as a well-defined Inner Circle or Shadow Cabinet or Bobby Brain Trust. "You know what he's like," observed Joe Dolan. "Robert Kennedy knows somebody who knows a lot about any subject. He talks to a lot of people. Who he talks to depends on what he's doing at the time. He doesn't talk to John Galbraith about organized crime."

The Kennedy brain-picking network had a wide-ranging constituency. It included people who worked for John F.

Kennedy, people who worked with Bobby when he was Attorney General, and people he didn't know too well. Bobby was able to draw on top men from a number of academic centers. Thus, in early 1966, when the Fulbright Committee was preparing to hear testimony from various experts on Chinese affairs, Bobby told a friend-about-town, "I've gotta get smart about China. Why don't you see if you can get some people to dinner?" A few nights later, a China seminar was arranged, with Bobby asking the questions over roast beef and mashed potatoes at Hickory Hill.

The experts were Professor A. Doak Barnett of Columbia University, John K. Fairbank and Benjamin Schwartz of Harvard. Also present were friends, including Senator George McGovern of South Dakota, the former Food for Peace Director under John Kennedy; New Frontiersman Frederick G. Dutton; and three others who valued their jobs in the Johnson Administration enough not to want to be identified. To an outsider it might have looked like a secret gathering of the Kennedy government-in-exile. But it was "nothing of the kind," according to one of the participants. "It was not a strategy meeting. There was nothing subversive about it."

"They don't need a government-in-exile," said another friend. "They do quite well within the established order."

These friends insist that Bobby was just tapping human resources available to any Senator. But clearly these resources are a little more available to Bobby.

Meanwhile, rumors were being voiced around Washington about the soon-to-be-established Kennedy Institute of Politics at Harvard, the institution being created along the banks of the Charles by Dr. Richard E. Neustadt, author of *Presidential Power*. And as early as March 1965, in an article on Neustadt appearing in the *New York Herald Tribune*, Arnold Beichman reported: "During the Institute's development he will continue to work closely with Senator Robert F. Kennedy. (Political gossip has it that the Kennedy Institute under Neustadt will play the role of a brain trust to further Kennedy's Presidential ambition.) He is still a free-lance consultant to several government agencies and, of course, to the President."

Neustadt did not take kindly to the suggestion that the Kennedy Institute was planned as a nursery for an eventual Robert F. Kennedy national administration. In early 1966, while he was putting in considerable time as a member of an LBJ mediation panel to avert a then-threatened airlines strike, Neustadt said, "Just as I start to kill myself to serve for President Johnson, I have to explain that I'm not organizing a set of flunkies for Robert Kennedy."

The Institute opened its doors in October 1966 and all was serene until an enterprising British journalist decided to look more closely into its origins. On January 15, 1967, when Henry Fairlie published his findings simultaneously in the London *Sunday Telegraph* and the Washington *Post,* all hell broke loose.

Fairlie began his explosive articles: "Money moves in these times in mysterious ways its wonders to perform. There is no longer any reason for it to be openly corrupt or for those who accept it to be openly venal. It operates through bodies, whether foundations or trusts, whether endowments or grants, which are not only legal but respectable. Indeed, under taxation laws, they can claim to be more than respectable. They present themselves, and are accepted, as charitable.

"When it is Kennedy money or Kennedy-controlled money, which is involved, one would *a priori* expect to find this new system of wealth working with both exceptional directness and exceptional subtlety. When one gets to Harvard . . . this is exactly what one finds.

"What follows is not the exposure of a scandal or a racket. It is the exposure of the way in which, under the most discreet and respectable and legal arrangements, money today wields power and wields it expertly and deliberately."

In London, the *Sunday Telegraph* editorialized: "The disturbing story by Henry Fairlie about how the Kennedy family are using the great wealth under their control to gain political influence—and eventually recapture the White House—smacks more of 18th-century England than 20th-century America. The great aristocratic families here used to monopolise talent and form personal factions and cabals in the hope of gaining power, until the processes of democracy put an end to such practices.

"How strange to see an aristocratic evil that was rooted out of Britain over a hundred years ago growing up in democratic America, enthusiastically supported, believe it or not, by the flower of the American liberal establishment. What the Cecils and Cavendishes have long since been stopped doing here, the Kennedys are now beginning to get away with in America.

"Let us hope the land of the free will not long stand for that."

Kennedy partisans bitterly denied that "the Kennedys have established, with funds collected in the memory of John F. Kennedy, a recruiting college," but certain facts cited by Fairlie appeared unassailable. First, under the contract between the Kennedy Library Corporation and the Harvard Corporation, the Library Corporation—the governing body of the well-publicized Kennedy Memorial Library—agreed to give $3,500,000 to Harvard on condition that the thirty-year-old Graduate School of Public Administration be renamed the John Fitzgerald Kennedy School of Government. Never before had any department or school at Harvard been named after a benefactor or graduate; and, indeed, the Harvard Corporation had to go to court to change its charter and rename the school. More significant, the Institute of Politics, which was to be created within the new JFK School of Government, received $10,000,000 from the Kennedy Library Corporation, nearly three times the amount given the parent institution. Moreover, the Institute with its $10,000,000 was to be controlled by an independent "advisory committee," of which one member must always be a member of the Kennedy family.

Asked Fairlie: "Why should there be an Advisory Committee at all, if the Institute is a genuine part of Harvard University responsible to the Harvard Corporation?"

Also disturbing was the fact that very little of the money collected and held by the Kennedy Library Corporation was actual Kennedy money. Much of it had been collected from thousands of Americans eager to contribute to a memorial honoring the late President.

Fairlie conceded he was unable to determine exactly the role the Kennedys played in appointments to the Institute, but "one leading member admitted to me that there were certain problems which were taken to Robert Kennedy. But one hardly needs more confirmation than the list of main appointments themselves. Whether past members of the Kennedy circle, whether aspiring members of it, or whether men the Kennedys would like to attract into it, they are all potential members of any future Kennedy Administration."

Harvard officials reacted with unusual emotion to Fairlie's accusations. Although originally concerned about the relationship of the University to the Institute, President Nathan Pusey explained that the public-administration school had been renamed "to honor an especially illustrious alumnus and public figure whose career had evoked hope and lifting of spirit in idealistic young people in all quarters of the globe."

Dean Don K. Price, Jr., of the JFK School of Government did concede: "It is, I admit, unusual for Harvard to name a school for an individual, but then it is unusual to have a Harvard graduate assassinated while serving as President of the United States." And in a letter to the Washington Post, Dean Price contended that there were others at the Institute of Politics besides Kennedy Democrats. There were even Republicans.

"It is not an unsophisticated venture," Fairlie replied, "and one would expect to find good Republicans associated with it, lending it an air of respectability. There are." He also quoted some lines from an unknown poet:

> *You cannot hope to bribe or twist*
> *The American political scientist.*
> *But seeing what, un-bribed, he'll do,*
> *There really is no reason to.*

The Washington Post assigned reporter Laurence M. Stern to look further into the controversy. And Stern came up with some evidence that made an even stronger case than Fairlie's. He reported, for example, that under the endowment agreement Jacqueline Kennedy had the right to veto Harvard's first three choices for any successor to Dr. Neustadt as Director of the Institute. "This extraordinary grant of authority to a member of a donor family is not recorded in the public file on the endowment agreement," Stern added. "The agreement decrees to Harvard that 'you will appoint as the first director of the Institute Prof. Richard E. Neustadt.' As a Kennedy nominee, it might be asked would Neustadt's primary loyalties be to the family or to the university which pays his salary?"

Through all this, the Kennedys remained silent. They were having enough trouble with the Manchester affair. They had learned that every time they opened their mouths in a controversy of this sort it turned into embarrassing front-page news. Their friends, however, could hardly contain their anger. Averell Harriman, who had been named chairman of the "advisory committee" to the Kennedy Institute of Politics, upbraided Fairlie at a large cocktail party in Washington. According to society columnist Betty Beale, Averell told Fairlie with a steely glare, "Sir Winston Churchill once said that very few understand the politics of their own country and no one can understand the politics of another country. I regard this as the least of your faults. I regard you as a journalist incapable of accuracy and with no sympathy for the people and institutions that are dear to this country. You will no longer be welcome in my home or office."

"Thank you very much, sir," said Fairlie. Harriman seemed startled by the reply.

27

Hit-and-Run Senator

By 1966, Robert F. Kennedy had emerged as one of the most powerful men in the nation. So much so that political prognosticators—both pro and con—were beginning to view Bobby's occupancy of the White House as almost inevitable. In fact, William F. Buckley, Jr., wrote a column entitled "The Inevitability of Bobby Kennedy," which reported with some humor and without undue alarm that Bobby was headed for higher things.

"He is indestructible," wrote Buckley. "He can say silly things, as he did all over Latin America, and somehow not be taken as silly. He can say outrageous things, as for instance that he would not object to American blood flowing into Vietcong veins, and when the public winces, he will issue a torrent of explanations and modifications which are gratefully and instantly accepted, and emerge as the forward-looking thinker. He can back the machine and somehow escape the normal consequences. It is, so far, a winning combination. . . ."

That Bobby was seeking the Presidency was generally conceded by his friends. Joseph Alsop was ecstatic about it all: "Senator Kennedy has now reached the status of an unprecedented political phenomenon," the columnist reported on July 1, 1966. "The young Theodore Roosevelt, returning from Cuba with all eyes upon him, is the nearest you can get to a parallel; and it is not really very near. . . .

"Why does he drive himself so hard, as a mere junior Senator, with a very long way to go in the race against very heavy odds? His own answer is a remark of Robert Frost's, that 'You don't go onto a tennis court to see whether the lines are straight; you go on to play tennis.'

"And to this answer he generally adds a somber reflection, suggested to him by his own tragedy, that 'there's no use figuring out where you're going to be later on; you may not be there at all; so the sensible thing is to do the very best you can all the time.' "

Bobby was beginning to feel his strength. He had hit it real big in Manhattan's tangled politics by picking a winner in what otherwise would have been a dull race for surrogate. The Senator's previous entry into local politics—his endorsement of lackluster Abe Beame as against glamorous John V. Lindsay for Mayor—had proved a fiasco. But this time he had come out against the organization man, backed a Reform type, and won.

As Tom O'Neill of the Baltimore *Sun* observed: "Since the primary election jousting brought him into conflict only with the machine on Manhattan Island, the Tammany domain, his always good relations with other party bosses in New York City and upstate, always good, remain undisturbed.

"All machine men defer to demonstrated power, and a chastened Tammany is unlikely to present further problems to the new leader."

Or so it seemed at the time. There could be no doubt that Bobby had solidified his position among many Gotham liberals and Reformers. He kept saying the things they wanted to hear. He kept skirting the Vietnam issue in a way that made it appear he was taking issue with the Johnson Administration position. And he scored high with the ADA-ers by flying to South Africa where in the city of Durban he joined a crowd of sympathizers in singing the American civil rights song "We Shall Overcome."

As *The Nation* put it, Kennedy "was speaking not only to the Africans but to liberals, intellectuals, progressive labor and, in general, that part of America which is left of center. If he is to achieve higher office than the Senate, that grouping must be the nucleus of his support. If events favor, it can spread from these elements to the less differentiated electorate." And as if on cue, Norman Thomas announced that he preferred Bobby to LBJ, whom he had preferred to Barry Goldwater in 1964. The veteran Socialist leader said he was "happily surprised at what Kennedy has been doing.

"I think it's a lot better than what Johnson has been doing," Thomas added, "and I hope Kennedy will persevere in this because he shows evidence of being a better bet for the things we believe in than any other Senator."

On June 11, 1966, Richard Nixon, an ardent Bobby-watcher, told newsmen, "Bobby Kennedy will be the second most powerful man in the Democratic party in 1968. Whether he challenges the President or not will depend on the polls."

And the polls, as of then, did indicate that Bobby's popularity was increasing rapidly. But the one that really shook Washingtonians to their heels was the one released by George Gallup on August 21, 1966, showing that among Democrats and independents, the man they favored for the Presidential nomination in 1968 was not Lyndon Johnson but Robert F. Kennedy.

"The Kennedy rise in political appeal with the American people over the last several months has been spectacular," Dr. Gallup wrote. "Last November the Gallup Poll reported that he posed a threat to Humphrey for renomination as Vice President in 1968. Today he poses a threat to the President himself."

Louis Harris, in a survey released September 27, 1966, also showed Bobby running ahead. "Although both men have denied that they are in a power struggle," Harris wrote, "nearly two out of three Democrats believe a battle is going on behind the scenes for control of the Democratic party. They picture the rivalry between the two men in terms of issues like Vietnam and the anti-poverty program, but also in terms of intense personal antagonisms. By a forty-seven to forty-one percent margin, Democrats making a choice say they would prefer Kennedy rather than Johnson to win such a contest."

Other polls were even more startling. The public-opinion survey conducted by the Minneapolis *Tribune* showed that Minnesota voters, by almost a two-to-one margin, thought that Kennedy would be a stronger running mate for Lyndon Johnson in 1968 than would Hubert Humphrey. Minnesota, of course, is the Vice President's home state.

Needless to say, none of this was exactly greeted with joy at the White House. In fact, the Administration's political strategists couldn't quite figure out why Bobby could be more

popular than the President. The decline in the President's
ratings was commonly attributed to supposed resentment of
his strong civil rights stand and big spending for welfare
programs. "Yet," as John C. O'Brien pointed out in the
Philadelphia Inquirer, "Senator Kennedy in recent speeches
has sought to outdo the President. He has accused the President of curtailing and holding back programs for alleviating
the plight of the poor—a category that includes a high percentage of Negroes. He said last April that the Johnson
budget cuts would be felt most by those least able to afford
them. And he has contended that not enough is being done to
give the Negroes equality with the whites. . . .

"If the President is in bad with the voters for pushing civil
rights too fast and spending on too big a scale for welfare—
the war on poverty and the like—why, the White House
strategists ask, is a United States Senator who advocates doing
more for civil rights and spending for welfare given a higher
popularity rating than the President?"

It was a good question. One reporter who sought the answers was Ted Knap of the Scripps-Howard newspapers, who
traveled to Emmetsburg, Iowa, to find out. Emmetsburg is
the seat of a county that has picked the winner in every
Presidential election since 1896. Two days of interviewing in
his weather-vane county confirmed the pollsters' findings. But
the interviews showed that the reasons were emotional and
personal, rather than ideological. "Ironically," reported Knap,
"on issues like Vietnam, poverty programs and Government
spending, most opinions were closer to Mr. Johnson's than to
Senator Kennedy's."

A typical response came from a middle-aged pharmacist,
who told Knap he was opposed to the poverty program, rent
subsidies and "all that Government intervention, particularly
in education and housing." He had voted for Johnson in 1964
but preferred Bobby for 1968, and said he was not aware
that the Senator had called for tremendous increases in the
poverty program and Federal spending for education, housing
and cities.

A hospital laboratory technician who had voted for Johnson in 1964 and before that for John F. Kennedy, also said
he'd rather vote for Bobby Kennedy for President in 1968.
"I like Kennedy better because he's a young man, climbing

mountains and sailing down rivers. He's a fighter, a hero type."

But probably the most realistic comment from the Midwest came from a Democratic leader who told the *U.S. News & World Report:*

"The sudden surge of Kennedy popularity in this part of the country is due, first, to the fact that the President's communications are not very good with the people out here. I don't know how long this will last, but it is a fact now. It stems ninety percent from Administration statements last spring that seem to blame farmers for the nation's inflation, and ten percent from instability due to the Vietnam war.

"The second thing that has happened is that Bobby is benefiting from the martyr complex. Bobby's support traces more to his dead brother than to anything he has done. I can't see that he has done anything to mark him as presidential material. There is much doubt as to his maturity, and certainly as to his ability. He is simply an opportunist."

Bobby seemed to be downgrading the significance of such polls. "At their best, they are a transitory measurement," he said. "There are peaks and valleys of popularity, probably more so in politics than anywhere else." Nevertheless, his spectacular surge to the top—and, after all, he had held elective office for only twenty-one months—was without precedent in modern political history.

"I can recall," wrote Roscoe Drummond, "no incumbent President in fifty years who was so seriously challenged for renomination. Hoover had no trouble getting renominated in 1932 at the depth of the depression, and the few gestures that were made against Mr. Truman in 1948 were feeble and ineffectual. Bobby's rise in the political scales has not been accidental. He has been working at it furiously—and skillfully.

"He has steadily carved out for himself a series of political positions on big issues that set him apart from the Johnson Administration to give him self-visibility but not so far apart as to alienate his Party. He has been frequently critical of the President, but not so critical that he could not support Mr. Johnson if it seemed desirable. . . ."

Even before these findings were released, Murray Kempton had written: "There are signs that the President has already conceded Kennedy the 1972 succession; he has been heard peevishly to remark that Vice President Humphrey just does not measure up. Mr. Johnson, who was never likable when he was a success, is likely to come to 1968 needing a new face on the business. It would be by no means surprising if he dispensed with the loyal Hubert Humphrey and accepted the distrusted Robert Kennedy as his Vice Presidential candidate. We could not imagine a more unpleasant dose for him; but, after last week, we could no more imagine anything that this man would not do to make safe an election."

Johnson had heard the rumors. On August 31, 1966, at a White House dinner attended by 300 top labor leaders including AFL-CIO President George Meany, Johnson put his arm around Humphrey and quipped: "We're married to each other. As long as I'm President or running for President, I want him [Humphrey] by my side." The labor leaders were loud in their enthusiasm. Many of them could not quite get over their distrust of Bobby and his ambitions.

Nevertheless, Humphrey's friends warily scrutinized each and every Kennedy move for some hint of his future intentions. They saw nearly incredible cynicism in his pretenses of shyness and detachment. They claimed that as usual in any Kennedy operation, Bobby's political activities were being conducted at two levels—one strategic and one operational. Not only was he making certain of the 1972 nomination, following Lyndon Johnson's two terms, but he was also trying to assure his own nomination, instead of Humphrey's, in the event anything should happen to LBJ before that.

Bobby had always been sorely troubled by the ever-growing attempts to associate him with the Fulbright-Morse position on the war in Vietnam. As a political and Senate loner, Bobby simply didn't want to become too closely tied to the Fulbright-Morse views, fearing they might later come back to haunt him. Besides, he was playing a broader game. He had already informed both California Governor "Pat" Brown and Oregon senatorial challenger Robert Duncan—both considered hard-liners on the Vietnam issue—that he intended to campaign for them in the fall.

It was on the issue of foreign aid, of all things, that Bobby sought to disassociate his position from Fulbright and Morse. Both were doing everything possible to slash appropriations. The foreign aid bill provided a much safer way to register one's protest against Vietnam than a vote against appropriations to supply American troops there. When Vietnam critics were added to the conservative Democrats and Republicans, who were traditionally opposed to foreign aid, the resulting cuts in appropriations went very deep.

The counter-rebellion was opened by Senator Kennedy, who said that Fulbright's demonstrably capricious turnabout on foreign aid—a turnabout in which he now insisted on the very crippling restrictions which for years he had implacably opposed—was simply "a retreat from responsibility." But Bobby also chided the Administration for failing to go all out for a measure that was inadequate even as first submitted.

Democratic Senator John O. Pastore of Rhode Island popped up to praise the appeal for a larger aid program but expressed regret that Bobby had not spoken out before the Senate made its "very serious cuts in this bill, cuts which I consider to be most regrettable." To which Bobby conceded a "miscalculation. . . ." He said that he had not realized the Senate might adopt such damaging amendments.

Senator Fulbright, taking the floor, assured Kennedy he was not alarmed over a $250,000,000 loan reduction. Rather, he said, he was concerned over the manner in which the Administration was using bilateral aid as a justification or a means to intervene in the affairs of other countries. "This program has over the years accumulated some very serious political barnacles—among them the involvement in Vietnam," Fulbright said. "I'm not for undertaking a policy of hegemony."

Bobby said that while he had "serious misgivings" himself about Vietnam, he considered aid to Vietnam "pretty far down the list of errors" in that Southeast Asian nation, thus challenging the argument made by Fulbright that Congress should deal warily with foreign aid because Secretary Rusk had cited it as one of the bases for the current U.S. commitment to Saigon.

Wayne Morse of Oregon, who had fought foreign aid bills even in the JFK days, made the most spirited counterattack. He said that Bobby's "first obligation" should have been to stand shoulder-to-shoulder with lawmakers who were seeking to clean up "abuses" in the aid program.

Considerable mirth was generated on the Senate floor when Morse accused Kennedy of participating "in what is obviously a blitzkrieg on the part of the Administration to stop us from cleaning up foreign aid this year." Bobby replied, "I have been accused of many things in my life, and the Senator from Oregon said that I was participating in a blitzkrieg with the Administration. That is the first time I have been accused of that, and I thank the Senator from Oregon. Since I have been in the Senate, I have never heard that said about me."

Grinning broadly, Morse replied, "I did not make the speech. The Senator from New York did."

What Bobby was going to do was the number-one question Bobby-watchers were asking, not only in Georgetown gardens those warm summer evenings but around the country. Reported Tom Wicker in *The New York Times:* ". . . although the idea of Robert Kennedy as a Presidential candidate is as old as the Johnson Administration, the notion that he might actually 'take over' in 1968 instead of waiting until 1972 now is being taken seriously, at least in dinner-table conversation."

What Bobby thought wasn't at all clear. Certainly he was on record as saying he would not try in 1968 but would wait until 1972, but he could always change his mind. But what was interesting is how professional politicians were beginning to rate him. A member of President Johnson's Cabinet who had known Bobby fairly well since 1951 told an interviewer in late 1966 that Bobby had grown enormously in the nearly two years he was in the Senate. "He's matured as a politician, and he's become a much more attractive guy in the process. From 1951 until after the assassination, Bobby was deeply involved in politics, but he was decidedly uncomfortable with politicians." At first he was not very comfortable in the Senate. One reason that he had now grown more comfortable as a Senator was that he had begun to understand the latitude he had to be his own man.

"In the Senate," this Cabinet member went on, "he is no longer regarded as a shallow kid and, significantly, he is probably right now in his career far ahead of his late brother in development. I would honestly say that he is now approaching his brother Jack at the level of the man we knew as President. . . . I would say that the guy has a great deal going for him and there is really no comparison between Bobby Kennedy today and Bobby Kennedy two years ago. The change is truly remarkable. If there is any single reason for it I would say that it is his realization that he is on his own and doing damned well at it."

That was one point of view. Another was provided by a liberal Democratic Senator from the West, who occasionally was listed in "dope" stories as a member of the Kennedy bloc. He said there were perhaps half a dozen colleagues who had a special respect for Bobby as a shrewd, hard-hitting political tactician—but not as a leader of any so-called Senate bloc. Actually he was far more enthusiastic about Teddy Kennedy. He spoke glowingly of his progress, his industry and the solid place he was building for himself in the Senate.

He thought that Bobby hadn't been around long enough to prove that he was willing to work hard. At this point in his career, he was in danger of being labeled an Estes Kefauver or Dick Neuberger—someone who pops off quickly but doesn't show a willingness to take on the menial, drab work of the Senate. The Senator conceded, however, that Bobby had had little time to prove himself in the Senate.

"Sure he makes a lot of speeches about Vietnam and nuclear disarmament," he said, "but this isn't the way you earn brownie points in the Senate." And with respect to Bobby's efforts to carve out positions on issues slightly apart from those of the White House, the Senator observed that his younger colleague was really saying very little that hadn't been said before "downtown." "Because it is Bobby making the speech, the press plays up any slight variations from Administration policy. Anyone else would be listed as hewing to the White House line. . . ."

Still, Robert F. Kennedy could be considered the hottest political commodity in sight. His appearance anywhere in the hustings guaranteed swollen crowds. He had exceeded his own President in public-opinion polls. And many people viewed him as almost inevitably the next President of the United States. And whatever he seemed to do ended up in the front-page headlines.

For example, the way he went after General Motors and its top executives at hearings into automobile safety. The automobile company had been caught in a clumsy effort to have private detectives spy into the personal affairs of a young and obscure lawyer named Ralph Nader, whose book *Unsafe at Any Speed* had castigated the industry's safety policies in general and GM's in particular. GM's belated explanation was that they suspected there might have been some collusion between Nader and the attorneys for claimants suing for $40,000,000 involving the company's Corvair.

Bobby succeeded in prodding embarrassed GM executives into acknowledging that the scope of their harassment of Nader was more than routine, that some GM legal officers were aware of the prying nature of the inquiry, and that a GM statement absolving the company was "misleading and inaccurate." In the manner he had used in grilling crooked labor leaders, Bobby repeatedly hammered at GM's statement. As a solid bank of TV cameras recorded the dramatic scene, Bobby pointed his finger at GM president James M. Roche and said, "There were those in GM who ordered the investigation and permitted a false and misleading statement to go out to the general public and the Congress."

Roche, who had testified that he had not been informed of the Nader investigation until it was nearly over, contended that a "lack of communications" within the company prevented him from knowing the full details.

"I can't believe that General Motors would be so inefficient," Bobby commented, and in a wry voice added, "I like my GM car, but you shake me up."

The automobile industry generally remained silent in the face of this Kennedy-leveled barrage. But Harold A. Fitzgerald, publisher of the Pontiac, Michigan, *Press,* objected strenuously "to the attempt to ridicule current automobile standards by naïve personalities that don't know the difference between torque and torsion. Nader's amateurish statements have been seized upon and accorded publicity they never deserved or warranted. Safety has been an issue with the industry from inception and the never-ending quest continues today—just as it always has in the past.

"Of course people are killed in automobiles. They're killed in bathtubs—plenty of them. They're killed on the front lawn. . . . Alcohol is a much, much closer associate of the Big Man with the Scythe than automobile construction. Records show that more than 50 percent of the fatal accidents prove alcohol was involved. Has Nader castigated the makers of strong drink—some of whom have amassed untold millions personally—like the Kennedys?"

But nowhere was Bobby's propensity for hogging headlines more clearly demonstrated than at the Senate hearings chaired by Abe Ribicoff, on the plight of the cities. This was in the summer of 1966, and the Connecticut Democrat was quite understanding about it all. "Let's face it," said Ribicoff. "Bobby Kennedy is a fact of life. Wherever he goes, he makes news."

The Saturday before the hearings started, Senator Ribicoff had visited the White House to assure a skeptical President that the hearings were not aimed at his Administration. Lyndon had his doubts. Nevertheless, if anybody had to run the hearings, the President said he'd just as soon it be Abe. So when Bobby asked to testify as lead-off witness, Ribicoff was horrified. He knew that Bobby would immediately convert the hearings into another Kennedy-Johnson confrontation, and he tried to dissuade him.

But Bobby said that he had a statement prepared and come hell or high water he was going to read it. The best Ribicoff could do was to turn the whole first day over to Congressional witnesses, of whom Bobby was one. He, of course, got all the headlines. And, as was to be expected, the headlines screamed that Bobby had sharply criticized President Johnson.

Bobby had implied that the Administration was using the war in Vietnam as an excuse for not increasing Federal aid to troubled cities, and refuting contentions that the Government could not afford big domestic spending programs at this time, he said, "The demands of Vietnam, purportedly responsible for the cutbacks in vital education, housing and poverty programs, in fact still represent less than three percent of our [gross] national product." But even with expenditures in Vietnam, he continued, "the Federal Government is spending a smaller proportion of our gross national product than it did three years ago."

Commenting on Bobby's statement, the Washington *Post* observed that while "Federal aid to urban areas is an ideal vehicle on which to tie political aspirations . . . to insinuate that the Administration is using the war in Vietnam as an excuse for lassitude in the struggle for more habitable cities is most unfortunate. That charge confuses and distorts the real issues. The choice is not one of fighting in Vietnam or struggling to check the social disintegration of our cities. Both fights must be waged, and the problem is one of establishing a rational system of priorities, deciding which goals are most important and allocating the resources of Government accordingly."

The President, anticipating the attack, had called in several Cabinet members on the eve of the hearings for a strategy session. They were to accentuate the positive—notably the $16.8-billion Federal outlay for urban programs in the past year. Then he sent five of his top men off to the hearings—Health, Education and Welfare Secretary John Gardner; Housing and Urban Development Secretary Robert Weaver; Attorney General Nicholas Katzenbach; Labor Secretary Willard Wirtz; and Economic Opportunity Director Sargent Shriver.

Secretary Weaver fared least well under the withering fire of Robert F. Kennedy, who wasn't happy with much of what he was doing. Impatiently dismissing Weaver's recitation of the Administration's efforts to cure the ills of city slums, Bobby snapped, "If this is the answer, then maybe we'd better get off the ship." Present programs, he added, lacked imagination and coordination. What was actually needed was something along the lines of a domestic Marshall plan. He even clashed with Nicholas Katzenbach, his old friend from the Justice Department, who sharply disagreed with Bobby's charge that the Administration's programs were "a drop in the bucket."

Speaking of the teeming headaches of megalopolis, Katzenbach said finally in patient exasperation, "We're looking at all this as a whole for the first time in a generation. You have to crawl before you walk, and walk before you run."

"I'm just not satisfied," Bobby replied.

"You've made that quite clear, Senator," the then Attorney General replied wearily.

Then it was Sargent Shriver's turn, and suddenly the grilling let up. Bobby saluted his brother-in-law for his opening statement—"the best summary of problems the country is facing." At issue was the budget for Head Start. The Administration had allocated $327,000,000 for this project to prepare deprived children for their first school year.

As usual, Bobby wasn't "satisfied." He claimed Head Start would reach only 30 percent of the children who needed it. "Could you use $300,000,000 more?" he asked.

"We could use $200,000,000 more," replied Shriver. "We could help 210,000 more children."

Bobby paused for a moment, stared down at a paper, shrugged, and shook his head slowly. "It's a point that distresses me," he said. "We're spending more than $300,000,000 on a supersonic jet transport that will eventually cost $4 billion. But we can't help 210,000 more children. I just can't be content with that. It's an outrage."

During his appearance, HEW Secretary Gardner made clear he was not opposed to further Federal outlays. But he warned against trying to correct problems with indiscriminate cash outpourings. "We should be particularly wary of the old American habit of spending a lot of money to still our anxieties," he said. It reminded him, in fact, of an Indian rain dance. "The dance didn't bring rain, but it made the tribe feel a lot better."

The fact remains that despite allegations that the White House had adopted a penny-pinching and niggardly attitude toward urban problems, the Johnson Administration was already spending many times more on such problems—schools, medicare, rent subsidies, urban renewal, mass transit, anti-poverty and the rest—than any Administration in history, including that of the late President John F. Kennedy.

"The irony of all this is exquisite," wrote columnist William S. White. "President Johnson's unexampled largesse to megalopolis is in the deepest sense open to objective criticism—but for being far too large rather than much too small. He had expected an amplitude of trouble and skepticism from the conservative side, and should have got it, in one columnist's opinion. But what he gets is trouble from the ultra-liberal side.

"The common explanation for this instance of the world turned upside down is that though Robert Kennedy as a powerful member of his brother's Cabinet surely did not demand urban schemes of the staggering scope he now contemplates, Robert Kennedy as a Senator sees a need to differentiate himself sharply from the Johnson Administration in pursuit of presidential ambitions. It may well be, too, that the years in between have changed his mind as to the gravity of the urban mess.

"Still, what is happening here goes far beyond all such considerations. For the effect of the actions of the Kennedy group is to draw an increasingly sharp line everywhere between city sheep and non-city goats by insisting upon such vast outpour-

ings to the cities as would make them the incredibly privileged
relief clients of the rest of the Nation.

"This is a politics of megalopolis first, second and always
that could become bitterly divisive and also could, by over-
pressing and overdemanding, produce not bread but stones
from a predominantly non-megalopolis Congress."

After chiding the Cabinet-level official for failing to do
enough for urban America, Ribicoff and Kennedy summoned
the men who actually run the cities—the mayors—and took
them to task. Some of the mayors took umbrage.

One was New York's tanned, young Mayor Lindsay, who
could barely suppress his annoyance when Bobby kept pressing him for a price tag on how much was needed in Federal
funds to alleviate Gotham's enormous problems. Finally,
Lindsay came up with a $50-billion figure over a ten-year pe-
riod to make New York "thoroughly livable." Bobby could
hardly believe it. It was, he said, a "totally unrealistic"
figure. Bobby said that Washington was "not about to increase
its aid to New York City at that rate."

Bobby took the same tack with Democratic Mayor Jerome
P. Cavanagh of Detroit who estimated that his city, with
one-half the population of New York, could use $15 billion
during the next decade. "There's just not going to be those
sums available," Bobby said chidingly. But the Kennedy treatment of either was mild compared with the going-over he
handed out to Mayor Samuel P. Yorty of Los Angeles.

Yorty, of course, was a logical Kennedy target. The
maverick Mayor, though a Democrat, had supported Richard
M. Nixon in the 1960 Presidential election. He had also
committed the unpardonable sin in the more recent California gubernatorial primary by drawing over a million votes
away from Governor Edmund G. "Pat" Brown, who was
being backed by Bobby. Yorty had been making noises
about staying "neutral" in Brown's forthcoming contest with
Republican Ronald Reagan.

The stage was set for a bitter confrontation—and bitter
it was. There were heated exchanges as Bobby relentlessly
questioned Yorty on the quality of his leadership. Bobby
wanted facts and figures on unemployment, Head Start
classes, training projects and other programs, particularly
in the explosive Watts area of Los Angeles. Yorty complained that Bobby was being "extremely unfair" because

many of the programs did not fall under his jurisdiction. The lines of jurisdiction in his city are very diffuse. The Mayor has all of the responsibility but none of the authority.

"But you are Mayor of all the people of Los Angeles," Bobby said icily. "If they have a problem, don't they look to you for leadership?"

Yorty, who had won re-election the previous year by a two-to-one margin over James Roosevelt, snapped, "They showed it in the last election."

Several thousand stern words later, Bobby said to Yorty, "You might not have the responsibility in each one of these fields, but you certainly are Mayor of the city and therefore we need some leadership."

"I don't need a lecture from you on how to run my city," Yorty retorted angrily.

When Bobby asked for Yorty's assessment of racial problems generally, the Mayor replied, "Politicians run around making promises that can't be kept, and people reach out for help that doesn't come. Sometimes, when people reach out, police have to stop them." Despite Watts, the Mayor added, Los Angeles enjoyed as good race relations as any city in the country.

This did not satisfy Bobby, who said, "The fact is that these people in trouble expect a better life, expect to have as much of a chance as you and I."

Yorty, who had made it the hard way, looked at Bobby, whose family fortune approaches the $400,000,000 mark, and snapped, "Certainly, Mr. Senator, they won't have the chances you had, but I hope they have the chance I had."

Yorty left the hearing room seething and the next day, back in Los Angeles, charged that he had been caught in a well-laid trap. "Kennedy played the prosecutor," he went on. "I got caught in the cross fire of Bobby Kennedy's attempt to undermine President Johnson. Bobby is an upstart who is trying to ride on his brother's fame and his father's loot and take over the United States of America."

Asked how Kennedy's criticism of Los Angeles could be connected with undermining Johnson, Yorty replied that Bobby wanted to "destroy all the friends he [Johnson] has. Kennedy wants either to see President Johnson defeated in 1968 or so weakened he can't name a successor in 1972. Bobby wants to be President and that's for sure."

Yorty had plenty of hometown allies. The City Council, the Bar Association and the Chamber of Commerce stood up in righteous indignation. A City Council resolution was drawn up admonishing "Washington legislators" to "mind their own damn business."

The reaction of Governor Pat Brown, then in an uphill battle to hold onto the governorship, appeared to be a few nervous coughs. Yorty's support—or lack of it—could have a bearing on Brown's chances against Reagan. Reagan, not so nervous, assailed the hearings as "one of the most arrogant displays I've ever seen."

That the subcommittee hearings constituted a made-to-order sounding board for Senator Kennedy could not be argued. What could be argued was how much they contributed to public understanding of the matters under inquiry. The Washington *Star* made these observations:

"In the last two weeks Senator Kennedy has treated the country to a kind of senatorial entertainment which adds nothing to his stature. The junior senator from New York, assisted by the junior senator from Connecticut, has summoned cabinet members and the mayors of large cities before him as if they were errant schoolboys and he their properly indignant teacher.

"He has, unfortunately, very little to teach anyone on the subject in hand except the extent of his animosity in several directions and the lengths to which he will go to vent it. The ostensible subject of the hearings is not the ineptness of the Johnson administration nor the alleged negligence of mayors nor even the new and different charm of Bobby in anger.

"The sincerity of the senator can be judged in several passages. One was his encounter with Mayor Lindsay of New York. The mayor specifically stated that he had no figures and wished to engage in no guessing games as to how much money New York would need from the federal government to alleviate its distress in several areas. The senator pressed and pressed again and finally elicited the figure of $50 billion over the next decade. Immediately he became an economy-minded guardian of the Treasury, taking the mayor to task for his grandiose notions. Yet only a few days earlier he had himself denounced the administration for its alleged 'drop in the bucket' expenditures upon the problems of the cities. Given that contrast, it seems safe to assume that had Mayor Lindsay been more modest in his estimate he would have been promptly denounced as penurious with the poor. . . .

"President Johnson, naturally, is a prime target in the general assault being conducted by the senator from New York, though so far the President has been struck at chiefly through his cabinet members. It is grossly unfair to portray this administration as unconcerned with the problems of the cities. It has created, at last, the long talked about Department of Urban Affairs at cabinet level. It has made funds available for urban experiments in human and material rehabilitation. Hopefully, it will soon put into effect the demonstration cities program which is in itself a lot more than a drop in anyone's bucket, and which also offers the promise of discovery of effective means toward an end that surely all agree on. . . ."

One Senate veteran, a liberal, put it this way: "Bobby is not a Senator's Senator. He understands very well the limitations of achieving a national identity if you keep your nose close to the legislative grindstone. That's not his objective. And, you know, you can't call that wrong. It's exactly what his brother Jack did. About the only important bill that Jack got through was the Fair Labor Standards Act.

"Now his brother Teddy is exactly the opposite. Teddy is conscientious. He spends considerable time studying a bill and its strategy. But Bobby has chosen the Senate as a springboard. And he sees his Senate role as the place for a dramatic confrontation, such as the confrontation with the President of General Motors or with Mayor Sam Yorty of Los Angeles.

"Look, if he really wanted to win that battle on the poverty bill, he'd have stayed right here in town for the past six weeks, buttonholing Senators, explaining the reasons for the increases and nailing down their votes. He'd have been on the phone for a solid week, coordinating pressure groups all over the country. He could easily have won that fight.

"Bobby was beaten trying to defend an increase over the President's budget of some $700 million. The next day Wayne Morse came in with a school bill that exceeded the President's budget by more than a billion. Ev Dirksen tried to cut this one back, too. But Wayne won because he had done his homework inside and outside the Senate.

"I would call Bobby a hit-and-run Senator. He'll come into a committee room where the TV cameras are, take a slug at General Motors and leave. The drudgery and shepherding a bill are left to someone else.

"If you're running for President, you don't have time to do anything of real substance on the legislative front. . . ."

Another Senator, one noted for his wit and philosophic bent, put it this way: "Bobby is an existentialist politician. Wherever the action is, he goes. Like Cape Town, where he denounced apartheid; and Kraków, where he talked about freedom. He can make bigger headlines shooting the rapids and climbing mountains than we can making floor speeches. Maybe that is the proper role for successful politicians. I certainly can't fault him for it. His interests are outside the Senate. Oh, I know he views the Senate as a good place to make a speech on occasion and a committee room as a good place to excoriate someone's shortcomings. All right, so he chewed out Sam Yorty for not doing a better job as Mayor. But what did this have to do with getting a bigger poverty bill through the Senate?"

A more sympathetic, but just as knowledgeable, source said, "He lends a presence to any hearing in which he participates. This cannot be denied. Bobby can put a Committee investigation on page 1 by his cross-examinations. This is important in the legislative process since the enactment of legislation, if controversial, demands a public involvement. And Bobby does have some influence with the young Turks in the Senate. If he makes an issue *his* issue, it becomes a different issue. . . .

"Bobby has no power in the Senate if you think of it in terms of the pork barrel. Bobby speaks beyond the Senate; he speaks to a national audience."

While Bobby was riding high on the national scene, he discovered anew the vagaries of involving himself in local politics. As New York's most influential Democrat, widely touted as a future Presidential candidate and honored for his stunning victory in Manhattan's surrogate race, it was generally assumed that his would be the most decisive voice in picking the Democratic candidate for Governor in 1966. It was also generally assumed that Kennedy's choice was

Eugene Nickerson, a smooth, handsome type who was County Executive in suburban Nassau, a "new face" in the New Frontier tradition who had demonstrated he could win in Republican territory. Nickerson certainly had been led to believe that Bobby would publicly endorse him.

Another who believed he had Bobby's imprimatur was Franklin Delano Roosevelt, Jr., who had resigned as chairman of the Federal Equal Employment Opportunity Commission to return to New York politics. A third active hopeful was Howard J. Samuels, a graduate engineer who had made a postwar fortune in the upstate plastics company he had founded. A public-spirited citizen, with a frequently unconventional approach to politics, Samuels confided, "Whatever I do, I'll have to do for myself." Which is pretty much the way it turned out.

And the man Robert Kennedy wanted least as his party's gubernatorial standard-bearer was Frank O'Connor, who had been described by *Time* as "a seasoned, big-city Irishman . . . who knows all the machine-made political tricks that Bobby learned up in Boston." O'Connor was much more. In the 1965 municipal elections he outpolled everybody else, including Mayor Lindsay, to become President of the City Council and the opinion polls showed him as the man most likely to beat Nelson Rockefeller.

The roots of hostility between Kennedy and O'Connor are old. As Attorney General, Bobby played a part in blocking O'Connor from getting the gubernatorial nomination in 1962. As a result, O'Connor never became a member of Bobby's fan club. "The Senator is jealous of his liberal image," wrote Mary McGrory, "and he does not feel that O'Connor, the former district attorney of Queens County and an old-school politician, enhances it in any way."

O'Connor did have trouble living down his conservative past. During the McCarthy era, he had supported a loyalty-oath bill and, as a state senator, he had once introduced a bill requiring two years' residence for people seeking relief payments. In more recent years, he had sought to atone for these misdeeds, but to no avail. The Liberal party just wasn't buying the "new look." What made the Liberal party position ludicrous was the fact that two years previously its leaders had proved quite willing to overlook Bobby Kennedy's Mc-

Carthyite background and anoint him as one of the great progressives of all time.

Earlier in the year, Bobby had made it clear that he expected to influence the ultimate gubernatorial choice. But he said he would not try to handpick the candidate. Later, in the flush of victory in the surrogate race, he indicated he might have more to say about the gubernatorial nomination than he had originally planned.

Several weeks before the state convention, Franklin Roosevelt unloosed a bombshell. He charged that a year before, the county "bosses," including Charley Buckley of the Bronx and Stanley Steingut of Brooklyn, had promised O'Connor the nomination provided he withdrew from the 1965 mayoral race.

"Mr. O'Connor's personal probity is not in doubt, but a candidacy founded upon an alliance of the Steingut and Buckley organizations and the noisome O'Connell machine in Albany cannot command public confidence," said *The New York Times*. "If the air is to be cleared, it is essential that responsible party leaders investigate the Roosevelt charges and set forth their findings."

At a news conference in Washington, Bobby asserted that the charges and countercharges could be "very harmful to those mentioned and to the Democratic party." Few Democrats, and even fewer Republicans, would have disagreed with him. But the New York *Post* was annoyed that Bobby had given "the impression that he was more concerned about the impact of the charges than their substance."

Realizing that he could not safely oppose his party regulars and that O'Connor had the nomination sewed up, Bobby beat a quiet retreat. Almost to the last, Eugene Nickerson had expected Bobby to publicly endorse him. Instead, Bobby disclosed that he would support whomever the state convention nominated.

That did it. Gene Nickerson withdrew from the race. Then Franklin Roosevelt abandoned his bid for the nomination. He made no secret of his anger at the Senator for failing to support his ambitions. He claimed Bobby had encouraged him originally to make the race. Conceding the nomination to O'Connor, Roosevelt said that Bobby "could have played a decisive role and we might have had another nominee." By this time, Howard Samuels was the only other candidate remaining in the race.

The Democratic State Convention finally convened in Buffalo on September 8—its results a foregone conclusion. About the only excitement on that sultry first day was generated by a group of Reformers who wanted to incorporate an anti-war plank into the party platform.

But the plank threatened the surface tranquility of the convention. There were frantic behind-the-scenes negotiations. Bill vanden Heuvel, embodying the great sovereign power of Robert F. Kennedy, handed down the Senator's dictum that a plank dealing with the Vietnam War had no place in the state Democratic platform. Vanden Heuvel, who was chairman of the platform committee, added, "Senator Kennedy does not want anything in the platform that would embarrass President Johnson and hurt the situation in Vietnam."

The Reformers, at first, were not buying any compromise. But after being advised of the embarrassing situation developing in Buffalo, President Johnson ordered Ambassador-at-large Averell Harriman to crush the revolt. Pleading with the Reformers, Harriman said, "You can't rat on our boys in the trenches." And finally, after a fierce debate, the Reformers voted 52 to 14 to agree to a compromise acceptable to the White House. As finally adopted, it stated support and commendation for President Johnson as "a man of peace," and urged all citizens to back the President, Senator Kennedy and others "in their efforts to end hostilities."

Later that night, according to Jack Newfield, Senator Kennedy approached a Reform Assemblyman and chided him as follows: "You gave up too easily. That resolution praised the President." The Assemblyman wondered whether he had heard correctly.

There remained only the formality of nominating Frank O'Connor for Governor. That's what Bobby thought as he whiled away the day in his air-conditioned suite at the Statler-Hilton. He had made no secret of his absolute boredom with the kaleidoscopic tribalisms of New York politics as he watched the convention proceedings on television. He wanted to do what had to be done and get away from Buffalo, a city he never particularly cared for anyway. Bobby was lying on the bed when Steve Smith came in to announce that

Howard Samuels had phoned to report his people were insisting on having his name put in nomination. This meant a long and dreary roll call, and Bobby, who had been waiting to introduce O'Connor to the convention, could hardly contain himself. He snapped, "You tell Samuels that if he can't trust his people, he had better find people he can trust."

Finally, Frank O'Connor was nominated. Howard Samuels had obtained 137 votes in the balloting before he moved to make O'Connor's nomination unanimous. Later O'Connor was quoted as wisecracking that his first-ballot victory was "easy —I just rounded up all the people Bobby Kennedy asked to run for Governor, and that was more than enough." It now became Bobby's burden to introduce O'Connor to the assembled delegates. This he did with hardly a trace of enthusiasm. He also called on all Democrats to unite, comparing their problems with the Liberal party with those Harry S Truman had confronted in 1948. (The Liberal party that day had begun the process of nominating Franklin D. Roosevelt, Jr., as its gubernatorial candidate by the democratic process of issuing a press release to that effect. The reason given by the Liberals for withholding their traditional endorsement of the Democratic candidate was that O'Connor had been picked by the "bosses.")

After O'Connor's acceptance speech, the convention adjourned for a long night of bargaining over the rest of the ticket. The bargaining centered on a choice for Lieutenant Governor, the number-two spot. Howard Samuels' name was suggested. But the negotiators rejected the idea after an intermediary relayed word that Bobby could not abide the upstater. The intermediary gave no reasons, indicating they were personal.

Senator Kennedy, meanwhile, flew back to New York aboard the *Caroline*. He had remained longer than he had expected. The crowd roared its approval when it was announced from the rostrum that Robert F. Kennedy would serve as the honorary chairman of the O'Connor campaign. All through the convention, the delegates had cheered Bobby lustily, had stood in jammed hallways for sweaty hours just to catch a glimpse of him, and had waved banners proclaiming HOORAY, HOORAY FOR RFK.

When the convention resumed, the hall was in an uproar with caucuses and demonstrations by Samuels' supporters.

Ray Jones put in a phone call to Samuels. He said he was not going to nominate Samuels unless Samuels was willing. Samuels was willing. The candidate, whose wife and eight children had been packing to leave town, ordered a television set sent up quickly from downstairs and watched the goings-on at the convention. Three taxicabs were called to stand by outside the hotel.

Rather than face an open roll-call fight and the possibility of defeat, the O'Connor forces finally decided to throw the nominations for second place open to the floor. It was clear by then that this would mean a Samuels victory. The delegates then unanimously nominated Samuels for Lieutenant Governor. Samuels, who had arrived at the hall half an hour after his nomination, happily accepted.

A Kennedy spokesman said that "whoever suggested" that Kennedy had vetoed Samuels "is not telling the truth." But that's not what the delegates thought as they roared through their nomination of Samuels. Ray Jones voiced the prevalent sentiment when he told reporters, "I'm tired of being told what to do."

In any case, Robert F. Kennedy experienced a mild setback. Though he was still the leader of his party, more disastrous events were soon to follow.

28

Campaign 1966

The wiry young man from New York squinted through the television lights that bathed the stage of the ancient Orpheum Theater in Sioux City, Iowa. Finally his eyes focused on the pretty blond in a green suit who had risen to ask the first question. "Have you ever thought about running for President?" she asked nervously.

The crowd of several thousand broke into earsplitting cheers. The young man, his fingers running through an unruly forelock, paused dramatically. He waved for silence. The crowd waited expectantly. Then he said simply, "Yes." And the crowd let loose a roar. The young man, of course, was Robert F. Kennedy. And that day, as James M. Perry reported in *The National Observer*, "it didn't seem so much that he was just *thinking* about the Presidency but that he was already *running* for it."

"I just want to be a good United States Senator," Bobby had said when asked about his future Presidential aspirations at Alverno College in Milwaukee during his opening Midwest swing of the 1966 campaign. But Kennedy dispatched teams of advance men including the energetic Jerry Bruno all over the country to prepare for his arrival. Nothing was left to chance. A Kennedy trip was as well planned as a Presidential trip. The advance man coordinated signals with local politicians, mapped out swift routes, advised local police on crowd control, arranged for getting out the crowds. Some local officials had the feeling of having been "run over."

"The Kennedy advance men came swarming in here about a week ahead of his visit," said one Mayor. "I've never seen anybody quite so arrogant. They wanted this, and they wanted that, and they wanted it all yesterday. At one point I was ready to pull the police and everybody else out of the picture and tell the Kennedy boys to handle the affair by themselves since they knew so much. But I wound up being a good guy. We put out flags, provided a police escort and all the rest."

This hard work paid off. Almost everywhere Bobby went he drew Presidential-size crowds. At airports, it seemed to at least one White House correspondent, a Kennedy arrival was almost indistinguishable from a Presidential arrival. It had everything but "Hail to the Chief." The hand-printed signs everywhere told the story: AMERICA NEEDS KENNEDY IN '68, WE'LL WAIT FOR YOU TIL '72, KEEP HARASSING LBJ, and RFK MINUS LBJ IN '72.

All this, of course, did not just happen. At Fresno, California, a $25 prize was offered by Bobby's advance man for the best "homemade" sign.

And at the Seattle Airport, another advance man told a state trooper not to restrain the crowd too much. "They'll muss him up a little," he said, "but he doesn't mind it." Ostensibly Bobby was campaigning for Democratic candidates across the nation. These consisted of his Congressional colleagues who had worked early and hard for JFK in 1960. But as the U.S. correspondent of *The Economist* reported: "Sometimes the local candidates felt that they had been helped; sometimes some of them felt like early Christians getting a nod of encouragement upon being thrown to the lions; a few even felt that the visiting Senator's entourage of ruthless young men from the East was treading over their prostrate forms in pursuit of a distant, glittering goal."

Most correspondents were impressed by the numbers of young people who turned out. There seemed to be a deep need on the part of the teenagers to touch Bobby. It was almost like the hysteria that greeted the Beatles or the Rolling Stones. If there were no restraining barriers, as was often deliberately the case, the youngsters would stampede to get close—to shake his hand, claw at his clothes or grab at his overflowing locks. "Did you touch him?" was one of the most frequently heard remarks in the wake of any appearance.

His appearance in Portland, Oregon, provided an excellent example of the planning skills that went into the tour. The

Senator had made it clear he wanted no empty seats anywhere on his itinerary, so the rally that had been originally scheduled for Memorial Coliseum—capacity 10,000—was switched at the last minute to the Labor Center, which holds only 1,200. The move had the desired result. So crowded was the Labor Center that Senator Kennedy himself had difficulty getting in.

Not all those who turned out to greet Bobby were youngsters. There were those who wanted to catch a glimpse of the man who might one day be President. A fireman, holding his son above his head, told a reporter at the Dubuque Airport, "How often do you get to see a President in our part of the country? Roosevelt came through here once, and maybe my son and I are seeing another President today." Many wanted to see the man they knew had been closest to John F. Kennedy. In the boondocks they still remembered the late President. They were still grieving over his untimely death. Somehow they wanted to make their feelings known to the younger Kennedy.

What he said was pretty much the same wherever he went. And that wasn't too much. In the party were Bobby's new press secretary, Frank Mankiewicz, and his speech-writer, Adam Walinsky. Any changes in the "basic" speech were mimeographed and handed out to the press, whose numbers were almost as great as those who traveled with the President. In the campaign's later stages, their corps included reporters and cameramen from newspapers and television networks in Canada, Sweden, Britain, South Africa, West Germany and the Netherlands.

Generally, the speeches were New Frontier Revisited, with repeated references to John F. Kennedy's 1960 crusade to get the country moving again. Bobby began each with the same kind of self-deflating wit that was the trademark of his late brother. Noting that Kennedy's speechmaking relied heavily on borrowed phrases from ancient literary figures, Peter Simple wrote in the London *Daily Telegraph:* "It would be better, as well as fairer to all those helpless writers, to draw on the resources of his own mind. This would at once reduce him to almost total silence, a relief to many and a welcome bar to his further political advancement."

Writing from Portland, James Reston reported: "This, however, is not so much a trip to expound Kennedy's policies as it is to exploit Kennedy's personality, gain publicity, and win influential supporters in the Democratic ranks. He remains ambiguous about Vietnam, but the main impression he leaves is that he is for peace, for composing differences with the Soviet and the Chinese, for escalating the war on poverty rather than the war in Vietnam, and always, while saying an occasional good word for President Johnson, he talks about his brother and takes up a position a little to the left of Mr. Johnson's policies both at home and abroad. Nineteen sixty-six, then, is obviously a training ground for a Kennedy Presidential bid in the future. . . ."

President Johnson, meanwhile, was taking a different tack in his speeches. He was campaigning on the theme that the Great Society had brought manifold benefits to the American people. In a Labor Day speech in Lancaster, Ohio, he told the crowds over his bullhorn, "Count your blessings. Don't wail and groan and make a martyr of yourself. No people ever had so much to be grateful for as we do."

Yet two weeks later, Bobby told an audience in Cincinnati, "I come here to you today as President Kennedy came in 1960 . . . to say this country can do better, it must do more . . . to make the world we hand to the next generation a better world than we received from the last."

If President Johnson was annoyed by such indirect criticism, he did not show it publicly. From the transcript of the President's press conference of September 21, 1966:

"*Question:* Senator Kennedy of New York has suggested it is a mistake for you to dwell so much on the accomplishments of your Administration and the prosperity of the country. He said you ought to focus more on the things that still need to be done. Could you comment, sir?

"*Answer:* Yes. We're trying to do that every day. We have submitted a program on things that need to be done and we're doing them. We have passed about 70 measures this year on things that need to be done and we have some 10 yet to be acted upon. And I agree that we ought to have a program and that we ought to try to get it passed if possible, and I'm rather pleased at the success that we have achieved so far and I'm very grateful for the cooperation of all the members of the Congress."

That Hubert Humphrey was more than annoyed was quite obvious and perhaps understandable. As Gerald Griffin noted in the Baltimore *Sun:* "Humphrey, who came to the Senate with a reputation as a red-hot liberal, is out defending the Johnson-style consensus and being booed as a Nazi because he supports the President in Vietnam. Kennedy, who was long regarded with distrust by the red-hot liberals, now is accepted as their hero as he stakes out positions to the left of the Johnson-Humphrey Administration."

In an unguarded moment, Humphrey let himself take a public swipe at Bobby during a television interview in Los Angeles. Asked to comment on Mayor Yorty's remark that Bobby was making a conscious effort to undermine the President, Humphrey said, "I don't think Senator Kennedy is out to get President Johnson—as such. I think he takes a different point of view than President Johnson. But I believe President Johnson's point of view is a little more mature, a little more responsible, a little more in the public interest."

In subsequent press dispatches, it was reported that Hubert felt he might have gone too far in criticizing Bobby. But it could be safely assumed that he did not feel that way a few days later when he read, in the October issue of *Harper's,* an article suggesting that Bobby's intention in 1968 was "to muscle Hubert Humphrey aside and take second place on the ticket." The article—"The Making of President Robert Kennedy"—was written by the well-informed William V. Shannon.

Bobby immediately denied any intention of forcing his way onto the 1968 national ticket. He said that such reports were a reflection on his political intelligence. In background interviews, he pointed out that it would be foolish for any Democrat, however popular nationally, to challenge either an incumbent President or the man he wanted as his Vice President. Moreover, as Vice President, he would not have the same flexible independence in stating his views as he had in the Senate.

But, as Warren Weaver, Jr., reported in *The New York Times:* "The Senator concedes that his candidate-style of national campaigning does put him in a position of strength if some unforeseen circumstances—death or disability of one of the principals or some national disaster—should suddenly alter the entire picture in the Democratic party."

Bobby answered that the real reason for his moving around the country was a sincere desire, as a loyal Democrat, to aid selected candidates. "When the requests come in," he said, "you have a choice: You can sit on your back or go out and try to help. I can't just answer 'That's your problem, not mine.' I'd have a tough time defending myself if I refused these requests because I'd rather stay home in McLean or go to the theater in New York." But despite these disclaimers, the number of correspondents covering his tour increased as the campaign went into its final stages, and even included, for the first time, Theodore H. White, gathering material for *The Making of the President 1968*.

For Tom Wicker of *The New York Times* the 1966 campaign brought back richly nostalgic and sad memories.

"It has been much like 1960 all over again," he wrote, "traveling the campaign routes this year with Richard M. Nixon and Senator Robert Kennedy. . . . Lyndon Johnson has been out of it all these past few weeks, just as he was in 1960, and one cannot help thinking that we have only been marking time, waiting for an old battle to be rejoined.

"There are differences, of course. The age gap is greater. If anything, the emotional frenzy into which the sight of Bob Kennedy drives his audiences is greater than anything John Kennedy caused six years ago. Nixon is more relaxed and easier going, a more likable human being. Neither is running for any office; neither seems to know quite what he is after; and if Bob Kennedy, like his brother, is the more exciting personality, Nixon now seems in a remarkable turnabout to be the more serene man, perhaps the more willing to let fate work its will on his fortunes.

"But the basic similarity is there: it is the same old Kennedy-Nixon campaign. In much the same voice, the same words, the same gestures, with the old intensity and vigor, sometimes even with the same quotations, Bob Kennedy is delivering the message of 1960. . . ."

Each man was acutely aware of the other's presence in the campaign. Nixon cracked about Bobby's hairdo or said, "I've seen some of those Democratic birds flying out of Washington. Lyndon is flying around electing his candidates for 1966. Bobby is flying around lining up his delegates for 1968. But poor Hubert—he's just flying around."

In California, shortly after the former Vice President had finished campaigning in that state, Bobby protested that the historical interchange between New York and the Golden

State had taken an unfair turn. "New York sent you your first settler, John Bidwell," he said. "We sent the motion-picture industry to California. We sent the Dodgers to California. You were kind enough to send us Richard Nixon. Some people out East feel we didn't get the right kind of deal."

In California, Bobby discovered it was not enough to be a Kennedy. In Mayor Yorty's home town he was plainly on the defensive. Yorty himself had left for Mexico after issuing a statement charging that Bobby was a "ruthless, egotistical young man campaigning for the Presidency," whose visit "might hurt rather than help Governor Brown." At his press conference, Bobby denied that he had ever implied criticism of the city or people of Los Angeles. He said that his difficulties with the Mayor were over differences in approach, "but there is nobody in any part of the country who can point a finger at somebody else, because none of us—Senators, Governors or Mayors—has done enough to deal with the great social problems of our cities. . . .

"I gather Mayor Yorty is not one of my greatest admirers," Bobby observed, "but he's entitled to his opinion. Of all the bad things he's said about me, he's said worse about President Kennedy."

On the lighter side, Bobby was asked if he could explain "the Bobby boom, the enormous popularity you seem to enjoy around the country," and he replied, "I always say it's because I have charm and wit, and personality and ability." He flashed a toothy grin. "But there may be something else to it."

Once he quit the woeful precincts of Los Angeles, he was no longer on the defensive. His mission in behalf of Pat Brown took on the more customary Presidential character as he traveled northward to San Francisco. At every stop, there were larger, more fervent crowds and placards demanding BOBBY FOR '68. He captured his audiences with his joshing, bantering style in which he exchanged quips with members of the throngs. When somebody called out in San Jose, "Bobby for President," he replied, "I know one person who wouldn't like to hear you say that." The audience whooped with joy. Then he added, "My younger brother wouldn't like to hear you say that." The crowd, which had been expecting to hear the name of Lyndon Johnson, roared.

Through it all, Pat Brown basked warmly in the Kennedy

glow. In his introduction of the Senator the Governor strove for as much benefit from the Kennedy mystique as possible. And he certainly needed it. The campaign was going badly. Racial problems in California, particularly recent riots in the Negro districts of Oakland and San Francisco, were working against him.

The high point of Bobby's two-day California visit was his appearance at the University of California at Berkeley. This was to be his principal confrontation of his Western expedition. The campus had become an outpost of the Far or New Left, and considerable time had been spent on his speech. Dick Goodwin had collaborated with Adam Walinsky to prepare a statement dealing largely with the most excruciating problem facing the people of California—the so-called white backlash. Some 13,000 people had jammed into the steep-sided Greek amphitheater, a gift to the University from William Randolph Hearst's mother, and overflowed onto the surrounding lawn.

On a campus where student dissent had become an overshadowing political and intellectual issue, Bobby began his speech by observing, "You are the first college to become a major political issue since George III attacked Harvard for being a center of political rebellion and subversion." And he was right.

"As for me," he continued, "I am glad of Berkeley, and I am glad to be here with you. For I am sympathetic, and I welcome the passionate concern with the condition and future of the American nation which can be found on this campus. It is not enough to allow dissent. We must demand it, for there is much to dissent from."

The major problem facing the American people revolved around race, and Bobby warned that while Negro violence could not be tolerated, "white backlash" against Negro progress could only become a national disaster. He said that opposition to violence is "the justified feeling of most Americans, white and black. But that 'backlash' which masks hostility to the swift and complete fulfillment of equal opportunity and treatment . . . is wrong, shameful, immoral, and self-defeating."

On a campus whose highly vocal peaceniks violently deplored President Johnson's Vietnam policy and demanded de-escalation of the conflict, Bobby got in another of his subtle digs at the Administration. "Recently we solemnly and dramatically declared an all-out war on poverty, yet in a country which will produce more than $700 billion of wealth this year, where $60 billion will be spent on defense, and where individuals spend $3 billion annually on dogs, we are devoting less than $2 billion to help eliminate American poverty. The war on poverty is one war where success demands immediate escalation."

Bobby concluded his speech by saying, "In your hands, not with Presidents or leaders, is the future of your world and the fulfillment of the best qualities of your own spirit."

It was Bobby's first serious address of the whole tour, wrote David Broder in the Washington *Post:* "Had he ended on the note of idealism in the last paragraph . . . and exited to the students' cheers and the stirring strains of 'America the Beautiful,' he would have had an unalloyed triumph.

"But the intoxication of the moment got him, and he decided to answer questions off-the-cuff. What emerged was a hip-shooting display of verbal carelessness, worthy of Barry Goldwater at his New Hampshire primary worst.

"In its final uncomfortable moment, Bobby stood mute at the microphone while hostile students booed the name of the President of the United States."

At that moment, President Johnson was meeting in Manila with the heads of state of the nations allied with the United States in Southeast Asia. Asked his views on ending the Vietnam War, Bobby drew cheers when he replied, "I agree with the slogan I heard from this campus: 'It's better to make love than to make war.' "

Asked to disassociate himself from President Johnson, Bobby answered with a flat "No." He then suggested that the American bombing of North Vietnam be ended simply because it was "not accomplishing a military purpose" and might actually be strengthening the North Vietnamese will to resist. "The people of South Vietnam should have the right to decide their own destiny. Personally, I don't think they want General Ky, just as it is clear they don't want the Communists either."

David Broder approached Bobby's press secretary, Frank Mankiewicz, and asked whether the Senator would care to elaborate on his remark about General Ky. Mankiewicz, who had been hired to try to keep the Senator's foot out of his mouth, said he'd see what he could do. And at the next stop, Bobby unexpectedly came into the press room where about twenty reporters were busily beating their typewriters. The Senator seemed upset. He said he understood some of "the boys" had something to ask him.

Broder said he had a question. Did the Senator think his remarks at Berkeley might have some effect on the Manila Conference?

"No, I don't think so," Bobby replied, "that is, of course, if you don't sensationalize it." Then he stomped out of the room, after once again exhibiting the abrasive qualities he had been trying so hard to eradicate. He then had Dick Goodwin telephone Benjamin Bradlee, who had become managing editor of the Washington *Post,* to complain. But Bradlee, despite his friendship with the late John F. Kennedy, refused to alter the Broder story when it came in. It was published just as it had been written.

Editorially, the Washington *Post* sniped: "Senator Kennedy was hardly constructive in his West Coast approach to Ky. The debate over the general's political popularity and credentials might happily have been deferred during the Manila meeting."

Even Joseph Alsop, writing glowingly about the Bobby tour, wrote: "The only hint of doubt about the durability of the Kennedy phenomenon came in the question period. There was danger when Kennedy said things about Vietnam that were not well founded, and did not reflect his own hard-headed comprehension of the nature of our national interests. In his speech, he had warned against self-indulgence. Yet it is self-indulgence to say these things which happen to suit his book at the moment, and then to explain they merely spell out, in a more realistic way, what President Johnson has said in his 'peace offensives' whose real character Kennedy well knows. Here, perhaps, is the chief threat to the Kennedy phenomenon."

Not so kind was William S. White. The columnist, who was reputed to be close to President Johnson, noted: "To join publicly with the beatniks and peaceniks at Berkeley at an hour that President Johnson is attempting to forward the American position in a fateful Asian summit conference is to embarrass not simply Brown and Johnson and the Democratic party, but rather the United States of America.

"Few would say that former Vice President Nixon is unduly soft on Johnson, on Brown or on the Democratic party. Yet the Nixon who also is campaigning in California has refused repeatedly to go so far as to embroil the Manila conference itself."

Back in New York, Bobby headed for Oneida County Airport where he was to meet Frank O'Connor, the Democratic candidate for Governor, and begin their first campaigning together. Their greeting was not exactly memorable.

"Hi, Bob," said O'Connor.

"Hi, Frank," replied Bobby.

Then they headed for a rally in Rome, at which the Senator compared O'Connor with his Republican opponent, Governor Nelson Rockefeller. "One offers new promises for the future; the other the stale forgotten promises of the past. One searches for new answers to the troubling and difficult problems of the day; the other searches only to repair the broken dreams of ambition."

By the time O'Connor took over, the crowd had already thinned. And that was to prove the story for the rest of the day. The excitement, as usual, was all because of Bobby. The last stop was Troy. There, at the airport, Sister Anne Patrice of St. Luke's Convent in Schenectady was waiting in the pelting rain holding a sign which read: THIS IS WHAT THE SISTERS SAY: ALL THE WAY WITH RFK.

"Have you told the bishop about this?" Bobby asked.

"Yes, sir," she replied. What's more, she added, the Mother Superior had driven her to the airport.

It was 10:00 P.M. when Bobby got back to New York. But the long, tiring day was not yet over. He was due to make a midnight appearance at a postal employees' dinner in Manhattan.

Rarely had there been a more confusing campaign. Actress Shelley Winters, long a Democratic activist, who had just returned from Hollywood, summed it up to Leonard Lyons: "If you leave New York for a few months, everything suddenly becomes confusing. I read that the Democratic candidate for Governor is a reactionary, the Republican candidate is a liberal, and the Liberal candidate is a Roosevelt. I got a letter from Bobby Kennedy, but I don't really know whom he's for." And to add to the confusion, the Conservative party's Paul L. Adams, the dean of obscure Roberts Wesleyan

College in North Chili, New York, and a political newcomer, concentrated his fire exclusively on Nelson Rockefeller, whom he characterized, in effect, as a "phony Republican."

Bobby had no choice but to work for O'Connor. A gracious, quiet, smallish man, O'Connor was further handicapped by what was probably the most bewildered campaign organization ever entrusted with a major undertaking. Its specialty appeared to be delivering the candidate to the wrong place at the wrong time. To bring order out of chaos, and to establish his own credentials as a loyal party man, Bobby assigned brother-in-law Steve Smith to "coordinate" the O'Connor campaign.

But the major complaint one heard around O'Connor's campaign headquarters those brisk fall days was a lack of money. Wherever O'Connor went, he talked bitterly about running a campaign without adequate financing while Rockefeller was trying to "buy" the election with his family wealth. "If we don't put some sort of limit on spending, then it will permit a few rich families to monopolize public offices in this country," he told a news conference. Later, his aides were forced to explain that O'Connor was not referring to the Kennedy family.

Once in Bobby's presence he berated Rockefeller for his "famous name" and his "billions," and Bobby turned to the gubernatorial candidate and quipped, "Careful, Frank. We're not against *all* famous names or *all* wealthy candidates, are we?"

Why no money? One reason was that Bobby wanted no part in raising any. True, he had assigned Steve Smith to the campaign, which was publicized as evidence that whatever Bobby's misgivings, he was doing all he could to put O'Connor in the Governor's chair, but what went unpublicized was that before taking the job Smith had set one condition—no fund-raising. This led David Broder to comment: "There are some who are unkind enough to suggest that having Steve Smith manage the campaign but not underwrite it, is approximately as useful as getting Bobby Mitchell to play on your football team providing he does not have to catch passes."

Wherever O'Connor campaigned, he was asked about his relations with Bobby. At Cornell University, for example, a student said, "There's a report in the *Cornell Sun* that Bobby Kennedy is anxious to see you defeated."

"I don't think there's a word of truth in it," O'Connor replied. "Bobby and I are going steady these days." That drew a laugh and he then continued: "Seriously, though, Bobby Kennedy is too big a man to engage in petty thinking." But when asked whether he would support Bobby for President in 1968 or 1972, O'Connor hedged.

Internecine warfare between the two groups soon broke out. "The Kennedy people aren't really helping very much," an O'Connor man told Marianne Means. "They are just warming chairs so that Kennedy can't be accused of defeating Frank."

As the campaign progressed, the Kennedy people became less and less guarded in their criticisms. They leaked stories to personal press contacts disavowing any Kennedy control of the O'Connor campaign. They also planted articles pinning blame for campaign mistakes wholly on O'Connor's associates. "They're going to lose this thing," one Kennedy aide told the *Times,* "and then they're going to blame it on Steve and the Senator. That's a bum rap. You can't do anything with these people, they're hopeless."

Bobby was also being indiscreet. At a campaign rally in Eastern Montana College in Billings, while talking about New Yorkers who had gone West, he said, "I wish they had stayed in New York—we would have run them for public office." It was, as Mary McGrory reported, "a spontaneous slur on New York's current hapless candidates he may wish he had not made."

Meanwhile, Mayor Lindsay was in real trouble over the issue of a civilian-dominated police review board, a hot issue with liberals, led by Lindsay, who supported such a body empowered to hear citizens' complaints about "police brutality." The conservatives, who believed that this would hamper police efficiency and morale, forced the issue on the ballot and were campaigning hard against it. Bobby privately told reporters he expected the project would be clobbered by three or four to one.

What he did not say was that he was trying desperately to avoid getting directly involved in the controversy. But Senator Javits had announced that he would campaign with Mayor Lindsay on the issue, and this forced Bobby into the fray. He agreed to join Javits as an honorary co-chairman of

FAIR—the Federated Association for Impartial Review—
but explained that because of a heavy schedule he would
have to limit his active participation.

In early October an angry interchange over FAIR's campaign broke out between Bobby and Lindsay, with Jack Javits
somewhere in the middle. The dispute reached its loudest
after Lindsay said he would attend a weekend strategy meeting on the review-board issue only if "Senator Javits promises he will physically produce Senator Kennedy." Lindsay,
who had been campaigning in the streets for the issue, had
made little secret of his annoyance over Bobby's providing
little more than lip service.

Three hours later, Bobby's office in Washington telephoned
New York's newspapers with a statement: "Senator Javits
spoke to me yesterday about a meeting on this matter and I
agreed to meet on Saturday in New York City, provided the
Senate was not in session.

"I was not informed at that time that I was to be 'physically produced' by anyone.

"My dealings with Senator Javits are always characterized
by candor and decency. When and if similar good manners
and courtesy are learned at City Hall, I would be happy to
meet with the Mayor."

Three hours later, the Mayor telephoned the Senator to
apologize. And they finally met, along with Senator Javits.
Kennedy and Javits then released a joint statement claiming
that the Birch Society was playing a secret though active role
in the campaign to abolish the board. "We believe," they said,
"it is important for the public, whatever its decision may be
on election day, to know of the extensive John Birch Society
role in the current campaign."

The *World-Journal-Tribune,* which also supported a civilian
board, denounced the two Senators for singling out the Birch
Society as the villain. "This is," the paper reported, "as
misleading and irrelevant as the reverse argument that Communists are behind the effort to preserve the board. These are
diversionary tactics that further befog a controversy that can
scarcely stand any more fog."

That Bobby had given up on the civilian review board was
apparent from his lackadaisical attitude. That he had also
given up on Frank O'Connor was also apparent by his canceling several days of final campaigning.

After casting his vote, Robert Kennedy spent three hours on election night watching the returns in the company of—of all people—the Soviet poet, Yevgeny Yevtushenko. They had met earlier in the day and Bobby had invited Yevgeny to rejoin him, after dinner, at the Steve Smiths' Fifth Avenue apartment. Yevtushenko dined with the John Steinbecks. A few months before, he and Steinbeck had exchanged letters about the war in Vietnam. Yevtushenko had asked the novelist to protest the war and Steinbeck had replied, "I am against this Chinese-inspired war. I don't know a single American who is for it. But, my beloved friend, you asked me to denounce half a war, our half. I appeal for you to join me in denouncing the whole war."

At the Steve Smiths', the conversation turned to Vietnam, China and U.S.-Soviet relations. "A darn good exchange," a Kennedy aide later said. "An awful lot of some quick exchanges. There's one thing they both have in common: a sense of humor. They can talk about the future of man and not start weeping. Yevtushenko was concerned that there was some form of major war in the making, and that it was up to young leaders like the Senator to do something about it."

Bobby and Yevie got along famously. Bobby knocked off a couple of bourbons, his visitor some Scotch. Bobby recited some Tennyson remembered from his school days. Yevtushenko recited Yevtushenko. All the while Bobby watched the returns on three television sets and checked the Board of Elections on a special telephone line.

Pretty early in the evening it was apparent that the civilian review board had suffered a stunning defeat, though not so bad as Bobby had predicted. And it was also pretty obvious that Frank O'Connor had too. Bobby's failure to show up at O'Connor's campaign headquarters thus far that evening had also not been unnoticed. A Kennedy spokesman said, "Why should he be down at the mess at the Commodore? There's no place for him to stay down there. It's always a madhouse on election night."

But, at 1:30 in the morning after O'Connor conceded defeat, Bobby did put in a brief appearance. The two men spent about ten minutes together in O'Connor's fifteenth-floor suite. "Hi, Bob, thanks for coming over," O'Connor said on greeting him. And on his way out Bobby told reporters he had come because "I just wanted to shake hands with him."

He then went off to a plush East Side restaurant, where his party of ten included Dick Goodwin and State Democratic Chairman John Burns. They were a somber group, but there was laughter and gaiety at the next table. "Do you think Governor Rockefeller is sitting over there?" Bobby asked jokingly. "Maybe we ought to join *that* party."

The next morning he and Ethel flew to the Bahamas for a much-needed vacation. On arriving in Nassau, Bobby told reporters that he planned to do some serious thinking about possible changes in the Democratic party's outlook. After a week's soaking in the sun and hard thinking, Bobby returned to New York to announce his solution: "The party must nominate candidates who can win."

That LBJ was in deep trouble was one of the messages in the midterm 1966 debacle. LBJ, previously considered invulnerable, now looked as if he just might be taken. Vice President Humphrey had also emerged with diminished prestige, having lost his own state of Minnesota. But Bobby was also hurt.

The casualty list was enormous. In California, where Bobby had campaigned for Pat Brown, Ronald Reagan won by a landslide. In Illinois, where he had spoken out for veteran Senator Paul Douglas, Republican Charles H. Percy was an easy victor. In Michigan, Republican Robert P. Griffin eliminated former Governor "Soapy" Williams, whose cause Bobby had espoused. In Oregon it was the same: the man Bobby had come to help, Robert Duncan, was vanquished by Republican Mark O. Hatfield. In Wyoming, Bobby had amused audiences by shouting, "How many are for Teno Roncalio for the Senate?" but when the votes were counted, Republican Clifford P. Hansen emerged the victor. And in Florida, Republican Claude Kirk scored a big upset over Democrat Robert K. High, whom Kirk had dubbed "Bobby's boy." He had even lost in Massachusetts, where the Kennedys were supposed to have taken over from the Lowells and the Cabots, if not the Deity.

According to *The New York Times,* only eighteen of the forty-six candidates for whom Bobby had campaigned won. He had had particularly bad luck with Governors; only two of the ten for whom he campaigned made it—Kenneth M. Curtis of Maine and John W. King of New Hampshire.

Nevertheless, some Washington pundits were more convinced than ever that Bobby would inevitably nudge Hubert Humphrey out of the Vice Presidency in 1968. They had argued for some time that if Johnson were troubled by a fall-off in popularity, he would betray no hesitancy in dumping Humphrey. And the 1966 election certainly indicated a decline in popularity.

"I am not in the least interested in running for Vice President in 1968," was Bobby's reaction to such speculation.

But, as Lyndon Johnson once said, "I hate that kid. But if I thought for one minute that I needed him, I'd take him. If I don't need him, he'll never get the job."

29

Wiretapping

Following the 1966 elections, some of Robert F. Kennedy's best friends advised the Senator that, whatever his personal instincts, his political interests called for him to tone down his publicity and to soften the thrust of his opposition to President Johnson.

"The reason why this change of pace is required," wrote columnist Joseph Kraft, a former JFK speech-writer, "springs from the strange condition of his being a man with abundant popularity but almost no power. Kennedy lacks the power that is available to Presidents, Governors, congressional leaders and even candidates. He lacks the power to generate occasions for action. He must wait on events.

"Precisely because he cannot act, Kennedy's popularity can easily wear thin. His voice can become just another broken record. The obvious way to avoid becoming a bore is to change pace. . . .

"Ceaseless opposition . . . would open a gulf between the Senator and the President that some other leader could readily fill. It would lay Kennedy open to the charge that he puts his personal interest above all other things, that he acts to divide his Party.

"The way around that danger is to fade into the background, to take on the protective coloring of being just another member of the Senate. As just another Senator, Kennedy could lay off the controversial issues."

But, while advice along these lines poured in on Bobby, his immediate future was no longer subject to personal decisions. For he was engaged in a behind-the-scenes wrangle with an obscure writer named William Manchester and was preparing for an inevitable showdown with none other than Director J. Edgar Hoover of the Federal Bureau of Investigation. And there would be no way that he could stop the extraordinary headlines which greeted both disputes.

The origins of the Kennedy-Hoover dispute lay in a long-smoldering, little-publicized feud dating back to the very first days of the New Frontier. Following President Kennedy's assassination, their relationship ended abruptly. Their only contacts were through formal correspondence and the orders each man issued through his intermediaries. When Bobby resigned as Attorney General in the summer of 1964, it seemed predestined that one day there would be a formal airing of their differences.

Fred B. Black, Jr., who had been a next-door neighbor of Lyndon Johnson and a former business associate of Johnson's former "right-hand man" in the Senate, Bobby Baker, was convicted of evading $91,000 in income taxes in 1966. But even though the conviction had been obtained on evidence developed by Internal Revenue Service agents without the use of any "tainted" methods such as eavesdropping, the Justice Department suddenly felt the urge to confess. In a memorandum filed by then Solicitor General Thurgood Marshall, the Supreme Court was informed that the FBI had placed a listening device in Black's suite at the Sheraton-Carlton in Washington. And the memorandum led the Supreme Court to throw out the case.

The Black case, of course, was a hangover from the days when Bobby Kennedy, as Attorney General, was gunning for Lyndon Johnson by probing Bobby Baker's involved financial shenanigans. And this unexpected government admission of what appeared to be an irrelevant technicality led to speculation that the White House desired to scuttle the case because it could only embarrass the President. By "admitting" the use of electronic eavesdropping devices, the Supreme Court, predictably, would grant Black a new trial.

The indefatigable Republican Representative from Iowa, H. R. Gross, issued this statement: "A few weeks ago Black, the friend of Bobby Baker, was indicating he was about to talk about Bobby [Baker] and high officials. The heat was on and the day seemed to be approaching when there would be a real test of whether Black would sing like a bird about high officials or go quietly to prison."

But even more important for LBJ, the Justice Department had publicized in neon lights that extensive "bugging" had taken place during Robert Kennedy's reign as Attorney General. Bobby was left with only one obvious out—that these illegal activities were unauthorized—and he rose to the bait. His office issued a statement saying that the Senator had no knowledge of any installation of a listening device in Black's hotel suite. And a month later, June 26, 1966, in an interview on the American Broadcasting Company's *Issues and Answers,* Kennedy blandly denied having ever authorized any illegal "bugging." It was a remarkable performance:

QUESTION: Senator, there have been recent disclosures indicating that a lot more wiretapping was done by the FBI in recent years than any of us knew about, some of it during the period when you were Attorney General. Did you authorize the FBI wiretaps of gamblers' telephones in Las Vegas in '62 and '63?

KENNEDY: No, I did not.

QUESTION: Did you ever authorize any wiretaps as Attorney General, except in national security cases?

KENNEDY: I did not.

QUESTION: Well, as Attorney General weren't you supposed to have supreme authority to approve any wiretaps that were made by the Justice Department?

KENNEDY: Yes.

QUESTION: Would this mean that wiretaps were made by someone at the Justice Department without your knowledge?

KENNEDY: Well, if there were any wiretaps that took place outside of national security cases, then they were.

QUESTION: Do you think this might mean the FBI was doing some wiretapping that you didn't know about?

KENNEDY: Well, I expect that maybe some of those facts are going to be developed. The only time I authorized or was ever requested to authorize wiretapping was in connection with national security cases under an arrangement that originally had been made by President Roosevelt and Attorney General Biddle.

Thus, Bobby sought to put all responsibility for illegal eavesdropping on the FBI. J. Edgar Hoover was infuriated, but he was not saying anything publicly—for the moment. What Bobby was also doing was taking advantage of a semantic opening. In their questions, the reporters had repeatedly used the terms "wiretaps" and "wiretapping." They were clearly unaware of the distinct technical differences between wiretaps and microphone-type listening devices—such as the "bugs" which the FBI installed in Black's hotel suite and in a number of offices and hotels in Las Vegas during the years of Bobby's "war" against the underworld. Thus when Bobby was asked whether he had authorized any Las Vegas wiretap, he gave a technically correct answer when he said "no." It was a bug, a device which is neither designed nor intended to monitor telephone conversations.

"In the absence of an elucidation from the former Attorney General, one is left to speculate," wrote William F. Buckley, Jr. "It is reasonable to suppose that J. Edgar Hoover would not jeopardize his reputation or that of the FBI in pursuit of a felon in Las Vegas, and it is unreasonable to suppose that if asked permission to use the bug, Attorney General Kennedy would have denied it, since he has never denied using the tap during his tenure. Perhaps the Senator's memory is defective. Perhaps he sought refuge in the technicality. In due course the matter should be cleared up. One supposes that the FBI, which is a highly efficient organization, could, if absolutely necessary, prove that Attorney General Kennedy had knowledge of the Las Vegas incident. One doubts it will come to that."

For a time, it appeared that the whole thing would be forgotten. But Bobby knew better, and he expected the worst. Reminding friends that the FBI director had long been a close friend of President Johnson, Bobby said, "Hoover is out to get me; he hates my guts."

A portent of things to come occurred shortly when Bobby declared that while he "would not absolutely bar members of the Birch Society from serving on a police force" he would bar members "of any extremist group" from the

FBI and the Secret Service. "I believe the questions of the FBI and the Secret Service are a different matter," he said. "These agencies have special responsibilities in the field of national security and . . . it does not seem to me to be wise to allow members of an extremist group to serve on them."

An FBI spokesman in Washington commented coldly, "The Senator had no basis for mentioning the FBI. There are no FBI agents who belong to the John Birch Society."

Then J. Edgar Hoover really blew the whistle on Bobby. He charged that Robert F. Kennedy, as Attorney General, not only knew of FBI eavesdropping in criminal cases but had in fact stepped it up. What had happened was that on December 5, 1966, Congressman H. R. Gross had written a letter to Hoover:

DEAR MR. HOOVER:

It has come to my attention that there have been many news stories that have indicated that the FBI has engaged in "eavesdropping" and wiretapping without authorization from the Attorney General. . . .

It had been my impression in the past that the FBI engaged in "eavesdropping" only with authority from the Attorney General. . . . I would appreciate it if you would send me any documentation that you have that authorized the FBI "eavesdropping."

Gross was astonished by the speed of Hoover's reply. It was hand-delivered by an FBI agent two days later when he was visiting relatives in Mississippi. "My dear Congressman," wrote Hoover. "Your impression that the FBI engaged in the usage of wiretaps and microphones only upon the authority of the Attorney General of the United States is absolutely correct. . . . Full documentation exists as proof of such authorizations.

"All wiretaps utilized by the FBI have always been approved in writing, in advance, by the Attorney General.

"As examples of authorization covering the period in which you were specifically interested, you will find attached to this letter a communication signed by former Attorney General Robert F. Kennedy, in which he approved policy for the use of microphones (bugs) covering both security and major criminal cases.

"Mr. Kennedy, during his term of office, exhibited great interest in pursuing such matters and, while in different metropolitan areas, not only listened to the results of microphone surveillances (bugging) but raised questions relative to obtaining better equipment. He was briefed frequently by an FBI official regarding such matters.

"FBI usage of such devices, while always handled in a sparing, carefully controlled manner and, as indicated, only with the specific authority of the Attorney General, was obviously increased at Mr. Kennedy's insistence while he was in office."

Enclosed with the letter was a photostat of an August 17, 1961, communication sent from the FBI to the Attorney General. It said in part: "If we are permitted to use leased telephone lines as an adjunct to our microphone surveillances, this type of coverage can be materially extended both in security and major criminal cases.

"Accordingly, your approval of our utilizing this leased-line arrangement is requested." And at the bottom was typed the word "approved," followed by Robert F. Kennedy's signature.

Bobby was at P.S. 305 in the Bedford-Stuyvesant section of Brooklyn, announcing his plans to redevelop the slum-ridden area, when the news broke. Asked for a comment, the Senator replied, "You can get a statement from my Washington office. I have nothing to say now."

The Senator's office then issued a statement accusing Hoover of being "misinformed." It had obviously been prepared well in advance, since it showed no awareness of the embarrassing memorandum countersigned by Kennedy.

Newsman Clark Mollenhoff, who had worked closely with Bobby during the labor rackets investigations, implied that the Senator was not as innocent of eavesdropping practices as he made out. "The whole matter has presented a difficult political problem for Kennedy, who is currently pursuing the most liberal wing of the Democratic party which includes many who have an inherent dislike for any type of eavesdropping or wiretapping by law-enforcement officers."

Still denying everything, Bobby shortly released a document—a letter from Courtney A. Evans, a retired FBI assistant director who had served as liaison between the Bureau and Attorney General Kennedy. It had been written at Bobby's request on February 17, 1966, further evidence that Bobby anticipated a public confrontation with Hoover. The substance was that Evans had never discussed with Kennedy the use of bugging devices, since Department practice had been to obtain the Attorney General's consent only in wiretapping, as opposed to eavesdropping, cases. "Nor do I know of any written material that was sent to you at any time concerning this procedure, or concerning the use, specific location or other details as to installation of any devices," Evans wrote. There was no mention in this letter of the general authorization which Kennedy had signed on August 17, 1961.

Hoover replied the next day—December 11—by saying it was "absolutely inconceivable" that either the Senator or Evans could make such a statement: "Official records of the FBI not only reflect discussions between former Attorney General Kennedy and Mr. Evans concerning the FBI's use of microphone surveillances, but also contain documents—including some bearing Mr. Kennedy's signature or initials—showing that the FBI's use of microphone and wiretap surveillances was known to and approved by Mr. Kennedy."

The FBI then produced two memorandums from Courtney Evans to Alan H. Belmont, assistant to J. Edgar Hoover. One read: "The Attorney General was contacted this morning, July 7, 1961, relative to his observation as to the possibility of utilizing 'electronic devices' in organized crime investigations." Evans described Kennedy as "pleased we had been using microphone surveillances . . . wherever possible in organized crime matters." He further quoted Bobby as saying that "for his own information he would like to see a list of the technical surveillances now in operation."

In the other, Evans told of presenting Kennedy with the August 17, 1961, communication in which the FBI sought permission to use leased phone lines to improve "microphone surveillance." According to Evans, Kennedy "approved the proposed procedure in this regard and personally signed the attached memorandum evidencing such approval." Evans, who might have cleared up the ambiguities, was not available for comment. Now an attorney in Washington, he had flown off to Puerto Rico.

Despite increasing evidence that his memory was failing him, Bobby Kennedy fought back. On December 11, 1966, he issued this statement: "It may seem 'inconceivable' to Mr. Hoover that I was not aware of the 'bugging' practices of the FBI during my term as Attorney General, but it is nonetheless true.

"Perhaps I should have known, and, since I was the Attorney General, I certainly take the responsibility for it, but the plain fact of the matter is that I did not know." Bobby further contended that "there is no indication that Mr. Hoover ever asked me for authorization for any single bugging device, in Las Vegas, New York, Washington or anywhere else." He conceded, however, that "on two occasions, I listened to what appeared to be recorded conversations with respect to organized crime," but he had no idea "that these had been obtained illegally, or that they had been obtained by any federal agency."

Bobby concluded his statement by hurling this challenge at J. Edgar Hoover: "Since Mr. Hoover is selectively making documents public, I suggest that he make his entire file available, and indicate under which Attorney General this practice began, whether any prior Attorneys General authorized it, and whether or not they were as uninformed as I was."

Of course, this was an empty challenge. The FBI had no intention of opening its confidential files to public scrutiny. And as a former Attorney General, Bobby knew it. In response to the challenge, an FBI spokesman replied, "I think we've released just about all the information we expect to."

Senator Edward Long of Missouri said he would invite Kennedy and Hoover to testify before his subcommittee investigating invasions of privacy. "Now that some of the principal participants have opened up these matters," he said, "we feel that an on-the-record airing is necessary." James Wechsler, an abject defender of Bobby Kennedy, wrote: "It can be safely prophesied that an inquiry conducted under Long's direction will be planned as a playground for Mr. Hoover."

To prove his point, Wechsler engaged in a bit of guilt by association: "Long's dedication to the cause of civil liberties can be most clearly measured by the identity of the man who wines and dines him when he visits New York. His name is Roy Cohn, the longtime manipulator of the late Senator McCarthy and, most recently, the presiding officer at a dinner honoring such pillars of progressivism as Everett Dirksen and William Buckley in the name of the late George Sokolsky."

The fact that Senator Long was not present at the dinner, sponsored by the American Jewish League Against Communism, did not deter Wechsler from identifying others: "The guest list," Wechsler revealed, "included President Johnson's political ambassador to New York, Edwin Weisl, and Senator Thomas Dodd." Others named by Wechsler included Assistant FBI Director John F. Malone, in charge of the New York office, and Louis B. Nichols, formerly a deputy to J. Edgar Hoover.

Then Wechsler put the sinister pattern together: "The fact to which these remarks are addressed is that Cohn has steadily maintained his connections with the FBI; that Mr. Hoover's New York emissary and Mr. Johnson's envoy did not consider it improper to take part in a tribute to the Dirksen-Buckley duo; and that, in the light of Cohn's close ties to Long, any hearing he conducts into the Hoover-Kennedy clash will almost surely be rigged in Hoover's favor."

Wechsler added it was "reasonable to assume that Long would not have projected such hearings without Hoover's assent and that Cohn, long one of Kennedy's least favorite people, encouraged the venture. In fact, there are now well-founded reports in Washington that Long was one of those who arranged the Hoover-Representative Gross exchange that touched off the public battle. No doubt, Mr. Kennedy will be able to take care of himself. . . ." Wechsler may have welcomed such a confrontation; but Robert Kennedy most assuredly did not.

As far as *The Nation* was concerned, however, "the one bright spot" in the controversy was Senator Long's "announcement that he means to get to the bottom of the whole wiretapping and bugging machinery and the federal government's role in what that quaint, old-fashioned liberal, Justice Oliver Wendell Holmes, called 'a dirty business.' Things have gone so wrong now that a showdown cannot be avoided."

James Reston thought otherwise. Writing in *The New York Times,* the columnist predicted—correctly, as it turned out—that the Long investigation was "not likely to get very far. The subject is too delicate to be discussed in specific detail at a public hearing. Mr. Hoover obviously cannot put all the papers on the table, as Senator Kennedy knows very well. . . .

"The Kennedy testimony now certainly does not jibe with what the Kennedys were saying at the beginning of the Kennedy Administration. . . . At that time President Kennedy explained privately that Mr. Hoover would be following much stricter orders in the new Administration than he had under President Eisenhower. And the Justice Department at that time explained that henceforth Attorney General Kennedy would supervise the activities of the FBI and would be the personal liaison on FBI matters with the President. . . ."

According to columnist Richard Wilson, J. Edgar Hoover's "documentation in the dispute is thus far quite obviously much stronger than Robert F. Kennedy's. . . . What underlies this dispute is that Kennedy had permitted himself to become a carrier or sounding-board for the entirely unjustified accusation that the FBI had gotten out of control and is tapping telephones and bugging private citizens by the thousands. What could be better proof of this than that such a puritanical Attorney General as Kennedy was in the dark, as he claimed, in some of the more sensational cases? For months, Hoover smoldered under this implication!"

The years-old reputation of the FBI for integrity was at stake. Also at stake, as many political observers in Washington saw it, was the political image—and possibly the ambitions—of Robert F. Kennedy.

Writing about the controversy, Richard Harwood reported in the Washington *Post:* "Senator Kennedy's Presidential fortunes are involved. If, as Director Hoover has insisted, Attorney General Kennedy was not only cognizant of but encouraged the illegal eavesdropping in which the FBI has been engaged for years, his political position is hardly enhanced. His credibility would be damaged, for he has denied the Hoover claim without reservation.

"His position with the liberal intellectual establishment

would likewise be impaired, for eavesdropping is inconsistent with prevailing concepts of civil liberty in the United States.

"If, as Kennedy insists, he was both opposed to and unaware of the FBI's eavesdropping practices, his executive competence could be brought into question. Because of his unique relationship to the White House, he was in a far better position than any of his predecessors or successors to assert the authority of the Attorney General over the FBI.

"Furthermore, ignorance of what Hoover and his men were doing would be a serious indictment of the communications process in the Department during Kennedy's tenure."

Licking his wounds after this painful battle, Bobby was quoted as lamenting that quarreling with the bulldog-tough FBI chief was "like having a fight with St. George." Behind the scenes, however, he was making every effort to defuse his quarrel with Hoover. It was a battle he knew he could not win. "Accordingly," the Washington *Post* reported, "a Kennedy operative last week discreetly approached two highly placed White House staff members to elicit their aid in dampening the controversy. The Johnson men offered their sympathy but said the President 'can't control' Hoover. Now the Senator is awaiting fresh charges from Hoover that his former boss knew all about the 'bugging.'"

President Johnson's public posture, meanwhile, was that he wanted no part of the feud. The President, reported James Reston, was "managing to restrain his grief over seeing the Senator in an embarrassing situation with Kennedy's new-found liberal supporters." There were those who believed that Lyndon Johnson had given Bobby the most brutal beating of his young life. The question was even raised as to whether Hoover had obtained the President's approval before writing his letter to the Republican Congressman from Iowa. Assistant White House press secretary George Christian appeared to give an inconclusive reply. He said he was "not aware" of any contact between the President and Hoover on the matter.

But there could be no doubt that Lyndon Johnson was enjoying Bobby's discomfiture. In his State of the Union message of January 10, 1967, the President left Bobby squirming when he denounced all wiretapping and bugging, public and private, "except when the security of the nation itself is at stake." The President also told Congress, "We should exercise the full reach of our Constitutional powers to outlaw electronic 'bugging' and 'snooping.' " As Ted Lewis observed: "The so-called liberal Democrats have always found any kind of wiretapping obnoxious. And instead of their natural political leader, Bobby Kennedy, demanding a halt to such 'invasion of privacy,' there is Lyndon Johnson offering himself as their new champion on this issue."

Obviously Bobby didn't like it. Sitting sphinxlike, the Senator was the only person in range of the TV cameras who did not applaud when the President attacked wiretapping. In all, the President spoke seventy minutes, and was interrupted forty times by applause. As the Baltimore *Sun* noted: "Senator Kennedy declined to applaud the remarks about wiretapping, but joined in at other points. One thing about Bobby we never understood is, he's a skier, football player, mountain climber and all, but he claps like Casper Milquetoast."

The controversy was briefly revived over the New Year's holiday when an enterprising reporter interviewed Edwyn Silberling, chief of the Organized Crime and Racketeering Section of the Justice Department when Bobby Kennedy reigned supreme. Silberling told Leslie M. Whitten of the New York *World-Journal-Tribune* that despite his claim to the contrary Bobby was well aware of FBI "bugging" practices during his three and a half years as Attorney General. Silberling claimed he distinctly recalled Bobby's urging the FBI to use more "technical equipment" in the fight against organized crime.

"Everybody at the meeting knew [Kennedy] was talking about electronic surveillance—parabolic microphones, spike microphones, bugs—that is, micro-transmitters—the whole thing." Silberling added that the meeting took place in Bobby's fifth-floor office at the Justice Department. Among those present was Courtney A. Evans, the FBI liaison with Kennedy. And Silberling recalled that Bobby, who wanted faster results in the anti-gangster program, had told Evans without qualification he wanted the FBI to use more "technical equipment" in order to get information.

Silberling's statement was important, Whitten observed, because it constituted "the first break in the phalanx of Senator Kennedy and his former assistants who insist that Kennedy had no knowledge of FBI 'bugging.' "

Two weeks later, interviewed in his Mineola law office by Arthur C. Egan of the New Hampshire's Manchester *Union Leader,* Silberling was asked if he feared Kennedy's wrath. "I have to tell the truth," he replied, "and let the chips fall where they may. I am not taking sides—I am not saying who is right and who is wrong in this dispute between Hoover and Kennedy—I am only telling you my recollections and the truth." Asked why Bobby was now insisting he knew nothing about FBI "bugging" during his tenure as Attorney General, Silberling said, "Since Bobby wants to be President of the United States—and to this end has attached himself to and progressively becomes more associated with the liberal elements in this country—he is almost forced to disclaim his role in the bugging operations and its source of authorization."

Silberling flatly predicted that neither Kennedy nor Hoover would ever appear before any Senate committee. He said he did not even believe that Senator Long would ask the two men to testify. "Senator Long is too much afraid of political reprisals by the Kennedy faction in Congress to risk calling Bobby to testify in the dispute with Hoover—and that is a shame."

Senator Long, having seen the interview, said he was considering calling Silberling before his subcommittee. But asked if he intended to call Bobby Kennedy and J. Edgar Hoover to testify, he replied, "I have repeatedly extended an invitation to both men to appear. But I can't very well subpoena a United States Senator or the FBI director. In any case, the committee is not interested in 'who done which,' but in uncovering the extent of these practices. The invitation to Senator Kennedy and to J. Edgar Hoover is still open, if either of them wants to testify."

On its face, the great controversy should have damaged Bobby's political future. "But," as Ernest B. Furgurson observed in the Baltimore *Sun,* "it is possible that not even complicity in eavesdropping, illegal or otherwise, will diminish [Bobby's] peculiarly personal magnetism among those young activists who are his great admirers.

"Many of those who have watched Kennedy campaign believe that attraction is related less to issues than to his manner, his semi-Beatle haircut and the fact that he is the late President's brother."

30

Books and History

On March 26, 1964, the Justice Department issued a press release announcing that "the Kennedy family has authorized William Manchester to write an extensive account describing the events of and surrounding the death of President Kennedy on November 22, 1963."

Ironically, in view of later events, the statement spoke of an authorized version "in the interest of historical accuracy and to prevent distortion and sensationalism." For his part, Manchester pledged he would regard the project as a "sacred trust."

Manchester had been selected to do the book because in 1962 he had published what was described by one prestigious reviewer as an "adoring" book about President Kennedy. Entitled *Portrait of a President: John F. Kennedy in Profile,* it was an adulatory, immensely readable study, well peppered by gossip, of the President.

The author was compared to "the dazzled artist [who] has gazed upon the subject with loving eyes and found redeeming beauty in his every flaw" in a *New York Times* Book Review by Tom Wicker, chief of the Washington bureau. Wicker raised an interesting point: "The question is whether any President is well served by the sort of adulation that Mr. Manchester allows himself and Mr. Kennedy has too often been accorded in the press. May it not tend to give both him and the public a sense of euphoria? And when trouble comes, as it always will, the fall from glory will be just that much harder. President Kennedy deserves better of his chroniclers. . . ." (Ironically, *Portrait of a President* was one of a number of books borrowed from a public library by Lee Harvey Oswald.)

What Bobby and Jacqueline Kennedy had hoped to do, by cooperating with Manchester, was to discourage undesirable writers who they felt were seeking to "exploit" the story of President Kennedy's death. Later Bobby was to say that "a lot of books were being written, information was coming out in bits and pieces, and much of it inaccurate. A lot of people were trying to make money out of it. So we thought perhaps that it might be better if everything were made available to one person."

It was Pierre Salinger who had suggested Manchester. Prior to this the Kennedys had sought to interest Theodore H. White or Walter Lord. White had rejected the idea. He had already done a piece on the assassination for *Life* and the pain in writing it was overwhelming. Moreover, he was already working on *The Making of the President 1964*.

Lord, who had written *A Night to Remember* and *Day of Infamy*, best-selling reconstructions of the *Titanic* disaster and the attack on Pearl Harbor, had then been asked by Edwin Guthman whether he'd be interested. At first he said no, but added he would think it over. Guthman never called back.

"I don't want anybody to make a [financial] killing out of my brother's death," Bobby told Manchester at their first meeting. To which the writer replied, "I'm not going to negotiate about your brother's death—you dictate your terms."

"One truth that emerged from the great book dispute," wrote John Corry in *The Manchester Affair*, "is that the Kennedys are really not very good in dealing with people who have other commitments; they are, in fact, vulnerable to them." And it was this vulnerability that led to the incredible series of misjudgments and misunderstandings that made the entire nation take a new look at the Kennedy family and its pretensions and ambitions.

Perhaps the first big mistake was the so-called "Memorandum of Understanding" signed March 24, 1964, by Bobby and Manchester. In retrospect, it was not an overly professional document, and it led some members of the bar to wonder just how good a lawyer Bobby really is. It consisted of eleven points, the third of which—and probably the most important—was: "The completed manuscript shall be reviewed by Mrs. John F. Kennedy and Robert F. Kennedy, and the final text shall not be published unless and until approved by them."

There was to be "no motion picture or other TV adaptation . . . based on the book. Other rights may be disposed of by William Manchester, with the approval of Mrs. John F. Kennedy and Robert F. Kennedy, though it is not the intention to prevent the sale of serial option rights to a responsible publisher." Other clauses provided that the book would not be published before November 22, 1968—the fifth anniversary of the assassination—unless Mrs. Kennedy approved; that for five years "members of the Kennedy family shall not cooperate with any other author who wishes to deal with the subject"; that Bobby would see that material was available only to Manchester, and that the material he obtained would be treated "with discretion." The publisher was to be Harper & Row; and if Jacqueline and Robert Kennedy became incapable of giving final approval to the text, "such approval shall be given by Senator Edward M. Kennedy or someone he designates."

Another of the Kennedys' early mistakes—as they later came to realize—was in refusing to cooperate with Jim Bishop, who wanted to write another version of the assassination. Experienced in the ways of politics, Bishop would have known how much weight to attach to some of the more hysterical anti-Johnson deliverances of Jacqueline Kennedy and Kenneth O'Donnell. This the inexperienced Manchester obviously did not know how to do.

Bishop, who had written the best-selling book *The Day Lincoln Was Shot,* had notified Mrs. Kennedy of his desire to do his account of her husband's death for Random House. But in a handwritten letter to Bishop dated September 17, 1964, the President's widow pleaded with Bishop not to continue the project. "The idea of it is so distressing to me, I can't bear to think of seeing—or of seeing advertised—a book with that name and subject—one that my children might see or someone might mention it to them."

Then she informed Bishop bluntly, "I hired William Manchester—to protect President Kennedy and the truth. He was to interrogate everyone who had any connection with those days—and if I decide the book should never be published—

then Mr. Manchester will be reimbursed for his time. Or if I decide it should be—I will decide when it should be published. . . .

"All the people he [Manchester] spoke to were asked not to discuss those days with anyone else, and they have all kept that faith, and will continue to do so. So that leaves nothing but the Warren Commission report—which will be public anyway—for an author like yourself to base a book on."

Bishop's immediate reaction was: "She's trying to copyright the assassination." He went ahead anyway. But he found doors closing so fast that, as he recalls it, "you could hear them clicking all over the place." Evelyn Lincoln, JFK's personal secretary, whom Bishop had met while researching *A Day in the Life of President Kennedy* (written at the invitation of JFK himself), declined to see him. George Thomas, JFK's valet, informed Bishop that he had promised not to talk. Even Cardinal Cushing was unavailable.

Meanwhile, Bobby Kennedy, described by Bishop as "the man who hoards his enemies," met with two executives of Random House to dissuade them from publishing "the Bishop book." Later, Bishop discovered that a weeping Mrs. Jacqueline Kennedy had sat at lunch with Bennett Cerf, chairman of Random House, and pleaded with him not to publish the book. As Cerf put it, Mrs. Kennedy "was terribly disturbed." He tried to explain to her, as tactfully as possible, that he believed it was pointless to turn down the book because "fifty other publishers" would grab it.

Bishop acknowledged Mrs. Kennedy's letter by noting that many books "would be written about the tragic day in Dallas. They will be written, whether you stand in the doorway to history or not. . . . To say that one man may write history, but another may not, amounts to a personal copyright. . . . If you want to deny me any personal assistance, I will respect your wishes, but I ask, in fairness, that you reopen the doors to the other parts of the story."

Back came a stern reply—this time typed, not handwritten: "I would like to reiterate that I meant exactly what I wrote you earlier. None of the people connected with November 22nd will speak to anyone but Mr. Manchester. That is my wish and it is theirs also. . . . I will not discuss those events with anyone else—nor will I 'reopen the doors to other parts of the story.'

"I chose Mr. Manchester because I respect his ability and because I believe him capable of detachment and historical accuracy . . . ," she continued. "I exercise no surveillance over what he is doing, and I do not plan to. He will present his finished manuscript and it will be published with no censorship from myself or from anyone else. I have too much respect for history to tamper with the results of his research.

"I have no wish to decide who writes history. Many people will write of last November for years—but the serious ones will wait until after Mr. Manchester's book appears. This book will be the one that historians will respect. What I am dedicated to is the accurate history of those days and that will come from Mr. Manchester."

Bishop said he intended to write the Kennedy book. "It is tasteless and cruel to profit by a lady's personal agony, but the official Kennedy family goes on publishing," he observed. "My book will not be published when the pain is fresh. It's a long way off. By the same token, no one will be able to pay me a retainer to suppress it."

Bishop was not the only author to have felt the effects of Kennedy family disapproval. A series of flaps over editing and publication—involving such diverse books as governess Maud Shaw's *White House Nannie—My Years with Caroline and John Kennedy, Jr.*, and Theodore Sorensen's *Kennedy*—led some critics to refer disparagingly to the family as "Keepers of the Flame."

For some reason, Miss Shaw had not been asked to sign the statement pledging she would not write about the Presidential family that other White House employees had been asked to sign. The British-born governess had gone to work for the Kennedys when Caroline was eleven days old and she remained nannie, as she put it, for "seven and a half dramatic, moving and happy years." Then she retired to England, where she lives, in part, on a Kennedy pension of about $40 a month.

Soon after her retirement, Miss Shaw had been asked by American publishers to write of her experiences. Miss Shaw, who obviously could have used the money, wrote to Jacqueline Kennedy asking if she would have any objections. "I'd rather you didn't do it," Mrs. Kennedy wrote back. "It would make capital out of the children." Three months later, approached by a British publisher, Miss Shaw decided she had a nice story to tell that could not possibly harm the Kennedys. The publisher who convinced her was Michael Borissow, managing director of Angley Books and chairman of Southern News Services, Ltd. As Borissow pointed out, other White House people—among them Schlesinger, Sorensen and Evelyn Lincoln—were busy grinding out their versions of Kennedyana, and he assigned writer Peter Whittle to the project.

When Mrs. Kennedy heard that the book was well under way, she made efforts to prevent its publication. She enlisted the aid of Sol M. Linowitz, top executive of the Xerox Corporation, and according to Michael Borissow, Linowitz telephoned him in the fall of 1965, saying he was in London on other business but had been asked while there to speak to him about Miss Shaw's book.

"He had a copy of the manuscript," Borissow recalled. "I don't know where he got it, but I think in Italy, from someone to whom we had offered it for serialization."

Borissow told Linowitz that Miss Shaw was well within her rights in doing the book, insofar as she had never promised not to write one.

During the conversation, according to Borissow, "there was some threat of an injunction against publication of the book." Borissow informed Linowitz, "I don't think you'd succeed, and I don't think it would be proper for you to try." He did assure Linowitz that he would try to accommodate Mrs. Kennedy "as far as I thought reasonable." And he did promise to go to New York to "discuss it with Mrs. Kennedy, because we were anxious not to upset her unnecessarily."

In New York, Borissow never did get to see Mrs. Kennedy or any member of the Kennedy family. Instead, he conferred with three Kennedy representatives at the Hotel Pierre. They included Linowitz, Mrs. Kennedy's secretary, Pamela Turnure, and "a man from the Attorney General's office—I don't remember his last name—a very nice chap."

As a result of the conference, according to Borissow, "about one hundred words were deleted, small details, nothing important, principally about how the children were told about the assassination."

On a trip to New York to promote her book in the spring of 1966, Miss Shaw had hoped to see the children at their Fifth Avenue apartment. "I wrote to Mrs. Kennedy that I'll visit here," she told an interviewer, "but I don't know what will come of that." The invitation never came.

Another to suffer Mrs. Kennedy's anger was, of all people, Paul B. (Red) Fay, one of JFK's closest personal friends and a former Undersecretary of the Navy. Fay had served with JFK in the Navy during the war and his *The Pleasure of His Company* was a lighthearted memoir of their friendship of twenty-one years. But in serving up his casual reminiscences of life with JFK from the Pacific war days to the White House, "Grand Old Lovable"—as JFK called him—revealed the President to have been a man who occasionally became discouraged, used slang words and sometimes ate his dinner in hotel rooms in his rumpled underwear. This was classified by the Kennedys and their friends as in bad taste and trivia.

In defense, Fay contended he was not trying to write history, but to provide "a personal view of Kennedy as a friend." He felt that Kennedy had commissioned the book by telling him, "Redhead, you've had an exposure to the Presidency that few people have had. You've got an obligation to write about it." In fact, the late President himself suggested that he keep notes in order to write such a book.

Ironically it was Bobby who helped get him a publisher, Harper & Row, a firm that had had close connections with the Kennedy family. Fay, by now back in his family's San Francisco construction firm, submitted a manuscript of some 180,000 words to the publisher. Copies went to the Kennedys. Jacqueline asked several friends including John Kenneth Galbraith to read the manuscript. Galbraith, who liked the book, later said his suggestions for revisions were minor. But Jacqueline "hated" the book.

According to Fay, she wanted to make certain "that history would not have an unkind view" of her husband. And she demanded extensive cuts. Fay finally agreed to chopping out some 90,000 words—about half the book—but drew the line when Bobby insisted on further cuts.

Columnist Jimmy Breslin, who happened to read a manuscript copy of the Fay book, discovered handwriting in Bobby's "bold hand" on various pages. One notation, on an early page, read: "Mr. Kennedy should not be called Joe, Big Joe, but Ambassador or Mr. Joseph Kennedy." On another page he found another notation: "I would like to see Red Fay write this story if my father was not ill—I think it is an outrage."

"Right now there is a determined effort by guardians of the legend of John F. Kennedy to stamp out the best personal account that has been written of the late President," reported Hugh Sidey in *Life*. "It is all utter nonsense, of course, because Fay's portrait is one of warmth and humanness, the very things that make Kennedy worthy of legend." *

Soon word spread that "Red" Fay was to be shunned. But what hurt Fay even more was Bobby Kennedy's refusal to talk to him. And Jacqueline Kennedy's angry refusal to accept a $3,000 contribution to the Kennedy Memorial Library. She called the donation "hypocritical." As one of Fay's few remaining friends put it, "The Kennedys sure know how to hurt a guy."

Another book the Kennedy family had sought to curb was *Kennedy Campaigning*, by Dr. Murray B. Levin, a political science professor at Boston University. "This book," the author wrote, "is about the Kennedy system of campaigning, the Kennedy style, and how it was used in 1962 with Edward Kennedy. In some ways, the 1962 campaign of Edward Kennedy provided the acid test of the Kennedy campaign system because the Kennedys attempted what many knowledgeable politicians thought was impossible, i.e., to 'convert' a twenty-nine-year-old novice who had never been elected to public office into a Senator of the United States. In retrospect, it was an impressive feat." It was indeed, and, as a reviewer in *The New York Times Book Review* put it, "This is an impressive book. . . ."

The trouble was that the Kennedys didn't think so; and, as a result, Dr. Levin had considerable trouble getting the book published.

The Kennedys didn't always exert direct pressure. As in the case of Jim Bishop, they attempted to dry up sources of information. A spokesman for New American Library says, "When Richard J. Whalen was researching his book *The Founding Father: The Story of Joseph P. Kennedy*, there was

---

* Sidey himself was the author of a generally sympathetic book on JFK's White House years: *John F. Kennedy, President*.

no attempt at interference, at least not in the same manner as with the Manchester book. Yet no member of the family would talk to him or even answer written inquiries for information." The Whalen book, published in 1964, became a best seller, selling over 70,000 hardback copies.

According to William Manchester, even Ted Sorensen catered to the Kennedy family's whims in order to obtain their approval for his *Kennedy*. "Like Pierre Salinger the following year," Manchester said, "Ted took the easy way, giving way on point after point and weakening what should have been a great volume. I had a small stake in Ted's book. I worked on the epilogue, and I spent two hours begging him to hold his ground. He refused. He was a public figure, not a writer; he couldn't see the principle involved." Manchester also claims to have interceded with Mrs. Kennedy when he heard that Arthur Schlesinger, Jr., was having a "chilly" July after refusing to budge on some proposed cuts in *A Thousand Days*.

"The issues of what should and should not be said are very real," Manchester wrote Mrs. Kennedy. "Unquestionably some things should be left unsaid. I, for one, am becoming an expert with the eraser. But I try to use it frugally. Eliminating all controversy would be the gravest sort of offense. It would be worse than just missing the truth. It would be telling a lie. And we can do better than that. If some bruises are inflicted, that is sad, but better bruises than history without flesh."

Though Manchester mentioned no names, he thought Mrs. Kennedy got the message. For in her reply of August 9, she conceded she had been upset by the Kennedy books, but she was sure Manchester had been "a comfort to Arthur." And Manchester said he "was left with the distinct impression that I had strengthened the case for *A Thousand Days*."

Only one "inside" book written by a member of the Kennedy circle emerged unscathed. That was *My Twelve Years with John F. Kennedy* by Evelyn Lincoln, who had been the President's private secretary. Mrs. Lincoln refused to submit the manuscript to the Kennedy family for approval. However, after the book was in galleys, she allowed the Kennedys to see the proofs. Whereupon the family asked her to delete some material. But, Mrs. Lincoln explained, it was too late to make requested cuts. And the Kennedys leaked the story that JFK had long wanted to get rid of her but that she refused to go.

However, no battle in the history of book publishing was so sensational as the storm that blew up around, and nearly swallowed, the Manchester book in the winter of 1966. On one side were Bobby Kennedy, Jacqueline Kennedy and a phalanx of lawyers, friends, advisers and sycophants. On the other side were Manchester; his literary agent Don Congdon; the executives of *Look* who had contracted to serialize the book; the book's publishers, Harper & Row; and another phalanx of lawyers.*

It had taken Manchester two years of working around the clock to complete the 700-page book. "Writing it was a distressing experience," he confided. On one occasion he had had to be hospitalized because of extreme exhaustion. This, incidentally, was later picked up by the Kennedy faction as evidence that Manchester "was off his rocker." Other equally vicious rumors were spread.

Hardly had the manuscript been completed when rumors swept the publishing world that the Kennedys objected strenuously to Manchester's jaundiced portrayal of Lyndon Johnson. The Kennedys feared, so the rumors had it, that they would be accused of character assassination—and that the backlash might do harm to Bobby's White House ambitions. There could be little doubt that the manuscript, in its original form, painted an almost unrelieved portrait of President Johnson as an unfeeling and boorish man.

Manchester himself conceded that he had tried—unsuccessfully—to purge himself of certain biases. In a letter to Mrs. Kennedy dated July 29, 1966, he wrote: "Though I tried desperately to suppress my bias against a certain eminent statesman who always reminded me of someone in a grade D movie of the late show, the prejudice showed through. This was cheap of me, but I suppose there is a little meanness in all of us. This man had lied to me twice, among other things; he is not what my father called . . . a gentleman. . . . So that, among other things, was cut. The result is a stronger, more dispassionate book. . . ."

Exactly how Johnson had "lied" to Manchester the author

* John Corry's *The Manchester Affair* gives an excellent account of the Battle of the Book.

never explained. Possibly this was a reference to Manchester's claim that the President had twice reneged on seeing him.

The President probably barred the door because he had been warned that Manchester was far from a Johnson admirer. The President obviously felt the Manchester book was "a Kennedy project from start to finish" and he saw no reason to be a party to it.

Though Manchester has since denied it, the first draft, then entitled *Death of Lancer* (after the Secret Service code name for JFK), was so anti-Johnson that his editor, Evan Thomas, suggested considerable rewriting. In a letter to Kennedy's advisers, Edwin Guthman and John Seigenthaler, Thomas observed: "The book was in part tasteless and gratuitously insulting to President Johnson and even to the memory of the late President Kennedy. The marvelous Irish politician who became one of the world's great statesmen is almost deprived of his miraculous self, seen, as the child of Arthur and Guinevere, while Black Jack Bouvier's daughter is somehow deprived of her hard-won stature by being born of elves in a fairy glade, by being dressed in magic cloth of gold. . . . The Texans in their polka dot dresses and bow-ties are seen as newly-arrived scum plucked from the dung heap by magical Jack." Thomas also noted "that Manchester wants so badly to present Oswald as a product of the Dallas-Birch sickness" that it "intrudes to the point of suspicion."

However, Thomas concluded that "this is such a good book, I can't see any publisher leaving any stone unturned, no matter what the consequences, and there will be bloody consequences when truly-dedicated Manchester comes across my markings. . . ." And Arthur Schlesinger, Jr., who read the first draft at Manchester's request, stated in a memorandum to the author: "I think this is a remarkable and a potentially great book," but warned that the depiction of Lyndon Johnson "too often acquires an exaggerated symbolism— so much so that some critics may write that the unconscious argument of the book is that Johnson killed Kennedy (that is, that Johnson is an expression of the forces of violence and irrationality which ran rampant through his native state and were responsible for the tragedy of Dallas)."

Evan Thomas succeeded in persuading Manchester to eliminate some of the offending material, including the opening pages which had Lyndon Johnson virtually forcing a reluctant President Kennedy to kill a deer at the ranch so it could be mounted for his office. As an opening scene, it had the effect, as Schlesinger noted in his memorandum, "of defining the book as a conflict between New England and Texas, decency and vulgarity, Kennedy and Johnson." The episode, in a toned-down version, was less conspicuously inserted in *The Death of a President*.

But Manchester's recasting of the book failed to satisfy the Kennedys. They now found fault with his use of material on Jacqueline's reaction to the assassination. In talking to Manchester, Jackie had been totally unguarded; but she had expected him to use judgment in sorting out what should and should not be used. According to the Kennedys, his judgment was poor.

While gathering material for the book, Manchester had interviewed Mrs. Kennedy twice, recording about ten hours of conversation on four reels of tape. An intense, emotional man, he became so immersed in his subject that he began referring to his own wife, Julia, as "Jacqueline." As a result of the pressures, he became ill, was hospitalized and treated by the same psychiatrist who tended F. Scott Fitzgerald's wife Zelda. In writing his book, he said, "I knew for the first time what it was like to live in an absolute monarchy. It was like she [Jacqueline Kennedy] was Marie Antoinette, completely isolated from the world around her by her court— her advisers."

Manchester's admiration for John F. Kennedy had been unbounded. He admits that he had transferred his feelings about the late President to his widow and Robert F. Kennedy, and that had been a great mistake. "They don't understand contemporary history," he told an interviewer. "John Kennedy did."

At one point, in the summer of 1966, Manchester was led to believe that the Kennedy family had finally approved the book. That was when Bobby sent him a telegram saying "members of the Kennedy family will place no obstacle in the way of publication."

"I was told by Harper's representative," Bobby explained, "that Manchester was becoming ill from an obsession with the thought that the book might never be published."

After receiving the telegram, Manchester wrote Kennedy, "Your telegram to me was superb. It covered everything and was airtight." So Manchester's agent, Don Congdon, began accepting magazine bids for serialization. Late in July 1966, Manchester called to tell Bobby that when the bids were opened all magazines but *Life* and *Look* had quickly been eliminated. "If you pick *Look*," the Senator told Manchester, "you don't have to check with me, but if it's *Life*, I want to talk to you about it."

The next day, *Look* bought the serialization rights, paying a record $665,000.

Mrs. Kennedy had spent the month of June in the Hawaiian Islands with her children. She returned to Newport in time to celebrate her thirty-seventh birthday on July 28. Three days later, Bobby Kennedy told her about the $665,000 deal. The next day, August 1, Evan Thomas called Manchester to report that Mrs. Kennedy was distressed over the amount of money involved in the sale. Thoroughly confused by now, Manchester tried to reach Bobby at Hyannis Port. Instead, he got Ethel Kennedy, whom he had grown to like very much. One reason was that, unlike the other Kennedys, she was absolutely without guile and unassumingly friendly. And Ethel reassured Manchester that although Jackie had been upset, she and Jean Smith had calmed her down. She thought everything would be all right now.

But everything was not all right. Apparently Bobby himself was having second thoughts. The July 28 telegram stating that "members of the Kennedy family will place no obstacle in the way of publication," he now insisted, "contained neither a waiver nor any of the approval rights." After consultations with his advisers, he had decided that the Manchester book should never see the light of print.

His decision had not been an easy one. "After all," as John Corry wrote in *The Manchester Affair*, "there is an assumption about the Kennedys: they are arrogant. There is truth to this, of course, although the political Kennedys usually carry arrogance with grace and flair. Without it they might be just uppity Boston Irish with money. Still, arrogance has its limitations, and in itself it does not win elections. Robert Kennedy knows this and he knows there is this picture of the arrogant, ruthless Bobby Kennedy, without grace and flair, who crushes everyone who gets in his way. He is not a notably impetuous man and he would rather not be thought of as arrogant. It may be assumed that he thought it over rather carefully before August 10, 1966, when he decided to try to prevent the publication of *The Death of a President."*

On that day Bobby sent the following telegram to Evan Thomas of Harper & Row: UNDER THE PRESENT CIRCUM-STANCES, WITH THE SITUATION AS DIFFICULT AS IT IS, I FEEL THE BOOK ON PRESIDENT KENNEDY'S DEATH SHOULD NEITHER BE PUBLISHED NOR SERIALIZED. I WOULD APPRECIATE IT IF YOU WOULD INFORM BILL MANCHESTER.

AS YOU KNOW ONLY TOO WELL, THIS HAS BEEN A TRYING SITUATION FOR EVERYONE AND I UNDERSTAND THE PROBLEMS THIS SITUATION HAS CAUSED YOU AND THE AUTHOR.

IT JUST SEEMS TO ME THAT RATHER THAN STRUGGLING WITH THIS ANY LONGER WE SHOULD TAKE OUR CHANCES WITH JIM BISHOP.

Needless to say, consternation swept through the executive offices of Harper & Row, which had long enjoyed a close relationship with the Kennedy family. Ever since the firm brought out John F. Kennedy's *Profiles in Courage,* the Kennedys and their friends had favored Harper & Row as the publisher of their books. And there were other connections. Cass Canfield, the head of Harper & Row, was genuinely fond of Jacqueline Kennedy. Mike Canfield, his stepson, had once been married to Mrs. Kennedy's sister, Lee Bouvier. Though the marriage ended in divorce, Cass Canfield had remained friendly with the Kennedys. But when the Manchester book was first offered to them, they had not been particularly enthusiastic. As Evan Thomas explained, the firm had not wanted to commercialize the death of President Kennedy.

After signing the *Look* contract on August 12, 1966, Manchester, accompanied by Thomas, flew to Washington in a chartered plane, hoping to effect a reconciliation. Kennedy was in his office, as was John Seigenthaler. The next three hours were "the most uncomfortable" Manchester had ever spent. "At the outset," he later said, "I was trying to find out what had gone wrong. It was futile. Like [Jacqueline], he appeared to be wholly irrational. He accused me of raising my voice. He pretended to leave the room, hid in an alcove, and leaped out, pointing an accusing finger at me. Once he beckoned Evan aside and held a whispered conversation with him, glaring meantime at me." The meeting had apparently got off to a bad start when Manchester said, "Well, Bob, I guess we should be facing each other with dueling pistols and swords."

Pacing tigerlike across the room in his shirt-sleeves, Bobby asked, "Why can't we stop this *Look* thing?" Manchester said that would be impossible; he had just signed a contract. "You have a contract with me, too," Kennedy shouted. "You must tell them that. Or tell me who the man up there is and I'll tell him myself. Give me his name. I'll call him now."

Manchester mentioned John F. Harding, *Look's* vice president, and Bobby stalked out of the room to call him. Bobby then told Harding that since he and Mrs. Kennedy had never approved the manuscript, *Look* would have to cancel the serialization. But Harding stood fast. Then Kennedy asked for a postponement of publication. Harding said he would discuss it with his boss, Gardner Cowles.

After the meeting was over, Manchester remained shaken. "This was the vicious Bobby Kennedy I heard so much about through the years," he said, and aboard the chartered plane, he cried all the way back to New York. Evan Thomas was annoyed: "Stop acting like an old woman."

A few weeks later Jacqueline invited Manchester to Hyannis Port. The understanding was that Bobby would not be there, so that there could be a calm discussion without "emotionalism." On September 6, the confrontation took place. Also present was Richard Goodwin. And after lunch on the porch, there was a three-hour discussion.

Jacqueline talked and talked about many things. The reason for Bobby's hostility toward Manchester in Washington, she said, was because he felt guilty, "like a little boy who knows he's done wrong." Commenting on "all those rats at *Look,*" she said that the behavior of Cowles and Harding was unforgivable. But, she insisted, she still liked Manchester. Looking directly at him, she said, "It's us against them. Your whole life proves you to be a man of honor." All Manchester would say to their entreaties was "I'll see Cowles. I'll see what I can do." This, of course, was an evasion; but it nevertheless seemed to relieve Mrs. Kennedy.

By now, Goodwin was deeply involved in all the frenzied negotiations and was busily editing the manuscript. He wanted to delete the material about the last night Mrs. Kennedy spent with her husband in a Fort Worth hotel. He wrote that "Mrs. JFK feels very strongly about this. Their sleeping arrangements, embracing, etc., will all be reprinted by *Modern Screen*, etc., sensationalized, cheapened. Asks if you will please take this out. . . ."

There were also other things that Goodwin wanted deleted, and Manchester says, "Dick tried to emasculate the *Look* galleys. He was editing largely for political reasons—material about Robert Kennedy and Johnson."

Another effort at reconciliation was made at Hickory Hill on October 10, when Manchester spent part of an evening with Bobby and Goodwin. "It was a weird experience," the author recalls. For one thing it was chilly, in more ways than one. "But Bobby being Bobby, he had to put on a bathing suit and go swimming. . . . Bobby would say something, and then he'd duck underwater. I'd turn to answer him, and he'd be gone. I'd start to say something, and he'd pop up behind me, his hair streaming over his face, and he'd ask another question."

Bobby said he had thought of filing suit, but had decided against it because that would mean "I'd be in the business of suppressing a book. I can't win that kind of fight." Then Bobby asked him to consider the changes in the *Look* serialization suggested by Goodwin. The author was deliberately evasive. "Bill," Bobby said, "you have the vagueness of a genius."

The meeting was to be the last direct confrontation between the two.

A week later, Bobby did call Manchester to invite him to meet again. He wanted to talk about rumors of how *Look* was intending to sensationalize the material. But Manchester, who by now had had his fill of all these paranoiac ravings, declined the invitation. The month of October passed with no meetings between the *Look* people and Senator Kennedy; and William Attwood, who had just been named editor, hoped the worst was over. He was in a decidedly uncomfortable position. He had been a friend of President Kennedy and at times had worked closely with the then Attorney General Kennedy on sensitive matters.

But the worst was not over. At a party given by author

John Gunther, Attwood encountered an old friend, Arthur Schlesinger, Jr. Artie snarled, "There will never again be a Kennedy by-line or my by-line in *Look*."

On November 15, Manchester and his wife Julia were in New York preparing to leave for London. They stayed at a suite maintained by *Look* for its executives at the Berkshire Hotel. Manchester spent the night revising and correcting proofs. He had registered under the name of his literary agent in order to avoid any of the Kennedys or their friends who he believed were looking for him.

Manchester completed his task about 7:00 A.M., took a bath, and with the proofs under his arm, went downstairs to have breakfast with Evan Thomas. Just as they finished ordering, Dick Goodwin and Burke Marshall walked in. Both sat down at the table uninvited. The first thing Goodwin said was, "Well, it looks as if we'll all be sailing on the *Queen Mary* together." Manchester nearly choked on his coffee.

Marshall, who is not given to small talk, got right down to business. He wanted to know whether Manchester would agree to changes in the serialization if *Look* did. Manchester said he would. Then Marshall asked, "Will you associate yourself with any further changes?"

Manchester, who by now knew that when you retreat with the Kennedys you continue to retreat, abruptly left the table and fled to his suite, the dignified Evan Thomas in hot pursuit.

When they got there, he turned on the man he thought was his friend. "You told them I'd be there."

"No, no," Thomas replied.

"You betrayed me."

"Bill, believe me, I did not betray you."

This dialogue was interrupted by the ringing of the doorbell. Manchester and Thomas said nothing. The bell rang and rang again. Finally a voice said, "Bill, are you in there?"

"My God," Manchester whispered, "it's Bob."

And so it was. Bobby kept ringing the doorbell. Then angrily, he pounded at the door. "Bill, Bill," the Senator shouted, "I know you're in there."

The commotion awakened Cowles editor Bob Jones, who was occupying one of the bedrooms in the suite. Jones went to the door, saw it was Senator Kennedy and returned to ask Manchester what to do. "Tell him I'm not here," Manchester said.

Nevertheless, Manchester did agree to some changes in the *Look* serialization. But *Look* refused to show its galleys to the Kennedys, so an impasse was reached. Jacqueline Kennedy decided to sue. She notified *Look* and Harper & Row that she intended to go to the courts to secure an injunction against publication.

Mrs. Kennedy then issued a statement through her office. Written by Ted Sorensen, it described the Manchester book as "in part both tasteless and distorted," and replete with "inaccurate and unfair references to other individuals [obviously President Johnson] in contrast with its generous references to all members of the Kennedy family." Moreover, to expose "all the private grief, personal thoughts and painful reactions which my children and I endured in those terrible days does not seem to be essential to any current historical record."

Two days later Jacqueline Kennedy lowered the boom. Her lawyers, most notably Simon Rifkind and Edward Costikyan (who had been called back from a much-needed vacation), prepared the papers which sought to prevent publication on the grounds of breach of contract. The papers were filed with Saul S. Streit, of the state Supreme Court.

"I have never seen Manchester's manuscript," Mrs. Kennedy said in her affidavit. "I have not approved it, nor have I authorized anyone else to approve it for me." Though she had "never seen Manchester's manuscript," she had previously labeled it "tasteless" and "distorted" and "unfair." Some people wondered how a book that was "never seen" could be judged so completely.

There was also a five-page affidavit from Bobby: "I categorically state that at no time did I ever give my approval or consent to the text of the manuscript, to any publication thereof, or to any time of publication; nor did I ever say or do anything from which the defendants could reasonably have believed that I did. To my knowledge, neither did plaintiff."

Up to now, Manchester had maintained public silence.

He wasn't feeling too well and, eventually, had to be hospitalized with a pneumonia infection in the lower left lung. Now confronted with a lawsuit, he decided to reply. In a statement he declared: "John Kennedy was my President. To suggest that I would dishonor his memory or my association with him is both cruel and unjust." He denied he had jumped the gun on the publication date or that "I have broken faith with Mrs. Kennedy." Though he said he had made substantial changes at the request of the Kennedys, he insisted that "in the last analysis, this is my book."

From Sun Valley, where Bobby and his family had gone for a vacation, the Senator responded: "If Manchester couldn't abide by the agreement, he should have said so [in 1964], not now, not two-and-one-half years later. But the arrangement was made and he said it was satisfactory. I agree there is a legitimate argument over whether the agreement should have been entered into. But it should have been brought up then, not now. If he said then that he would be the final judge, that would have been the final, deciding factor. But he didn't say that. . . . He kept saying he didn't want to make a penny out of it. Apparently $650,000 makes a difference. . . ."

James Reston looked upon the developing imbroglio with sadness. He wrote that though "Mrs. Kennedy could easily win her case in the American courts," she would inevitably "lose it in the world." Moreover, "if she is worried about Manchester's frank disclosures about what the Kennedys thought about Johnson during the assassination crisis, she can forget it, because Bill D. Moyers, the President's press secretary, has already read the offending passages, and no doubt the President has been told what he already knew or suspected before Mr. Manchester ever got involved in this unhappy incident.

"So much for the practical reasons of not trying to stop the unstoppable," Reston continued. "The personal aspects are even more interesting. Mrs. Kennedy naturally wants to emphasize everything that perpetuates the good and minimizes the bad in the Kennedy story. . . .

"What she is faced with is the death of Camelot, the killing of the myth. It is intolerable but also inevitable, and the lawsuit is only going to make the inevitable even more intolerable, especially for such a private person."

There can be little doubt that President Johnson was disturbed by the reports of his behavior following the assassination. Indeed, some incredible stories were circulated.

Time delivered the ultimate irony: "There are already signs that the shabby treatment of Lyndon Johnson might create a backlash of public sympathy for him." And there were also signs that the old image of Bobby Kennedy—ruthless, unforgiving, and brutal—was again emerging.

Just before the hearings on the lawsuits, there were out-of-court settlements. The first came with *Look*, whose executives breathed easier since their first installment of the Manchester series was already on the presses. But the Senator, still skiing at Sun Valley, had to be consulted on every aspect. Sometimes, perhaps because he was on the slopes, he was not readily available. The Senator's own lawyers were embarrassed by his conduct.

"Every comma, every goddam comma, had to be checked," said the *Look* negotiators, "with the Sun Valley command post."

After an agreement was reached, *Look's* Bill Attwood outraced Mrs. Kennedy's counsel, Simon Rifkind, to the TV microphones to get the magazine's position on record first. He explained that *Look* had sacrificed only 1,600 words out of a projected 80,000 and everybody was happy that the issue had been settled.

Mrs. Kennedy's statement, as read by Rifkind, contained a paragraph which *Look's* people could hardly have been expected to endorse: "I have been told there are historical inaccuracies and unfair references in this book. That they have been written is unfortunate. However, it was clear before bringing this suit that historical judgments, even if inaccurate, could not properly be suppressed by a court of law. In time, history will deal fairly and justly with this period."

For many years, Attwood had exchanged Christmas cards with the Kennedys. Christmas 1966 came and went, however, without cards from either Jackie or Bobby. Attwood had been unceremoniously dumped from their lists.

But, astonishingly, he received a Christmas card from Teddy Kennedy—for the first time. And it made Attwood nervous.

"I wonder if he's trying to tell me something," he said.

In its settlement, Harper & Row, as *Look* before them, also agreed to revise some of the passages dealing with Mrs. Kennedy. Meanwhile, there were reverberations from West Germany, where the popular weekly *Der Stern*, which had bought the serial rights from *Look*, announced that it intended to publish the unexpurgated edition it had contracted for. Things apparently were not aided when a Kennedy emissary, William vanden Heuvel, flew over to argue with editor Henri Nannen.

At this point, Henri Nannen began to feel political pressure. Nannen told an interviewer that Bobby "tried to use the influence of German politicians who desired to maintain the Senator's friendship. Kennedy even tried to get Chancellor Kurt Georg Kiesinger to intervene. But Kiesinger came to my defense by saying, 'Is this a democracy we are living in, or not?'" Finally, a civil court in Hamburg, where *Look* sought an injunction against *Der Stern*, also upheld the German magazine's right to publish the unexpurgated version.

But a few days later Nannen announced: "What I could not do under political censorship or pressure of legal actions, I gladly consent to do voluntarily. . . . *Der Stern* will from now on voluntarily abridge a few passages from William Manchester's report, a few passages in which Mrs. Kennedy revealed personal problems to the author and whose omission she had requested. But *Der Stern* refuses to submit to the political censorship of Senator Robert Kennedy. More of the politically and historically interesting passages to which he objected will not be omitted."

And so the graceless battle came to its inevitable end.

As Gore Vidal wrote, "Manchester's contribution to history may prove not to be the writing of the book so much as being the unwitting agent who allowed the innocent millions an unexpected glimpse of a preternaturally ambitious family furiously at work manipulating history in order that they might rise."

The Manchester affair hurt Bobby's image badly, and the polls showed voters no longer favored him over the President. Almost on the spur of the moment, Bobby told his friends, "I gotta get out of the country." And he did.

31

Peace Feelers

Actually, Bobby's trip to foreign climes had been suggested by some of his most influential counselors, who felt that a change of scenery was imperative in view of his declining political fortunes. His quarrels with J. Edgar Hoover and William Manchester had once again shown Bobby as the tough, ruthless and arrogant man that he was. His advisers recalled that his highly publicized trips to various parts of the world had demonstrated a good new Bobby, warm and likable. But before the trip was over, he had opened himself up to charges of conducting irresponsible, extra-governmental diplomacy at a time when secret Vietnamese war negotiations might have been in progress. And once again he was to stand accused of seeking to undermine Lyndon Johnson. At least, the President thought so.

But this was the last thing in the world Bobby had wanted to do. He had had no intention of upstaging President Johnson. "To the contrary," wrote Rowland Evans and Robert Novak, "it was a spontaneous by-product of the restlessness, impatience and a large dose of improvisation that mark the Kennedy method today."

A pretext for the trip was readily provided when brother Teddy suddenly decided he was too busy to attend (along with sixteen other members of Congress) a seminar on Anglo-American affairs at Ditchley Park in England. Teddy, who had attended the 1966 sessions, claimed he was too deeply involved in delicate negotiations to free a constituent, Vladimir Kazan-Komarek, from a Czechoslovak prison. Kazan-Komarek, a Cambridge, Massachusetts, travel agent, had been arrested in Prague and sentenced to eight years in prison on charges of subversion.

Two weeks before the conference, Bobby agreed to take his place, and the sponsors were more than happy about the substitution. Then he hurriedly piled on other engagements across Europe, not leaving much time for the closed-door conference. On January 25, 1967, Bobby flew off to London well ahead of his Congressional colleagues. On this expedition, unlike his previous ones, he traveled without retinue. Only Bill vanden Heuvel, the indefatigable bag carrier, accompanied him.

At London's Heathrow Airport, Bobby was asked the inevitable questions, including one about his views on Vietnam. He said, "On such matters I will speak only at home," and apparently that was his resolve, but two days later he was speaking about Vietnam at Oxford University.

Bobby made clear that he opposed United States bombing of military targets in North Vietnam. And he agreed with suggestions that Americans had made a number of mistakes in handling Vietnam. But he said he was convinced that President Johnson was sincere in wanting peace and being willing to negotiate whenever Hanoi showed a reasonable willingness.

Then, speaking of the quest for peace, Bobby said, "I think the next three or four weeks are critical and crucial." He stated that secret talks were then going on and insisted that they must be carried out that way and not in the glare of publicity. Within the hour his remarks were carried to the far corners of the earth. The *World-Journal-Tribune* in New York bannered its story: BOBBY BARES SECRET VIET TALKS.

To say that the Johnson Administration was irritated would be putting it mildly. The word from Hanoi had been that it was willing to talk only if secrecy could be assured. Now Bobby had blabbed, and a White House spokesman charged "mischievous interference." Eugene V. Rostow, speaking for the State Department, had this to say about Bobby's indiscretion: "If he didn't know what he was talking about, then he was acting irresponsibly. But if he did know what he was talking about, then he was also acting irresponsibly."

What Bobby had talked about was highly classified material he had obtained in what was described as a "much too precise briefing" from his good friend Ambassador-at-Large Averell Harriman. The other Senators who had come to Ditchley had also been briefed, but—except for Bobby—all had kept the sensitive information to themselves.

The day after his *faux pas* Bobby was still busy explaining. He said he had not described the forthcoming talks as secret, but had simply referred to the coming visit to Britain of Soviet Premier Aleksei Kosygin, talks between U.S. officials and representatives of the enemy on war prisoners, and contacts being made by various third parties. But he repeated that the next "few" weeks would be "crucial and critical." As for the Ditchley conference, he largely ignored it. Instead, he found time to talk with Prime Minister Harold Wilson and other Government and opposition leaders about problems "all over the world."

Commented London's *Daily Sketch:* "Senator Kennedy, starting a seven-day tour of Europe, said . . . that, looking ahead a few years, he was confident of a satisfactory result. He was talking about Britain's negotiations to enter the Common Market, but the words are equally appropriate to his own ambition: to become President of the United States."

Bobby then flew to Paris for a three-and-a-half-day visit. At Orly Airport, the Senator was engulfed by about two hundred autograph seekers, including some Americans. Wherever he went, flashing his shy, slightly pained smile, Bobby was trailed by photographers, hailed by teen-agers shouting "Bob-bee, Bob-bee," and mentioned in gossip columns. In a sense, he was playing at being President, for as one Paris journalist wrote: "He's making the kind of trip that LBJ would like to make but cannot because of Vietnam."

Bobby made it his business to see almost every high official in (and out) of the French Government. He talked almost exclusively about Vietnam. And in France, as elsewhere on his European trip, he made contact with the Left. Bobby obviously hadn't forgotten that the late John F. Kennedy had been the first American President since Roosevelt to win the confidence of the European Left. In Paris, he sought out Pierre Mendes-France, François Mitterrand, Jean Lecanuet and other members of the Gaullist

opposition, even though he had been forewarned that de
Gaulle might be resentful. As Bernard Kaplan, NANA's
Paris correspondent, reported: Kennedy "understands the
value to an American leader that a left-of-center image
possesses in European eyes; Lyndon Johnson's example has
proven to him that this can't be acquired purely through
domestic attitudes on questions like civil rights, but has to be
sought in European terms."

At his request, U.S. Ambassador Charles "Chip" Bohlen
arranged a luncheon with three sophisticated, English-
speaking French journalists—André Fontaine, foreign editor
of the influential *Le Monde;* Michel Gordey of the mass circulation *France-Soir;* and Raymond Aron, the sociologist
who writes a Lippmann-like column for *Le Figaro.*

After some chit-chat, Bobby began asking questions. He
wanted to know whether the journalists believed that Great
Britain would get into the Common Market "this time
around." All three said they didn't think so—and Bobby
nodded agreement. And when Gordey, a long-time friend of
America, lamented what he termed the lack of a U.S. policy
in Europe, coupled with a decline in U.S. prestige largely
because of Vietnam, Bobby also heartily agreed. He told the
journalists he did not believe that U.S. bombings in North
Vietnam served any useful military purpose. He said they
ought to be stopped—but not in such a way as to encourage
false hopes for negotiations. "The next two or three weeks,"
he again said, would be decisive.

Later, one of the journalists said that he and his colleagues,
after comparing notes, had the impression that Bobby was
making the trip for purely political reasons. "Bobby wants
to get his pictures in the papers at home," he said. "After
the Manchester fracas, the polls showed his popularity declining. That's why he's in Europe. He's seeking to recoup
his losses. He's also trying to familiarize himself with the
mechanics of Vietnam diplomacy—perhaps he intends, again,
to take a position slightly to the left of Lyndon Johnson."

But the highlight of Bobby's trip was his 70-minute meeting
with Charles de Gaulle. Bobby gave the French President a
de luxe edition of *Profiles in Courage,* inscribed by Jackie,
and for a few minutes they discussed the late President Kennedy. Then the conversation turned to Vietnam. "He was
very grand and very sweeping," Bobby later told Murray

Kempton. "He just kept saying that America was a very great power, financially and spiritually. She could do what she wanted to do." She could, de Gaulle had suggested, simply withdraw from Vietnam.

Bobby recalled replying that it was not quite that simple. Though he had some differences with the Johnson Administration, Kennedy told de Gaulle, still he had been part of it. Though he was disturbed by the war, still, once he had been engaged in it, what was he to do?

"There was a long silence for the translation," Bobby added, and then de Gaulle answered, "You are a young man, and I am an old man and I have fought many battles and I carry many scars. I will tell you: Don't involve yourself with the problem."

In and of itself, the de Gaulle-Kennedy confrontation mattered little in the course of events. The fact of the meeting, as Marshall McLuhan might have observed, was more significant than its content. But Bobby made it sound awfully exciting when he left de Gaulle's offices in the Élysée Palace and was surrounded by fifty or more newsmen. Though France's main contribution to the war had been to urge unilateral U.S. withdrawal from Vietnam, Bobby predicted that "France and General de Gaulle are going to play an important role in any successful effort we undertake to find a solution to the trouble in Vietnam. If that's not recognized in Washington we are in great difficulty."

The White House again made no secret of its annoyance, apparently considering Bobby's séance with de Gaulle a downright insult to LBJ, who had not seen the French President since JFK's funeral. Back in Washington, Bobby's press agent Frank Mankiewicz tried to calm things down by contending that there had been some overreaction to the Senator's comments in both England and France. As for Bobby's bouquet to de Gaulle, Mankiewicz contended that his boss had for some time refused "to join in the spitting on the French" so popular in Washington these days. Bobby, he added, had always been charitable to de Gaulle on a broad range of issues, including NATO.

Three hours after seeing de Gaulle, Bobby staged one of those incongruous happenings that defy ready explanation. At an off-the-record briefing for some thirty American newspapermen, Bobby said flatly that de Gaulle was not really interested in seeking peace in Vietnam because while the United States was preoccupied there he had a freer hand to shape the kind of Europe he wanted. In short, far from de Gaulle's having an "important role" to play in securing peace in Vietnam, the French were really not unhappy about seeing the war continue.

Bobby began his briefing by saying it was his impression that there were "tremendous differences" within the French Government over the role Paris should play in Southeast Asia. There was, he continued, a "lack of understanding" in the upper echelons as to "what the top [i.e., de Gaulle] is thinking."

"What is the top thinking?" a reporter asked.

"The top," Bobby replied almost casually, "doesn't want the struggle in that part of the world to terminate. For all the obvious reasons . . . France and de Gaulle are more important in world affairs because of Vietnam. Our prestige has diminished in this part of the world . . . de Gaulle only wants the conflict to be terminated when it is to *his* best interests. . . . The French Government has no interest in negotiations at this time."

What made all this sound so incredible was not that others had not come up with the same conclusion, but that Bobby was saying it, only three hours after seeing de Gaulle, to a group of sophisticated journalists who, he must have known, would spread the word immediately.

Bobby's off-the-record views, needless to say, reached de Gaulle in a matter of hours. According to the London *Daily Express:* "His comments have so angered the General that it is doubtful if, while he remains only a Senator, he will ever be received in the Élysée Palace again. . . . One emotion President Johnson and General de Gaulle have in common at the moment is a certain distaste for Senator Bobby Kennedy." Besides, de Gaulle felt, among other things, "that to impugn French motives while technically a guest of the French was an unpleasant breach of manners."

Otherwise Bobby did the correct things while in Paris. He placed a bouquet on General Alphonse Juin's coffin. He also began burnishing his "cultural" image. "Up to now," NANA's Bernard Kaplan reported, "Continentals have thought of him as lacking his brother's wider mind and intellectual grace.

And these were essential to Europe's appreciation of the Kennedy style."

Though not previously known to be overly interested in the world of art, Bobby turned up at the Grand Palais for an exhibit by Pablo Picasso, and was duly photographed admiring some of the paintings. That night, according to a Scripps-Howard dispatch, Bobby set off for an impromptu visit to student hangouts in the Latin Quarter. He was accompanied by a reporter and a photographer from *France-Soir* and a photographer from the weekly *Paris-Match*.

Nicole Alphand, the wife of Herve Alphand (who was now the number-two man at the Quai d'Orsay), assembled Paris society for a dinner party in Bobby's honor. Invited were several of the leading lights of the *"Tout Paris"* intellectual wing including, of course, Françoise Sagan. Also there were Pierre Cardin, the couturier, and a judicious sprinkling of high-ranking diplomats and politicians. Movie stars Shirley MacLaine, Catherine Deneuve and Candice Bergen also added glamour. Candy, who was shooting a film in Paris, had been invited by Mme. Alphand at Bobby's request. (Bobby, like his father before him, is a great admirer of feminine pulchritude.) The French newspapers, obviously impressed, reported that *le sénateur* had spent most of the evening in deep conversation with Françoise Sagan. They could hardly imagine Lyndon Johnson doing that.

Nor could they imagine President Johnson dining alone with a lovely movie star like Candice Bergen. But as Edgar Schneider reported in *Paris-Presse* of February 4, 1967, "Senator Kennedy could not resist the pleasure of seeing Candice" his last night in Paris. "Tired of the official banquets and political meetings, Mr. Kennedy decided that nothing could be more agreeable to end his stay in Paris than an intimate dinner in a cozy place in Saint-Germain-des-Prés. So Bobby very candidly asked Miss Bergen to share his last evening."

They dined at the Cris de Paris, one of the fashionable restaurants on the Left Bank. According to Schneider: "It was Candice who made the reservation. For two. In fact, they were three, Miss Bergen being accompanied by 'Mousse,' a tiny white dog from the Canary Islands. . . . The dinner ended at 11:30 P.M., with a little acrobatic act, very much appreciated by the other diners. Bobby Kennedy dived under the table on his hands and knees to pull out Miss Bergen's dog. Mousse, completely forgotten, had fallen fast asleep."

So long as Bobby discussed world affairs with movie stars, the White House maintained serenity. But top figures in the Johnson Administration were definitely irritated at him for continuing to discuss Vietnam policy with heads of state and in other ways involving himself in what are normally Presidential matters. In West Germany, Bobby visited with Chancellor Kurt Kiesinger and Foreign Minister Willy Brandt. In Italy, Bobby talked to Premier Aldo Moro and Foreign Minister Amintore Fanfani. And wherever he went, he repeated his belief that North Vietnam's "hard line" showed signs of weakening and that the weeks ahead would be "critical."

As usual, Bobby found time to visit with assorted "beautiful people." In Rome, it was Elizabeth Taylor and Richard Burton; and he was photographed during a shopping tour with the beautiful American-born Countess Consuelo Crespi, who was brought up in New York City as Consuelo O'Connor. Bobby bought gifts for his wife and children.

On his last day in Europe, he had an audience with Pope Paul for thirty-five minutes. According to Bobby, he and the papal leader discussed "in great detail" ways of finding peace in Vietnam. But any comment on a possible new papal peace move, he told reporters, must come from the Vatican.

All in all, it was quite a busy week for the junior Senator from New York—a round of top-level conferences the likes of which were unprecedented in American history. Rarely had any American in high position, no matter how much he might have differed with United States foreign policy, ever entered into what some Administration officials described as negotiations with foreign leaders over the heads of the President and the Secretary of State. These officials were of the opinion that he had gone far beyond the Senate's traditional "advise and consent" role and had intruded directly into the making of foreign policy. "We didn't like it when Joe McCarthy did it," said one official. "Why should we like it now?"

Of course, this was not the Bobby Kennedy who, back in 1962, had enthusiastically proclaimed in Saigon, "We are going to win in Vietnam. We will remain here until we do win. . . . I think the American people understand and fully support this struggle."

Bobby's lack of restraint was further demonstrated on landing at Kennedy International Airport. He hurriedly left his own press conference to dash over and have his picture taken with Vladimir Kazan-Komarek, the Massachusetts travel agent rescued from Czechoslovakia after being sentenced to eight years on charges of subversion. Bobby attributed the release to the "personal efforts" of his brother Teddy, and he noted that Czechoslovakia had more than once shown great friendliness to the Kennedys. Whether intended or not, this was construed at the White House as a gratuitous and unparalleled slap at the State Department and the President. Bobby also overlooked the efforts of another Senator from Massachusetts, the Republican Edward M. Brooke, in seeking Kazan-Komarek's release.

While in Paris, it later developed, Bobby had been saved from an outright *gaffe* that could have had dangerous consequences not only for him but—even more important—for the United States. Bobby had to be dissuaded from meeting with Mai Van Bo, the North Vietnamese envoy to Paris. Apparently he was of the opinion that he could work out a peace with the Communists all by himself. Somehow the United States Embassy got it through Bobby's head that it was not *de rigueur* for a Senator to meet with the enemy. So Bobby had settled instead for a visit to the French Foreign Office. Accompanied by the ever-faithful vanden Heuvel and the U.S. Embassy's Vietnam expert, John G. Dean, Senator Kennedy had met instead with Étienne Manac'h, Director of Asian and Oceanic Affairs at the Quai d'Orsay.

Manac'h, who in the past had provided U.S. diplomats with information picked up by French officials in Hanoi and Peking, told Kennedy that Mai Van Bo had informed him that the North Vietnamese were willing to negotiate a settlement in three stages: 1) bilateral discussions of U.S.-North Vietnamese relations; 2) discussions of the future U.S. role in South Vietnam; 3) negotiations aimed at an overall settlement in Vietnam. Manac'h, speaking in French, said that this understanding was that such negotiations could begin if the United States would agree to halt the air bombings of North Vietnam.

At first, Bobby did not understand the significance of the

information dumped in his lap by the top French official. For one thing, he doesn't speak French. He had difficulty following the conversation even when it was translated for his benefit by John Dean.

Dean, who could hardly contain his excitement, cabled the substance of the conversation to the State Department. Foggy Bottom cabled back to ask whether Manac'h's information constituted a "message" from Hanoi. The French said the Americans could interpret the information any way they liked. "Only hours after the Kennedy encounter—and days before the story broke—the most elaborate sensing and prob-ing apparatus that this government has ever assembled had followed that lead back, like countless others, and found it disappeared into familiar thickets," reported *Life's* Hugh Sidey.

Thus President Johnson was able to tell a press conference with some assurance that he was aware of no "serious effort" by Hanoi to stop the war. Privately, he said, he hoped that a real signal would come to start peace talks. "I chase every peace feeler," he said, "just like my beagle chases a squirrel."

Somehow, *Newsweek's* veteran diplomatic correspondent, Edward Weintal, learned the details of the Kennedy-Manac'h conversation. Publication of the three-stage proposal caused an international sensation. As a consequence, Bobby was widely reported to have returned home with a "peace feeler" from Hanoi.

Apparently Bobby was amazed. As *Newsweek* put it: "His middleman role in a Hanoi-to-Paris-to-Washington peace re-lay turned out to have been more a case of inadvertence, if not innocence, abroad. He had missed the point when he first heard it; he realized its full impact only after he came back from Europe and found Washington excitedly debating wheth-er it was a 'message,' a 'signal,' or a 'feeler,' or merely a Gallic fantasy. In the aftermath, Bobby was certain only that he had sampled the olive branch—and found it full of thorns."

The White House thought the story had been "leaked" by the Senator himself, in an effort to get a share of the favor-able publicity surrounding efforts to bring an end to the Vietnam War. As the Detroit *News's* Washington correspond-ent J. F. Ter Horst put it: "What upset Mr. Johnson was his feeling that Kennedy was using the world's hunger for peace to enhance his own political importance. The President doesn't claim to know the thought processes of Hanoi's leaders. But if they want a serious reaction from him, he figures they are too smart to entrust a peace bid to an anti-American like de Gaulle for transmission to the White House by a Johnson rival like Kennedy."

At any rate, according to *Newsweek's* Ken Crawford: "In the Johnson circle, it was accepted as self-evident that Bobby Kennedy, smarting from loss of face and standing in a public opinion poll resulting from the unseemly brawl over William Manchester's book, had tried to muscle in on peace negotiations to change the subject and stage a comeback.

"In the Kennedy camp, it was confidently assumed that Bobby in fact had made a significant contribution to the peace effort by relaying Bo's proposal but that the Administration, because it didn't want peace badly enough to cut a rival in on the credit, was doing everything it could do to belittle the Kennedy mission in Paris."

On arriving back in Washington, Bobby had telephoned the White House for an appointment. The White House announced that Undersecretary of State Nicholas Katzenbach would be delighted to hear the Senator's report. "From a Kennedy view, the White House announcement . . . must have been a cold rebuff, hardly retrieved by the President's belated decision to grant Kennedy an audience," reported Wechsler of the New York *Post.*

The upshot was a bitter White House confrontation on February 6, 1967, between the President and the Senator. The only others present were Katzenbach and Walt Rostow. Dispensing with preliminaries, the President bluntly accused Bobby of having "leaked" the story of the peace proposal to *Newsweek,* thus interfering with delicate behind-the-scenes negotiations. Kennedy denied the accusations, suggesting that the story might have come from *"your* State Department." The President was indignant. "It's *your* State Department, not mine," he shot back. "It was rough," said Rostow, shaking his head as he departed from the Johnson-Kennedy showdown. "It was very rough."

Exactly how rough was to become the subject of a rash of rumors and speculations. A month later, *Time* published some extraordinary details. According to the magazine, the President had not only castigated Kennedy for his position on Vietnam, but warned, "If you keep talking like this, you won't have a political future in this country within six months." Finally, he told Bobby, "I never want to hear your views on Vietnam again. I never want to see you again."

According to *Time,* Bobby replied by calling the President an "s.o.b.," adding, "I don't have to sit here and take that——." The magazine did not print the last word of the sentence, but it took little imagination to figure it out.

From all accounts, the President insisted that Bobby go before the press to deny that the United States had ever received a genuine peace feeler from Hanoi. Bobby, at first, refused. He said he would have to look at all the pertinent communications before he could make such a statement. "I'm telling you that you can," Johnson told him coldly.

In the White House lobby, an obviously subdued Bobby capitulated. "I did not bring home any peace feelers," he meekly told newsmen. He also said that "I never received the impression in any of the conversations" on his European trip "that I was the recipient of any peace feelers."

The President wasn't saying anything—publicly. But by his actions he demonstrated his overwhelming dislike for the junior Senator from New York. Only later did Johnson and Kennedy try to de-escalate their private war. Both sides agreed that while the private confrontation between LBJ and Bobby had not been exactly friendly, it was not so stormy as *Time* had reported.

"I wouldn't say it was amiable," said Bobby's press aide. "But just because it wasn't amiable doesn't mean that they were shouting insults at each other."

In a later interview, Bobby denied that either he or the President had used profanity. He also denied that the President had said he never wanted to talk to him again. Asked if the President had said the Senator had no political future because of his stand on Vietnam, Bobby replied, "I don't want to talk about that."

Precisely what was said at the February 6 meeting will probably remain in dispute unless, as columnist Ted Lewis suggested, a transcript is eventually published. "Johnson has been careful in any previous delicate talks of this kind to see that what happened wasn't twisted," commented Lewis. "There is a recording device available at all times. One sits on his office desk. . . . Kennedy has a special knowledge of the value of recording devices."

Bobby had begun to play down his differences with LBJ by joking about them. At the Gridiron dinner, where he represented the Democratic party, Bobby avowed he could not understand all the reports of disagreements between him and LBJ. "Why," protested Bobby, "Lyndon and I were very friendly during the first part of the Kennedy Administration. But then, as we left the inaugural stand . . ."

At political gatherings, Bobby regaled audiences with another account of his set-to with LBJ: "We had a long serious talk about the possibility of a cease-fire, the dangers of escalation, and the prospects for negotiations—and we agreed that the next time we met, we'd talk about Vietnam." And when he spoke at the University of Oklahoma in March, Bobby quipped that the university's president was "one of the friendliest presidents I have seen in a long time," a remark that was greeted with loud laughter and applause.

On February 8, two days after his heated meeting with the President, Robert F. Kennedy flew off for a speech before a conference of China experts at the University of Chicago. The speech had been scheduled for the night before in the university's huge Mandel Hall. But a heavy snowstorm kept Bobby in Washington, and he asked if he couldn't fly out the next day and give his speech. The university was delighted, but the best hall it could provide was the Law School Auditorium which seats only about 1,000. Chaos raged around the door as nearly three times that number sought to get in.

The speech, Bobby's aides said, had been eighteen months in preparation. It echoed Senator J. William Fulbright, who had condemned the United States for what he viewed as its "arrogance of power." Using more words to make the same point, Bobby counseled against "the self-righteous assertion of sweeping moral principles as a substitute for policy" in attitudes toward Asia. He insisted that Communism in Vietnam was "basically a native growth with its own revolutionary tradition and dynamism" and was neither inspired nor directed by Communist China. He also dismissed "attempts to portray Vietnam as a Chinese-inspired conflict"—thus raising an indirect challenge to President Johnson, whom he did not name, and the broad framework of the Administration's Southeast Asia policies.

"For many years," he said, "we have disposed our forces,

made commitments and conducted our enterprises, virtually without conscious policy and direction, unaware of what we seek and the price we are prepared to pay. . . ."

The most curious passage in the 6,000-word speech dealt with Thailand. "Of course," said the Senator, "we must keep our commitments and obligations." Then, after saying it was necessary to know "toward what ends those commitments are made" and what means are used to gain them, Bobby said, "Thus it is one thing to defend a commitment in Vietnam, yet it is something else indeed to fulfill that commitment by extending military operations to Thailand in return making a new commitment to that nation as well."

Jerry Greene of the New York *Daily News* termed this passage "fuzz of the thickest kind," adding:

"As his late brother's principal policy adviser, Kennedy surely had a piece of the fateful decision when JFK in 1962 in a dramatic maneuver rushed a battalion of Marines and an Army battle group into Thailand to guard against possible Communist attack.

"That's when the commitment of forces was really made. Most of the troops left after a time (to be replaced by other types), but enough heavy equipment was left in stockpile to fit out a brigade for emergency action."

About this time there developed a controversy over the Central Intelligence Agency's covert financing of student groups, labor unions and other private organizations. The controversy had been touched off by an exposé in the New Left monthly *Ramparts,* which told of CIA subsidization of the National Student Association. The practice had begun during the Truman Administration and had been continued through the Eisenhower and Kennedy Administrations. And Robert F. Kennedy not only knew all about it as his brother's overseer of CIA activities, but had pressed the intelligence agency to expand the subsidies. In fact, it had been Bobby's pressures that had led to an extension of payments to NSA and like groups.

As far as can be determined, President Johnson had no knowledge of the subsidies until word of the projected *Ramparts* article reached S. Douglas Cater, Jr., a Presidential assistant. In January 1967, Cater had been visited by W. Eugene Groves, president of the National Student Association, who was terribly worried about what the article would do to NSA's reputation.

After learning of the secret fund, President Johnson ordered that all such programs be stopped. "His first impulse," wrote James Reston, "was to deal not with the problem but with the politics of the problem. Senator Eugene McCarthy, who has been critical of the CIA, was telephoned in Florida; Senator William Fulbright . . . was told privately what was coming; and the Administration was especially careful to head off any public criticism by Senator Robert Kennedy, who knew all about the fund when he was Attorney General and therefore reacted prudently."

Bobby "reacted prudently," that is, up to a point. He held a background press conference to state his views on the CIA, which he termed an "invaluable organization." And he told the reporters on a not-for-attribution basis that it was unfair for Vice President Humphrey and other top Administration officials to let the CIA "take the rap." With a rueful grin about "getting into another controversy," Bobby in effect absolved the CIA of ultimate responsibility for its dabbling in student affairs, noting, "These basic decisions were not made unilaterally by the CIA but by the executive branch—in the Eisenhower, Kennedy and Johnson Administrations. All relevant government agencies are contacted for their approval. That includes the White House. If the policy was wrong, it was not the product of the CIA but of each Administration. . . . We must not forget that we are not dealing with a dream world, but with a very tough adversary."

It was an "admirable statement," according to *Newsweek's* Kenneth Crawford. "But then he spoiled the effect by suggesting, not for attribution, that President Johnson knew all about the student manipulations and thus deserved to share in the blame."

The stories flowing from this off-the-record briefing were, at first, attributed to "one of the highest officials in both the Kennedy and Johnson Administrations." A week later the identity of the source was disclosed by Drew Pearson and Jack Anderson. "The incident," the columnists reported, "has not helped improve relations between the President and the young man who wants to be President—namely, Senator Robert Kennedy."

On March 2, 1967, a little over a year after his original

speech breaking with the Administration on Vietnam, Robert F. Kennedy returned to the subject on the Senate floor. Bobby had remained relatively uncommunicative about his feelings toward the war, confining his dissent to "reservations" and "regrets" about the bombing of North Vietnam and occasional disrespects to the military government of then South Vietnamese Premier Nguyen Cao Ky. As a result, he had been increasingly criticized in "peace" circles for his failure to make his position clear.

Then, in a Lincoln Day speech about the time Bobby returned from Europe, Jacob Javits broke outright with the President on Vietnam. The Republican Senator called for an end to the bombing of the North and suggested that the Vietcong be permitted "to participate in the political and governmental life in South Vietnam." The Javits defection was a serious blow to President Johnson. For one thing, as Murray Kempton noted, the President "has long cherished Javits as a force in being against Robert Kennedy. . . . And Javits has broken what until now had been a Republican consensus which had enabled the President to contain the dissident Democrats in the Senate. What Javits has done is to indicate that to withdraw from the President's position is to take a posture well beyond anything that Kennedy has said directly until now; he has made opposition to the war respectable." The liberal pressures finally got to Bobby. "I've got to say something," he told Murray Kempton. "I have to speak out."

For weeks it was widely advertised in advance that Bobby would make a major statement. Peter Lisagor reported in the Chicago *Daily News* that Kennedy was about to "cross the Rubicon" in his tense relations with President Johnson. And Mary McGrory also reported that the Senator would risk an open break with the Chief Executive by voicing his opposition to the bombing of North Vietnam.

In preparing the speech, Kennedy consulted with such longtime advisers as Arthur Schlesinger, Jr., and Richard Goodwin. Finally the speech was written by the Senator's chief ghost, Adam Walinsky. It was also Walinsky who arranged for Bobby to invite New Left spokesmen Staughton Lynd and Tom Hayden to his United Nations Plaza apartment to discuss their illegal trip, along with Communist theoretician Herbert Aptheker, to North Vietnam. Bobby also spoke at length to peace activist Allard K. Lowenstein, who was to emerge as the leader of a campaign aimed at dumping President Johnson from the 1968 Democratic ticket.

Theodore Sorensen, who read an early text of the speech, sharply questioned its wisdom. But Arthur Schlesinger, Jr., insisted that the Senator deliver the speech. The Johnson Administration, deeply troubled, dispatched Ambassador-at-Large Averell Harriman to urge Bobby not to make the speech. The Presidential emissary laid it on the line. He contended that intelligence intercepts indicated that Hanoi was hurting badly and that the Communist regime at last seemed to be impressed by Washington's firmness. Harriman impressed on Bobby that Hanoi had come to realize that it was losing the war in South Vietnam, that it couldn't possibly win; and what the Red leaders were now counting on was sowing confusion and division in Washington. Harriman also pointed out that a high-level North Vietnamese delegation had flown to Burma to meet with United Nations Secretary General U Thant. U.S. Ambassador Arthur Goldberg, who was traveling in Asia, was in close touch with U Thant, and there was some slight hope in Washington that something would come out of these backstage developments.

Again Averell Harriman pleaded with Bobby "in the national interest" not to make the speech. But Kennedy said it was too late to turn back. The speech was already written and the texts were in circulation. He had no choice but to deliver it as advertised. The Presidential envoy returned to the White House saying that his old friend was "heedless."

On the afternoon of March 2, Bobby finally delivered the speech. The galleries were about three-quarters full. About thirty Senators were present at the onset because a roll call had just been completed, and the only Senator who remained through the entire performance was Teddy Kennedy. Bobby appeared somewhat tense. But his voice was resonant. At the outset, he was at pains not to seem to be baiting the President.

"As he must make the ultimate decisions, he is also entitled to our hopeful sympathy, our understanding, and our support in the search for peace. Nor are we here," he went on, "to curse the past or to praise it. Three Presidents have taken action in Vietnam. As one who was involved in many of these decisions, I can testify that if fault is to be found or responsibility assessed, there is enough to go around for all—including myself."

Yet the speech, in effect, accused President Johnson of intensifying the war just when "opportunity for settlement has been at hand." Bobby's penchant for giving with one hand and taking away with the other was again being exhibited.

The heart of the Kennedy speech was a proposal for a three-point peace program: First, the United States should halt the bombing and announce its readiness "to negotiate within the week." Second, the negotiators should start with an agreement "that neither side will substantially increase the size of the war in South Vietnam—by infiltration or reinforcement." To police such an agreement, Bobby proposed the creation of an international border, port or highway patrol. And as a third step, he proposed an "international presence," presumably under UN control, that would gradually replace United States troops while the two sides worked out a settlement permitting all major political interests—including the Communists—a role in creating a new South Vietnamese Government. Should the enemy use the negotiations merely as a cover for retooling its war machine, Bobby argued, the United States could always break off the talks and re-examine our position. If we then resumed bombing, we would enjoy "far clearer international understanding [of] our motives and necessities."

The Kennedy speech was emotional in content and contained references to the slaughter of innocent women and children by American bombs: "We are not in Vietnam to play the part of an avenging angel pouring death and destruction on the roads and factories and homes of a guilty land. It should be clear by now that bombing of the North cannot bring an end to the war in the South; that, indeed, it may well be prolonging the war."

When he concluded, Democratic Leader Mike Mansfield leaped to his feet "to compliment and commend the Senator on a most thoughtful and soul-searching speech . . . a necessary speech." Apprehensive over how Hanoi might interpret it, however, Mansfield claimed it did not represent a break "between the Senator from New York and the Administration." In fact, "there is a good deal of agreement between the

Administration and the Senator. . . ." But Mansfield was almost alone in that opinion.

One thing was certain. The White House did not share Mansfield's opinion. Kennedy, who had promised to send a copy to the White House well in advance of delivery, instead had sent it only an hour before he began speaking on the Senate floor. Moreover, he had sent it to Mike Manatos, a White House aide who had been appointed during the Kennedy years.

Bobby was a cinch to dominate the nation's front pages with his speech. But a few hours before Bobby began to speak, the President suddenly decided to hold a news conference and he casually dropped the news that Moscow had agreed to talks on "means of limiting the arms race in offensive and defensive nuclear missiles."

Then LBJ paid a surprise visit to Howard University, where he made an unscheduled speech at a celebration of the predominantly Negro school's 100th anniversary. In it the President recommitted his Administration to equal opportunity for Negroes. And, that same day, Secretary of State Rusk noted that proposals "substantially similar" to Senator Kennedy's had already been explored with the Communists "without result." And in Saigon, General Westmoreland, then American commander in Vietnam, issued an impassioned plea for the continuation of U.S. bombing raids in North Vietnam. "As long as the enemy continues to move large quantities of men and war supplies from North Vietnam to South Vietnam," he said, "a bombing pause will cost many additional lives and probably prolong the conflict. I don't want to pay one drop of blood for a pig in a poke."

In some quarters, all this Presidential activity was being described as a case of "political overkill." But the White House insisted that the President's extraordinary sense of timing was a coincidence. Despite the denials, the activity had all the earmarks of an Administration effort to blanket Kennedy. After months of staying away from the press and public, President Johnson made a public appearance every day of the week after the Kennedy speech.

Senator Javits, who along with others had made peace proposals similar to those enunciated by Bobby, said that "the political and emotional problems" between the President and Kennedy "cannot and should not be permitted to affect our national policy on Vietnam." He added that it was generally believed that the relationship between the two men involves other emotional and political factors than the search for a policy in Vietnam. "The speed with which [Kennedy's] suggestions were rejected by the Secretary of State, by the White House and by other Administration spokesmen, plus the fevered activity of the Administration last Thursday, would indicate to me that these proposals were hardly given the consideration they deserve."

Top Administration spokesmen quickly denied this. The proposals had not been rejected because of Presidential antipathy to Bobby. These officials, some of whom had been in the JFK Administration, claimed they saw literally nothing new in the Kennedy proposals. "I read it carefully twice," one official said, "and I'm still wondering why he made the speech. We've worked awfully hard to bring North Vietnam to the conference table, and met a blank wall. Then we find Senator Kennedy coming up with a formula with nothing new in it. Why?" Administration spokesmen also took issue with Bobby for having quoted British Prime Minister Wilson as having remarked the week before, "One single simple act of trust could have achieved [peace]."

"Incidentally," wrote James Reston, "British officials here support the Administration on the interpretation of this last point. The 'simple act of trust,' they explain, was that Hanoi should agree to some military concession to match the U.S. offer to end the bombing, and this proposal—which was apparently supported by Premier Kosygin of the Soviet Union —was rejected by the Hanoi Government." Later, in the House of Commons, the Prime Minister also made it clear he was talking about Hanoi alone.

Hanoi, needless to say, took great satisfaction in the Kennedy speech. *Nhan Dan*, official organ of the North Vietnam Communist Party, said that Kennedy had placed the Johnson Administration in an "awkward and embarrassing position." But the Soviet newspaper *Izvestia* neither praised nor criticized Bobby's speech. Warning that "one should not exaggerate the extent of disagreement between Kennedy and Johnson," *Izvestia* declared: "Such a halfway policy is characteristic of the Senate opposition on Vietnam. It is irresolute and its numbers are small. It does not influence the course of the White House."

Arthur Schlesinger, Jr., echoed Bobby's speech in considerably blunter terms by accusing the Administration of deliberately misrepresenting Hanoi's negotiating proposals because it "does not wish to negotiate now." The instant historian supported Bobby's contention that Washington had hardened its terms for talks since the previous year.

The continued sniping by the Kennedy forces convinced many Washington observers that Lyndon Johnson was ready to chew up Bobby Kennedy and his Presidential ambitions. The house was packed for the President's March 9 press conference. The assembled newsmen, however, found the President mounting a peace offensive aimed at stilling the Senator with kindness.

"I don't want to quarrel with anyone," the President announced grandly. He was dismayed at the thought that anyone would think that "personalities or politics" had tinged his rejection of the Kennedy peace proposals. "We have help and suggestions from members of the Senate," the President purred. And "I have no particular fault to find or criticism to make of others. . . . I must grant to them the same sincerity that I reserve for myself."

But privately, Lyndon Johnson was seething. According to Life's Hugh Sidey, the President "is almost convinced that Bobby Kennedy plans to make a try for the 1968 Presidential nomination. He probes his visitors these days. Eyes narrowed, hunched forward, LBJ asks: 'What's Kennedy really up to?' The evidence available suggests that about the last thing Kennedy wants to do is run in 1968. But if the Senator decides to take his halt-the-bombing proposal to the stump, the President's suspicions will harden."

How the President really felt seeped out at a supposedly private dinner of the Democratic National Committee on March 9, 1967. Though he named no names more current than Neville Chamberlain's, the President obviously referred to Bobby when he said, "Peace . . . must not be bought at the price of a temporary lust for popularity." He said the one thing the American public would not tolerate was "a dishonorable settlement disguised as a bargain for popularity purposes eighteen months before the election." Then he read a letter to the grieving sister of a soldier killed in Vietnam: "Your brother was in South Vietnam because the threat to the Vietnamese people is, in the long run, a threat to the free world community." It was signed, the President said, so slowly that few could have missed the point, by John F. Kennedy.

Bobby was also attacked from the Far Left. Robert Scheer of *Ramparts* came to New York to argue the merits of the Kennedy speech on television with Bill vanden Heuvel. The bearded editor laced into Kennedy as "a rather ordinary, ambitious politician, no different than the other men in the Senate, and there's been a certain amount of delusion about his gutsiness, and his leadership, and so on, and he hasn't demonstrated his capacity to lead. I think the issue of Vietnam is one on which he could lead. . . ." Moreover, Scheer could not see the logic of Bobby's criticizing the Johnson Administration "unless he criticizes his own past action, which was one of wholehearted support for the war. . . ."

Vanden Heuvel replied that Bobby, in his speech, did indeed "take his portion of the blame for the events in Vietnam. . . . But I think that the most important thing that he is concerned about is bringing a negotiated end to the hostilities in Vietnam. He is not interested in a political situation that is going to enhance his particular situation right now, or his future reputation . . . and I would think that probably a lot of his advisers said to him that there were political negatives in his giving a speech on this subject at this time; nevertheless, he chose to speak out on a very difficult subject. . . ."

Scheer responded by saying that if Senator Kennedy were sincere he would publicly break with the Johnson Administration on Vietnam. He also said that people like vanden Heuvel had felt it was "obscene" for the Russians to demand "good faith" of the Hungarian Freedom Fighters before the Russians stopped mowing them down with their tanks. "I think that this is the position of the United States in Vietnam: there's something obscene about asking people who are being bombed to show good faith, and there is something obscene about their saying that the man who has directed that bombing is a man of peace, and—"

"I agree with you," said vanden Heuvel.

But a lot of old-line Democrats didn't agree. They were dismayed over what Bobby and his spear-carriers were saying

about the President. They believed that the purpose of the
Kennedy speech had been political, though it was difficult for
them to determine what the Senator thought he might gain
from it.

According to Marianne Means, "the speech widened a
slowly emerging estrangement between Kennedy and a large
segment of New York Democratic Party regulars. Officials,
shaken by the 1966 elections, are now rallying around the
Johnson flag on the realistic assumption that if the party is
divided it will lose the White House in 1968. A number of
powerful party leaders who once flirted with the possibility of
a Kennedy candidacy in 1968 are now irritated by his failure
to join a united front behind President Johnson."

The concern among Democratic regulars was then made
manifest by an anti-Kennedy speech delivered by the party's
elder statesman, James A. Farley, at a Jefferson-Jackson Day
dinner in Hartford, Connecticut. The audience, including
Senator Ribicoff and Democratic National Chairman John
M. Bailey, was stunned. Almost everyone was aware that
Farley, a close friend of the Kennedy family, had backed
John F. Kennedy's campaign for the Presidency and Bobby
Kennedy's campaign for the Senate. Except for two loud
boos, they sat in stony-faced silence as the former Postmaster
General, never one for double-talk, bluntly assailed Bobby
Kennedy's "soaring ambition." Farley claimed that if Presi-
dent Kennedy were alive he would strongly support Johnson
instead of undermining him.

Bobby's private remarks about Farley, needless to say,
were unprintable. Publicly, however, he turned the other
cheek. Through a spokesman, Bobby said, "Mr. Farley has
served the Democratic Party and his country with distinction
over the years." He had no further comment.

In late March, Hanoi inexplicably released an exchange
of letters between Lyndon Johnson and Ho Chi Minh. President Johnson, without publicity, had written a studiously
noninflammatory letter to the Vietnamese dictator, exhorting
him to come to the peace table. The Johnson letter was dated
February 2, 1967, and was delivered to a North Vietnamese
representative in Moscow on February 8.

"If we fail to find a just and peaceful solution, history will
judge us harshly," Johnson wrote. The President offered to
end the bombing of North Vietnam and to suspend any

further U.S. troop buildup in the South "as soon as I am assured that infiltration into South Vietnam by land and by sea has stopped."

The letter was delivered to Ho on February 10. His reply of February 15 was a flat rejection, embellished with ritualistic Communist insults. The Red dictator reiterated Hanoi's demand for "unconditional" cessation of the bombing and "all other acts of war" against the North. Only then would Hanoi "enter into talks and discuss questions concerning the two sides." He also included a needling reference to President Johnson's fragmented war image at home and abroad: "Our just cause enjoys strong sympathy and support from the peoples of the whole world, including broad sections of the American people."

Release of Ho's back-of-the-hand reply should have quieted critics who were savagely condemning President Johnson for not having done enough to convince Hanoi of our sincerity in wanting to end the war. As Ken Crawford put it: "Now it develops that Mr. Johnson could have documented a devastating answer to the Kennedyites had he chosen to do so. He didn't so choose because he was convinced—still is—that peace negotiations, if they are to succeed, must be conducted away from the goldfish bowl of publicity. . . ."

But if members of the Kennedy circle were disconcerted by Ho's unexpected revelations, they refused to acknowledge it. The Senator himself obviously had not had the slightest inkling of the Ho-Johnson exchange when he set forth his "peace" proposals. Now he was caught in an extremely embarrassing position. What to do? Bobby's decision was to issue another statement. Although most Washington observers felt the letter underscored the President's earnest good intentions, Bobby insisted that the Johnson letter had imposed new and harsher conditions for peace talks. The President had upped the ante by demanding "evidence that Hanoi has already ceased infiltration before we stop the bombing." The President did not deign to reply, but others in the know called the Kennedy statement pettifoggery.

"It must be said for the Kennedys that when they get launched on a wrong course they stick with it doggedly," wrote columnist Richard Wilson. "Kennedy's obtuse version of events has so little relation to the substance involved as to raise doubts that he really can be serious.

"What would lead anyone to think that Ho is a benevolent old man who will come to the conference table and be reasonable if only the United States will let up on the pressure? Is there anything in the history of U.S. relations with the Communist world that would conceivably cause Kennedy to think otherwise than that Communist leaders respect only force? His own experience as an adviser to his brother, John F. Kennedy, should have convinced him of that. . . .

"What is of more importance than Kennedy's self-justification is why Ho so bitterly and sententiously rejected a Johnson offer couched in the most conciliatory tones. . . . A guess is offered here. Ho has once again concluded that internal ferment in the United States will get him off free on the bombing. He might have even foreseen Kennedy's reaction."

Bobby's interpretation of the Johnson letter was not shared by many on Capitol Hill. Majority Leader Mike Mansfield, who usually sided with Kennedy on Vietnam, regarded the Johnson letter as "conciliatory." In Senate debate, Senator Gale McGee made a thinly veiled attack on Kennedy. From the hindsight provided by Ho's letter, said the Wyoming Democrat, "the meddling of our amateur diplomats now appears to have been even more foolish and irresponsible and even a bit more shabby than it did at first brush."

With such reactions flowing in, Bobby Kennedy decided it was time to begin mending fences in his own party. On June 3, a "Salute to Johnson" dinner was held at the Americana Hotel by New York Democrats. President Johnson was the main speaker. Bobby Kennedy, who arrived late after a flight from England (where he had attended the funeral of the wife of Lord Harlech, British Ambassador to the United States during the Kennedy years), said of the President, "He has poured out his own strength to renew the strength of the country . . . he has sought consensus, but has never shrunk from controversy . . . he has gained huge popularity, but never hesitated to spend it on what he thought important. . . . He has led us to build schools, homes, clinics, hospitals, to rebuild the cities, to clean water, to reclaim the beauty of the countryside, to educate children, to comfort the oppressed on a scale unmatched in history."

Sitting on the podium at Bobby's left, President Johnson followed every word intently and looked anything but displeased. For the first time in three years, a reunion between the Kennedy and Johnson wings of the Democratic party appeared possible.

32

Future

There were, in Jules Feiffer's words, the Good Bobby and the Bad Bobby. The Good Bobby sympathized with peace marchers, worried about all the money Americans spend on dogs while children go hungry, got indignant over conditions in the ghettos and condemned the Vietnam War as "immoral." The Bad Bobby was the Bobby who refused to match his eloquent speeches with deeds.

And until mid-March 1968, according to the liberals, the Bad Bobby was in the ascendancy. For he steadfastly refused to contest Lyndon Johnson for the Democratic nomination for President in 1968. Prudence thus prevailed over passion. The pragmatist in Bobby Kennedy had clearly won out over the ideologue, dictated by what he conceived to be the interests of the public, the party and—most important—his own personal interests. "I must examine the issue in relation to my concern about my own future," Bobby said.

An unsuccessful challenge to President Johnson in 1968, he reasoned, would create enemies who would make it almost impossible for him to get the nomination in 1972. Or, even more immediately, any such move would most definitely remove him from any consideration by President Johnson as a Vice Presidential running mate. For, as *Newsweek* put it so well: "Kennedy can and does leave the impression that he might find second spot on an LBJ ticket in 1968 surprisingly comfortable."

But Kennedy's statement supporting LBJ's reelection was deliberately designed to leave open the option of running should any development or decision take President Johnson out of the race. The Kennedy intellectuals were sharply divided on whether their paladin should challenge President Johnson. Schlesinger, for example, argued that the Senator should take the risk. Ted Sorensen, however, insisted Bobby would be courting political oblivion if he did so. "If he got the nomination," said Sorensen, "it would be at the cost of alienating large parts of the Democratic organization, on whose help he would have to rely in the general election campaign." And even Dick Goodwin, who rarely errs on the side of caution, said, "They want him to jump out of the window, but they are not telling him what floor it is on."

"About the only thing," reported James Reston of *The New York Times*, that Kennedy's advisers "all agree on is that President Johnson should go down in history as a political accident between the two Kennedy Presidencies, and that Senator Kennedy should at least get ready to run, just in case President Johnson decides at the last minute not to seek re-election." And the London *Observer* reported a Saturday night visit by some earnest friends to Hickory Hill, Bobby's meditative pad. "His demeanor," the *Observer* recounted, ranged "from 'tempted' to 'tormented' "—but obviously neither tempted nor tormented enough to stick his neck out. Courage, of course, is much easier to write about than to practice.

"Here is a guy who made a moral issue of the war," one of Bobby's personal friends told *Newsweek*. "This is the man who has to swim in the cold waters, ski the toughest slopes, take on the mountain. He cannot go to South Africa and stay out of New Hampshire."

But stay out he did and, as a consequence, Eugene McCarthy emerged from the Granite State's primary as a knight in shining armor to many thousands of men and women, particularly those in the colleges, who had believed Bobby to be a courageous young man willing to battle for the things he believed in. What Artie Schlesinger had feared soon came to pass. The New Left, many of them the future voters Bobby had been cultivating for years, turned on him with a passion. At Brooklyn College, he was greeted by signs reading: BOBBY BIRD; STOP PUSSYFOOTING AROUND; RFK JOKES WHILE HANOI CHOKES; LYNDON'S BOY.

The surprise entry of Senator McCarthy into the Presidential sweepstakes—coupled with his not too subtle hints that he would like Bobby's endorsement—presented the New York Senator with a quandary. McCarthy really hit Bobby where it hurt. "There are some Americans," he said, of his colleague from New York, "who have not yet spoken as their minds and consciences dictate. In some cases, they have not done so for reasons of personal or political convenience. These are a few, I suspect, who are waiting for a kind of latter-day salvation. Four years is too long to wait."

But Bobby appeared to be willing to wait.

It had not been an easy or comfortable decision for Bobby. He was prepared for recriminations from those critics of the Vietnam War who had counted on him to contest Johnson's renomination. He had had warning from his would-be biographer, Jack Newfield. "Kennedy is now torn about what to do," Newfield wrote in *The Village Voice*. "The part of him that is the cold, cynical political manager with an instinct for arithmetic majorities thinks he can't win, that even if he wrests the nomination from LBJ, the party would be so split he could never win in November. This is the 'Bad Bobby' Jules Feiffer so brilliantly satirized a few months ago. It is conventional, safe, ambitious. And, if it finally comes to dominate the rest of Kennedy, and kill off the other, subterranean Kennedy, our hopes for him will turn to ashes.

"But there is another Kennedy. It is the Kennedy who sounds like Fidel Castro when he is moved by the sight of peasants subsisting on crabs that live off excrement in Brazil. It is the Kennedy who emotionally told the girls at Marymount College that America is doing to the Vietnamese what the Germans did to the Jews. It is the Kennedy who can read Camus and suddenly discover he no longer believes in capital punishment.

"If Kennedy does not run in 1968, the best side of his character will die. He will kill it every time he butchers his conscience and makes a speech for Johnson next autumn. It will die every time a kid asks him if he is so much against the Vietnam war, how come he is putting party above principle? It will die every time a stranger quotes his own words back to him on the value of courage as a human quality.

"Kennedy's best quality is his ability to be himself, to be authentic in the existential sense. This is the quality the best young identify with so instinctively in Kennedy. And it is this quality Kennedy will lose if he doesn't make his stand now against Johnson. He will become a robot mouthing dishonest rhetoric like all the other politicians.

"To everything there is a time, to everything there is a season. This is a time of plague and a season for courage. . . ."

The only courage demonstrated, however, was seemingly against McCarthy. As Jerry Tallmer reported in the New York *Post,* the language in Kennedy circles regarding McCarthy grew more sulphurous: "He's lazy. But why is he in there if he's lazy? Nobody can figure the man out, this great ADA liberal (McCarthy resigned as an ADA member in 1960) with a voting record of what—sixty-two percent or something? He's unreliable. He bombs out on every occasion. And then, just to observe him, he's physically laconic, just the way he walks around at half-speed. . . ."

For despite Lyndon Johnson's reference to the Kennedy-McCarthy opposition he faced, the two Senators had been less than friendly for many years. Bobby had not forgotten McCarthy's role in attempting to stop his brother's nomination in 1960. At that time McCarthy's suggestion that he be nominated for President was widely quoted: "I'm twice as liberal as Humphrey, twice as bright as Symington and twice as Catholic as Kennedy."

"Of all the people who were stinking mean about President Kennedy at Los Angeles and long thereafter," wrote Joe Alsop, "the meanest by a fairly long chalk was Senator McCarthy."

McCarthy has never liked the Kennedys. In the late fifties, when the Landrum-Griffin labor bill was being debated, the late Jack Kennedy let him take an exposed position and then backed away from it. "Since then," he told columnist Joseph Kraft, "I've had my guard up against the Kennedys."

As for Bobby, McCarthy vowed in January 1968 that the New York Senator would "have a fight on his hands" if he tried to seize control of the war protest faction at the Democratic National Convention. In *Look* he wrote: "It has been suggested that after I have fought through the primaries and it gets close to convention time . . . Kennedy will step in and pick up all the pieces. I doubt it. If that is his plan, he will have a fight on his hands to see who has the most strength. I will not step aside voluntarily. And I think it will be difficult for him to stay on the sidelines and then make an eleventh-hour bid. . . ."

So Bobby Kennedy, who had been cultivating the peace vineyards for several years, watched with frustration as McCarthy, never his ally, harvested the grapes. The strain was beginning to show. "I have a feeling that I am not accomplishing a great deal," Bobby said at one point, and rarely had any politician made such a confession of futility. The cautious politician had won out over the impassioned idealist.

At the Gridiron Club dinner in March 1968, Presidential aspirants in both parties were joshed by Washington newsmen. To the tune of "Stand Up, Stand Up for Jesus," a club member, in the role of Robert F. Kennedy, sang:

> Stand up, stand up for Lyndon,
> We must be firm and true.
> Believe me, I admire him,
> The gossip's just not true.
> I'm not like Gene McCarthy
> Or Fulbright's careless crew.
> I will stand up for Lyndon,
> There's nothing else to do.

Then a few days later came Gene McCarthy's strong showing against President Johnson in the New Hampshire primary. He drew 42 percent to Johnson's 49 percent of the Democratic vote. His effort could no longer be dismissed as a futile exercise. It was obvious that there was a strong potential in the anti-war movement and all-out opposition to President Johnson.

Late on primary night, Bobby telephoned McCarthy to congratulate him. "Wasn't that nice of him to call!" McCarthy said.

Four days later, on March 16, before a packed audience in the Caucus Room of the Old Senate Office Building—where his late brother had made a similar announcement eight years before—Bobby declared, "I am announcing today my candidacy for the Presidency of the United States. I do not run for the Presidency merely to oppose any man, but to propose new policies."

Although faced with Bobby's formidable opposition, Gene McCarthy insisted he was in the contest to stay. And he rejected Bobby's offer to support him in the Wisconsin primary as an effort "to fatten me up for the kill." He described Bobby's style as a belated "crash course in great ideas." As for his rival's popularity, he said, "I don't have the enemies in the party that Bobby has—or in the country, for that matter."

In discussing other differences between himself and Bobby, McCarthy joshed, "He plays touch football; I play football. He plays softball; I play baseball. He skates in Rockefeller Center; I play hockey."

Murray Kempton, a strong McCarthy supporter, excoriated Bobby. The New York *Post* columnist noted that Bobby in January had approved a resolution pledging New York Democrats to "continued loyalty and vigorous support" of LBJ. "He did that from cowardice; nothing has happened since, except that President Johnson was bloodied in New Hampshire; and Senator Kennedy is just as much a coward when he comes down from the hills to shoot the wounded."

"He has," Kempton continued, "in the naked display of his rage at Eugene McCarthy for having survived on the lonely road he dared not walk himself, done with a single great gesture something very few public men have ever been able to do: In one day, he managed to confirm the worst things his enemies have ever said about him. We can see him now working for Joe McCarthy, tapping the phones of tax dodgers, setting a spy on Adlai Stevenson at the U.N., sending good loyal Arthur Schlesinger to fall upon William Manchester in the alleys of the American Historical Association.

"I suppose that I would prefer him as President to poor Mr. Johnson; it is not easy to think of a public man I wouldn't. But Senator Kennedy is otherwise only a bitter thought, and I blame myself, not him, for all the years he fooled me."

Such comments annoyed Bobby, who believed he actually had more guts than McCarthy because he had more to lose. And he began to tell people that McCarthy is "a vain man who could easily turn into another Henry Wallace."

Publicly, however, Bobby largely ignored McCarthy. At first he concentrated his fire on President Johnson. "Who is it that is truly dividing us?" he asked. And the only divider he named was "the President of the United States, President Johnson." And he clearly implied that, because of his failures of leadership, the President bore some personal responsibility for the alienation and drug addiction among American youth, for the anarchy of the ghetto riots and for other social ills.

And, in calling for the right of dissent, Bobby observed, "Every dictatorship has ultimately strangled in the web of repression it wove for its people. . . ." Asked privately if he meant to associate the Johnson Administration with "dictatorship," Bobby said, "No." But the question remains as to whom or what he was talking about.

Bobby played games with the truth when he deliberately misstated facts about the Vietnam War, the most notable being that "when we draft our eighteen- and nineteen-year-olds, the least we can ask of South Vietnam is that they draft theirs." Called on this by newsmen, Bobby did concede somewhat grudgingly that the Saigon regime was, indeed, drafting its young men.

"This has led to widespread criticism among the large retinue of journalists traveling with him," Richard Harwood reported to the Washington *Post* on March 28, 1968. "The word 'demagogue' crops up constantly in their conversation."

But Bobby was well on his way. He succeeded in pulling together a campaign organization that put McCarthy's relatively amateurish effort to shame. And he attracted huge crowds wherever he went. About which *The New York Times* commented editorially: "Senator McCarthy tends to understate his ideas and avoid harsh appeals to emotion. By contrast, Mr. Kennedy seeks to evoke ever stronger outbursts of crowd frenzy. He runs the risk of caricaturing the issues he is trying to develop. 'Sock it to 'em, Bobby!' the slogan which his audiences have begun to shout, has demagogic undertones that ill comport with the seriousness of the questions before the nation."

On March 31, 1968, Lyndon Baines Johnson surprised the nation by announcing, "I shall not seek and I will not accept the nomination of my party as your President." Acknowledging there was "division in the American house," LBJ withdrew in the name of national unity, which he said was "the ultimate strength of our country." At the same time, the President announced an open-end suspension of the bombings of large areas of North Vietnam.

Driving in from Kennedy Airport after he heard the news,

Bobby Kennedy wondered out loud, "I wonder if he would have done it if I hadn't come in."

At his United Nations Plaza apartment, he met with some of his advisers and staff trying to figure out how to pay tribute to a man he had been savaging for several weeks. The next morning, Bobby told a press conference that the President's actions reflected "both courage and generosity of spirit" and that he had asked to see him "in the interest of national unity." But he made clear he would continue his campaign for the Presidency.

There could be little doubt that the Kennedy campaign was moving, but in a year of surprising political developments no one really knew where it would end. At stake was the perpetuation of the dynasty. And for a Kennedy, nothing was of more importance.

33

End

> Just as I went into politics because Joe died, if anything
> happened to me tomorrow, my brother Bobby would
> run for my seat in the Senate. And if Bobby died, Teddy
> would take over for him.
>
> —JOHN F. KENNEDY

On June 4, 1968, Bobby Kennedy was dejected, fatalistic and withdrawn. He had pushed himself almost beyond the brink of exhaustion in his California campaign; and now —along with his usual coterie of friends—he was awaiting the primary results. He was aware that even if he trounced Gene McCarthy, the Presidential nomination might still be beyond his grasp. Most pundits were already conjecturing that Vice President Hubert Humphrey, who had entered none of the primaries, had the nomination sewed up.

Bobby was looking beyond California. He was prepared to stump from one end of New York State to the other in the forthcoming primary. "It'll mean a bloodbath in New York, but I've got to have it."

And he was thinking of a whirlwind trip to Europe in July. It would have been a historical "first"—the first time any Presidential candidate had ever traveled abroad to demonstrate his extraordinary popularity with foreigners and thus seek to convince the Democratic kingmakers of his stature on the global scene. On his tentative itinerary were Germany, France, Britain and Italy. He was also considering a dramatic foray behind the Iron Curtain, perhaps Poland where he had been so well received in years gone by.

Also on his mind in his final hours was Gene McCarthy's

485

refusal to step aside from his own Presidential quest to join forces against the common foe—Vice President Humphrey. McCarthy was just not buying the argument of his colleague from New York—namely, that Bobby was much better equipped politically and financially to obtain the nomination at the Democratic Convention.

The Kennedy juggernaut had indeed overwhelmed McCarthy's tattered and unpaid legions in Indiana and Nebraska. But in Oregon, much to everyone's surprise, the juggernaut faltered. McCarthy scored an impressive victory, one that not only gave the Minnesotan a tremendous lift but shattered the myth of the Kennedys' invincibility. It was the first electoral defeat of any Kennedy; and though there is nothing that says a man has to win all the time, with Bobby it was an article of faith.

Also painful was the fact that Gene McCarthy's legions were composed largely of dedicated young people from the nation's campuses. Bobby was envious. He agreed that the McCarthy youngsters were "better" than his volunteer workers; that they were brighter and far more committed. "I understand their hating me," he said. "You have to hate to run a good campaign. I wish I had some of them."

Many liberals were still unwilling to forgive Bobby for belatedly entering the Presidential race, after McCarthy's success in New Hampshire. "Indeed," lamented Arthur Schlesinger, Jr., in the *New Republic,* "I find myself puzzled by the hostility to Robert Kennedy which appears to rage in so many liberal breasts. I do understand, of course, why people were upset, or irritated, by the mode of Kennedy's entry into the 1968 Presidential contest. But I really do not think too much significance should be read into this."

There were other reasons. Many people just didn't cotton to the idea of the Kennedys' throwing all their weight and money around. Their worst fears were confirmed when Mrs. Rose Kennedy disarmingly observed that if the family had the money, why shouldn't Bobby spend his way into the White House? "It's our money, and we're free to spend it any way we please," said Bobby's mother.

"It's part of this campaign business," she continued. "If you have money, you spend it to win. And the more you can afford, the more you'll spend. The Rockefellers are like us.

We both have lots of money to spend on our campaigns. It's something that is not regulated. Therefore, it's not unethical."

In the wake of the Indiana primary, Governor Roger Branigan, runner-up to Senator Kennedy as the "favorite son" candidate, remarked, "You can't beat two million dollars."

On March 25, 1968, the Washington *Post* reported on the Kennedy campaign: "Staff members are racing around the country on the credit cards of Joseph P. Kennedy and various family enterprises." (Obviously the rich are able to campaign on credit.)

Then came Drew Pearson's column confirming the worst fears about Bobby. Pearson disclosed, with full documentation, that in 1963 while Bobby was Attorney General he had ordered the FBI to at first "bug" and later wiretap the telephone of the Reverend Dr. Martin Luther King. According to the columnist, his reason was that King "was in touch with various Communists and was being influenced by them."

Bobby did not deny the charge. Instead, he sought to evade questions concerning it. But he was put on the spot during a television debate with Senator McCarthy when he was asked whether he had ordered the wiretap. His response was that while he was the nation's chief law officer he had, indeed, authorized eavesdropping procedures in "national security" cases. By law, he insisted, he could not discuss any of these cases. Thus again he evaded answering a most embarrassing question.

The irony of all this was that some weeks before, Bobby had chartered a jetliner to return Dr. King's body from Memphis, where the civil rights leader had been assassinated, to his home city of Atlanta. The episode had been well publicized. As was Bobby's appearance at the funeral.

Also dismaying to the liberals were Bobby's appeals, particularly in Indiana and Nebraska, to conservative-minded voters. He even trimmed his overflowing locks. But, perhaps more importantly, he trimmed his views on race and social welfarism.

Not only was he demanding "law and order" in so-called white-backlash areas; Kennedy also spoke out repeatedly against the Federal welfare formula and called for a return of decision-making powers to states and local communities. "The welfare system," he said, sounding like Barry Goldwater, "does nothing. It gives somebody a dole; it's a payoff."

Assessing the Indiana primary, one TV pundit noted in bewilderment that Bobby had run as a "states rights" candidate.

"I get the feeling that I've been writing some of his speeches," exclaimed an amazed Governor Ronald Reagan, one of the nation's leading exponents of conservatism. "When he gets before a Chamber of Commerce he talks like Barry Goldwater. But before some left-wing students at Berkeley, he sounds like Bettina Aptheker."

And Richard Nixon complained that Kennedy had expropriated some of his down-the-line Republican ideas. "Bobby and I have been sounding pretty much alike," observed the Republican nominee.

Nelson Rockefeller couldn't resist assailing "the junior Senator from New York, whom we call the junior Senator from Massachusetts," as talking from both sides of his mouth on major issues in the Presidential campaign. According to Rockefeller, Kennedy seemed "able to change his rhetoric as fast as he once changed his residence. As you know, he recently campaigned through Indiana and Nebraska—a study in conspicuous conservatism." *

Gene McCarthy wasn't making things easier when he zeroed in personally on Bobby and his practice of "the old politics." The Minnesotan took a dig at his opponent's "same old rhetoric" from the 1960 John F. Kennedy campaign— "We're going to do better, we're going to get the country moving, we're going to do more . . . but beyond that no specification as to which way the country's going to move, or what we're going to do more of, or what we're going to do better."

He also discounted what he termed the return of Kennedy's "knights of the round table," including Theodore Sorensen, Lawrence O'Brien, Kenneth O'Donnell and Arthur Schlesinger, Jr. Kennedy has "even brought his cocker spaniel into the campaign. Nothing new, nothing surprising. The use of the cocker spaniel goes back to 1952 in America."

* This was less than two weeks before the assassination. Following Bobby's death, Governor Rockefeller—in his desperate campaign to forestall Nixon's almost-certain nomination in Miami Beach in August—wrapped himself in RFK's mantle by insisting not only that the late Senator was "a man who cared" but that he (Rocky) felt a personal responsibility to make Bobby's "unfulfilled dreams" of peace and social justice come true. Those who knew Rocky's true feelings toward Bobby before his death were amazed at the Governor's sudden admiration.

And even Bobby's emotional forays into the nation's ghettos were discounted by liberals such as Murray Kempton. Comparing the Kennedys to the Bonapartes, the McCarthy-supporting columnist declared, ". . . they identify with the deprived, being the radical foes of all authority when they are out of power. . . ."

The closing days of the make-or-break California primary were not happy ones in the Kennedy camp. Defeat in Oregon plus near exhaustion had gutted the candidate's spirit. Jack Newfield was with Bobby on that final Sunday. According to the future RFK biographer, that day he "seemed somber and withdrawn as he looked blankly out of the window of his . . . campaign jet. Normally Kennedy would gossip and joke with me on a campaign trip." But all he said was that he hoped that a mutual friend would win his Congressional primary fight in Long Island. Then he turned his worn-out face to the window. "On Monday he was drained and his speeches flat, and he got sick to the stomach in the middle of his final campaign speech in San Diego. The press whispered about a premonition of defeat."

Defeat in the Golden State would have meant the end of Robert Kennedy's hopes for the Presidency in 1968—if not forever. Everything that counted rode on how the voters reacted on Tuesday. And while the polls showed him ahead, they also indicated that Gene McCarthy was coming up fast. Thus, Bobby's somber mood on Election Day.

He had driven himself that last week with a frenzy rarely seen in American politics. And the crowds reacted in kind. Except for a former FBI agent, security was virtually non-existent. Bobby refused the aid of police wherever he went. As a consequence, no police were accompanying him that fateful Tuesday night. "We were not there because we were not wanted," a dejected police official later observed. "Senator Kennedy told us on several occasions that he didn't want us around."

And he didn't want them around because he feared the police would inhibit his personal contacts with the public as well as be resented by the cop-hating youngsters he sought to attract to his appearances. "The name of the game," a top Kennedy aide explained, "was to have those TV cameras pan on the cheering mobs, tousling his hair, tugging at his clothes, even though he was a very private person and hated to be handled by people, to have people put their arm around him, for example."

Bobby himself was aware of the dangers. Almost fatalistically he told a reporter, "I play Russian roulette every time I get up in the morning. I just don't care. There's nothing I can do about it anyway."

On that fateful Tuesday night, a party was going on in Suite 511 of the Ambassador Hotel. But, as the early TV returns showed Gene McCarthy running solidly ahead, Bobby remained secluded in a bedroom, receiving calls and talking to his advisers. For several hours Kennedy brooded.

Then, while McCarthy still led in the vote tally, NBC joined CBS in projecting Kennedy as the victor in the California primary. At the same time, he scored heavily in South Dakota where Hubert Humphrey had been expected to win. A smile lit Bobby's face.

Puffing happily on a thin cigar, Bobby began discussing *The New York Times,* whose treatment of his candidacy he felt lacked objectivity. One reason for its bias, he said, was its "anti-Catholicism." And he intended to attack the *Times* on television when he returned to New York on Thursday or Friday, he said.

"Their idea of a good story is 'More nuns leave convents than ever before,' " Bobby said. Minutes later he vowed "to chase Hubert Humphrey's ass all over America."

Looking young and tanned, Bobby went into the living room to greet dozens of celebrity friends who had come to celebrate the victory. The word went out that the "real big" party would be celebrated in Hollywood's gayest, most "in" nightclub, The Factory. The Senator would be there after he made his victory statement.

Before hundreds of cheering, shouting supporters in the Ambassador's jam-packed Embassy Room, Robert Francis Kennedy made his final speech. "Sock it to 'em, Bobby," the crowd chanted. Kennedy did not. First he introduced family members and other celebrities on the platform. Then he began: "I want to thank all of you, all of you who are here. Mayor Yorty has sent the message we've been here too long already. Now it's on to Chicago—and let's win there!"

Then he made it clear that, as far as he was concerned, the race for the Presidential nomination had narrowed down to himself and Hubert Humphrey. "I would hope now that the California primary is finished that we might have a dialogue or debate between the Vice President and myself about which direction we're going to go."

To the ear-ringing sounds of cheers and applause he stepped off the podium and walked to the rear. There, in a serving pantry, beside tables stacked with dishes, glasses and bottles, he was shot by an assassin. Early Thursday morning, Robert Francis Kennedy was dead.

And hardly had he been buried at Arlington, close to the grave of the late John F. Kennedy, when talk began that Senator Edward M. Kennedy could have the Vice Presidential nomination on a Humphrey ticket if he wanted it. As Arthur Schlesinger, Jr., put it, Ted Kennedy "will be a very important factor in the country for years to come." The Kennedy torch had been passed to the youngest brother.

Sources

CHAPTER 1 BOBBY

Reilly's pickets: *The Village Voice*, March 9, 1967; Bobby's Vietnam speech on March 2, 1967: *Congressional Record*, March 2, 1967, pp. S–2995–3012; meeting with Staughton Lynd and Tom Hayden: Andrew Kopkind, "Waiting for Lefty," *New York Review of Books*, June 1, 1967; *The New York Times*, May 7, 1967; Schlesinger on JFK escalation of Vietnam War: *A Thousand Days* (Boston: Houghton Mifflin Company, 1965), p. 451; JFK sent 25,000 troops: JFK press conference, September 12, 1963, as quoted in *Congressional Record*, February 24, 1966, p. S–3822; Philip Geyelin, *Lyndon B. Johnson and the World* (New York: Frederick A. Praeger, Inc., 1966), p. 50; Bobby on winning Vietnam War: Robert F. Kennedy, *Just Friends and Brave Enemies* (New York: Harper & Row, Publishers, 1962), pp. 9–10; *New York Herald Tribune*, February 19, 1962; *Washington Star*, February 19, 1962; *The New York Times*, February 19, 1962, and March 19, 1968; Bobby wanted to be ambassador to Vietnam in 1964: *The New York Times*, June 18, 1964; Vidal on JFK–Vietnam: "The Holy Family," *Esquire*, April 1967

Peregrine Worsthorne opinions: London *Sunday Telegraph*, September 4, 1966; audit of tax of federal judge: *Newsweek*, March 28, 1963; Bobby poked Bowles: *Time*, February 16, 1962; Bobby and mayor who touched him: *Newsweek*, October 24, 1966; Mrs. Longworth story: private sources; Sorensen on Bobby: *Newsweek*, October 24, 1966; Guthman on changing: Richard Reeves, "Kennedy, 2 Years After His Election," *The New York Times Magazine*, November 14, 1966; Manchester on Bobby: John Corry, *The Manchester Affair* (New York: G. P. Putnam's Sons, 1967), p. 107; JPK on Bobby hates the way I do: Anderson and Fred Blumenthal, "Washington Brother Act," *Parade*, April 28, 1957; Bobby and Lindsay: Dick Schaap, with picture editor Michael O'Keefe, *R.F.K.* (New York: The New American Library, Inc., 1967), p. 77; Bobby and questions: William V. Shannon, *The Heir Apparent* (New York: The Macmillan Company, 1967), pp. 59–60; Bobby and Luce during Manchester controversy: Frank Getlein, Washington *Star*, March 15, 1967; Jim Bishop's 1960 comments: Longview *Daily News*, October 25, 1960; John O'Hara on Bobby's charm: *Town & Village*, July 15, 1965

Guthman on working for Bobby: Richard Reeves, "The People Around Bobby," *The New York Times Magazine*, February 12, 1967; secretary quit and vanden Heuvel defense of Bobby: Barry Farber, host, *What Is Kennedy Really Like?* WABC–TV, September 28, 1967; Gerald Gardner a joke writer in 1964: Nick Thimmesch and William Johnson, *Robert Kennedy at 40* (New York: W. W. Norton & Company, Inc., 1965), p. 190; I. F. Stone comment: *I. F. Stone's Weekly*, October 19, 1964; staff and New Leftists: Andrew J. Glass and Leroy F. Aarons, "A Young Crew Around Young Robert," Washington *Post*, February 12, 1967; Scheer on staff: "A Political Portrait of Robert Kennedy," *Ramparts*, February 1967; Newfield on Bobby: "The Bobby Phenomenon," *The Nation*, November 14, 1966; *The New York Times* report: May 26, 1966; Peregrine Worsthorne comment: *op. cit.*

"electric socialism": Robert Scheer, *Ramparts, op. cit.; Human Events*, April 23, 1966; Gilder in *The New Leader:* "Kennedy Through GOP Glasses," December 18, 1967; quoting JFK: *Time*, as quoted by Walter Winchell, New York *Mirror*, May 17, 1962; *To Seek a Newer World* (Garden City: Doubleday & Company, Inc., 1967); Kempton on speeches: New York *Post*, December 12, 1966; *Cheetah* quote: John Speicher, "The New Heroes," November 1967, p. 28; Crawford on fogies: *Newsweek*, November 7, 1966; Shannon quote: *op. cit.*, pp. 248–49; debating Buckley: *The Wall Street Journal*, January 31, 1967; *Time*, April 8, 1966; Reagan debate: *National Observer*, July 3, 1967

LBJ on Bobby: Robert Sherrill, *The Accidental President* (New York: Grossman Publishers, Inc., 1967), p. 12; Bobby on LBJ: *Time*, March 17, 1967; LBJ on Young Knight: Stewart Alsop, "The Kennedy Hurricane," *The Saturday Evening Post*, August 27, 1966; Bobby as a Senator: *Newsweek*, October 24, 1966; Richard Reeves, *op. cit.*, November 14, 1966; New York politician: *ibid.*

CHAPTER 2 RUN

Vidal's 1963 attack: "The Best Man, 1968," *Esquire*, March 1963; Bobby and AAU vs. NCAA: *Newsweek*, March 18, 1963; Patterson photo: *Newsweek, ibid.*; Senators on future President: *The Wall Street Journal*, October 17, 1966; Richard Reeves, *op. cit.*, November 14, 1966; Bobby a basket case: *Time*, September 16, 1966; Bobby's denials of seeking Presidency: Washington *Post*, January 31, 1968; *The New York Times*, January 31, 1968; *The New York Times* on Bobby's not running: February 1, 1968

Paul Hope remark: Washington *Star*, March 18, 1968; LBJ expected it: *Time*, March 22, 1968; McCarthy's response: *Newsweek*, March 25, 1968; Bobby's people: William Nicholas, *The Bobby Kennedy Nobody Knows* (New York: Fawcett World Library, 1967); footnote on Texans: Washington *Star*, October 29, 1967; Camelot: *Newsweek*, October 24, 1966; Otten comments: *The Wall Street Journal*, October 17, 1966; Fordham speech: text; Ethel's tastes: *Newsweek*, March 18, 1963; Bobby's tastes: *David Susskind Show*, October 2, 1966; Tacitus boo-boo: *Congressional Record*, April 25, 1967, p. S–5775; Marion, Iowa, lady: *Newsweek*, October 24, 1966; Perry in *The National Observer:* October 17, 1966; Boorstin on pseudo-events: *ibid.*

Mount Kennedy climb: *The New York Times*, March 25, 1965; *Newsweek*, April 5, 1965; "Kennedy on Top of Mount Kennedy," *Life*, April 2, 1965; Wechsler on Mount Kennedy climb: New York *Post*, March 23, 1965; Bobby's *Life* article: "Our Climb up Mt. Kennedy," April 9, 1965; Teddy's reaction: Richmond *News Leader*, March 25, 1965; *Time* on Explorers' Club reaction: as quoted in *Human Events*, April 24, 1965; Amazon Valley trip: Andrew J. Glass, "The Compulsive Candidate," *The Saturday Evening Post*, April 23, 1966; Perry on hair combing: *op. cit.*; chauffeur and physical fitness: William Nicholas, *op. cit.*; protecting Jackie: Marquis Childs, "Bobby and the President," *Good Housekeeping*, May 1962; Joey Gallo meeting: *Newsweek*, March 18, 1963

Bobby canceled speech: *The New York Times*, October 5, 1967; New York *Daily News*, October 5, 1967; Roger Mudd interview: CBS–TV, June 20, 1967; rudeness: Penn Kimball, "Kennedy," *Life*, November 18, 1966; Wechsler's version: New York *Post*, November 17, 1966

CHAPTER 3   FAMILY

JPK on top dollar: Richard J. Whelan, *The Founding Father* (New York: The New American Library, Inc., 1964), p. 104; Florabel Muir comment: New York *Daily News*, April 29, 1966; Kennedy's greedy: New York *World-Telegram & Sun*, November 12, 1959; *Newsweek*, November 23, 1959; Weisl grudge: Arnold Beichman, "Pipeline to the President," *New York Herald Tribune Sunday Supplement*, January 17, 1965; Weisl on Bobby: New York *Daily News*, March 23, 1968; JPK on go where money is: Ann Geracimos, "Bobby Kennedy Was Here," *New York Herald Tribune*, October 11, 1964

Bobby visits Riverdale: *The New York Times*, October 8, 1964; Bronxville estate: *The New York Times*, June 6, 1929; Mrs. JPK remark to Queen: Robert Curran, *The Kennedy Women* (New York: Lancer Books, Inc., 1964), p. 23;

Reader's Digest quote: Jerome Beatty, "Nine Kennedys and How They Grew," April 1939; JFK letter to parents: Gene Schoor, *Young John Kennedy* (New York: Harcourt, Brace & World, Inc., 1963), p. 37; Bobby and Teddy on JPK: *The Fruitful Bough: Tributes to Joseph P. Kennedy*, privately published by the Kennedy family, 1965, as quoted in *Newsweek*, November 1, 1965; Mrs. JPK on hot water: New York *Post*, November 8, 1964; Mrs. JPK on ruler: Washington *Star*, May 17, 1966; JFK and headmaster: *JFK, The Childhood Years*, CBS News, October 31, 1967; excerpts, New York *Post*, November 4, 1967

Bobby on Joe Jr.: Robert E. Thompson and Hortense Myers, *Robert F. Kennedy: The Brother Within* (New York: The Macmillan Company, 1962), p. 64; Eunice and Hail Mary: William J. Duncliffe, *The Life and Times of Joseph P. Kennedy* (New York: Macfadden-Bartell Corp., 1965), p. 76; Kennedys vs. Cape Codders: Leo Damore, *The Cape Cod Years of John Fitzgerald Kennedy* (Englewood Cliffs, N.J.: Prentice-Hall, Inc., 1967), pp. 39–41; Billings on Bobby; Thompson and Myers, *op. cit.*, p. 45

CHAPTER 4   CHILDHOOD

JFK met Bobby: William Manchester, *Portrait of a President: John F. Kennedy in Profile* (New York: Macfadden-Bartell Corp., 1964), p. 124; friends on Bobby: William Nicholas, *op. cit.*; Mrs. JPK on Teddy: undated AP dispatch from Newport, 1963; Bronxville school: Washington *Star*, February 23, 1962; Ann Geracimos, *op. cit.*; Bobby and magazines and Porky: Thompson and Myers, *op. cit.*, p. 67; Teddy's recollections: Ann Geracimos, *op. cit.*; Luella R. Hennessey: "Bringing Up the Kennedys," as told to Margot Murphy, *Good Housekeeping*,

August 1961; Mrs. JPK memoirs: "Leaves from Our Lives," as serialized by New York *World-Journal-Tribune,* October 2, 1966; table debates: *Time,* July 11, 1960

Moley on JPK–FDR: *The First New Deal* (New York: Harcourt, Brace & World, Inc., 1966), pp. 381–82; JPK book: *I'm for Roosevelt* (New York: Reynal Hitchcock, 1936); FDR note to JPK: Leo Damore, *op. cit.,* p. 43; Richard J. Whelan, *op. cit.,* p. 186; Bobby letter from FDR: Dick Schaap, *op. cit.,* p. 26; *Life* on Kennedys: as quoted by John Henry Cutler, *Honey Fitz* (New York: The Bobbs-Merrill Co., Inc., 1962), p. 279; JFK on musical: James Mac-Gregor Burns, *John Kennedy: A Political Profile* (New York: Harcourt, Brace & World, Inc., 1960), p. 37; Luella Hennessey on "Kick": *op. cit.;* meeting celebrities: Thimmesch and Johnson, *op. cit.,* p. 35; London press: Richard J. Whelan, *op. cit.,* p. 211; visit Pope: *New York Herald Tribune,* March 14, 1939; JPK remark: Walter Vincent Carty, "Kennedy's Father," *This Month,* February 1962

CHAPTER 5   WAR

LBJ comparisons: *The New York Times,* December 5, 1967; Baltimore *Sun,* July 14, 1960; *The New York Times,* July 14, 1960; *Liberty* article: May 21, 1938; JPK re Czechs: John Morton Blum, *From the Morgenthau Diaries: Years of Crisis, 1928–1938* (Boston: Houghton Mifflin Company, 1959), p. 518; Kennan quoted: *Memoirs: 1925–1950* (Boston: Little, Brown and Company, 1967), as quoted by Robert Gottlieb, *Book World,* October 22, 1967; Churchill remark: Nigel Nicolson, ed., *Harold Nicolson: Diaries and Letters: 1930–1939* (New York: Atheneum Publishers, 1966), as quoted in *The Wall Street Journal,* January 5, 1967; JPK call to FDR: Joseph Alsop and Robert Kintner, *American*

White Paper: The Story of American Diplomacy and the Second World War (New York: Simon & Schuster, 1940), p. 68; Randolph Churchill: London *Sunday Times,* June 20, 1965; Mrs. Harold Laski comment: Washington *Post Sunday Supplement,* December 3, 1967; Washington *Post,* December 9, 1967; New York *Post,* December 8, 1967; JFK remark in 1960: Randolph Churchill, *op. cit.;* JPK interview: Joseph F. Dinneen, *The Kennedy Family* (Boston: Little, Brown and Company, 1959), p. 84; Cummings: as quoted in *The New York Times,* December 7, 1940

CHAPTER 6   SCHOOL

Pearl Harbor day: *Newsweek,* December 12, 1966; Curran comment: *Time,* May 4, 1942; Bobby's view: Thompson and Myers, *op. cit.,* p. 135; Milton classmate: *Time,* October 10, 1960; JFK letter to Bobby: Robert J. Donovan, *PT 109* (New York: Fawcett World Library, 1962), p. 152; Joe Jr.'s last words: Samuel Eliot Morison, "Death of a Kennedy," *Look,* February 27, 1962; Torres comments: interview, January 4, 1968; Billings on Bobby: William Manchester, *Portrait of a President, op. cit.,* pp. 25–26; Considine interview: New York *Journal-American,* December 1, 1963; John Hersey article: "Survival," *Reader's Digest,* August 1944, reprinted from *The New Yorker,* June 17, 1944

CHAPTER 7   HARVARD

Democrat Bobby: Thompson and Myers, *op. cit.,* p. 55; Harvard football games: Boston *Herald,* Sunday sports sections, September–November, 1946–47; Boston *Post* articles: June 3, 4, 5 and 6, 1948; decision on law school: Thompson and Myers, *op. cit.,* pp. 46–47; Thimmesch and Johnson, *op. cit.,* p. 38; law school marks: St. Louis *Post-Dispatch,* February

24, 1957; professors on Bobby: Margaret Laing, *The Next Kennedy* (New York: Coward-McCann, Inc., 1968), pp. 112–13; McCarthy at Student Legal Forum: Charlottesville *Progress*, May 17, 1951; other forum speakers: Charlottesville *Progress* (Arnold) September 30, 1950; (Krock) October 19, 1950; (Douglas) November 15, 1950; (Richardson) December 1, 1950; (Joseph P. Kennedy) December 13, 1950; (Hughes) December 15, 1950; (Congressman John F. Kennedy) February 21, 1951; (Bunche) March 27, 1951; (Landis, Eban and Sarper) April 12, 1951; (Folsom) April 18, 1951; text of JPK speech: *Congressional Record*, December 15, 1950, p. A–7723

Ethel: *Newsweek*, March 18, 1963; Helen Thomas, "The Other Kennedy Women," UPI series, 1963; Marguerite Higgins, "The Private World of Robert and Ethel Kennedy," *McCall's Magazine*, February 1962; Judy Michaelson, "Woman in the News: Ethel Kennedy," New York *Post*, June 25, 1966; Bobby on swinging higher: Joe McCarthy, *The Remarkable Kennedys* (New York: The Dial Press, Inc., 1960), p. 29; Ethel on competitiveness: Helen Thomas, *op. cit.*; William Manchester, *Portrait of a President, op. cit.*, p. 23; Kathleen and Joey: UPI dispatch, *Philadelphia Inquirer*, March 25, 1963

CHAPTER 8 LODGE

Buckley on McCarthy: "Why Not Teddy?" *National Review*, October 9, 1962; JPK on JFK–Lodge race: *Time*, July 11, 1960; Richard J. Whalen, *op. cit.*, p. 419; JPK wanted Bobby as manager: Rose Kennedy, "Leaves from Our Lives, II," Washington *Star*, October 10, 1966; Eunice quoted: Thimmesch and Johnson, *op. cit.*, p. 111; JFK announcement: William Manchester, *Portrait of a President, op.*

cit., p. 126; Bobby's arrival: Ed Linn, "The Truth About Joe Kennedy," *Saga*, July 1961; Boston politicians: Joe McCarthy, *op. cit.*, p. 134; Hugh Sidey, "Brother on the Spot, Robert Kennedy," in *The Kennedy Circle*, Lester Tanzer, ed. (Washington: Robert B. Luce, 1961), pp. 197–98; Dever in campaign: Hugh Sidey, *op. cit.*, p. 198; Ed Linn, *op. cit.*; Bobby's behavior: Thimmesch and Johnson, *op. cit.*, p. 113; Eisenhower on money: William J. Miller, *Henry Cabot Lodge* (New York: James J. Heineman, Inc., 1967), p. 253; Bobby on workers: Ralph Martin and Ed Plaut, *Front Runner, Dark Horse* (Garden City: Doubleday & Company, Inc., 1960), p. 184

JPK in campaign: *ibid.*, p. 167; courting Taftites: Ralph Blagden, "Cabot Lodge's Toughest Fight," *The Reporter*, September 30, 1952; William S. White, *The Taft Story* (New York: Harper & Row, Publishers, 1954), p. 182; courting Jews: Martin and Plaut, *op. cit.*, pp. 172–73; Richard J. Whelan, *op. cit.*, p. 426; Gardner Jackson episode: James MacGregor Burns, *op. cit.*, pp. 109–10; New York *Post*, January 12, 1961; Martin and Plaut, *op. cit.*, pp. 139–40; JPK dealings with Fox: Joe McCarthy, *op. cit.*, pp. 139–40; election night: Hugh Sidey, *op. cit.*, pp. 198–99; Martin and Plaut, *op. cit.*, p. 182

CHAPTER 9 McCARTHY

Bobby on McCarthy: Thompson and Myers, *op. cit.*, p. 100; Marguerite Higgins on Bobby: New Rochelle (New York) *Standard-Star*, November 15, 1965; Bobby on Communism: Thompson and Myers, *op. cit.*, p. 106; JFK's bill on East–West trade: Boston *Traveler*, May 9, 1951; Bobby's testimony: *Newsweek*, June 1, 1953; Bobby and letter to Ike: Sherman Adams, *First-Hand Report* (New York: Harper & Row, Publishers, 1961), pp. 140–41; Arthur Krock,

The New York Times, May 5 and July 19, 1953; The New York Times, May 5, 23, 24, 26 and 29, 1953, and July 19, 1953; Boston Traveler, May 26, 1953; and private sources; Bobby's criticism in The Enemy Within (New York: Popular Library, Inc., 1960), p. 291; Bobby and Matthews appointment: The New York Times, June 19, 1953; Bobby did not quit in anger: Boston Post, August 1, 1953

Bobby on Hoover Commission: Thompson and Myers, op. cit., pp. 112–13; private sources; Bobby's letter to The New York Times: February 3, 1954; Ike on Bricker Amendment: Mandate for Change 1953–1956 (New York: The New American Library, Inc., 1963), p. 348; The New York Times editorial on Bricker Amendment: January 24, 1954

Anna Lee Moss before Committee: Time, March 22, 1954; Thompson and Myers, op. cit., pp. 114–15; new information on Mrs. Moss: Washington Post, May 23, 1958; New York Daily News, October 30, 1958; "Schine plan": The New York Times, June 12, 1954; Cohn to reporters: Baltimore Sun, March 5, 1965; Bobby prepared summary: Thompson and Myers, op. cit., p. 117; Bobby on McCarthy: ibid., p. 121; Dirksen proposal: Edward Bennett Williams, One Man's Freedom (New York: Popular Library, Inc., 1964), pp. 61–62; JFK on censure: New York Post, July 30, 1956

CHAPTER 10   McCLELLAN

Bobby's work on Peress case: Boston Post, January 21, 1955; The New York Times, January 25, 1955; McClellan reopened case: Newsweek, April 4, 1955; Drury in The New York Times: "The Man Who Replaces McCarthy," The New York Times Magazine, February 20, 1955; Committee report: Lionel Lokos, Who Promoted Peress? (New York: Bookmailer, 1961), p. 107; Fort Monmouth summary: Ralph de Toledano, R.F.K.: The Man Who Would Be President (New York: G. P. Putnam's Sons, 1967), p. 73; Mrs. Hort story: The New York Times, May 26, 1955

Trip to Russia: Boston Herald, February 28 and September 16, 1955; Boston Traveler, September 29, 1955; Boston Post, October 11, 1955; U.S. News & World Report, October 20, 1955; New York Daily News, December 12, 1955; Robert F. Kennedy, "The Soviet Brand of Colonialism," The New York Times Magazine, April 8, 1956; William O. Douglas, Russian Journey (Garden City: Doubleday & Company, Inc., 1955)

Trade schools investigation: Boston Post, September 24, 1955; strategic items: Boston Herald, February 22, 1956; Bobby's letter to The New York Times: March 17, 1956

Bailey Report: U.S. News & World Report, August 1, 1960; Catholic opposition to JFK: Arthur Schlesinger, Jr., A Thousand Days, op. cit., p. 6; Profiles in Courage reference: (New York: Harper & Row, Publishers, 1956), p. 8; Kazin comment: "The President and Other Intellectuals," American Scholar, Autumn 1961; JFK contribution to Nixon: San Diego Union, July 20, 1960; Harvard seminar: John P. Mallan, "Massachusetts: Liberal and Corrupt," The New Republic, October 13, 1952; Bobby challenged as delegate: Boston Herald, March 10 and 16, 1956

Bobby at convention: Theodore C. Sorensen, Kennedy (New York: Harper & Row, Publishers, 1965), p. 88; Sorensen–McCarthy encounter: ibid., p. 89; Martin and Plaut, op. cit., p. 90; Bobby angry: Theodore C. Sorensen, op. cit., p. 91; Douglass Cater, "The Cool Eye of John F. Kennedy," The Reporter, December 10, 1959; Bobby's later appraisals: Hugh Sidey, *op. cit.*, p. 201; Martin and Plaut, *op. cit.*, p. 185; Bobby in 1956 campaign: Anthony Lewis, "What Drives Bobby Kennedy?" *The New York Times Magazine*, April 7, 1963; Boston *Globe*, October 9, 1956; Bobby on singing "Dixie": Boston *Herald* (AP dispatch), September 26, 1956

CHAPTER 11   HOFFA

Mollenhoff on Bobby: *Tentacles of Power: The Story of Jimmy Hoffa* (Cleveland: The World Publishing Company, 1965), pp. 128–29; Mollenhoff convinced Bobby: *ibid.*, p. 124; Bobby at Teamsters' headquarters: Robert F. Kennedy, *The Enemy Within, op. cit.*, pp. 16–17; Mollenhoff's forecast: Mollenhoff, *op. cit.*, p. 149; Cheasty dinner: Mollenhoff, *ibid.*, pp. 147–49; Des Moines *Register*, July 7, 1957; Robert F. Kennedy, *op. cit.*, pp. 44–51; Williams on parachute: Mollenhoff, *op. cit.*, p. 213; New York *Post*, March 26, 1964; Sheridan–Louis encounter: Robert F. Kennedy, *op. cit.*, p. 66; Hoffa–Bobby Minifons encounter: Dan Wakefield, "Bob," *Esquire*, April 1962; Bobby–Anthony West encounter: *International Teamster*, April 1959, pp. 16–17; Bickel article on Bobby: "The Case Against Him for Attorney General," *The New Republic*, January 9, 1961; criticism of Rogers: Chicago *Daily News*, January 5, 1961; Goldblatt episode: *Hearings before the Select Committee on Improper Activities in the Labor or Management Field*, 86th Congress, 1st Session, Pursuant to Senate Resolution 44, 86th Congress, "Investigation of Improper Activities in the Labor or Management Field," Part 56, July 10, 13 and 14, 1959, pp. 19609–13; Paul Jacobs article: "Extracurricular Activities of the McClellan Committee," *California Law Review*, Vol. 51, 1963, pp. 296–310;

Rauh on Bobby: Wakefield, *op. cit.;* Milone meeting: Jacobs, *op. cit.*

CHAPTER 12   GOLDWATER

McClellan background: AP Biographical Service Sketch 4124, September 1, 1962; Goldwater recollections: interview, December 13, 1966; Kennedy–Reuther friendship: *Newsweek*, July 22, 1957; cost of wiretapping Hoffa: Walter J. Miller Jr., "Bobby and Jimmy: Round Six," *The Nation*, April 7, 1962; Bobby's Notre Dame speech: Boston *Globe*, February 23, 1958; Bobby's Knights of Columbus speech: Boston *Sunday Advertiser*, April 20, 1958; political career for Bobby: St. Louis *Post-Dispatch*, February 24, 1957; Boston *Herald*, April 9, 1959; *Look*, August 6, 1957; *The New York Times* profile: March 13, 1956; *Parade* article: "Washington Brother Act," April 28, 1957; Republicans on UAW strikes: *Time*, March 16, 1959; The Report of the Minority, February 1960, New Hampshire *Sunday News*, January 24, 1960; Washington *Star*, June 20, 1959; New York *Daily News*, June 19, 1959; Baltimore *Sun*, February 17, 1960; Campaigne interview: January 1967; William Moore quotation: *Chicago Tribune*, November 13, 1960

CHAPTER 13   PLANS

JFK gossip: *Time*, January 20, 1961; Carpozi book: *The Hidden Side of Jacqueline Kennedy* (New York: Pyramid Publications, Inc., 1967), p. 39; Barnett report: North American Newspaper Alliance (NANA), July 21, 1957; Cunningham on 1958 race: Theodore C. Sorensen, *op. cit.*, p. 77; Teddy as campaign manager: Washington *Post-Herald*, August 18, 1958; Teddy met Joan: Stephen Hess, *America's Political Dynasties* (Garden City: Doubleday & Company, Inc.,

1966), p. 518; JFK election: James MacGregor Burns, *op. cit.*, p. 223

Stevenson on Kennedy money: *Newsweek*, February 29, 1960; Patterson announcement: Washington *Star*, June 17, 1959; Sorensen on Patterson: *op. cit.*, p. 158; Bobby and Patterson: *The New York Times*, May 23, 1961; JFK shock at Patterson endorsement: Washington *Star*, June 19, 1959; George Wallace on Patterson: Richmond *News Leader*, May 12, 1967; Roy Wilkins on Patterson endorsement: *The New York Times*, May 23, 1960; Thurgood Marshall on endorsement: *The New York Times*, July 13, 1960

Bobby resigned: *The New York Times*, September 11, 1959; rumors that Seigenthaler wrote *The Enemy Within*: Richard Reeves, "The Men Around Bobby," *The New York Times Magazine*, February 12, 1967; Seigenthaler's denial: *The New York Times Magazine*, February 26, 1967; Telford Taylor review: *New York Herald Tribune Book Review*, February 28, 1960; JPK made deal with Fox for movie: Richard J. Whelan, *op. cit.*, p. 469; meeting at Bobby's house: *Time*, February 15, 1960; Theodore H. White, *The Making of the President 1960* (New York: Atheneum Publishers, 1961), pp. 49–58; Theodore C. Sorensen, *op. cit.*, pp. 119–21

CHAPTER 14 PRIMARIES 1960

Bobby barked at Reformers: Oliver Pilat, "Kennedy on His Own," *The Progressive*, November 1964; DiSalle for JFK: Michael V. DiSalle, with Lawrence G. Blochman, *Second Choice* (New York: Hawthorne Books, Inc., 1966), pp. 198–99; W. H. Hessler, "How Kennedy Took Ohio," *The Reporter*, March 3, 1960; *Knickerbocker News*, July 20, 1960; New York *Post*, February 9, 1960; Providence *Journal*, January 6, 1960; Des Moines *Register*, January 6, 1960;

Newsweek, May 16, 1960; O'Connell support: *New York Herald Tribune*, November 23, 1963; New York *Post*, January 4, 1961; Washington *Post*, March 22, 1960; Buckley support: New York *World-Journal-Tribune*, January 23, 1967; *The New York Times*, January 23, 1967; Hamill comment: New York *Post*, January 26, 1967

JFK "underdog" in Wisconsin: Washington *Star*, February 10, 1960; *The Wall Street Journal*, January 22, 1960; San Diego *Union*, January 31, 1960; Kempton comment: New York *Post*, February 12, 1960; Humphrey on brother: Washington *Post*, March 1, 1960; McCarthy on JFK: Washington *Star*, December 3, 1967; Kennedy clan campaigning: *Newsweek*, March 28, 1960; *U.S. News & World Report*, March 14, 1960; Washington *Post*, March 25, 1960; HHH on glamour: *Time*, March 28, 1960; Sahl blacklisted: Denver *Post*, July 25, 1967; Washington *Daily News*, March 6, 1963; *New York Herald Tribune*, May 30, 1962; *Barry Gray Show*, WMCA (New York), August 21, 1967; *The New York Times*, November 11, 1967; *Variety*, January 3, 1968; Teddy campaigning: *Newsweek*, March 28, 1960; HHH on rackets: *The Wall Street Journal*, March 9, 1960; Sinatra "out": New York *Mirror*, March 23, 1960; New York *Journal-American*, April 11, 1960; *Knickerbocker News*, July 11, 1960; Los Angeles *Mirror*, July 14, 1960; Jackie Robinson on Bobby: New York *Post*, March 16, 1960; Lippmann comment: Madison *Capital Times*, April 8, 1960; Miles McMillin comment: as quoted in the New York *Post*, March 27, 1960

Marquis Childs on anti-Catholic literature: Washington *Post*, March 25, 1960; *National Review* on Corbin: December 16, 1961; Wisconsin election night; New York *Post*, April 7, 1960; Arthur Edson quoted: Newark *Star Led-*

ger, July 19, 1960; Hoffa: *New York Herald Tribune,* May 6, 1960

FDR Jr. calls HHH a draft-dodger: Washington *Star,* April 28 and 30, 1960; *New York Herald Tribune,* May 7, 1960; Washington *Post,* May 1, 1960; New York *Journal-American,* May 7, 1960; *The New York Times,* May 9, 1960; Baltimore *Sun,* May 7, 1960; *Time,* February 8, 1963; New York *Post,* September 10, 1966; Muriel Humphrey's reaction: Warren Weaver, Jr., "One of Them Will Probably Be Next in the White House," *The New York Times Magazine,* May 22, 1966; vote-buying charges: Baltimore *Sun,* May 13, 1960; *Time,* June 6, 1960; *Newsweek,* June 6, 1960; St. Louis *Post-Dispatch,* August 7, 1960; *Washington Post,* August 9, 1960; *Chicago Tribune,* November 24, 1960; *New York Post,* August 23, 1967

lis *Star,* July 13, 1960; Sanford announcement: *Newsweek,* July 18, 1960; Kennedy deal with Vandiver: Baltimore *Sun,* May 10, 1961; Troutman activity: Pearson, *ibid.,* and April 6, 1962; Schlesinger and Minnesota delegation: Arthur Schlesinger, Jr., *op. cit.,* p. 31; Schlesinger's other problems: *Time,* December 17, 1965; Kennedy machine: *Newsweek,* July 18, 1960; Sinatra and Rat Pack: New York *Daily News,* August 14, 1960; *Human Events,* August 25, 1960; *The New York Times,* July 12, 1960; Bobby interviewed on TV: Morrie Ryskind, "The Rover Boys in Los Angeles," *National Review,* July 30, 1960; Bobby on civil rights: Stan Opotowsky, *The Kennedy Government* (New York: E. P. Dutton & Co., Inc., 1961), p. 59; family arrivals: Luella R. Hennessey, *op. cit.;* LBJ arrival in L.A.: *New York Herald Tribune,* July 9, 1960; Cincinnati *Enquirer,* July 11, 1960

CHAPTER 15 CONVENTION 1960

JFK–Stevenson meeting: William Attwood, *The Reds and the Blacks* (New York: Harper & Row, Publishers, 1967), p. 5: Stevenson biographer: Herbert J. Muller, *Adlai Stevenson: A Study in Values* (New York: Harper & Row, Publishers, 1967), pp. 242–43; JPK on Stevenson: Kenneth S. Davis, *The Politics of Honor: A Biography of Adlai E. Stevenson* (New York: G. P. Putnam's Sons, 1967), p. 427; JFK would walk out: William Attwood, *op. cit.,* p. 6; dinner in Georgetown: *ibid.,* pp. 6–7; Truman speech: *Chicago Tribune,* July 3, 1960; *Newsweek,* July 11, 1960; Janeway on LBJ: *The Economics of Crisis* (New York: Weybright & Talley, Inc., 1968), p. 274; Luce luncheon: *New York Herald Tribune,* July 27, 1960; two Bobbys meet: Pearson, Washington *Post,* July 15, 1960; LBJ announcement: *The New York Times,* July 6, 1960; *The New York Times* comment, July 9, 1960

Pearson on Sanford: Indianapo-

Bobby on Stevenson: Baltimore *Sun,* July 14, 1960; Stevenson speech: Kenneth S. Davis, *op. cit.,* p. 435; Bobby on Brown: Washington *Post,* October 28, 1966; Bobby on Hubert: Baltimore *Sun,* July 14, 1960; LBJ last minute attacks: *The New York Times,* July 14, 1960; Baltimore *Sun,* July 14, 1960; JFK on McCarthy censure vote: *Newsweek,* September 26, 1960; McCarthy nominates Stevenson: Kenneth S. Davis, *op. cit.,* pp. 437–38; Bobby's call to JFK: *Time,* July 25, 1960; Bobby and voter registration: *Newsweek,* July 25, 1960; Bobby on Stevensonians: Arthur Schlesinger, Jr., *op. cit.,* p. 32

Monroney on v.p.'s: *ibid.,* p. 31; Washington *Post* story: James A. Wechsler, "The Two-Front War: Johnson vs. Kennedy," *The Progressive,* May 1967; Spivack story: *The Spivack Report,* December 5, 1966; Salinger on choosing LBJ: Pierre Salinger, *With Kennedy* (Garden City: Doubleday & Company, Inc., 1966), p. 46; Kiker article: "Robert Kennedy and the What If Game," The Atlantic, October 1966; Bobby on LBJ selection: Thimmesch and Johnson, op. cit., pp. 119–20; JFK meeting with Southerners: "If Kennedy Hadn't Picked LBJ—" U.S. News & World Report, August 2, 1965; Ribicoff: ibid.; JFK on wanting to win: William Manchester, Portrait of a President, op. cit., p. 117; RFK and LBJ: Newsweek, July 25, 1960; Theodore H. White, op. cit., pp. 172–77; Arthur Schlesinger, Jr., op. cit., pp. 36–48; private sources; Sorensen on Meet the Press: Washington Star, February 25, 1964; Galbraith on LBJ: Arthur Schlesinger, Jr., op. cit., p. 48; LBJ nomination: Time, July 25, 1960; JPK on LBJ selection: Arthur Schlesinger, Jr., op. cit., pp. 48–49

CHAPTER 16   CAMPAIGN 1960

Jackson as manager: Time, October 10, 1960; Louchheim ouster: Washington Star, July 16, 1960; private sources; Bobby takeover: Time, op. cit.; registration drive: Newsweek, October 15, 1960; New Frontier slogan: New York Herald Tribune, March 5, 1961; JFK on Sorensen: Richard Nixon, Six Crises (Garden City: Doubleday & Company, Inc., 1962), p. 407; visit to Byrd: New York Herald Tribune, August 6, 1961; Charleston (South Carolina) News and Courier, October 29, 1960; JFK on Bobby: Hugh Sidey, op. cit., p. 209; Irwin Ross interview: New York Post, October 10, 1960; objection to calling JFK "Jack": Evelyn Lincoln, My Twelve Years with John F. Kennedy (New York: Bantam Books, Inc., 1965), pp. 140–41; Bobby on Jackie: Robert Curran, op. cit., p. 56; Eunice: Robert A. Liston, Sargent Shriver: A Candid Portrait (New York: Farrar, Straus & Giroux, Inc., 1964), p. 59
"People Machine": Ithiel de Sola

Pool, Robert P. Abelson and Samuel Popkin, Candidates, Issues and Strategies: A Computer Simulation of the 1960 and 1964 Presidential Elections (Cambridge: The M.I.T. Press, 1965); Thomas B. Morgan, "People Machine," Harper's, January 1961; JFK links Hoffa to Nixon: The New York Times, August 7, 1960; Red Fay on JFK–Nixon friendship: Paul B. Fay, Jr., The Pleasure of His Company (New York: Harper & Row, Publishers, 1966), p. 62; Chicago Tribune editorial: September 13, 1960; Bobby on GOP anti-Catholic spending: New York Herald Tribune, October 24, 1960; Houston ministers meeting: Theodore C. Sorensen, op. cit., pp. 189–93; "Speech of John F. Kennedy, Greater Houston Ministerial Association, Rice Hotel, Houston, Texas, Monday Evening, September 12, 1960," The Speeches of Senator John F. Kennedy, Presidential Campaign of 1960 (Washington: Government Printing Office, 1961), pp. 206–18; Buckley on Houston speech: "A Long Way from Rome," The New York Times Book Review, May 14, 1967; Clinton Green story: Thompson and Myers, op. cit., pp. 207–9; Coffin article: "New Man in Town," New Leader, January 30, 1961; National Conference on Constitutional Rights and American Freedom: New York Post, September 27, 1960
Barry Gray Show: transcript, WMCA, New York, August 24, 1960; New York Post, August 26, 1960; JFK apology to Southerners: Charleston (South Carolina) News and Courier, September 4, 1960; Quemoy–Matsu: New York Journal-American, October 15, 1960; The Joint Appearances of Senator John F. Kennedy and Vice President Richard M. Nixon, Presidential Campaign 1960 (Washington: Government Printing Office, 1961), pp. 162–64 (October 7) and pp. 204–5 (October 13)
Bobby on Cuba: transcript, Face

the Nation, CBS-TV, September 25, 1960; JFK on Cuba: "Speech of Senator John F. Kennedy, Hemming Park, Jacksonville, Florida, October 18, 1960," *The Speeches of Senator John F. Kennedy, Presidential Campaign of 1960, op. cit.,* p. 1168; JFK statement on intervention in Cuba: "Following Is the Text of a Statement on Cuba by Senator John F. Kennedy, October 20, 1960," *ibid.,* p. 681; Nixon reaction: Richard M. Nixon, *op. cit.,* pp. 354–57; Kempton reaction: New York *Post,* October 7, 1960

Wofford appointment: Washington *Post,* March 16, 1960; Theodore C. Sorensen, *op. cit.,* p. 172; Powell support of JFK: New York *World-Telegram & Sun,* September 21, 1960; Bobby dropped charges against Powell (Pearson–Anderson), New York *Post,* January 17, 1968; St. Louis *Post-Dispatch,* April 14, 1961; Dr. Martin Luther King episode: Theodore H. White, *op. cit.,* pp. 322–23; Robert A. Liston, *op. cit.,* pp. 104–5; Arthur Schlesinger, Jr., *op. cit.,* p. 61; New York *Post,* December 24, 1960; *The New York Times,* December 14, 1960; private sources; Nixon on King episode: Simeon Booker, "What Republicans Must Do to Regain the Negro Vote," *Ebony,* April 1962; *The Nation* editorial: November 19, 1960

election eve: *Time,* November 16, 1960; Theodore H. White, *op. cit.,* p. 18; New York *Post,* November 9, 1960; election results: *1962 World Almanac,* p. 417

vote frauds: Richard Wilson, "How to Steal an Election," *Look,* February 14, 1961; *Hearing Before the Subcommittee on Privileges and Elections of the Committee on Rules and Administration, U.S. Senate,* 87th Congress, 1st Session, July 13, 1961; New York *Herald Tribune,* December 5 and 6, 1960; *Chicago Tribune,* December 11 and 15, 1960; Chicago *Daily News,* December 16, 1960; *Chicago Tribune,*

March 7, 1962; Los Angeles *Times,* December 3, 1960; Los Angeles *Times,* February 16, 1961; Washington *Post,* December 14, 1960; pressure on Nixon to challenge: Richard M. Nixon, *op. cit.,* pp. 412–13; JFK–Nixon meeting: *ibid.,* pp. 409–11; Paul Martin, "What Jack Told Dick: He'll Ignore More Radical Planks in Party's Platform," Elmira *Star-Gazette,* January 5, 1961

Bobby in Mexico: New York *Journal-American,* November 26, 1960; Rayburn on Bobby: *Newsweek,* March 18, 1963; Bobby visits Rogers, Hoover and Douglas: Hugh Sidey, *John F. Kennedy: President* (New York: Atheneum Publishers, 1963), pp. 14–15; *The New York Times* editorial: November 23, 1960; *Chicago Tribune* editorial: December 17, 1960; Sokolsky comment: Washington *Post,* December 23, 1960; Bobby on JFK remark: William Manchester, *Portrait of a President, op. cit.,* pp. 110–11; Bobby before Senate Committee: *Hearing Before the Committee of the Judiciary, U.S. Senate, 87th Congress, 1st Session, on Robert F. Kennedy, Attorney-General Designate,* January 13, 1961; Keating questions: *ibid.,* pp. 37–38; Senate approval: Washington *Post,* January 14, 1961; Maxine Cheshire story: Washington *Post,* December 17, 1960

CHAPTER 17   ATTORNEY
GENERAL I

Bobby on divorcing self from politics: New York *Herald Tribune,* January 6, 1961; Day on Bobby running patronage: J. Edward Day, *My Appointed Round: 929 Days as Postmaster General* (New York: Holt, Rinehart & Winston, Inc., 1965), pp. 8–9; judgeships: Washington *Post,* October 22, 1967; Pat Anderson, "Robert's Character," *Esquire,* April 1965; *The New York Times,* June 21,

1961; *Time,* November 6, 1964; Schlesinger's rationale: Arthur Schlesinger, Jr., *op. cit.,* p. 582; Paul Corbin and Bobby: *Newsweek,* September 4, 1961; Corbin hearings: *Hearings Before the Committee on Un-American Activities, House of Representatives, 87th Congress, 1st Session, Testimony by and Concerning Paul Corbin,* September 6 and 13, 1961; November 13, 27 and 28, 1961; and March 15 and July 2, 1962 (Washington: Government Printing Office, 1962), pp. 1235–1465

Silberling appointment: Baltimore *Sun,* February 2, 1961; Manchester *Union Leader,* January 17, 1967; Bobby's early 1961 view on wiretapping: Peter Maas, "Robert Kennedy Speaks Out on Civil Rights, Wiretaps, Organized Crime, Anti-Trust Suits, and Subversive Activity," *Look,* March 28, 1961; Bobby's authorizations of bugging: *The Wall Street Journal,* April 4, 1967; Caplin memorandum: *ibid.;* confidential squad: *Chicago Tribune,* December 21, 1966; Silberling on mob convictions: Manchester *Union Leader, op. cit.;* Bobby's wiretapping bill to Congress: *The New York Times,* April 4, 1962; *Washington Post,* April 6, 1962; ACLU opposition: New York *Post,* March 24, 1964

Anderson's impression of Bobby: *Esquire, op. cit.;* Bobby on night of Bay of Pigs failure: Marquis Childs, "Bobby and the President," *Good Housekeeping,* May 1962; JFK speech to ASNE: *The New York Times,* April 21, 1961; JKF's despondency: *Time,* November 29, 1963; JPK remark: Richard J. Whelan, *op. cit.,* p. 474

CIA investigation: *Newsweek,* March 18, 1963; Getlein on Bobby's interest in counter-insurgency: Washington *Star,* January 31, 1968; JFK's interest in guerrilla warfare: Theodore C. Sorensen, *op. cit.,* pp. 632–33; Bobby on Vietnam: *The New York Times,* February 11, 1962; Washington *Daily News,* February 20, 1962; Bobby in Saigon: Robert F. Kennedy, *Just Friends and Brave Enemies, op. cit.,* pp. 9–10; *New York Herald Tribune,* February 19, 1962; Washington *Star,* February 19, 1962; *The New York Times,* March 19, 1968; Galbraith on troop buildup in Vietnam: *Time,* February 16, 1968; Bobby's view on leaving Justice Department: William Shannon, *The Heir Apparent, op. cit.,* p. 114; Mary McGrory interview: New York *Post,* August 2, 1961

Bobby denied JFK reneged on Bay of Pigs air cover: *Newsweek,* February 4, 1963; Washington *Star,* January 21, 1963; Gore of Florida on JFK briefing: AP dispatch, January 26, 1963; Pentagon on war-gamed: *Newsweek,* February 4, 1963; Salinger on 1960 press reports of brigade: Pierre Salinger, *op. cit.,* p. 146; ANPA speech: text, *Chicago Tribune,* April 28, 1961; JFK remark to Catledge: Washington *Post,* June 2, 1966; Congressman Wilson's report: *Congressional Record,* April 11, 1962, p. H–5884; Jim Bishop audit: New York *World-Journal-Tribune,* March 24, 1967; Nixon and Finch audits: private sources

JFK–Bobby relationship: Marquis Childs, *Good Housekeeping, op. cit.;* Bobby and Trujillo assassination: Hugh Sidey, *John F. Kennedy: President, op. cit.,* pp. 187–88; *Time,* February 16, 1962; JFK–Bobby at Berlin Wall crisis time: *ibid.;* Schlesinger on Bobby: Wakefield, "Bob," *Esquire,* April 1962; Lerner criticism: New York *Post,* April 16, 1962; Ruark comment: New York *World-Telegram & Sun,* December 21, 1960; JPK insists Teddy be Senator: *Time,* September 28, 1962; Teddy's campaign: Paul Driscoll, "Jack Was Asking About You," *The New Republic,* June 4, 1962; Murray B. Levin, *Kennedy Campaigning* (Boston: Beacon Press, 1966); *Time,* September 28, 1962; *The*

New York Times, September 21, 1962

CHAPTER 18   ATTORNEY
GENERAL II

Wechsler observations: New York *Post,* November 27, 1961; National Crime Commission: Robert F. Kennedy, *The Enemy Within,* op. cit., p. 251; Hoover's opposition: Chicago *Daily News,* March 22, 1961; Bobby not civil rights crusader: biographical sketch by Robert E. Clark, Washington *Star,* January 13, 1961; *Look* interview by Peter Maas: op. cit.; McClellan on Bobby: Robert Sherrill, "How to Succeed on the Potomac: Be an Investigator," *The New York Times Magazine,* October 8, 1967; Hoffa's phones tapped: Thimmesch and Johnson, op. cit., p. 77; Starnes comment on Hoffa: New York *World-Telegram & Sun,* January 26, 1961; Hoffa conviction: Syracuse *Post Standard,* June 30, 1963; Chicago *Daily News,* March 22, 1961; Washington *Star,* December 13, 1966; Richmond *News Leader,* December 16, 1966; *Time,* December 23, 1966

Bobby's book on world trip: *Just Friends and Brave Enemies,* op. cit.; Cleveland *Plain Dealer* editorial: January 29, 1962; Lindsay letter: text, *Congressional Record,* February 7, 1962, p. H–1865; *New York Herald Tribune,* February 8, 1962; Rusk's reply: *Chicago Tribune,* February 9, 1962; *Baltimore Sun,* February 9, 1962; New York *World-Telegram & Sun* editorial: February 12, 1962; *The Reporter* comments: March 15, 1962; Bobby in Berlin: *New York Herald Tribune,* February 23, 1962

Keating on Cuban missile crisis: James Daniel and John G. Hubbell, *Strike in the West: The Complete Story of the Cuban Crisis* (New York: Holt, Rinehart & Winston, Inc., 1963); Keating feared bugging: New York *Post,* January 5, 1967; New York *World-Journal-*

Tribune, January 5 and 6, 1967; ExComm sessions: Kenneth S. Davis, op. cit., p. 478; Sulzberger on missile crisis: *The New York Times,* June 18, 1967; Alsop-Bartlett article: *The Saturday Evening Post,* December 8, 1962; repercussions of article: Kenneth S. Davis, op. cit., pp. 485–87; Stevenson on *1984: ibid.,* p. 461

Kennedys on civil rights: *Time,* June 21, 1963; Bobby and Baldwin meeting: New York *Post,* May 28, 1963; *The Village Voice,* June 6, 1963; London *Sunday Telegraph,* June 2, 1963; "Kennedy and Baldwin," *The New Republic,* June 15, 1963; New York *Post,* May 27, 1963; Washington *Star,* May 26, 1963; Baldwin's fears of wiretapping: Fern Marja Eckman, *The Furious Passage of James Baldwin* (New York: M. Evans & Co., Inc., 1966), p. 194; General Aniline: *New York Herald Tribune,* March 24, 1962; Washington *Post,* March 5, 1963; New York *Post,* October 20, 1964; Pearson in New York *Post,* May 18 and 19, 1964; Washington *Daily News,* May 20, 1961; Binghamton *Press,* December 14 and 22, 1961, and January 7, 1962

Bobby vs. LBJ: Leonard Baker, *The Johnson Eclipse* (New York: The Macmillan Company, 1966), pp. 160–61; voodoo doll: *Life,* November 18, 1966; Ribicoff recollection: Vera Glaser, NANA, March 22, 1966; Beichman on LBJ: "Pipeline to the President," *New York Herald Tribune Sunday Supplement,* January 17, 1965; JFK to drop LBJ: Evelyn Lincoln, *Kennedy and Johnson* (New York: Holt, Rinehart & Winston, Inc., 1968), p. 205

CHAPTER 19   AFTERMATH

Lahey column: Detroit *Free Press,* December 13, 1963; mission to see Sukarno: *The New York Times,* January 19, 25 and 29, 1964; *Chicago Tribune,* January

26, 1964; Hugh Sidey, "Grief: R.F.K.'s Mission to Asia," *Life,* January 31, 1964; Sidey visit with Bobby: *ibid.;* Bobby call to NANA: James Shevis, NANA, December 16, 1966; new inscription in White House: *New York Herald Tribune,* January 11, 1964; *The New York Times,* January 11, 1964; Reston on New Frontier: *The New York Times,* November 15, 1963; *The New Republic* on New Frontier: "Kennedy as Target," June 1, 1963

Corbin busy for Bobby in New Hampshire: *The New York Times,* March 11, 1964; *Washington Post,* March 12, 1964; Victor Lasky, NANA, March 14, 1964; *Denver Post,* March 16, 1964; *Newsweek,* March 16, 1964; *Washington Star,* March 18, 1964; *Time,* March 20, 1964; *Newsweek,* March 23, 1964; LBJ buildup of Shriver: Tom Wicker, "The Big Political Sprint," *The Saturday Evening Post,* April 25, 1964; Lippmann opposes Bobby for V.P.: *New York Herald Tribune,* April 23, 1964; St. Louis *Post-Dispatch* editorial: as quoted in the New York *Post,* April 30, 1964; Schlesinger and Bailey conversation: William Manchester, *The Death of a President* (New York: Harper & Row, Publishers, 1967), p. 450; O'Brien a renegade: New York *Post,* February 15, 1967; Galbraith a "rat fink": *Time,* February 16, 1968; Bobby on Bundy: Chicago *Daily News,* July 27, 1965; Jackie cold-shouldered LBJ: Marguerite Higgins in *Park East,* August 19, 1965; Pearson in New York *Post,* May 26, 1965, and Washington *Post,* December 22, 1966; LBJ dumps Bobby: *New York Herald Tribune,* August 21, 1964

CHAPTER 20   DECISION

Bobby on forming new country: Marguerite Higgins in New Rochelle (New York) *Standard-Star,* August 15, 1964; Bobby on note to Cabinet officials: *The New York Times,* August 7, 1964; Kraft col-

umn: Washington *Star,* July 31, 1964; Higgins column: New Rochelle *Standard-Star, op. cit.;* Wicker report: *The New York Times,* July 31, 1964; second meeting: Theodore H. White, *The Making of the President 1964* (New York: Atheneum Publishers, 1965), p. 278; Crotty announcement: Baltimore *Sun,* August 1, 1964; Bobby thought V.P. would go down to wire: *Newsweek,* August 24, 1964; other support: New York *Post,* August 7, 1964; Washington *Star,* August 8, 1964; Bobby on visiting New York zoo: "Talk of the Town," *The New Yorker,* June 24, 1961; bosses for Bobby: *The New York Times,* August 17, 1964; Bobby delegate from Massachusetts: Baltimore *Sun,* August 14, 1964; *The New York Times,* August 22, 1964

Wagner reluctant: *New York Herald Tribune,* August 1, 14, 16, 21 and 22, 1964; Bobby on Wagner support: Washington *Star,* August 11, 1964; *New York Herald Tribune,* August 11, 1964; *The New York Times* editorial: August 12, 1964; Stratton opposition: *The New York Times,* August 8, 9 and 12, 1964; *New York Herald Tribune,* August 17, 1964; Washington *Post* editorial: August 24, 1964; *New York Herald Tribune* editorial: August 20, 1964; Wagner endorsement: *The New York Times,* August 22, 1964; *New York Herald Tribune,* August 22, 1964; *Philadelphia Inquirer,* August 22, 1964; *New York Herald Tribune* editorial: August 22, 1964; *The New York Times* editorial: August 22, 1964

Bobby enters race: New York *Journal-American,* August 25, 1964; *The New York Times,* August 26, 1964; *Philadelphia Inquirer,* August 26, 1964; Bobby declares: *The New York Times,* August 26, 1964; *New York Herald Tribune,* August 26, 1964; Keating offers map: *The New York Times,* August 26, 1964; Baltimore *Sun,*

August 26, 1964; Harriman party at Atlantic City: *The New York Times,* August 26, 1964; New York *Post,* August 26, 1964; Washington *Post,* August 26, 1964; Buckley stayed away later: Pete Hamill, New York *Post,* January 26, 1967 meeting re taking convention by storm: New York *Post,* August 26, 1964; Oliver Pilat, "Kennedy on His Own," *The Progressive,* November 1964; Jackie at Atlantic City: Washington *Daily News,* August 28, 1964; *Chicago Tribune,* August 28, 1964; Washington *Star,* August 28, 1964; Bobby's speech: New York *Post,* August 28, 1964; *Newsweek,* September 7, 1964; Mary McGrory comments: Washington *Star,* August 28, 1964; New York State Convention: *The New York Times,* September 2, 1964

CHAPTER 21   CAMPAIGN 1964

Bobby's departure as Attorney General: *The New York Times,* September 4, 1964; Washington *Daily News,* September 4, 1964; Des Moines *Register,* September 4, 1964; *Newsweek,* October 24, 1966; launching campaign: *The New York Times,* September 7, 1964; Bobby's techniques: Robert G. Spivack in the *New York Herald Tribune,* October 4, 1964; Marquis Childs in the *New York Post,* September 10, 1964; aura of JFK invoked: Albany *Times-Union,* September 10, 1964; Bigart in *The New York Times:* October 9, 1964; Schlesinger in *The New Republic,* October 10, 1964; Bobby castigates actor Paul Newman: Gore Vidal, "The Best Man 1968," *Esquire,* March 1963; Newfield in the *New America:* as quoted in *The Village Voice,* November 24, 1966; "intellectuals" party: *Time,* October 23, 1964; *The New York Times,* October 15, 1964; Jonathan Aitken and Michael Beloff, *A Short Walk on the Campus* (New York: Atheneum Publishers, 1966), pp. 50–51

Bobby's nostalgic visit: New York *Post,* October 7, 1964; New York *Journal-American,* October 7, 1964; *New York Herald Tribune,* October 8, 1964; Susskind on Bobby: New York *World-Telegram & Sun,* October 28, 1964; Jack English's defense of Bobby: Bob Waters, *Bobby Kennedy: Next President of the United States* (Rockville Center: G. C. London, 1965), p. 32; Kennedy women in campaign: Marquis Childs, New York *Post,* October 27, 1964; Bobby in Polish parade: *The New York Times,* October 5, 1964; *New York Herald Tribune,* October 5, 1964; Washington *Post,* October 5, 1964; New York *Post,* October 5, 1964; Buffalo parade: AP dispatch, October 12, 1964; John Roosevelt ad: *The New York Times,* November 2, 1964; civil rights issue: *New York Herald Tribune,* September 6 and 9, 1964; New York *Post,* September 9, 1964; *The New York Times,* September 10, 1964; Bobby not using New York as stepping-stone: *The New York Times,* October 1, 1964

Keating popular in Jewish areas: *Newsweek,* October 12, 1964; Bobby–Bigart story: *The New York Times,* October 1, 1964; Bobby campaigning in Jewish areas: *Newsweek,* October 12, 1964; *New York Herald Tribune,* September 21, 1964; New York *Post,* October 2, 1964; Spivack column: *New York Herald Tribune,* October 4, 1964; Keating on General Aniline: *New York Herald Tribune,* September 21, 1964; Bobby and Italians: *New York Herald Tribune,* September 9, 1964; *The New York Times,* October 11, 12 and 13, 1964; Marvin R. Pike, AP dispatch, Buffalo, October 11, 1964; Drew Pearson, Bell–McClure Syndicate, October 10, 1964; Lynn report: October 26, 1964; Ernst in *The Villager:* October 8, 1964

Bobby reaching for LBJ coattails: New York *Post,* October 14, 1964; New York *Journal-American,*

October 26, 1964; Higgins column: New Rochelle *Standard-Star*, October 16, 1964; Marianne Means report: New York *Journal-American*, November 22, 1964; Bobby called Keating conservative: New York *Daily News*, October 27, Felknor, *Dirty Politics* (New York: 1964; Felknor book: Bruce L. W. W. Norton & Company, Inc., 1966), pp. 175–98; Javits on distorting Keating record: New York *Post*, November 1, 1964; "The Myth of Keating's Liberalism" document: New York State Democratic Committee, Statler–Hilton Hotel, William McKeon, State Chairman; *The Reporter* on Kennedy "mythmakers": November 5, 1964; Marilyn Monroe pamphlet: *The Wall Street Journal*, October 28, 1964; the "debate": New York *Journal-American*, October 28, 1964; New York *World-Telegram & Sun*, October 28, 1964; *Newsday*, October 28, 1964; New York *Post*, October 28, 1964; *The New York Times*, October 30, 1964

CHAPTER 22   JUNIOR SENATOR

election night: New York *Journal-American*, November 4, 1964; New York *Post*, November 4, 1964; Washington *Star*, November 4, 1964; *New York Herald Tribune*, November 5 and 8, 1964; *Newsweek*, November 9, 1964; Robert Ajemian, "Two Kennedys Sweep Two States," *Life*, November 13, 1964; victory statement: New York *World-Telegram & Sun*, November 4, 1964; Betty Beale on etiquette: Washington *Star*, November 8, 1964; Starnes comment: New York *World-Telegram & Sun*, November 4, 1964; Keating in *U.S. News & World Report*: November 16, 1964; official count: New York *Daily News*, December 8, 1964; *The New York Times* editorial: November 4, 1964; Weisl's reaction: Thimmesch and Johnson, *op. cit.*, pp. 224–25; Bartlett column: Washington *Star*, November 5, 1964; Bobby's pre-election interview: *Newsweek*, November 16, 1964; *The New York Times* on Salinger defeat: November 4, 1964

visit to Defense Secretary: *The New York Times*, November 6, 1964; closing of Brooklyn Navy Yard: Baltimore *Sun*, November 20, 1964; Wagner's wait for Bobby: *Newsweek*, November 16, 1964; Bobby sworn in as Senator: *The New York Times*, January 5, 1965; *New York Herald Tribune*, January 5, 1965; New York *Post*, January 7, 1965; *Newsweek*, January 18, 1965; New York *World-Telegram & Sun*, February 19, 1965; LBJ's State of the Union speech: *Newsweek*, January 18, 1965; Bobby's Ethel–Bird joke: New York *Journal-American*, January 7, 1965; Bobby–Teddy competition: *Newsweek*, January 18, 1965

Desmond on patronage: "Albany Hippodrome: Wagner, Rocky and the Kennedy Act," *The Nation*, February 22, 1965; leadership fight in legislature: *The New York Times*, February 5, 1965; *Time*, February 5, 1965; *The New York Times*, February 21, 1965; Desmond comment: *The Nation*, *op. cit.*; Bobby's comment: *Newsweek*, February 15, 1965; Bobby's letters to Zaretzki and Travia: *The New York Times*, February 11, 1965; New York *World-Telegram & Sun*, February 11, 1965; Washington *Star*, February 11, 1965; *The New York Times* editorial: February 12, 1965; replies to Bobby: *The New York Times*, February 12, 1965; *New York Herald Tribune*, February 12, 1965; *The Reporter* letter: February 25, 1965; Rocky–Bobby feud: New York *Daily News*, February 6, 1965; *Time*, February 12, 1965; *The New York Times*, February 16, 1965; Javits–Bobby feud: New York *Post*, February 17, 1965; New York *World-Telegram & Sun*, February 19, 1965; New York *Daily News*, Feb-

ruary 22, 1965; *Newsweek,* March
1, 1965; Drummond comment:
New York Herald Tribune, February 8, 1965; cementing relations
with Eastland: Drummond, *ibid.;*
The Village Voice, November 19,
1964; New York *Daily News,*
December 23, 1964

CHAPTER 23   FEUD WATCHING

Bobby before Long Committee:
New York *Daily News,* March 3,
1965; *The New York Times,* March
4, 1965; Washington *Star,* March
3, 1965; *Chicago Tribune,* March
3, 1965; Baltimore *Sun,* March 4,
1965; *New York Herald Tribune,*
March 3 and 4, 1965; New York
Post, March 4, 1965; New York
World-Telegram & Sun, March 10,
1965; *Time,* March 12, 1965; *Newsweek,* March 15, 1965; Washington
Star editorial: March 6, 1965;
Wechsler in New York *Post:* March
9, 1965; *Chicago Tribune* editorial:
March 4, 1965; Mesta–Kennedy
parties: New York *Post,* June 25,
1965; Washington *Star,* June 26,
1965; Washington *Daily News,*
June 26, 1965; *The New York
Times,* June 26, 1965; *New York
Herald Tribune,* June 27 and July
8, 1965; New York *World-Telegram
& Sun,* July 3, 1965; Kennedys'
guerrilla warfare on voting-rights
bill: New York *Post,* April 8, 1965;
Richmond *News Leader,* May 15,
1965; New York *Daily News,* May
21, 1965; *Chicago Tribune,* May 24,
1965; *Time,* May 21, 1965; *Human
Events,* May 22, 1965; Alexander
M. Bickel, "The Kennedy–Javits
Voting Amendment," *The New Republic,* June 5, 1965; *The Nation,*
June 14, 1965; "Washington Report," *Life,* May 21, 1965; Thimmesch and Johnson, *op. cit.,* pp.
260, 265–66
Bobby and Dominican Republic: Rowland Evans and Robert
Novak, *Lyndon B. Johnson: The
Exercise of Power* (New York: The
New American Library, Inc.,
1966), pp. 510–29; *New York Her-*

ald Tribune, May 5, 1965; New
York *Post,* May 20, 1965; *News-
week,* July 26, 1965; New York
Post, November 7, 1965; *Time,*
November 11, 1966; John Bartlow
Martin, *Overtaken by Events* (Gar-
den City: Doubleday & Company,
Inc., 1966), pp. 705–7; Buckley on
Bobby: Richmond *News Leader,*
May 15, 1965; John O'Hara com-
ment: *Human Events,* July 24,
1965
Bobby's altered speech on Viet-
nam: New York *World-Telegram
& Sun,* July 9, 1965; *The New York
Times,* July 10, 1965; *New York
Herald Tribune,* July 10, 1965;
Newsweek, July 26, 1965; Bobby
on sending blood to North Viet-
namese: *New York Herald Trib-
une,* November 6, 1965; New York
Daily News, November 7, 1965;
New York *Post,* November 8,
1965; *Chicago Tribune,* November
10, 1965; New York *Journal-American,* November 14, 1965; *National
Review Bulletin,* November 23,
1965; *Human Events,* November
20, 1965; Bobby's speech on nuclear weapons: Washington *Star,*
June 23, 1965; *The New York
Times,* June 25, 1965; New York
Post, July 1, 1965; "Kennedy and
China," *The New Republic,* July 3,
1965; Boston *Globe,* July 6, 1965;
Newsweek, July 5, 1965; *Time,*
July 23, 1965; Spivack comments: New York *Journal-American,* July 8, 1965; Higgins comments: New Rochelle *Standard-
Star,* November 15, 1965; Bobby
on *Meet the Press:* transcript

CHAPTER 24   LATIN TRIP

Michael Davie book: *LBJ: A
Foreign   Observer's   Viewpoint*
(New York: Duell, Sloan & Pearce,
1966), pp. 29–30; Robin Douglas–
Home article on Jackie: *Queen,*
February 1967; Douglas–Home remarks: New York *Post,* February
10, 1967; Bobby–Zaretzki exchange: Thimmesch and Johnson,
op. cit., pp. 239–40; vanden Heuvel

not appointed: *New York Herald Tribune*, March 31, 1965; *Newsweek*, March 22, 1965; New York *Post*, September 5, 1965; Kempton on Beame–Lindsay contest: "Shouting for Help," *The New Republic*, September 25, 1965; *The New York Times* editorial: October 27, 1965; Beame campaign: *New York Herald Tribune*, September 15, 1965; New York *Post*, September 30, 1965; New York *Daily News*, October 28, 1965; *Chicago Tribune*, October 29, 1965; *The New York Times*, November 2, 1965; Murray Kempton, "Running Against Buckley, Lindsay Beats Beame," *The New Republic*, November 13, 1965; *New York Herald Tribune* on Bobby's campaign style: November 2, 1965; Wechsler comment: New York *Post*, November 3, 1965; Steingut remark: William V. Shannon, *op. cit.*, p. 166; Bobby's voting-rights challenged: *The New York Times*, November 3, 1965; private sources; election night: New York *Post*, November 3, 1965; Mary McGrory comments: New York *Post*, November 8, 1965; *The New York Times* quote from South America: November 20, 1965; O'Connor disagrees: *The New York Times*, November 22, 1965; Peluso in the New York *Daily News*: November 29, 1965

Bobby–Vaughn clash: Washington *Post*, November 18, 1965; New York *Post*, November 19, 1965; Washington *Star*, Nov. 19, 1965; Glass on Latin trip: "The Compulsive Candidate," *The Saturday Evening Post*, April 23, 1966; footnote on Bobby's bills: private sources; Latin trip: *The New York Times*, November 14, 1965; New York *Post*, November 16 and 22, 1965; *New York Herald Tribune*, November 16 and 30, 1965; *The Wall Street Journal*, November 18, 1965; Baltimore *Sun*, November 21 and 22, 1965; New York *World-Telegram & Sun*, November 22, 1965; *The New York Times*, November 25, 26 and 28, 1965; New York *Daily News*, November 26, 1965; *The New York Times*, December 1, 1965; New York *World-Telegram & Sun*, December 2, 1965; *Newsweek*, December 6, 1965; *National Guardian*, January 1, 1966; Wechsler on invitation for briefing: New York *Post*, December 7, 1965; Bobby on trip: *Newsweek*, December 6, 1965; Spivack comment: New York *Journal-American*, November 27, 1965; Bobby's long Latin speech: New York *Post*, May 11, 1966; *The New York Times*, May 10 and 11, 1966; Baltimore *Sun*, May 12, 1966; *The New York Times*, May 15, 1966; Washington *Star*, May 15, 1966; Eder in *The New York Times*: May 12, 1966; Mexican criticism: *Chicago Tribune*, May 22, 1966; Briggs criticism: Baltimore *Sun*, October 13, 1966; New York *Daily News*, October 13, 1966; Richmond *Times-Dispatch*, October 13, 1966; *Human Events*, October 22, 1966

CHAPTER 25   MOVING
            LEFTWARD

Wechsler on Bobby on a spot: New York *Post*, January 6, 1966; letter to editor: *New York Herald Tribune*, January 12, 1966; TV newscaster comment: Peter Jennings, ABC–TV, as quoted in the *New York Herald Tribune*, January 6, 1966; Buchwald comment: *New York Herald Tribune*, January 16, 1966; strike end: *New York Herald Tribune*: January 26, 1966; Bobby–Lindsay and Bronx Park: *The New York Times*, January 22, 1966; New York *Post*, January 24, 1966; New York *World-Telegram & Sun*, January 24, 1966; New York *Daily News*, January 24, 1966; *The New York Times*, January 25 and February 28, 1966; New York *Post*, March 3, 1966; Bobby–Javits feud: *New York Herald Tribune*, February 21, 1966; *The New York Times*, February 22, 1966; *Time*, July 22, 1966; Ted Lewis comment: New York *Daily News*, April 14, 1966;

Bobby–Rocky feud again: (NHRR) *New York Herald Tribune*, January 25, 1966; New York *Post* (retarded), February 5, 1966, and (primary bill) May 13, 1966; *The New York Times* (Con-Con), September 26 and (addicts) November 3, 1966

Bobby calls for coalition with Vietcong: *The New York Times*, February 20, 1966; Baltimore *Sun*, February 20, 1966; *New York Herald Tribune*, February 20, 1966; reactions: New York *Post*, February 22, 1966; *New York Herald Tribune*, February 23, 1966; *Chicago Tribune*, February 23, 1966; *Time*, March 4, 1966; *Newsweek*, March 7, 1966; Bobby bailed out: *Chicago Tribune*, February 23 and 24, 1966; *The New York Times*, February 23, 1966; *New York Herald Tribune*, February 23, 1966; New York *Daily News*, March 2, 1966; New York *Post*, February 23, 1966; Bobby and Lincoln: Peoria *Journal Star*, February 25, 1966, as quoted in *Congressional Record*, March 3, 1966, pp. A–1122–23; Humphrey and Bundy reactions: *The New York Times*, February 21, 1966; *New York Herald Tribune*, February 21, 1966; Baltimore *Sun*, February 21, 1966; Ted Lewis comment: New York *Daily News*, March 4, 1966; *Worker* comment: February 27, 1966; Bobby on commitment and bombings: *New York Herald Tribune*, February 23, 1966; Lerner comment: New York *Post*, February 3, 1966; Crawford comment: *Newsweek*, March 7, 1966

LBJ Freedom House speech: *The New York Times*, February 24, 1966; *New York Herald Tribune*, February 24, 1966; New York *Post*, February 24, 1966; New York *Journal-American*, February 26, 1966; *The New York Times*, February 27, 1966; Atra Baer comment: New York *Journal-American*, February 24, 1966; Bobby–LBJ on poverty budget: *The New York Times*, April 20, 21 and 23, 1966; New York *Post*, April 20,

1966; McNamara speeches: Richmond *News Leader*, June 4, 1966; Bobby–LBJ no-feud: *Newsweek*, June 13, 1966; *The New York Times* editorial: May 28, 1966

no visas for newsmen: *The New York Times*, May 25, 1966; Washington *Post* comment: June 5, 1966; Bobby goes to South Africa: "The Kennedy Reception," *The New Republic*, June 11, 1966; Washington *Star*, June 2 and 5, 1966; Washington *Post*, June 5 and 9, 1966; Baltimore *Sun*, June 5, 1966; New York *Post*, June 9, 1966; *The New York Times*, June 12, 1966; *Time*, June 17, 1966; *Newsweek*, June 20, 1966; George Laing in the New York *Daily News:* June 18, 1966; visit to Robertson and bugging: George Laing, *ibid.*; New York *Post*, May 12, 1966; Richmond *News Leader*, July 20, 1966; Roanoke *Times*, September 8, 1966; University of Cape-town: text, *Congressional Record*, June 6, 1966, pp. S–11838–39; New York *Daily News*, June 7, 1966; Washington *Star*, June 7, 1966; Reuters (June 10), as quoted in the *Chicago Tribune*, June 11, 1966; Washington *Star*, June 10, 1966; New York *Post*, June 8, 1966; Coetzee comment: Washington *Star*, June 8, 1966; London *Express* comment: *Time*, June 17, 1966; Meredith shot: *The New York Times*, June 7, 1966; student asked about God's being black: Baltimore *Sun*, June 8, 1966; New York *Daily News*, June 18, 1966; Bobby's *Look* article: "Suppose God Is Black," August 23, 1966; Angus Deming in *Newsweek*, June 27, 1966

Bobby in Tanzania: *The New York Times*, June 10, 1966; New York *Daily News*, June 10, 1966; Baltimore *Sun*, June 10, 11 and 12, 1966; Washington *Post*, June 11 and 12, 1966; New York *Post*, June 11, 1966; Washington *Star*, June 12, 1966; Bobby in Kenya: *The New York Times*, June 15, 1966; New York *Daily News*, June 15,

1966; Bobby in Ethiopia: New York *Daily News*, June 16, 1966; *The New York Times*, June 16, 1966; *The Reporter* comment: June 30, 1966; Bobby returns: *The New York Times*, June 20, 1966; Washington *Star*, June 20, 1966; *Chicago Tribune*, June 20, 1966; Washington *Post*, June 20, 1966; *U.S. News* report: June 20, 1966; Muggeridge comments: *Esquire*, November 1966

Bobby backs liberal wing in surrogate race: New York *Post*, May 24, 1966; *The New York Times*, May 26, 27 and 28, 1966; *The Village Voice*, May 26, 1966; New York *Daily News*, May 30, 1966; behind-scenes maneuvers: *The New York Times*, June 1, 2, 5 and 13, 1966; New York *Daily News*, June 3, 1966; New York *Post*, June 8 and 13, 1966; *Human Events*, June 18, 1966; Rose statement earlier: *The New York Times*, July 3, 1966; Crotty sponsored by Bobby: *The New York Times*, June 25, 1966; Nolan in *The New Republic*: "The Kennedys at Home Have a Few Problems," June 25, 1966; surrogate battle: *The New York Times*, June 20, 23 and 24, 1966; New York *Post*, June 20, 22 and 27, 1966; New York *Daily News*, June 23, 1966; *Chicago Tribune*, June 25, 1966; Washington *Post*, June 26, 1966; election of surrogate: *The New York Times*, June 29, 1966; New York *Post*, June 29, 1966; *Time*, July 8, 1966; *Newsweek*, July 11, 1966; Bobby's new power: Washington *Star*, June 29, 1966; *The New York Times*, June 30, 1966; Evans and Novak comment: Washington *Post*, July 1, 1966; rafting trip: New York *Post*, July 5, 1966; *Time*, July 15, 1966

CHAPTER 26   GOVERNMENT-IN-EXILE

Look editors on Bobby's "goon squad": Richard Reeves, "The People Around Bobby," *The New York Times Magazine*, February 12, 1967; backgrounds of Seigenthaler, Marshall and Goodwin: Richard Reeves, *ibid.*; Andrew J. Glass and Leroy F. Aarons, "A Young Crew Around Young Robert," Washington *Post*, February 12, 1967; additional Goodwin background: Washington *Post*, April 3, 1962; *The New York Times*, November 22, 1963; *Time*, July 15, 1966; *The New York Times*, September 18, 1966; Washington *Star*, September 28, 1966

Schlesinger: Richard Reeves, *op. cit.*; *Time*, December 17, 1965; *Chicago Sun-Times*, August 1, 1965; Washington *Post*, October 11, 1967; Schlesinger offered to resign: *A Thousand Days*, *op. cit.*, p. 537; Roche on Schlesinger: Washington *Post*, March 13, 1967; *Chicago Tribune*, March 23, 1967; Schlesinger a swinger in New York: *Time*, March 3, 1967; Schlesinger's disclosure on Rusk: *New York Herald Tribune*, August 3, 1965; *The Nation*, August 2, 1965; *National Review*, July 27, August 10 and 24, 1965; New York *Post*, August 31, 1965; *Newsweek*, December 20, 1965; Rusk's replies: Department of State, Press Release No. 184, Secretary Rusk's News Conference of August 2, 1965; New York *Journal-American*, January 10, 1966; Muggeridge on Schlesinger: *Esquire*, February 1966

Sorensen on his book: Richard Reeves, *op. cit.*; Terence Smith, "The New New Frontier of Ted Sorensen," *The New York Times Magazine*, March 26, 1967; Sorensen one of first to leave LBJ: Washington *Star*, January 16, 1964; LBJ nice to him: Terence Smith, *op. cit.*; Sorensen busy in New York: *The New York Times*, January 15, 1967; *The Village Voice*, August 4, 1966; Sorensen denial of running for office: *The New York Times*, March 13, 1967; Sorensen against Bobby's running in 1968: *The New York Times*, November 24, 1966; New York

Daily News, November 25, 1966;
Sorensen close to Bobby: The New
York Times, January 15, 1967

Alsop on Edelman and Walinsky: New York World-Journal-Tribune, January 23, 1967; Scheer in
Ramparts: February 1967; Walinsky brash: Glass and Aarons, op.
cit.; Edelman less controversial:
Reeves, op. cit.; Mankiewicz and
others: Reeves, ibid.; Glass and
Aarons, op. cit.; private sources

China seminar: Newsweek, May
16, 1966; Beichman on Neustadt:
New York Herald Tribune, March
21, 1965; Neustadt's complaint:
Newsweek, May 16, 1966, and Oc-
tober 31, 1966; Henry Fairlie ar-
ticle: London Sunday Telegraph,
January 15, 1967; Washington
Post, January 15, 1967; debate on
article: The New York Times,
January 22, 1967; William S.
White in the New York World-
Journal-Tribune, January 18 and
February 3, 1967; Baltimore Sun,
January 29, 1967; Congressional
Record, January 30, 1967, pp. S–
1112–14; Time, February 3, 1967;
Dean Price letter to Washington
Post: January 19, 1967; Fairlie's
reply: Washington Post, January
23, 1967; Neustadt's reply: ibid.;
Stern in Washington Post: Febru-
ary 5, 1967; Harriman–Fairlie ex-
change: New York World-Journal-
Tribune, February 19, 1967

**CHAPTER 27 HIT-AND-RUN
SENATOR**

Buckley on the inevitability of
Bobby: New York Journal-Ameri-
can, March 31, 1966; Alsop ec-
static: Washington Post, July 1,
1966; O'Neill in Baltimore Sun:
July 1, 1966; The Nation com-
ment: July 4, 1966; Gallup
Poll: Washington Post, August
21, 1966; Harris Poll: New
York Post, September 27, 1966;
Minneapolis Tribune Poll: The
New York Times, August 14, 1966;
LBJ reaction to polls: New York
Post, August 26, 1966; The New

York Times, September 20, 1966;
O'Brien in the Philadelphia Inquirer: August 25, 1966; Ted Knap
comment: Washington Daily
News, August 25, 1966; U.S. News
& World Report interview: September 26, 1966; Drummond comment: Washington Post, August
24, 1966; Kempton comment: New
York Post, July 7, 1966; LBJ–HHH
married: Washington Star, September 20, 1966

Bobby separates self from Ful-
bright–Morse on foreign aid: Con-
gressional Record, July 21, 1966,
pp. S–15801–34; July 22, 1966,
pp. S–16015–42; July 25, 1966, pp.
S–16145–48   and   S–16159–76;
Washington Post, July 22, 24 and
26, 1966; The New York Times,
July 22, 1966; Baltimore Sun,
July 22, 1966; New York Post,
July 26, 1966; Wicker in The New
York Times: August 26, 1966;

Bobby goes after GM: The Nation,
March 21, 1966; New York Post,
March 22, 1966; New York Her-
ald Tribune, March 23, 1966; The
Wall Street Journal, March 25,
1966; James Ridgeway, "GM
Comes Clean," The New Republic,
April 2, 1966; Time, April 8,
1966; Fitzgerald in Pontiac Press:
as quoted in Chicago Tribune,
May 21, 1966

Ribicoff on Bobby: The New
York Times, August 29, 1966;
Washington Star, August 26, 1966;
Bobby testifies at hearings: Wash-
ington Post, August 16, 1966; The
New York Times, August 16, 1966;
New York Post, August 16, 1966;
Washington Post comment: Au-
gust 22, 1966; Administration re-
buttal: The New York Times, Au-
gust 25, 1966; Time, August 26,
1966; The New York Times, Au-
gust 17, 1966; Washington Star,
August 29, 1966; Washington
Post, August 23, 1966; Katzenbach
on stand: Washington Post, Au-
gust 18, 1966; Baltimore Sun, August 18, 1966; Washington Post,
August 23, 1966; Shriver on stand:
New York Daily News, August 20,

1966; *Newsweek*, August 29, 1966; White comments: *Washington Post*, August 23, 1966; Mayors Lindsay, Cavanagh and Yorty on stand: *Washington Star*, August 23, 24, 25 and September 5, 1966; *Washington Post*, August 24, 1966; *The New York Times*, August 24, 25 and 30, 1966; *Roanoke Times*, August 27, 1966; *Chicago Tribune*, August 28 and 29, 1966; *Newsweek*, September 5, 1966; *Washington Star* comments: August 28, 1966

Bobby's choice for governor: *Time*, August 26, 1966; FDR Jr. a choice for governor: *The Wall Street Journal*, July 7, 1966; Mary McGrory on Bobby–O'Connor: *New York Post*, September 10, 1966; Liberals against O'Connor: *New York Post*, August 19, 1966; FDR Jr.'s bombshell: *The New York Times*, July 29, 1966; *The New York Times* comment: August 12, 1966; *New York Post* comment: July 29, 1966; Democratic State Convention: *Washington Star*, September 8, 13 and 14, 1966; *The New York Times*, September 11 and 12, 1966; *Newsweek*, September 19, 1966; Vietnam plank: *New York Daily News*, September 8, 1966; *The Village Voice*, September 15, 1966; O'Connor on how he won: *Time*, September 16, 1966; FDR Jr. nominated by Liberals: *Baltimore Sun*, September 8, 1966; Samuels nominated in anti-Bobby revolt: *New York Post*, September 8 and 9, 1966; *The New York Times*, September 9 and 10, 1966; *Long Island Press*, September 9, 1966

CHAPTER 28   CAMPAIGN 1966

Bobby in Sioux City: *The New York Times*, October 10, 1966; Perry in *The National Observer*: October 17, 1966; advance men: *U.S. News & World Report*, November 7, 1966; signs and crowds: *The New York Times*, op. cit.; *Washington Post*, October 10, 1966; *U.S. News*

& World Report, op. cit.; speech texts: Jules Witcover, "Robert Kennedy on Tour," *The New Republic*, October 1, 1966; Reston from Portland: *The New York Times*, October 26, 1966; LBJ vs. Bobby in Ohio: *Washington Post*, September 20, 1966; transcript of LBJ press conference: *The New York Times*, September 22, 1966; Griffin in the Baltimore *Sun*: October 3, 1966; Humphrey in Los Angeles: *The New York Times*, September 27, 1966; *Washington Post*, September 27, 1966

Bobby's denial of Presidential ambitions: *The New York Times*, September 2, 1966; Weaver in *The New York Times*: October 19, 1966; Wicker nostalgic: *Roanoke Times*, November 3, 1966; Nixon on Democrats: *The New York Times*, October 2, 1966; Bobby on Nixon: *The New York Times*, October 23, 1966

Bobby–Yorty exchange: Baltimore *Sun*, October 23, 1966; *New York Daily News*, October 23, 1966; *The New York Times*, October 23, 1966; *Washington Post*, October 23, 1966; campaigning in rest of California: *New York Post*, October 24, 1966; Bobby's popularity: *The New York Times*, July 3, 1966; *Long Beach Independent*, October 24, 1966; Bobby at Berkeley: *The New York Times*, October 24, 1966; *Baltimore Sun*, October 24, 1966; *Washington Post*, October 24, 1966; *New York Daily News*, October 24, 1966; *Human Events*, November 5, 1966; Broder in *Washington Post*: October 25, 1966; Alsop's and White's comments: *New York World-Journal-Tribune*, October 26, 1966

Bobby campaigns for O'Connor: *Baltimore Sun*, October 2, 1966; *Washington Post*, September 14, 1966; *The New York Times*, October 2, 1966; Shelley Winters: *New York Post*, September 12, 1966; Bobby assigned Steve Smith: *The New York Times*, Sept. 24, 1966; O'Connor on rich families: *The*

New York Times, October 11, 1966; Broder on no fund-raising: Washington Post, October 18, 1966; O'Connor at Cornell: New York Post, September 27, 1966; Marianne Means' interview: New York World-Journal-Tribune, November 1, 1966; Bobby's aides blame O'Connor's aides: The New York Times, October 25, 1966; Bobby at Eastern Montana College: Washington Star, October 30, 1966

civilian review board: The New York Times, July 13, October 7 and November 3 and 4, 1966; New York Post, October 27 and November 8, 1966; New York Daily News, November 4, 1966; New York World-Journal-Tribune, November 9, 1966; New York World-Journal-Tribune editorial: October 28, 1966; election night: New York World-Journal-Tribune, November 9, 1966; New York Post, November 9 and 12, 1966; Bobby's thoughts from Nassau: The New York Times, November 11, 1966; Washington Post, November 18, 1966; Bobby's candidates' failures: New York Post, November 10, 1966; The New York Times, November 13, 1966; Washington Post, November 14, 1966; Newsweek, November 21, 1966; The New York Times on winners: November 13, 1966; LBJ on taking Bobby as V.P.: "He Drives to Bring About 'The Restoration,'" Life, November 18, 1966

CHAPTER 29   WIRETAPPING

Kraft comment: Washington Post, November 14, 1966; government and Black: Richmond News Leader, June 2, 1966; The New York Times, July 14 and November 16, 1966; Washington Star, November 17, 1966; New York Post, November 17, 1966; Time, December 23, 1966; National Observer, November 14, 1966; Representative Gross statement: Richmond News Leader, June 2, 1966; Bobby on Issues and Answers program:

as quoted by Allen–Scott Report, New Rochelle Standard-Star, December 12, 1966; Buckley on wiretaps and bugs: Richmond News Leader, August 1, 1966; Bobby on FBI and Birchers and FBI denial: Washington Post, December 2, 1966; Hoover on Bobby's step up of eavesdropping: The New York Times, December 11, 1966; New York World-Journal-Tribune, December 11, 1966; Baltimore Sun, December 11, 1966; Washington Star, December 11, 1966

round two of charges: The New York Times, December 12, 1966; New York World-Journal-Tribune, December 12, 1966; Baltimore Sun, December 12, 1966; Wechsler defense of Bobby: New York Post, December 19, 1966; The Nation comment: December 26, 1966; Reston in The New York Times: December 14, 1966; Richard Wilson comment: Washington Star, December 14, 1966; Harwood in Washington Post: December 18, 1966; Bobby on fighting Hoover: Time, December 23, 1966; Washington Post report: December 26, 1966

LBJ aloofness: The New York Times, December 13, 1966; Baltimore Sun, December 13, 1966; LBJ embarrassed Bobby on wiretapping: New York Post, March 23, 1967; Ted Lewis comment: New York Daily News, January 12, 1967; Baltimore Sun comment: January 12, 1967; Manchester Union Leader interview with Silberling: January 17, 1967; Long on calling Bobby and Hoover to testify: Human Events, February 11, 1967; Furgurson in the Baltimore Sun: December 14, 1966

CHAPTER 30   BOOKS AND HISTORY

announcement: John Corry, The Manchester Affair (New York: G. P. Putnam's Sons, 1967), p. 32; Wicker review of first Manchester book: *The New York Times Book Review*, September 30, 1962; Bobby on selecting one person: New York *World-Journal-Tribune*, November 30, 1966; Lord and White rejected job: John Corry, *op. cit.*, p. 19; Corry on Kennedys vulnerable: *ibid.*, p. 29; memorandum: *ibid.*, pp. 29–31; Bishop letter: Washington *Post*, September 17, 1966; Bishop's column: Philadelphia *Bulletin*, August 11, 1965; Bishop–Kennedy exchanges: *The New York Times*, September 18, 1966; Washington *Star*, September 18, 1966; New York *Daily News*, September 18, 1966; *Newsweek*, October 3, 1966

Maud Shaw book: *White House Nannie—My Years with Caroline and John Kennedy, Jr.* (New York: The New American Library, Inc., 1966); Washington *Post*, November 20, 1965; Jim Shevis, NANA, December 16, 1966; New York *Post*, April 24, 1966; *Book Week*, April 17, 1966; *The New York Times*, December 22, 1966; private sources

Paul Fay book: Paul B. Fay Jr., *The Pleasure of His Company* (New York: Harper & Row, Publishers, 1966); Jim Shevis, *op. cit.*; New York *Post*, October 1, 1966; *Time*, October 28, 1966; Hugh Sidey, "The Presidency: Nobody's Rumpled, Nobody's Real," *Life*, December 9, 1966; Breslin on Bobby's handwriting: New York *World-Journal-Tribune*, December 15, 1966; Jacqueline's reaction to Fay book: New York *Post*, December 6, 1966

Levin book: Murray B. Levin, *Kennedy Campaigning: The System and the Style as Practiced by Senator Edward Kennedy* (Boston: Beacon Press, 1966); Jim Shevis, *op. cit.*; *The New York Times Book Review*, October 23, 1966; private sources; Manchester on Sorensen and Salinger: "William Manchester's Own Story," *Look*, April 4, 1967; Mrs. Lincoln's book: *My Twelve Years with John F. Ken-*

nedy (New York: David McKay Co., Inc., 1965)

Manchester book controversy: John Corry, *op. cit.*; Manchester, *op. cit.*; *The New York Times*, December 17 and 23, 1966, January 30, 1967; New York *Post*, December 15, 19, 22 and 24, 1966, January 23 and 28, 1967; William H. Rudy, "Manchester vs. The Kennedys," series January 30–February 4, 1967; and April 5, 1967; New York *World-Journal-Tribune*, December 16, 1966, January 24, 29 and 31, February 2, and March 1, 1967; Washington *Post*, January 29, February 7 and March 20, 1967; *Time*, December 23, 1966, January 20 and May 5, 1967; *Human Events*, December 17, 1966; Washington *Star*, December 20, 1966; Richmond *News Leader*, December 24, 1966; George Sherman, "The Book of the Century," *This Week*, January 8, 1967; *Chicago Tribune*, January 10, 1967; New Rochelle *Standard-Star*, January 31, 1967; *Newsweek*, February 6, 1967; *The Reporter*, February 8, 1967; Baltimore *Sun*, January 10 and February 1, 1967

LBJ thought book a Kennedy project: New York *Daily News*, December 23, 1966; Manchester on living in an absolute monarchy: *The New York Times*, January 23, 1967; Reston on the death of Camelot: *The New York Times*, December 18, 1966; exchange of Christmas cards: New York *World-Journal-Tribune*, February 14, 1967; Vidal on preternaturally ambitious family: *Book Week*, April 9, 1967

CHAPTER 31   PEACE FEELERS

Evans and Novak on Kennedy method: New York *World-Journal-Tribune*, February 10, 1967; Bobby on arrival in London: New York *Post*, January 26, 1967; Bobby on Vietnam at Oxford: New York *World-Journal-Tribune*, January 29, 1967; *The New York Times*, January 29, 1967; Baltimore *Sun*,

January 29, 1967; Bobby's "clarification": *The New York Times*, January 31, 1967; *Daily Sketch* comment: *U.S. News & World Report*, February 13, 1967

Bobby greeted by teenagers in Paris: *Newsweek*, February 13, 1967; Kaplan report: NANA, February 7, 1967; Kempton on Bobby–de Gaulle meeting: New York *Post*, February 15, 1967; Bobby on de Gaulle just after meeting: New York *Daily News*, February 1, 1967; *Chicago Tribune*, February 1, 1967; Bobby's off-the-record briefing three hours later and de Gaulle's anger: New York *Daily News*, February 9, 1967; London *Daily Express*, as quoted in San Francisco *Chronicle*, March 19, 1967; Kaplan on Bobby's cultural image: *op. cit.;* visit to Latin Quarter: New York *World-Journal-Tribune*, February 19, 1967; Alphand party: *The New York Times*, February 5, 1967

Bobby in Bonn: New York *Post*, February 2, 1967; Washington *Post*, February 3, 1967; New York *World-Journal-Tribune*, January 29, 1967; Bobby in Rome: *Chicago Tribune*, February 3, 1967; *The New York Times*, February 3, 1967; Baltimore *Sun*, February 4 and 5, 1967; New York *World-Journal-Tribune*, February 4 and 21, 1967; Bobby's return to New York: New York *Daily News*, February 5, 1967; Washington *Star*, February 5, 1967; *The New York Times*, February 5, 1967

Bobby's meeting with Étienne Manac'h: New York *World-Journal-Tribune*, February 10 and 11, 1967; *Time*, February 10, 1967; *The New York Times*, February 12, 1967; *Newsweek*, February 13, 1967; Sidey's comment: *Life*, February 17, 1967; *Newsweek's* Weintal: February 13, 1967; signal or no-signal: New York *Post*, February 6, 1967; New York *World-Journal-Tribune*, February 8, 1967; Washington *Post*, February 10, 1967; *Newsweek* on innocence

abroad: February 20, 1967; Ter Horst in Detroit *News:* NANA, February 9, 1967; Wechsler on White House appointment: New York *Post*, February 7, 1967

LBJ–Bobby meeting on February 6: *Time*, March 17, 1967; *The New York Times*, February 7 and March 15, 1967; Washington *Post*, February 7, 1967; Baltimore *Sun*, February 7 and March 15, 1967; *Chicago Tribune*, March 15, 1967; New York *World-Journal-Tribune*, March 15, 1967; New York *Post*, March 15, 1967; LBJ and photographers: New York *Post*, March 7, 1967; Ted Lewis on transcript: New York *Daily News*, March 16, 1967; Bobby's joke on cease-fire: *The Wall Street Journal*, March 17, 1967

Bobby's China speech: *The New York Times*, February 9, 1967; Baltimore *Sun*, February 9, 1967; New York *Post*, February 9 and 10, 1967; Washington *Star*, February 11, 1967; text, *Congressional Record*, February 20, 1967, pp. H–1533–35; Greene comment: New York *Daily News*, February 10, 1967; CIA flap: *The New York Times*, February 15 and 22, 1967; New York *World-Journal-Tribune*, February 21 and 24, 1967; Washington *Star*, February 21, 1967; New York *Post*, February 22, 1967; New York *Daily News*, February 24, 1967; Reston on LBJ's impulse: *The New York Times*, February 17, 1967; Crawford comment: *Newsweek*, March 6, 1967; Pearson and Anderson on Bobby's off-the-record briefing: Washington *Post*, February 21, 1967; Kempton on Javits–Bobby–LBJ on Vietnam: New York *Post*, February 14 and 15, 1967; Lisagor report: (CDN) New York *Post*, February 22, 1967; Mary McGrory comment: Washington *Star*, February 17, 1967; Lynd and Hayden visit Bobby: *Time*, March 17, 1967; *The Village Voice*, March 2, 1967

Bobby's end-the-bombing speech on Vietnam: *The New York Times*,

March 3, 1967; Washington *Post*, March 3, 1967; Baltimore *Sun*, March 3, 1967; *Chicago Tribune*, March 3, 1967; New York *Post*, March 3, 1967; *Time*, March 10, 1967; Bobby's rudeness to LBJ in delivery of text: *Life*, March 17, 1967; LBJ activity day of Bobby's speech: *The New York Times*, March 3, 1967; New York *World-Journal-Tribune*, March 3, 1967; Savannah *Evening Press*, March 3, 1967; Javits on LBJ–Bobby emotions: *The New York Times*, March 6, 1967; Washington *Post*, March 6, 1967; Administration spokesmen critical: Baltimore *Sun*, March 7, 1967; Reston on British support for LBJ: *The New York Times*, March 3, 1967; Hanoi and Moscow reactions: *The New York Times*, March 5, 1967; Schlesinger backs Bobby: *The New York Times*, March 9, 1967; New York *Daily News*, March 9, 1967; LBJ's press conference: *The New York Times*, March 10, 1967; Washington *Star*, March 10, 1967; Washington *Post*, March 10, 1967; Sidey comment: *Life*, March 17, 1967; LBJ at Democratic National Committee dinner: Baltimore *Sun*, March 11, 1967; *Newsweek*, March 20, 1967; Scheer and vanden Heuvel on TV: Newsfront, WNDT-TV, New York, March 2, 1967; Marianne Means comment: New York *World-Journal-Tribune*, March 7, 1967; Farley speech: *The New York Times*, February 26, 1967; New York *Post*, February 27, 1967; New York *World-Journal-Tribune*, February 27, 1967; New York *Daily News*, February 27 and 28, 1967; Hartford *Courant*, as quoted in the *Chicago Tribune*, March 5, 1967

Hanoi release of LBJ–Ho letters: *The New York Times*, March 22, 1967; Washington *Star*, March 22 and 25, 1967; Crawford in *Newsweek*: April 3, 1967; Bobby's new statement: New York *World-Journal-Tribune*, Mar. 22 and 23, 1967; Baltimore *Sun*, March 22,

1967; *The New York Times*, March 23, 1967; Richard Wilson comment: Washington *Star*, March 24, 1967; Senator Mansfield comment: New York *World-Journal-Tribune*, March 23, 1967; Senate debate: Baltimore *Sun*, March 24, 1967; Bobby praises LBJ at dinner: *The New York Times*, June 4, 1967; text, *Congressional Record*, December 6, 1967, pp. A–6026–27

CHAPTER 32   FUTURE

Bobby the pragmatist: Washington *Post*, January 31, 1968; Bobby on his future: *The New York Times*, January 9, 1968; *Newsweek* on LBJ–RFK in 1968: January 29, 1968; Sorensen and Goodwin remarks: A. James Reichley, "He's Running Himself Out of the Race," *Fortune*, March 1968; *Observer* report: as quoted in *National Review Bulletin*, November 7, 1967; *Newsweek* quote: January 29, 1968

McCarthy victory in New Hampshire: *The New York Times*, March 13, 1968; McCarthy rapped Bobby: New York *Post*, January 6, 1968; Newfield on the Bad Bobby: *The Village Voice*, December 28, 1967; Tallmer in the New York *Post*: February 26, 1968; McCarthy's 1960 remark: *The Wall Street Journal*, November 16, 1967; Alsop on McCarthy–Kennedy: Washington *Post*, November 6, 1967; Kraft on McCarthy: Washington *Post*, November 12, 1967; *Look* magazine: as quoted in the Baltimore *Sun*, January 23, 1968; Gridiron dinner song: *The New York Times*, March 10, 1968

Bobby enters 1968 Presidential race: Washington *Post*, March 17, 1968; McCarthy's reaction to Bobby: *Time*, March 29, 1968; *Newsweek*, April 1, 1968; Kempton comments: New York *Post*, March 26, 1968; Bobby on McCarthy vanity: Richard Reeves, "The Kennedy Machine Is Moving: The Making of a Candidate 1968," *The New York Times Magazine*, March 31, 1968; Bobby's wild attacks on LBJ: Washington *Star*, March 24, 1968; *The New York Times* editorial: March 31, 1968; Bobby's reactions to LBJ's announcement: as quoted by Jimmy Breslin, New York *Post*, April 1, 1968; Bobby's press conference: Washington *Star*, April 1, 1968

CHAPTER 33   END

JFK statement: Joe McCarthy, *The Remarkable Kennedys* (New York: Dial Press, 1960), p. 116; Bobby to take trip to Europe: private sources; Bobby on McCarthy's campaigners: *The National Observer*, June 10, 1968; Schlesinger in *The New Republic*: "Why I Am For Kennedy," May 4, 1968; Rose Kennedy on money: *Chicago Tribune*, May 11, 1968; Pearson vs. Bobby re wiretap of Martin Luther King: New York *Post*, May 27, 1968; Washington *Post*, June 4, 1968; *Chicago Tribune*, May 26, 1968; Carl Greenberg, New York *Post*, May 31, 1968; TV debate with McCarthy: Washington *Star*, June 2 and 3, 1968; Washington *Post*, June 2, 1968; Bobby's conservative speeches in Indiana: *The New York Times*, May 3, 1968; Kenneth

Crawford, "The Man to Beat," *Newsweek*, May 20, 1968; Reagan on Bobby's speeches: *The New York Times*, May 21, 1968; Richard Wilson, Washington *Star*, May 10, 1968; Nixon on Bobby: *The New York Times*, June 2, 1968; Rockefeller on Bobby: *The New York Times*, June 12, 1968; *Chicago Tribune*, June 17, 1968; McCarthy on Bobby: Washington *Post*, May 27, 1968; Baltimore *Sun*, May 27, 1968; Kempton on Bobby: as quoted in *Newsweek*, June 17, 1968

Newfield on last days of California primary: *The Village Voice*, June 13, 1968; Bobby refused police protection: Walter Winchell, New York *Daily Column*, June 19, 1968; Kennedy aide on crowds: *The National Observer*, June 10, 1968; Bobby on Russian roulette: Richmond *News Leader*, June 6, 1968; Bobby on *The New York Times*: Jimmy Breslin, " 'Bonnie and Clyde' Revisited," *New York*, July 8, 1968; Bobby on chasing Humphrey: Jack Newfield, *op. cit.*; Bobby's victory speech: *The New York Times*, June 5, 1968; Washington *Star*, June 5, 1968; Washington *Post*, June 5, 1968; New York *Post*, June 5, 1968; Schlesinger on Teddy: *The New York Times*, June 10, 1968

Index

HOW
IT
WORKS
**From color camera
to color
1,071
two-color
drawings**
Easy-to-understand
explanations

HOW IS color television transmitted? (See page 166 of THE WAY THINGS WORK.) How does a helicopter fly? (See page 560.) How does "dry cleaning" clean? (See page 407.)

THE WAY THINGS WORK is a lucid encyclopedia of technology, an endlessly fascinating anthology of descriptions and diagrams that unravel the mystery of common mechanisms and today's technological marvels. It's a book to delight everyone intrigued with the way things work.

We invite you to mail the coupon below. A copy of THE WAY THINGS WORK will be sent to you at once. If at the end of ten days you do not feel that this book is one you will treasure, you may return it and owe nothing. Otherwise, we will bill you $9.95, plus postage and handling. At all bookstores, or write to Simon & Schuster, Inc., Dept. W-3, 630 Fifth Ave., New York, N.Y. 10020.

78013

And don't forget the other seven Robbins' blockbusters with sales totaling over 70,000,000 copies!

AT YOUR BOOKSTORE OR MAIL THE COUPON BELOW

Mail Service Department
POCKET BOOKS, Dept.5
A Division of Simon & Schuster, Inc.
1 W. 39th St./New York, N.Y. 10018

Please send me the following:

No. of Cps.	Amt.		Price	Title
....	....	78502	($1.50)	THE INHERITORS
....	....	78014	($1.25)	THE ADVENTURERS
....	....	78015	($1.25)	THE CARPETBAGGERS
....	....	78016	($1.25)	THE DREAM MERCHANTS
....	....	78017	($1.25)	NEVER LOVE A STRANGER
....	....	78018	($1.25)	A STONE FOR DANNY FISHER
....	....	78019	($1.25)	WHERE LOVE HAS GONE
....	....	78020	($1.25)	79 PARK AVENUE

Plus 25¢ ....for mailing and handling.
Please enclose check or money order. We are not responsible for orders containing cash.

TOTAL AMOUNT............

(PLEASE PRINT CLEARLY)

Name...

Address...

City..

State.. Zip....................

78013

2 P7/1

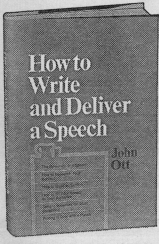